LISA R BIXENSTINE

D1130011

Hiram College Library

Gift of

Lisa Safford

Miss E. Blackstone

THE DAGUERREOTYPE IN AMERICA

by
Beaumont Newhall

THIRD REVISED EDITION

WITHDRAWN
HIRAM COLLEGE LIBRARY

DOVER PUBLICATIONS, INC., NEW YORK

2.120
3 New

Preface to the Dover Edition

This third edition has been expanded by the addition of sixteen more pages of plates; corrections and minor revisions have been made in the text; and the Bibliography has been brought up to date to include reprints of obscure and long out-of-print manuals, and microfilms of periodicals. I thank Dover Publications, Inc., for bringing the book back into print; it is my hope that it will not only be useful to scholars, collectors and the general reading public, but that it will also stimulate further research into one of America's most lasting contributions to the history of photography.

October 1975   BEAUMONT NEWHALL

Copyright © 1961, 1976 by Beaumont Newhall.
All rights reserved under Pan American and International Copyright Conventions.

Published in Canada by General Publishing Company, Ltd., 30 Lesmill Road, Don Mills, Toronto, Ontario.
Published in the United Kingdom by Constable and Company, Ltd., 10 Orange Street, London WC 2.

This Dover edition, first published in 1976, is a revised and enlarged edition of the work first published in 1961 by Duell, Sloan & Pearce.

International Standard Book Number: 0-486-23322-7
Library of Congress Catalog Card Number: 76-691

Manufactured in the United States of America
Dover Publications, Inc.
180 Varick Street
New York, N.Y. 10014

Contents

Plates

following page 112

1. The family daguerreotype, about 1850.
2. Self-portrait. By Henry Fitz, Jr., probably 1839.
3. King's Chapel Burying Ground, Boston. By Samuel Bemis, 1840.
4. Merchants' Exchange, Philadelphia. By Walter R. Johnson, 1840.
5. Old Patent Office, Washington, D. C. By John Plumbe, Jr., about 1846.
6. Third Street at Chestnut, Philadelphia. By George Read, 1842.
7. Chestnut Street, Philadelphia, about 1844.
8. John Quincy Adams. By Philip Haas, 1843.
9. Andrew Jackson. Probably by Dan Adams, before 1845.
10. Zachary Taylor, about 1850.
11. John Tyler, about 1845.
12. State Street at Main, Rochester, New York. By Edward Tompkins Whitney, about 1852.
13. Ruins of the American Hotel, Buffalo, New York, about 1850.
14. Man sitting on sofa with dog, about 1850.
15. Butterfly collector, about 1850.
16. Mrs. Joseph Elisha Whitman, Sr., and her son Joseph Elisha, Jr., born 1853.
17. Cobbler, about 1850.
18. Tole ware maker, about 1850.
19. Frederick Warren, city marshal of Worcester, Massachusetts, about 1850.
20. "The Woodsawyer's Nooning." By George N. Barnard, 1853.
21. Seamstress, about 1850.
22. Woman with sheet music, about 1850.
23. Henry Brewer, of the H. & J. Brewer Drug Store, Springfield, Massachusetts, about 1850.
24. Ship in dry dock, Boston Navy Yard. By Southworth & Hawes, about 1852.
25. Locomotive "Hoosac."
26. Train wreck on the Providence and Worcester Railroad. By L. Wright, 1853.
27. Burning mills at Oswego, New York. By George N. Barnard, 1853.
28. Woodward Woolen Mill, Woodstock, Vermont, about 1850.
29. Steamship in dry dock, Boston. By Southworth & Hawes, about 1855.
30. Quaker sisters, about 1850.
31. Dog. By Sheldon Nichols, about 1855.
32. Girl, about 1850.

Illustrations in the Text

Introduction

PHOTOGRAPHY first came to America in 1839 in the form of the daguerreotype. For twenty years it is through the daguerreotype that we see the men and the places of the United States. In galleries all over the country silvered copper plates were polished mirror bright; fumed straw yellow and rose red with vapors of iodine, chlorine, and bromine; exposed in bulky wooden cameras; developed over heated mercury; fixed, gilded, washed, and fitted like jewels in cases. Thousands earned their livelihoods with Daguerre's invention; hundreds of thousands of Americans, rich and poor, famous and unknown, proud and meek, young and old, faced the mesmeric lens of the daguerreotypist's camera for the eternity of twenty to forty seconds of immobility.

More daguerreotypes have survived than would be imagined. Fortunately the process is relatively permanent. In their velvet-lined cases daguerreotypes are precious objects, which no one wants to throw carelessly away. In spite of the fact that many were melted down for their silver, and many others were ruined in bungling attempts to clean their tarnished surfaces, thousands remain in pristine condition, eloquent yet forgotten remembrances of the past.

No other pictorial technique was more popular in America in the 1850's: as Horace Greeley said, "In daguerreotypes we beat the world." There were more daguerreotype galleries in New York City than in all of England in 1853, and more on Broadway alone than in London. Americans were more grateful to Daguerre than Frenchmen. When he died, he was mourned by the daguerreotypists of New York, who voted to wear crape on their left sleeves for the space of thirty days. "Ah, what regard for immortality, what sentiment!" exclaimed the vice-president of the Société Libre des Beaux-Arts at a memorial service to Daguerre in the French town of Bry-sur-Marne, where he died in 1851. "America has shown herself grateful to our illustrious countryman, when French photographers were forgetful. . . . "

11

Introduction

In writing this history, my first debt is to the collectors who have preserved and generously made available to me not only daguerreotypes but documents and notes about some of the men who made them: the late Alden Scott Boyer of Chicago, who during his lifetime gave his entire collection on the history of photography to the George Eastman House, and who for five years sent me daily bulletins of "plucks and culls" from his extensive reading in the books he had collected; Mrs. Zelda P. Mackay of San Francisco; Helmut and Alison Gernsheim of London; Señor Julio F. Riobò of Buenos Aires; Dale Walden of Boise, Idaho; A. R. Phillips, Jr., of Los Angeles; Richard B. Holman of Boston; and Walter Scott Shinn of New York. I was made welcome with typewriter and copying camera in many libraries, historical societies, and museums. I thank in particular the Trustees of the Camera Club, New York; Mr. Clarence S. Brigham, retired Director of the American Antiquarian Society in Worcester, Mass.; Mr. R. W. G. Vail, retired Director of the New-York Historical Society; Mr. Walter M. Whitehill, Director and Librarian of the Boston Athenaeum; Mr. A. Hyatt Mayor, Curator of Prints, The Metropolitan Museum of Art, New York; Miss Grace Mayer, Special Assistant to the Director of Photography of the Museum of Modern Art, New York; Dr. Louis Walton Sipley, Director of the American Museum of Photography, Philadelphia; Mr. Paul Angle, Director of the Chicago Historical Society; and Mr. Charles Van Ravenswaay, Director of the Missouri Historical Society. Friends and colleagues have encouraged me by sharing their research and pointing out untapped sources of pictures and information: I am particularly grateful to Ansel Adams, Albert Boni, Roger Butterfield, I. Bernard Cohen, Marshall Davidson, Jay Leyda, and Ferdinand Reyher. The late John A. Tennant was my sole direct link with the past: he knew men who were daguerreotypists; from his vast knowledge of more than three quarters of a century's activity as writer, editor, and publisher he gave me help I could not have found elsewhere.

My wife Nancy has accompanied me every step of the way into the past and in the task of organizing the fruits of this research. She made the final selection of daguerreotypes for reproduction and the sequence of their presentation.

BEAUMONT NEWHALL

PART I

An Art and an Industry

1. *A Wonder from Paris*

AMERICA first heard about Daguerre's invention from Samuel F. B. Morse, the painter and inventor. He was in Paris in the winter of 1838-39, when he presented his electric telegraph to the Academy of Sciences, and held weekly demonstrations. "I am told every hour," he wrote his brother, "that the two great wonders of Paris just now, about which everybody is conversing, are Daguerre's wonderful results in fixing permanently the image of the *camera obscura* and Morse's Electro-Magnetic Telegraph."[1]

Just before he left Paris for home, Morse visited Daguerre, saw his daguerreotypes, and wrote about them on March 9, 1839, in a letter to his brother which was published in the New York *Observer*.

> They are produced on a metallic surface, the principal pieces about 7 inches by 5, and they resemble aquatint engravings; for they are in simple chiaro oscuro, and not in colors, but the exquisite minuteness of the delineation cannot be conceived. No painting or engraving ever approached it. For example: In a view up the street, the distant sign would be perceived, and the eye could just discern that there were lines of letters upon it, but so minute as not to be read with the naked eye. By the assistance of a powerful lens which magnified fifty times, applied to the delineation, every letter was clearly and distinctly legible, and so also were the minutest breaks and lines in the walls of the buildings; and the pavements of the streets. The effect of the lens upon the picture was in a great degree like that of the telescope in nature. . . . The impressions of interior views are Rembrandt perfected.[2]

All who saw Daguerre's pictures for the first time were equally impressed. They marveled that skill of hand played no part in their creation, and the amount of detail which was, so to speak, automatically recorded seemed almost beyond belief. No pictures like them had ever before been seen.

Many had already tried to accomplish what was now a reality: the fixation of the image of the camera. Morse must have shared the feelings of the German

15

scientist who, reading of the discovery, "felt something like the enviers of Columbus, when he made the egg stand on its end."[3] For Morse, years before, had made experiments while he was at Yale University "to ascertain if it were possible to fix the image of the Camera Obscura."[4] Like most others, he did not succeed. "Finding that light produced dark and dark light, I presumed the production of a true image to be impracticable, and gave up the attempt. M. Daguerre has realized in the most exquisite manner this idea."[5] The method by which Daguerre achieved this long-sought-for end remained his secret during the time that Morse was in Paris.

Like Morse, Louis Jacques Mandé Daguerre was a painter. Since 1822 one of the popular Parisian spectacles was his "Diorama"—a theater without actors. Scenery alone, of the most illusionistic kind, provided the amusement. There were three separate stages inside the Diorama around a circular auditorium, the floor of which was a great turntable that revolved to face, in turn, the stages, where were shown huge paintings, seventy-two by forty-eight feet in size. When illuminated from the top, the front alone of each picture could be seen; when lighted from behind, another picture, painted on the back, became visible through the semi-transparent canvas. By controlling the lighting, the pictures dissolved one into another. Parisians paid admission to see such make-believe scenes as an Alpine village before and after its destruction by an avalanche, or Midnight Mass at the Church of St.-Etienne-du-Mont. The latter was one of the most popular of the presentations: as night fell the church gradually darkened, the devout came to take their places, and, to the peals of an organ and the fumes of incense, choir boys lit candles. The Mass was sung, the faithful disappeared, the candles were extinguished, and daybreak illuminated the stained-glass windows. The illusionism was so perfect that a lad from the country threw a coin onto the stage "to find out if it really was space in front of him." When an art student set up an easel and began to paint the Diorama of Napoleon's Tomb, Daguerre said to him, "Young man, come as often as you want to, but don't work here, because you'll be making nothing but a copy of a copy. If you want to study seriously, go out doors."[6]

The success of the Diorama depended almost entirely on its scenery. To assist him in obtaining exact perspective, Daguerre, like so many other artists of the day, used a camera obscura. This instrument was simply a box, with a lens

16

at one end and a ground glass at the other, on which the lens formed an image. By laying thin paper over the glass, the image could be traced.

It is difficult to establish exactly when Daguerre first had the idea of recording the camera image chemically, rather than by the laborious use of pencil and paper. It is likely that by 1826 he was well along the way to discovering this technique, which was to be known as photography. At least Charles Chevalier, the Parisian optician who supplied him with lenses, recollected that Daguerre said to him in that year: "I have fixed the images formed in the camera obscura."[7] At the suggestion of Chevalier, Daguerre began to correspond with a fellow countryman, Nicéphore Niépce, who, the optician said, was working along the same lines. After three years of mutual distrust and suspicion, the two became partners. Daguerre later recollected: "I contributed a camera, which I modified for this use and which, by extending greater sharpness over the larger field of the image, had much to do with our later success. Certain important modification which I had applied to the process, added to the further research of M. Niépce, led us to predict a happy conclusion when [in 1833] death tore from me this man, whose heart was as great as his knowledge profound. . . . Overwhelmed by this loss, I gave up our work for the time being; but soon I followed it up with zeal and attained the goal we had aimed for."[8] The first of his successful pictures which now exists is a view of the corner of his studio, showing statues, pictures, a wicker-covered bottle, bric-a-brac. The original, dated 1837, is in the collection of the Société Française de Photographie in Paris.

Daguerre kept his technique a secret.

By the fall of 1838 he was ready to market his invention. He announced an exhibition of his daguerreotypes, to open on January 15, 1839. The show never took place, for in the meantime François Arago, one of France's most distinguished scientists, Secretary of the French Academy of Sciences, and a Deputy in the Chamber from the Department of Pyrénées-Orientales, had become deeply interested. On January 7 he lectured about the daguerreotype to the Academy, and suggested that the French Government reward Daguerre for his invention and donate it to the entire world. He announced that he would make this request to the Minister of the Interior or the Chambers as soon as Daguerre proved to him that the process was indeed practical, inexpensive, simple, and portable.

Only a few months before, Morse had presented his electric telegraph before

17

the Academy, and had gained the respect of Arago and other distinguished Academicians. For this reason he had no difficulty in arranging the rendezvous with Daguerre which he reported to his brother.

Daguerre paid Morse the compliment of a return visit at noon on March 8, climbed the three flights to the apartment Morse shared with the Rev. Edward Kirk on the Rue Neuve-des-Mathurins, and spent over an hour examining the new invention. It was an unlucky hour for him: across the city the Diorama was in flames. Before word of the fire reached Daguerre, the building had burned to the ground. Everything was destroyed, Morse said, "all his beautiful works, his valuable notes and papers, the labor of years of experiments."[9] Happily the government was already making plans to award Daguerre, now left without means of support, a pension.

On his return to America, Morse persuaded the National Academy of Design, of which he was president, to elect Daguerre an honorary member. To our knowledge this recognition of photography as an art by an official body of painters is unique. "When I proposed your name," Morse wrote Daguerre. "it was received with wild enthusiasm, and the vote was *unanimous*. . . . I hope, before this reaches you, that the French Government, long and deservedly celebrated for its generosity to men of genius, will have amply supplied all your losses by a liberal sum. If, when the proper remuneration shall have been secured to you in France, you should think it may be for your advantage to make an arrangement with the government to hold back the secret for six months or a year, and would consent to an exhibition of your *results* in this country for a short time, the exhibition might be managed, I think, to your pecuniary advantage."[10]

Daguerre answered in July: "I am very proud of the honor which has been conferred upon me. . . . The transaction with the French Government being nearly at an end, my discovery shall soon be made public. This cause, added to the immense distance between us, hinders me from taking advantage of your good offer to get up at New York an exhibition of my results."[11]

The plan which the French Government adopted was to grant Daguerre a yearly pension of six thousand francs in return for a complete disclosure of his process. Isidore Niépce, who had succeeded to the partnership on the death of his father, was to receive four thousand francs. The bill was passed by both Chambers of government and it was announced that the disclosure would be made at a

18

special joint meeting of the Academy of Sciences and the Academy of Fine Arts in Paris on August 19, 1839.

By three o'clock on the afternoon of that day, every seat in the auditorium of the Palace of the Institute was taken, and two hundred stood outside in the courtyard. It was expected that Daguerre would explain the process, but Arago spoke in his stead. He began with an apology: "I have to express my regret that the inventor of this most ingenious apparatus has not himself undertaken to explain all its properties," he said. "Only this morning I begged the able artist to accede to a wish which I well knew was universal; but a bad sore throat—fear of not being able to render himself intelligible . . . proved obstacles which I have not been able to surmount."[12] Beyond these words, no transcript exists of the speech. But it was widely reported.

The London *Literary Gazette* for August 24 stated that Arago spent a good deal of time recounting the history of the discovery, "a subject already pretty well known to the public." After giving a résumé of Niépce's work, his partnership with Daguerre, his death, and Daguerre's subsequent discovery of "entirely new methods," the correspondent summarized Arago's description of the process "as now used by the author" in the following words:

> A sheet of copper, plated with silver, is washed carefully in a solution of nitric acid, which removes from it all the extraneous matters on its surface, and especially any traces of copper from the silver surface. A slight degree of friction is requisite in this process, but it must not be applied always in the same direction. M. Daguerre has observed, that with the friction used in a particular manner, a sheet of copper thus plated with silver answered better than a sheet of silver alone; and he infers from this, that voltaic agency is not unconnected with the effect. When the sheet is thus prepared, it is placed in a closed box and exposed to the vapour of iodine. This vapour is made to pass through a very fine sheet of gauze, to render its distribution more equable over the surface of the silver, and in order to effect this object (which is quite indispensable) more certainly, the sheet has a small metallic rim raised all around its edges. A thin coating, of a yellow colour, is thus formed on the surface of the sheet, which is estimated by M. Dumas* at not more than a *millionth part of a millimetre* in thickness. The sheet, when covered with this substance, is of the most excessive sensibility to light; and is thus ready for the camera obscura. M.

*Jean-Baptiste-André Dumas (1800-1884), French chemist.

19

Daguerre, in the instrument which he uses, employs a piece of unpolished [i.e., ground] glass, which he brings first of all into the focus of the lens, in order to determine the exact point at which the sheet should be placed; and, as soon as this is determined, the sheet is placed accordingly. A few seconds, or minutes, according to the time of day, the state of the atmosphere, &c., suffice for form-ing the photogenic image; but it is hardly, if at all, visible on the surface of the sheet. To make it so, the sheet is placed in another box, and exposed to the vapour of mercury, heated to 60° Reamur, or 167° of Fahrenheit. One of the most curious circumstances attending this part of the process is, that the mer-cury must act at a certain angle. If the drawing is intended to be seen ver-tically, it must be suspended over the mercury at an angle of 45°; if it is to be seen at an angle of 45°, it must be suspended horizontally. On being taken out from the mercury-bath, the sheet is plunged into another bath of hypo-sulphite of soda; this solution attacking the parts upon which the light has not been able to act, and respecting the light parts,—being the very inverse of the action of the mercury. It may be supposed, therefore, observed M. Arago, that the light parts of the image are formed by an amalgamation of mercury and silver, and the dark parts by a sulphuret of silver at the expense of the hypo-sulphite of soda. M. Arago observed, that no satisfactory reason has yet been given for this latter part of the process. The sheet is finally washed in distilled water, and the operation is terminated. The drawing, thus obtained, is perfectly insensible to the action of light, but it is liable to injury, just like a crayon or pencil-drawing, and requires to be preserved under a glass. The effect of the whole is miraculous: and as an instance, we may mention that one of the drawings exhibited by M. Daguerre, on Monday, was the view of a room with some rich pieces of carpet in it; the *threads* of the carpet were given with mathematical accuracy, and with a richness of effect that was quite marvellous. . . .

We need hardly say that the most enthusiastic cheers responded from the grave benches even of the Academy, on the termination of M. Arago's descrip-tion, and the President, M. Chevreul,* complimented M. Daguerre in the warmest terms.[13]

Once the secret of how to make a daguerreotype was announced, a fever for photography ran high in Paris. Marc-Antoine Gaudin, a young scientist who had invented a pneumatic pump, was in the audience. Years later he told how eager he and his friends were to try making daguerreotypes themselves. He rushed

---

*Michel-Eugène Chevreul (1786-1889), French chemist; later director of the Gobelins tapestry works; famous for his theories of color vision.

20

out to buy iodine right after the meeting, and was disappointed that the sun was already setting and that he would have to put off the trial until the next morning. "As soon as day broke," he recollected, "my camera was ready. It consisted of an ordinary lens of three-inches focal length, fixed in a cardboard box. After having iodized the plate while holding it in my hand, I put it in my box which I pointed out of my window, and bravely waited out the fifteen minutes that the exposure required; then I treated my plate, inclined at the normal 45° angle, with mercury, heating the glue pot which contained it with a candle. The mystery was done at once: I had a Prussian blue sky, houses black as ink, but the window frame was perfect! . . ."[14] Gaudin could hardly wait to show his picture to his friends; they were all getting the same kind of result; nobody had anything to compare with the poorest of Daguerre's pictures.

The process was not as easy as it looked. At the request of the government and in response to popular demand, the inventor gave a series of public demonstrations, and an instruction manual was published.

The book, titled *Historique et description des procédés du Daguerréotype et du Diorama,* first appeared in Paris under the imprint of Alphonse Giroux et Cie. on August 21, 1839. It was a paper-covered pamphlet of seventy-nine pages, containing lucid instructions and detailed scale drawings of the needed apparatus. Almost at once, English, German, Italian, Spanish, and Swedish translations were published; by the end of the year it had appeared in more than thirty variant editions.[15]

From this booklet Morse, like others all over the Western world, learned Daguerre's technique. "The first brochure which was opened in America at the bookseller's containing your exposé of your process, I possess," he wrote Daguerre.[16]

2. *First Trials*

IN HIS LETTER to Daguerre, Morse did not say when he received the published instructions and began to attempt to duplicate the pictures which had so impressed him in Paris. The *American Journal of Science and Arts* in its October, 1839, issue stated that Daguerre's book had arrived on September 20 via the crack steamer *British Queen,* seventeen days out of Liverpool. By the twenty-eighth, Morse exhibited a view of the Unitarian church, taken from the third story of New York University. The time of exposure, he recollected, was fifteen minutes.

This daguerreotype, which apparently no longer exists, was hailed by the *Journal of Commerce* as "the first fruits of Daguerre's invention, as put in practice in this country."[1] On reading this report, Morse at once wrote to the editor: "If there is any merit in first producing these results in this country, that merit I believe belongs to Mr. D. W. Seager of this city, who has for several days had some results at Mr. Chilton's* on Broadway. The specimen I showed you was my first result."[2]

Of D. W. Seager we know but little. On November 7, 1839, he presented to the American Institute "a specimen of the Daguerreotype which I produced in the month of September and exhibited at your last fair."[3] In the letter of transmittal which we have quoted, now in the George Eastman House, he claimed that his first result was on September 16—four days before the arrival of the *British Queen.* How he learned to make daguerreotypes is something of a mystery. There is a picturesque story, related by the brother of George W. Prosch, who built Morse's camera and later became a daguerreotypist, that Seager was in England when the news of Daguerre's secret technique was made public. Just as the ship in which Seager was sailing to America was leaving the dock in London, a friend threw him a copy of Daguerre's manual, fresh from the press. Was it this choice of a *bon voyage* gift which brought the daguerreotype to America?

*James R. Chilton, 263 Broadway, New York; chemist and, later, daguerreotypist.

No work by Seager exists. On October 5 he lectured on the process at the Stuyvesant Institute; the announcement stated that "the following gentlemen have given permission to be referred to as being familiar with the process and its extraordinary results: President Duer,* Columbia College; Professor Morse; James R. Chilton, Esq.; Jno. L. Stephens, Esq.†"[4] As the meeting was scheduled for 7:30 P.M., it is most unlikely that Seager was able to demonstrate the process. Full sunshine was practically a necessity, so weak in light sensitivity were plates made from Daguerre's specifications.

America's first photographer disappeared from the scene almost as soon as he arrived. He was in Mexico in 1867, where for more than ten years he had been economic adviser to the government; apparently he had long given up his photographic interests.[5]

Morse, who was one of America's most skilled and respected portrait painters, almost immediately began to attempt what Daguerre had told him was impossible: the taking of portraits by the daguerreotype process. He recollected that toward the end of September or early in October he succeeded in making "full length portraits of my daughter, single, and also in groups with some of her young friends. They were taken out-of-doors, on the roof of a building, in the full sun-light, and with the eyes closed. The time was from ten to twenty minutes."[6] The only trace of these experiments is a crude wood-engraving of a double portrait, printed by America's first photographic historian, Marcus A. Root, in his *The Camera and the Pencil.* The draftsman who copied the daguerreotype drew the eyes open.

At about the same time Morse's friend, John W. Draper, began identical experiments. As a scientist he had long been interested in the chemistry of light, and had used light-sensitive materials in the study of the solar spectrum. When William Henry Fox Talbot's "photogenic drawing" process was published in the spring of 1839, Draper repeated the Englishman's experiments, and discovered that by using lenses of large aperture and short focal length, exposures could be reduced. When Daguerre's instructions arrived, he applied this principle. "I

*William Alexander Duer (1780-1858): judge, N. Y. Supreme Court; President of Columbia College.

†John Lloyd Stephens (1805-52): traveler and author; took daguerreotypes in Yucatán in 1841 (see pp. 73-75.)

resorted to a lens of five inches diameter and seven inches focus [i.e., $f/1.4$], which I still have. I dusted the sitter's face with flour and pushed the back of the camera to the violet focus."[7]

Draper sent a sample of his portraiture to the English scientist, Sir John F. W. Herschel, on July 28, 1840; it was a portrait of his sister, taken at an exposure of 65 seconds. The daguerreotype was in existence until 1933, when the image was washed away in an attempt to clean it. It has been widely reproduced as the world's first portrait photograph. Draper made no such claim. In his letter to Herschel he simply stated that it was "no better in point of execution than those ordinarily obtained."[8]

He did, however, claim that he was the first to take a portrait by Daguerre's technique. "I believe I was the first person here who succeeded in obtaining portraits from the life," he wrote Herschel; and he later stated: "How any doubt can now be entertained as to who took the first sun-portrait, passes my comprehension."[9]

Morse was more modest. In 1849 he wrote: "If mine were the first, other experimenters soon made better results, and if there are any who dispute that I was the first, I shall have no argument with them; for I was not so anxious to be the *first* to produce the result, as to produce it in any way. I esteem it but the natural carrying out of the wonderful discovery, and that the credit was after all due to Daguerre. I lay no claim to any improvements."[10]

Others in America were taking daguerreotypes in these first weeks of enthusiasm. Joseph Saxton of the United States Mint in Philadelphia threw together a magnifying glass and a "seegar" box to make a camera and with other home-made equipment somehow succeeded in taking a recognizable picture of the Central High School. The daguerreotype, which Saxton said he took on October 16, 1839, and which was described in the *United States Gazette* on October 24, is now in the collection of the Pennsylvania Historical Society in Philadelphia. It is the only existing American daguerreotype that can be surely documented as having been taken in 1839. Its small size (1¾ by 2⅜ inches), its lack of detail, and its short tonal scale—the image is hardly more than a silhouette—are in marked contrast to Daguerre's results. If it is typical of what was being produced elsewhere in the country, Americans had much to learn.

Saxton had his plates made by Robert Cornelius, a lamp maker and metalworker skilled in plating. Almost at once Cornelius himself became interested in the daguerreotype, learned the process, and added his claim of priority in portraiture to those of Morse and Draper. He took, he said, a self-portrait in his backyard. "I was alone and ran in front of the camera," he told Julius F. Sachse, historian and editor of the *American Journal of Photography*, some thirty years later.[11] The portrait, now in the private collection of Mrs. Joseph Carson, is obviously an early experiment, but its 1839 production date cannot be documented. Even Sachse, the most ardent champion of Cornelius, had to admit that "unfortunately the exact date of this successful experiment at portraiture has not come down to us, nor is Mr. Cornelius able to recall it to a certainty."[12] The records of the American Philosophical Society state that Cornelius showed a daguerreotype at the December 6, 1839, meeting, but the subject is not specified. Had it been a portrait, the fact would surely have been noted.

In the winter or spring of 1840 Cornelius established the first portrait gallery in Philadelphia; it was patterned on the New York studio of John Johnson and Alexander S. Wolcott which the New York *Sun,* in its issue of March 4, 1840, called "the first daguerreotype gallery for portraits."

John Johnson recollected that he brought Alexander Simon Wolcott of New York a description of Daguerre's discovery on October 6, 1839, and that they at once made a camera and took a "profile miniature" on that very day.[13] As proof, he offered the entry in his daybook of the purchase of chemicals. The camera was miniature; 4 by 2 by 2 inches. Instead of a lens they used a concave mirror. The light-sensitive silvered plate was placed in front of the mirror, in the focus of the rays it reflected. Johnson said he sat in a beam of sunlight for five minutes; the result was "a profile miniature on a plate not quite ⅜ in. square."[14]

Wolcott and Johnson were encouraged and by the end of the year built a larger camera of the same design with the assistance of Henry Fitz, Jr., a telescope maker who had just returned from a trip to England in November. Experiments were tried on 2-by-2½-inch plates "with tolerable success." One of these experiments is believed to be the self-portrait of Fitz with eyes closed, now in the Smithsonian Institution, Washington (Plate 2). Wolcott patented this camera on May 8, 1840,[15] just after he and Johnson moved their gallery in New York from 52 First Street to the Granite Building on the corner of Broadway and Chambers Street.

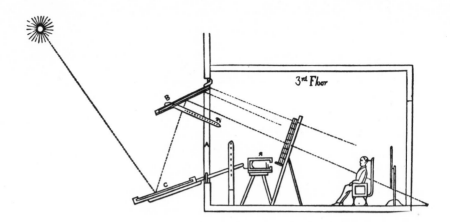

Their studio was an unusual sight. Hanging out of an upper-story window, right over the street, were two huge mirrors. The lower mirror reflected the sun's rays upwards to the surface of the second mirror which, in turn, bounced the sunbeam directly onto the face of the sitter, who was seated in a posing chair, his head held immobile by an iron clamp. To soften somewhat this harsh light, Wolcott and Johnson intercepted the sunbeam with a rack of glass bottles filled with a blue solution of copper sulphate.

Wolcott's camera was introduced to England by Johnson's father, and was used by Richard Beard in his portrait studio in London.

> *London Morning Chronicle, Sept. 12, 1840.* By this new process the time required for a person to sit for his portrait is reduced so that under the different circumstances of the intensity of light, &c., a likeness may be taken in from one to four minutes. At the same time the pain of sitting exposed to the direct rays of the sun is greatly diminished as the light is modified, by being transmitted through coloured glass, so that any person even with the weakest sight can bear it without any inconvenience.

Despite the claims of Morse, Draper, Wolcott, and Johnson, Americans were not the first to make portraits by photography. Before details of the technique had crossed the Atlantic, portraits were already being taken in France. They were probably no better—nor worse—than the corpse-like images Morse produced of his daughter and her friends, with whitened face and closed eyes, or the tiny miniatures of Wolcott and Johnson which would not cover a thumbnail. In the Parisian satirical magazine *Charivari* for August 30, 1839, we learn how it was done. We translate: "You want to make a portrait of your wife. You fit her head in a fixed iron collar to give the required immobility, thus holding the world still for the time being. You point the camera lens at her face; but, alas, you make a mistake of a fraction of an inch [in focusing], and, when you take out the portrait it doesn't represent your wife—it's her parrot, her watering pot—or worse."

An edition of Daguerre's manual published by Susse Frères and Lerebours before November, 1839, gave more serious advice; "To make a portrait, you must have access to bright light, and this is even more important with subjects whose complexion is vivid, for red is, so to speak, the equivalent of black. Success will only come in exposing the sitter to the sun, in the open air, with reflectors of white cloth. You can, as Arago has shown, put in front of the sitter a large pane of blue glass; this will eliminate the fatigue which causes the inevitable closing of the eyes. . . ."

François Gouraud, a pupil of Daguerre's who was visiting America, wrote that "within fifteen days after the publication of the process of M. Daguerre in Paris, people in every quarter were making portraits. At first they were all made with *the eyes shut*. M. Susse, of the Place de la Bourse, was one of the first amateurs who succeeded in making them in the most satisfactory manner."[16]

Gouraud arrived on the S.S. *British Queen* on November 23, 1839. He came to America as the agent of Alphonse Giroux & Cie., the Paris firm which sold not only Daguerre's manual but also the only daguerreotype apparatus personally endorsed by him. The visitor's mission was to establish a central overseas agency for the sale of cameras and apparatus so that "the artists and amateurs of the two Americas should enjoy the same advantages that are offered to France by the new discovery of Mr. Daguerre, and to guard them from the frauds of a reckless competition prejudicial to the process."[17]

Although English translations of Daguerre's manual were readily available in America,[18] written instructions, however lucid and specific, were no substitute for personal demonstrations. This François Gouraud supplied. He also showed examples of Daguerre's work in New York, Boston, and Providence which so excelled anything that had been done in America that Morse and other pioneers became his eager pupils.

3. *Daguerre's Agent*

MONSIEUR Gouraud lost no time. Within a week after landing he called at the office of the newspaper which had published Morse's first account of Daguerre's discovery.

New York Observer, November 30, 1839. THE DAGUERREOTYPE.

We have been favored with the sight of a large number of pictures from a collection of the exquisitely beautiful results of this wonderful discovery, just arrived from Paris; several of them *taken by Daguerre himself.* The collection is in the hands of M. Gourraud [sic], a gentleman of taste, who arrived on Saturday in the British Queen. . . . M. Gourraud is on his way to the Havana for the purpose of transmitting to Paris, photographic views of the scenery of that part of the world.

Our readers may suppose that, after reading the highly wrought descriptions of the new art, which we have transferred to our paper from European points, we were prepared to form something like an adequate conception of its power; but we can only say as the Queen of Sheba said after examining the exhibition of the glory of Solomon, "The half was not told us." We can find no language to express the charm of these pictures, painted by no mortal hand. . . . We are told that the shop-windows in Paris, in which the photographic pictures are exhibited, are so beset by the crowd that the streets are impassable in their vicinity. . . . We hope M. Gourraud will stay so long among us as to give us a few practical lectures, and also to furnish an opportunity for our citizens to see this collection of Nature's own paintings.

The editor's hope was fulfilled when Gouraud sent prominent New Yorkers a lithographed invitation to a private viewing of the collection on December 4 at the Hotel Francois, 57 Broadway.

He exhibited some thirty pictures. From eyewitness accounts, the daguerreotypes must have been similar to those Daguerre showed in Paris during the previous winter and spring—brilliant, highly detailed images on silvered copper plates 6½ by 8½ inches in size. To the French subjects, Gouraud added a few

28

taken by himself in New York. Philip Hone, onetime mayor of New York City, wrote in his diary that the exhibition consisted of "views in Paris, and an exquisite collection of objects of still life. . . . Every object, however minute, is a perfect transcript of the thing itself; the hair of the human head, the gravel on the roadside, the texture of a silk curtain, or the shadow of the smaller leaf reflected upon the wall, are all imprinted as carefully as nature or art has created them in the objects transferred; and those things which are invisible to the naked eye are rendered apparent by the help of a magnifying glass."[1]

On December 20 Gouraud moved the collection uptown to the more accessible Granite Building on the corner of Chambers Street and Broadway. He reduced the admission fee from $1.00 to 50 cents, and gave lessons. Samuel F. B. Morse became an eager student, hoping that from the personal instruction of Daguerre's pupil he would master details of manipulation which were unclear in the inventor's instruction manual. On January 14, 1840, he noted: "Nothing particular in the polishing, except that the acidizing process is more essential than I had supposed, and requires greater delicacy in the manipulation."[2]

His technique improved so that the *Evening Post,* on February 18, praised one of his daguerreotypes as "remarkable for its strength and distinctness, quite as much so as the best of those executed by Daguerre himself, which has been brought to this country." Morse took this daguerreotype with a camera he built himself. On the twenty-first there appeared this letter in *The Evening Star:*

> Mr. Editor—I am glad to learn, from a respectable journal of this city, that Professor Morse has executed a specimen of photogenique drawing as distinct as it could be done by Mr. Daguerre himself, and that he has, from Mr. Daguerre's work, constructed the instrument with great nicety himself. Having endeavored, during two months, to give to Mr. Morse all the instructions in my power, I am naturally pleased to hear of his success, as I should of the success of all the numerous amateurs who have attended my private or public instructions of the process of Daguerreotype.
>
> I remain, sir, your obedient servant,
>
> FRANÇOIS GOURAUD
> Pupil of Mr. Daguerre

Morse replied that before Gouraud had arrived in the United States, he had already made daguerreotypes from the instructions in Daguerre's book. He had eagerly taken the opportunity of studying with Gouraud, but the two months' instruction led to nothing. "He revealed nothing *new* to me. . . . All the instruction professed to be imparted by M. Gouraud, I have felt it necessary to forget."[3] A few days later Morse publicly accused Gouraud of degrading the name of Daguerre by selling toilet articles at his exhibition of daguerreotypes.

In the midst of this exchange of letters, Gouraud left New York for Boston; he apparently had given up his project of going to Cuba. On March 6, 1840, he held a private opening of his collection of daguerreotypes at the Tremont House; on the eleventh the public was invited to view them at Horticultural Hall, and on the twenty-fourth he began a series of four lectures at the Masonic Temple.

> *Boston Daily Evening Transcript, March 28, 1840.* The explanation of the process of producing the Daguerreotype pictures, gave the utmost possible satisfaction to an audience of five hundred ladies and gentlemen, the number of whom would have been twice or thrice increased if the lecturer had not judiciously limited the issue of tickets, to prevent confusion and give every auditor a full opportunity to hear and see. During his lecture Mr. Gouraud prepared a plate, describing the mode of operation as he proceeded, which, when finished, was placed in the camera obscura, and the whole apparatus being then set on a window of the hall commanding a view of Park Street from the Church to Beacon Street, including a portion of the Common—a most beautiful and perfect picture was produced in *ten minutes,* to the delight and astonishment of the spectators.

Edward Everett Hale, who was to become famous as the author of "The Man Without a Country," was one of Gouraud's pupils. He tried to make a portrait on April 15, with the help of his cousin, Frank Durivage. "Took a view of Mr. Mott's Church," he wrote in his journal. "I stood in the picture myself, getting Frank to open and close the camera at the right time. But this operation was rather a failure, for having stood mostly against a strong dark shade, nothing could be seen but my white shirt bosom and face and my two legs, which came against a light in the picture. It seemed really more wonderful than ever to think that the picture took itself so entirely that I, who was the artist if any one was, was represented (and correctly) in the drawing."[4]

On the very day that young Hale was making this experiment, Gouraud sold a complete apparatus to another student, a Boston dentist named Samuel Bemis. The outfit, neatly packed in the original wooden case in which it was delivered, is now in the George Eastman House, Rochester—the camera, its brass-mounted lens and ground-glass screen; the iodizing box with its wooden cup for the particles of iodine; the slotted box to hold the plates; the silvered copper plates themselves, 6½ by 8½ inches in size; the mercury bath, a tapered box on four legs with an iron bottom, a thermometer on its side, curtained window, and inside a sloping rest for the plate; the alcohol lamp with which to heat the mercury and dry the plate after washing.

Dr. Bemis paid Gouraud $51 for the apparatus, $2.00 apiece for twelve plates, and $1.00 for freight; the receipted bill is preserved with the camera. Four days after he had bought the equipment he made a daguerreotype of King's Chapel Burying Ground (Plate 3). On the back of the homemade frame is the handwritten note:

> *Boston, April 19 1840. –S. A. Bemis's first daguerreotype experiment.—Iodizing process 25 mts. (apparatus new), camera process 40 mts.—Wind N.W., sky clear, air dry and very cold for the season.—Lens Meniscus Daguerr's apparatus.—Time 4.50 to 5.30 p.m.; N. Y. plate, ordinary.*

The state of the weather was noted because so little was known about the factors which influence exposure. Later on, daguerreotypists learned that their plates were more sensitive in dry weather than in damp, and that just before a thunderstorm broke, their exposures were the shortest.

The picture which Dr. Bemis made on that April day in 1840 is an excellent record. Like all early daguerreotypes, it is a mirror image: the buildings are laterally reversed. The doctor photographed with an eye for detail, and yet the picture hangs together; miraculously we behold the very atmosphere of Boston over a hundred and twenty years ago.

Only a dozen more daguerreotypes by Dr. Bemis are known to exist. They are all in the George Eastman House collection. Most of them are other views of King's Chapel and the Burying Ground, taken probably in the winter of 1840-41, for changes are discernible in the buildings, and a heavy snow has fallen. One is most curious: it is on silver paper. Presumably it is an experiment, for the image is so faint that it is barely visible.

While in Boston, Gouraud published, under the title *Description of the Daguerreotype Process,* a condensation of Daguerre's manual.[5] In it he reprinted from the *Boston Daily Patriot and Advertiser* of March 26, 1840, an account of how to take portraits by the daguerreotype. Before he had left Paris—which must have been before November 1, 1839, when the *British Queen* sailed from Liverpool—Abel Rendu, "a young man in the employment of the Minister of Public Instruction," had shown him portraits taken on daguerreotype plates with a simple, uncorrected meniscus lens. Rendu was dissatisfied with the results, for they lacked "the positively mathematical perfection which M. Daguerre required." Gouraud stated that he did not bring any examples with him from Paris, thinking that he would take portraits in America. It is not known if he did so; no examples of his work in this field have come to light. Yet Philip Hone, on seeing the collection which Gouraud exhibited in New York, praised the exquisite detail of the daguerreotypes by pointing out that "the hair of the human head" could be distinguished in them. And the painter George Fuller wrote to his father from Boston, on April 11, 1840, that he proposed to purchase a camera from Gouraud and take lessons from him. "But two minutes' time is required to leave a complete impression of a man's countenance, perfect as nature can make it," Fuller wrote, and concluded, "We can afford to take a perfect likeness for $7.00; the plate and glass will cost $2.00, leaving $5.00. With custom enough fifty could be taken in one day."[6]

Abel Rendu himself came to America, sent by Alphonse Giroux to find out why Gouraud did not pay his bills. Gouraud was in financial distress. His New York landlord sued him for rent, and it is said that his personal effects were seized in April. In May we find Gouraud in Providence, Rhode Island, showing a collection at Union Hall. In 1842 he was in Buffalo: Walker's *Buffalo City Directory* of that year listed "Gonraud, Francois, daguerreotype." The typesetter must have misread *u* as *n,* for Samuel F. B. Morse met the Frenchman at Niagara Falls; all was forgiven, and Gouraud served as Morse's guide.

From Buffalo, Gouraud toured the country, lecturing to audiences of thousands on a bewildering yet spectacular memory system. He wrote a manual on the subject and a dictionary. He died before his book on shorthand, *Practical Cosmophonography,* appeared in 1850. He called himself François Fauvel-Gouraud then, and had long since abandoned the daguerreotype. What he thought of it he summed up in a terse sentence in his *Phreno-Mnemotechny:* "The Daguerreotype will hardly . . . afford subsistence for satisfying a tame hare."

32

4. *The Shaping of an Industry*

WHEN Gouraud reached his discouraging conclusion in 1845, daguerreotypes were so popular in America that the word was assimilated, not without difficulty, into everyday language. If the French had difficulty spelling it (the magazine *L'Artiste* wrote "Daguérotype," and the newspaper *Gazette de France*, "Daguerr-otype"), Americans could be excused, though Edgar Allan Poe sternly pointed out "this word is properly spelt Daguerréotype, and pronounced as if written Dagairraioteep. The inventor's name is Daguerre, but the French usage requires an accent on the second e, in the formation of the compound term."[1] But the four-syllable pronunciation was already American usage.

> *New York Observer, December 7, 1839*. THE DAGUERREOTYPE. We have been asked how this novel name is pronounced. Some truly mangle it most sadly. *Dog-gery-type*, says one,—*Dag-gery-type*, says another,—*Daygwerryotype* says a third. We have endeavored to procure the right pronunciation.
> *Daguerre* is the name of the distinguished discoverer of this wonderful art. His name has been given to this process by the savants of Paris. His name, spelt in our language, will be *Dargair;* the accent on the last syllable. If to this be added the latter part of the word, *o-type*, the word is easily pronounced, and might be spelt to conform to the sounds of our language *Dar-ger-row-type*, mak-ing *g* hard before *e*, and putting the accent on the second syllable.—*J. of Com.*

Although an adjective, *daguerréotypical*, was made of the word by William Makepeace Thackeray, in common usage the inventor's name alone was used to form the adjective, which was spelled "Daguerreian," "Daguerrean," "Daguerrian," and "Daguerran." This adjective also served as a noun, synonym-ous with "daguerreotypist" or "daguerreotyper." The word "daguerreotype" was used frequently outside of its technical meaning; the Boston publication *The Daguerreotype: A Magazine of Foreign Literature and Science* was not a professional journal about photography. Its publisher set forth in a prospectus that the mag-azine was intended "to supply . . . a series of striking pictures of the constantly-varying aspect of public affairs . . . and is, therefore, not inaptly, called the Daguerreotype."

Within a decade, daguerreotyping was recognized as an industry. The Commonwealth of Massachusetts officially reported in 1855 that 403,626 daguerreotypes had been taken in the state during the past twelve months, the work of 134 "Daguerreotype Artists" and 260 hands.[2] In 1860, at the end of the daguerreotype era, the United States Census reported 3,154 photographers. Every major city and town had at least one gallery—as the studios were universally called— and itinerant daguerreotypists traveled to remote backwoods and frontier areas in their horse-drawn "saloons," or floated down the rivers in houseboats. From Louisville, Kentucky, came the report in 1855: "There is not a place of one hundred inhabitants in any of the Southern or Western states that have not been visited by from one to any number of itinerants."[3]

Very little is known about most of these pioneer photographers. From city directories we can produce hundreds of names, for the classification "Daguerreotype Miniatures," or "Daguerreian Artists" began to appear in the 1840's, just above "Dentists," which they sometimes outnumbered. From these records we can gain knowledge of the periods of activity and the wanderings of a host of daguerreotypists. Occasionally an obituary or a newspaper article enables us to visualize a personality. But, with rare exceptions, we can seldom study a sufficient number of daguerreotypes known to be made by one person to attempt to distinguish individual style. Daguerreotypes were unique; nothing, neither negative nor proof, was left behind when the picture had been delivered; and although museums were suggested, no action was taken. Except for the thousands of extra daguerreotypes kept by Albert Sands Southworth and Josiah Johnson Hawes in their Boston gallery, no contemporary collections exist. Such extraordinary collections of daguerreotypes as the "National Portrait Gallery" of Mathew B. Brady, who was to win fame for his photographic documentation of the Civil War, or the three hundred daguerreotypes of California mining operations taken by Robert H. Vance are lost.

Daguerreotyping had its Vasaris in the persons of two devoted journalists, Samuel Dwight Humphrey and Henry Hunt Snelling, who independently and in competition founded the world's first photographic magazines. Humphrey was a daguerreotypist from Canandaigua, New York, who had moved to New York

City. On November 15, 1850, he began publication of *The Daguerreian Journal.* When he changed the title two years later to *Humphrey's Journal Devoted to the Daguerrean and Photogenic Arts* he claimed a circulation of two thousand. Snelling already had publishing experience when he went to work for Edward and Henry Tiebout Anthony in the New York stockhouse of photographic goods; while still working there he began publishing, in January, 1851, his *Photographic Art-Journal.* Three years later he changed the title to *Photographic and Fine Art Journal.* Both magazines were similar. They contained original contributions, reprints from English textbooks, translations from the French, and lively news from "the fraternity." If we lack exact biographical data about the men who established photography in America as a profession, we can vividly reconstruct their problems, their techniques, and their professional careers from the pages of these journals. We shall allow Humphrey and Snelling to speak frequently and freely in our account of daguerreotyping in America.

Yankee ingenuity transformed Daguerre's technique to a perfection undreamed of in Europe, and daguerreotypists in France and England boasted in advertisements that they worked "The American Process." At the Great Exhibition in the London Crystal Palace in 1851, Americans took three of the five medals in daguerreotyping. Editorials in the London and Paris press praised the American contributions with enthusiasm matched only by their praise for the yacht *America* and the exceedingly light construction of our racing sulkies. We have been able to reconstruct the American Process in detail, thanks again to Humphrey and Snelling, who published instruction manuals as well as their periodicals. This technical account forms Chapter 14 of this book.

In brief, the improvements that were worked out in America were largely mechanical. The silvered copper plates were re-silvered or "galvanised" by electrotyping. They were polished or "buffed" with more efficient tools, often power driven: twenty patents were issued for devices to hold the plate during this operation. The boxes used to sensitize or "coat" the plates first with iodine fumes and then with fumes of chlorine and bromine, separately or in combination, were functionally designed. Cameras became more compact: the first application of the accordion-like bellows to make the camera box collapsible was due to the ingenuity of William Lewis and William Henry Lewis of Daguerreville, near Poughkeepsie, New York, in 1851. Development over hot mercury, or "mercurial-

35

izing," was done in cast-iron pots. Apparatus was standardized, and mass-produced in factories.

Plate sizes were standardized.

4/4 or whole plate	6½ by 8½ inches
1/2 or half plate	4¼ by 5½ inches
1/4 or quarter plate	3¼ by 4¼ inches
1/6 or sixth plate (medium)	2¾ by 3¼ inches
1/9 or ninth plate	2 by 2½ inches

Cases to contain the finished pictures were manufactured in quantity. They were at first made of pressed paper, to imitate leather. The daguerreotype was covered by a brass cut-out mat. On top of this was placed a thick piece of plate glass of identical size. The sandwich was bound together with gummed paper or goldbeater's skin, and often enclosed in a delicate frame of gilded brass called a "preserver." The assembly fitted snugly into the boxlike case. Highly ornate, plastic "Union cases" became popular at the end of the daguerreotype era; their manufacture is the first recorded industrial use of thermoplastic in the world.

Most importantly, by improved sensitizing techniques developed in England, and by the use of imported Viennese and Parisian lenses of relatively large aperture, and consequently of greater light-passing power, exposures were reduced from minutes to seconds: the average portrait sitting lasted from twenty to forty seconds.

To learn to daguerreotype well enough to hang out a shingle took only a little instruction and a modest investment. George Reed, for example, bought a camera in February, 1844, from Anson Clark, a daguerreotypist in West Stockbridge, Massachusetts, and took instruction from him. By March he was in business, and in one month had cleared the sum of sixty dollars.[4]

Hundreds answered advertisements such as appeared in the *New York Herald* in 1852:

> WANTED, fifty young men to learn the art of daguerreotyping. Instruction given in a few days, and a whole set of apparatus furnished for $50. Direct "Broadway Post Office" will meet with immediate attention.

The students came from all walks of life: masons, engravers, grocers, express men, window-shade manufacturers, locksmiths, jewelers, carpenters, writing masters, and railroad men are in the roster of those who, at one time or another, were professional cameramen. Many of them were jacks-of-all-trades; one of them, Frank Gage, wrote in 1858: "Today you will find the Yankee taking daguerreotypes; tomorrow he has turned painter; the third day he is tending grocery, dealing out candy to the babies for one cent a stick."[5]

Not all were serious; the majority quickly dropped daguerreotyping as a profession. The Boston directories for the years between 1840 and 1861 listed 180 names under the heading "Daguerreotype Miniatures." Of these only seven stayed in business for ten years or more, and seventy-seven are listed for one year only. Too many saw in daguerreotyping a quick road to riches. John H. Fitz-gibbon of St. Louis, who spent a lifetime in photography, echoed the concern of the handful of men who were dedicated to the art of Daguerre in *The Western Journal* for 1851:

> Many young men, suddenly captivated with a love for the Fine Arts, take it into their heads that they are destined to make a figure, or *figures* in the world, consequently their genius must no longer be hidden under a bushel, but expand its wings in a higher intellectual atmospheric region. Or, what is still more likely, they are lured into this pursuit by a prospect of an *easy* and rapid accumulation of money. Instantly they repair to an itinerant *professor* and for *ten, twenty* or *thirty dollars* are regularly manufactured in the short space of from three to six days into full-bred professors of the photographic art. Is it then to be wondered at that we find so many awful, ghost-like looking shadows poured out upon the world by a host of ignorant pretenders? Not at all![6]

The profession was divided into three classes, Snelling said: "Those who deservedly stand pre-eminent in the art; those who are not so successful in its practical details, but who aim at a higher standard; and those who have taken it up merely for the sake of a precarious and easy livelihood."[7] He was writing in 1853, but the schism had existed ever since daguerreotyping swept through the country.

Boston, Philadelphia, and New York were from the outset the centers of the daguerreotyping industry. In these cities the finest daguerreotypes the world has known were produced, in galleries where new techniques were constantly being developed, which their students spread throughout the country. In these cities, too, the cheapening of the process and the lowering of standards first began, which led to the replacement of the daguerreotype by the negative-positive processes on which present-day techniques are founded.

37

5. *Boston Pioneers*

Two galleries opened in Boston in 1841, the United States Photographic Institute of John Plumbe, Jr., and the Artists Daguerreotype Rooms of Albert Sands Southworth and Co. The careers of their proprietors and the fortunes of their enterprises are in sharp contast, and form a pattern which was to be followed elsewhere. Plumbe took up daguerreotyping to make money. As soon as he could he hired others to do the work, and established a chain of galleries in various cities. His name, stamped on the products of these galleries, was a trademark rather than a signature. His prices were low. His venture was short-lived. Southworth and his partners looked upon daguerreotyping as an art. They boasted that they did not employ cameramen, but personally posed their sitters. Their prices were high, and they refused to lower them in the face of competition. The studio was active throughout the entire daguerreotype era, and one of the partners, Josiah Johnson Hawes, continued in business at the same location for the rest of the century.

John Plumbe, Jr., was a railroad man. Born in Wales in 1809, at twenty-three he was superintendent of the railroad between Richmond, Virginia, and Roanoke, North Carolina. He was one of the first to dream the great American dream of a railroad linking the Atlantic and the Pacific. In 1838 Congress gave him $2,000 to survey the route from Milwaukee to Sinipee, Wisconsin. When the money was gone he was back in Washington where, Plumbe later recollected in the one and only issue of his magazine, *The Plumbeian,* "we continued to press the matter upon Congress—until, after having devoted nearly all our time, for upwards of three years, upon the line—exhausting all our means (pecuniarily)—we, at last, after being laughed at as a madman, were obliged to resort to taking Daguerreotype likenesses, in order to keep up the soul of our undertaking by supporting our body."[1]

By February, 1841, he was in Boston, "Professor of Photography" at Har-

38

rington's Museum. Where, or from whom, he learned to daguerreotype is not known. Within months he moved to a hall over the Whig Reading Room where he opened the United States Photographic Institute. He was quick to take advantage of each new technical development. He met Daniel Davis, Jr., who was to write the first book on electricity in America, and who was already experimenting with Daguerre's technique along with his brothers Ari and Asahel. Ari demonstrated the process at the Lowell Institute in February; in June he advertised cameras for sale. One of his employees, Elias Howe (who later invented the sewing machine), cut the metal mats.

Despite the official ring of its name, the United States Photographic Institute was a private enterprise. Plumbe took portraits, sold apparatus and materials, and gave instruction. His portraits were so popular that he had to keep a register of sittings, and require appointments. There is no trace of this early work, but it greatly impressed the public, to judge from the press notices which the Professor reprinted in a circular headed DAILY MAIL—EXTRA and datelined United States Photographic Institute, Boston, September, 1841. The *Bay State Democrat* wrote that Plumbe "takes the very life from a man, and transfers it to his silver plate. We saw one of KRANTZ the other day, taken by the Professor's Daguerreotype, so faithfully that he has not looked well since."

At the Institute Plumbe also sold apparatus and gave instruction. He forthrightly appealed to the pocketbook:

> The price of a Daguerreotype miniature, of medium size, including the morocco case, in this city, is five dollars; and I supply my pupils with a similar *plate and case* for one dollar (when a considerable quantity is wanted); thus leaving *four* dollars to pay for the *trouble* of taking a likeness, less the cost of the other articles used, which would be so little, as to render it difficult to compute the amount upon a single picture. . . . No one can possibly fail to acquire knowledge of the art, whose perseverance will extend to a few hours' application, every day for a month; and there is no reason why the very *first* trial may not result in the production of a good picture.[2]

One of Plumbe's cameras, now in the George Eastman House, is a crudely built reduced model of Daguerre's camera, with removable ground glass to which a mirror is hinged, so that the image can be seen by looking down on the camera. To measure the extension of the telescoping boxes, a metal scale is affixed to the top of the inner box. The units, which range from 90 to 200, are purely arbitrary, for the scale was intended for a thermometer. It bears the first seven letters of the name "J. S. F. Huddleston," an instrument maker. He may well have built the camera. He was himself a daguerreotypist; three of his pictures were exhibited at the Massachusetts Charitable Mechanic Association in 1841.

The cases which Plumbe sold were made by William Shew who, with his brothers Myron, Jacob, and Trueman, learned daguerreotyping from Samuel F. B. Morse; built the first gallery in Ogdensburg, New York; worked for a while in Rochester and Geneva, New York; and formed the L. P. Hayden Company in New York for the manufacture and sale of daguerreotype material.

Plumbe rapidly expanded his operations. He bought from Daniel Davis his patent for a way to color daguerreotypes by electroplating selected areas of the silver surface with various metals, and peddled it to daguerreotypists in New England. Lucius H. Cathan wrote Southworth from Townshend, Vermont: "Mr. Plumbe has filled the country people's heads full, with the idea of his 'colored photography,' as I have seen but few of them I could discover nothing so 'wonderful' or 'astonishing' in those, I should be pleased to have your view upon the subject."[3] Plumbe sent Trueman Shew to superintend a gallery in Philadelphia in 1842. He was in New York in 1843. A New Yorker wrote Southworth in that year, "Mr. Plumbe is here making quite a stir in the Dag^e line. Pictures are taken here for $1.00 and case included."[4] Jacob Shew went to Baltimore to open a Plumbe gallery there. In 1845 Plumbe boasted of fourteen galleries in New York; Boston; Saratoga Springs; Louisville, Kentucky; Petersburg, Virginia; Alexandria, D. C. (now Virginia); Philadelphia; Baltimore; Harrodsburgh Springs, Kentucky; Newport, Rhode Island; Dubuque, Iowa; Cincinnati; and St. Louis.

His was the first of many chains of galleries. The product of every branch was stamped "PLUMBE," no matter what photographer had taken the picture. The pattern which was thus established was quickly followed by other daguerreotypists, to the confusion of the historian. With only a few exceptions, the names of those who took specific daguerreotypes remain unknown, lost in the blanket credit given to the proprietors of the galleries which employed them.

Plumbe pioneered in another field. He was the first to collect portraits of celebrities. In 1846 he began publication of *The National Plumbeotype Gallery,* a collection of lithographs based on daguerreotypes—"transferred," he called them, though they are clearly hand drawn. He announced on November 2 a new series:

> The Proprietor of the Plumbe National Daguerrian [sic] Gallery, having discovered a method of transferring beautiful copies of Daguerreotypes to paper —proposes, by this means, to publish a *daily Portrait* of some interesting public character on fine quarto paper, constituting an appropriate ornament to the centre table, &c., &c., commencing January 1st, 1847.[5]

But the empire of John Plumbe was short-lived. He sold his New York gallery to William H. Butler, his head man there, in 1847, and the other galleries soon changed ownership, though the name "Plumbe's Daguerrean Gallery" was retained as late as 1852 in Boston (John P. Nichols, proprietor), and 1850 in Washington (Blanchard P. Paige, proprietor).

In 1849 Plumbe went to California. He had not forgotten his dream of a transcontinental railroad, and on the way overland he made a preliminary survey of a southern route. Back in Washington he met bitter opposition from Asa Whitney, who favored a northern route. In deep discouragement he locked himself in a room in his brother's house in Dubuque, Iowa, on the morning of May 29, 1857, and cut his throat with a razor.[6]

Albert Sands Southworth was born in West Fairlee, Vermont, in 1811. He recollected that he first became interested in daguerreotyping on attending one of Gouraud's demonstrations in Boston.

> His illustrative experiment resulted in his producing a dimmed and foggy plate, instead of the architectural details of buildings and the definite lines and forms of street objects. It happened to be a misty day, attended with both snow and rain. The professor appeared highly elated, and exhibited his picture with great apparent satisfaction that he had it in his power to copy the very mist and smoke of the atmosphere on a stormy day.
>
> Mr. Pennell* had a few months previously graduated at Bowdoin College, in his native town. He had gone to New York for the purpose of prosecuting a professional course of study, and had been led to interest himself in Professor Morse's experiments for the purpose of procuring pecuniary assistance by some employment of his leisure hours. He had been my former school and room mate, and had written me to visit New York and learn respecting the new art. He in-

---

*Joseph Pennell, friend of Southworth, a student and assistant of Samuel F. B. Morse, apparently unrelated to the internationally famous illustrator or the Kansas City photographer of the same name.

vited me also to join him as an associate in business for the purpose of making likenesses. He introduced me to Professor Morse, and from him we received all the information and instruction he was able to give upon the subject. . . . I do not remember that Professor Morse had then made any likenesses. Very clear, distinct views of Brooklyn buildings in the distance and the roofs in the foreground, taken from the top of buildings in Nassau-street, were upon his table. I do remember the coil of telegraph wire, miles in length, wound upon a cylinder, with which he was experimenting. . . .[7]

They formed a partnership, bought a camera and the needed apparatus, and returned to Massachusetts, where they opened a studio in Cabotville (now Chicopee). Southworth wrote his sister Nancy in May, 1840:

I cannot describe all the wonders of this Apparatus. Suffice it to say, that I can now make a *perfect* picture, in one hour's time, that would take a Painter Weeks to draw. The picture is represented *light and shade,* nicer by far than any Steel engraving you ever saw. . . . We have improved it much since we commenced, so much so that we have been high complimented by good judges. We have already sent some specimens to Europe.[8]

In September he wrote of further improvements:

I have succeeded in managing the Daguerreotype so as to make perfect likenesses. . . . In a fair day it requires three minutes sitting and we positively know that we can have an apparatus that will not require more than thirty seconds.[9]

They sent twenty-two miniatures to the 3rd Exhibition of the Massachusetts Charitable Mechanic Association; the judges voted them "the best exhibited."

In April, 1841, the partners moved to Boston, where they opened a gallery under the name "A. S. Southworth & Co." They had need of a helper, and Southworth asked his sister to join them: "I must have some one to wait upon ladies when they call upon us—to frame miniatures, and assist me in the process. There is nothing but what would be termed light work about our establishment." Nancy came; her brother paid $2.62½ per week for her board in July, we learn from the account books of the firm.

The dateline "Boston" first appears in the ledger on June 3, 1841; cash receipts are recorded over the past three months for seventy-three miniatures at prices varying from $2.00 to $5.00 each. Like Plumbe, they sold apparatus; more than a thousand dollars' worth was posted in the books up to the end of October.

42

Each customer paid $25 tuition in addition to the cost of the camera, apparatus, and basic supplies.

They sold imported lenses from France at $30. ("We warrant them superior to anything for that price.") Cameras cost from $50 up. ("We don't get up any cheap setts, $50 is the lowest, does good work, $60 is better finish. . . . We will warrant the Camera satisfactory, the Lenses set in a Brass Tube and the focus adjusted with a set screw. The Camera shall be elegant and the Brass work Bronzed. . . . If you send us $20.00 we will wait three months for the rest. . . .")[10]

They contracted for the manufacture of plates and cases, and a supply of chemicals. In this enterprise they were in direct competition with Plumbe, who seems to have been not wholly satisfactory. Gardner Warren, of Woonsocket, Rhode Island, asked the price of plates: "I lately purchased a lot of Mr. Plumbe . . . which were of very inferior quality."[11] L. C. Smith of Sharon, Vermont, complained: "I have ordered some Bromine on Plumbe and forwarded him $6.00. He sent me Bromide. I sent him five dollars for a few plates, he sent me plates of his own make which are worthless."[12] Southworth & Co. did not escape criticism themselves, however. Henry Moore wrote from Lowell that he could not use a plate "more than five times."[13] B. Foster, of Portland, Maine, complained that the gilding solution he received was not good: rush me more, he asked, "but let it be ever so much better." He was disappointed at the second shipment and asked to have his money returned.[14] They got into an unfortunate tangle with J. W. Talbot, of Petersborough, New Hampshire, who claimed he had been incorrectly billed. "I have paid you nearly $1400.00 for apparatus & stock, and I thought you intended to deal fairly. I hope so still. The difference of $5 is no great affair at any rate but right is right."[15]

In 1844, Pennell left Southworth to teach at a private school in the South; he did not abandon daguerreotyping, however, for he ordered from Charleston plates and cases. He later took a job in the daguerreotype platemaking department of J. M. L. & W. H. Scovill in Waterbury, Connecticut, from whom Southworth purchased material.

His place in the firm was taken by Josiah Johnson Hawes. Like Southworth, Hawes had determined to become a daguerreotypist on seeing one of Gouraud's demonstrations in Boston. He was by trade a carpenter, by avocation a painter: "I practiced painting on ivory, likewise portraits in oil, landscapes, etc., with no

43

teacher but my books. About this time—1840—the excitement of the discovery of the daguerreotype took place; some specimens of it which I saw in Boston changed my course entirely. I gave up painting and commenced daguerreotypy."[16]

Exactly when Hawes joined Southworth is not clear. He was already in business as a professional daguerreotypist, to judge from a trade card reading "Superior Colored Daguerreotypes by Hawes & Somerby" in the Hawes papers; nothing is known of the enterprise, nor of Somerby. Pennell was no longer with Southworth in 1844, and it is probable that the new partnership was formed in that year, when a new studio was built in the building owned by Amos Lawrence at 5½ Tremont Row (later renumbered 19), where Horatio Greenough, William Wetmore Story, and other Boston artists had their studios. For the past three years Southworth had leased space at $25 per quarter. On June 12, 1844, Southworth wrote to his landlord, proposing to lease the upper rooms in the building "provided we can put Skylights in the Roof. . . . Our plan is to take off the flat part of the Roof and put up a Roof-Sash 15 feet by 12, the width of the flat roof. The pitch of the sash to be 5 feet on a base of 6 feet or vary as may be best, over Room 15." The permission was granted. By 1845 the name of the firm was changed to Southworth & Hawes.

The business became a family affair in 1847, when Hawes married Southworth's sister Nancy.

The portraits produced by Southworth & Hawes are remarkable for the bold, simple presentation of the personality of the sitters. They avoided the stereotyped poses so characteristic of their competitors, and often broke convention. Southworth said:

> What is to be done is obliged to be done quickly. The whole character of the sitter is to be read at first sight; the whole likeness, as it shall appear when finished, is to be seen at first, in each and all its details, and in their unity and combinations. Natural and accidental defects are to be separated from natural and possible perfections; these latter to obliterate or hide the former. Nature is not at all to be represented as it is, but as it ought to be, and might possibly have been; and it is required of and should be the aim of the artist-photographer to produce in the likeness the best possible character and finest expression of which that particular face or figure could ever have been capable. But in the result there is to be no departure from truth in the delineation and representation of beauty, and expression, and character.[17]

44

When Chief Justice Lemuel Shaw of the Massachusetts Supreme Court came to the gallery, one of the partners met him at the entrance to the skylight studio or, as it was called, "operating room." A ray of sunlight threw the judge's massive features into strong relief, and they took him where he stood (Plate 95). Daniel Webster was brought to the gallery by William Willard, a portrait painter, who wanted to spare the aging statesman the long sittings that would be required to make a painting of him. What Southworth & Hawes produced will live long after the paintings which Willard made from the daguerreotype. They sought the unusual pose: Lola Montez, the adventuress who fled from Bavaria to America, from king's mistress to entertainer of the forty-niners in San Francisco, with a cigarette between her gloved fingers (Plate 54); Harriet Beecher Stowe, the author of *Uncle Tom's Cabin,* beside a sensitive plant (Plate 100). They pushed the medium to the utmost of its limits to take "available light" exposures in a schoolroom crowded with girls (Plate 57) and in a hospital operating room (Plate 64).

They daguerreotyped Boston from their studio; three daguerreotypes exist of the funeral of Abbott Lawrence in 1855 showing the cortege arriving and leaving the Brattle Square Church. They photographed ships in drydock (Plates 24 and 29), a proud clipper lying at an East Boston wharf (Plate 69), and even a ship at sea. The *Boston Daily Atlas* for May 20, 1854, in describing the cabin decorations of the clipper ship *Champion of the Seas,* noted that "over the transom sofa are three panels, which contain daguerreotype pictures. The first is a representation of the ship 'Great Republic,' under all sail by the wind, the second is the outline of the 'Champion of the Seas' as she now lies broadside on, and other objects in the background, and between the two ships is a picture of Mr. Donald McKay, their builder. These pictures were taken by Messrs. Southworth and Hawes, and are about the best of the kind we have seen."

The daguerreotype of the *Great Republic* we have not been able to locate, but the picture of the *Champion of the Seas* may well be the daguerreotype in the collection of Richard Parker (Plate 69), and the portrait of McKay may be the splendid whole plate in the Metropolitan Museum of Art which we reproduce (Plate 67), or the "mammoth," but blurred, plate in the same collection.

Whole-plate daguerreotypes of Niagara Falls in winter, with fantastic ice sculpture, and a rather dull set of views of Mt. Auburn Cemetery, along with a number of portraits, were made in pairs, with the camera moved slightly be-

45

tween exposures, for viewing in a stereoscope. As early as 1852, Southworth & Hawes showed a stereoscopic daguerreotype of the Greek sculpture "The Laocoön" in the Boston Athenaeum; the June issue of the magazine *To-day* found "the illusion . . . absolute. The spectator sees the copy of this celebrated group in complete relief, standing off from the curtain behind it; and has nothing whatever to confirm his judgement, which informs him that he looks on reflections from a perfectly flat surface. . . . The effect of the Laocoön in this stereoscope is really finer than one often gains in looking at the statue."

They built a "Grand Parlor and Gallery Stereoscope" which resembled a piano and contained a dozen pairs of stereoscopic daguerreotypes which the visitor changed by turning a crank. Admission was 25 cents; a season ticket, 50 cents. One of the pictures which visitors particularly admired was of a bride. This "tableau" inspired a poem in the *Boston Daily Atlas* for April, 1854. The partners reprinted it on the back of the ticket. We quote the last lines:

> A portrait so true no canvas can bear—
> O let it forever stand lingering there;
> Whatever the changes the far years betray,
> Still, still keep her *there,* a bride e'en for aye.

Southworth & Hawes boasted that they never employed operators (as cameramen were then called), but that "one of the partners being a practical artist," sitters could be assured of personal attention. Undoubtedly the reference was to Hawes, who gave up painting for photography in 1840. Certainly daguerreotypes made in the gallery in 1850 and 1851 were his work, for Southworth was in California, where he sought unsuccessfully to make his fortune in the gold fields. He was in poor health when he returned, and appears to have been less active in the firm than his partner. He was probably more mechanically gifted than Hawes, and was undoubtedly responsible for the two patents which were issued jointly to him and to Hawes.[18] A third patent, No. 12,700, dated April 10, 1855, was taken out by Southworth alone. It became infamous. It was titled "Plate-Holder for Cameras." The specifications read:

> The object of my invention is to bring in rapid succession different parts of the same plate or different plates, of whatsoever material prepared, for photographic purposes into the center of the field of the lens for the purpose of either

46

timing them differently, that the most perfect may be selected, or of taking different views of the same object with the least delay possible, or of taking stereoscopic pictures upon the same or different plates with one camera.

The device was not new, and photographers were indignant when they were sued for using similar apparatus not manufactured by Southworth. But time and again the validity of the patent was upheld by the courts. The patent was reissued in 1860; Southworth sold part rights to Simon Wing of Waterville, Maine, who was thus enabled to secure U. S. Patent 30,850 (December 4, 1860) for his greatly improved sliding plate holder, with which he claimed he could make 616 half-inch-square negatives on one plate. Southworth left Hawes in 1861; ten years later, the Supreme Court invalidated the patent. In the last years of his life Southworth was a handwriting expert. He died in 1894.

Hawes continued at the Tremont Row gallery. A manuscript in his hand, on a letterhead of the *Boston Daily and Weekly Globe,* dated 1877, is in the Hawes papers. It is obviously copy, apparently fragmentary, for an advertisement:

THE ANNOUNCEMENT

which Mr. J. J. Hawes of the old firm of Southworth & Hawes makes to the patrons of that old and popular establishment, located at 19 Tremont Row, will be read with interest by thousands of people. Mr. Hawes has all the negatives at this place, some fifty thousand in number, and also ten thousand daguerreotypes of prominent citizens of Boston, ladies and gentlemen, extending back to *1843.*

A newspaper reporter interviewed him in 1886:

Now and then Mr. Hawes takes from its box some striking daguerreotype and makes from it a large photograph, life-size, or nearly so. The sad-eyed Webster, looking tired and baffled, and with stern lips, is one of his; and he has just finished one of Webster far more impressive; a front face, dark and strong, and far from saintly, but full of intellect and will; no light in the deep-set eyes, no sweetness in the firmly shut mouth, no aspiration in the face. And yet one cannot get away from it. . . . More magnificent than any other is a large standing photograph of Chief Justice Shaw, taken from an old daguerreotype. It is wonderfully artistic, with brilliant lights and deep shadows, as if it were taken from a marble statue. It is a majestic picture with "the front of Jove himself," and the masses of wavy hair are very effective. It is one of the most remarkable photographs in existence. . . . There is a singular charm in these old pictures,

47

especially in the brilliant daguerreotypes. Most of them will never be reproduced, one day they will all be destroyed, but it is worth while to get now those
that can be bought, for pictures keep their popularity but a little while, and
drift out of the market.[19]

Happily the prediction was untrue. When Josiah J. Hawes died in 1901, on a
brief vacation trip to New Hampshire, the collection was inherited by his son,
Dr. Edward S. Hawes. He put them on public sale in 1934. It was a unique collection, in size and quantity; nothing else like it has survived from the daguerreotype era. The cream of the collection, including the finest portraits of celebrities,
was acquired by the Metropolitan Museum of Art in New York. Another group
is now in the Boston Museum of Fine Arts. Upward of a thousand portraits of
unidentified sitters are in the George Eastman House, Rochester, New York, together with business letters, invoices, receipts, and account books, through the
combined generosity of the late Alden Scott Boyer, Holman's Print Shop, Boston,
and the Hawes family.

6. *Innovations from Philadelphia*

WHEN John Plumbe, Jr., opened his Philadelphia branch in 1842, Robert Cornelius had abandoned his gallery. For two years this pioneer had been taking portraits, using the lighting scheme devised by Wolcott and Johnson in New York. "His laboratory was conspicuous. On the outside could be seen a large mirror swung on a bracket, for illuminating his sitters with reflected sunlight."[1] But few of Cornelius's portraits have survived; they are distinguished by the solid brass frames in which they were encased.

To judge from the city directories, Plumbe had at first no competition, for no other daguerreotypist is listed in 1842. But in the following year the entry appears: "LANGENHEIM, W. & F., daguerreotypers."

Frederick Langenheim and his brother William were born in Germany. William, who was the elder by two years, came to America in 1834, at the age of twenty-seven. He settled in Texas. When hostilities broke out with Mexico, he joined the patriot army, which won the independence of Texas. Although he escaped the massacre at the Alamo, he was captured by the Mexicans, and languished in prison for upward of a year, until a truce was established. He continued a military career: in 1837 he served as commissary sergeant in the campaign against the Seminole Indians in Florida. On his discharge three years later he joined his brother Frederick in Philadelphia. They joined the staff of the German language newspaper *Die Alte und Neue Welt*.

The Langenheims became involved in daguerreotyping by pure chance. Back home in Brunswick, Germany, their sister Louisa had married Johann Bernhard Schneider, a teacher in the Carolo Wilhelmina Polytechnic Institute. Schneider's fellow student in Vienna, Peter Friedrich Wilhelm Voigtländer, was building daguerreotype cameras and lenses. He sent an outfit to Schneider who, after mastering its use, sent it to his brothers-in-law in Philadelphia. It was a small camera, for plates barely an inch in diameter; with it the Langenheims took a portrait of their employer, John Schwakke, editor and publisher of *Die*

49

Alte und Neue Welt.[2] Soon they became American agents for Voigtländer's all-metal camera and his portrait lens, designed by Josef Petzval. The lens was revolutionary. It was greater in diameter than any other lens of the same focal length: by today's nomenclature it would be marked *f*/3.6. Consequently it passed more light than other lenses, and by its use exposures could be greatly reduced.

The all-metal camera took circular pictures 2½ inches in diameter. It was at once a success; by 1842, six hundred had been sold. It resembled a spyglass, recollected Alexander Beckers, a daguerreotypist who worked for the Langenheims. "The camera rested on a candlestick-like tripod, with three set screws for adjustment, and was placed on an ordinary table. To interchange the ground glass and round daguerreotype plate, it was necessary to unscrew a flanged ring, and replace the same by reverse motion. For the adjustment of the focus, there was the rack and pinion, as Voightlander's [sic] instruments still have. . . ."[3]

The new apparatus was expensive. Charles G. Page of Washington wrote Southworth, on January 12, 1843, that he had received from Philadelphia a new camera imported from Vienna. "I paid—$275.00—I can hardly say if the results will warrant this great expense . . . but from a single trial I am satisfied that the pictures will surpass anything I have ever seen. (Nous verrons.)"[4]

On the twenty-fourth he reported: "My new lenses work admirably. They require 40 seconds to 25 with your apparatus [i.e., camera], but it takes magnificent large pictures."[5] He discarded the camera, the workmanship of which he reported to be crude. But Voigtländer's lenses became famous—so famous that they were counterfeited. Daguerreotypists were warned that the signature of Voigtländer was being forged on tubes of local manufacture by unscrupulous dealers.

In 1845 the Langenheims took eight sets of five daguerreotypes of Niagara Falls. They framed them side by side to form panoramas, and sent sets to President Polk, Daguerre, Queen Victoria, the Duke of Brunswick, and the kings of Prussia, Saxony, and Wurtemberg. The eighth set was formerly in the American Museum of Photography in Philadelphia, together with letters and medals from the illustrious recipients of the other sets. These letters the Langenheims printed in a broadside, to promote their enterprise.

More than any other daguerreotypists in America, the Langenheims kept in touch with European developments. In 1846 Frederick bought, and patented in the United States as assignee, a technique for coloring daguerreotypes invented by a Swiss miniaturist and pioneer daguerreotypist, Johann Baptist Isenring.[6] It was so simple a trick that it is a wonder that its validity was not challenged by the patent office. A sheet of glass was laid over the daguerreotype, and the outline of the area to be colored was traced on the glass with a fine brush and India ink. Next, tracing paper was put on the glass and the outline marked with a lead pencil. The outline was followed with a sharp knife. The stencil thus produced, covering all of the area except that to be colored, was fastened on the daguerreotype, which was shaken up with dry pigment in a closed box. For years, daguerreotypists had achieved the same results applying the colors with a brush.

John Edward Mayall, a competitor in Philadelphia who had received a similar patent in 1843,[7] wrote Southworth: "I should like to hear your opinion of Langenheim's patent. I intend to learn if he can legally substantiate it and if not shall resist. Otherwise I must agree."[8] A few days later he wrote: "First about the Langenheim patent for coloring backgrounds. He has got one and served me a notice to desist. I have written to the Patent Office in Washington but their answer is that if I have any redress it is in the Courts of Law. Mr. Van Loan [his partner] brought this process from England but we can not swear to having colored any until Mr. L. began it and I am afraid we could not sustain our claim legally. . . . I am so busy with Daguerreotype that I cannot attend to anything else at present."[9]

Mayall, with Samuel Van Loan, pioneered in making daguerreotypes of those allegorical subjects which are usually the province of painting: his most famous production was a set of ten daguerreotypes each representing a line of the Lord's Prayer. He moved to London in 1846. His Philadelphia gallery was bought by Marcus A. Root, a writing master turned photographer. Mayall became the most fashionable portraitist in London; his are the finest portraits of Queen Victoria. He later moved to Brighton; for one year he was mayor of the city. He died not far from there in 1904, aged ninety-one.

William Langenheim visited England in 1849 to negotiate with William Henry Fox Talbot for the purchase of his United States patent for making photographs with paper negatives. Talbot had discovered, four years before Daguerre's process had received public notice, and without knowledge of his work, a totally different photographic system. On reading the report of Arago's address in January, 1839, to the Academy of Science in the *Comptes Rendus* of that official body,

51

Talbot found himself "in a very unusual dilemma (scarcely to be paralleled in the annals of science)." He hastened to send, first to the Royal Institution and then to the Royal Society, an account of his invention, the results of which seemed in theory to duplicate Daguerre's work. It turned out that Talbot's technique was different from Daguerre's. Instead of silvered copper plates, Talbot used sheets of paper; instead of sensitizing them with fumes of iodine, he soaked the paper first in an aqueous solution of sodium chloride and then in silver nitrate solution. Instead of a unique, direct positive, Talbot secured a negative—from which a limitless number of positive prints could be made. Modern photographic techniques are based on Talbot's discovery; Daguerre's process became obsolescent twelve short years after its publication. Because Daguerre had patented his process in England, Talbot patented his improved "calotype" or "talbotype" process in England, France, and the United States.[10]

Edward Anthony, the stock dealer, was the first to inform Talbot in 1847 that he had been granted a United States patent, and asked for an option to purchase the rights. Two months later, Anthony wrote that he was no longer interested; and for two years there were no takers. Then, in the spring of 1849, William Langenheim went to visit Talbot in the village of Lacock, Wiltshire, where he lived. From the Red Lion Inn, Langenheim wrote Talbot that he would pay him a thousand pounds for the American rights to the patent. The deal was closed on May 11, 1849.[11]

But Americans would have nothing to do with the English process, even though the Langenheims circulated a thousand copies of a brochure pointing out the advantages:

> The common method of taking Daguerreotype Portraits on silvered copper-plates, although very valuable, is liable to many objections which are avoided by this process. In the first place a paper surface is substituted for the highly polished metallic one, and in consequence the pictures can be seen in any direction, and at a considerable distance. After obtaining the first (negative) impression, *any required number of* (positive) *Copies can be procured, all equally perfect, at any time thereafter, without another sitting, and, at a very trifling expense.* . . . As the pictures are not only on paper, but even penetrate into the mass of the paper itself, they cannot be rubbed out, and can, therefore, be enclosed in a letter and sent by mail.[12]

They offered to take portraits at from $5.00 to $12 per dozen, depending on the

52

sizes, which ranged from 4½ by 6 inches to 8 by 10½ inches. Despite these inducements, the new process did not capture the public's fancy.

To judge from existing examples of the Langenheims' "Portraits from Life on Paper," the public's apathy is understandable, for the pictures are weak, poorly lighted, and with none of the quality seen in the product of even a journeyman daguerreotypist. They painted out the background to silhouette the figures, which were monotonously alike: head, shoulders, and one arm propped on a side table or on the top of a truncated, fluted column. Photographers were disinterested, for they were reluctant to pay for the use of any restricted process; they looked upon payment of the license fee as a needless expense, and they saw no reason to abandon the daguerreotype process, which the American public was most enthusiastically endorsing.

The Langenheims became financially embarrassed. Less than a year after they bought his patent, the brothers wrote Talbot that they had not sold a single license. They suggested that accounts might be settled if Talbot were to purchase rights to *their* patent, a technique for making negatives on glass.

This process was a modification of an invention by Niépce de Saint-Victor, the nephew of Daguerre's partner, by which light-sensitive silver salts were bound to the surface of a glass plate by white of egg. The Langenheims called glass positives made from these negatives "hyalotypes."[13] For this invention they received a United States patent on November 19, 1850.[14]

It was not new, and daguerreotypists knew that it should not have been allowed. It hardly differed from the albumen plates of John Adams Whipple, for which a patent[15] had been granted just a few months earlier, and which Whipple called "crystalotypes." But from the practical standpoint, the Langenheims scored a novelty: they used the material to make slides for the magic lantern. To them goes the credit for producing the first photographic transparencies for projection; from this invention rose a thriving industry, which gradually merged into the motion pictures. They exhibited a collection of their hyalotypes at the Great Exhibition in London in 1851.

The Langenheims also pioneered in stereoscopic photography, and founded the American Stereoscopic Company for the sale and distribution of paper prints and transparencies produced from hyalotype negatives.

Just when they began to expand in this field is not clear. Root states that they produced stereoscopic pictures in 1850. By 1854 they were producing them in quantity.

> *Photographic Art-Journal, September, 1854.* We had the pleasure of a call from Mr. Langenheim, who has just returned from Europe, and of seeing a few of his beautiful stereoscopic pictures. . . . These pictures surpass anything of the kind we have ever seen, and we do not think they can be excelled.

The Library of Congress owns a scrapbook, obviously intended as a catalogue, of twenty-four paper stereographs of views in Pennsylvania and New York, with the manuscript title, "Photographic Views at Home and Abroad, taken and published by F. Langenheim, 188 Chestnut St., Philadelphia, 1856."

Stereoscopic daguerreotypes were not uncommon. Besides Southworth and Hawes, there were others who invented viewing devices. John F. Mascher, a Philadelphian, described in the *Scientific American* for June 13, 1852, a box stereoscope which he made for two half-plate daguerrotypes; a year later he patented a folding daguerreotype case which contained, on a flap hinged to the inside cover, two spectacle glasses.[16] A similar daguerreotype case was patented by John Stull, also of Philadelphia: the lenses were set in holes pierced in the cover which, instead of being hinged, was fastened to the bottom by folding arms in such a way that it always remained parallel to the twin daguerreotypes.[17]

But the daguerreotype was not a satisfactory technique for the stereoscope. The pictures were expensive, fragile, and bulky. It was difficult to look at them through magnifying lenses, because of the highly polished surface. The Langenheims' paper prints and glass transparencies became at once popular. They soon faced competition when the London Stereoscopic Company opened an American branch and sent a cameraman here. Edward and Henry T. Anthony began in 1859 to publish paper prints in vast quantities, printed from negatives made by the wet collodion process which soon displaced the hyalotype technique. By the time of the Civil War the Langenheims were putting all their attention into the production of lantern slides. When William Langenheim died in 1874, his brother Frederick retired.

For a while the Langenheims had a branch gallery in New York, in partnership with Alexander Beckers. So, too, did M. A. Root, in partnership with his brother Samuel. For New York in the 1850's was the center of the daguerreotype industry.

54

7. *The Broadway Galleries*

"THERE is probably no city in the United States where the Daguerreian art is more highly appreciated and successfully practiced than New York," Humphrey wrote in 1850.[1] There were 77 rooms, he said, employing 127 operators at $10.00 a week, 11 ladies at $5.00 a week, and 46 boys at $1.00 a week. In 1853 it was estimated that a thousand New Yorkers made their living by daguerreotyping. There were eighty-six portrait galleries in the city then, and thirty-seven of these were on Broadway.

Broadway was the favored location of daguerreian artists, not only because it was the center of business, but because it was fashionable to promenade along the thoroughfare when the week's work was done. "Broadway is in full force through Sunday, and with an increased power on Sunday evening," a New Yorker wrote in 1853.[2] "It is then that the nice dressing of New Yorkers is to be seen in the highest perfection—a perfect Mississippi, with a double current up and down, of glossy broadcloth and unblemished DeLaines. . . . There are hundreds and thousands in New York who cannot live out of Broadway: who must breathe its air at least once a day, or they gasp and perish." As a hit tune of the era put it:

> The O.K. thing on Saturday
> Is walking down Broadway
> The festive, gay, Broadway

A popular diversion, while walking down Broadway, was to drop into a daguerreotype gallery. To choose which one was baffling. Daguerreotypists advertised in the newspapers, hung banners outside their galleries, and arranged display cases with samples of their work at the street entrance to entice promenaders to climb the flights of stairs. For all the galleries were walk-ups, since the great skylights essential to indoor portraiture in those days had to be built on the upper floors, and elevators were not yet common. It was hardly possible to choose a gallery in advance, and make an appointment for a sitting, because only if the

55

day was fair could daguerreotypes be taken. If promenaders dropped into a gallery and found a lot of people waiting their turns, the temptation would be to seek another, less popular establishment. So daguerreotypists took pains to make their reception rooms as comfortable and attractive as they could.

The most famous of the Broadway galleries were those of Mathew B. Brady, Martin M. Lawrence, and Jeremiah Gurney.

Brady was a jewel-case manufacturer who had just taken on a new line, miniature cases, when Southworth's pupil L. C. Champney visited him in 1843. At Champney's suggestion, he wrote Southworth on June 17, 1843:

Sir:
I beg leave of communicating these few lines soliciting your attention, I being informed by L. Champney and several of your frends [sic] that you are one of the most successful prof. of daguerreotype and doing the most extensive

56

business in Boston and invariably use a great number of miniature cases. I have been engaged some time past in manafucturing [sic] miniature cases for some of the principal operators in this city and recently in business for myself and anxious for engagements. I have got up a new style case with embossed top and extra fine diaframe [sic]. This style of case has been admired by all the principal artists in this city. If you feel desirous to see my style of cases if you will favor me with an answer I will send them by Horse Express. If my style of cases should suit you I can supply you on reasonable terms.[3]

In 1844 Brady opened a Daguerrean Miniature Gallery at 205 Broadway, just below Fulton Street. His success was immediate, and on March 19, 1853, he opened a branch "uptown" at 359 Broadway, over Thompson's Saloon. On the very same day his competitor, Martin M. Lawrence, opened *his* new gallery at Number 381. Humphrey was invited to both openings. He partook of "a collation of the choicest supplies of good things in the most epicurean order," and inspected the galleries in detail. The two establishments were almost identical. He described Brady's:

Humphrey's Journal of the Daguerreotype, June 15, 1853. The floors are carpeted with superior velvet tapestry, highly colored and of a large and appropriate pattern. The walls are covered with satin and gold paper. The ceiling frescoed, and in the center is suspended a six-light gilt and enamelled chandelier, with prismatic drops that throw their enlivening colors in abundant profusion. The light through the windows is softened by passing the meshes of the most costly needleworked lace curtains, or intercepted, if occasion requires, by shades commensurate with the gayest of palaces, while the golden cornices, and festooned damasks indicate that Art dictated their arrangement. The harmony is not the least disturbed by the superb rosewood furniture—tête-à-têtes, reception and easy chairs, and marble-top tables, all of which are multiplied by mirrors from ceiling to floor. Suspended on the walls, we find Daguerreotypes of Presidents, Generals, Kings, Queens, Noblemen—and *more nobler men* —men and women of all nations and professions.

Past the reception room was an office and a ladies' parlor, all in gold and green, with rosewood furniture. Two operating rooms led from the reception room—one with a northern, the other with a southern exposure. Humphrey, who was writing for the profession, does not waste words on these rooms: "To go into a description of the apparatus and arrangements, would be repeating what every

first-class operator is familiar with." A wood engraving of the gallery, which Brady used for advertising and on his billhead, shows the reception room in exaggerated perspective. Far in the distance can be seen a camera on a tripod and a man standing beside it.

To assume that this cameraman is M. B. Brady himself, would be a mistake. Like all the other Broadway daguerreotypists, Brady employed operators to do the work of photographing. Otherwise he could not have managed two galleries on Broadway and a third in Washington. Nor could he have taken off eighteen months for a trip to Europe in 1851-52, leaving George S. Cook in charge. His position was made clear in the *Photographic Art-Journal,* March, 1851: "Brady is not an operator himself, a failing eyesight precluding the possibility of his using

58

the camera with any certainty, but he is an excellent artist nevertheless—understands his business so perfectly, and gathers around him the first talent to be found." This observation was repeated in 1854: "Although Mr. Brady is not a practical operator, yet he displays superior management in his business and consequently deserves high praise for the lofty position he has attained in the Daguerreian fraternity."[4]

The operators were journeymen, and it was a problem to keep a good one. Some left the employ of the big houses to start their own galleries. Brady's first operator, James A. Brown, set up for himself on Broadway in 1848. Polycarp von Schneidau, the Swede who was the first to make a daguerreotype of Jenny Lind in Brady's gallery, opened in Chicago and became famous for his memorable portrait of Abraham Lincoln. Others were snapped up by rival proprietors. Edwin Bronk left Brady to take charge of the St. Louis gallery of T. C. Dobyns, who ran a chain of daguerreotype galleries in the South. He recruited his cameramen in New York. "Principles, take bonds on your operators to remain with you," Humphrey warned, "or you lose them. Mr. D. will never take an operator in the actual employment of any establishment, but when they resign he picks them up."[5] Lawrence yielded his chief operator, Edwin Church, to Dobyns for his Memphis, Tennessee, gallery. And Gurney lost his man Litch to England. Of the daguerreotypists whose skill brought fame to Brady and his competitors, we know but little. Only those whose activities made copy for the trade papers can even be named.

It is not difficult to visualize the operating rooms at Brady's, which Humphrey took for granted. There would be, of course, a slanting skylight, preferably dirtied over to diffuse the light. There would be a number of iron headrests, either the plain cast-iron model or the newly introduced Jenny Lind model with ornate base and fluted column. There would be a simple background of dark Roman ocher, moleskin color, or bluish gray. (Elaborate painted backdrops did not come into general use until the time of the Civil War.) There would be a movable reflector, or screen to bounce light into the shadow side of the face. Except for the camera on its tripod there would be nothing else in the operating room. The preparation of the plates, their polishing and sensitizing before exposure, their development by hot mercury, and the final fixing, gilding, and coloring, would be taken care of in the mechanical department on the fourth floor.

Martin M. Lawrence, Brady's neighbor in the next block, was particularly noted for two specialties: the extra large (12-by-15-inch) daguerreotypes called "mammoth," and allegorical subjects. His "Past, Present, and Future," three young ladies facing to the left, front, and right, had won for him a prize at the 1851 Great Exhibition in the Crystal Palace, London—an honor he shared with Brady. (Gossip had it that the daguerreotype was in fact the work of Lawrence's operator Gabriel Harrison, late of Plumbe's gallery, who soon left him to establish his own business in Brooklyn. There he took a daguerreotype of an unknown poet named Walt Whitman, who used an engraving from it as a frontispiece to his volume *Leaves of Grass.*)

Humphrey described Lawrence's gallery with the same detail as Brady's. It was almost identical: a reception room on the third floor, richly furnished; two 25-by-30-foot operating rooms on the fifth floor, with 16-foot ceilings and skylights each 12 by 15 feet.

Jeremiah Gurney boasted that his was "the oldest and most extensive establishment in the world," having been founded in 1840. The only biographical information we have of Broadway's most popular daguerreotypist is a profile in the New York *Star* for November 6, 1887, which states that Gurney was a jeweler in Saratoga, New York, in 1839. There he met an Englishman named Shaw, from whom he bought a camera in exchange for a watch.

He brought this crude affair to New York and started in the daguerreotype in connection with his jewelry business. He opened a jewelry shop at No. 189 Broadway and in his show case put four daguerreotypes. They were small affairs, but he charged $5 each for a portrait. The first day he had one sitter, the second two, and from then on success was assured. Daguerreotypes were the rage, and the public clamored for them as loudly as they do now for first night seats at the debut of a society belle.

In 1852, when the gallery of Jesse H. Whitehurst at 349 Broadway was destroyed by fire, Gurney bought it, refurnished it, and operated it as a branch of his downtown gallery. In the following year he sent daguerreotypes in competition with Brady and Lawrence to the Exhibition of the Industry of All Nations, New York's answer—complete with Crystal Palace—to the London Great Exhibition. He won only honorable mention, against the bronze medals awarded to Brady and Lawrence.

Winning the Anthony pitcher, first prize in America's first strictly photographic competition, however, more than made up for this disappointment. In an effort to raise the standards of daguerreotyping, Edward Anthony, owner of the nation's largest stockhouse of daguerreotype materials, apparatus, and cameras, had offered in 1851 a $500 prize for the best set of daguerreotypes. To his dismay, not one daguerreotypist entered, "probably in consequence of the natural mod-

61

THE ANTHONY PRIZE.

esty of inventors," he wrote, and went on to explain: "Inasmuch, however, as the money has been offered, I myself consider that it no longer belongs to myself but to Art. Therefore . . . I have decided to invest the above amount in a MASSIVE SILVER PITCHER, of appropriate design, to be awarded as a prize for the *best four daguerreotypes* that shall be offered for competition previous to November 1st, 1853."[6]

The pitcher was described in *Gleason's Pictorial Drawing-Room Companion:*

On one side is the sun rising over a beautiful landscape, with a daguerreian apparatus, seemingly ready to catch the most interesting features of the picture, as it throws its golden rays over the scene. On the other side is represented a chemical laboratory —showing that to chemistry the art is chiefly indebted; and on the two front tablets are portraits of those two illustrious artists — Daguerre and Niépce. On the handle we have again the vine, in which is a lizard creeping to the mouth of the pitcher, the whole finished with a most exquisitely chased base.[7]

The pitcher was awarded to Gurney for his whole-plate portrait of his daughter. The second prize, of two silver cups, went to Samuel Root, brother of Marcus. The prizes were awarded by Anthony at Gurney's gallery four days before Christmas, 1853. Professor James Renwick of Columbia College, one of the judges, was chairman; letters from Samuel F. B. Morse and J. W. Draper, the two other judges, were read; toasts were made; and the party went on to "a second edition . . . the corks, toasts, bottles and tumblers were as thick as fog on a damp morning."[8]

Encouragement of the kind Anthony offered was needed, for a vicious price war was going on all over the country and on Broadway in particular. Humphrey and Snelling were constantly writing editorials against the price cutters; mutual-protection societies were formed; but all in vain. Snelling attacked the morals of what he called the "two shilling operators": "Their rooms are frequently the resort of the low and depraved, and they delight in nothing more than desecrating the Sabbath by daguerreotyping these characters in the most obscene positions."[9]

The price charged for a medium-sized daguerreotype at such a first-rate gallery as Brady's was, in 1853, $2.00. At the same time, in the "picture factories" of Reese & Co., Rufus Anson, and Carden & Co., the cost was but 50 cents. Miniature sixteenth-size (1⅝ by 1⅝ inch) daguerreotypes could be had for 25 cents. The two-shilling operators were a constant threat to those daguerreotypists who, often not without reason, called themselves artists. Brady stated his position in an advertisement in the *New York Tribune* for April 10, 1854: "I wish to vindicate true art, and leave the community to decide whether it is best to encourage real excellence or its opposite; to preserve and perfect an art, or permit it to degenerate by inferiority or materials which must correspond with the meanness of price."[10] Yet he was to announce that "by a new arrangement" of his downtown gallery he would "make better pictures for from 50 cents to $1, than have ever been made before at these prices."[11]

The reason for the success of the 50-cent men was not only the relaxation of standards, the pushing of smaller size, and aggressive advertising, but especially the division of labor and industrial organization which they introduced. Established daguerreotypists saw only their sloppy workmanship, and called them "the blue bosom operators" because they did not have skill enough to record a white shirt white: their careless technique brought about solarization, which in the daguerreotype process renders the highlight areas blue. Humphrey said they exhibited at the American Institute Fair only to get a free pass.

Reese and Company, of 289 Broadway, claimed to have inaugurated the mass-production system. In a thirty-six-page brochure published by the firm with the somewhat misleading title *Daguerreotype Directory,* it is explained that Professor Reese was a political refugee from Germany, and that on coming to America in 1852 he introduced the "German system" of daguerreotyping. The principle of division of labor was carried out to a greater degree than in other galleries. The establishment was divided into departments: polishing, two sky-lights north and south, mercurializing, gilding, and coloring, each the charge, if we are to believe the Professor, of Ph.D.'s and baronets, for he names them: "Dr. Dutton Van Skoik, Sir John Clark, Prof. Marat." He claimed in his booklet that "300 to 500 or even 1000 portraits were made daily"—a production far above that of the older galleries. (Humphrey, for instance, boasted that on the day after Christmas, 1853, he made sixty-four portraits between 9:30 and 4 o'clock.)

In contrast to the big Broadway galleries, with their emphasis on the palatial splendor of the reception rooms, the picture factories were bare and unadorned. There were no delicate rosewood tête-à têtes; the customers sat on wooden benches, "forms," as a British visitor, John Werge, wrote:

> I had a dollar's worth of these "factory" portraits. At the desk I paid my money, and received four tickets, which entitled me to as many sittings when my turn came. I was shown into a waiting room crowded with people. The customers were seated on forms placed around the room, sidling their way to the entrance of the operating room, and answering the cry of "The next" in much the same manner that people do at our public baths. I being "the next," at last went into the operating room, where I found the operator stationed at the camera, which he never left all day long, except occasionally to adjust a stupid sitter. He told the next to "sit down" and "look thar," focussed, and putting his hand into a hole in the wall which communicated with the "coating room," he found a dark slide [i.e. plate holder] ready filled with a sensitized plate, and putting it into the camera, "exposed," and saying "that will dew," took the dark slide out of the camera, and shoved it through another hole in the wall communicating with the mercury or developing room. This was repeated as many times as I wanted sittings, which he knew by the number of tickets I had given to a boy in the room, whose duty it was to look out for "the next" and collect tickets. The operator had nothing to do with the preparation

64

of the plates, developing, fixing, or finishing of the picture. He was responsible only for the "pose" and "time," the "developer" checking and correcting the latter occasionally by crying out "Short" or "Long" as the case might be. Having had my number of "sittings," I was requested to leave the operating room by another door which opened into a passage that led me to the "delivery desk," where, in a few minutes, I got all my four portraits fitted up in "matt, glass, and preserver,"—the pictures having been passed from the developing room to the "gilding" room, thence to the "fitting room" and the "delivery desk," where I received them. Thus they were finished and carried away without the camera operator ever having seen them. Three of the four portraits were as fine Daguerreotypes as could be produced anywhere.[12]

Professor Reese was a man of marked prejudice. That he should attack the established daguerreotypists with violent sarcasm is understandable, but his unchivalrous blast at the few lady daguerreotypists then active is not so readily explained. "Much has been said, written and whistled with regard to females being capable of taking daguerreotypes . . . it's all gammon . . . we shall yet believe that female Daguerreans are out of place, pants or no pants."

Already, by the time this was written in 1854, the daguerreotype was doomed. Its place was soon to be taken by an entirely different technique, the wet-collodion process, invented by Frederick Scott Archer in England, and published by him in *The Chemist* for March, 1851.

Archer's process, like Whipple's crystalotypes and the Langenheims' hyalotypes, was basically a modification of H. Fox Talbot's calotype process. The negatives were on glass. To sensitize them, Archer first coated the glass with collodion, a viscous solution of guncotton which dries to form a hard, skinlike film. In this collodion, potassium iodide had been dissolved. While the coating was still tacky, he plunged the plate into a bath of silver nitrate solution. By this action, light-sensitive silver iodide was produced in suspension within the collodion coating. After exposure the plate was developed by pouring over it a solution of pyrogallic acid and silver iodide. It was fixed with sodium thiosulphate (then called "hyposulphite of soda"), washed, and dried. Prints were made from these negatives with paper sensitized by Talbot's process, or with albumen paper, which had been coated with white of egg. In the daguerreotype days the word "photography" was reserved for this new collodion process. By the outbreak of the Civil War, photographs became cheaper than mass-produced daguerreotypes.

65

Snelling warned of the coming revolution. In August, 1853, he complained that "the daguerreotypists of America have so long heard their praises sung, and so long been tickled with the assertion of their superiority in the art, that they seem to think that there is no possibility of their ever being surpassed. . . . They even laugh at the idea that paper photographs can ever equal the daguerreotype." He saw the end of Daguerre's invention as a parlor ornament: "Enlarge the daguerreotype above that of 9 x 11 inch size and it becomes coarse and unsightly, whereas the paper photograph is improved in its details, its sharpness, and its beauty; and does not deteriorate in softness of tints or brilliancy of tone."[13] By March, 1854, he reported that there was "more apparatus, &c., sold in the United States within the last three months for paper manipulation than during the whole previous time since its discovery."[14] Of the Broadway daguerreotypists who had switched to paper and glass, Snelling named Brady, Gurney, and Lawrence. "In view of the hosts of 25 cent galleries springing up in all quarters, our most respectable artists begin to look to the crystalotype to redeem their artistic skill from the odium cast upon the daguerrean art by its prostitution to such paltry results."

The paper processes were introduced to the daguerreotypists by a new class of operator. Brady employed Austin A. Turner, who while in the employ of the Boston daguerreotypist Marcus Ormsbee was sent to learn the crytalotype process at Whipple's gallery. Having learned the technique, Turner held out for higher wages, striking every few weeks, until he was earning $36 a week—more than three times the average operator's pay. He finally left for New York, learned the collodion process, taught it at $50 a lesson, and wound up in Brady's gallery.

Lawrence obtained the services of Caleb Hunt.

Gurney was joined in 1853 by his former pupil Charles DeForest Fredricks, who had picked up the new technique in Paris, where it was already well established. The partnership was short-lived, for in 1855 Fredricks opened his own gallery at 585 Broadway. Over the entrance, spelled out in a semicircle of giant wooden letters, were the words PHOTOGRAPHIC TEMPLE OF ART. The days of the Broadway Daguerreian Galleries were drawing to a close.

8. *Itinerants and Travelers*

FROM shore to shore the motto,

> Secure the shadow 'ere the substance fade,
> Let Nature imitate what Nature made!

was blazoned forth on handbills and in newspaper advertisements by the proprietors of daguerreian galleries named Sunbeam, Apollo, National, Premium. In their advertising they appealed to sentiment:

> Nobody who travels knows that he shall return. Therefore he ought to leave something behind for his friends to remember him by. What can be more appropriate than a Daguerreotype? because nothing can represent the features so well and so accurately. At LANGENHEIM'S establishment, Exchange, 3d story, good ones can be procured.[1]

While some daguerreotypists scorned advertising—Lawrence said, "I prefer to write my own advertisements on well-prepared and polished plates"[2]—most of the proprietors had a keen and ingenious sense of publicity. Brady hung a huge dummy camera, surmounted by an eagle, on the side of his building. Banners were strung up and the walls of buildings covered with signs. Gurney had handbills printed to resemble in size and typography paper money; in each corner were the figures 100 in large type; beneath, written out in fine print, were the words "and forty nine"—the address of his Broadway gallery. Premiums were offered; the first person to appear each morning was given a free sitting. William A. Pratt, of Richmond, Virginia, offered shares in a $30,000 "donation" of real estate, which could be purchased either in cash or in the cash value of daguerreotypes taken by him. Even "tie-in deals" were offered: a New York hatter inserted free a daguerreotype in the lining of each hat sold.

Galleries in the smaller cities rivaled the luxury and elegance of Broadway establishments. In 1851 Charles Cist, the historian of Cincinnati, stated that there were thirty-seven daguerreotypists and seventy-eight assistants in that city; they did an $80,000 business. He proudly reported: "Our daguerreian artists stand high everywhere. Reed, the artist, who carried portraits taken by Hawkins and Faris* to Europe, states, in a letter home, that their works were recognized at a glance in Florence, by Frenchmen and others, as American productions, and superior to anything produced on the continent of Europe."[3]

The most elaborate of the Cincinnati galleries was James P. Ball's Great Daguerreian Gallery of the West, opened in 1853. "There are nine artists employed in this gallery," Ball boasted, "consequently visitors are not obliged to wait a whole day for a picture, but can get what they desire in a few minutes."[4] A wood engraving of the gallery appeared in *Gleason's Pictorial Drawing-Room Companion* for April 1, 1854, with a description. It was twenty feet wide by forty feet long.

> The walls are tastefully enamelled by flesh-colored paper, bordered with gold leaf and flowers. The panels on the south side and west end are ornamented with ideal figures. . . . On the ceiling is a centre piece representing the aerial regions, in which Venus, the goddess of Beauty, is sitting recumbent on a splendid throne. . . . The very seat on which you sit and the carpet on which you tread seem to be a gem culled from the fragrant lap of Flora. . . .

Even the smaller cities and towns had show places. Anson Clark fitted up the rooms adjacent to his West Stockbridge, Massachusetts, gallery "for a cabinet of minerals and natural curiosities," he wrote in 1842. "It already contains several hundred specimens of minerals together with models of machines—the pictures of all the heathen Gods and Goddesses—eggs of various kinds of birds several hundred—shells of various kinds—and other natural and artificial curiosities among which are—the cane that kill'd Abel and one of the Rams horns that blow'd down the walls of Jericho, etc. etc."[5] Andrew Wemple Van Alstin, active in Worcester, Massachusetts, went around the world collecting birds, which he mounted and displayed in his daguerreotype rooms.

Platt D. Babbitt, of Niagara Falls, reversed this pattern. Instead of bringing natural curiosities to his gallery, he set up an outdoor studio with the nation's most popular tourist attraction as a background. By arrangement with the man-

*Ezekiel C. Hawkins and Thomas Faris were partners in Cincinnati from 1844 to 1849, when Hawkins opened his Apollo Gallery and Faris his Melodeon Gallery.

ager of the American side of the falls, he set up a daguerreotype camera on a permanent tripod, pointing straight at the Horseshoe Falls across Prospect Point. Above the camera he built a hip-roofed pavilion—as much to advertise his presence as to protect his equipment from the elements. When visitors stood on the brink of Prospect Point to admire the falls, he took their pictures. Dozens of daguerreotypes exist, all identical except for the people (Plate 34). Babbitt continued at his stand from 1854 well into the last quarter of the century, making group photographs in all the techniques which followed the daguerreotype. He held a monopoly: when a Scotsman, William Thompson, attempted to photograph the falls from Prospect Point, "Mr. Babbitt would not have it. . . . Every time Mr. Thompson made an attempt to take the cap off the camera for an exposure, Mr. Babbitt and his forces would stand between the camera and the falls swinging large-sized umbrellas to and fro, thus preventing Mr. Thompson from getting a picture. The war between the two men came to such a pitch that Mr. Babbitt was finally forced to vacate and thereafter the Scotch artist held the fort."[6]

Where galleries had not been established, traveling daguerreotypists set up their cameras in rented rooms, or drove their wagon-studios into town, unhitched the teams, and set up shop in a vacant lot or public square. All of the needed apparatus, including a tripod and a headrest to clamp on the back of a chair, could be packed into a small trunk. Any well-lighted room would serve as a studio, and a blanket across the corner of the room would serve as a darkroom. Southworth's pupils traveled up and down New England.

> *L. C. Champney to A. S. Southworth, Bennington, Vermont, March 9, 1843.* I think I shall stay up this way for the present. They all say that my pictures are the best that they ever saw. I have tride the light as you proposed, but they do not like the dark on one side of the face, and I cant sell a picture that where one side of the face is darker than the other, altho it seems to stand out better and look richer.

Business was going well with Champney when, on April 13, he ordered more plates. They did not arrive when he needed them, and he wrote again nine days later: "I have bin watering ever since for the plates, and one day seems one week to me. Please forward directly." In July he wrote that he had been to New York. He bought some cases from Brady. "I thought they were as good as yours when

69

I was there, but to come back and compare them I found they would not be durable. They will never know the difference in the country." Champney was not long a customer. In reply to a dun in 1844 he wrote: "I was unfortunate in the Daguerreotype Business. I was obliged to drop it and go to work at my Traid."[7]

The itinerants went from town to town. Sarah Holcomb, also a pupil of Southworth's, left Saxonville (near Boston) for Manchester, New Hampshire, in the winter of 1846. There she found that someone had already set up a gallery, so she went on to Concord. A storm held her up. At Claremont, New Hampshire, she found that there had been no operator for a year. The prospects were good but, "on unpacking my things, found all my chemicals frozen. The bottle of bromide . . . burst and made sad work for me. . . . I can do nothing till I get more," she wrote Southworth.

Enterprising daguerreotypists fitted up wagons as "Daguerreotype Saloons," hitched teams of horses to them, and drove around the countryside.

> *New York Mirror, October 31, 1846.* There is a chap traveling in Connecticut, who has fitted up a large double wagon into a sort of saloon, with a daguerreotype apparatus, and is going about like a tin pedlar, calling at houses and taking pictures here and there, as he can find customers.

Humphrey called these wagons "rotary establishments," and noted in 1852 that there were four working out of Syracuse, New York. In the nearby town of

70

Lockport, E. R. Graves and Henry Pruden built a "mammoth Daguerreotype Gallery on wheels" in 1853 at a cost of $1,200; "it was 28 feet long, 11 feet wide and 9 feet high, with a beautiful skylight and tastefully furnished."[8] Along the riverways, floating galleries were not uncommon. John R. Gorgas spent three years on the Ohio and Mississippi Rivers, "the happiest of my life, with a handsome boat 65 feet long, well appointed, a good cook, with flute, violin and guitar, had a jolly time, did not need advertising, and never did any Sunday work."[9]

The itinerants traveled far and wide. The history of the daguerreotype in South America is a record of American travelers; for even though Daguerre's process first came to South America directly from France, it was not followed up. The Franco-Belgian school-ship *La Orientale,* on a trip around the world, touched at Rio de Janeiro in 1840. The chaplain, Louis Compte, who had mastered the daguerreotype process in France just before the ship sailed, gave a demonstration to the citizens.

> *Journal de Commercio, January 17, 1840.* One must have seen the thing with one's own eyes to have an idea of the rapidity and the result of the operation. In less than nine minutes the fountain of Paço Square, Peixe Park, and the monastery of São Bento and all surrounding objects were reproduced with such fidelity, precision and detail that they really seem made by the very hand of nature, almost without the intervention of the artist.[10]

Compte made similar demonstrations in Baía and, on February 27, in Montevideo.[11] But not until a handful of adventurous American daguerreotypists traveled to South America was the daguerreotype established there as an industry.

In 1842 Augustus Morand of New York visited South America. Shortly after arriving in Rio de Janeiro, where he set up rooms in the Hotel Pharoux, he was invited by the Emperor, Dom Pedro II, to demonstrate the process. The Emperor was entranced, learned the process himself, and commanded Morand to take views of the Imperial residence at São Cristóvão and portraits of the royal family. In a biographical sketch of Morand in the *Photographic Art-Journal,* the Rev. D. P. Kidder tells of a triumph of photographic skill:

> It was the custom of the Emperor to visit, every Saturday morning, his Palace in the city. One of these occasions he conceived to be an excellent opportunity for producing a fine picture of the Emperor with his body guard and splendid equipage. Having prepared his plates at an early hour, he awaited their arrival.

71

At the usual time the guard drew near in advance of the Emperor's carriage; the instant it halted, and while the Emperor was in the act of stepping out of his carriage, Mr. M. exposed his plate, and in a second of time, procured a picture truly beautiful.

The body guard composed of 40 horsemen, were with but one or two exceptions all perfect, also the "Major Domo" in the act of kneeling to kiss the Emperor's hand as he stepped from the carriage. The likeness of the Emperor himself was very correct.

The whole time consumed in taking, finishing, and framing the picture was less than forty minutes from the time he arrived at the Palace. The Emperor doubted the fact, until his attention was called to the carriage in the plate, when he immediately assented, for it was the one presented to him by Queen Victoria, and one that he had not used for several months previous. The Emperor was in raptures with the picture and ordered that it should be hung in the Imperial Gallery, where it now remains, a testimonial of the enterprise and skill of our American artist. Mr. M's studio was enriched by many views taken from the most beautiful sites around Rio de Janeiro— and but for feeble health, a complete Daguerrean Panorama would have been the result of his abode within the tropics.[12]

Morand returned to the United States in April, 1843. He traveled through the southern states and then opened a gallery in New York in 1848.

John A. Bennett, whose Mobile, Alabama, gallery was purchased by M. A. Root, was in Buenos Aires in 1845. He had changed his first name to Juan sometime during his travels in Colombia, the Antilles, and Venezuela. He was in competition with his compatriots Tomás C. Helsby, Henrique North, Guillermo Weston, and Carlos D. Fredricks.

The latter was the very same Charles DeForest Fredricks who was Gurney's partner on Broadway. In 1843, when he was twenty years old, he went to Venezuela to join his brother, who was a trader there. Just before sailing he bought a complete daguerreotype outfit from Gurney and learned how to use it. When he arrived at Angostura (the present Ciudad Bolivar), the customs officials made such a fuss over this strange apparatus, and demanded such exorbitant duty for its importation, that he left it on the dock, to be returned to New York. Fredricks was the guest of the leading merchant in town. During his visit the merchant's son died. The brokenhearted father had no portrait of the child. He offered to clear Fredricks' outfit through customs if he would take a posthumous daguerreotype. The daguerreotypist agreed, and at the first trial succeeded. The inhabitants had never seen the like before; they demanded that he take their portraits; in three weeks he ran out of materials and had earned $4,000. He sent to New York for plates and chemicals, joined his brother in San Fernando, and made his way up the Orinoco River to Brazil and down the Amazon, daguerreotyping all the way. At the rapids of the Mapuera, deep in the jungle, the Indian guides ran off with the canoes and provisions. There was nothing to do but wait for help. For twenty-two days they subsisted on sour mandioc, an Indian food, until they were rescued by a party of government officials and soldiers.

Fredricks returned to New York to recuperate, but the next year, 1844, he was back. Except for quick trips to New York he traveled all over South America for the next nine years. He ran a gallery in Belim (Para), then moved to Maranhão, Baía (Salvador), Rio de Janeiro, and Porto Alegre. On a trip through the province of Rio Grande, en route to Montevideo and Buenos Aires, he traded a horse for each picture: "our photographer arrived at his journey's end in patriarchal style, surrounded by an immense drove of horses, which he finally sold, at $3 each."[13] The Governor of Corrientes pressed upon Fredricks a live tiger in exchange for a daguerreotype portrait. The beast was chained securely to the boat, and Fredricks planned to bring this bounty to New York, but the tiger did not survive captivity. Fredricks lived in Buenos Aires and Montevideo for about a year; a few of his daguerreotypes, stamped "Carlos D. Fredricks & Co." exist, including a whole plate of the harbor. He went to Paris in 1853 to learn the new glass-plate process, which he brought back to his former teacher, Jeremiah Gurney; he never again visited South America.

John Lloyd Stephens, travel writer and explorer, sailed to Central America on October 3, 1839, where he and Frederick Catherwood made a study of the ancient ruins there. In his report of the expedition, *Incidents of Travel in Central America, Chiapas and Yucatan,* he regretted that he had left New York too soon to take along a daguerreotype camera. He knew of it, for he sponsored Seager's demonstration, which took place just two days after he left New York.

On his second trip, in 1841, Stephens and Catherwood had a complete daguerreotype outfit. It proved to be of little use for their objective.

At Uxmal, Mr. Catherwood began taking views, but the results were not

73

sufficiently perfect to suit his ideas. At times the projecting cornices and orna-
ments threw parts of the subject in shade, while others were in broad sunshine;
so that, while parts were brought out well, other parts required pencil drawings
to supply their defects. They gave a general idea of the character of the building, but would not do to put into the hands of the engraver without copying
the views on paper . . . which would require more labor than that of making
at once complete original drawings. He therefore completed everything with his
pencil and camera lucida, while Doctor Cabot [the third member of the party]
and myself took up the Daguerreotype; and, in order to ensure the utmost accuracy, the Daguerreotype views were placed with the drawings in the hands
of the engravers for their guidance.[14]

But if the daguerreotype proved unsatisfactory for scientific purposes, it
offered the party much satisfaction of another sort.

The process was still a novelty in Yucatán, although even at that early date
someone had been there with a camera. They set up a portrait studio in their
quarters in Mérida and for a while met with great success. Their first subject
was "a delicate and dangerous blonde, simple, natural, and unaffected, beautiful
without knowing it, and really because she could not help it." She was posed by
Stephens, "and as this required great nicety, it was sometimes actually indispensable to turn the beautiful little head with our own hands, which, however, was a
very innocent way of turning a young lady's head." The exposure was "eternity":
one minute and thirty seconds by the watch. While Catherwood processed the
plate, Stephens "took occasion to suggest that the process was so complicated,
and its success depended upon such a variety of minute circumstances, it seemed
really wonderful that it ever turned out well. The plate might not be good, or
not well cleaned; or the chemicals might not be of the best; or the plate might
be left too long in the iodine box, or taken out too soon; or left too long in the
bromine box, or taken out too soon; or a ray of light might strike it putting it
into the camera or in taking it out; or it might be left too long in the camera or
taken out too soon; or too long in the mercury bath or taken out too soon; and
even though all of these processes were right and regular, there might be some other
faults of omission or commission which we were not aware of; besides which, climate and atmosphere had great influence, and might render all of no avail."
But happily Stephens did not need to catalogue the sources of failure, "for the
young lady's image was stamped upon the plate and made a picture which en-

chanted her and satisfied the critical judgment of her friends and admirers. Our experiments upon the other ladies were equally successful . . . our reputation increased, and we had abundance of applications."

A few days later all that Stephens had feared occurred. They had gone, upon invitation, to a private house.

It was our intention to go through the whole family, uncles, aunts, grand-children, down to Indian servants, as many as would sit; but man is born to disappointment. I spare the reader the recital of our misfortunes that day. It would be too distressing. Suffice it to say that we tried plate after plate, sitting after sitting, varying light, time, and other points of the process; but it was all in vain. The stubborn instrument seemed bent upon confounding us; and, covering our confusion as well as we could, we gathered up our Daguerreotype and carried ourselves off. What was the cause of our complete discomfiture we never ascertained, but we resolved to give up business as ladies' Daguerreotype portrait takers.[15]

9. *Facing the Camera*

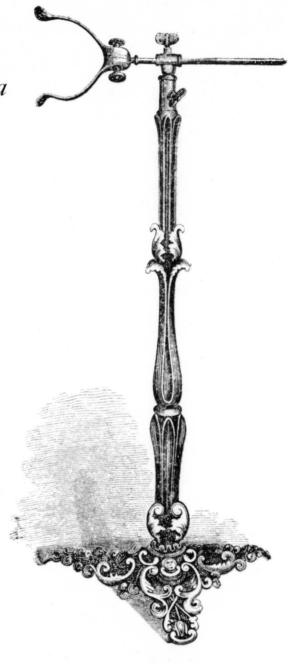

WITH an exposure of approximately twenty seconds, it was an ordeal to sit for one's likeness, whether in Central America or in a luxurious Broadway gallery. Absolute immobility was required during the time that the lens was uncovered, and to help the sitter hold still, heavy iron headrests were provided, with adjustable horns forming a semicircle to accommodate the back of the head. These were not clamps; the head was not held rigid; they were rests against which one could lean. The heavier they were, the better, and one daguerreotypist found that moving them around his gallery was a healthy daily exercise. Ralph Waldo Emerson entered in his journal for October 24, 1841:

> Were you ever daguerreotyped, O immortal man? And did you look with all vigor at the lens of the camera, or rather, by direction of the operator, at the brass peg a little below it, to give the picture the full benefit of your expanded and flashing eye? and in your zeal not to blur the image, did you keep every

HEAD-REST

76

finger in its place with such energy that your hands became clenched as for fight or despair, and in your resolution to keep your face still, did you feel every muscle becoming every moment more rigid; the brows contracted into a Tartarean frown, and the eyes fixed as they are fixed in a fit, in madness, or in death? And when, at last you are relieved of your dismal duties, did you find the curtain drawn perfectly, and the hands true, clenched for combat, and the shape of the face or head?—but, unhappily, the total expression escaped from the face and the portrait of a mask instead of a man? Could you not by grasping it very tight hold the stream of a river, or of a small brook, and prevent it from flowing?[1]

Emerson's disappointment in his likeness was a not uncommon reaction. When a sitter complained to Abraham Bogardus, "My picture looks like the *Devil*," the Broadway daguerreotypist said, "I told him I had never seen that personage and could not say as to resemblance, but sometimes a likeness ran all through families."[2]

Snelling urged his readers to avoid stilted poses.

Photographic Art-Journal, February, 1851. "Look right into the camera," is a direction often given to the sitter by the Daguerreotypist, which cannot be too highly censured; for a more palpable error, where grace and ease is desired, could not be committed.

That the position of every portion of the sitter's person should be carefully studied, may be illustrated by a single incident that came under our observation but a short time since. A gentleman had a daguerreotype of his wife taken by one of our best artists, and so far as the tone and boldness of the picture was concerned, it could have no superior—still, when it was delivered, he expressed himself dissatisfied, declaring that it had no more resemblance to his wife than to any other lady. We were appealed to to decide, and gave our opinion as above expressed, but nothing could move his decision, although he acknowledged that he perfectly agreed with us, as to its merits in other respects, and as he could not censure the artist, he willingly took the daguerreotype, deciding to make another trial at a future day. We then explained the cause of his disappointment, and he was satisfied that the fault was with the lady, although we, in our mind, were positive it was with the artist. The fact was, she had elevated her eyebrows to such a degree, as to give her eyes a very disagreeable stare, and produce a contraction in other portions of her features.

Had the operator paid attention to his subject, he would have studied her face more minutely, detected the defect, and watched his opportunity to secure the impression of the image, at the moment when a more pleasing expression

77

crossed the features. This he might readily have produced by some pleasant re-mark, or delicate compliment.

Yet all could not be left to the operator. The sitter had to be something of an actor. "Some of us know better than others how to put on the best look," N. P. Willis, the novelist, observed. "Some are handsome only when talking, some only when the features are in repose; some have more character in the full face, some in the profile; some do the writhings of life's agonies with their hearts and wear smooth faces, some do the same work with their nostrils. A portrait-painter usually takes all these matters into account, and, with his dozen or more long sittings, has time enough to make a careful study of how the character is worked out in the physiognomy, and to paint accordingly. But in daguerreotyping, the sitter has to employ this knowledge and exercise this judgment for himself."[3]

The comparison with the portrait painter was inevitable. Samuel F. B. Morse, himself a distinguished portraitist with the brush, had already pointed out that the daguerreotype should prove to be valuable to the artist. "How narrow and foolish the idea which some express that it will be the ruin of art, or rather artists, for every one will be his own painter," he wrote to his fellow artist, Washington Allston.[4] The painter Rembrandt Peale, however, expressed concern: "Daguerreotype and photographs all have their relative merit; and as memorials of regard, are not to be despised. The task of the portrait painter is quite another thing—an effort of skill, taste, mind and judgment . . . to render permanent the transient expression of character which may be the most agree-able."[5]

Yet painters did not hesitate to make use of daguerreotypes, particularly when their assignment was to make portraits of famous people. William Willard's solution to the problem of painting the aged Daniel Webster by having a daguerre-otype made of him by Southworth & Hawes was a common practice. A painting of Webster in the Memorial Art Gallery of the University of Rochester, New York, is from a daguerreotype by F. DeBourg Richards of Philadelphia—even though it is signed "G. W. Merrick." Plumbe's daguerreotype of Washington Irving (Plate 61) was used by several painters as a substitute for the presence in their studios of that illustrious writer. The painting by Henry F. Darby in the Sleepy Hollow Restorations, Tarrytown, New York, is clearly copied from the daguerreotype. Plumbe's image appears again, copied in every detail, in the

78

group portrait of "Irving and his Friends" in the same collection by Christian Schussle. It is likely that this painting is based entirely on daguerreotypes, for the features of James Fenimore Cooper bear a striking resemblance to the daguerreotype which was made in Brady's gallery for the *International Magazine* in 1851—the very same daguerreotype from which Charles Eliot Loring derived the painting which now hangs beside Schussle's in the Tarrytown museum.

This use of daguerreotypes appeared entirely legitimate in the middle of the nineteenth century, when photography was considered an automatic process. Photography was called the pencil of Nature, the child of light, Nature's amanuensis: daguerreotypes were advertised as sun-drawn miniatures. "It is a work of Nature, not of Art—and as far surpassing the production of the pencil as all Nature's effort do those of man."[6] The professional press noted with pride that painters were using the work of daguerreotypists.

> *Humphrey's Journal, April 15, 1852*. Thomas Faris of Cincinnati has made a portrait of Kossuth full length from which Eaton* is to paint a portrait.

> *American Journal of Photography, November 1, 1860*. Edgar A. Poe's daguerreotype, in the possession of Ossian E. Dodge, has been enlarged to life size in a copy, taken from it by a Cleveland photographer, and painted in oil by Walcutt,† the western artist.

It is surprising that today art historians, with their delight in probing into the prototype of every artist's work, should so generally fail to recognize that photography has been ever since 1839 both a source and an influence to hosts of painters. Nor was the role of photography unnoticed by critics of the day. Théophile Gautier, reviewing the 1861 Salon, remarked that "the daguerreotype, which has been given neither credit nor a medal, has nevertheless worked hard for the exhibition. It has yielded much information, spared much posing of the model, furnished many accessories, backgrounds and drapery which had only to be copied and colored."[7]

Illustrated magazines began to reproduce daguerreotypes by means of wood engravings, steel engravings, or other graphic arts techniques. The demand for portraits of celebrities was so great that Humphrey warned his readers:

*Probably Joseph Oriel Eaton, active in Cincinnati in 1853.
†Probably William Walcutt, who was in Cleveland 1859-60.

It is no uncommon saying by our first men, that they "wish there was no such discovery as Daguerre's, for it is so annoying that it is impossible to go to New York, Boston or Philadelphia, without being tormented by a dozen invitations to sit for a daguerreotype likeness." This we heard from a gentleman, who, during a stay of a single day in this city, received no less than TWENTY-ONE "very polite invitations" to allow the ARTIST "the gratifying pleasure of adding a portrait of his most honorable sir to their collection."[8]

The first of these collections of celebrities was The National Daguerreotype Miniature Gallery, founded by Edward Anthony in partnership with Jonas Edwards, Howard Chilton, and J. R. Clark. Humphrey was impressed by the effort which the firm made to obtain portraits. "Mr. Anthony," he wrote in 1852, "went from this city to the residence of *Gen. Andrew Jackson,* for the purpose of securing a likeness of the old hero before his death." The national Capitol itself was invaded; the firm succeeded in having a committee room set aside for their use as a studio. The most famous product of the gallery was a 27-by-36-inch mezzotint, "Clay's Farewell to the Senate," drawn by J. Whitehorne "from Daguerreotype likenesses," and published in 1846. It contains ninety-six portraits: who made them is not stated. An engraving of Daniel Webster, copied from a daguerreotype by John Adams Whipple and published by the firm, was so popular that it was recopied by the daguerreotype process.

The originals, with countless others, were lost when the gallery, then owned by Daniel E. Gavit, burned to the ground on February 7, 1852. "The next day," Humphrey wrote, "as some gentlemen were looking over the ruins where all seemed a mass of ashes, coals, melted glass, brass, copper, and silver, all were startled by the announcement 'Here is a perfect specimen'; and what added more to the happy feeling of all present, it was immediately recognized as the likeness of *John Quincy Adams,* as pure and unspotted as himself. The enthusiasm manifested on this occasion, can be better imagined than described. Should that *good* man appear in person before the living Representatives of our country, no greater surprise could be manifested than was on the finding of his perfect likeness in *these* ruins."[9]

Undoubtedly inspired by Anthony—it is no accident that his first New York gallery was in the same building as Anthony's shop—Mathew B. Brady began in 1845 to make a similar collection of portraits of celebrities, a project which he pressed with such vigor that his gallery was to be called the "Valhalla of America." In 1850 he announced the publication of twenty-four lithographs by Francis D'Avignon, drawn from daguerreotypes. Only twelve were published, in a folio volume titled *The Gallery of Illustrious Americans*. Although it was clearly stated on the title page that the illustrations were "From daguerreotypes by Brady, engraved by D'Avignon," beneath the portrait of William Ellery Channing appears the credit: "S. Gambardella pinx." Other portraits in Brady's collection, not reproduced in the 1850 publication, originated from other galleries. The portrait of Edgar Allan Poe (Plate 62), so often reproduced as the work of Brady, was taken in the Providence, Rhode Island, gallery of Masury & Hartshorn on November 9, 1848; the operator was a Mr. Manchester,—either Henry N. or his brother Edwin H., who took over the gallery in 1850. Poe was persuaded by a friend to sit for his daguerreotype in the gallery a few days after he had attempted suicide. The cause of Poe's acute distress was his failure to win the hand of Mrs. Sarah Helen Whitman in marriage, for which purpose he visited Providence. He gave Mrs. Whitman the daguerreotype, which she considered "wonderful . . . all the stormy grandeur of that Via Dolorosa had left its sullen shadow on his brow, but it was very fine."[10] Three identical daguerreotypes exist, all of which can be traced to Mrs. Whitman. They are without doubt copies of a now lost original.

Four identical daguerreotypes of Henry Clay have been located: one in the Southworth & Hawes collection, one with the name LAWRENCE stamped on the mat, a third from Brady's studio, and a fourth—undocumented—in the A. Conger Goodyear collection. We do not know who took the portrait of John Howard Payne, the author of "Home, Sweet Home"; identical daguerreotypes are in the Southworth & Hawes collection, in the George Eastman House, and in the Goodyear collection (in a frame bearing the label of J. Vannerson).

It was a widespread custom for daguerreotypists to publish daguerreotype copies of daguerreotypes. Apprentices did the duplicating. "Thinking that perhaps Daguerreotypists in the country would like to have a copy of Jenny Lind," Frederick DeBourg Richards advertised in the *Daguerreian Journal*, August, 1851, "and as it is allowed by all that my picture is the best in America, I will sell copies at the following prices:—one sixth, $2; one-fourth, $4; one-half, $6." Daguerreotypists exhibited copies without disclosing their authorship, a practice that has led to utter confusion in the attribution of daguerreotypes to individual makers. Direct provenance from a known gallery is not evidence that the daguerreotype was the work of the proprietor.

When the collodion process replaced the daguerreotype, Brady copied his entire collection on glass negatives. E. and H. T. Anthony sold photographs from these plates. Although these "cartes-de-visite" are plainly marked on their backs "Published by E. & H. T. ANTHONY, 501 Broadway, New York, from photographic negative in BRADY'S National Portrait Gallery," historians have assumed that Brady himself posed the sitter and was responsible for the photograph. Brady's activity was the counterpart of the present-day picture agency's. He both commissioned photographs and collected them. He followed a practice that was fully accepted in the day.

The lack of concern on the part of daguerreotypists and public alike for exact credit makes it impossible to study the work of individuals, as one studies the oeuvre of a painter, or the opera of a composer. Even in the work of Southworth & Hawes, who boasted that they never employed operators, there are daguerreotype copies of daguerreotypes that are quite likely the work of others.

Mathew B. Brady, because of the extraordinary documentation of the Civil War, an outgrowth of his *Gallery of Illustrious Americans*, which he had the imagination and daring to accomplish, has rightfully won a place as a pioneer photographic historian. Yet, as proprietors of galleries, neither he nor his competitors can be judged as photographers. The late Robert Taft summed it up in his book, *Photography and the American Scene* (1938):

> I have no sympathy with some of the pseudo-critics of the modern day who see in any photograph bearing Brady's imprint the hand of the artist. Although it is true that, during his early years, Brady worked long and diligently to master his art, once this mastery had been achieved, and his competence assured, Brady left the actual photographic work to others. He kept abreast of his times, however, employed only the most competent operators, and did not hesitate to spend money upon the introduction of new devices or new methods. But he was absent from his business for long intervals, and during such periods the quality of the work turned out by his galleries did not suffer. Even during the Civil War, when actually engaged in photographic work, he employed a large number of operators, and many of the photographs, in fact a large proportion, of those credited to Brady were made by his employees. The credit which is

82

due Brady is for his original idea as a photographic historian, his persistence in
this idea, and for sufficient business acumen and management to carry it out—
and not for any artistic merit his work may possess. One judges an artist by the
work of his own hand, not by the work turned out by his employees. This is
not to say that some of the work turned out from Brady's studio may not have
artistic value, but in most instances we do not know who deserves the praise
for such merit.[11]

Brady constantly maintained the highest ideals of taste. He was deeply concerned
with the status of photography as an art. He wrote Samuel F. B. Morse on February 15, 1855:

> Permit me to request your opinion in reference to the aid which the progress
> of Daguerreotyping has afforded the kindred arts of painting drawing & engraving. As the first successful introducer of this rare art in America, the first
> President of the National Academy of Design, and in virtue of your long &
> distinguished artistic experience your views upon this topic will be received by
> the public & the world of art with high consideration.
>
> The influence which Daguerreotyping has exercised upon the social amenities, universalizing as it has the rarest & most subtle of artistic effect, placing
> within general reach the results which before its introduction were laboriously
> & slowly wrought with the pencil, is understood and appreciated. The fact that
> it has found its way where other phases of artistic beauty would have been disregarded is recognized. During my experience, however, I have endeavored to
> render it as far as possible an auxiliary to the artist. While the other features
> of its development have not been disregarded I have esteemed this of paramount importance. How far I have succeeded & whether the recognition of the
> effort among Artists has been commensurate with the aid they have derived
> from it I know of none so eminently qualified to judge as yourself.[12]

Only a handful from the thousands of daguerreotypes, by daguerreotypists
known and unknown, have the magic inner life which distinguishes a work of
art. Emerson could write "'Tis certain that the Daguerreotype is the true Republican style of painting. The artist stands aside and lets you paint yourself."[13]
His friend Henry David Thoreau was more perceptive: "Nature is readily made
to repeat herself in a thousand forms, and in the daguerreotype her own light is
amanuensis. . . . Thus we may easily multiply the forms of the outward; but to
give the within outwardness, that is not easy."[14]

83

10. *The Explorers*

ALTHOUGH the overwhelming majority of daguerreotypes taken in America during the two decades when the process flourished were portraits, daguerreotypists took pictures of everything on which the sun shone—and the sun itself. They turned their cameras on cities and landscapes; they invaded the gold fields; they planted their tripods on summits of the Rocky Mountains and on the island of Okinawa, and in Japan.

Most daguerreotypists were frequently called upon to take pictures out-of-doors. These were universally called "views," and required the use of lenses better corrected than those made for portraiture, where sharpness of field was sacrificed for speed. Since a daguerreotype image is normally reversed, as in a mirror, a prism or mirror had to be placed over the lens—unless the daguerreotype served as a model for an engraver, who needed a reversed image. While portraits were wholly acceptable when reversed—the sitter knows his own features only in a mirror—city views with signs reading backward were not acceptable, particularly if merchants had commissioned them.

With one exception, the face of every major city of America can be studied in daguerreotypes. Views of New York City do not exist. They were taken; wood engravings from some of the daguerreotypes were published in *Putnam's Magazine* in 1853. Not one of them has survived.

The finest city views are panoramas, made by taking a series of pictures from one position by turning the camera exactly the angle of view of the lens between each exposure. The finished daguerreotypes were framed with the edges butting.

Charles Fontayne and William Southgate Porter set up their whole-plate camera in Newport, Kentucky, opposite Cincinnati, in 1848. They took eight plates which embrace two miles of the Ohio River from the village of Fulton to the foot of Vine Street in Cincinnati (Plates 37-38). The magnificent panorama is now owned by the Cincinnati Public Library. It won fame for Fontayne and

84

Porter when they exhibited it at the Franklin Institute, the Maryland Institute, and the Great Exhibition in London, 1851. So detailed is this striking panorama that the river craft have been identified.

But of all American cities, San Francisco was the most frequently daguerreotyped. Its rapid growth, the pride of its citizens, and international curiosity about the City of Gold created a demand for pictures, and this demand the daguerreotype satisfied in part.

Daguerreotypists flocked to San Francisco along with the gold hunters. A. S. Southworth was there, not with his camera, but to seek his fortune in the mines. Other, wiser, daguerreotypists found that fortunes could be made by sticking to their trade. There were fifty of them in San Francisco between 1850 and 1864. The earliest was a lady, Mrs. Julia Shannon; but she was not in business long, for her profession is listed in the 1852 directory as "accoucheur." Cameramen came from Massachusetts, South Carolina, Florida, and New Brunswick, Canada. Their prices were high, yet they did a thriving business. Henry Bradley, formerly of Wilmington, South Carolina, "practised his art on the west side of Montgomery, between Washington and Jackson. His prices were from eight dollars upward, according to the size and style of the portrait and frame. The courteous artist was hardly allowed time to breathe, much less to eat, or take a moment's rest or two before the departure of a steamer. Californians were so anxious that their friends in civilized countries should see just how they looked in their mining dress, with their terrible revolver, the handle protruding menacingly from the holster, somehow, twisted in front, when sitting for a daguerreotype to send to the States! [Plate 77] They were proud of their curling moustaches and flowing beards; their bandit-looking *sombreros;* and our old friend Bradley accumulated much *oro en polvo* and many yellow coins from private mints."[1]

The most memorable work of the San Franciscan daguerreotypists were the panoramas they made of the city.

In 1852 William Shew, who had given up his Boston gallery and case factory and settled in San Francisco, made a panorama of five plates of the city from Rincon Point (Plates 70-74). This vivid document is now in the Smithsonian Institution in Washington. The inner harbor is choked with ships abandoned by their crews and left to rot or become floating storehouses. Later the area was filled in; it now forms downtown San Francisco. Five other panoramas exist, all looking toward the Bay.[2] Who took them is not known. Perhaps one, or more, can be ascribed to S. C. McIntyre, dentist turned daguerreotypist from Tallahassee, Florida, who took a panorama described in the *Alta California* for February 1, 1851, as the first of its kind:

DAGUERREOTYPE OF SAN FRANCISCO.—Decidedly the finest thing in the fine arts produced in this city, which we have seen, is a consecutive series of Daguerrean plates, five in number, arranged side by side so as to give a view of our entire city and harbor, the shipping, bay, coast and mountains opposite, islands, dwellings and hills—all embraced between Rincon Point on the right, to the mouth of our beautiful bay on the left, included between lines proceeding from the hills to the west of the city as the point of vision.

This picture, for such it may be termed, although the first attempt, is nearly perfect. It is admirable in execution as well as design. It is intended for the "World's Industrial Convention" in London. We venture the assertion that nothing there will create greater interest than this specimen of Art among us, exhibiting a perfect idea of the city which all of the world carries with its name abroad more of romance and wonder than any other. It is a picture, too, which cannot be disputed—it carries with it evidence which God himself gives through the unerring light of the world's great luminary.

The people of Europe have never yet seen a picture of this, to them, the most wonderful city. This will tell its own story, and the sun to testify to its truth. . . . The views were taken by Mr. McIntyre of this city. He proposes, if his efforts meet with sufficient encouragement, to finish and furnish duplicates of this excellent and artistical picture to the lovers of art, at one hundred dollars. It may be seen at this office.

There is no record that the panorama was shown at the Great Exhibition of the Works of Industry of All Nations in London. But Europeans soon became familiar with a similar panorama of San Francisco in an etching, measuring 39 by 9½ inches, made by the French artist Charles Méryon from a set of five daguerreotypes in 1856. Charles Baudelaire, poet and art critic, considered the print Méryon's masterpiece. The commission was irksome to the artist. He found it difficult to resolve the perspective, for each daguerreotype had its own vanishing point. Méryon was not content to copy the plates; he wanted to produce a picture as if he had drawn it on the spot, and used the daguerreotypes as documents, rather than as models. They were confusing: some areas contained too much detail, other areas were so indistinct that it took him days of study to disentangle one building from another.[3]

86

Humphrey praised McIntyre's panorama; he was especially enthusiastic about a set of six half-plates of gold mining, "picturing 'all sorts'—men, with spade and tin pan in hand, eagerly looking after dust; some examining a lump just found, others up to their knees in water, and, among the rest is, in a bent position, a man, pan in hand, looking up with a grin, exhibiting 'something' in his pan which he no doubt would try to make us believe was the metal."[4] (Cf. Plate 85)

Eduard Vischer, in a report of a trip to the mining regions in 1859, wrote:

> The daguerreotype is especially suited to reproduce all these mechanical mining devices. In the mining region nature, too, seems bare of all cheerful embellishment, with a stark contrast between the naked masses of rock and the thin, straggly pine woods. Luxuriant foliage is seen but rarely. Rich material for observation is offered in the photographic views of the American River region exhibited in Vance's Panorama. Similar photographs of other mining regions would complete a picture gallery the inspection of which would almost be a substitute for a visit to the places themselves.[5]

A large number of these documentary daguerreotypes exist (Plates 85-87). Who made them we do not know. Robert H. Vance, whose "Panorama" Vischer praises, specialized in them and put three hundred on exhibition in New York in 1851. In the catalogue he wrote:

> These Views are no exaggerated and high-colored sketches, got up to produce effect, but are as every daguerreotype must be, the stereotyped impression of the real thing itself.
>
> They embrace among a variety of others, a splendid Panoramic View of San Francisco. . . . Also, views of Stockton, Coloma, Carson's Creek, Makelame Hill, the Old Mill where the gold was first discovered, Nevada, Gold Run, Marysville, Sacramento, Benicia, &c., &c. Also, a large collection of views taken of the miners at work, in different localities; also a likeness of Capt. Sutter, and a large collection of sketches of the different tribes of Indians on the Pacific Coast.[6]

This magnificent collection no longer exists. How or when these historical documents disappeared is not known. The exhibition was not a financial success, and Vance offered the daguerreotypes for sale in 1852. They were bought by Gurney, but a year later he sold them to John H. Fitzgibbon of St. Louis, who had them on display in his gallery in 1856. Perhaps they disappeared when Fitzgibbon sold his gallery in 1861 and moved to Vicksburg, Mississippi. It was an unlucky move for him, for he was captured by the Union Army and sent to a prisoner-of-war camp in Cuba. On his release he made his way back to St. Louis and reopened his gallery. In 1877 he retired, and began publication of a magazine, *The Saint Louis Practical Photographer,* in which he presented reminiscences of the pioneers and his own early experiences as a daguerreotypist. In spite of his historical interest, he gave no clue in the magazine to the disappearance of the Vance collection.

Curiously, and to the despair of the historian, not one daguerreotype is known to exist from those that were taken under even more difficult conditions by the handful of daguerreotypists who accompanied official government expeditions and exploring parties to little-known parts of the country.

Edward Anthony was the first to serve as official photographer on a government survey. When Professor James Renwick of Columbia College was appointed by the President chairman of a commission to survey and explore the northeast boundary of the United States and Canada, he invited his former pupil, Anthony, to accompany him and take daguerreotypes of terrain. On March 28, 1842, the commission submitted its report, together with supporting documentation, including "copies of some daguerreotypes."[7]

Perhaps influenced by this official acceptance of daguerreotypes as topographical documents, Colonel John Charles Frémont took a camera with him on his first government expedition to explore the Oregon Trail from the Mississippi to Wyoming. Charles Preuss, the German cartographer of the expedition, noted in his diary on August 2, 1842: "Yesterday afternoon and this morning, Frémont set up with daguerreotype to photograph the rocks; he spoiled five plates that way. Not a thing was to be seen on them. That's the way it often is with these Americans. They know everything, they can do everything, and when they are put to a test, they fail miserably."[8] Five days later Frémont again failed. Preuss commented: "Today he said the air up here is too thin; that is the reason his daguerreotype was a failure. Old boy, you don't understand the thing, that is it."[9] No record exists of Frémont's daguerreotypes—nor any other reference to them.

In making preparations for his fifth crossing of the Rocky Mountains in 1853, Frémont decided to leave photography to a professional. He chose Solomon

88

N. Carvalho, a daguerreotypist from Charleston, South Carolina, after a contest with another candidate, a certain Bomar, for the position of photographer. The daguerreotype process was already threatened by the negative-positive process, and Frémont did not know which technique would be better suited to the rigors of mountain travel. As a practical test, he ordered a contest between the two. "In half an hour from the time word was given," Carvalho recounted in his *Incidents of Travel and Adventure in the Far West,* "my daguerreotype was made; but the photograph could not be seen until next day, as it had to remain in water all night, which was absolutely necessary to develop it."[10] Evidently Bomar was far from skilled in the art of paper and glass photography, for no such all-night processing time is specified in the technical literature.

Carvalho joined the party, and soon was setting up his camera at a Cheyenne village on Big Timber to photograph the daughter of the Great Chief. "She attired herself in her most costly robes, ornamented with elk teeth, beads, and colored porcupine quills—expressly to have her likeness taken. I made a beautiful picture of her." He touched her brass bracelet with quicksilver: "it instantly became bright and glittering as polished silver."[11] To the Indians, it was magic.

Around New Year's Day, 1854, the party was high in the Rockies. Carvalho climbed to mountain peaks with Frémont and photographed the landscape.

> To make daguerreotypes in the open air, in a temperature varying from freezing point to thirty degrees below zero, requires a different manipulation from the processes by which pictures are made in a warm room. My professional friends were all of the opinion that the elements would be against my success. Buffing and coating plates, and mercurializing them, on the summit of the Rocky Mountains, standing at times up to one's middle in snow, with no covering above save the arched vault of heaven, seemed to our city friends one of the impossibilities—knowing, as they did, that iodine will not give out its fumes except at a temperature of 70° to 80° Fahrenheit. I shall not appear egotistical if I say that I encountered many difficulties, but was well prepared to meet them by having previously acquired a scientific and practical knowledge of the chemicals I used, as well as of the theory of light: a firm determination to succeed also aided me in producing results which, to my knowledge, have never been accomplished under similar circumstances.
>
> While suffering from frozen feet and hands, without food for twenty-four hours, travelling on foot over mountains of snow, I have stopped on the trail, made pictures of the country, repacked my materials, and found myself . . . frequently some five or six miles behind camp, which was only reached with

89

great expense of bodily as well as mental suffering. The great secret, however, of my untiring perseverance and continued success, was that my honor was pledged to Col. Frémont to perform certain duties, and I would rather have died than not have redeemed it.[12]

The going became even more difficult. All fifty pack animals fell several hundred feet to the bottom of a ravine; two were killed, and the tent poles were smashed. The men "had to sleep out upon the open snow, with no covering but our blankets." Provisions got low, they were forced to slaughter the horses for food; twenty-seven were butchered. To save themselves, Frémont ordered all superfluous baggage buried in the snow, including the daguerreotype apparatus. The party finally arrived at Parawan in Little Salt Lake Valley, southern Utah, on February 8, 1854. One of them died. Carvalho was too ill to continue. He and F. W. Egglofstein, the topographical engineer, left the party and proceeded by foot to Salt Lake City.

The daguerreotypes which cost Carvalho such great effort have never been found, although Mrs. Frémont, in the introduction to her husband's memoirs, states that he managed to save them and sent them to Brady to be copied.[13]

While Frémont, at his own expense, was exploring for a route for the proposed transcontinental railroad straight across the Rocky Mountains, four official government surveys were being made for alternate routes. Isaac I. Stevens left St. Paul in June, 1853, to explore a northern route to Fort Vancouver (now Vancouver, Washington), where he arrived in December. John Mix Stanley, the most celebrated painter of Indians since George Catlin, was a member of the party. He had a camera. The official United States War Department report states that on September 4, 1853, "Mr. Stanley commenced taking daguerreotypes of the Indians with his apparatus. They were delighted and astounded to see their likenesses produced by the direct action of the sun. They worship the sun, and they considered that Mr. Stanley was inspired by their divinity, and he thus became in their eyes a great medicine man."[14]

Stanley's daguerreotypes shared the fate of Carvalho's. Perhaps they perished in the fire in the Smithsonian Institution which destroyed Stanley's entire collection of paintings.

The daguerreotype flourished in an age of government expeditions. When a fleet of vessels of war sailed around the world under the command of Commodore Matthew Calbraith Perry on the delicate mission of opening diplomatic relations with the empire of Japan, there were but two civilians on board the flagship: William Heine, a painter from Dresden, and E. Brown, daguerreotypist.

Perry was besieged by scientists and explorers who wished to accompany him, for it was planned to make a complete report of the flora and fauna of the island of Japan and the life and customs of the people. On the grounds that military discipline, which he considered essential to the success of the mission should the Japanese prove hostile, could be enforced only with regular, trained Navy personnel, Perry refused these requests. The only exception was for the two artists, who were added to the crew of the U.S.S. *Mississippi* as acting master's mates.

The *Mississippi* set sail in 1852, bound for Japan by way of the Cape of Good Hope, Mauritius, Singapore, and Shanghai. At Lew Chew, as the island of Okinawa was then called, Brown was settled in a house on the outskirts of Tumai; his companion drew him photographing, with a whole-plate camera on a cast-iron studio stand, four Lew-Chewans in front of a temple. The picture appears as a lithograph in the richly illustrated, three-volume report issued by the United States government.[15] Twenty-one lithographs and thirteen wood engravings in the report are based on Brown's daguerreotypes; the remainder are either signed by Heine or bear the double credit, "From life by Heine. Figures by Brown." It is not improbable, therefore, that Brown's daguerreotypes served as models for these pictures. Most of the daguerreotypes credited to Brown are portraits; a few are temples and buildings.

Perry's fleet, numbering four ships and 560 men, entered Uraga Bay, Japan, in July, 1853, and lay at anchor there. The Japanese were thrown into confusion; never had they seen so many western vessels. Ten days later, after demanding an audience with the Emperor's representatives and announcing that he would return in the spring, Perry steamed away. In February he returned with ten ships and two thousand men. He was welcomed, presents were exchanged, exploring parties organized, and a treaty signed in which Japan agreed to allow foreign vessels to obtain stores and provisions.

The diplomatic success of the expedition, which marks the beginning of the rise of Japan as a national power, has overshadowed its scientific and ethnological significance. No comparable description of the life and customs of the Japanese and the natural resources of their country had ever been published. The reliance on photographs in the pictorial documentation published in the report pointed the way to the future.

11. *A Tool for Scientists*

BESIDES its use on scientific expeditions, the daguerreotype was found of great value by astronomers.

Humphrey reported that the solar eclipse of May 26, 1854, had been photographed by John Campbell, John Kelsey in Rochester, New York, C. Barnes in Mobile, Alabama, George E. Hale in Detroit, and by the Langenheims in Philadelphia.[1] Snelling added M. A. Root and Victor Prevost.[2] All used the daguerreotype process except Prevost, a Frenchman who had just come to America, bringing with him an adaptation of the calotype paper-negative technique. In the literature of astronomy yet another photographer is recorded, Professor William Holmes Chambers Bartlett of West Point, who took four daguerreotypes.[3]

Never before had so many people been able to take astronomical photographs. Solar eclipses had been photographed before—first, without much success, in Milan by G. A. Majocchi on July 8, 1842. Though only partially visible in the United States, the eclipse of July 28, 1851, was daguerreotyped by John Adams Whipple at Harvard College Observatory.[4]

Whipple was scientifically trained. He was a chemist by profession when the daguerreotype process came to America, and supplied chemicals to daguerreotypists. But the manufacturing processes proved detrimental to his health and in 1843 he took up the camera as a profession in partnership with Albert Litch until, in 1846, Litch left to become Gurney's operator. Whipple had great mechanical ingenuity. To produce a vignette effect in his portraits he interposed between the camera and the sitter a circular mask; he patented this technique, which he called "crayon portraiture" in 1849.[5] Humphrey visited him in Boston.

Daguerreian Journal, July, 1851. Whipple is going it by steam . . . a large fan is so arranged and worked by steam that it keeps a cool and rather inviting breeze and prepares the complexion of the sitter for one of his best, even in the warmest weather; by steam he cleans his plates, heats his mercury, distils water and *steam like* sits his picture—hence we conclude that Mr. W. lives by steam.

92

VIEWS OF THE RECENT ECLIPSE.

[Engraved for Moore's Rural New Yorker, from Daguerreotypes taken by John Kelsey.]

Whipple used a wood engraving of a steam engine in the advertisement of his Washington Street gallery in the *Boston Almanac for the Year 1851*. He said that it was one horsepower, with 3¼-inch bore and 6-inch stroke. The boiler was 18 inches by 5 feet; coal to run it cost 25 cents a day.[6]

Professor William Cranach Bond, and his son George Phillip Bond, the director of Harvard College Observatory, found Whipple an ideal technician to realize their desire to daguerreotype the heavenly bodies with their great 15-inch telescope, then the largest in the world. To do this, the delicate adjustments of the telescope had to be altered, and the eyepiece removed: the telescope itself was

93

used as a camera. Experiments were begun in 1848, with indifferent success, Bond reported. On December 18, 1849, the astronomers recorded in the observatory log book the visit of Whipple and his assistant William B. Jones "to take a Daguerreotype of the Moon." Normal observations were interrupted, and the astronomers were vexed: "very much against our inclinations we unscrewed the Micrometer (for the first time for more than a year past I should judge)."[7]

On the night of July 16/17, 1850, the micrometer was again taken off. A star was daguerreotyped, the star Alpha Lyrae—the first star (except the sun) ever to be photographed. A newspaper marveled at this accomplishment; it calculated that the light by which the daguerreotype was taken "took its departure from the star more than twenty years ago, long before Daguerre had conceived his admirable invention."[8]

Whipple and Jones continued in March, 1851, and by altering the focus of the telescope by half an inch, to compensate for chromatic aberration, succeeded in obtaining a daguerreotype of the moon which, Bond wrote, was "a better representation of the Lunar surface than any engraving of it, that I have ever seen."[9]

They sent a copy of the moon daguerreotype to Humphrey. It was a quarter plate, and must have been of extreme interest to the editor for, while he was living in Canandaigua, New York, he had tried the same thing. On the night of September 1, 1849, he took nine exposures on a single plate, moving the plate holder between each, ranging in time from 2 minutes 10 seconds to less than a second. His camera was an ordinary portrait camera with a relatively short focal-length lens: the moon was recorded as a disk one tenth of an inch in diameter. Snelling pasted in each copy of the July, 1853, issue of the *Photographic Art-Journal* a copy of one of Whipple's moon daguerreotypes made by Whipple himself with his crystalotype process (Plate 66). It won for him a prize medal at the Great Exhibition in London in 1851. Bond sent two other daguerreotypes by Whipple to Sir John F. W. Herschel; they are now in the Science Museum, London.

Other natural phenomena were daguerreotyped. Both Alexander Hesler of Chicago and T. M. Easterly of St. Louis captured the flash of lightning on daguerreotype plates. W. H. Goode of Yale University wrote in 1840, "I have taken proofs of microscopic objects magnified 600 times, by receiving images from a solar microscope on the iodized surface. Perfect images of insects and

94

other small objects are thus obtained."[10] Microphotography—the reduction of printed matter to minute size, for reading under magnification— was accomplished:

> *Philadelphia Public Ledger, December 30, 1843.* A copy of the Boston Transcript has been daguerreotyped of the size of an inch by an inch and a half. The heading, capital letters, and pictorial figures are clear to the naked eye, and by the aid of a twelve-power microscope the letter press may be read with ease.

Had the unknown experimenter sent this daguerreotype to the Great Exhibition in London, 1851, he might have won a medal. The jury was disappointed to find "no miniature of printed books (holding out the promise of future publications in miniature), or that of condensing in volume for preservation in museums, etc., the enormous mass of documentary matter which daily more and more defies collection from the mere impossibility of storage, but which will one day become matter of history."[11]

12. *A Quest for Color*

WHEN Daguerre first showed his daguerreotypes in 1839, the public regretted that the colors of nature were not recorded in the wonderfully autographic manner that light and shade was reproduced. To fill this deficiency, the only recourse was to tint the daguerreotype by applying color to its delicate surface. Plumbe and Langenheim peddled their patented techniques for accomplishing this coloring by electroplating or by the use of stencils; two other similar processes were patented.[1] But for the most part daguerreotypists applied dry powdered pigment directly to the metal surface with a finely-pointed camel's-hair brush. A very slight amount of isinglass dissolved in water was first applied to the surface. It was allowed to dry and then was made tacky by breathing on it. Diamonds were made to shine by digging into the surface of the plate with the sharp point of an awl, laying bare a point of silver. Jewelry was painted gold. The delicacy of the surface of a good daguerreotype made any handwork beyond tinting impractical; retouching was out of the question, for it was impossible to imitate by hand the fine detail and rich tonal scale of a well-made plate.

The best daguerreotypists preferred to leave their work uncolored.

Photographic Art-Journal, April, 1854. Although some of our finest artists use this style of coloring, they must in their own minds condemn it, as they know that they are working to please the bad tastes of the community and not their own. What is finer in the daguerreian art than a fine, sharp, bold picture without color (or a slight flesh tint,) or a drab background, not killed with too much mercury?

The judges of the 1848 Exhibition of the Massachusetts Charitable Mechanic Association in Boston had this to say of Nancy Southworth's handiwork on her brother's daguerreotypes: "The coloring is managed so as to diminish the regret that it should be attempted." Their judgment coincided with that of the French critic Louis Figuier, who wrote in the same year (we translate): "To color a daguerreotype plate is as ridiculous as to illuminate an engraving by Reynolds

96

or Rembrandt. The essential merit of photographic images rests in the beautiful gradations of tone and in a harmony of light and shade so perfect that it defies the engraver's burin. All these qualities become submerged in this absurd paste of colors."[2]

But the public demanded that their likenesses be colored. When they read in newspapers the announcement that a daguerreotypist by the name of Rev. L. L. Hill had discovered a method of color photography, they put off having their pictures taken, waiting the promised day when they could have them in full color. Hill had issued in November, 1850, a technical manual, *The Magic Buff*. On the last page he wrote:

NATURAL COLORS

Several years' experiments have led us to the discovery of some remarkable facts, in reference to the process of daguerreotyping in the *colors of nature*. For instance, we can produce *blue, red, violet,* and *orange* on one plate, at one and the same time. We can, also, produce a landscape, with these colors beautifully developed—and this we can do in only one-third more time than is required for daguerreotype. The great problem is fairly solved. In a short time it will be furnished to *all* who are willing to pay a moderate price for it. Our friends will please keep us apprized of their P.O. address.

Levi L. Hill was known to daguerreotypists as the author of *A Treatise of Daguerreotype*,[3] published in Lexington, New York, in 1849. It was an excellent manual; three thousand copies were said to have been sold. He was former pastor of the Baptist Church in Westkill, New York, and a publisher of religious tracts; his *Baptist Library* had seven thousand subscribers in 1843. He renounced the cloth because of acute bronchitis, which prevented him from preaching. By accident he found that the fumes of bromine and chlorine he inhaled when visiting a daguerreotypist's shop were beneficial, so he took up daguerreotyping. He began his color experiments, he said, in 1847.

Snelling congratulated Hill in the January, 1851, issue of the *Photographic Art-Journal* with a certain reserve: "We learn with pleasure that Mr. L. Hill has succeeded in impressing the image upon the daguerreotype plate in all the beauty and brilliance of the natural colors. If this be true, we congratulate Mr. Hill on his success. . . . Mr. Hill, however, is not the first who has made experiments towards its investigation."

97

Hill replied in a letter dated February 4, 1851, which Snelling printed,[4] that some two years before he had discovered *"a singular compound"* (the italics are Hill's) the vapors of which he used instead of mercury to develop a *"latent colored image* on a prepared sensitive surface." The process was different from Daguerre's and that of Alexandre Edmond Becquerel, who was experimenting toward the same end in Paris. "All is perfectly simple," Hill wrote, "and a good Daguerreotypist would master the process in one day." He listed among his forty-five specimens:

1. *A view,* containing a *red house, green grass and foliage,* the *wood-color of the trees,* several cows of different shades of *red* and *brindle,* colored garments on a clothesline, *blue sky,* and the *faint blue of the atmosphere,* intervening between the camera and the distant mountains, very delicately spread over the picture, as if by the hand of a fairy artist.
2. *A sun-set scene,* in which *the play of colors upon the clouds* are impressed with a truthfulness and gorgeous beauty which I cannot describe.
3. *Several Portraits,* in which I have the *true complexion of the skin,* the *rosy cheeks and lips, blue and hazel eyes, auburn, brown and sandy hair,* and every *color of the drapery. Changeable silk* is given in all its fine blending of colors, and delicate richness of hues. I not only get red, blue, orange, violet &c., but their *various tints.*

Hill stated that he had not completed his experiments; yellow was still difficult to obtain. "I am *fully resolved,"* he concluded, "to carry my process *as far as I can,* before making it public. Till then, all will be kept a profound secret. My wife and myself alone know the process, and not a scrap or item shall ever be communicated until I am made *perfectly sure* of a suitable compensation." To finance his experiments, he announced that he planned to write a new book.

Daguerreotypists were impatient; already news of the discovery was hurting their business. Anthony made a suggestion:

Edward Anthony to L. L. Hill, February 13, 1851. You deserve a liberal reward for a discovery so perfect as your article describes it to be. Make up your mind what sum of money would be a fair equivalent, so that you could freely give the benefit of it to the whole world.

Let a subscription list be started, to which all who are interested in the progress of the art, shall be invited to contribute, . . . no money to be paid over until all is subscribed, and until certain gentlemen selected as judges—say Draper, Morse, &c., shall pronounce the discovery true, and in all its parts as represented. . . .

98

I will be happy to head the list with a subscription of one hundred dollars.[5]

L. L. Hill to Edward Anthony, March 28, 1851. Since arriving home I have been very unwell—my old bronchial difficulty, excited by a severe cold. I have not done a day's work, and it has been a sore affliction to me. I am now somewhat better, and hope to resume my wonted labors in a day or two.

It has been a question with me—How shall I get through? I am a poor man, and must have means of supporting my family, without embarrassment, or I cannot work. In New York offers of money were made to me—I have received the same from other sources—but which I have been all along fearful to do, I am now fully resolved not to do, viz: to receive advances on a process, in the disposition of which I *will* act independently. After much deliberation, therefore, and seeing no other way short of *committing myself,* I am about getting up another book.[6]

Humphrey visited Hill and rushed back to New York to announce that the reverend had accepted his invitation to become co-editor of his magazine. He inserted in the May 15, 1851, issue an engraving of the new editor, from a daguerreotype he had taken of him. Humphrey editorialized: "Could Raphael have looked upon a *Hillotype* just before completing his Transfiguration, the palette and brush would have fallen from his hand, and this picture would have remained *unfinished.*"

Samuel F. B. Morse now added his enthusiastic praise. He wrote Anthony on May 29: "My Dear 'Son of Art'—Yours of the 27th inst. I have this day received, and in reply would say that I visited Mr. Hill some days since, and was much gratified with my visit, although you are misinformed in regard to my having seen his results. From my conversations with him, however, *I have no doubt whatever of the reality of his discovery.*"[7] He concluded that he advised Hill to sell his new book at $100 a copy. Anthony answered that he thought the price "a moderate one."

But Morse found it difficult to defend Hill.

Samuel F. B. Morse to L. L. Hill, June 21, 1851. The publicity of the fact that I have visited you, has occasioned correspondence between some of the Daguerreotypists and myself evincing on their part a very natural anxiety and curiosity to know if the discovery is indeed a fact. I have been questioned also by some who follow the *trade,* not the *profession,* of Photography, in a way that required some effort on my part to keep down my rising indignation. Among others a Mr. Clark who was formerly, not now, with Messrs Anthony & Edwards, whom

99

I had never before seen, but who accosted me in the street respecting you in a manner which at once put me on my guard. 'Well, sir, I hear you have been to see Mr. Hill, the thing is all humbug, I suppose.' He used an oath with it, and apologized for the expression, to which I replied 'there was no need of an apology. . . .' Mr. C. spoke very patronizingly towards you, however, he thought of visiting you, could render you very valuable assistance, although not now in the profession, having left it and become a merchant, &c., &c. I told him you refused all visitors and therefore he had better not lose his time, and as for assistance, you did not need it. Another, Mr. Haas, is among the incredulous, especially when I told him I *had not seen* the *results*. This was proof positive that there was nothing to it, and he seemed to exult for a moment, but when I told him that the results existed nevertheless, whether he chose to believe it or not, and that I had no doubt of the reality of the discovery, he seemed sobered and thoughtful.[8]

Humphrey assured his readers, in the July 15 issue of the *Daguerreian Journal,* that he had complete confidence in Hill; he hoped to arrange an exhibition in New York of hillotypes "on or before September next." In the meantime Hill asked to be left alone. Snelling, in the August issue of the *Photographic Art-Journal,* was less patient. He stated that Hill was under moral obligation to produce, having caused such injury to the daguerreotype industry by his premature announcement.

On September 29, Hill was forced to write Humphrey that he could no longer serve as joint editor of the *Daguerreian Journal.* He further stated: "The information . . . that I would finish my experiments in September, I will not be able to fulfill."[9] Humphrey went to see Hill. He came back disillusioned. "We cannot see that Mr. H. has advanced a single step for the last six months. . . . We do not wish to deprecate Mr. Hill's alleged discovery. . . . We can only give the reader the facts in relation to what we and others have seen, and leave him to draw his own conclusions."[10]

The New York State Daguerreian Association—formed to present a solid front to the competition of cheap operators—held a special meeting in Brady's gallery on November 11, 1851. Humphrey reported that he saw only copies, and no pictures made from life. He was not shown the originals which Hill had copied, and so could not judge the quality of the colors. A committee was appointed: D. D. T. Davie, J. M. Clark, and William A. Tomlinson. Brady was in Europe.

100

The daguerreotypists went to Westkill. Hill, they said, received them courteously, but refused to show them anything.

Hill's account was somewhat different:

> The *"Committee"* of the miserable apology for a "New York State Daguerre-ian Association" who visited me during this stage of the proceedings well il-lustrated, in their course, the character of justice I received. . . . Three men— D. D. T. Davy [sic], "Phot." of Utica, Clark of New York, and Tomlinson of Troy—came to my house. . . . This Davy, after a liberal effusion of flattery, and after a kind reception from me, proceeded to threaten me with exposure as a humbug, and more than intimated that a banditti of ruffians, like himself, would visit this quiet valley with the laudable purpose of *breaking into my labora-tory.* . . . I candidly confess that I was afraid of the threatened attack.

Hill procured a revolver, the loan of a watchdog, and the offer by neighbors to serve as the "Westkill Police." In case of trouble, he was to sound a watchman's rattle.

> One dark night we were alarmed by the terrific barking of the faithful dog. I immediately rose from bed, and after listening for a few moments at one of the doors, I became satisfied that the enemy was around. . . . I forgot all about the "rattle," and the thought of summoning the "Police" did not enter my mind. . . . With no other soldier but the dog, I opened the door, rushed upon the enemy ——when, lo and behold, instead of meeting the chivalrous "Phot" and his ruffian army—instead of having a chance to display our valor, and to spit out the fire of our patriot souls—we encountered *our old cow.*[11]

Back in New York, the committee made their report, which was released to the New York *Times.* Their conclusion was shattering:

> They have found no evidence to satisfy them that any person has ever seen any picture colored by any process, new to the scientific world, at the hands of Mr. Hill. On the contrary they are of the opinion that the pictures in colors which have been exhibited by Mr. Hill are mere transfers of colored prints. . . . Your Committee have come to the conclusion that Mr. L. L. Hill has not only deluded many Professors of the Daguerrean Art, but that he has deluded him-self thoroughly and completely—that the origin of the discovery was a delusion —that the assumed progress and improvement of it was a delusion—and that the only thought respecting it, in which there is no delusion, is for everyone to abandon any possible faith in Mr. Hill's abilities to produce natural colors in Daguerreotypes—of which the whole history has been an unmitigated delusion.[12]

101

Hill wrote to the *Tribune:* "Allow me, through your journal, to ask the public to give me time to present some *authentically* established facts. At present my health is very poor; I hope that Divine Providence will grant me the strength to complete my labors."[13]

"We pity Mr. Hill, but we do not censure or abuse him," Snelling wrote, and then reprinted from a Philadelphia newspaper a devastating exposé signed "A Practical Daguerre," charging that the color announcement was a means of promoting the sale of Hill's books. The letter was translated in *La Lumière,* the French professional journal, with the note: "Dear Readers: You will hear nothing further about Mr. Hill."

But the reverend was not crushed by the report of what he called the "self constituted and rowdy committee." He wrote Morse, asking if, in his position as a respected artist and scientist, he would write a certificate. Morse offered sound advice in his reply.

> *S. F. B. Morse to L. L. Hill, February 28, 1852.* If the result be shown to a few friends, who can testify that they have seen it, although the process be concealed, yet this is such a publication as will secure to you the honor of the discovery, but if result as well as process is concealed your simple declaration cannot be permitted by the world to stand in the way of others' discovery, and others' results.[14]

In further correspondence, Hill explained over and again to Morse that he could not do as he suggested. On September 24, 1852, he wrote Morse that he was sick, feared death, and needed Morse's name in testimony. He implored Morse to come to Westkill. Morse came, saw twenty hillotypes, and was convinced. He wrote the *National Intelligencer:*

> The colors in Mr. Hill's process are so fixed that the most severe rubbing with a buffer only increases their brilliancy, and no exposure to light has as yet been found to impair their brightness. They are produced in twenty seconds. . . . Mr. Hill has made a great discovery. It is not perfected . . . who have a right to demand him to reveal it to the public now? Who, indeed, have a right to demand it at any time?[15]

The New York operators again made overtures to Hill. James P. Weston and Alexander Beckers went to Westkill, offering to raise by subscription $50,000 to $100,000.

Hill's answer came in the form of a circular, *To the Daguerreotypists of the United States and to the Public at Large,* in which he again stated that the invention he announced was his own, and all he had ever claimed for it. The delay in publication was due to difficulties, "invisible goblins of a new photogenic process." To raise funds, he announced the sale of chemicals and "a new edition of *Photographic Researches.*"

This was too much for the daguerreotypists. Wrote "Mercury" in the *Photographic Art-Journal,* December, 1852: "I fear his 'child of light' will, at no distant day, discombulate his flobnolix without any compunctious scruples of conscience." And when Hill persuaded the Patents Committee of the United States Senate to publish an official "Memorial,"[16] endorsing the process and testifying to Hill's priority, the *Scientific American* commented:

> Mr. Hill comes out with a Report of the Senate Committee on Patents, and would compel the world, *nolens volens,* to acknowledge his right to the title of discoverer of Heliochrome. To do this will require, however, something more than a Senate Report, and we must be convinced by deeds, and not by words, before we can place implicit reliance upon what has been affirmed. . . . Instead of taking the proper steps to substantiate his claims as an inventor in the Patent Office, he exhibits a few specimens of what he calls sun-coloring, to a committee in no ways suited, either professionally or otherwise, to give an opinion upon the subject, and imagines that, by a favorable report, his claims as the discoverer is confirmed.[17]

For a whole year, the hillotype lay dormant. Then, in December, 1854, through the medium of the professional press, Hill asked daguerreotypists who wanted to know of his plans of publishing his heliochromatic process to write him. They got in response a circular, offering a reflector at $5.00, to invert the image in taking views, and five formulas. About color photography they read only another testimonial by Morse—and an appeal for funds. He had mastered, Hill said, the reproduction of all colors, but still was not satisfied with yellow. Whereupon "R.R." suggested to Humphrey that a procession of believers should march on Westkill wearing chrome-yellow breeches. The Liverpool (England) Photographic Society read the circular. It had been sent to them from New York by William Ross, with a letter.

William Ross to the Liverpool Photographic Society, July 10, 1855. I have been given to understand that doubts exist in Britain as to whether *any one* ever issued such a circular as has been imputed to Hill, or if such has been issued, it could never have emanated from any one claiming to be a Christian, far less a *clergyman;* yet such is the fact; a pity, to be sure, but still a fact, painful though it may be.[18]

Ross, in a second letter, praised the society for reading the circular, "for it would be a great pity so much valuable information should not be widely diffused." He hoped the members might "be induced to erect in their hall a statue of *brass* in his honor."[19]

At last, in 1856, came the announcement which, for six years, daguerreotypists had awaited. In a twenty-page pamphlet "in the genuine well known style Hillesque," Hill offered the process for sale in a book at $25.

But by then the furor had died down; daguerreotypists were taking up new processes—the ambrotype, the tintype, and paper photographs. The book, *A Treatise on Heliochromy; or, The Production of Pictures by Means of Light in Natural Colors,* appeared, with the imprint of Robinson and Caswell, New York. It is a curious publication, part autobiographical, part technical—if the confused, wordy, and seemingly interminable account of his experiments can be taken seriously.

What did Hill produce? His pictures were seen and praised by trained daguerreotypists: Fitzgibbon, Marcus A. Root and his brother Samuel, Whipple, Caleb Hunt from Gurney's gallery, and Gurney himself. Morse specifically stated that the colors were vivid and resisted buffing—which no hand-colored plates could withstand.

From the perspective of a hundred years, we now realize that in a bungling, inefficient way, Hill must have stumbled on the phenomenon of the color sensitivity of photochlorides. There is more than one recorded instance where a daguerreotypist noted that he had obtained colors upon the silvered plate. P. H. Van der Weyde in Holland found a distinct blue tint in the skies of landscape daguerreotypes.[20] The "blue bosom" operators got their nickname because the shirt fronts of their sitters turned out to be blue instead of white.

It is the property of certain silver salts to assume the colors of the light thrown upon them. In 1810 Thomas Johann Seebeck pointed this out to Johann Wolfgang von Goethe: "I found the chloride of silver changing as follows,—It had become red-brown in the violet—occasionally more violet, at other times more blue—and this colouration reached also beyond the line of the violet designated before, but was not deeper than in the violet. In the blue of the spectrum the

104

chloride of silver became true blue, and this color, decreasing and gradually getting lighter, extended into the green. In the yellow I found the chloride of silver mostly unchanged. Sometimes it appeared to me more yellow than before; however, in the red, and often a little beyond the red, it had taken the red of a rose."[21]

Sir John Herschel, apparently unaware of what Seebeck had written, and inspired by the work of Fox Talbot, noted the same phenomenon: "When a slip of sensitive paper is exposed to a highly concentrated spectrum, a picture of it is rapidly impressed on the paper, not merely in black, but in colour. . . . I have not been able to fix these tints. They are, however, susceptible of half-fixing by the mere action of water, and may be viewed at leisure in moderate daylight or by candlelight."[22]

These experiments were upon paper. In France the scientist Alexandre Edmond Becquerel was working along the same lines when he discovered that the identical phenomenon occurred with daguerreotype plates. He reported to the Academy of Sciences on February 7, 1848: "When a well-polished metal plate, either of silver or silver plated, is put a few centimeters above the surface of chlorinated water, it assumes at the end of several minutes a whitish tint due to the formation of a chloride of silver; if there is thrown upon its surface a concentrated solar spectrum, a few centimeters in length, before long a photographic impression is obtained which covers all the visible part of the spectrum."[23]

Becquerel noted that the plate assumed colors analogous to the spectrum. Orange was the first to appear. Where red rays fell on the plate, it became reddish-purple; green was slightly yellow and turned gradually to blue and to violet. On prolonged exposure, the colors darkened until, in an hour or two, they disappeared.

Becquerel improved his technique for sensitizing the plate to colors by electroplating with platinum; he found that if these plates were exposed while heated to 212°F., the color sensitivity was further increased. He made color reproductions by this "photochromatique" technique, simply by placing the colored print face down on the sensitized plate and exposing it to light through the back. He tried his photochromatic plates in a camera, but the time required was hopelessly long: "ten or twelve hours were required to obtain a good image of a colored engraving put 4 ft. 10 in. in front of the lens, even though the print was exposed to full sunlight during this time."[24] The colors were good—better than contact prints from engravings. He failed to get satisfactory landscapes, however, for the plates were less sensitive to green than to white light. "Perhaps with practise, working often, one will succeed; for my part, I have looked upon this as secondary and I have stopped working with it, knowing that, at present, one cannot make use of this process in the arts."[25]

For there was no way to fix the images so that they would be no longer affected by light. "I have tried every kind of reaction in the attempt to render the images inalterable to light, but I have not succeeded."[26] Hill knew of Becquerel's work: he admitted so in his first description of the process in the *Photographic Art-Journal* for February, 1851. He also knew of the work Niépce de Saint-Victor was doing. This French experimenter, the nephew of Daguerre's partner, repeated Becquerel's experiments and achieved partial success. One of his color daguerreotypes, of a colored, geometrical drawing, is now in the George Eastman House.[27] It was made in 1867. It is kept in the dark and seldom looked at, for it is feared that the colors are unstable; only the reds and blues appear, and they are pale.

It is, therefore, entirely possible that Hill could have taken daguerreotypes in color by a similar photochloride process. But how he fixed these images to bear exposure to light, as Morse testified, remains his secret. Probably the only explanation of the whole affair was that offered by John Towler, editor of *Humphrey's Journal,* when Hill died in 1865: "He always affirmed to this writer that he *did* take pictures in their natural colors, but it was done by an *accidental* combination of chemicals which he could not, for the life of him, again produce!"[28]

106

13. *Photography Triumphant*

THE WORD "photography" was reserved by daguerreotypists to refer to the wet-plate, or collodion, process invented by Frederick Scott Archer in England in 1851. Although it was introduced to America within a year, photography did not become a serious threat to the daguerreotype until it was used to make imitation daguerreotypes on glass.

These glass positives were called "ambrotypes"—a name coined by Marcus A. Root, meaning, he said, "imperishable picture." They were popularized by James A. Cutting, a Boston daguerreotypist, and his partner Isaac A. Rehn of Philadelphia in 1854.

Basically an ambrotype is a glass negative backed with black, to make it appear positive. The areas of a negative representing the shadows of the subject are relatively transparent; having received but little light, only a small portion of the sensitive material has been reduced to opaque silver. Consequently the black backing becomes visible. The highlights, on the other hand, having received the maximum amount of light, are converted by processing to opaque silver, which hides the black backing.

The backing was various: a piece of black velvet, or black cardboard, or blackened tin was common. Other ambrotypists used black paint, or black asphalt varnish. Frequently the glass itself was of a deep violet tint; no backing was needed.

Ambrotypes were made in the same sizes as daguerreotypes, bound up with ornamental brass mats, and put into cases made for daguerreotypes. They are often confused with daguerreotypes. The test is simple. Take the picture out of the case and examine the back. If it is copper, or copper lightly silver plated, the picture is a daguerreotype.

Cutting was granted three United States patents.[1] Two were for the composition of the collodion; the third was for a technique for cementing the cover glass to the developed photographic plate by the use of Canada balsam. He and his

107

partner Rehn rigidly enforced their patents. It was impossible for anyone to produce photographs by the collodion process without making use of some of the "improvements" specified in the patents. In vain photographers complained to the courts that potassium iodide and potassium bromide had long been used in photography. Not until the patents expired in 1868 could photographers use the collodion process without either paying a royalty or facing the likelihood of court action.

Ambrotypes enjoyed a short period of popularity. Robert Taft, in his *Photography and the American Scene,* notes that of the 123 wood engravings in *Frank Leslie's Illustrated Newspaper* for 1856 drawn from photographs, 100 were reproduced from ambrotypes, 10 from paper photographs, and only 13 from daguerreotypes.

Veteran daguerreotypists deplored the trend. They pointed out that the ambrotype cannot match the quality of a daguerreotype—an observation with which we most certainly agree. J. H. Fitzgibbon wrote the editor of the *American Journal of Photography:*

> I was glad to see by your Journal that there is a chance once more of the star of Daguerre shining forth again. I fought hard once for it till it got entirely obscured by a black cloud called Ambrotype, which laid me in the shade as well as the Daguerreotypes; but the black, nasty, filthy, ghastly, dead, inanimate, flat, shade of shadows, are beginning to burst, break, peel, turn, change all colors (but the natural one) and must in time die out without any other exertion than their own selves.[2]

They were already dead when Fitzgibbon wrote the editor in 1861; their place was taken by the tintype, known in its day as the "melainotype," or, more commonly, the "ferrotype."

The process was invented by Professor Hamilton L. Smith, of Kenyon College, Gambier, Ohio. He patented his invention in 1856;[3] it was bought by William Neff and Peter Neff, Jr., of Cincinnati, who baptized the process "melainotype." It was a modification of the ambrotype; instead of flowing collodion on a glass surface, sensitizing it, developing it, and backing the resulting negative with black, Smith used a sheet of thin iron, japanned black, as the support of the sensitized collodion. No backing was needed. The Neffs' chief competitor in the manufacture of plates was Victor M. Griswold; he called his product "ferrotype plates." The word tintype is a misnomer. As one ferrotypist remarked, the only tin in a tintype is "the 'tin' that goes into the happy operator's pocket."[4]

At first cased like daguerreotypes and ambrotypes, tintypes were soon delivered in inexpensive cut-out paper mats. They were indestructible and needed no protection; they were light in weight; they could be sent in an ordinary letter through the mails. They could be cut with tinsnips into circles and ovals to be fitted into jewelry. During the Presidential campaign of 1860, lapel buttons bearing the portraits of the candidates appeared by the hundreds.

At the outbreak of the Civil War tintypes suddenly became extremely popular. Soldiers sent back home their portraits, taken at camp by itinerants who posed them against painted backgrounds of tents, cannons, and battle scenes. They carried into combat precious likenesses of their loved ones. The "cheap operators" found the tintype more suited to economical production than the daguerreotype. Established galleries preferred photography on paper, and "cartes-de-visite" in particular.

This style of photograph came from France. In 1854 a Parisian photographer, Adolphe-Eugène Disdéri, conceived the idea of using a camera with four lenses to record several images at a time, or in rapid succession, upon one plate. A single print from this negative was then cut up into small prints, which were mounted on cards 2¼ by 4 inches, about the size of a visiting card: hence the name, which Americans retained when they began to produce them in 1859.

Humphrey's Journal, February 15, 1861. These portraits, as we shall call them—for they are indeed nothing more than full-length miniatures of the human face and form—are generally taken in a standing position. . . . A great degree of the beauty of the picture is obtained by the backgrounds which are used. The usual stereoscopic camera with two tubes is the one generally employed—the advantage is that by a new and beautiful arrangement of the box, an operator is enabled to produce four or more of these negatives upon one glass plate, thereby facilitating their rapid production. . . . In most cases these portraits are taken in a standing position and with outdoor dresses, overcoats, hats, shawls, etc.

The sale of portraits became lucrative. When Fort Sumter was attacked, George S. Cook took an ambrotype of the commander, Major Robert Anderson. The Anthonys bought the portrait, copied it, and were making a thousand prints a day in January, 1861. Daguerreotypes of famous people were multiplied by the carte-de-visite: Brady's *National Portrait Gallery* was published by the Anthonys; people began to collect portraits of kings and emperors, soldiers and statesmen, poets and musicians, and put them in albums along with family portraits and pictures of friends.

The daguerreotype era was over. "Ten years ago we had here (in the North) only Daguerreotypes, now not one," the editor of the *American Journal of Photography* wrote in the October 15, 1861, issue. "The Daguerreotype had many friends, but it was doomed; we shall not hear of it again—peace to its ashes! . . . The series of fashions we have had in the art are steps of progress—the daguerreotype, ambrotype, 4-4 [i.e. whole plate] photograph, stereoscope, and at last the card portrait." Joseph H. Ladd, the new editor of *Humphrey's Journal*, protested: "We believe that the march of improvements is *onward*, and that even the card pictures will have their rivals for the favor of the fickle public. But as for the daguerreotype, the first in the race, we affirm that the time has not yet arrived when it is to be considered as 'doomed.' "

But Daguerre's beautiful process was already obsolete. Veterans looked back to it with fondness. "I shall always remember with pleasure the good old daguerreotype," said Abraham Bogardus. "No glass to clean and albumenize; no black fingers; few or no re-sittings; no retouching; no proofs to show for his grandmother, and his sister, and his cousins, and his aunts to find fault with; no waiting for sunshine to print with; no paper to blister, and no promising of the pictures next week if the weather was good. The picture was gilded, finished and cased while the lady was putting on her bonnet; delivered, put in her pocket, and you had the money in your pocket."[5] The anonymous author of *Sunlight Sketches,* a popular manual published by Snelling in 1858, wrote that a well-exposed collodion plate should be developed and defined in all its parts, "like the beautiful daguerreotype . . . beautiful as the light of heaven can make it,"[6] and then paid tribute to the obsolete process of Daguerre:

"O sad fate of the beautiful daguerreotype! l would to heaven I could forget it. But it lingers in my soul like fond remembrance of a dear departed friend."

110

PART II

Plates

No attempt to eliminate the marks of age has been made in reproducing the original daguerreotypes. Over the years the delicate surfaces of many of the most striking daguerreotypes were marred by scratches, tarnish, and corrosion which defy restoration. It was felt that any attempt to eliminate these blemishes by even the most skillful hand retouching would be unwarranted. Occasionally we have trimmed away blank areas along the edges of the plate, the better to reveal the main subject. In this cropping we have followed the custom of the period, for daguerreotypists invariably put the plates behind gilded mats of varying format.

The size of each original is indicated by the size of the plate.

Whole plate	6½ by 8½ inches
Half plate	4½ by 5½ inches
Quarter plate	3¼ by 4¼ inches
Sixth plate	2¾ by 3¼ inches
Ninth plate	2 by 2½ inches

1. THE FAMILY DAGUERREOTYPE, ABOUT 1850.
Sixth plate; daguerreotypist not known. International Museum of Photography, Rochester, N. Y.

2. SELF-PORTRAIT OF HENRY FITZ, JR., PROBABLY 1839.
Ninth plate daguerreotype. Smithsonian Institution, Washington, D. C.

3. KING'S CHAPEL BURYING GROUND, BOSTON, APRIL 19, 1840.
Whole plate daguerreotype by Samuel Bemis. International Museum of Photography, Rochester, N. Y.

4. MERCHANTS' EXCHANGE, PHILADELPHIA, FEBRUARY, 1840.
Whole plate daguerreotype by Walter R. Johnson. Franklin Institute, Phila-delphia.

5. OLD PATENT OFFICE, WASHINGTON, D. C., ABOUT 1846.
    Half plate daguerreotype by John Plumbe, Jr. The Library of Congress,
    Washington, D. C.

6. THIRD STREET AT CHESTNUT, PHILADELPHIA, JULY, 1842.
Sixth plate daguerreotype by George Read. International Museum of Photography, Rochester, N. Y. (Zelda P. Mackay Collection.)

7. CHESTNUT STREET, PHILADELPHIA, ABOUT 1844.
Sixth plate; daguerreotypist not known. International Museum of Photography, Rochester, N. Y.

8. JOHN QUINCY ADAMS, SIXTH PRESIDENT OF THE UNITED STATES, 1843.
*Half plate daguerreotype by Philip Haas. The Metropolitan Museum of Art,
New York. (Gift of I. N. P. Stokes and the Hawes family.)*

9. ANDREW JACKSON, SEVENTH PRESIDENT OF THE UNITED STATES, BEFORE 1845.
*Sixth plate daguerreotype, probably by Dan Adams. International Museum
of Photography, Rochester, N. Y. (Gift of A. Conger Goodyear.)*

10. ZACHARY TAYLOR, TWELFTH PRESIDENT OF THE UNITED STATES, ABOUT 1850.
Whole plate; daguerreotypist not known. Chicago Historical Society, Chicago.

11. JOHN TYLER, TENTH PRESIDENT OF THE UNITED STATES, ABOUT 1845.
Whole plate; daguerreotypist not known. Chicago Historical Society, Chicago.

12. STATE STREET AT MAIN, ROCHESTER, NEW YORK, ABOUT 1852.
*Whole plate daguerreotype by Edward Tompkins Whitney. International
Museum of Photography, Rochester, N. Y.*

13. RUINS OF THE AMERICAN HOTEL, BUFFALO, NEW YORK, MARCH, 1850.
*Whole plate; daguerreotypist not known. Buffalo Historical Society, Buffalo,
N. Y.*

14. MAN SITTING ON SOFA WITH DOG, ABOUT 1850.
Sixth plate; daguerreotypist not known. Northampton Historical Society, Northampton, Mass.

15. BUTTERFLY COLLECTOR, ABOUT 1850.
Sixth plate; daguerreotypist not known. International Museum of Photography, Rochester, N. Y.

16. Mrs. Joseph Elisha Whitman, Sr., and her son Joseph Elisha, Jr., born 1853.
Sixth plate; daguerreotypist not known. The Society for the Preservation of New England Antiquities, Boston.

17. COBBLER, ABOUT 1850.
Location of original not known.

18. TOLE WARE MAKER, ABOUT 1850.
Sixth plate; daguerreotypist not known. International Museum of Photography, Rochester, N. Y. (Zelda P. Mackay Collection.)

19. FREDERICK WARREN (DIED 1858), CITY MARSHAL OF WOR-
CESTER, MASSACHUSETTS, WITH PRISONER, ABOUT 1850.
*Half plate; daguerreotypist not known. American Antiquar-
ian Society, Worcester, Mass.*

20. "THE WOODSAWYER'S NOONING," 1853.
*Whole plate daguerreotype by George N. Barnard. Location of original not
known; 1908 photocopy courtesy Onondaga Historical Association, Syracuse,
N. Y.*

21. SEAMSTRESS, ABOUT 1850.
Sixth plate; daguerreotypist not known. Minnesota Historical Society, St. Paul, Minn.

22. WOMAN WITH SHEET MUSIC, ABOUT 1850.
Sixth plate; daguerreotypist not known. Society for the Preservation of New England Antiquities, Boston.

23. HENRY BREWER, OF THE H. & J. BREWER DRUG STORE, SPRINGFIELD, MASSA-
CHUSETTS, ABOUT 1850.
*Half plate; daguerreotypist not known. Connecticut Valley Historical Mu-
seum, Springfield, Mass.*

24. SHIP IN DRY DOCK, BOSTON NAVY YARD, ABOUT 1852.
Whole plate daguerreotype by Southworth & Hawes. International Museum of Photography, Rochester, N. Y.

25. LOCOMOTIVE "HOOSAC," OWNED BY FITCHBURG RAILROAD, 1854–62.
Half plate; daguerreotypist not known. Collection of the late Frank R. Fraprie, Boston.

26. TRAIN WRECK ON THE PROVIDENCE AND WORCESTER RAILROAD NEAR PAW-
TUCKET, RHODE ISLAND, AUGUST 12, 1853.
*Half plate daguerreotype by L. Wright. International Museum of Photog-
raphy, Rochester, N. Y. (Zelda P. Mackay Collection.)*

27. BURNING MILLS AT OSWEGO, NEW YORK, JULY 5, 1853.
Sixth plate daguerreotype; copy of a whole plate daguerreotype by George
N. Barnard. International Museum of Photography, Rochester, N. Y.

28.   WOODWARD WOOLEN MILL, WOODSTOCK, VERMONT, ABOUT 1850.
*Detail of half plate; daguerreotypist not known. International Museum of
Photography, Rochester, N. Y.*

29. STEAMSHIP IN DRY DOCK, BOSTON, ABOUT 1855.
Whole plate daguerreotype by Southworth & Hawes. Collection Richard Parker, Marblehead, Mass.

30. QUAKER SISTERS, ABOUT 1850.
Sixth plate; daguerreotypist not known. International Museum of Photography, Rochester, N. Y. (Zelda P. Mackay Collection.)

31. DOG, ABOUT 1855.
Sixth plate daguerreotype by Sheldon Nichols. International Museum of Photography, Rochester, N. Y. (Zelda P. Mackay Collection.)

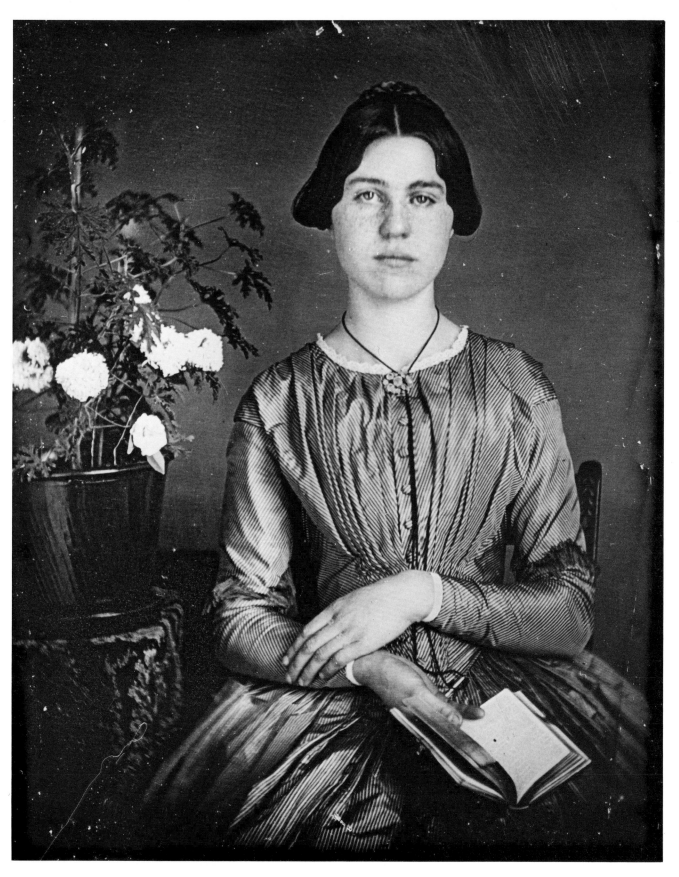

32. GIRL, ABOUT 1850.
Sixth plate; daguerreotypist not known. Collection Estate of Edward Weston, Carmel, Calif.

33. Suburban house, about 1850.
Half plate; daguerreotypist not known. Collection Emmanuel Weil, Albany, N.Y.

34. GROUP AT NIAGARA FALLS, ABOUT 1855.
*Whole plate daguerreotype by Platt D. Babbitt. International Museum of
Photography, Rochester, N. Y.*

35. GALENA, ILLINOIS, BETWEEN 1852 AND 1854.
Whole plate daguerreotype by Alexander Hesler. Chicago Historical Society, Chicago.

36. BALTIMORE, FROM FEDERAL HILL, LOOKING NORTH-NORTHWEST, BETWEEN 1853
AND 1854.
Whole plate daguerreotype by H. H. Clark. The Peale Museum, Baltimore.

37–38. CINCINNATI WATERFRONT, 1848.
Two of eight whole plate daguerreotypes forming a panorama, by Charles Fontayne and William Southgate Porter. The Public Library of Cincinnati and Hamilton County, Cincinnati, Ohio.

39. Dan Bryant, minstrel, about 1855.
   Half plate daguerreotype, probably by John H. Fitzgibbon.
   Chicago Historical Society, Chicago.

40. Brass ensemble, about 1850.
   Half plate; daguerreotypist not known. International Museum of Photog-
   raphy, Rochester, N. Y.

41. ST. LOUIS LEVEE, ABOUT 1855.
Whole plate; daguerreotypist not known. Missouri Historical Society, St. Louis.

42. SUSPENSION BRIDGE OF ST. ANTHONY, CONNECTING MINNEAPOLIS WITH NICOLET
ISLAND; OPENED JANUARY 27, 1855.
*Half plate; daguerreotypist not known. Minnesota Historical Society, St.
Paul, Minn.*

43. Maungwudaus, chief of the Ojibway tribe of Pennsylvania, about 1850. *Quarter plate; daguerreotypist not known. International Museum of Photography, Rochester, N. Y.*

44. ABRAHAM LINCOLN, ABOUT 1847.
Quarter plate daguerreotype by N. H. Shepard. The Library of Congress, Washington, D. C.

45. Daguerreotype gallery of Joel Emmons Whitney, corner of Third and Cedar Streets, St. Paul, Minnesota, about 1852.
Whole plate daguerreotype, probably by Joel Emmons Whitney. Minnesota Historical Society, St. Paul, Minn.

46. FRANCIS PARKMAN, AMERICAN HISTORIAN, ABOUT 1850.
*Quarter plate daguerreotype by Southworth & Hawes. The Metropolitan
Museum of Art, New York. (Gift of I. N. P. Stokes and the Hawes family.)*

47. INDIAN CAMP ON SITE OF DOWNTOWN MINNEAPOLIS, 1854.
*Quarter plate; daguerreotypist not known. Minnesota Historical Society,
St. Paul, Minn.*

48. SLEEPING BABY, ABOUT 1850.
*Whole plate daguerreotype by Southworth & Hawes. Collection Ansel Adams,
Carmel, Calif.*

49. Mother and child, about 1850.
Sixth plate; daguerreotypist not known. Collection Beaumont Newhall, Santa Fe, New Mexico.

50. DANIEL WEBSTER SITTING OUTDOORS AT HIS MARSHFIELD, MASSACHUSETTS, HOME, ABOUT 1848.
Half plate; daguerreotypist not known. International Museum of Photography, Rochester, N. Y. (Zelda P. Mackay Collection.)

51. COMPANION OF DANIEL WEBSTER, ABOUT 1848.
*Half plate; daguerreotypist not known. Collection Charles Swedlund, Buffalo,
N. Y.*

52. ELDERLY COUPLE, ABOUT 1850.
*Whole plate daguerreotype by Southworth & Hawes. International Museum
of Photography, Rochester, N. Y. (Gift of Alden Scott Boyer.)*

53. UNIDENTIFIED MAN, ABOUT 1850.
*Sixth plate daguerreotype by Southworth & Hawes. International Museum
of Photography, Rochester, N. Y. (Gift of Alden Scott Boyer.)*

54. LOLA MONTEZ, IRISH-BORN DANCER, ACTRESS, ADVENTURER, ABOUT 1852.
*Whole plate daguerreotype by Southworth & Hawes. The Metropolitan
Museum of Art, New York. (Gift of I. N. P. Stokes and the Hawes family.)*

55. MRS. JAMES R. VINCENT, BOSTON ACTRESS, ABOUT 1852.
Whole plate daguerreotype by Southworth & Hawes. Society for the Preservation of New England Antiquities, Boston.

56. UNA AND JULIAN HAWTHORNE, CHILDREN OF NATHANIEL
HAWTHORNE, ABOUT 1850.
*Sixth plate; daguerreotypist not known. The Boston Athe-
naeum, Boston.*

57. GIRLS' SCHOOL, ABOUT 1855.
*Whole plate daguerreotype by Southworth & Hawes. The
Metropolitan Museum of Art, New York. (Gift of I. N. P.
Stokes and the Hawes family.)*

58. HENRY WADSWORTH LONGFELLOW, AMERICAN POET, ABOUT 1850.
Quarter plate daguerreotype by John Adams Whipple. The Museum of
Modern Art, New York. (Gift of A. Conger Goodyear.)

59. WILLIAM HICKLING PRESCOTT, AMERICAN HISTORIAN, PROBABLY 1842.
Half plate daguerreotype by Southworth & Hawes. The Metropolitan Museum of Art, New York. (Gift of I. N. P. Stokes and the Hawes family.)

60. ASHER B. DURAND, AMERICAN PAINTER, ABOUT 1855.
*Half plate; daguerreotypist not known. The New-York Historical Society,
New York.*

61. WASHINGTON IRVING, AMERICAN WRITER, ABOUT 1849.
Half plate daguerreotype by John Plumbe, Jr. The New-York Historical Society, New York.

62. EDGAR ALLAN POE, AMERICAN WRITER, 1848.
Quarter plate daguerreotype by Henry N. or Edward H. Manchester. American Antiquarian Society, Worcester, Mass.

63. THE BOSTON ATHENAEUM, ABOUT 1855.
*Whole plate daguerreotype by Southworth & Hawes. International Museum
of Photography, Rochester, N. Y.*

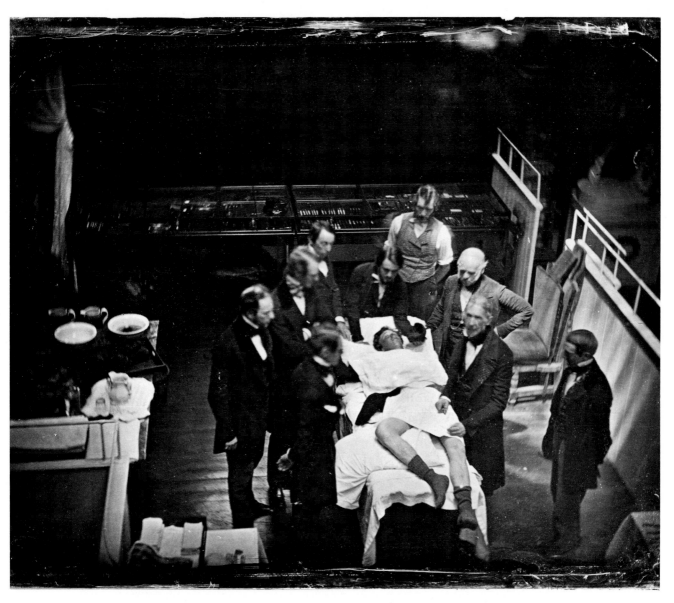

64. OPERATING ROOM OF THE MASSACHUSETTS GENERAL HOSPITAL, BOSTON;
RE-ENACTMENT OF THE DEMONSTRATION OF ETHER ANESTHESIA BY W. T. G.
MORTON ON OCTOBER 16, 1846.
Daguerreotype by Southworth & Hawes. Location of original not known.

65. ELIHU BURRITT, AMERICAN LINGUIST AND ADVOCATE OF INTERNATIONAL PEACE, ABOUT 1850.
Half plate; daguerreotypist not known. American Antiquarian Society, Worcester, Mass.

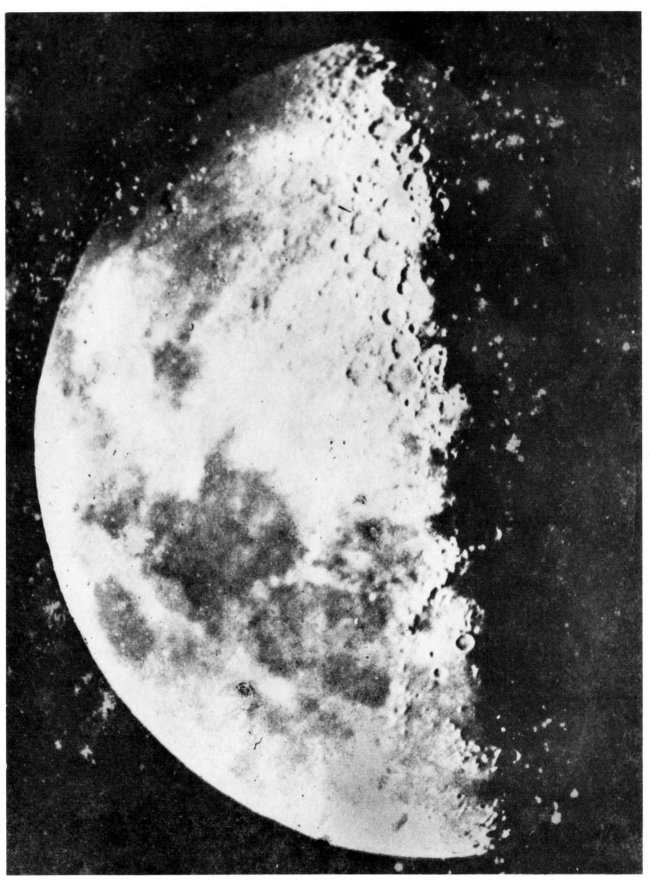

66. THE MOON, 1851.
Daguerreotype by John Adams Whipple. Location of original not known; reproduced from an original calotype copy in The Photographic and Fine Arts Journal, *July, 1853.*

67. DONALD McKAY, CLIPPER SHIP BUILDER, ABOUT 1855.
Whole plate daguerreotype by Southworth & Hawes. The Metropolitan Museum of Art, New York. (Gift of I. N. P. Stokes and the Hawes family.)

68. SHIPYARD, PROBABLY DONALD MCKAY'S, EAST BOSTON, ABOUT 1855.
Whole plate daguerreotype by Southworth & Hawes. Collection Richard Parker, Marblehead, Mass.

69. CLIPPER SHIP "CHAMPION OF THE SEAS," ABOUT 1858.
Whole plate daguerreotype by Southworth & Hawes. Collection Richard Parker, Marblehead, Mass.

70–74. SAN FRANCISCO FROM RINCON POINT, ABOUT 1852.
Panorama of five whole plate daguerreotypes by William Shew. Smithsonian Institution, Washington, D. C.

75–76. SAN FRANCISCO, LOOKING NORTHEAST TOWARD YERBA BUENA ISLAND, ABOUT 1851.
Plates 5 and 6 of a panorama of six whole plates; daguerreotypist not known. California Historical Society, San Francisco.

77. SOLOMON YEAKEL, '49ER, ABOUT 1850.
Sixth plate; daguerreotypist not known. The Bancroft Library, University of California, Berkeley; reproduced by permission of the Director, The Bancroft Library.

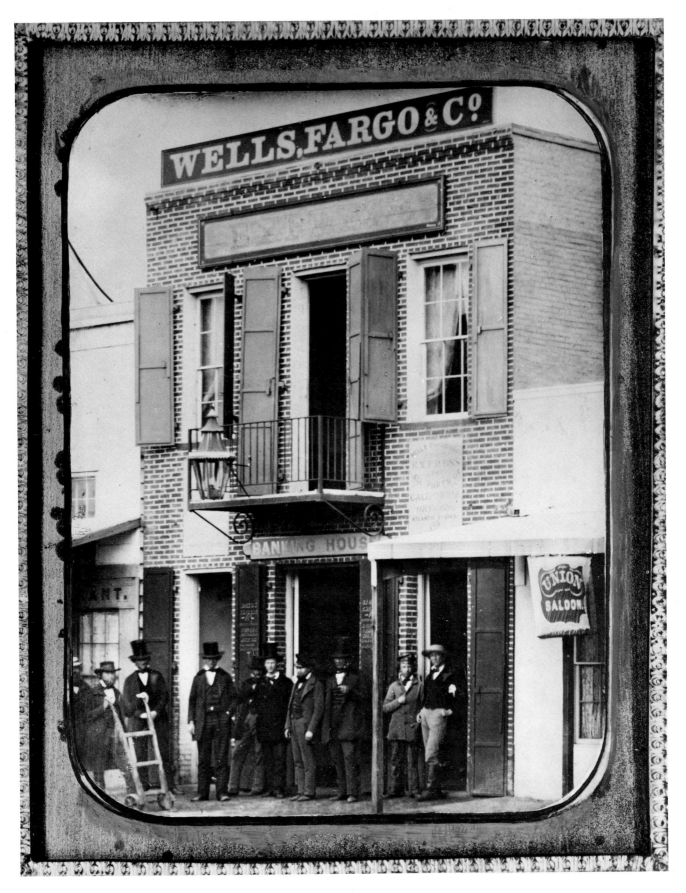

78. WELLS FARGO BANK, SAN FRANCISCO, 1852.
Whole plate; daguerreotypist not known. Wells Fargo History Room, San Francisco.

79. San Francisco, about 1855.
   *Whole plate; daguerreotypist not known. American Antiquarian Society,
   Worcester, Mass.*

80. Montgomery Street looking north, San Francisco, 1850.
Half plate daguerreotype by Fred Coombs. International Museum of Photography, Rochester, N. Y.

81. MONTGOMERY STREET LOOKING SOUTH, SAN FRANCISCO, 1850.
Half plate daguerreotype by Fred Coombs. International Museum of Photography, Rochester, N. Y.

82. THE TRAVELING DAGUERREOTYPE WAGON OF WILLIAM SHEW, SAN FRANCISCO, 1851.
Whole plate daguerreotype probably by William Shew. Collection of the Exchange National Bank, Chicago.

83. SMITH & PORTER'S COFFEE HOUSE, SAN FRANCISCO, ABOUT 1852.
Whole plate; daguerreotypist not known. The Bancroft Library, University of California, Berkeley; reproduced by permission of the Director, The Bancroft Library.

84. Rix family house, San Francisco, August 20, 1855.
Whole plate daguerreotype by Robert H. Vance. The Oakland Museum, Oakland, Calif.

85. Gold miners, California, about 1852.
   Quarter plate; daguerreotypist not known. The Bancroft Library, University of California, Berkeley; reproduced by permission of the Director, The Bancroft Library.

86. GOLD MINING, HORSESHOE BAR, NORTH FORK OF THE AMERICAN RIVER, CALIFORNIA, ABOUT 1853.
Half plate; daguerreotypist not known. Collection A. R. Phillips, Jr., Los Angeles.

87. GOLD MINING; IN DISTANCE, GRIZZLEY FLAT, CALIFORNIA, ABOUT 1853.
Half plate; daguerreotypist not known. The Bancroft Library, University of California, Berkeley; reproduced by permission of the Director, The Bancroft Library.

88. TOWN, PROBABLY IN CALIFORNIA, ABOUT 1852.
Whole plate; daguerreotypist not known. Collection Mrs. Violet Mayborn Schenk, Rochester, N. Y.

89. YREKA, CALIFORNIA, ABOUT 1850.
   Half plate; daguerreotypist not known. Collection Edwin Grabhorn, San Francisco.

90. GRAVE OF ROBERT BARNARD, DIED 1856.
Half plate daguerreotype by J. M. Ford, San Francisco. The New-York Historical Society, New York.

91. HENRY CLAY, BEFORE 1852.
*Copy on collodion plate of a daguerreotype from the gallery of Mathew B.
Brady. The Library of Congress, Washington, D. C.*

92. SAM HOUSTON, PRESIDENT OF THE REPUBLIC OF TEXAS, ABOUT 1850.
Sixth plate; daguerreotypist not known. International Museum of Photography, Rochester, N. Y. (Gift of Alden Scott Boyer.)

93. ALBERT SANDS SOUTHWORTH, ABOUT 1850.
*Sixth plate daguerreotype from the gallery of Southworth
& Hawes. The Metropolitan Museum of Art, New York. (Gift
of I. N. P. Stokes and the Hawes family.)*

94. JOSIAH JOHNSON HAWES, ABOUT 1850.
*Sixth plate daguerreotype from the gallery of Southworth
& Hawes. The Metropolitan Museum of Art, New York.
(Gift of I. N. P. Stokes and the Hawes family.)*

95. LEMUEL SHAW, CHIEF JUSTICE OF THE MASSACHUSETTS SUPREME COURT, 1851.
Half plate daguerreotype by Southworth & Hawes. The Metropolitan
Museum of Art, New York. (Gift of I. N. P. Stokes and the Hawes family.)

96. CAESAR, THE LAST NEGRO SLAVE OWNED IN NEW YORK STATE, 1851.
*Sixth plate; daguerreotypist not known. The New-York Historical Society,
New York.*

97. NEGRO WOMAN, ABOUT 1850.
   Sixth plate; daguerreotypist not known. The International Museum of
   Photography, Rochester, N. Y. (Zelda P. Mackay Collection.)

98. WILLIAM LLOYD GARRISON, AMERICAN ABOLITIONIST, ABOUT 1850.
Half plate daguerreotype by Southworth & Hawes. The Metropolitan Museum of Art, New York. (Gift of I. N. P. Stokes and the Hawes family.)

99. JOHN BROWN, ABOLITIONIST, WINTER OF 1856–57.
Detail of half plate daguerreotype by John Adams Whipple and James
Wallace Black. The Boston Athenaeum, Boston.

100. HARRIET BEECHER STOWE, AMERICAN AUTHOR, ABOUT 1850.
Quarter plate daguerreotype by Southworth & Hawes. The Metropolitan
Museum of Art, New York. (Gift of I. N. P. Stokes and the Hawes family.)

101. STEPHEN A. DOUGLAS, ABOUT 1853.
Whole plate; daguerreotypist not known. International Museum of Photography, Rochester, N. Y. (Zelda P. Mackay Collection.)

102. DANIEL WEBSTER, 1850.
*Whole plate daguerreotype by Southworth & Hawes. The Metropolitan
Museum of Art, New York. (Gift of I. N. P. Stokes and the Hawes family.)*

103. CHARLES SUMNER, UNITED STATES SENATOR, ABOUT 1850.
Whole plate daguerreotype by Southworth & Hawes. The Metropolitan Museum of Art, New York. (Gift of I. N. P. Stokes and the Hawes family.)

104. ABRAHAM LINCOLN.
Quarter plate daguerreotype, copy of a portion of a paper print made in 1858. Daguerreotypist not known. Collection America Hurrah Antiques, New York.

PART III

A Technique and a Craft

14. *The American Process*

DAGUERRE'S technique was so greatly modified by Americans that within a decade European daguerreotypists advertised that they worked "The American Process." At first daguerreotypists jealously guarded their trade secrets. John H. Fitzgibbon, who was a student in 1841, recollected that every operator had a "secret process—the gilding, the bromide, the quick, the galvanizing, the magic buff, the crayon, the coloring . . . all of which we poor *beginners* had to pay for to keep up with the times and produce as good work as our brother artists."[1]

Soon manuals began to appear. In 1849 Humphrey, Snelling, and Hill brought out standard works which went into several editions and were followed by other treatises. (See Bibliography, p. 169.) From them, and from *Humphrey's Journal* and the *Photographic Art-Journal,* we can reconstruct in detail every step of the process.

CAMERAS AND LENSES

The equipment required to set up a permanent gallery represented a fair amount of capital. Snelling, in his *A Guide to the Whole Art of Photography* (1858), printed a list of everything needed, down to the carpet, furniture, and window shades: the inventory totaled $453.82. The most expensive item was the lens—or "tube," as it was familiarly called—at $75. Snelling recommended either Harrison's or Holmes, Booth and Hayden's. He might well have recommended the Voigtländer lens, which the Langenheims imported.

Snelling itemizes "Improved rose wood camera box" at $18.00. He does not specify the make, but they were all similar, whether manufactured by W. and W. H. Lewis at Daguerreville, by Palmer and Longking, by Holmes, Booth and Hayden, or by E. and H. T. Anthony. A pioneer daguerreotypist, James F. Ryder, had fond recollections of this type of camera.

> I can see its rosewood veneer, the edges at front and back chamfered to an Angle of forty-five degrees; its sliding inside box, with the focusing glass which was drawn up and out of the top through open doors and the plateholder was

115

A CAMERA

ALLEN'S CAMERA BOX

A UNION CAMERA STAND

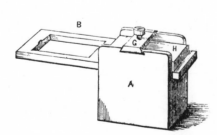

A COATING BOX

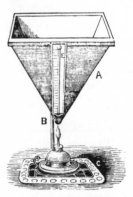

A MERCURY BATH

slid down into its place. These doors were hinged to open one toward the front and the other toward the back, each having a little knob of turned bone by which to lift it, and there were two little inset knobs of the same material turned into the top of the box upon which the knobs of the door should strike, and the concussion of these bone knobs more than fifty years ago is remembered today as plainly as though I had been hearing them every day from then until now; while the odor of iodine from the coated plates in that dear old box lingers with me like a dream.[2]

In 1851 W. and W. H. Lewis brought out their newly patented camera embodying two improvements. It was fitted with a bellows "making it very compact, which is a very essential requisite, particularly for packing in transit or for traveling operators."[3] This is, to our knowledge, the first use of the bellows for a photographic camera; it soon became a universal feature of camera design. It was not, however, this improvement which the Lewis brothers sought to protect by patent. They fitted a sliding panel on the back of the camera, on one end of which was a ground glass for focusing and on the other the plate holder.

U. S. Patent 8,513, November 11, 1851. The advantages of this mode of constructing cameras over the old and usual methods are that in cameras that open at the top the light from the skylight particularly is apt to enter the joint of the lid, that allows the glass to be removed and the plate to be put in; but in ours the top of the camera is perfectly tight. . . . In the old cameras the ground glass had to be withdrawn and then the plate and frame put in, which occupied much more time than in our arrangement, in which by merely sliding the frame across the camera the ground glass is removed at the same time the daguerreotype-type plate is put into place, and the speed with which daguerreotypes are taken is a great object, particularly with children, as they as well as others are apt to move if too much time is employed, thereby spoiling the picture.

The "tripod camera stand" listed by Snelling at $3.20 was wooden: three turned legs screwed into an iron collar through which passed an upright wooden shaft that could be fastened at any height by a set screw. Cast-iron camera stands were also popular in the 1850's.

PLATES

The budding daguerreotypist was advised by Snelling to budget $20 for "an assortment of plates." They were made by silversmiths, who brazed a sheet of pure silver to a block of copper and ran the composite block again and again between rollers until it was a sheet approximately .02-inch thick. They cut it up into standard sizes:

Whole plate, or 4/4	6½ by 8½ inches
Half plate	4¼ by 5½ inches
Quarter plate	3¼ by 4¼ inches
Sixth, or medium plate	2¾ by 3¼ inches
Ninth plate	2 by 2½ inches
Sixteenth plate	1⅜ by 1⅝ inches

The fractions of the standard whole plate were approximate, for the pieces were trimmed to preserve more or less the proportion of 1:1.3. One ingenious Yankee found a way to cut ten ninths from a whole.

Oversize plates were occasionally used. These "mammoth" plates, sometimes called double or 8/4, were not made in standard sizes. Southworth & Hawes boasted that their 13½ by 16½-inch daguerreotype of Hiram Power's popular sculpture, "The Greek Slave," had "nearly 100 more square inches than any plate shown outside of our rooms."[4] But, if we are to believe the statement that Gouraud showed, in Boston in 1840, plates of 480 square inches, made by Daguerre, their boast was idle.[5]

American daguerreotypists preferred French plates. Like all silverware, each French plate was stamped on the edge with official government hallmarks. Usually there were three: (1) a star; (2) a number denoting the proportion of silver to copper (thus *40* indicated that 1/40 of the thickness was silver and 39/40 copper); and (3) a design, varying with the individual maker but always enclosed in a rectangle often incorporating the word *doublé* (plated). The practice of stamping plates with names or initials was adopted by American platemakers, although it was not required by law. In a few instances enough is known about the American makers to establish the date when certain brands of plates were introduced, and this evidence is of value in the dating of finished daguerreotypes that bear these hallmarks. The largest manufacturer was the firm of J. M. L. and W. H. Scovill, of Waterbury, Connecticut, and New York City. Joseph Pennell, who left Southworth to work with Scovill, wrote his former partner in 1848 that they were "getting out 1000 plates per day all winter thus far and there is prospect of a hard year's work ahead in this line of business."[6]

118

1

Anthony

2

3

A.B. & P.

4

L.B. BINSSE & C? N.Y.

5

L B B & C?

6

CORDUAN & C? N.Y.

7

B.F. 40

8

H B H

9

JONES & CO.

10

PEMBERTON & CO.
CONN.

11

SCOVILLS

12

SCOVILLS N?2

13

SCOVILL MFG. CO.
EXTRA

14

FINEST QUALITY N?1 E WHITE MAKER N.Y.

1, 2 Anthony, Clark and Company, New York. In business, 1846-51.

3 A. Beckers and V. Piard, New York. In business, 1851-55.

4, 5 L. B. Binsse and Company. Used by C. G. Page, 1843[7]; advertised price list of P. N. Horseley, New York, 1847.

6 Joseph Corduan, New York, Advertised, N.Y. *Observer,* Feb. 29, 1840; won diploma for plates, American Institute, 1843.

7 Benjamin French, Boston. Began to deal in daguerreotype materials, 1848.

8 Holmes, Booth and Hayden, New York.

9 Jones and Co., New York.

10 Pemberton and Co., Connecticut.

11-13 J. M. L. and W. H. Scovill; Scovill Manufacturing Co., Waterbury, Conn. Began manufacture of plates, 1842; name changed to Scovill Manufacturing Co., 1850.

14 Edward White. Began manufacture, 1844.[8]

Plates at first were expensive. Dr. Samuel Bemis paid Gouraud $2.00 apiece for whole plates in 1840, and Plumbe charged 67½ cents for a single quarter plate in 1841. By 1850, however, the price had come down and the best imported "star, phoenix or crescent" plates of the popular medium (sixth) size cost $2.00 a dozen; American plates of the same size cost $1.37½ a dozen.

The plates were seldom used just as they came from the stockhouse, for daguerreotypists liked to add more silver to them by electroplating them or, as they called the process, "galvanizing," a technique invented at the same time as the daguerreotype process itself. This method of plating one metal upon another by electric action was described by Daniel Davis, Jr., in his *Manual of Magnetism,* the first American book on electricity, published in Boston in 1842. The article to be plated is attached to a wire and suspended at one end of a tank filled with potassium cyanide solution; a block of the other metal, attached to a second wire, is suspended at the other end of the tank. When both wires are connected to the terminals of a wet battery, molecules of metal are transferred by electrolytic action from the block to the article. In the second edition of his *Manual* (1847), Davis specifically described silver plating daguerreotype plates.

Galvanizing soon became standard practice. "I would as soon think of making hay without sunshine as daguerreotypes without galvanized plates," declared D. D. T. Davie in 1853.[9] A wet battery was a part of the kit of every first-rate operator; Snelling included one at $3.00 in his inventory, plus "1 plate of silver for galvanic battery" at $8.00.

Warren Thompson of Philadelphia introduced galvanizing to France as a part of "le procédé américain," and the firm of Christofle began to manufacture in 1851 their "scale" plates, so-called because of the hallmark, a pair of scales, the government symbol for electroplated wear. Their product was endorsed by Thompson in a letter dated March 20, 1851, which Christofle reprinted in an advertisement in the French professional photographers' magazine, *La Lumière.* We translate: "It is well known by almost all experienced operators that silver deposited by the galvanic process is highly favorable for daguerreotypes, the whites being much less liable to solarize* and the darks more transparent and more per-

---

*"Se solidariser" in the original; probably a typographical error for "se solariser," or "to solarize"—a technical term for the reversal of tones on overexposure, to which daguerreotypes were prone.

120

fect in their details. Almost all the best operators in America for the past five years have galvanized their plates themselves. I did the same until I began to use yours which, I find, allow me to dispense with this process that has given me so much bother. . . ."

BUFFING

Immediately before use each plate, whether galvanized or not, had to be polished to a brilliant, mirror-like finish. To hold the plate while he polished it, the daguerreotypist first turned over the edges with a plate bender ($2.00) just enough so that the plate could be gripped by the plate block ($4.50), two wooden blocks which expanded by springs or a screw. He then fastened the plate block in the plate vise ($2.50).

The daguerreotypist now began the long, tedious operation of buffing. He sprinkled the plate with rottenstone (56 cents per bottle) or pumice, and polished it with a buff stick (three for 38 cents) covered with buckskin ($2.00). The buff was a swordlike wooden blade, upward of two feet long exclusive of its wooden handle. He polished with slow, deliberate strokes, always parallel to one of the edges, alternating from the shorter to the longer dimension. If the buff became clogged with the abrasive, he cleaned it with a buff brush (25 cents). Some daguerreotypists heated the buffs in a can on the stove until they were almost charred. After the plate seemed well polished, the daguerreotypist picked up a second buff, identical to the first but covered with canton flannel (four yards, 75 cents) or perhaps silk, and with the finest of jeweler's rouge (25 cents per ounce) finished the polishing. By now the plate had no longer a silver appearance, but seemed black. The daguerreotypist took care to give the final strokes in a direction parallel to the bottom of the finished daguerreotype—that is, crosswise for the usual vertical portrait, lengthwise for a group or landscape. This was done so that the tiny scratches, which even the most skillful buffing could not eliminate, would be parallel to the viewing light, and would cast no shadows.

There were tricks of the trade. Some daguerreotypists claimed that lamp-black was better than rouge; others made their own abrasive by calcining flour in homemade crucibles. There were those who put tallow on their buffs, "not quite enough to grease a griddle."[10] Hill in his pamphlet, *The Magic Buff*, instructed the daguerreotypist to spread on the buff leather a mixture of silver oxide and spermaceti, suet or lard.

121

Yankee ingenuity soon led to the construction of machines to lighten the labor of buffing. Alexander Beckers claimed to have made the first of these buff wheels when he was with the Langenheims in 1843. "It was constructed like an ordinary grindstone," he recollected, "the wheel being cushioned and covered with buckskin."[11] To make a seamless leather covering, daguerreotypists sometimes cut a strip right around the carcass of a calf, had this endless strip tanned, and then built a wheel to fit it. In Boston, John Adams Whipple ran his buff wheel with his steam engine; elsewhere foot power was the rule.

COATING

Once buffed, the plate was made light sensitive. Nothing like total darkness was required; "a hiding place," Beckers said, was all that was necessary. Humphrey told his readers to build a framework in the corner of a room and cover it with dark muslin; it should have a window in it covered with white paper. Two specially constructed pieces of apparatus were now needed, called "coating boxes" ($11 the pair), identical except that one was not the height of the other. Each was a wooden box containing a blue-green, hand-blown glass jar. The cover was a piece of ground glass fitted to the underside of one end of a board; a recessed opening at the other end held the daguerreotype plate. The taller of the two coating boxes contained a small amount of iodine crystals (75 cents per ounce); the shorter, a mysterious substance called "quickstuff," "the quick," or "dry sensitive" (50 cents the bottle), the exact formula of which was each daguerreotypist's secret, but which always contained bromine and chlorine compounds. In 1839 John Frederick Goddard, who was working Wolcott's camera in London, discovered that by subjecting the plate to other haloids as well as iodine, its sensitivity was increased.[12] His improvement in the process marked a turning point in the technique, for exposures were reduced radically.

G. W. Prosch to A. S. Southworth, March 30, 1841. Last Saturday I tried Bromine with the Iodine and was able to take pictures in an ordinary room with diffused light in 25 seconds, without the Bromine it required 4 minutes.[13]

The plates were put into position over these chemicals simply by sliding the lid. They changed color over the iodine: yellow, then orange, red, violet, blue, green, and again yellow. Humphrey recommended that the plate be left over the iodine from fifteen to sixty seconds until it was orange-yellow, then over quickstuff to a deep rose; then back again over the iodine for one tenth of the time of the first coating.

The stench of a daguerreotype workroom was overpowering. Iodine, bromine, and chlorine compounds at normal room temperature continually release vapors and still today, more than a hundred years later, coating boxes give forth a marked odor. Daguerreotypists tried to make their boxes airtight, and tested them by dropping pieces of burning paper inside. If smoke came out when the lid was closed, the coating box was unsatisfactory. Humphrey advised a correspondent who complained of the strong odor of bromine in his rooms to "sprinkle freely about the floor acqua ammonia."[14]

On cold days coating was impossible without specially warming the equipment. A friend wrote Southworth that Martin M. Lawrence couldn't take his portrait on the day he called at the Broadway daguerreotypist's gallery because "his stove was down and the temperature of his room was below 70°, and he could not operate at a temperature less than this."[15] Alexander Beckers complained that his employer, Edward White, would not allow a fire in his gallery overnight, and consequently it became impossible to take pictures during the winter. There were other despairs. Turpentine fumes were certain to interfere with coating, and it was impossible to work in a freshly painted room, or even in a building where house painting was going on in other rooms. One luckless daguerreotypist had just started business when a hatter moved next door; the dust which flew about when the furs were whipped into felt "caused such a commotion among the operator's chemicals, and covered everything about his room so completely, that he was unable to get a picture at all, and was obliged to abandon his premises."[16]

The daguerreotypist put the now sensitized plate into a "plate holder" or "plate shield"—a wooden frame with a removable back held in place by a wooden button, and sliding panel on front. Its purpose was to protect the plate from light while it was not in the camera. It fitted inside the camera in place of the ground-glass focusing panel. The slide was pulled out, and then the exposure made by uncapping the lens.

EXPOSURE

Only experience taught the daguerreotypist how long to expose his plates. There were three variables to be taken into account: the strength of the light, the

123

light-passing power of the lens, and the sensitivity of the plate. The first two could be measured; as early as 1839 light meters of the actinometer type were in use: the time taken by sensitive material to darken to a standard tint was used as a measure of the intensity of the illumination. There is no evidence, however, that American daguerreotypists ever resorted to exposure meters. Lenses were not fitted with adjustable diaphragms. The sensitivity of the plate varied enormously. It was hardly possible to duplicate results, even though attempts were made to standardize coating techniques. Daguerreotypists noticed that the relative humidity of the air affected sensitivity. Before a thunderstorm the plates were especially "fast," and it was suggested that electricity played a part in the phenomenon. Experiments were made in passing an electric current through the plate while exposing.

In the early days, exposures were measured in minutes. D. W. Seager published an exposure table in the appendix to a reprint of Daguerre's manual which appeared in the *American Repertory of Arts, Sciences and Manufactures* for March, 1840. The shortest exposure is five minutes and the longest is seventy minutes. This corresponds almost exactly to an exposure table published in France by Daguerre's assistant, Hubert, as an appendix to Macedoine Melloni's *Rapport sur le Daguerréotype* (Paris, 1840).

With the introduction of Voigtländer's large-aperture lenses and quickstuff, exposures were reduced to seconds. The average sitting required from twenty to forty seconds, to judge from the few records which have survived:

Date	Daguerreotypist	Exposure time
Mar. 20, 1841	George W. Prosch	25 sec.
Aug. 26, 1841	Elias Howe	20-30 sec.
Jan. 24, 1843	Charles G. Page	25-40 sec.
Mar. 29, 1843	Henry Moore	30 sec.
Feb. 11, 1844	E. H. Baker	30-45 sec.
Mar. 6, 1846	J. E. Mayall	3-9 sec.

Children were always a problem, for they would not sit still. E. T. Whitney, of Rochester, New York, found a way to trick them into periods of immobility long enough to allow an exposure of sorts to be made. "I use, with good success," he wrote in 1855, "a little toy bird, that I make sing inside the camera, occasionally showing a part of it to attract attention to the instrument."[17]

124

Outdoors, snapshots were occasionally obtained. Alexander Hesler of Galena, Illinois, set up his camera on the deck of the steamboat *Nominee* in 1851 and photographed the river landings on the Mississippi from Galena to St. Paul, to be used as illustrations for a guidebook. He claimed that he gave instantaneous exposures with a shutter driven by a rubber band. Years later he exposed his secret: the plates were coated two or three weeks before use. "The longer they were kept, the more rapid they became," he wrote, and added that they "could be exposed and developed at any future time."[18]

MERCURIALIZING

It was not the usual practice, however, to postpone the processing of the exposed plate, and most daguerreotypists developed them at once. The process was called "mercurializing." The mercury bath ($2.50) was an inverted, truncated hollow pyramid of cast iron, supported on an iron stand over an alcohol or spirit lamp (two for 62 cents). Along the side of the bath was the scale of a thermometer, the bulb of which lay inside the pot where a quarter pound of mercury (94 cents) had been poured. On coming to work in the morning, the daguerreotypist lit the alcohol lamp so that the mercury would vaporize; it was kept hot all day at a temperature between 70° and 80° C. (158° to 176° F.). This custom of quoting in the centigrade rather than the Fahrenheit system caused confusion. "You told me the mercury should not rise above 70°," a student wrote to Southworth in 1844, and asked, "But if the atmosphere was warmer than that—what is to be done? Would it require the lamp at all?"[19] When the plate was put face down over the mercury, the vapors formed an amalgam on it in proportion to the amount of light received by it in the camera. Development ranged from two to four minutes; George Barnard noted that his daguerreotype "Woodsawyers' Nooning" (Plate 20) was over the mercury two minutes. Humphrey furnished a table of effects produced by mercurializing:[20]

Time Mins.	Effect
½	Deep blue.
1	Ashy and flat—no shadows, linen deep blue.
1½	Coarse and spongy—shadows muddy—drapery dirty reddish brown.
2¼	Soft—face scarcely white, shadows neutral, drapery fine dark brown, linen somewhat blue.

Time Mins.	Effect
2½	Clear and pearly, shadows clear and positive, of a purple tint, drapery jet black, with the dark shade slightly frosted by the mercury.
2¾ to 3	Hard and chalky—shadows harsh, drapery roughened and misty with excess of mercury.

The average daguerreotypist's rooms were poorly ventilated, and the air was so charged with mercury vapor that gold watch chains became coated with amalgam. Humphrey, concerned over the health of his readers, tested the purity of the atmosphere in his own workroom by hanging a piece of gold foil "four feet above, and two from the perpendicular, at the side of the bath; and in two days the leaf began to turn slightly white, and at the expiration of the fifth day it was so alloyed as to cause the amalgam to drop."[21] He was much concerned, for he reported that his friend Jeremiah Gurney "has been confined to his bed by his system being charged with *mercury*—he has suffered the most acute pain, and been unable to move his limbs; his legs and arms have been swollen to nearly double the ordinary size, and his situation has been of the most perilous nature. We have known several instances of effects produced by mercury, but never to such an extent. No operator can observe too much caution in being exposed to the vapors of this metal."[22] L. L. Hill urged his readers "to ventilate your mercury—its fume is loaded with rheumatism, sciatica, lumbago, toothache, neuralgia and decrepitude."[23] Everything used in processing was toxic; the vapors of mercury, the gasses of chlorine, iodine, bromine, solutions of potassium cyanide. Some died; it is a wonder that more did not.

FIXING AND GILDING

The plate was finished by washing it with a 10 per cent solution of sodium thiosulphate (then called "hyposulphite of soda"—50 cents a pound) which removed the unexposed coating of silver halide. The plate was not immersed, but the solution was poured over it while it was held over an alcohol lamp with a pair of pliers (50 cents). Humphrey gives explicit directions:

> First, light your spirit lamp, then, with your pliers take the plate by the lower right hand corner, holding it in such a manner that the pliers will form in a line with the upper left hand corner; pour on, slowly, the hyposulphite solu-

126

tion, slightly agitating the plate, until all the coating is dissolved off, then rinse off with clean water.[24]

By the same manipulation, the plate was washed with a 1.25 per cent solution of gold chloride (42 cents per bottle) mixed with a 2 per cent solution of sodium thiosulphate. "Gilding," as this gold-toning technique was called, was invented by the Frenchman Hippolyte-Louis Fizeau in 1840; it was the first significant improvement on Daguerre's original process, and was at once universally adopted. It increased the brilliance of the image. Fizeau explained that "silver has been dissolved, and gold has been precipitated upon the silver, and also upon the mercury; but with very different results. The silver, which by its polish, forms the dark parts of the picture, is in some degree browned by the thin coating of gold which covers it, whence results an increased intensity in the black parts; the mercury, on the contrary, which, under the form of infinitely small globules, forms the whites, increases in strength and brilliancy, by its amalgamation with gold, whence results a greater degree of fixity, and a remarkable augmentation in the light parts of the image."[25] Humphrey notes that at first the plate became cloudy when treated with the gilding solution. "This is generally the best sign that the gilding will bring out the impression with the greatest degree of distinctness," he wrote. "Soon the clouds gradually begin to disappear, and 'like a thing of life' stands forth the image, clothed with the brilliancy and clearness that the combined efforts of nature and art can produce."[26]

All that was now required of the daguerreotypist was to rinse the plate in water, dry it over the alcohol lamp, put it into a case, and hand it to the customer.

CASES

The surface of a daguerreotype was so fragile—Arago, when describing Daguerre's first results, compared them to the wings of a butterfly—that immediate protection of the plate was imperative. On the Continent, daguerreotypes were framed like drawings, behind large cut-out mats of the style called by the French "passe-partout." Often the cover glass was painted white, brown, purple, or black on the underside; frequently the maker put his name in a lower corner.

In England, and particularly in America, daguerreotypes were put into cases designed for miniatures: two shallow boxes hinged on one side, with a fastening on the other.

127

The standardization and mass-production techniques which characterized the American daguerreotype process were highly developed in the manufacture of cases. They were sold to the daguerreotypists by stockhouses along with plates and chemicals; the price a sitter paid for his likeness varied according to the case which he chose. Most daguerreotypists kept a large variety on hand. Some had their names stamped on the lining of the cover. While it is tempting to consider the presence of a gallery name and address as documentation of the maker, it must be remembered that the cases throughout the daguerreotype period were interchangeable; a sixth-plate daguerreotype can readily be fitted into *any* sixth-plate case with no more trouble than putting a book into a slip case. Over the years families and collectors have put treasured daguerreotypes in better cases than the original ones. Thus the design of a case can only help in the attribution and dating of a daguerreotype; it cannot determine it.

Leather miniature cases were more expensive than daguerreotypes: Southworth paid the Boston case maker J. H. Smith $17 for one of goatskin in 1845. They were replaced by imitations, made of paper, pressed in dies to resemble tooling. Among the earliest manufacturers was William Shew, the Boston daguerreotypist. His cases often have a delicate design of roses. Frank Roy Fraprie, for years editor of *American Photography* and an ardent collector of daguerreotype cases, found twenty-six different designs of the rose case. He put forth the ingenious hypothesis that the number of leaves on the lower branches secretly indicated the date that the case was made: one lower branch invariably showed four, indicating the decade; the number of leaves on the opposite branch indicated the year in the decade. Other, identical cases bear the label of H. Studley, Boston.

Brady designed a case with a harp while he was a case manufacturer; it is one of the few paper cases which are signed. This may well be the pattern which Southworth's pupil L. C. Champney bought at $5.00 per dozen in 1843.

At first the covers were lined with padded silk; later velvet was used. The date of the change in style can be judged by correspondence of Southworth with a pupil:

Henry Moore to A. S. Southworth, April 1, 1843. I enclose five dollars and should like to have you send me a dozen plates and a doz. cases—8 cases the size of the one you sent and 4 smaller. I like those that are lined with silk velvet better than those lined with silk.[27]

128

Southworth to Moore, not dated. We have no velvet lined cases now. We have Satin of different colors—Blue—and Purple or Claret. You shall have them at $5.00 per doz.[28]

On April 14 Moore returned Southworth's letter endorsed, "Please send a doz. cases lined with purple and claret—half each." Southworth's customers found that designs with roses and harps sold best.

Before they were put into these cases the daguerreotypes were bound up with a gilded mat, or border. At first the material was paper, then gilded brass was substituted. The rectangular opening gave way to fancy shapes:

J. M. L. and W. H. Scovill to A. S. Southworth, October 30, 1843. After about two weeks we shall have Fig[d] Border Oval & Octagon & Acorn &c., &c.[29]

Snelling illustrated in his *Dictionary of the Photographic Art* four types of mats: the "elliptic" (curved top), "double elliptic" (rounded corners top and bottom), the "oval," and the "non-pareil" of rococo ornateness. He recommended the double elliptic and the oval.

The daguerreotype, border, and glass were bound together with goldbeater's skin or gummed paper. Often the sandwich was surrounded by the "preserver," a thin frame of highly malleable oroide brass. The unit was simply pushed into the bottom of the case, which had velvet sides to make a snug fit.

About 1853 an entirely new style of daguerreotype case was introduced, made of plastic. It was called the "Union case." The earliest reference to it in the professional press is Humphrey's description of Mascher's stereoscopic viewer in the June 15, 1853, issue of his *Journal.* Referring to a wood engraving, he wrote, "The view is perspective, and exhibits the attachment to a Union Daguerreotype case."

These molded cases were produced in a great variety of designs. A check list, which is by no means complete, of the various designs is given in K. M. McClintock's *Handbook of Popular Antiques* (1946): 110 are described. These are the cases commonly referred to as hard rubber or gutta-percha. They are nothing of the sort, but are true thermoplastic products. Samuel Peck, who invented a way of strengthening them by pressing gilded paper against the composition, described the plastic in the specification for his U.S. Patent 11,758, granted October 3, 1854: "The composition of which the main body of the case is made, and to which my invention is applicable, is composed of gum shellac and woody fibers or other suitable fibrous material dyed to the color that may be required and ground with shellac between hot rollers so as to be converted into a mass which when heated becomes plastic so that it can be pressed into a mold or between dies and made to take the form that may be imparted to it by such dies." Peck made no claim to the invention of the composition, or to its use to form daguerreotype cases.

Just twenty-seven days after Peck had received his patent, his brother-in-law Halvor Halvorson filed another patent *identical* to Peck's which he assigned to one Horace Barnes. The specifications of the Halvorson patent (No. 13,410, granted August 7, 1855) repeat those of Peck's verbatim, except that Peck's "nonporous" has become, incorrectly, "porous," and his "combined" is written "confined," which is meaningless in the context. It would appear that Halvorson literally copied out Peck's words. Why this duplication? There was no competition, for there is no record that Halvorson manufactured cases. Were the brothers-in-law trying out the validity of the patent? Did they feel that a second patent made assurance doubly sure? We know from the label pasted in a number of Union cases that the patents were merged, and that the unknown Mr. Barnes dropped out:

GENUINE UNION CASE
Improved

———

Fine Gilt and Burnish-
ed Hinge.

———

S. PECK'S PATENT,
Oct. 3d, 1854

———

H. HALVORSON'S PATENT,
Aug. 7th, 1855,
Assigned to S. Peck.

In 1856 Peck filed another patent (No. 14,202): "Fastening for the Hinges of Daguerreotype Cases." Again he takes for granted the plastic composition. The specifications read: "Daguerreotype and other similar cases are now largely manufactured of a plastic material the base of which is gum shellac." What Peck sought to protect was a means of imbedding brass strips in the plastic, to which hinges could be fastened. "Hitherto the hinges have been fastened by rivets through the material . . . nearly thirty percent of the cases were spoiled by breaking them in rivetting on the hinges."

Samuel Peck was a typical Yankee Jack-of-all-trades—carpenter, storekeeper, grocer, theater owner, undertaker, daguerreotypist. In 1850 he patented a device to hold daguerreotype plates while polishing them. And in the same year he began the manufacture of daguerreotype cases. He formed the firm of Samuel Peck & Co. in 1855. Five years later he withdrew and the assets of the company were sold to Scovill and Co., the photographic stockhouse.

The third to patent an improvement on plastic daguerreotype cases was Alfred P. Critchlow, who began to make cases in 1852 in Florence, Massachusetts. He was granted U. S. Patent 15,915 on October 14, 1856 (re-issued April 21, 1857), for "embracing rivetted hinges." Instead of fastening the hinges to the sides or walls of the case, he fastened them to the top and bottom.

Critchlow formed a partnership with Samuel L. Hill and Isaac Parsons in 1853; in 1857 David G. Littlefield joined the firm. The company claimed the plastic case as its invention. A case in the writer's collection bears the label:

A. P. CRITCHLOW & CO.

Manufacturers of

Daguerreotype Cases

A. P. C. & Co.

Are the **Original Inventors** of the
Composition for the **Union Case** (so
called,) including all the various
shades of color and fineness of texture peculiar to their manufacture
and of the **Embracing Rivited Hinges**,
thus securing them from breaking out
as do others that are inserted with
or without a metal brace.

131

But in his patent Critchlow made no such claim, for he wrote: "the kind of daguerreotype or picture case for which I have particularly devised my improvement is that which is common and well known as being made of composition."

Critchlow left the company in 1858; the firm name Littlefield, Parsons & Co. was then adopted. The name of the firm was again changed to Florence Manufacturing Company and, more recently, the Pro-Phy-Lac-Tic Brush Company. The original die of the proudest of the company's productions, an 8-by-10-inch case for whole-plate daguerreotypes bearing a bas-relief from the painting "Washington Crossing the Delaware" by Emmanuel Leutze, is still owned by the Pro-Phy-Lac-Tic Brush Company. A brilliant impression of it was made with modern thermoplastic material for the George Eastman House collection.

The dies for this case were cut by F. B. Smith and Hartmann, New York. They also cut for Peck a whole-plate case from the painting "The Landing of Columbus" by John Vanderlyn in the rotunda of the Capitol, Washington, D.C. Raphael's "Madonna of the Chair" served as model for Henning and Eymann. Perhaps the finest of all Union cases is the utterly simple transcription into bas-relief of Sir Thomas Lawrence's "The Calmady Children," a painting now in the Metropolitan Museum of Art. It is the only die signed by H. W. Hayden. Four cases are signed "Goll," probably Frederick Goll, listed in the New York City directory for 1853-54 as die-sinker: the designs show the Washington Monument in Richmond, Virginia, a medallion of George Washington, a horse race, and a copy of the painting by Asher B. Durand, "The Capture of Major André." Other less impressive cases are signed "A. Schaefer" and "J. Smith."

Some of the finest cases are unsigned; many, such as "American Country Life; Summer's Evening" from the Currier and Ives lithograph by F. F. Palmer of 1855, exist in several variants. For each variation a separate set of dies must have been made; the investment in the case industry must have been substantial.

Besides those of Peck, Critchlow, Littlefield, Parsons & Co., and the Florence Manufacturing Co., other labels are found inside Union cases: Holmes, Booth & Hayden; Scovill Manufacturing Co.; Wadhams Manuf'g Co. (Kinsley & Parker's Hinge, Patented June 1, 1858). The products of these firms are indistinguishable.

Modern experts marvel at the quality of these pioneer plastic products. Significantly, the largest collection of them is in the possession of the Waterbury Companies, one of the leading plastic manufacturers of the country.

Papier-mâché cases, inlaid with mother-of-pearl, and handsomely painted with landscapes or flowers, were also popular, and a great variety of lockets, brooches, and other jewelry was designed to hold small daguerreotypes cut into oval or circular shapes.

RESTORATION

Like all objects made of silver, daguerreotypes tarnish. They cannot be cleaned by friction, for the image would then be rubbed off. Daguerreotypists knew how to clean even those which were completely hidden beneath tarnish. Abraham Bogardus told the Society of Amateur Photographers in 1889:

"Only a few years ago a lady came to me with a half-sized picture, and you could not see anything at all upon it. She wanted to know if I could clean it. . . . In about five minutes I brought it to her . . . she fainted dead away. . . . It was her husband who had been dead twenty years, and she had not seen the picture in fifteen years. It was so completely covered with a film that there was nothing to be seen, and I brought it up as good as it was originally. As I say, the lady fainted immediately. It was just as if her husband had been brought back from the grave for her to see."[30]

Daguerreotypists cleaned the plate by washing it with a solution of potassium cyanide. For years this deadly poison was the only known solvent for the tarnish. It is not a chemical to be used by the layman. A grain of it will kill a man if taken internally.

Fortunately a nontoxic technique has been recently discovered by Mrs. Ruth K. Field, assistant curator of the Missouri Historical Society, St. Louis.

Remove the daguerreotype from the case, unframe it, and wash it in distilled water to remove surface dirt. Drain and immerse, until the discoloration is washed away, in the following solution:

Distilled water	500 cubic centimeters
Thiourea	70 grams
Phosphoric acid (85%)	80 cc.
Non-ionic wetting agent (e.g. Kodak "Photo-Flo" Solution)	2 cc.
Distilled water to make	1000 cc.

133

Remove plate from bath and rinse under running water. Place in a mild solution of ordinary soap and water and agitate briefly. Rinse again with tap water, then distilled water. Immerse in 95% grain alcohol; drain; dry over alcohol lamp.

Provided it does not suffer physical damage, no photograph is more permanent than a daguerreotype. The image will bear the action of light, for the light-sensitive salts were completely removed in processing. Heat, however, must be avoided, for it will drive out the mercury which, in amalgam with the silver, forms the highlights. For this reason, daguerreotypes should not be exposed to sunlight or kept near radiators or hot electric bulbs.

COPYING DAGUERREOTYPES

The successful copying of daguerreotypes with modern photographic materials depends upon properly illuminating them, and shielding the camera to eliminate reflection. Daguerreotypists built velvet-lined boxes, one end open, the other closed, with two slits on each side to admit light. The daguerreotype was laid against the closed end. The lens of the camera was put inside the open end.

We have found that excellent results are obtained simply by shielding the camera during exposure with a three-foot square of black velveteen, with a hole in its center the diameter of the lens, suspended in front of the camera from a stand for photographic lamps to which a cross bar is fixed by a laboratory clamp. An ordinary lens hood painted black is slipped through the hole in the velvet and over the lens mount.

Camera equipment is optional. We use a 4-by-5-inch view camera of ancient vintage, medium-speed panchromatic film, and a 6-inch Goerz Dagor lens, usually set at $f/22$.

The majority of the copies in this book were made by daylight, since photographing was done in private homes and museum galleries. When copying, it is essential to orient the daguerreotype in the position in which it was intended to be viewed. This is because, in the buffing, daguerreotypists always finished with strokes horizontal to the dimension of the plate which was to be the bottom of the final picture. Vertical scratches, under normal illumination, are more conspicuous than horizontal ones.

The density scale of a daguerreotype is approximately that of conventional

134

modern developing-out paper. The densities of a typical Southworth & Hawes portrait measured

$$D \min = 0.36$$
$$D \max = 1.70$$

Thus the density scale of this sample is 1.34.

Pragmatically, it has been found that the best results are secured with a development 50 per cent beyond normal.

We calculate exposure with a standard gray card as used in color photography placed in the position of the daguerreotype, from which we take a reading with a photo-electric exposure meter. Due allowance must be made, of course, for bellows extension.

A portable copying stand made of elements from a discarded view camera has proved most convenient for traveling. The double-extension bed is clamped onto the end of the copying camera bed. The rising front of the discarded view camera was converted to an easel, fitted with two ledges between which a daguerreotype in its case can be held. Grooves in the ledges enable us to hold a naked daguerreotype plate. It is strongly urged that, whenever possible, the daguerreotype be removed from its case and cover glass.

Experiments were made with polarizing the incident light and photographing through a polarized filter. No practical advantage was gained. A technique described by Truso Leslie in *Photo Era,* XXIV (1910), 250, was also tried with little success. Leslie recommends using a white, rather than a black, shield over the camera to secure a positive image on the film. He states that more evenly lighted and brilliant results are thus obtained. Our experiments did not bear out this claim.

Excellent results have been obtained by the use of color film, not only for tinted originals, but for monochromatic daguerreotypes: the characteristic deep-brown tint of a well-gilded plate is beautifully reproduced on modern multi-layer reversal films.

Since daguerreotypes have no grain—a 3,000X magnification by an electron microscope reveals only a pitting of the surface—they stand enlargement excellently well, particularly when thrown on a screen by a lantern slide projector.

135

The photographic quality of a well-made daguerreotype is beyond compare. We cannot imagine that they ever were more brilliant, more detailed, more beautiful. Through them we can see the past with the eyes of the past. It is not by chance that they are endowed with this evocative power; daguerreotypists had the future in mind. Humphrey urged his readers to make each daguerreotype "worthy of preserving as a remembrance of the past. It would call to mind the men of generations gone by. For such let every ambitious Daguerreotypist strive."[31]

PART IV

Biographies and Notes

Standard abbreviations, as listed in *Webster's New Collegiate Dictionary*, are used throughout, plus the following:

AJP	*American Journal of Photography*
APB	*Anthony's Photographic Bulletin*
dag'type	daguerreotype
DAB	*Dictionary of American Biographies*
DJ	*The Daguerreian Journal*
Exh. London 1851	Exhibited at the Great Exhibition of the Works of Industry of All Nations in the Crystal Palace, London, 1851.
Exh. N. Y. C. 1853-54.	Exhibited at the Exhibition of the Industry of All Nations in the Crystal Palace, New York City, 1853-54.
GEH	George Eastman House Collection.
HJ	*Humphrey's Journal.*
PAJ	*The Photographic Art-Journal* and its continuation, *The Photographic and Fine Art Journal.*
Taft	Robert Taft, *Photography and the American Scene* (New York: The Macmillan Company, 1938; reprinted New York: Dover Publications, 1964).

Biographies

ADAMS, DAN
Active Nashville, Tenn., 1845.

ANSON, RUFUS
Active N. Y. C., 1851-67.

ANTHONY, EDWARD
Born N. Y. C., 1818. Studied civil engineering at Columbia College, N. Y. C. Taught dag'type process by S. F. B. Morse. Photographer, U. S. Govt. survey of Canadian border, 1842. Proprietor of "National Daguerreotype Miniature Gallery," N. Y. C., with Jonas M. Edwards, Howard Chilton, J. R. Clark: (Anthony, Edwards & Chilton, 1843; Anthony, Edwards & Co., 1844-45; Anthony, Clark & Co., 1846-47). Opened dag'type stockhouse, N. Y. C., 1847. Partnership with bro., 1852. Offered prize for best dag'types, 1852-53. Died N. Y. C., 1888. *Wilson's Photographic Mag.*, Jan. 5, 1889; *HJ,* IV (1852), 12-13; *Photographic Times,* XVIII (1888), 631 (portrait).

ANTHONY, HENRY T.
Born 1814. Joined bro. Edward in his photographic stockhouse, 1852. Discovered instantaneous process with wet plates, 1858; as a consequence the firm went into business making stereoscopic pictures. Died N. Y. C., 1884. *APB,* XV (1884), 52-53, 453; *Phila. Photog-*

rapher, XXI (1884), 341; *Yearbook of Photog.,* 1885; Taft, 463.

BABBITT, PLATT D.
Active Niagara Falls, 1854—c. 1870. Taft, 96.

BAKER, E. H.
Active in Providence, R. I., 1884.

BALL, JAMES P.
Active Cincinnati, 1853-59; to Europe, 1856.

BARNARD, GEORGE N.
Active in Oswego, N. Y., 1851-54? Secretary, N. Y. State Daguerreian Assoc., 1853. Purchased Clark's gallery in Syracuse, 1854. Hon. Mention, Anthony's Prize Competition, 1854. During Civil War, official photographer at Chief Engineer's Office, Division of the Mississippi, U. S. Army; documented Sherman's campaign (61 photographs, published in portfolio, 1865). *HJ,* V (1853), 190, 320; Taft, 230, 232, 486.

BARNES, C.
Active in Mobile, Ala., 1850-54.

BEALS, A. T.
Active, N. Y. C. Exh. N. Y. C. 1853-54.

BECKERS, ALEXANDER

Born Germany. To Phila., 1836. Learned dag'type process from Frederick Langenheim, 1842. To N. Y. C., 1843: operator for E. White, 1844. Partner of Langenheims, N. Y. C., 1848; of Victor Piard, 1849. U. S. Pat. 6,812 (block for holding dag'type plates), 1849. Sold dag'type business, 1858. U. S. Patents for cabinet stereoscope: 16,962 (1857); 23,438 (1859); 23,543 (1859); 24,855 (1859); 26,407 (1859). U. S. Pat. 23,342 (hinge for stereoscope reflectors) issued to Alen Beckers, 1859, claimed by Alexander Beckers. *St. Louis & Canadian Photographer*, XXIII (1899), 324 (portrait); Reminiscences: *British Jour. Photog.*, XXVI (1889), 510-11; *Wilson's Photographic Mag.*, XXVI (1889), 182-84; *Photographic Times*, XIX (1899), 131-32.

BEMIS, SAMUEL

Born 1789. Jeweler, dentist, amateur photographer. Learned dag'type technique from François Gouraud, 1840. Died Boston, 1881. Boston *Evening Transcript*, May 25, 1881.

BENNETT, JOHN A.

Active Mobile, Ala., 1844 and (under name Juan A. Bennett) Buenos Aires, 1845, Montevideo, 1842-43, Bogota, 1852. J. F. Riobó, *Daguerrotipos . . . en Buenos Aires* (1949).

BISBEE, A.

Active Dayton, O. Exh. N. Y. C., 1853-54.

BLACK, JAMES WALLACE

Learned dag'type process from John Lerow, Boston, 1845. Partner of J. A. Whipple, 1856-59. Took first aerial photographs in U. S. from balloon, 1860. Taft, 186. Reminiscences: *St. Louis Practical Photographer*, I (1877), 220.

BOGARDUS, ABRAHAM

Born, Dutchess Co., N. Y., 1822. To N. Y. C., 1837; dry goods clerk. Learned dag'type process from G. W. Prosch, 1846. Opened gallery, N. Y. C., 1846. First president, Natl. Photographic Assoc., 1868-74. Made dag'types of bank note designs for Amer. Bank Note Co., 1873. Gave up photog., 1887. Died Brooklyn, 1908. *Phila. Photographer*, VIII (1871), 313-15 (portrait); *St. Louis & Canadian Photographer*, XXII (1899), 324; *Photo-Miniature*, No. 72 (1905), 664-65 (portrait); Boston *Evening Transcript*, Mar. 24, 1908; Taft, 332, 416. Reminiscences: *APB*, XV (1884), 62-67; *British Jour. Photog.*, XXXVI (1884), 183-84, 200-201; *Century Mag.*, new series, XLVIII (1904), 84-91.

BRADLEY, HENRY W.

Born Wilmington, N. C. To San Francisco. Partner of W. H. Rulofson, 1863-?

BRADY, MATHEW B.

Born Warren Co., N. Y. 1822 (?). To N. Y. C. with William Page, painter, 1837. Manufacturer of jewel and dag'type cases, 1843-45. Opened dag'type gallery, 205 Broadway, 1844: James A. Brown, operator. Published *Gallery of Illustrious Americans* (12 lithographs after dag'types), 1850. Opened Washington gallery, 1847. To Europe, Jul. 1851-May 1852: George S. Cook in charge N. Y. C. gallery. Exh. London, 1851 (Prize Medal); N. Y. C., 1853-54. Opened 2nd N. Y. C. gallery, 359 Broadway, 1854; 26 employees ("artists, operators, salesmen") in 1858. Put

Alexander Gardner in charge of Washington gallery, 1856. N. Y. C. gallery moved to 785 Broadway, 1860. Organized "photographic corps," Civil War, 1861-65. Lost ownership of negatives, 1870's. Exhibited Phila. Centennial Exhibition, 1876. Died, N. Y. C., 1896. Taft, 465; J. D. Horan, *Mathew Brady* (1955); R. Meredith, *Mr. Lincoln's Camera Man* (1946); C. L. Edwards in *PAJ*, I (1851), 36-40 (portrait). Obituary: *Wilson's Photographic Mag.,* XXXIII (1896), 121-23 (portrait).

BRONK, EDWIN

Active N. Y. C. (operator for Brady); St. Louis (operator for T. C. Dobyns); Winchester, Columbus, O.

BROWN, E.

Probably active N. Y. C. Accompanied U. S. Navy expedition to the China Seas and Japan, 1852-54.

BROWN, JAMES A.

Born 1819. Active N. Y. C. (operator for Brady, 1843; own gallery, 1848-54). Exh. N. Y. C. 1853-54. U. S. Pat. 10,255 (ornamenting and embellishing dag'types), 1853. *Wilson's Photographic Mag.,* XXX (1893), 235.

BURGESS, NATHAN G.

Learned dag'type process in Paris, 1840. Active N. Y. C., 1844-59. Author: *The Ambrotype Manual* (1856), 2d ed., 1856; 3rd ed., 1857; 4th to 7th eds. (titled *The Photograph and Ambrotype Manual*), 1858, 1859, 1861; 8th ed. (titled *The Photograph Manual*), 1862. *AJP*, new series, I (1858), 10.

BUTLER, WILLIAM H.

Active N. Y. C. (operator for Plumbe; own gallery, 1847-53).

CAMPBELL, JOHN

Took dag'type of eclipse of sun, 1854. Active in Jersey City, N. J., 1860. *PAJ*, 3rd series, XI (1860), 148.

CARDEN & CO.

Active N. Y. C., 1853-54. (Carden & Norton, 1854).

CARVALHO, SOLOMON N.

Born Charleston, S. C., 1815; painter there. Took up dag'type, c. 1850. Invented technique of enameled dag'types, 1852; employed by Jeremiah Gurney, 1853. Cameraman on Frémont expedition across Rocky Mts., 1853-54. N. Y. C., 1862. Died there, 1899. Author: *Incidents of Travel and Adventure in the Far West with Col. Frémont's Last Expedition* (1860). *Natl Mag.,* II (1853), 572; *PAJ*, III (1852) 256; *HJ* IV (1853), 383; Taft, 490; A. W. Rutledge, *Trans. Amer. Philosophical Soc.,* XXXIX (1949), 164-65.

CATHAN, LUCIUS H.

Born 1817. Active Townshend, Vt., 1843-?; Boston, 1848-50; Townshend 1851-? Died c. 1890.

CHAMPNEY, L. C.

Learned dag'type process from A. S. Southworth; itinerant in Mass., Vt., 1842-44.

CHAPIN, MOSES SANFORD

Born Milford, Mass. Cabinetmaker. Active as dag'typist in Worcester, Mass., 1850-c.

1865. E. F. Coffin in *Worcester Hist. Soc. Publication,* new series, I (1935), 432-39.

CHILTON, HOWARD

Proprietor of "National Daguerreotype Miniature Gallery," N. Y. C., with Edward Anthony and Jonas M. Edwards, 1843.

CHILTON, JAMES R.

Born 1810. Chemist, pioneer dag'typist. Active N. Y. C. 1839-43(?). Died 1863. *AJP,* new series, VI (1863), 71.

CHURCH, EDWIN

Active St. Louis; sold gallery there to Dobyns, 1851. To N. Y. C.; operator for Lawrence; left to join Dobyns in Memphis, Tenn. *DJ,* II (1851), 338; *HJ,* V (1853), 190.

CLARK, ANSON

Born 1788. Active West Stockbridge, Mass., 1841-44. Died 1847. Hartford, Conn., *Courant,* Jan. 2, 1849; *Berkshire Whig,* Mar. 4, 1847.

CLARK, DAVID

Active New Brunswick, N. J. Exh. N. Y. C., 1853-54.

CLARK, J. M.

Member, N. Y. State Daguerreian Assoc.; on committee to investigate L. L. Hill's alleged color process, 1851.

CLARK, J. R.

Proprietor of "National Daguerreotype Miniature Gallery" with Edward Anthony, 1846-47.

COOK, GEORGE SMITH

Born Stratford, Conn., 1819. Boyhood in Newark, N. J. Traveled in South, 1838; settled in New Orleans; studied painting. Opened dag'type gallery in New Orleans, c. 1845. To Charleston, 1849. In charge of Brady's N. Y. C. gallery while Brady was in Europe, 1851-52. Returned to Charleston. Photographed Civil War from Confederate front. N. Y. C., 1874-75. To Richmond, Va., 1880. Died Bel Air, nr. Richmond, 1902. A. D. Cohen in *PAJ,* I (1851), 285-87 (portrait); A. L. Kocher & H. Dearstyne, *Shadows in Silver* (1954).

COOMBS, FRED

Active St. Louis, 1846; Chicago, 1849; San Francisco, 1850.

CORNELIUS, ROBERT

Born 1809. Lamp-shade manufacturer. Began dag'typing, 1839. Gallery in Philadelphia, 1840-42. Died, 1893. *AJP,* XIV (1893), 420 (portrait); Taft, 457-58.

CUTTING, JAMES A.

Inventor. Secured patent for beehive, 1842. Moved to Boston. Three U.S. Patents (11,213, 11,266; 11,267) for modification of collodion process, including ambrotype, 1854. Yachtsman: collected from his yacht *Ambrotype* aquatic specimens which he exhibited at "The Aquarial Gardens," Boston (later acquired by P. T. Barnum). Died in Insane Asylum of Worcester, Mass., 1867. *Worcester Daily Spy,* Aug. 12, 1867.

DAVIE, DANIEL T.

Born 1819. Began photog., 1846. Active

Utica, N. Y., 1848-51. Member N. Y. State Daguerreian Assoc.; on committee to investigate L. L. Hill's alleged color process, 1851. Took portraits "of all officers of government and Congress" in Washington. Opened Syracuse, N. Y., gallery, 1852. Author: *Photographer's Pocket Companion* (1857); *Secrets of the Dark Chamber* (1870). *PAJ*, II (1851), 165-66 (portrait); III (1852), 320, 351; *DJ*, I (1850), 29, 64.

DAVIS, ARI

Instrument maker, active in Boston with bro. Daniel, Jr., 1834-? Took dag'types in Boston and Lowell, Mass., 1841.

DAVIS, ASAHEL

Instrument maker, active in Boston with bro. Daniel, Jr. To Philadelphia to work in Plumbe's establishment. E. Z. Stone in *Contributions of the Old Resident's Assoc., Lowell, Mass.,* V (1892), 165-88.

DAVIS, DANIEL, JR.

Instrument maker, pioneer dag'typist, electrical experimenter. Born Princeton, Mass., 1813. Active in Boston with bro. Ari as instrument maker, 1834-52. Learned to dag'type from François Gouraud, 1840; made apparatus and took dag'types same year. U. S. Pat. 2,826 (improvements in coloring dag'type pictures), 1842, assigned to John Plumbe, Jr. Author: *Manual of Magnetism* (1842), first U. S. book on electricity. Retired, 1852. Died Princeton, Mass., 1887. E. F. Blake, *History of the Town of Princeton* (1915), II, 75-76; *Boston Weekly Transcript,* Mar. 29, 1887.

DOBYNS, T. C.

Established chain of dag'type galleries: New Orleans, Vicksburg, Louisville (1850); Nashville, St. Louis (1851); Memphis (1854). N. Y. C. gallery, 1853-? *HJ*, V (1853), 190, 222.

DRAPER, JOHN WILLIAM

Scientist, pioneer dag'typist. Born England, 1811. To U. S., 1832. Prof. Chemistry, N. Y. University, 1837-81; president, 1850-73. First dag'type experiments, 1839. Died Hastings, N. Y., 1882. *AJP*, I (1852), 2; M. A. Root, *The Camera and the Pencil* (1864), 340. See also his *Scientific Memoirs,* XIII, 197; *Amer. Repertory of Arts, Sciences and Manufactures,* I (1840), 401-404.

EASTERLY, THOMAS M.

Born Brattleboro, Vt., 1809. Active Liberty, Missouri, with F. F. Webb, 1846-47; St. Louis, 1848-82. Died, 1882. *APB*, III (1872), 611; C. Van Ravenswaay in *Bul. of the Missouri Hist. Soc.,* X (1953), 56-57; *Practical Photographer,* VI (1882), 144.

EDWARDS, JONAS M.

Proprietor of "National Daguerreotype Miniature Gallery," N. Y. C., with Edward Anthony, Howard Chilton, 1843-45.

EVANS, O. B.

Active Buffalo, N. Y., 1850 or earlier. Advertised as "oldest practical Daguerreian in America" in Buffalo Business Directory, 1855. Exh. London, 1851. *DJ*, I (1850), 29.

FARIS, THOMAS

Began dag'typing 1841. Active Cincinnati, 1844-52; N. Y. C., 1858-?

FITZ, HENRY

Telescope maker, pioneer dag'typist. Born Newburyport, Mass., 1808. To N. Y., 1818. Assisted Wolcott and Johnson in making their 1839 dag'type portraits. Gallery in Baltimore, 1840-42. To N. Y.; concentrated on making telescopes, including world's biggest (16 inches). Died N. Y. C., 1863. *AJP*, new series, VI (1863), 215.

FITZGIBBON, JOHN H.

Born London, 1816 (?). To N. Y. C. while a child. Apprenticed to saddler, then ran a hotel nr. Lynchburg, Va. Began to dag'type, 1841. Opened St. Louis gallery, 1846. Purchased from J. Gurney the R. H. Vance collection of dag'types of Pacific Coast, 1853. Exh. N. Y. C., 1853-54 (Hon. Mention). Moved to Vicksburg, 1861; captured by Union Army; prisoner of war in Cuba. Returned to St. Louis, 1866. Retired, 1876. Editor and publisher *St. Louis Practical Photographer* (first issue, 1877). Died on train en route to Convention of Photographers' Assoc. of America, of which he was president, 1882. *AJP*, new series, VI (1863), 143; *HJ*, V (1853), 299; *PAJ*, VII (1854), 104, 192; VIII (1855), 32; IX (1856), 128; *Photographic Mosaics,* 1871, p. 45; *St. Louis Practical Photographer,* I (1877) front. to no. 1 (portrait); C. Van Ravenswaay in *Bul. of the Missouri Hist. Soc.,* X (Oct., 1953), 58-60; Taft, 488.

FONTAYNE, CHARLES H.

Born 1814. Began photog. in Baltimore. To Cincinnati, 1846. Made, with W. S. Porter, 8-plate dag'type panorama of Cincinnati waterfront. Exh. London, 1851. Life-size photographs, 1854; 5½ x 7 ft. enlargements,

1855. Invented machine for bulk printing, 1858. Died Clifton, N. J., 1858. *AJP*, new series, III (1860), 104, 112; *PAJ*, VII (1854), 192; VIII (1855), 96, 192; X (1857), 349; *Wilson's Photographic Mag.,* XXXVIII (1901), 192; M. A. Root, *The Camera and the Pencil* (1864), 385-86.

FORD, J. M.

Active San Francisco and Sacramento, Calif., 1854-56.

FOSTER, B.

Active Portland, Me., 1843.

FREDRICKS, CHARLES DeFOREST

Born 1823. Taught dag'type process by J. Gurney. To Venezuela, 1843; traveled through S. America dag'typing, 1843-c.52. To Paris, 1853. To N. Y. C.; partner of J. Gurney, 1855-56; own gallery 1857-? *APB*, XII (1881), 110-12; Taft, 134.

GAGE, FRANKLIN B.

Active in St. Johnsbury, Vt., 1851-? Author: *Theoretical and Practical Photography on Glass and Paper* (1859). E. T. Fairbanks, *The Town of St. Johnsbury, Vt.* (1914), p. 488.

GAVIT, DANIEL E.

Born, 1819. Active Albany, N. Y., 1850; N. Y. C., 1850-52. Purchased "National Daguerreotype Miniature Gallery" of Anthony, Clark & Co., 1850. Exh. London, 1851. Delegate to formation meeting of N. Y. State Daguerreian Assoc., 1851. Gave up photog., c. 1852. Publisher of newspaper in Jersey City, 1853. Died N. Y. C., 1875. *New England Hist. & Geneal. Register,* Jan., 1923; *DJ*,

I (1850), 51; II (1851), 31; *HJ*, V (1853), 190; *PAJ*, II (1851), 123.

GORGAS, JOHN M.

Began photog. Pittsburgh, Pa., 1847. To Madison, Ind., 1853; floating gallery on Ohio and Mississippi Rivers, 1853-56. Reminiscences: *St. Louis & Canadian Photographer,* XXIII (1899), 327.

GOURAUD, FRANÇOIS

Full name: Jean-Baptiste François Fauvel-Gouraud. Arrived N. Y. C. from France, Nov. 23, 1839, purporting to be pupil of Daguerre and agent of Alphonse Giroux. Exhibited dag'types, taught, N. Y. C., 1839-40; Boston, 1840; Providence, R. I., 1840. To Buffalo, 1842. Began to lecture on memory training, 1842. Published three books on subject and a shorthand manual. Died c. 1848. Manuscript biography by J. E. Rockwell in N. Y. Public Library.

GRAVES, E. R.

Itinerant, working out of Lockport, N. Y., 1853.

GRISWOLD, VICTOR M.

Began to dag'type with bro. M. M. Griswold in Tiffin, O., 1850. Active Lancaster, O., 1852. Learned collodion process from S. D. Humphrey, 1853 (?) According to his son, devised technique for putting collodion emulsion on any surface, including tin. Began manufacture of "ferrotype" (i.e. tintype) plates, 1856. Author: *A Manual of Griswold's New Ferro-Photographic Process for Opal Printing on the Ferrotype Plates* (1866). Died Peekskill, N. Y., 1873. E. P. Griswold, "How the Tin-

type was Invented," *Amer. Amateur Photographer,* I (1889), 235-36; Obituary by M. M. Griswold in *Photographic Times,* II (1872), 107, 118-19.

GURNEY, JEREMIAH

Began to dag'type while a jeweler in Saratoga, N. Y., 1839(?). Active N. Y. C., 1840-after 1865. Bought Whitehurst's gallery, 1852. Exh. N. Y. C. 1853-54 (Hon. Mention). Won Anthony Prize Competition, 1853. Partner of Charles D. Fredricks, 1855-56. Author: *Etchings on Photography* (1856). *DJ*, I (1850), 51; II (1851), 340; III (1852), 66, 257; *HJ*, IV (1852), 127, 240; V (1853-54), 246, 273-78; *PAJ*, III (1852), 66, 257; VII (1854), 6; N. Y. *Star*, Nov. 6, 1887.

HAAS, PHILIP

Active N. Y. C., 1846, '48, '50-57. Exh. N. Y. C. 1853-54.

HARRISON, CHARLES C.

Active as dag'typist, N. Y. C., 1851; gallery purchased by George S. Cook; became camera maker (pupil of Henry Fitz). Exh. London, 1851; N. Y. C., 1853-54 (Bronze Medal). Died, N. Y. C., 1864. *AJP*, new series, III (1861), 279 (portrait); *DJ*, I (1851), 127; II (1851), 180; *HJ*, V (1854), 299; XVI (1865), 240, 256; *PAJ*, II (1851), 127; *Phila. Photog.,* II (1865), 16, 97.

HARRISON, GABRIEL

Born Philadelphia, 1817. To N. Y. C., 1822; worked for father printing bank notes. Brief career as actor (1838), painter. Learned dag'-type process in Plumbe's N. Y. C. gallery; became assistant, later operator, for William

Butler, 1844-48. Operator for M. M. Lawrence, 1849-52. Own gallery, Brooklyn, N. Y., 1852; N. Y. C., 1859. Exh. N. Y. C., 1853-54 (Hon. Mention). *PAJ,* I (1851), 169-77 (portrait); III (1852), 320; *HJ,* IV (1852), 63; H. R. Stiles, *History of King's County* (1884), p. 1151-58.

HARTSHORN, W. S.

Active in Providence, R. I., with S. Masury, 1848; sold out to Manchester Brothers, 1850.

HAWES, JOSIAH JOHNSON

Born East Sudbury (now Wayland), Mass., 1808. Apprenticed to a carpenter; self-taught painter. On seeing Gouraud's demonstration of dag'type, took up process, 1840. Joined A. S. Southworth, Boston, 1844. Died, Crawford Notch, N. H., 1901. *Boston Herald,* Aug. 9, 1901; *Photo Era,* VII (Sept. 1901), 119; XVI (1906), 104-07; *Worcester Spy,* Jan. 6, 1888; also references under SOUTHWORTH, ALBERT SANDS.

HAWKINS, EZEKIEL C.

Active in Cincinnati, 1844-60. Exh. N. Y. C., 1853-54. *DJ,* I (1850), 29; II (1851), 242.

HELSBY, TOMAS C.

American, active in Buenos Aires, 1846. J. F. Riobó, *Daguerrotipos . . . en Buenos Aires* (1949).

HESLER, ALEXANDER

Born Montreal, Canada, 1823. Boyhood in Vermont. To Racine, Wisc., 1833. Learned photog. Buffalo, 1847; opened gallery in Madison, Wisc., 1847. To Galena, Ill., 1848; dag'typed Mississippi River from Galena to St. Paul from S.S. *Nominee,* 1851. Took dag'-type of Minnehaha Falls which inspired Longfellow to write "Hiawatha," 1852. To Chicago, 1853. Exh. N. Y. C., 1853-54 (Bronze Medal). Died "in harness—during the photographing of a group by flashlight," Evanston, Ill., 1895. *APB,* XXVI (1895), 259; *HJ,* V (1854), 299; *PAJ,* VII (1854), 384; Evanston, Ill., *Index,* July 6, 1895; Taft, 98, 471; B. Newhall in *Minnesota History,* XXXIV (1954), 28-33. Reminiscences: *Photographic Times,* XIX (1889), 130-31.

HILL, LEVI L.

Born Athens, N. Y., 1816. Father murdered, 1828. Apprentice printer, *Hudson Gazette,* 1829-31. To N. Y. C., and then Kingston, N. Y., as printer, 1831, in office of *Ulster Plebeian.* Joined Baptist Church; studied at Hamilton (N. Y.) Literary and Theological Seminary, 1833-34. Preacher, Baptist Church, New Baltimore, N. Y., c. 1836; Married, 1836. Settled in Westkill as pastor, 1836-45. Published *The Baptist Library* (3 vols., 1843), *The Baptist Scrapbook* (1845). Set up printing shop with bro. R. H. Hill in Prattsville, N. Y., c. 1844. Returned to Westkill, 1845: became dag'typist. Published *Treatise on Dag'type,* 1849 (2nd printing, 1850; 3rd printing, titled *Photographic Researches,* 1851; 4th printing, 1851; 2nd ed., 1854). Announced color process, 1850. Investigated by committee of N. Y. State Daguerreian Assoc., 1851; declared a humbug. Published *Treatise on Heliochromy,* 1856. To Hudson, N. Y., 1856. Died N. Y. C., 1865. A. J. Olmsted in *Jour. Photographic Soc. of America,* XI (1945), 164-66; obit., *British Jour. Photog.,* XII (1865), 155; *HJ,* XVI (1865), 315-16.

HILLS

Active with Gabriel Harrison, Brooklyn, 1853-?

HOLCOMB, SARAH

Taught dag'type by A. S. Southworth. Itinerant in Mass. and N. H., 1846.

HOLMES, S. A.

Active N. Y. C., 1855. *HJ,* VI (1855), 295, 327.

HOVEY, DOUGLAS

Born Hampton, Conn., 1828. To Grandville, O., c. 1836. To Philadelphia, c. 1849, to work in dag'type gallery of Samuel Root. To Rochester, N. Y., 1854 (partner of John Kelsey, 1854-55; of Henry G. Hartman, 1857-63; own business, 1866). Began to manufacture albumen paper, 1868. Died Rochester, N. Y., 1886. *Rochester Morning Herald,* Feb. 10, 1886; *PAJ,* VIII (1855), 59.

HOWE, ELIAS

Inventor of sewing machine. Born, Spencer, Mass., 1819. Instrument maker in shop of Daniel Davis, Jr., Boston. Worked for J. A. Whipple manufacturing dag'type supplies, 1841; own dag'type gallery, Cambridgeport, Mass., 1841-? U. S. Pat. 4,750 (sewing machine), 1846. Died Brooklyn, 1867. DAB; *Photographer's Friend,* III (1873), 70; *Boston Weekly Transcript,* Mar. 29, 1887.

HOWE, GEORGE M.

Active Portland, Me. Exh. N. Y. C., 1853-54.

HUDDLESTON, J. S. F.

Instrument maker in Boston. Built apparatus for J. Plumbe, Jr. (?) Exhibited dag'types, 1841.

HUMPHREY, SAMUEL DWIGHT

Active Canandaigua, N. Y., 1849, when he dag'typed moon. To N. Y. C., 1850, as dag'-typist and editor and publisher of world's first magazine devoted to photog., the *Daguerreian Journal* (1850-51; title changed to *Humphrey's Jour.,* 1852). Stockdealer, c. 1854-58. Resigned editorship of *HJ,* 1859. Author: *A System of Photography* (1849; 2nd ed. same yr.); *American Handbook of the Daguerreotype* (1853; 5th ed. 1858); *Practical Manual of the Collodion Process* (2nd ed., 1856; 3rd ed., 1857).

HUNT, CALEB

Operator for J. Gurney. Active in Cleveland, 1854. *HJ,* V (1854), 335.

JOHNSON, JOHN

Made pioneer portrait dag'types with A. S. Wolcott, 1839. U. S. Pat. 2,391 (buff wheel), 1841. *AJP,* new series, VI (1864), 343; *DJ,* II (1851), 56-57, 73-80; see also references under WOLCOTT, ALEXANDER SIMON.

JOHNSON, WALTER R.

Prof. of Physics and Chemistry, Univ. of Penna., 1839-43. Brought dag'type apparatus from abroad to Phila., 1839; lectured about process and took dag'types, 1839-40. Died Phila. 1852. *U. S. Gazette,* Oct. 22, 1839; Jan. 31, Feb. 11, 1840; *Appleton's Cyclopaedia of Amer. Biography;* Taft, 457.

JONES, WILLIAM B.

Active in Boston; assistant to J. A. Whipple, 1849-50; co-patentee of crystalotype (U. S. Pat. 7,458), 1849.

KELSEY, C. C.

Active Chicago. Exh. N. Y. C., 1853-54.

KELSEY, JOHN

Active Phila. (operator for M. Shew); to Rochester, N. Y., 1853 (partner of James Heath, 1853; of Daniel Hovey, 1854-55). Dag'typed eclipse of sun, May 26, 1854.

KIMBALL, J. A.

Active N. Y. C. Exh. N. Y. C., 1853-54.

LANGENHEIM BROTHERS

WILLIAM LANGENHEIM. Born Brunswick, Germany, 1807. To U. S.; in Texas, 1834-36. To Phila., 1840, where he was associated rest of life with bro. Frederick. Died Phila., 1874.

FREDERICK LANGENHEIM. Born Brunswick, Germany, 1809. To Phila., 1840; after brief career as newspaperman for German language *Alte und Neue Welt* opened dag'type studio with bro. William, c. 1842. N. Y. C. gallery (with Alexander Beckers), 1845-48. Assignee of Johann B. Isenring's U. S. Pats. 4.369 and 4,370 (coloring dag'types), 1846. Purchased W. H. F. Talbot's U. S. Pat. 5,171 (calotype process), 1849. Invented albumen plates (hyalotypes); U. S. Pat. 7,784, 1850. Exh. London, 1851. Pioneers in stereoscopic photog.; by 1854 in business selling them under name "American Stereoscopic Company." Introduced photographic lantern slides; sold business to Caspar Briggs, 1874. Died Phila., 1879. F. Roemer, *Texas, with Particular Reference to German Immigration*

(1935), p. 167ff; L. W. Sipley, *Penna. Arts & Sciences,* II (1937), 25-29, 58-59; M. A. Root, *The Camera and the Pencil* (1864), pp. 355-56; 363.

LAWRENCE, MARTIN M.

Born 1808. Active N. Y. C., 1842-? Exh. London, 1851 (Prize Medal); N. Y. C., 1853-54. *DJ,* I (1851), 215; *HJ,* IV (1852), 63; V (1853), 10, 190; *PAJ,* I (51), 103-106 (portrait).

LITCH, ALBERT

Active Boston; partner of J. A. Whipple, 1844-46. Operator for J. Gurney; to England, 1853. *HJ,* IV (1853), 383.

LONG BROTHERS

ENOCH LONG. Born Hopkinton, N. H., 1823. H. H. LONG. Students of R. Cornelius, 1842. Gallery in Augusta, Ga. To St. Louis, 1846-65. Enoch L. operated galleries in Alton, Quincy, and Galena, Ill. Exh. N. Y. C., 1853-54. Enoch L. in business as "solar printer" Quincy, Ill., 1891. C. Van Ravenswaay in *Bul. of the Missouri Hist. Soc.,* X (1953), 63-64.

McDONNELL, DONALD & CO.

Active Buffalo, N. Y., 1850-? Exh. N. Y. C., 1853-54.

McINTYRE, S. C.

Dentist in Tallahassee, Fla.; advertised as dag'typist, 1845. To San Francisco, 1850. *DJ,* II (1851), 115.

MANCHESTER BROTHERS

HENRY N. MANCHESTER, EDWIN H. MANCHESTER. Active Providence, R. I., 1848-60

148

(operators for Masury & Hartshorn, 1848; Manchester & Co., 1850-51; Manchester & Chapin, 1853; Manchester & Brother, 1860).

MASCHER, JOHN F.

Active Phila. Pioneer in stereoscopic phot., 1852. U. S. Pats. 9,611 (stereoscope), 1853; 12,257 (stereoscopic medallion), 1855; 16,600 (imitation tortoise-shell dag'type case), 1857. *HJ*, VII (1855), 139.

MASURY, SAMUEL

Active Providence, R. I.; in partnership with Hartshorn, 1848; sold out to Manchester Bros., 1850. To Boston; partner of George M. Silsbee, 1852-54; of Silsbee & J. G. Case, 1855-57; own business, 1858-60. Exh. N. Y. C., 1853-54 (with Silsbee).

MAYALL, JOHN JABEZ EDWIN

Born (Birmingham, England?), 1810. To Phila. Learned dag'type process from Paul Beck Goddard and Hans Martin Boyé, 1840; partner of Samuel Van Loan, 1845-46. To England, 1846; established chain of galleries in London and provinces. British Pat. 193 (vignetting device), 1853. To Brighton, 1864; mayor, 1877-78. Died 1901. *AJP*, new series, III (1861), 260-63; VI (1864), 343; XIV (1893), 373-74; *British Jour. Photographic Almanac*, 1892; *Brighton Gazette & Hove Post Special Illustrated Edition*, June 30, 1904; *DJ*, I (1850), 46; II (1851), 32; *HJ*, IV (1853), 315; *PAJ* II (1851), 127-28.

MEADE, CHARLES RICHARD

Active Albany, with bro. Henry, 1842. Sent dag'types of Niagara Falls to King of France and Emperor of Russia. To Europe, 1849; took six portraits of Daguerre. Exh. London,

1851. N. Y. C. gallery, 1852-? (with bro.) Exh. N. Y. C., 1853-54; Paris Exposition, 1855. Died St. Augustine, Fla., 1858. See references below.

MEADE, HENRY

Active Albany, with bro. Charles Richard, 1842. To Europe before 1849. Associated with bro. in N. Y. C. gallery and exhibited with him. Died, 1865. *Gleason's Pictorial*, II (1852), 377; *PAJ*, III (1852), 293-95; E. Lacan, *Esquisses photographiques* (1856), p. 147-49; *DJ*, I (1850), 51; *HJ*, IV (1852-53), 233, 314; V (1853), 299; VI (1854), 160; IX (1858), 352; XVI (1864-65), 304; *PAJ*, II (1851), 123; XI (1858), 128; C. W. Canfield in *Amer. Annual of Photog.*, 1891 and 1893.

MOISSENET, DOBYNS, RICHARDSON & CO.

Active in New Orleans, Exh. N. Y. C., 1853-54.

MOORE, HENRY

Active Lowell, Mass., 1843.

MORAND, AUGUSTUS

Learned dag'type, 1840. To Rio de Janeiro, 1842; took dag'types for Dom Pedro II. Returned to U. S., 1843; traveled through South. Opened gallery in N. Y. C., 1848. President, N. Y. State Daguerreian Assoc., 1851. Last appearance in N. Y. C. directory, 1856. *PAJ*, I (1851), 237-39.

MORSE, SAMUEL FINLEY BREESE

Artist, scientist, inventor of the electric telegraph, pioneer dag'typist. Born Charlestown, Mass., 1791. First photochemical experiments while student at Yale College, 1805-10. Studied painting with Washington Allston. Patented electric telegraph, 1837. To Europe, 1837. Showed Daguerre telegraph; in return Daguerre showed him finished dag'types, but did not disclose process, Mar. 7, 1839. Returned to U. S., April 1839. Nominated Daguerre hon. member, Natl Academy of Design, May, 1839; election unanimous. Took his first successful dag'type, Sept. 28, 1839. Opened studio with Draper, 1840. Although he shortly gave up photography as a profession, maintained an interest rest of life: supported L. L. Hill's claims, 1851-52; judged Anthony Prize Competition, 1853. Died N. Y. C., 1872. Carleton Mabee, *The American Leonardo; a Life of Samuel F. B. Morse* (1943); S. I. Prime, *The Life of Samuel F. B. Morse* (1875). Reminiscences: M. A. Root, *The Camera and the Pencil* (1864), pp. 344-48.

NEFF, PETER, JR.

Purchased, with bro. William, H. L. Smith's melainotype (i.e. tintype) patent, 1856.

NEFF, WILLIAM

See reference above.

NICHOLS, JOHN P.

Active Boston, 1849-51 (proprietor of Plumbe's dag'type gallery). *DJ*, I (1851), 256.

NICHOLS, SHELDON K.

Active Hartford, Conn., San Francisco. Exh. N. Y. C., 1853-54.

NORTH, ENRIQUE

American, active Buenos Aires, 1848. J. F. Riobó, *Daguerrotipos . . . en Buenos Aires* (1949).

NORTH, WILLIAM C.

Active Dayton, O. Exh. N. Y. C., 1853-54.

ORMSBEE, MARCUS

Active Boston, 1852-60.

PAGE, CHARLES G.

Active Boston with Daniel Davis, Jr., in manufacture of electrical machines. To Washington, 1839; examiner of patents, U. S. Patent Office. Took dag'types, Washington, 1843. *Boston Weekly Transcript,* Mar. 29, 1887.

PAIGE, BLANCHARD P.

Active Washington, D. C. (proprietor of Plumbe's National Gallery), 1850-65; sold out to S. C. Mills.

PECK, SAMUEL

Active New Haven, Conn., 1847-60? U. S. Pat. 7,326 (block to hold dag'type plates when polishing), 1850. Opened factory for making dag'type cases, 1850. U. S. Pat. 11,758 (Union cases), 1854. Samuel Peck & Co. founded, 1855. U. S. Pat. 14,202 (hinge for dag'type case), 1856. *DJ*, I (1850), 29.

PENNELL, JOSEPH

Pupil and assistant of S. F. B. Morse, N. Y. C., 1840. Partner of A. S. Southworth in Cabotsville (now Chicopee), Mass., 1840, and in Boston, 1841-44. To South; schoolteacher. To Waterbury, Conn., 1845, as plate maker for Scovill until 1848.

PLUMBE, JOHN, JR.

Born Wales, 1809. Surveyed RR, 1832. Superintendent, RR Richmond, Va., to Roanoke, N. C., 1832. Appropriation from U. S. Congress to survey route for transcontinental RR. 1838. To Washington, 1840; took up phot. when funds ran out. Opened gallery Boston, 1841, sold 1846. Maintained other galleries across the U. S.: Baltimore, 1841-?; N. Y. C., 1843-47; Phila., 1842-45; Lexington, Ky., 1845-?; Washington, D. C., 1846-50. Purchased from D. Davis, Jr., U. S. Pat. 2.826 (coloring dag'types), 1842. Published *Plumbeian*, 1846; *National Plumbeotype Gallery*, 1846. Gave up photog., 1849. Killed himself by cutting throat, Dubuque, Iowa, 1857. R. Taft in *Amer. Phot.*, XXX (1936), 1-11; *Boston Advertiser*, Feb. 2, 1841; DAB; *HJ*, IX (1857, 112; Taft 49, 462.

PORTER, WILLIAM SOUTHGATE

Born 1822. Active Phila. To Cincinnati, 1848; partner of Charles Fontayne. Exh. London 1851. Died 1889. See also references under FONTAYNE, CHARLES.

PRATT, E. W.

Operator of Plumbe. Own gallery, N. Y. C., 1845. *Sci. Amer.*, Sept. 11, 1845.

PRATT, WILLIAM A.

Born England, 1818. To U. S., 1832. Opened dag'type gallery in Richmond, Va., 1846. U. S. Pat. 4,423 (coloring dag'types), 1846. To Europe, 1851. Exh. London 1851. Built "Pratt's Castle," Gothic Revival studio, Richmond, 1853-54. Supt. of bldgs. and grounds, Univ. of Va., 1858. *Bul. of Valentine Museum*, Spring, 1949; M. W. Scott, *Houses of Old Richmond* (1941), p. 286; *PAJ*, I (1851), 189; II (1851), 63, 190, 235 (illus. of gallery).

PROSCH, GEORGE W.

Active N. Y. C., 1840-41; Canada, 1842-43; N. Y. C., 1846; Newark, N. J., 1850-55. *HJ*, VI (1854), 327; *Sci. Amer.*, Apr. 9, 1846.

PRUDEN, HENRY

Itinerant, working out of Lockport, N. Y., 1853.

READ, GEORGE

Active Phila., 1842.

REED, G. M.

Active N. Y. C., 1854.

REESE & CO.

Active N. Y. C., 1853-54. Author: *Daguerreotype Directory* (1854).

REHN, ISAAC A.

Active Phila. Painter, 1848. Bought from J. A. Cutting one-quarter interest in ambrotype patents. Taft, 125.

RICHARDS, F. DE BOURG

Active Phila., 1848-?

ROOT, MARCUS A.

Born Granville, O., 1808. Studied painting with Thomas Sully, 1835. Teacher of penmanship, Phila., 1840-48. Learned dag'type process from R. Cornelius, 1843. Active as dag'typist, Mobile, Ala., 1844; thence New Orleans, St. Louis (with Miller). Bought gallery of J. E. Mayall, Phila., 1846. Exh. London, 1851; N. Y. C., 1853-54 (Hon. Mention). Opened N. Y. C. gallery with bro. Samuel, 1849; sold it to him, 1851. Said to have coined name "ambrotype" for collodion positives, 1854. Died Phila., 1888. Author: *Philosophical Theory and Practice of Penmanship* (1842); *The Camera and the Pencil* (1864). *Phila. Press,* Apr. 16, 1888; *McClure's Mag.,* IV (1897), 945; *Photographic Times,* XVIII (1888), 195; *British Jour. Photographic Almanac,* 1889; *Sartain's Mag.,* V (1849), 189.

ROOT, SAMUEL

Born Ohio, 1819. Studied dag'type in Phila. Gallery in N. Y. C. with bro. Marcus, 1849-51; bought out gallery, 1851. To Dubuque, Iowa, 1857. Retired, 1882. Died Rochester, N. Y., 1889. Dubuque, Iowa, *Daily Times,* Mar. 15, 1889.

RULOFSON, WILLIAM HERMAN

Born nr. St. John, N. B., 1826. Began to take dag'types in St. John before 1846. To sea; shipwrecked; landed destitute in Liverpool; supported himself with his camera, 1846. Reopened St. John gallery, 1848. To California; arrived San Francisco, 1849; to Sonora, 1850 (partner of J. D. Cameron, 1850-51). To San Francisco, 1863 (partner of Henry W. Bradley). President, Natl Photographic Assoc., 1874. Alleged author of *The Dance of Death* by "William Herman," a work usually ascribed to Ambrose Bierce, 1877. Died from fall while inspecting skylight of gallery, San Francisco, 1878. R. Haas in *Calif. Hist. Soc. Quarterly,* XXXIV (1955), 289-300; XXXV (1956), 47-58.

RYDER, JAMES F.

Itinerant, 1847; settled in Cleveland, O., 1850. Introduced negative retouching to America, 1868, when he employed Karl

152

Leutgib, trained by H. W. Vogel in Germany. Retired, 1894. Died, Cleveland, 1904. Autobiography: *Voigtländer and I* (1902); also published by installments in *Photo Beacon,* XIII (1901). Taft, 326 (portrait); *Photo-Miniature* No. 62 (1904), 123-24.

SAXTON, JOSEPH

Employee of U. S. Mint, Phila. Took dag'-type before Oct. 24, 1839. *U. S. Gazette,* Oct. 24, 1839.

SEAGER, D. W.

Born England (?). In N. Y. C. when news of Daguerre's technique arrived. Claimed to have taken on Sept. 16, 1839, first dag'type in U. S. Lectured on dag'type, 1839-40. To Mexico as adviser to gov't on natl economy. Author: *The Resources of Mexico Apart from the Precious Metals* (1867).

SHEW, JACOB

Active Baltimore (in charge of Plumbe's gallery), 1841-?; Phila., 1850-? Purchased Van Loan gallery, 1851. San Francisco, 1854, 1860-62; 1863 (with Charles F. Hamilton); 1864-78. *DJ,* I (1850), 29; II (1851), 19.

SHEW, MYRON

Active Phila., 1841-51 or later. *DJ,* II (1851), 32.

SHEW, TRUEMAN

Active Phila., 1841-48.

SHEW, WILLIAM

Born nr. Watertown, N. Y. Pupil with bros. Jacob, Myron, and Trueman of S. F. B.

Morse. Hired by J. Plumbe to superintend his Boston gallery, 1841. Opened own gallery, Boston, 1845; began to manufacture dag'type cases and to sell photographic materials. To San Francisco, 1850; gallery there through 1903. Author: "Photography," *Pioneer, or California Monthly Mag.,* II (1854), 34-40. *Camera Craft,* V (1902), 101-107; *HJ,* IV (1852), 44.

SILSBEE, GEORGE M.

Active Boston, 1852-57 (with Masury, 1852-54; with Masury & Case, 1855-57). Exh. (with Masury) N. Y. C., 1853-54.

SIMONS, MONTGOMERY P.

Active Phila. Bought from Warren Thompson U. S. Pat. 3,085 (coloring dag'types), 1843. Casemaker, 1843-47. First listed in directory as dag'typist, 1848. Author: *Plain Instructions for Coloring Photographs* (1st and 2nd eds., 1857); *Photography in a Nut Shell* (1858); *Secrets of Ivorytyping Revealed* (1860).

SMITH, HAMILTON L.

Prof. of chemistry; inventor of tintype. Graduated from Yale Univ., 1839. Took dag'-types in Cleveland, O., 1840. Prof. of chemistry, Kenyon College, Gambier, O., 1853. Invented melainotype (i.e. tintype); U. S. Pat. 14,300 (1856). To Geneva, N. Y., 1867: Prof. of chemistry Hobart College (1867-1900) and president (1883-84). *Natl Cyclopaedia of Amer. Biography;* Taft, 154-55 (portrait); *Amer. Jour. Science and Arts,* XL (1841), 139.

SMITH, L. C.

Active Sharon, Vt., 1843.

SNELLING, HENRY HUNT

Born Plattsburg, N. Y., 1817. Early life in military camps; Council Bluffs, N. W. Territory. To N. Y. C.; genl sales manager of E. Anthony, 1843-57. Editor and publisher, *Photographic Art-Journal* (1851-54), *Photographic and Fine Art Journal* (1854-59). Employed by Internal Revenue Dept., 1860. Editor Cornwall, N. Y., *Reflector.* Became blind, 1887. Author: *The History and Practice of the Art of Photography* (1849; 2nd ed., 1850; 3rd ed., 1851; 4th ed., 1853); *A Dictionary of the Photographic Art* (1854); *A Guide to the Whole Art of Photography* (1858); *Memoirs of a Boyhood at Fort Snelling* (1939); *Memoirs of a Life* (3 vols., ms. in Newberry Library, Chicago); "Colored Glasses in the Relation to Photography and the Eye," *Internat. Ann. of Anthony's Photographic Bul.,* 1883, 490-95. *PAJ,* VIII (1855), front. (portrait by Brady); *The Camera,* XLVII (1933), 391-94; *AJP,* XIV (1893), 188.

SOMERBY

Presumably active Boston before 1844.

SOUTHWORTH, ALBERT SANDS

Born West Fairlee, Vt., 1811. Attended Phillips Academy, Andover, Mass. On seeing Gouraud's demonstrations of dag'type in Boston, 1840, went to N. Y. C. Learned process from S. F. B. Morse with his friend J. Pennell. Formed partnership with him; opened gallery Cabotville (now Chicopee), Mass., 1840. To Boston, 1841. Pennell left, 1844; partnership with J. J. Hawes, 1844-61 (firm name: "Southworth & Hawes" adopted 1845). To Calif., 1849-51. U. S. Pats. 11,304 (stereoscopic camera), with Hawes, 1854; 12,700 (plate holder), 1855; 13,106 (stereoscope), with Hawes, 1855. Died Charlestown, Mass., 1894. Author: "Address to Natl Photographic Assoc. of the U. S.," *Phila. Photographer,* VIII (1871), 315-23. I. N. Phelps Stokes, *The Hawes-Stokes Coll. of Amer. Dag'-types by Albert Sands Southworth and Josiah Johnson Hawes* (Metropolitan Museum of Art, 1939); B. Newhall in *Art News Annual 1948,* pp. 91-98, 168-72; *DJ,* II (1851), 114-15; *HJ,* V (1853), 223; *Western Photographer,* Apr. 1876, p. 233.

STANLEY, JOHN MIX

Painter of Indian scenes; occasional dag'-typist. Born 1814. Active as dag'typist in Washington, D. C., 1842 (Fay & Stanley). On gov't expedition under Isaac I. Stevens to explore route for transcontinental RR, 1853, took dag'types. DAB; Taft, 261-62.

STULL, JOHN

Active Phila. U. S. Pat. 12,451 (stereoscope), 1857.

TALBOT, J. W.

Active Petersborough, N. H.

THOMPSON, WARREN

Active Phila., 1840-46. U. S. Pat. 3,085 (coloring dag'types), 1843, assigned to Montgomery P. Simons. To Paris, 1847; active there through 1859. Pioneer in production of enlargements of extreme size, 1855. *PAJ,* new series, I (1855), 253.

TOMLINSON, WILLIAM AGUR

Born 1819. Active Poughkeepsie, N. Y., 1846; Troy, N. Y., 1850, 1853; N. Y. C., 1857-62. Member, N. Y. State Daguerreian

Assoc.; on committee to investigate L. L. Hill's alleged color process, 1851. Died 1862(?)

TURNER, AUSTIN A.

Operator for Ormsbee, Boston. Learned collodion process. Became operator for Brady. *PAJ,* VIII (1855), 129 (portrait), 160.

VAN ALSTIN, ANDREW WEMPLE

Born Canastota, N. Y., 1811. Pupil of George Adams, Worcester, Mass. In business there, 1843 to death, 1857. *Worcester Hist. Soc. Publications,* new series, I (1935), 433-39.

VAN LOAN, SAMUEL

Born England. Active Phila., 1844-54. Sold gallery to J. Shew, 1851.

VANCE, ROBERT H.

Produced over 300 dag'types of West Coast; exhibited them in N. Y. C., 1851; sold to Jeremiah Gurney, 1852. In San Francisco, 1854-61. Galleries in Sacramento and Marysville, Calif. Sold San Francisco gallery to Charles L. Weed, 1861. Left Calif., 1865. *DJ,* II (1851), 371; *HJ,* V (1853), 41, 89, 105; Book Club of Calif., *A Camera in the Gold Rush* (1946).

VANNERSON, J.

Active Washington, D. C. Exh. N. Y. C., 1853-54.

VON SCHNEIDAU, JOHN FREDERICK POLYCARPUS

Born Stockholm, Sweden, 1812. To U. S. as refugee (reason: he married a Jewess), 1842.

To N. Y. C., 1849; operator for Brady. Active Chicago, 1849-55. Appointed Vice Consul for Sweden, Norway, Denmark. Exh. N. Y. C., 1853-54. Died Chicago, 1859; cause believed poisoning from photographic chemicals. Chicago *Tribune,* June 10, 1947 (portrait); *HJ,* IV (1853), 287.

WARREN, GARDNER
Active Woonsocket, R. I., 1843.

WEBSTER & BROTHER
E. L. Webster. Israel B. Webster (born Plattsburg, N. Y., 1826). To Louisville, Ky., 1850. Exh. N. Y. C., 1853-54 (Bronze Medal). Israel B. W. retired, 1877. J. S. Johnston, ed., *Memorial History of Louisville,* I, 463.

WESTON, GUILLERMO
American; active Buenos Aires, 1849. J. F. Riobó, *Daguerrotipos . . . en Buenos Aires,* 1949.

WESTON, JAMES P.
Active, N. Y. C., 1851-52, '55-57.

WHIPPLE, JOHN ADAMS
Born Grafton, Mass., 1822. Manufactured chemicals for dag'typing. Opened gallery in Boston with Albert Litch, 1844-46. Dag'-type of moon, 1849; of star, 1850. U. S. Pats. 6056 (crayon dag'types), 1849; 7,458 (crystalotypes), with William B. Jones, 1849. Exh. London, 1851 (Council Medal); N. Y. C., 1853-54 (Silver Medal). Partner of J. W. Black, 1856. Gave up photography, 1874. Died Boston, 1891. *DJ,* II (1851), 83. 114-15, 210; *HJ,* IV (1853), 44; V (1854), 299; *PAJ,* II (1851), 94-95 (portrait); III (1852), 195,

271-72; *AJP,* new series, III (1860), 245, 319; VI (1864), 321-23; Boston *Evening Transcript,* Apr. 11, 1891; *Amer. Annual Photog.,* 1892, p. 242; *Natl Cyclopedia of Amer. Biography,* VII, 525 (portrait).

WHITE, EDWARD
Active N. Y. C., 1843, '44, '50. Dag'type platemaker as well as dag'typist.

WHITEHURST, JESSE H.
Born Virginia, c. 1820. Opened dag'type gallery in Norfolk, Va., 1844; also in Baltimore (opened 1844), Richmond, Va., Lynchburg, Va., Washington, D. C. (active 1850), N. Y. C. (destroyed by fire 1852; purchased by Lawrence). Exh. London, 1851; N. Y. C., 1853-54. Died Baltimore, 1875. *HJ,* IV (1852), 47; *PAJ,* III (1852), 257; *Phila. Photog.,* XI (1875) 300-01 (list of operators).

WHITNEY, EDWARD TOMPKINS
Born N. Y. C., 1820. Jeweler. Taught photog. by M. M. Lawrence, 1844. To Rochester, 1845; partner of Mercer, 1845-48; own gallery, 1849-51; partner of Conrad B. Denny, 1852-54. His photo. of Genessee Falls, Rochester, published *PAJ,* XI (1858), 254. To Norwalk, Conn., 1859. Reminiscences: *Photographic Times,* new series, XI (1881), 345-48.

WHITNEY, JOEL EMMONS
Born Phillips, Me., 1822. To St. Paul, 1850. Learned dag'type process from Alexander Hesler. Gallery in St. Paul, 1851-71. Exh. N. Y. C., 1853-54. Died St. Paul, 1886. T. M. Newton, *Pen Pictures of St. Paul* (1886), 243; B. Newhall in *Minnesota History,* XXXIV (1954), 28-33 (portrait).

WILLIAMSON, CHARLES H.

Active Brooklyn, N. Y. Exh. N. Y. C., 1853-54.

WOLCOTT, ALEXANDER SIMON

Optical designer, mechanic, pioneer dag'-typist. Active N. Y. C. Claimed to have taken portraits by dag'type process in Oct., 1839. Invented mirror camera: U. S. Pat. 1,582

(1840). Opened portrait gallery with John Johnson, 1840. Died Stamford, Conn., 1844. *AJP*, new series, IV (1862), 525.

WRIGHT, L.

Active Pawtucket, R. I., 1853.

ZUKY, ANTHONY

Active N. Y. C. Exh. N. Y. C., 1853-54.

Notes on the Text

1. A WONDER FROM PARIS

1. Morse to F. O. J. Smith, in Samuel Iraneaus Prime, *The Life of Samuel F. B. Morse* (N. Y.: D. Appleton and Co., 1857), p. 36.
2. *The Observer* (New York), April 20, 1839.
3. *Allgemeine Zeitung* (Augsburg), Jan. 27, 1839.
4. *The Observer, loc. cit.*
5. *Ibid.*
6. Charles Chevalier, *Guide du photographe* (Paris: Charles Chevalier, 1854), 3e partie, pp. 6-7.
7. Arthur Chevalier, *Etude sur la vie . . . de Charles Chevalier* (Paris: Bonaventure & Ducessois, 1862), pp. 18-19.
8. Louis Jacques Mandé Daguerre, *Le Daguerréotype.* An undated broadside, in GEH. Presumably issued in December, 1838, or January, 1839, since the opening of an exhibition of 40 daguerreotypes is announced for January 15, 1839. For facsimile and translation, see *Image,* VIII (1959), 32-36.
9. *The Observer, loc. cit.*
10. Prime, *Morse,* pp. 406-407.
11. *Ibid.,* p. 407.
12. François Arago, *Rapport sur le Daguerréotype* (Paris: Bachelier, Imprimeur -Libraire, 1839), pp. 5-6.
13. "The Daguerre Secret," *Literary Gazette* (London), No. 1179 (Aug. 24, 1839), 538-39. An almost identical account appeared in the *London Globe,* Aug. 23, 1839. It was widely reprinted in the United States (*National Intelligencer,* Sept. 25; *Niles' National Register,* Sept. 28; *Amer. Jour. of Science and Arts,* Oct.; *United States Mag. and Democratic Rev.,* Nov.).
14. Marc-Antoine Gaudin, *Traité pratique de photographie* (Paris: J. J. Dubochet, 1844), p. 6.
15. The first edition is known in only two copies, both in GEH. I am indebted to M. Pierre G. Harmant, archivist of the Société Française de Photographie, for establishing the exact date when this edition was published. For descriptions of the other editions and translations, see my bibliography in Helmut & Alison Gernsheim, *L. J. M. Daguerre* (New York, Dover Publications, Inc., 1968), pp. 198-205.
16. Prime, *Morse,* pp. 407-408.

2. FIRST TRIALS

1. *Journal of Commerce* (New York), Sept. 28, 1839. Reprinted in Carleton Mabee, *The American Leonardo: A Life of Samuel F. B. Morse* (N. Y.: Alfred A. Knopf, 1943), p. 229.
2. *Journal of Commerce,* Sept. 30, 1839. Mabee, *Amer. Leonardo,* p. 229.
3. *Image,* I (Jan., 1952), 2.
4. *Morning Herald* (New York), Oct. 3, 1839. Reprinted in Robert Taft, *Photography and the American Scene* (N. Y.: The Macmillan Co., 1938), pp. 16-17.
5. Seager wrote a 20-page booklet, *The Resources of Mexico Apart from the Precious Metals* (Mexico City: Printed by J. White, 1867), urging agricultural reforms through irrigation, storage of grain, and abolishment of local excise taxes on produce.
6. Letter, Morse to Marcus A. Root, Feb. 10, 1855: Prime, *Morse,* p. 403.
7. J. W. Draper in Marcus A. Root, *The Camera and the Pencil* (Philadelphia: M. A. Root, etc., 1864), p. 340.
8. Taft, *Photography,* p. 29.
9. Root, *Camera and Pencil,* p. 342.
10. Henry Hunt Snelling, *The History and Practice of the Art of Photography* (N. Y.: G. P. Putnam, 1849), p. 9.
11. Julius F. Sachse, "Early Daguerreotype Days," *AJP,* XIII (1892), 306-15.
12. *Ibid.*
13. *DJ,* II (1851), 56-57, 73-80.
14. *Ibid.*
15. U. S. Pat. 1,582 (May 8, 1840): "Method of taking likenesses by means of a concave reflector and plates so prepared as that luminous or other rays will act thereon."
16. François Gouraud, *Description of the Daguerreotype Process* (Boston: Dutton and Wentworth's Print, 1840), p. 14.
17. *The Observer* (New York), Dec. 14, 1839; quoted from *Journal des Débats* (Paris), Nov. 10, 1839.
18. Working directions were reprinted from the translation of Daguerre's manual by J. S. Memes (London: Smith Elder and Co., 1839) in: *The Observer* (New York), Nov. 3, 1839; *Amer. Repertory of Arts, Sciences and Manufactures,* I (Mar. 1840), 116-23; *The Family Magazine,* VII (1840), 415-23, and in Jacob Bigelow's *The Useful Arts* (Boston: T. Webb and Co., 1840), II, 350-67. A translation by J. F. Frazer appeared in *Jour. of the Franklin Inst.,* new ser. XXIV (Nov., 1839), 303-311. A condensation, by William E. A. Aikin, with facsimiles of the illustrations, was published in *Maryland Medical & Surgical Jour.,* I (April, 1840); it was reprinted as a brochure.

3. DAGUERRE'S AGENT

1. Philip Hone, *Diary* (N. Y.: Dodd, Mead & Co., 1927), I, 435.
2. Carleton Mabee, *The American Leonardo: A Life of Samuel F. B. Morse* (N. Y.: Alfred A. Knopf, 1943), p. 234.

3. *Evening Star* (New York), Feb. 24, 1840.
4. *Amer. Annual of Photog.* for 1894, p. 262.
5. François Gouraud, *Description of the Daguerreotype Process* (Boston: Dutton and Wentworth's Print, 1840).
6. [Josiah B. Millet], *George Fuller, his Life and Works* (Boston & New York: Houghton, Mifflin and Co., 1896), p. 14.

4. THE SHAPING OF AN INDUSTRY

1. Quoted from *Alexander's Weekly Messenger,* Jan. 15, 1840, by Clarence S. Brigham in his *Edgar Allan Poe's Contributions to Alexander's Weekly Messenger* (Worcester, Mass.: American Antiquarian Society, 1943), pp. 20-22.
2. Commonwealth of Massachusetts, *Statistical Information Relating to Certain Branches of Industry in Massachusetts for the Year Ending June 1, 1855* (Boston, 1856), p. 591.
3. *PAJ*, VIII (1855), 70.
4. Unpublished notebook of Anson Clark, Stockbridge, Mass., Public Library.
5. *HJ*, X (1858), 36.
6. *The Western Jour.,* VI (1851), 200-201.
7. *PAJ*, VI (1853), 63.

5. BOSTON PIONEERS

1. The only copy I have seen of *The Plumbeian*, Vol. 1, No. 1, Jan. 1, 1847, is in the N. Y. Public Library. It is uncatalogued but can be found bound with a miscellaneous collection of Plumbe's publications under the title *National Plumbeotype Gallery*.
2. Broadside, in Library of the Eastman Kodak Research Laboratories, Rochester, N. Y.
3. Unpublished letter, Apr. 14, 1843. GEH.
4. Unpublished letter from David Harris, Feb. 14, 1843. GEH.
5. Prospectus on back cover of sheet music published by Plumbe. In N. Y. Public Library, bound with *National Plumbeotype Gallery*.
6. *Daily Express & Herald* (Dubuque, Iowa), May 30, 1857.
7. *British Jour. of Photog.*, XVIII (1871), 530-31.
8. I. N. Phelps Stokes, *The Hawes-Stokes Collection of American Daguerreotypes by Albert Sands Southworth and Josiah Johnson Hawes* (N. Y.: The Metropolitan Museum of Art, 1939), p. 6.
9. *Ibid.*
10. Quoted by L. C. Champney in his unpublished letter to Southworth, Jul. 14, 1843. GEH.
11. Unpublished letter, Apr. 28, 1843. GEH.
12. Unpublished letter, Jul. 17, 1843. GEH.
13. Unpublished letter, Mar. 9, 1843. GEH.

14. Unpublished letter, Aug. 7 and 9, 1843. GEH.
15. Unpublished letter, Nov. 12, 1844. GEH.
16. *Photo-Era,* XVI (1906), 104-107.
17. *British Jour. of Photog.,* XVIII (1871), 583.
18. U. S. Pat. 3,085 (Jul. 11, 1854): "Improvement in taking daguerreotypes for stereoscopes."
    U. S. Pat. 12,700 (Apr. 10, 1855): "Plate-holder for cameras."
19. *Worcester Spy* (Worcester, Mass.), Jan. 6, 1886.

6. INNOVATIONS FROM PHILADELPHIA

1. *Wilson's Photographic Mag.,* XXVI (1889), 182-84.
2. In 1845, according to family records kindly sent us by Voigtländer A. G., Peter Friedrich Wilhelm Voigtländer married Nanny Langenheim, sister of Frederick, William, and Louisa Langenheim.
3. *Wilson's Photographic Mag.,* XXVI (1889), 182-84.
4. Unpublished letter. GEH.
5. Unpublished letter. GEH.
6. U. S. Pat. 4,369 (Jan. 30, 1846).
7. U. S. Pat. 3,085 (May 12, 1843).
8. Unpublished letter, Feb. 5, 1846. G.E.H.
9. Unpublished letter, Feb. 16, 1847. G.E.H.
10. British Pat. 8,842 (Feb. 8, 1841); French Pat. 10,627 (Aug. 20, 1841); U. S. Pat. 5,171 (Jun. 26, 1847).
11. Unpublished letters. Quoted by courtesy of Mr. Harold White, who is writing a definitive biography of H. Fox Talbot.
12. Undated broadside. GEH.
13. From the Greek, meaning "glass print." The word was used as early as 1840 by Fr. V. W. Netto in his *Die Glasdruckkunst, oder Hyalotypie* (Quedlinburg und Leipzig: Gottfried Bassel, 1840).
14. U. S. Pat. 7,784 (Nov. 19, 1850).
15. U. S. Pat. 7,458 (Jun. 25, 1850).
16. U. S. Pat. 9,611 (Mar. 8, 1853).
17. U. S. Pat. 12,451 (Feb. 27, 1855).

7. THE BROADWAY GALLERIES

1. *DJ,* I (1850), 49.
2. Cornelius Mathews, *A Pen-and-Ink Panorama of New York City* (N. Y., 1853), pp. 35, 37.
3. *Image,* I, No. 3 (Mar. 1952), 2.
4. *PAJ,* VII (1854), 103.
5. *HJ,* V (1853), 222.

6. *PAJ*, IV (1852), 384.
7. *Gleason's Pictorial Drawing-Room Companion*, IV (1853), 21.
8. *HJ*, V (1854), 273.
9. *PAJ*, VIII (1855), 76.
10. *HJ*, VI (1854), 15.
11. Undated trade card. GEH. Between Mar., 1853, and Dec., 1854, Brady operated two galleries in N. Y. C.
12. John Werge, *The Evolution of Photography* (London: Piper & Carter, 1890), pp. 200-203.
13. *PAJ*, VI (1853), 127-29.
14. *PAJ*, VII (1854), 96.

8. ITINERANTS AND TRAVELERS

1. From a clipping dated Mar. 4, 1848, in the Langenheim archives, The American Museum of Photography, Philadelphia.
2. *PAJ*, I (1851), 106.
3. Charles Cist, *Sketches and Statistics of Cincinnati in 1851* (Cincinnati: W. H. Moore & Co., 1851), p. 187.
4. *Cincinnati Daily Enquirer*, Jul. 15, 1854.
5. Unpublished letter, Anson Clark to Messrs. Bewell & Sizer, Feb. 17, 1842. Public Library, Stockbridge, Mass.
6. Reminiscences of Jacob J. Anthony, *Niagara Falls Gazette*, April, 1914.
7. Unpublished letters of L. C. Champney to Southworth, Nov. 2, 1844. GEH.
8. *Lockport Daily Courier*, Jul. 19, 1853.
9. *St. Louis & Canadian Photographer*, XXIII (1899), 327.
10. Quoted by Gilberto Ferrez, *A Fotografia no Brasil* (Rio de Janeiro: Privately published, 1953), p. 6. The three daguerreotypes taken by Compte are reproduced by Ferrez.
11. For a full account of the introduction of daguerreotyping by Louis Compte to S. America, see José Maria Fernández Saldaña, "La Fotografía en el Río de la Plata," *La Prensa*, Jan. 26, 1936; Julio F. Riobó, *La Daguerrotipia y los Daguerrotipos en Buenos Aires* (2d ed.; Rio de Janeiro: The Author, 1949).
12. *PAJ*, I, (1851), 239.
13. *APB*, XII (1881), 110-12.
14. John L. Stephens, *Incidents of Travel in Yucatan* (London: John Murray, 1843), I, 175.
15. *Ibid.*, pp. 100-105.

9. FACING THE CAMERA

1. Ralph Waldo Emerson, *Journals, 1841-1844* (Boston: Houghton Mifflin Co., 1911), pp. 100-101.
2. *APB*, XV (1884), 63.

3. Nathaniel Parker Willis, *The Convalescent* (N. Y.: Charles Scribner, 1859), pp. 286-87.
4. Samuel Iraneaus Prime, *The Life of Samuel F. B. Morse* (N. Y.: D. Appleton and Co., 1875), pp. 404-408.
5. *The Crayon,* IV (1857), 44-45.
6. Advertisement of H. N. Macomber in *Lynn Democrat* (Lynn, Mass.), Dec. 14, 1844.
7. Théophile Gautier, *L'Abécédaire du Salon de 1861* (Paris: E. Dentu, 1861), p. 297.
8. *DJ,* III (1851), 52.
9. *HJ,* IV (1852), 12.
10. Quoted in *N. Y. Times,* Oct. 8, 1933.
11. Robert Taft, *Photography and the American Scene* (N. Y.: The Macmillan Co., 1938), p. 59.
12. Unpublished letter. The Library of Congress.
13. Emerson, *Journals,* p. 111.
14. Henry David Thoreau, *Journal,* Walden ed. (Boston: Houghton Mifflin Co., 1906), I, 189.

10. THE EXPLORERS

1. T. A. Barry & B. A. Patten, *Men and Memories of San Francisco in the Spring of '50* (San Francisco: A. L. Bancroft and Co., 1873) pp. 143-44.
2. (1) Smithsonian Institution; (2) George Eastman House, Rochester, N. Y.; (3) Coll. Zelda P. Mackay, San Francisco (left hand half) and Library of Congress (right hand half); (4) American Antiquarian Society, Worcester, Mass.; (5) Coll. Mr. Billy Pearson, La Jolla, Calif.; (6) California Historical Society, San Francisco, Calif. Except for (1), which was taken by William Shew, the makers of the other plates are not known. In the Southworth & Hawes collection at the Metropolitan Museum of Art, New York, is a single plate, possibly taken by Southworth, which may well form part of a panorama.
3. No. 73 in Loys Delteil, *Le Peintre-graveur illustré, Tome second: Charles Méryon* (Paris, 1907).
4. *DJ,* II (1851), 115-16.
5. *Quarterly of the Calif. Hist. Soc.,* XI (1932), 229.
6. The only recorded copy is in the N. Y. Public Library: *Catalogue of Daguerreotype Panoramic Views in California, by R. H. Vance, on Exhibition at No. 349 Broadway* (New York: Baker, Godwin & Co., Printers, 1851). It is a pamphlet of eight pages (including cover-title), containing 131 entries for both single pictures and groups.
7. U. S. 27 Cong., 3 Sess., House of Representatives, Executive, Doc. No. 31.
8. Charles Preuss, *Exploring with Frémont,* translated and edited by Erwin G. and Elisabeth K. Gudde (Norman, Oklahoma: Univ. of Oklahoma Press, 1958), p. 32.
9. *Ibid.,* p. 35.
10. Solomon N. Carvalho, *Incidents of Travel and Adventure in the Far West with Col. Frémont's Last Expedition* (N. Y.: Derby & Jackson, 1860), p. 24.
11. *Ibid.,* p. 68.
12. *Ibid.,* pp. 20-21.
13. Robert Taft, *Photography and the American Scene* (N. Y.: The Macmillan Co., 1938), p. 267.
14. U. S. War Dept. *Reports of Explorations and Surveys . . . for a Railroad to the Pacific Ocean* (Washington, D. C., 1860), I, 103.

15. Francis L. Hawks, *Narrative of the Expedition of an American Squadron to the China Seas and Japan, performed in the years 1852, 1853, and 1854 under the command of Commodore M. C. Perry, United States Navy* (3 vols.; Washington, D. C.: A. O. P. Nicholson, Printer, 1856).

11. A TOOL FOR SCIENTISTS

1. *HJ*, VI (1854), 73.
2. *PAJ*, VII (1854), 224.
3. Dorrit Hoffleit, *Some Firsts in Astronomical Photography* (Cambridge, Mass.: Harvard College Observatory, 1950), p. 22.
4. *Ibid.*, p. 19.
5. U. S. Pat. 6,056 (Jan. 23, 1849).
6. *PAJ*, III (1852), 271-72.
7. Hoffleit, *Astronomical Phot.*, p. 25.
8. *Ibid.*, p. 27.
9. *Ibid.*
10. *Amer. Jour. of Science and Arts*, XL (1841), 139.
11. Great Exhibitions of the Works of Industry of All Nations, *Reports by the Juries* (London, 1852), p. 279.

12. A QUEST FOR COLOR

1. U. S. Pat. 2,522 (Mar. 28, 1842): Benj. R. Stevens and Lemuel Morse of Lowell, Mass., "Improvements in the mode of fixing daguerreotype impressions so as to allow of colors being applied to same." U. S. Pat. 3,085 (May 12, 1843): Warren Thompson, of Philadelphia, Penn., assignor to Montgomery P. Simons, "Improvements in coloring daguerreotype pictures."
2. Louis Figuier, "La Photographie," *Revue des Deux-Mondes*, XXIV (1848), 127.
3. No copy of the first edition has been located. A second edition appeared in 1850; it was published in four parts, of which the fourth was a pamphlet titled *The Magic Buff.*
4. *PAJ*, I (1851), 116.
5. *Ibid.*, p. 337.
6. *Ibid.*, p. 338.
7. *Ibid.*, p. 339.
8. Unpublished letter. The Library of Congress.
9. *DJ*, II (1851), 340.
10. *Ibid.*, p. 337-38.
11. Levi L. Hill, *Treatise on Heliochromy* (1856), pp. 28-30.

12. *New York Times,* Nov. 21, 1851.
13. The letter was translated into French in *La Lumière,* II (1852), 24.
14. Unpublished letter. The Library of Congress.
15. Quoted in *Scientific American,* Oct. 23, 1852.
16. U. S. 32 Cong., 2 Sess. Senate Report 427; Serial 671.
17. *Scientific American,* Apr. 2, 1853.
18. *Liverpool Photographic Jour.,* II (1855), 99-100.
19. *Ibid.*
20. *Amer. Jour. of Photog.,* new ser., IX (1867), 268-70.
21. *Yearbook of Photog.,* 1890, pp. 38-51.
22. *Ibid.*
23. Translated from *Annales de Chimie et de Physique,* 3ᵉ série, XXII (1848), 451-59.
24. *Ibid.*
25. Translated from *Annales de Chimie,* XXV (1849), 447-74.
26. *Ibid.*
27. A color reproduction of this unique color photograph appears in J. M. Eder, *Geschichte der Photographie* (Halle: Wilhelm Knapp, 1932), II, plate III.
28. *HJ,* XVI (1865), 315-16.

13. PHOTOGRAPHY TRIUMPHANT

1. U. S. Pat. 11,213 (Jul. 4, 1854), "Improvements in the preparation of collodion for photographic pictures." U. S. Pat. 11,266 (Jul. 11, 1854), "Improvement in compositions for making photographic pictures." U. S. Pat. 11,267 (Jul. 11, 1854), "Improvement in photographic pictures upon glass."
2. *AJP,* new. ser., IV (1861), 112.
3. U. S. Pat. 14,300 (Feb. 19, 1856): H. L. Smith of Gambier, Ohio, assignor to William Neff and Peter Neff, Jr., of Cincinnati, Ohio, "Photographic pictures on japanned surfaces."
4. Edward M. Estabrooke, *The Ferrotype and How to Make It* (Cincinnati, O., & Louisville, Ky.: Gatchel & Hyatt, 1872), p. 77.
5. *APB,* XV (1884), 62-67.
6. *Sunlight Sketches; or, The Photographic Text Book* (N. Y.: H. H. Snelling, 1858), p. 26.

14. THE AMERICAN PROCESS

1. *Photographic Mosaics,* 1871, p. 45.
2. James F. Ryder, *Voigtländer and I in Pursuit of Shadow Catching* (Cleveland: Cleveland Printing and Publishing Co., 1902), p. 16.

3. U. S. Pat. 8,513 (Nov. 11, 1851).
4. Advertisement in *The Massachusetts Register* (Boston: George Adams, 1852), p. 328.
5. *Daily Evening Transcript* (Boston, Mass.), May 30, 1840.
6. Unpublished letter, Jan. 25, 1848. GEH.
7. In a letter to Southworth, dated Apr. 14, 1843, Page states that he is using "Bince's" plates.
8. In a letter to Southworth, dated N. Y., Dec. 14, 1844, Edward White states: " . . . we have commenced manufacturing plates . . . $3.50 per doz. $36 per gross." On Dec. 20, White elaborated: "We import the metal, but it is rolled, planished, polished and finished in our own establishment. . . . The person who is working for us is the same person that showed Scovill first how to make plates (a Mr. Read)." Both letters in GEH.
9. *PAJ*, V (1853), 165-67.
10. Unpublished letter, A. E. Osborn to Southworth & Hawes, May 8, 1848. GEH.
11. *Wilson's Photographic Mag.*, XXVI (1889), 183.
12. The discovery of hypersensitizing the daguerreotype plate by the use of haloids other than iodine has also been credited to Paul Beck Goddard of Philadelphia by Julius F. Sachse, *Amer. Jour. of Phot.*, XIII (1892), 355-62. The Philadelphian, however, did not place his claim until Jan., 1842, more than a year after John Frederick Goddard described his process in the London *Literary Gazette* for Dec. 12, 1840. See "The Two Goddards and the Improvement of the Daguerreotype," *British Jour. of Photog.*, LXXXIV (1932), 58-59; J. Hughes, "The Bromine Question," *op. cit.*, XI (1864), 166-67.
13. Unpublished letter. GEH.
14. *DJ*, I (1850), 60.
15. Unpublished letter, A. E. Osborn to Southworth & Hawes, May 8, 1848. GEH.
16. *PAJ*, I (1851), 35.
17. *PAJ*, VIII (1855), 76.
18. *Photographic Times*, XIV (1889), 130-31.
19. Unpublished letter, C. K. Wentworth to Southworth, Oct. 7, 1844. GEH.
20. Samuel D. Humphrey, "The American Daguerreotype Process," in: Robert Hunt, *Photography* (N. Y.: S. D. Humphrey, 1852), pp. 229-51.
21. *HJ*, IV (1852), 288.
22. *Ibid.*
23. Levi L. Hill, *A Treatise on Heliochromy* (N. Y.: Robinson & Caswell, 1856), p. 25.
24. Samuel D. Humphrey, *A System of Photography*, (2nd ed.; Albany: Printed by C. Van Benthuysen, 1849), pp. 47-48.
25. Translated from Fizeau's memoir, read on Mar. 23, 1840, to the Academy of Science in N. P. Lerebours, *A Treatise on Photography* (London: Longman, Brown, Green, and Longmans, 1843), p. 55.
26. Samuel D. Humphrey, *American Hand Book of the Daguerreotype* (5th ed.; N. Y.: S. D. Humphrey, 1858), p. 47.
27. Unpublished letter, GEH.
28. Unpublished letter, GEH.
29. Unpublished letter, GEH.
30. *British Jour of Photog.*, XXVI (1889), 184.
31. *HJ*, V (1853), 201.

Notes on the Plates

6. Signed on back, "George Read, Phila.—July, 1842."

7. Philadelphia directories show that Ferdinand Arnold, 63 Chestnut Street, and W. W. Keene and Co., 61 Chestnut Street, were neighbors only in 1843-45.

8. The fine daguerreotype of John Quincy Adams was acquired by The Metropolitan Museum of Art, New York, from the estate of Josiah Johnson Hawes, and was catalogued as the work of the Southworth & Hawes gallery. The presence of the hallmark "SCOVILL MFG CO" on the upper right hand corner of the plate indicates that the daguerreotype was made after the death of Adams in 1848, for the firm of J. M. L. and W. H. Scovill did not adopt this name until 1850. It is thus clear that the daguerreotype is a copy. Recently I acquired a daguerreotype portrait of a certain Joseph Ridgway, seated in the identical chair, with the same carpet, table, lamp, fireplace and mantelpiece that appear in the Adams portrait. On the mat is printed "P. Haas. Washington City, 1843." My attribution of the Adams portrait to Haas is confirmed by the note in Adams's diary that he sat for Haas in October, 1843. Haas published a lithograph of a similar portrait of Adams "taken from a Daguerreotype" in the same year; it is an alternative pose, with the identical chair that appears in the Metropolitan Museum's daguerreotype. The discovery of the Ridgway portrait confirms the deductions of Marvin Sadik in his exhibition catalogue, *The Life Portraits of John Quincy Adams*, Washington, D. C., The National Portrait Gallery, 1970, plate 41.

9. Andrew Jackson's granddaughter, Mrs. Rachel Jackson Lawrence, was present when a daguerreotype almost similar to this was taken by Dan Adams of Nashville, Tennessee, on April 15, 1845. "I have a vivid recollection of the arrangement for taking this likeness," she wrote in *McClure's Mag.*, IX (1897), 803. "He was much opposed to having it taken and was very feeble at the time. I still have the old plates of some earlier daguerreotypes, but they are entirely faded out."

11. It is possible that this may be one of the daguerreotypes taken by Edward Anthony for his "National Daguerreian Miniature Gallery." See Paul M. Angle, "American Photography, 1845-1865," *Chicago History*, IV, No. 1 (1954), 2-5.

12. The penthouse is Whitney's gallery; the men standing on the roof are probably his assistants. Whitney moved into this new gallery in 1851; his neighbors Nelson Hawley, bookbinder, Brown and Williams, carpet ware, and James Z. Newcombe, dry goods, all moved out of the building in 1853.

166

19. Frederick Warren, city marshal of Worcester, Massachusetts, died November 13, 1858, by the accidental discharge of a revolver in the hand of the deputy sheriff of Charleston, South Carolina.

20. Barnard wrote in *PAJ*, VII (January, 1854), 9-10, that this daguerreotype "was made in my room by sky-light, on a scale plate. . . . It represents an aged Canadian Woodsawyer and his son, surrounded by the instruments and objects of their labor, enjoying their noon-tide meal. The old wood-sawyer is sitting on the buck, and on one end of the table, and the boy, in an attitude of overworked fatigue, is coiled up on the wheel-barrow, the instrument of his industry. . . ." It won honorable mention in Anthony's Prize Competition, 1854.

25. "The locomotive 'Hoosac' . . . was built by John Souther of Boston in 1854 for the Fitchburg R.R., at that time running between Boston and Fitchburg, Mass. . . . The locomotive had 16 x 20″ cylinders, 54″ drivers and weighed 54,000 lbs. . . . The Fitchburg R.R. sold this locomotive on March 15, 1862, to the United States Government and they placed the locomotive in service on the U. S. Military R.R. in Virginia. In 1865 it was sold to the Baltimore and Ohio R.R." From a letter to the author dated March 3, 1949, from Charles E. Fisher, President, Railway and Locomotive Historical Society, Inc.

26. A wood engraving from this daguerreotype was published in the *Illustrated News* (New York), August 27, 1853, with the note: "From an excellent daguerreotype by Mr. L. Wright of Pawtucket, R. I., taken a few minutes after the catastrophe." The collision between the trains, which were bound for Uxbridge and Providence respectively, happened on August 12, 1853. It was caused by miscalculation of the conductor—whose watch was slow. Fourteen were killed. Robert L. Wheeler, "Conductor's Watch Slow, 14 Die," *Providence Sunday Journal,* October 25, 1953.

37-38. The two daguerreotypes we reproduce are the second and third of the series of eight which form a panorama of two miles of the Ohio River, from the foot of Vine Street, Cincinnati, to the village of Fulton. The daguerreotypes were taken from Newport, Kentucky. All eight plates are reproduced in *Bul. of the Hist. and Philos. Soc. of Ohio,* VI (April 1948), 28-39, with identifications of the buildings by Carl Vitz. Capt. Frederick Way, Jr., has identified in detail the steamboats in a mimeographed report accompanying a set of twenty photographs, obtainable from the Steamboat Photo Company, 121 River Avenue, Sewickley, Pennsylvania. The panorama was exhibited at the Franklin Institute, Philadelphia, 1849 (highest premium); Maryland Institute, 1849 (highest premium); Great Exhibition of the Works of Industry of All Nations, London, 1851.

44. A photograph of this daguerreotype is reproduced as Figure 1 in F. H. Meserve and C. Sandburg, *The Photographs of Abraham Lincoln* (1944) with the note: "Believed to have been made by N. H. Shepherd in Springfield, Ill., in 1846. Mr. Robert Todd Lincoln, who owned the original, stated to the author that he believed it was made in Washington about 1848."

50. A wood engraving from this daguerreotype appears in *Harper's New Monthly Mag.* VI (1852), 88*.

54. Probably taken during Lola Montez's first American trip; she was in New York City from December 5, 1851, to January 19, 1853.

57. The school has been identified as the Emerson School, Boston. See I. I. Phelps Stokes, *The Hawes-Stokes Collection of American Daguerreotypes by Albert Sands Southworth and Josiah Johnson Hawes* (New York: The Metropolitan Museum of Art, 1939), p. 20.

58. From this daguerreotype a lithograph by F. D'Avignon, dated 1859, was published by C. H. Brainard, Boston.

61. A daguerreotype identical to this, except that it is a mirror image, is in the J. Pierpont Morgan Library, New York. A photograph of it, with the caption "Washington Irving—from Daguerreotype by Plumbe—1849—aet. 66" appears as an illustration in *Washington Irving: Mr. Bryant's Address on his Life and Genius* (New York: Putnam, 1860).

63. One of a stereoscopic pair, acquired by the George Eastman House with the original "Grand Parlor and Gallery Stereoscope" of 1854.

69. Tentatively identified as the ship *The Champion of the Seas,* by Mr. John Leavitt of Marblehead, Massachusetts.

80. Fred Coombs, whose name is stamped on the plate, appears as daguerreotypist in the San Francisco directory for 1850 only. In the following year the firms Sabatie and Maubec, and D. L. Ross, whose names appear on signs, moved from Montgomery Street, and Kendig and Wainwright changed their style to Wainwright, Byrne and Co. Hence this daguerreotype was undoubtedly taken in 1850, and is one of the earliest photographs of San Francisco in existence.

86. A wood engraving of this scene, "made in the fall of 1853," was published in *Gleason's Pictorial,* March 25, 1854. It is reproduced in J. H. Jackson, *Gold Rush Album* (New York: Charles Scribner's Sons, 1849), p. 192.

95. A wood engraving from this daguerreotype, with a short biography of Chief Justice Shaw, appears in *Gleason's Pictorial,* I (1851), 320.

96. In 1808 all slaves in New York State under sixty-five were freed. Caesar, owned by Francis Nicoll, was seventy-one at the time. The daguerreotype was taken in 1851, a year before his death at the age of 114. *N. Y. Genealogical and Biographical Record,* LVI (1925), 65-67.

99. A wood engraving from this daguerreotype in *L'Illustration* (Paris), XXXIV (December 17, 1859), 429, credits Whipple and Black as the photographers.

101. Dated "about 1854" by Robert Taft in his *The Appearance and Personality of Stephen A. Douglas* (reprinted from *The Kansas Historical Quarterly*, Spring, 1954). Taft knew the daguerreotype only from reproductions.

102. An almost identical daguerreotype is in the Museum of Fine Arts, Boston. An engraving of the head is reproduced in H. C. Lodge, *Daniel Webster* (Boston: Houghton, Mifflin and Company, 1899) with the note: "From a daguerreotype taken Apr. 29, 1850, by J. J. Hawes, Boston."

104. An image identical to this daguerreotype, but reversed, is reproduced as Fig. 9 in F. H. Meserve and C. Sandburg, *The Photographs of Abraham Lincoln* (1944) with the note: "A photograph of the daguerreotype believed to have been made by C. S. German in Springfield in 1860. Major William H. Lambert of Philadelphia, who owned the original, was unable to give the compiler its history, but he believed it was made in 1858."

Selected Bibliography

PERIODICALS

American Journal of Photography. New York: 1852–67.

Microfilm: Xerox University Microfilms, No. 4634.

The Daguerreian Journal. New York, 1850–51. Continued as *Humphrey's Journal, Devoted to the Daguerreian and Photogenic Arts* (1852–62), *Humphrey's Journal of Photography, Chemistry, and Pharmacy* (1862-63); *Humphrey's Journal of Photography and the Heliographic Arts and Sciences* (1863); *Humphrey's Journal of Photography and the Allied Arts and Sciences* (1863–70). New York: 1852–70.

Microfilm: Helios Microfilms, Daguerreian Era, Pawlet, Vermont.

The Photographic Art-Journal. New York: 1851–54. Continued as *The Photographic and Fine Art Journal*. New York: 1854–60.

Microfilm: Helios Microfilms, Daguerreian Era, Pawlet, Vermont.

DAGUERRE MANUAL

Daguerre, Louis Jacques Mandé. *Histoire et description du procédé nommé le Daguerréotype*. Paris: Giroux, 1839. 79 pp. + 6 plates.

This, now rare, first edition of Daguerre's manual is the basis of all others. It is reproduced, with one of the many translations into English, in facsimile by Winter House Ltd., New York, 1971. A bibliography of all known editions and translations in book form appears in the above work and in Gernsheim's *L. J. M. Daguerre*, cited below. The instructions were widely published in American periodicals: see p. 158, note 18.

AMERICAN MANUALS

The following titles are the most important. For a complete bibliography of books on photography published before the Civil War, see Albert Boni, *Photographic Literature*, New York; Morgan & Morgan, Inc., 1962, pp. 236–39.

Bisbee, Albert. *History and Practice of Daguerreotyping*. Dayton, O.: L. F. Claflin & Co., 1853. 104 pp.

Facsimile reprint: New York: Arno Press, 1973.

Croucher, John H. *Plain Directions for Obtaining Photographic Pictures by the Calotype and Energiatype . . . Also, Practical Hints on the Daguerreotype*. Philadelphia: A. Hart, late Carey & Hart, 1853. 224 pp.

Facsimile reprint: New York: Arno Press, 1973. This English manual also appeared under the imprint of H. C. Baird, Philadelphia, in editions dated 1855 and 1860.

Gilman & Mower. *The Photographer's Guide, in which the Daguerrean Art is Familiarly Explained*. Lowell, Mass.: Samuel O. Dearborn, printer, 1842, 16 pp.

Haley, W. S. *The Daguerreotype Operator. A Practical Work, Containing the Most Approved Methods for Producing Daguerreotypes*. New York: Printed for the Author, 1854. 80 pp.

Hill, Levi L. *A Treatise on Daguerreotype; the Whole Art Made Easy, and All the Recent Improvements Revealed.* Lexington, N. Y., Holman & Gray, Printers, 1850, 4 vols. in 1.

Facsimile reprint: New York: Arno Press, 1973.

2d ed., with title *Photographic Researches and Manipulations, Including the Author's Former Treatise on Daguerreotype.* Lexington, N. Y.: Holman & Gray, 1851. 2d ed. revised and enlarged, with same title: Philadelphia: Myron Shew, 1854.

Humphrey, Samuel Dwight. *A System of Photography; Containing an Explicit Detail of the Whole Process of Daguerreotype.* By S. D. Humphrey and M. Finley. Canandaigua, N. Y.: Printed at the Office of the Ontario Messenger, 1849. 82 pp.

Facsimile reprint in R. Sobieszek, ed., *The Daguerreotype Process: Three Treatises,* New York: Arno Press, 1973. Second edition, without by-line of Finlay: Albany, C. Van Benthuysen, 1849. 144 pp.

—— *American Handbook of the Daguerreotype.* New York: S. D. Humphrey, 1853. 144 pp.

Fifth ed., 1858. Facsimile reprint: New York: Arno Press, 1973.

Hunt, Robert. *Photography . . . with Additions by the American Editor.* New York: S. D. Humphrey, 1852. 290 pp.

Reprint of the most important English manual, with important original chapter by Humphrey.

Simons, Montgomery P. *Photography in a Nut Shell; or, The Experiences of an Artist in Photography, on Paper, Glass and Silver.* Philadelphia: King & Baird, 1858. 107 pp.

Snelling, Henry Hunt. *The History and Practice of the Art of Photography.* New York: G. P. Putnam, 1849. 139 pp.

Facsimile reprint: Hastings-on-Hudson, N. Y.: Morgan & Morgan, 1970. Second ed., 1850. 3rd ed., 1851. 4th ed., 1853.

—— *A Dictionary of the Photographic Art.* New York: H. H. Snelling, 1854. 236 pp.

—— *A Guide to the Whole Art of Photography.* New York: H. H. Snelling, 1858. 80 pp.

MODERN ACCOUNTS

Gernsheim, Helmut & Alison. *L. J. M. Daguerre: the History of the Diorama and the Daguerreotype.* New York: Dover Publications, 1968. 246 pp.

Contains a chapter on the daguerreotype in America.

Rinhart, Floyd and Marion. *American Daguerrean Art.* New York: Clarkson N. Potter, Inc., 1967. 140 pp.

Rudisill, Richard. *Mirror Image; the Influence of the Daguerreotype on American Society.* Albuquerque: University of New Mexico Press, 1971. 342 pp.

Sachse, Julius F. "Philadelphia's Share in the History of Photography." *Journal of the Franklin Institute,* CXXXV (1893), 271–87.

Taft, Robert. *Photography and the American Scene; a Social History, 1839–1889.* New York: The Macmillan Company, 1938. 546 pp.

Reprinted without change: New York: Macmillan, 1942, and (paperback) New York: Dover Publications, 1964.

Index

HIRAM COLLEGE

772.120973 New
Newhall, Beaumont,
 1908-1993,
The daguerreotype in America

772.120973 New
Newhall, Beaumont,
 1908-1993,
The daguerreotype in America

Annotated Instructor's Edition

Mittendrin

Deutsche Sprache und
Kultur für die Mittelstufe

CHRISTINE GOULDING
California State University, Chico

WIEBKE STREHL
University of South Carolina

WOLFF A. VON SCHMIDT
University of Utah, Emeritus

PEARSON

Boston   Columbus   Indianapolis   New York   San Francisco   Upper Saddle River
Amsterdam   Cape Town   Dubai   London   Madrid   Milan   Munich   Paris   Montreal   Toronto
Delhi   Mexico City   São Paulo   Sydney   Hong Kong   Seoul   Singapore   Taipei   Tokyo

Executive Acquistions Editor: Rachel McCoy
Editorial Assistant: Lindsay Miglionica
Publishing Coordinator: Regina Rivera
Executive Marketing Manager: Kris Ellis-Levy
Marketing Assistant: Michele Marchese
Associate Managing Editor: Janice Stangel
Senior Managing Editor for Product Development:
  Mary Rottino
Production Project Manager: Janice Stangel
Executive Editor. MyLanguageLabs: Bob Hemmer
Senior Media Editor: Samantha Alducin
MyLanguageLabs Development Editor: Bill Bliss
Development Editor: Katherine Gilbert/Harriet
  Dishman
Senior Art Director: Maria Lange
Interior Designer: PreMediaGlobal/Heather Marshall
Cover Designer: Suzanne Benehke

Art Manager: Gail Cocker
Art Studio: Peter Bull
Senior Operations Supervisor: Mary Fischer
Senior Operations Specialist: Alan Fischer
Photo Research Manager: Annette Lindner/Lee Scher
Photo Researcher: Jill S. Kelly
Composition/Full Service: PreMediaGlobal
Production Editor, Full Service: Jenna Gray
Cover Photo Credit: Gavin Hellier/Robert Harding
Printer/Binder: RR Donelley
Cover Printer: Lehigh Phoenix
Publisher: Phil Miller
Cover Caption: Road Bridge over Lake Sylvenstein with
  mountains.

Credits and acknowledgments borrowed from other sources and reproduced, with permission, in this textbook appear on the appropriate page beginning on p. xix.

Copyright © 2013, Pearson Education, Inc. All rights reserved. Manufactured in the United States of America. This publication is protected by Copyright, and permission should be obtained from the publisher prior to any prohibited reproduction, storage in a retrieval system, or transmission in any form or by any means, electronic, mechanical, photocopying, recording, or likewise. To obtain permission(s) to use material from this work, please submit a written request to Pearson Education, Inc., Permissions Department, 1900 E. Lake Ave., Glenview, IL 60025. For information regarding permissions, call (847) 486-2635.

10 9 8 7 6 5 4 3 2 1

Student Edition, ISBN-10: 0-13-1948806
Student Edition, ISBN-13: 978-0-13-194880-8
Annotated Instructor's Edition, ISBN-10: 0-205-78326-0
Annotated Instructor's Edition, ISBN-13: 978-0-205-78326-7

Contents

Scope and Sequence

KAPITEL 3 Thüringen

Einführung

Dialekttipp: Thüringisch

Lese- und Hörtexte

Lesetext 1: Auf den Spuren Johann Sebastian Bachs in Thüringen (Biografie)

Lesetext 2: Welterbe Wartburg (Buchtipp)

Hörtext 1: Tourismus im Thüringer Wald in Zeiten des Klimawandels (Radiobericht)

Lesetext 3: Deutschlands erstes Bratwurstmuseum (Interview)

Lesetext 4: Universitätsstadt Weimar (Stadtporträt)

Hörtext 2: Zwei Studentinnen in Weimar (Gespräch)

Kulturtipps: Barock, Sängerkrieg, Elisabeth von Thüringen, Martin Luther, Burschenschaften, Rennsteig, Wellness, Bauhaus, Deutsche Klassik, Weimarer Republik, Semesterticket

Grammatik

Noun cases (Kasus der Nomen)

    Nominative case (Nominativ)

    Accusative case (Akkusativ)

    Dative case (Dativ)

    Genitive case (Genitiv)

Articles: **der-** and **ein-**words (Artikel: **der-**Wörter und **ein-**Wörter)

Personal pronouns (Personalpronomen)

Word order: Accusative and dative objects (Wortstellung: Akkusativ- und Dativobjekte)

Immer weiter!

Weitere Themen

KAPITEL 4 Wien

Einführung

Dialekttipp: Wienerisch

Lese- und Hörtexte

Lesetext 1: Das 24. Donauinselfest: Eine rauschende Party – ganz ohne Promille (Artikel)

Hörtext 1: Ein Anruf beim Vienna Ticket Office (Telefongespräch)

Lesetext 2: Stephansdom (Internetseite)

Lesetext 3: Kaffee. Wien – Mit Leib und Seele (Reiseführer-Auszug)

Hörtext 2: Margarete Schachermeier: Eine Wienerin stellt sich vor (Interview)

Lesetext 4: „Das Fenster-Theater" von Ilse Aichinger (Kurzgeschichte)

Kulturtipps: Donauinsel, KünstlerInnen, Steckerlfisch und Gulasch, Zentralfriedhof, Gotische und romanische Architektur, Stammgast und Stammtisch, Biedermeier, Mocca und Einspänner, Sigmund Freud, Heuriger, Ringstraße, Prater, Matura

Grammatik

Prepositions (Präpositionen)

    Accusative prepositions (Präpositionen mit Akkusativ)

    Dative prepositions (Präpositionen mit Dativ)

    Genitive prepositions (Präpositionen mit Genitiv)

    Two-way prepositions (Wechselpräpositionen)

Da- and **wo-**compounds (**Da-** und **wo-**Verbindungen)

Weak nouns (Schwache Nomen)

Immer weiter!

Weitere Themen

Preface

Mittendrin is an intermediate-level German program designed to promote communicative and cultural competence. The program supports the development of the full range of language skills and modes of communication while offering a strong cultural orientation and a controlled review and expansion of introductory-level grammar. Carefully chosen reading and listening texts in each chapter introduce students to the multifaceted culture of German-speaking Europe. These texts provide the basis for comprehension activities, vocabulary acquisition, speaking and discussion opportunities, and research and writing assignments. Vibrant photographs and detailed maps further highlight the breadth and diversity of the German-speaking world. Rich audio-visual and language input and activities that engage students with cultural issues place students both linguistically and culturally "mittendrin"; they are fully immersed in the language and culture of German-speaking Europe.

The *Mittendrin* program offers an engaging, flexible curriculum that appeals to a wide variety of interests. It develops skills for immediate practical usage while at the same time providing students with a solid foundation for further study.

Highlights

Cultural orientation

Ten region-oriented chapters. Each chapter of *Mittendrin* focuses on a German-speaking region and its customs and traditions, geography, history, demographics, economic development, cuisine, and language. Centuries of geographical, political, and religious fragmentation in German-speaking Europe have resulted in cultural differences that persist to the present day. In numerous ways, German speakers still tend to identify with their regional cultural heritage rather than their nation. Globalization has even further strengthened people's sense of identification with their native area. The ten region-oriented chapters offer students a rich view of the varied German cultural landscape and an enhanced understanding of characteristic regional nuances.

The highlighted region in each chapter consistently informs the content. Nine of the ten chapters of *Mittendrin* feature a region in German-speaking Europe that constitutes a modern state (**Bundesland** or **Kanton**) or city-state. These political entities, which in many cases have existed only since 1945 or even 1990, are not presented as culturally homogeneous entities. Instead, they provide a basis for exploring both similarities and differences within and among the German-speaking regions.

Kulturtipps. In addition to the regional approach in each chapter, texts are accompanied by **Kulturtipps,** which highlight cultural references in the texts. **Kulturtipps** aid students' understanding of the texts, expand their knowledge of German culture, and demonstrate that cultural awareness and language comprehension are inseparably intertwined.

Dialekttipps. Each chapter further includes a **Dialekttipp** that introduces students to specific characteristics of a major German dialect spoken in the focus region. Students see samples of the dialect, learn about its usage and status among native speakers, and examine how the dialect differs from standard German in pronunciation, vocabulary, and grammar. Students will then encounter some of the described linguistic features of the dialect later in the chapter texts.

Variety of texts

Careful balance of authentic and author-generated texts. The majority of the reading and listening texts in *Mittendrin* are authentic texts in their original form or authentic texts that have been adapted; some additional texts have been author-generated. All texts in *Mittendrin* have been chosen with the goal of introducing relevant and interesting content, including a variety of text formats and styles, promoting language skills, and teaching the targeted structures. Through the accompanying activities, students practice and develop skills for navigating their way through a wide variety of German texts.

Lese- und Hörtexte. There are four **Lesetexte** and two **Hörtexte** in each chapter. The **Lesetexte** and **Hörtexte** provide the basis for skills practice and cultural exploration in each chapter. The written texts and audio texts expose students to a broad range of content and genres while still maintaining focus on the chapter region. These texts cover a variety of subject areas, including history, art, music, literature, education, technology, the environment, geography, cuisine, multiculturalism, sports, politics, business, economics, transportation, the working world, and contemporary life. The **Lesetexte** represent diverse text sources and types: autobiographical excerpts, biographies, newspaper articles, reviews, speeches, interviews, websites, blogs, brochures, press releases, job advertisements, and literary works, including short stories, excerpts from a novel, a drama, a poem, and a fairy tale. The **Hörtexte** use audio recordings derived from or modeled after authentic sources and represent a range of authentic situations, including conversations, interviews, news reports, radio programs, advertisements, and song. These reading and listening texts are the basis for comprehension activities and exercises that engage students in the critical analysis of genres. They also serve as models for students' own written and oral production.

Treatment of vocabulary

Neue Vokabeln. Each **Lesetext** is accompanied by a list of **Neue Vokabeln** that contains words intended for active mastery. These lists contain high-frequency words based on *A Frequency Dictionary of German* (Jones and Tschirner, 2006) and any additional words that are essential to the understanding and discussion of the texts. Students first see the words in context and then practice them actively in a **Vokabelarbeit** activity. To further aid mastery, new active vocabulary items are regularly recycled. The separate word list accompanying each **Lesetext** gives instructors flexibility in lesson planning and also allows students to quickly locate words associated with each reading and to learn them in context.

For easy reference, the four **Neue Vokabeln** lists in each chapter are compiled into a comprehensive list in the Student Activities Manual (SAM), where there are further opportunities for students to work actively with chapter vocabulary as well as to practice vocabulary expansion strategies.

Glossary and glosses. Relevant words appearing in listening and reading texts that are not typically learned in the first year and not intended for active mastery are glossed and/or available in the **German-English Glossary** in the back of the book. The **Glossary** also includes all vocabulary items introduced for active mastery throughout the book. Words from the **Neue Vokabeln** appear in the **Glossary** with chapter numbers to indicate where they are first learned.

Treatment of grammar

Basic and intermediate structures (Grammatik). *Mittendrin* helps students attain mastery of basic German grammar with a thorough review of introductory-level topics. At the same time, intermediate-level grammar topics (e.g., future perfect tense, passive voice, subjunctive II) are introduced and actively practiced. Grammar explanations and activities are all conveniently located in a single **Grammatik** section in each chapter.

Contextualized, flexible grammar. Grammar activities are always connected to the geographic region and related themes of the chapter. Because grammar activities are based immediately on chapter content, there is no break in continuity when shifting between the reading and listening texts and the grammar exercises. The placement and design of grammar exercises in *Mittendrin* allow for flexibility in lesson planning. Instructors may choose to incorporate the grammar units in whole or in part, as classroom activities or homework assignments.

Advanced structures and metalinguistic approaches (Sprachanalyse). While students practice beginning and intermediate grammar structures for productive acquisition in the **Grammatik** sections, they also gain exposure to advanced grammar topics (e.g., extended modifiers, passive voice alternatives, subjunctive I). These advanced topics are presented for receptive acquisition only in the **Sprachanalyse** feature located in each corresponding chapter of the Student Activities Manual (SAM). Here students also have the opportunity to examine German from a metalinguistic perspective (e.g., various uses of *werden,* German word order, writing style) and thus become familiar with characteristic structures of German. Learners' receptive abilities naturally outpace their productive abilities. Knowledge of these structures will improve their comprehension of the language well before they are ready to produce them.

Clear cross-references to relevant **Sprachanalyse** activities in the SAM appear in the text chapter. Each SAM chapter focuses on a single **Sprachanalyse** topic and contains a series of activities that draw examples of language usage from the chapter texts. The introductory **Sprachanalyse** explains a linguistic feature of German using examples from the chapter **Einführung.** Two to four additional activities in each SAM chapter take examples from the **Lesetexte** and guide students through the process of recognizing and accurately comprehending the usage of these structures in context. This unique component helps students develop reading strategies and language recognition skills that boost their comprehension of German.

Chapter Organization

Each chapter opens with a map of the region being studied, as well as second, smaller map showing the location of the region within German-speaking Europe. The chapter then continues with a series of distinctive features.

Einführung This section consists of a text introducing the region being highlighted in the chapter, followed by **Fragen zum Text.**

Dialekttipp Each chapter spotlights a major German dialect spoken in the focus region. Accompanying **Zum Dialekt** activities allow students to analyze some distinctive dialect features.

Lese- und Hörtexte This section contains four reading and two listening texts. Each of the six texts is fully supported by appropriate scaffolding, and contains a useful and engaging set of activities organized in a logical progression.

- The introduction to each text provides students with background information and is accompanied by instructor annotations with suggestions for activating students' prior knowledge, guiding them to actively think about the topic, and helping them to understand and engage with the information in the text introduction.
- **Vor dem Lesen / Vor dem Hören** sections provide pre-reading or pre-listening activities.
- **Beim Lesen / Beim Hören** exercises encourage students' active engagement with the text during the first reading or listening. **Beim Hören** sections also contain a preview of unfamiliar vocabulary not intended for active mastery to aid student comprehension during listening. These are given in order of appearance in the text so that students can easily follow along.
- **Lesetexte** and **Hörtexte** represent a variety of text types and cover a broad range of topics. English glosses of words critical to understanding the text but not intended for active mastery are provided for the **Lesetexte.**
- **Neue Vokabeln** follow each of the four readings. These sections list high-frequency words, which are essential to the discussion of the texts and are intended for active acquisition.
- **Kulturtipps** explain cultural references contained in the reading and listening texts. These support students' comprehension of the texts and of German culture in general.
- Post-reading and -listening activities begin with comprehension (**Textarbeit**) exercises, followed by a **Vokabelarbeit** activity, in which students actively use the **Neue Vokabeln.** Discussion and interpersonal speaking activities follow. Finally, writing, composition, Internet research, and presentation activities associated with the theme of the reading or listening selection complete the activity set.

Grammatik Each chapter covers a set of grammar topics that review introductory level structures and introduce intermediate structures. Detailed grammar explanations in English are followed by activities that incorporate the context and content of the chapter, fully integrating skills and grammar practice with cultural content. Some key elements of grammar are comprehensively reviewed in later chapters (such as cases in *Kapitel 7* and verb tenses in *Kapitel 8*). The activities can be done in tandem with the **Lesetexte** and **Hörtexte** and can be either assigned as homework or completed in class.

Immer weiter! This wrap-up section synthesizes the content of the chapter one final time. Discussion and writing tasks prompt students to describe, contemplate, and integrate what they have learned about the focus region throughout the chapter.

Weitere Themen Each chapter contains a list of twenty topics related to the focus region that can be used for further exploration.

Mittendrin and the ACTFL National Standards

The five Cs outlined in ACTFL's *National Standards for Foreign Language Learning in the 21st Century*—Communication, Cultures, Connections, Comparisons, and Communities—are actively integrated throughout the *Mittendrin* program.

Communication. *Mittendrin* emphasizes functional, purposeful, task-based language use. **Fragen zum Text** and **Textarbeit** activities guide students through understanding a wide range of reading and listening texts (*interpretive mode*). Pre- and post-reading activities, and **Immer weiter!** assignments actively engage students in meaningful conversation (*interpersonal mode*). Students present information and ideas orally and in theme-related writing assignments that consistently specify the purpose, form, and the audience to be addressed (*presentational mode*).

Cultures. Culture permeates *Mittendrin* and provides the organizational principle for the book. Students are exposed to a wide variety of cultural products (e.g., literary works, job ads, regional crafts), practices (e.g., festivals, leisure time activities, culinary habits), and perspectives (e.g., attitudes about education and German reunification). Every chapter contains ample opportunities for students to make connections between beliefs, behaviors, and cultural artifacts and achievements.

Connections. The content of *Mittendrin* embraces numerous disciplines: geography, politics, music, education, history, linguistics, business, environmental studies, and many more. Through their engagement with German in the text, students reinforce and further their knowledge of other disciplines. Through guided Internet research assignments, students access information and explore the distinctive viewpoints of German speakers that are accessible to them only through their knowledge of the language.

Comparisons. Opportunities for linguistic and cultural comparison are abound in *Mittendrin.* Students routinely explore the relationship between language use and meaning, between genre and content. **Dialekttipps** and particularly the **Sprachanalyse** activities focus students' attention on the structure of German. Personalization of the content impels students to compare German attitudes and practices, (e.g., responses to climate change, views on education, multilingualism and multiculturalism, favored modes of transportation) to their own and to understand culture as a reflection of historical, geographic, political, and economic conditions.

Communities. *Mittendrin* prepares students to participate in meaningful exchanges with other German speakers, both immediately in the classroom setting and with native speakers at home and abroad. Personalized, engaging activities stimulate students to use the language for personal enjoyment and the **Weitere Themen** encourage the use of the language for enrichment beyond the classroom.

Program Components

Instructor Resources

Annotated Instructor's Edition (AIE). This rich resource for both seasoned and novice instructors offers suggestions for presentation of new material and creative use of activities, including options for variations and expansion. Answers for activities are provided where appropriate. The AIE also contains useful notes on language and culture.

Instructor's Resource Manual. The IRM provides sample syllabi, sample lesson plans, and audio scripts. The IRM is available in a downloadable format on the Instructors' Resource Center, and in MyGermanLab.

Testing Program. A flexible testing program allows instructors to customize tests by selecting the modules they wish to use. This complete testing program includes chapter tests and comprehensive examinations that test reading, listening, writing, and speaking skills, vocabulary acquisition, grammar skills, and cultural knowledge. The testing program is available in a downloadable format on the Instructor's Resource Center, and in a test-generating format in MyGermanLab.

Audio Files for the Testing Program. All listening tests are recorded for the instructor's use in a classroom or laboratory setting on MyGermanLab™ and on CD.

Student Resources

Student Activities Manual (SAM). The SAM provides complete coordination with the structure and approach of the *Mittendrin* textbook, and offers an ample variety of writing and listening activities that are contextualized to coordinate with the chapter themes. It contains additional reading and listening comprehension activities for the texts in *Mittendrin,* vocabulary practice and expansion exercises as well as comprehensive chapter vocabulary lists, grammar practice, writing and speaking assignments, activities to assess cultural understanding, and activities to accompany an original audio text, found on the Audio Program. It also contains the unique **Sprachanalyse** feature that furthers students' comprehension of authentic language.

Answer Key for the SAM. This component is available for optional inclusion in course packages; it includes answers for all discrete and short answer exercises in the SAM.

Audio for the SAM. Students and instructors have access to the audio recordings for the SAM in several formats: on Audio CDs, via the Companion Website, and in MyGermanLab.

Audio for the Text. Students and instructors have access to the audio recordings for the listening activities in the core text. This audio is available in several formats: on the Audio CDs, via the Companion Website, and in MyGermanLab (which includes the pronunciation of vocabulary lists).

Online Resources

MyGermanLab™. This new, nationally hosted online learning system was created specifically for students in college-level language courses. It brings together, in one convenient, easily navigable site, a wide array of language-learning tools and resources, including an interactive version of the Student Activities Manual and all materials from the Audio program. Readiness checks and grammar tutorials presented in English individualize instruction to meet the needs of each student. Instructors can use the system to make assignments, set grading parameters, listen to student-created audio recordings, and provide feedback on student work. Instructor access is provided at no charge to adopting institutions. Students can purchase access codes online or at their local bookstore.

Companion Website. The Companion Website (CW) provides links for Internet activities and audio for listening activities in the textbook and in the Student Activities Manual. It is located at: http://www.pearsonhighered.com/mittendrin.

Acknowledgments

No textbook comes to fruition without the efforts of those working diligently behind the scenes. We would like to express our deep appreciation to all the people who contributed their talents to *Mittendrin*. We are especially grateful to Rachel McCoy, Executive Acquisitions Editor, for her unfailing enthusiasm, patience, and commitment to the success of this project and to Phil Miller, Pearson's Publisher for World Languages for his steadfast support.

Words cannot adequately express our gratitude to our Developmental Editor Katherine Gilbert, whose intelligent editorial suggestions, ability to anticipate production hurdles, and meticulous attention to detail brought about significant improvements in the text. Both Katherine Gilbert and Harriet C. Dishman, Foreign Language Development Director at PreMediaGlobal, expertly guided us throughout the revision process, acted as a sounding board for our ideas, helped find creative solutions to sometimes seemingly insurmountable problems, and supplied infinite patience and good humor. We are deeply indebted to both of them for their contributions. We are grateful also to Copyeditor Esther Bach for her thorough review of the manuscript, to Karen Hohner for her careful editing, and to Stephen Ingle for his preparation of the index. We thank our Project Manager Jenna Gray at PreMediaGlobal whose excellent communication and organizational skills kept the project on schedule.

A special thanks goes to Lindsay Miglionica, Editorial Assistant, who helped to keep the manuscript flowing from authoring to production. We greatly appreciate the work of Pearson's tireless production team. Janice Stangel, Associate Managing Editor, and Mary Rottino, Senior Managing Editor, effectively coordinated the work of the many people involved. Many thanks to Bob Hemmer, Executive Editor for MyLanguageLabs and Samantha Alducin, Senior Media Editor, for her implementation of MyGermanLab™, and to Bill Bliss, Developmental Editor for MyLanguageLabs™, for carefully overseeing the preparation of the Student Activities Manual and Testing Program. We also extend our gratitude to Kris Ellis-Levy, Executive Marketing Manager, and Michele Marchese, Marketing Assistant, for coordinating the materials for the marketing campaign. We would also like to sincerely thank cartographer Peter Bull Studio for their superb maps and the talented Gail Cocker for her keen attention to the creation of each and every map.

A special acknowledgment goes to our dear friend and previous co-author Karl F. Otto, Jr., Professor Emeritus of German, University of Pennsylvania, whose participation in the nascent stage of this project was invaluable.

We can never thank our families enough for their enduring patience and unconditional support.

We would like to thank the following colleagues who took time from their busy schedules to review the manuscript during its various stages of development.

Brigetta M. Abel, *Macalester College*

Rita Abercrombie, *Baylor University*

Shana Bell, *Arizona State University*

Lisa Barboun, *Coastal Carolina University*

Klaus Brandl, *University of Washington*

Monika Chavez, *University of Wisconsin-Madison*

Irene S. Di Maio, *Louisiana State University*

Anke Finger, *University of Connecticut*

Lisabeth Hock, *Wayne State University*

Deborah Horzen, *University of Central Florida & Rollins College*

Madelon Köhler-Busch, *University of Maine-Orono*

Douglas James Lightfoot, *The University of Alabama*

Patrick M. McConeghy, *Michigan State University*

Hannelore Mundt, *University of Wyoming*

Iulia Pittman, *Auburn University*

Stephen Pugh, *University of Texas at El Paso*

Brigitte Rossbacher, *University of Georgia*

Patricia A. Schindler, *University of Colorado at Boulder*

Johannes Schmidt, *Clemson University*

Bruce H. Spencer, *University of Iowa*

Nina Vyatkina, *University of Kansas*

Credits

Text Credits

p. 22: „Meine Kindheit": Thomas Mann, Gesammelte Werke in 13 Bänden, Band 11, Reden und Aufsätze 3. © 1960, 1974 Fischer Verlag GmbH, Frankfurt am Main.; p. 46: „Wir sind ein Volk": Bundeskanzler-Willy-Brandt-Stiftung; p. 51: Erinnerungen an den Mauerfall: Fünf Fragen an Brunhilde Heß (Interview): Bundeszentrale für Politische Bildung; p. 54: Berlin-Bärenstark! Knut tut der Wirtschaft gut: dpa Deutsche Presse Agentur GmbH, Mittelweg 38, 20148 Hamburg Germany; p. 59: Ein Wochenende in Berlin: © Tchibo GmbH; p. 80: Auf den Spuren Johann Sebastian Bachs in Thüringen: Thüringer Bachwochen e.V. (http://www.thueringer-bachwochen.de/); p. 93: Deutschlands erstes Bratwurstmuseum: "Deutschlands erstes Bratwurstmuseum", Author interview with Thomas Mäuer, with kind permission of Thomas Mäuer; p. 98: Universitätsstadt Weimar: Bauhaus-Universität Weimar; p. 127: Stephansdom: Verein "Unser Stephansdom"; p. 131: Kaffee. Wien – Mit Leib und Seele: auszugsweise aus Käthe Springer; Wien City Guide, mit freundlicher Genehmigung, Christian Brandstätter Verlagsgesellschaft m.b.H., Das Verlagsservice für Museen, Unternehmen und öffentliche Stellen, www.brandstaetter-verlag.at; p. 138: Das Fenster-Theater: Ilse Aichinger, Das Fenster-Theater from: Ilse Aichinger, Der Gefesselte. Erzählungen1. © 1953 by S. Fischer Verlag GmbH, Frankfurt am Main; p. 159: „Public Viewing macht die Festspiele nicht kaputt": Zeit Online; p. 169: Praktikum bei BMW (Interview): BMW Group; p. 182: „Das doppelte Lottchen": Erich Kästner: "Das doppelte Lottchen" 159. Auflage, Cecilie Dressler Verlag, Hamburg, 2008; p. 205: Zwei Farben Grau: Taz, die Tageszeitung © 2004; p. 214: Zwischen Comics und Nobelpreisträgern: Anne Wirth © 2009; p. 219: „Das Hochzeitsfoto": © 1992 by Dieter Zimmer vertreten durch AVA international GmbH Autoren- und Verlags-Agentur, München-Breitbrunn (www.ava-international.de).; p. 248: „Wir nennen uns Zoogler!": Wiederabdruck mit freundlicher Genehmigung der Greater Zurich Area AG; p. 252: Elizabeth Barton: Eine Ausländerin in Zürich (Personenporträt): Mit freundlicher Genehmigung der Greater Zurich Area AG (Text: ZÜRICH Magazine, Marius Leutenegger); p. 256: Umstrittenes Hochdeutsch im Kindergarten: Neue Zürcher Zeitung, 17. März 2008, Autorin: Katja Baigger; p. 260: Das ungleiche Paar: Universität und ETH in Zürich (Radiosendung): 2008 Schweizer Radio DRS; p. 264: „Andorra": "Andorra", S. 468–487 aus: Max Frisch, Andorra. Stück in zwölf Bildern. © Suhrkamp Verlag Frankfurt am Main © 1961.; p. 290: Daimler startet Mobilitätskonzept „car2go" in Ulm: Daimler startet Mobilitätskonzept „car2go" in Ulm © Daimler AG; p. 294: Die Popakademie Baden-Württemberg (Interview): © www.localheroes-radio.de; p. 306: „Das verlorene Taschenmesser": "Das verlorene Taschenmesse" aus: Hermann Hesse, Sämtliche Werke, Band 3, © Suhrkamp Verlag Frankfurt am Main 2001.; p. 339: Erster Türkischer Karnevalsverein gegründet: WDR.de; p. 373: Chaos am Flughafen: „Ein klarer Fall von höherer Gewalt": Frankfurter Allgemeine Zeitung; p. 381: Freizeit mit dem Rhein-Main-Verkehrsbund: Rhein-Main-Verkehrsbund; p. 386: Karoline von Günderode in Winkel (Radiobeitrag): © Hessischer Rundfunk, 2011 (1993)

Photo Credits

p. 1 (bottom left): Otmar Smit/Shutterstock; p. 1 (top left): lullabi/Shutterstock; p. 1 (top right): Shestakoff/Shutterstock; p. 1 (bottom right): Markus Gann/Shutterstock; p. 2: Frank Wasserfuehrer/Shutterstock; p. 4: sculpies/Shutterstock; p. 5 (top): Christine Goulding; p. 5 (bottom): Melanie Vollmert/Shutterstock; p. 6: Sascha Burkard/Shutterstock; p. 9: RicoK/Shutterstock; p. 14: thorabeti/Fotolia; p. 15: wiw/Fotolia; p. 16: Ingo Wagner/dpa/picture-alliance/Newscom; p. 18: crimson/Fotolia; p. 21: TCI/MARKA/Alamy; p. 22: Wiebke Strehl; p. 23: Wiebke Strehl; p. 25: AF archive/Alamy; p. 34: Corinna Strade/Fotolia; p. 37: Christine Goulding; p. 38 (bottom right): jan kranendonk/Shutterstock; p. 38 (top right): Nico Stengert/imagebroker/Alamy; p. 38 (left): paparazzit/Shutterstock; p. 41: Increa/Fotolia; p. 45: ITAR-TASS Photo Agency/Alamy; p. 48: Increa/Fotolia; p. 51: Kaiser/Caro/Alamy; p. 52: c/Shutterstock; p. 53: 360b/Shutterstock; p. 56: Senilm/Fotolia; p. 57: Beth Smith; p. 58: BerlinPictures/Shutterstock; p. 60 (top): Maree Stachel-Williamson/Shutterstock; p. 60 (bottom): Barbara Pheby/Fotolia; p. 61: Aleksandar Hajdukovic/Shutterstock; p. 63 (top): Interfoto/Alamy; p. 63 (bottom): lumen-digital/Shutterstock; p. 64: Art Kowalsky/Alamy; p. 71: IH-Images/Shutterstock; p. 76 (top left): Tobilander/Fotolia; p. 76 (bottom right): anyaivanova/Shutterstock; p. 76 (top right): twoandonebuilding/Shutterstock; p. 76 (bottom left): Henry Czauderna/Fotolia; p. 76 (center right): Nikada/iStockphoto; p. 79: Thomas Frey/Imagebroker/Alamy; p. 80: Getty Images/Photos.com/Thinkstock; p. 84: l-pics/Fotolia; p. 85: © Ulrich Kneise/Schnell & Steiner; p. 87 (right): Jozef Sedmak/Shutterstock; p. 87 (left): Getty Images/Photos.com/Thinkstock; p. 89 (top): Christine Goulding; p. 89 (bottom): Gerhard Köhler/Fotolia LLC; p. 90: Alexander Rochau/Fotolia; p. 92: Daniel Fleck/Shutterstock; p. 93: Courtesy 1. Deutsches Bratwurstmuseum; p. 94: Herkunftsverband Thüringer und Eichsfelder Wurst und Fleisch e.V.; p. 96: Schütze/Rodemann/Bildarchiv Monheim GmbH/Alamy; p. 98 (bottom): Bernd Kröger/Fotolia; p. 98 (top): Volker Z/Fotolia; p. 99: filosofin/Fotolia; p. 100: Hemera/Thinkstock; p. 102 (top): Henry Czauderna/Fotolia; p. 102 (bottom): amrita/Shutterstock; p. 107: Sebastian Köhler/Fotolia; p. 115 (top left): fritz16/Shutterstock; p. 115 (top right): Carmen Steiner/Fotolia; p. 115 (bottom right): Péter Gudella/Shutterstock; p. 115 (bottom left): 4FR/iStockphoto; p. 118: Hubert Dimko; www.donauinselfest.at; p. 121 (top): ksch/Fotolia; p. 121 (center): FK-Lichtbilde/Fotolia; p. 121 (bottom): Adrea Wilhelm/Fotolia; p. 124:

Lana Sundman/Alamy; p. 125: Bob Cheung/Shutterstock; p. 127 (top): jomare/Fotolia; p. 127 (bottom): Aleksandar Todorovic/ Shutterstock; p. 130: Margarete Schachermeier; p. 131 (left): Margarete Schachermeier; p. 131 (right): Margarete Schachermeier; p. 133: Everett Collection Inc/Alamy; p. 135: Margarete Schachermeier; p. 136: Pavol Kmeto/Shutterstock; p. 137: Interfoto/ Alamy; p. 147: fritz16/Shutterstock; p. 150 (top): Jorg Hackemann/Shutterstock; p. 150 (bottom): clearlens/Shutterstock; p. 154: irakite/Shutterstock; p. 155 (bottom right): Arnd Drifte/Fotolia; p. 155 (left): R.S.Jegg/Shutterstock; p. 155 (top right): Scirocco340/ Shutterstock; p. 158: Everett Collection Inc/Alamy; p. 159: fotobi/Fotolia; p. 164: Mirenska Olga/Shutterstock; p. 165 (top): Landshuter Hochzeit 1475; p. 165 (bottom): Soundsnaps/Shutterstock; p. 166 (top): Lazar Mihai-Bogdan/Shutterstock; p. 166 (bottom): Mirenska Olga/Shutterstock; p. 167: Rmbssk/Shutterstock; p. 169: Norbert A./Shutterstock; p. 172: Jörg Hackemann/ Fotolia; p. 173 (top): Lina_S/Shutterstock; p. 173 (bottom): Zyankarlo/Shutterstock; p. 175: andreanord/Shutterstock; p. 176 (top): Dmitry V. Petrenko/Shutterstock; p. 176 (bottom): Christa Eder/Fotolia; p. 179: Sean Nel/Shutterstock; p. 180: Norbert Probst/ imagebroker/Alamy; p. 181: Interfoto/Alamy; p. 183: Denis and Yulia Pogostins/Shutterstock; p. 196 (top): Andre Nantel/ Shutterstock; p. 196 (center): Pictures4you/Fotolia; p. 196 (bottom left): Kai Michael Neuhold/Fotolia; p. 196 (bottom right): OD/ Fotolia; p. 199: PeJo/Shutterstock; p. 203: Torsten Lorenz/Shutterstock; p. 204: sandy young/Alamy; p. 206 (top): Gerhard Richter 2012; p. 206 (bottom): Gerhard Richter 2012; p. 207: SuperStock/SuperStock; p. 210 (top): Bettmann/Corbis; p. 210 (bottom): Brian K./Shutterstock; p. 211: Olga Kolos/Shutterstock; p. 212 (left): Bartosz Koszowski/Shutterstock; p. 212 (right): Nobor/ Shutterstock; p. 214: Courtesy Anne Wirth; p. 216: Interfoto/Alamy; p. 217 (top): © Leipziger Messe GmbH/Leipziger Buchmesse; p. 217 (bottom): 1992 by Dieter Zimmer vertreten durch AVA international GmbH Autoren- und Verlags-Agentur, München-Breitbrunn (www.ava-international.de <http://www.ava-international.de/>); p. 218: Harald Lange/Fotolia; p. 221 (top): Deutsche Bundesbank, Frankfurt am Main, Germany; p. 221 (center): Deutsche Bundesbank, Frankfurt am Main, Germany; p. 221 (bottom): Andreas Schmidt; p. 224: Tino Thoß/Fotolia; p. 225 (left): Courtesy Dresden Marketing GmbH; p. 225 (right): jomare/ Fotolia; p. 232: Eyesart/Fotolia; p. 237 (bottom right): celeste clochard/Fotolia; p. 237 (top left): swisshippo/Fotolia; p. 237 (bottom left): celeste clochard/Fotolia; p. 237 (top right): Ulrich Mueller/Shutterstock; p. 241 (top left): Roman Sigaev/Shutterstock; p. 241 (top center): Roman Sigaev/Shutterstock; p. 241 (top right): National Geographic Image Collection/Alamy; p. 241 (bottom left): Roman Sigaev/Shutterstock; p. 241 (center left): Roman Sigaev/Shutterstock; p. 241 (center right): Roman Sigaev/Shutterstock; p. 241 (center right): Roman Sigaev/Shutterstock; p. 241 (bottom right): David R. Frazier Photolibrary, Inc./Alamy; p. 242 (top left): Roman Sigaev/Shutterstock; p. 242 (top right): Roman Sigaev/Shutterstock; p. 242 (bottom left): Roman Sigaev/Shutterstock; p. 242 (bottom right): Hiltl, Zurich, Switzerland; p. 243 (top): Roman Sigaev/Shutterstock; p. 243 (bottom left): Roman Sigaev/ Shutterstock; p. 243 (bottom center): Roman Sigaev/Shutterstock; p. 243 (bottom right): Roman Sigaev/Shutterstock; p. 244 (top): ExQuisine/Fotolia; p. 244 (bottom left): Jakub Niezabitowski/Fotolia; p. 244 (bottom right): Jean-Yves Roure/Alamy; p. 248: Greater Zurich Area AG - http://www.greaterzuricharea.ch; p. 250: Peter Wey/Shutterstock; p. 253: Olga Bogatyrenko/ Shutterstock; p. 255: Matka_Wariatka/Shutterstock; p. 261 (left): ETH Zurich (Swiss Federal Institute of Technology, Zurich); p. 261 (right): Alexander Chaikin/Shutterstock; p. 263: Interfoto/Alamy; p. 277: awdebenham/iStockphoto; p. 281 (left): Falk Kienas/Shutterstock; p. 281 (top right): Kuelcue/Dreamstime; p. 281 (bottom right): clearlens/Fotolia; p. 286 (top): Cogipix/ Shutterstock; p. 286 (bottom): Christian Jung/Fotolia; p. 287 (top): Jens Ottoson/Shutterstock; p. 287 (bottom): sybanto/ Shutterstock; p. 290 (top): steffenw/Fotolia; p. 290 (bottom): Daimler AG; p. 298 (top): mpgphoto/Fotolia; p. 298 (bottom): „Hochschwarzwald Tourismus GmbH – Tourist Information Schluchsee"; p. 300: SF photo/Shutterstock; p. 304 (left): Scirocco340/ Shutterstock; p. 304 (right): Kai Koehler/Fotolia; p. 305: Interfoto/Alamy; p. 309: Scirocco340/Shutterstock; p. Michael Kügler/ Fotolia; p. 320: jovannig/Fotolia; p. 323 (left): ThomasSaupe/iStockphoto; p. 323 (top right): seen/Fotolia; p. 323 (bottom right): vario images GmbH & Co.KG/Alamy; p. 326: Duncan Walker/iStockphoto; p. 329 (top): www.kallipos.de; p. 329 (bottom): Oliver Hoffmann/Shutterstock; p. 332 (left): rtem/Shutterstock; p. 332 (right): MichaelUtech/iStockphoto; p. 337: imago sportfotodienst/ Newscom; p. 339 (top): Val Thoermer/Shutterstock; p. 339 (bottom): Joern Wolter/vario images GmbH & Co.K/Alamy; p. 340: bezmaski/Shutterstock; p. 341: ZoneFatal/Shutterstock; p. 345: Guido Kollmeier; p. 348: Interfoto/Alamy; p. 352: c/Shutterstock; p. 363 (top left): Nathan Brandt/iStockphoto; p. 363 (top right): Corbis Bridge/Alamy; p. 363 (bottom right): C. Schiller/Fotolia; p. 363 (bottom left): Jeremy Edwards/iStockphoto; p. 366: Thomas Maier/iStockphoto; p. 369 (top): Axel Schmies/imagebroker/ Alamy; p. 369 (bottom): Gina Sanders/Fotolia; p. 372: AndreasWeber/iStockphoto; p. 373: nazarethman/iStockphoto; p. 377: Colour/Shutterstock; p. 378: Silberkorn/iStockphoto; p. 380: HarriesAD/iStockphoto; p. 381: Paolo Gianti/Shutterstock; p. 382: Christine Goulding; p. 382: Christine Goulding; p. 382: Christine Goulding; p. 382: Christine Goulding; p. 382: Christine Goulding; p. 382: Christine Goulding; p. 382: Christine Goulding; p. 383 (top): Christine Goulding; p. 383 (center): anweber/Shutterstock; p. 383 (bottom left): Christine Goulding; p. 383 (bottom right): Christine Goulding; p. 384 (top): ronfromyork/Shutterstock; p. 384 (bottom): Getty Images/Photos.com/Thinkstock; p. 387: Interfoto/Alamy; p. 388: LianeM/Shutterstock; p. 390 (top): Photos. com/Thinkstock; p. 390 (center right): severjn/Shutterstock; p. 390 (bottom center): severjn/Shutterstock; p. 390 (bottom left): severjn/Shutterstock; p. 390 (center left): severjn/Shutterstock; p. 390 (bottom right): severjn/Shutterstock; p. 390 (center): severjn/Shutterstock

KAPITEL

1

Norddeutschland

Note. Photo descriptions for chapter openers can be found on p. ii.

Sylt · DÄNEMARK · OSTSEE

Flensburg
Husum
SCHLESWIG-HOLSTEIN
Nord-Ostsee-Kanal ★ Kiel
Rügen
Stralsund
Travemünde
Lübeck
Wismar
Rostock
Greifswald
Cuxhaven
NORDSEE
MECKLENBURG-VORPOMMERN
Borkum
Wilhelmshaven
HAMBURG
Warnow
Emden
Bremerhaven
★ Schwerin
Neubrandenburg
Oldenburg
BREMEN
Lüneburg
Elde
Müritzsee
Weser
Elbe
BRANDENBURG
LÜNEBURGER HEIDE
POLEN
NIEDERSACHSEN
Celle
Aller
Wolfsburg
Mittellandkanal
★ Hannover
Braunschweig
Osnabrück
Salzgitter
Hameln
Hildesheim
Leine
SACHSEN-ANHALT
NIEDERLANDE
NORDRHEIN-WESTFALEN
Weser
Göttingen
50 km
50 mi
HESSEN · THÜRINGEN

Warm-up. To set the scene, have students look at the map and photos of Northern Germany and describe the geography of the region. Then ask them what they expect to find in a region bordering the sea: *Was findet man am Meer? Wie ist das Leben am Meer? Was macht man am Meer? Welche Berufe haben mit dem Meer zu tun?*

Background. Tell students that Northern Germany, like the rest of Germany, was divided for 40 years. Though differences arose and still exist between those who lived in West Germany and those who lived in East Germany (due to the different living conditions and experiences of residents of the two states during those years), studies following reunification showed that Germans in the northern states continued to identify and perceive themselves as *Norddeutsche*. Northern German identity is based on factors and conditions common to both Northeastern and Northwestern Germany.

Einführung

01-01 to 01-03

Read the *Sprachanalyse: Increasing vocabulary recognition* in SAM 01-02, which demonstrates strategies for deciphering unknown vocabulary in the *Einführung*. As you read the *Lesetexte* in this chapter, do the *Sprachanalyse* activities in the SAM 01-03, 01-06, 01-09, 01-13, 01-15, 01-19 to practice language recognition skills.

Sprachanalyse. Each chapter SAM features a *Sprachanalyse* topic that focuses students' attention on deciphering meanings in context. Each topic is introduced by having students more closely examine language features of the chapter *Einführung*. Then at least two *Lesetexte* in each chapter have an accompanying *Sprachanalyse* activity in the SAM. In the

coastal sandy heathland

Sprachanalyse in the *Kapitel 1* SAM, students develop strategies for recognizing unknown vocabulary and improving their reading comprehension. Students learn to read more quickly and efficiently and acquire techniques for expanding their vocabulary knowledge.

flatfish varieties

Note for *Einführung*. Draw students' attention to the names of the states that comprise northern Germany. Two of them are so-called *Bindestrichländer*. Have students surmise why these and four other states in Germany have hyphenated names.

Answers to *Fragen zum Text*. **1.** Dänemark, die Nordsee und die Ostsee; **2.** Sie sind durch Flüsse – die Weser und die Elbe – mit dem Meer verbunden. **3.** Es hat milde Winter und verhältnismäßig kühle Sommer und es regnet zu allen Jahreszeiten. **4.** Waren, Ideen, Menschen; **5.** Wegen der frischen Luft und der herrlichen Strände.

Norddeutschland umfasst fünf Bundesländer: Niedersachsen, Schleswig-Holstein, Mecklenburg-Vorpommern sowie die zwei Stadtstaaten Hamburg und Bremen. Die Landschaft und das Leben Norddeutschlands sind vor allem durch die Nähe zum Meer geprägt. Neben Dänemark bilden die Nordsee und die Ostsee den Großteil der nördlichen Grenze Deutschlands. 5 Die drei größeren Bundesländer haben Meeresküsten. Der Stadtstaat Hamburg, die nördlichste Millionenstadt Deutschlands, ist durch die Elbe, den zweitlängsten Fluss Deutschlands, mit dem Meer verbunden. Die Weser, ein schiffbarer Fluss, verbindet den Stadtstaat Bremen mit der Nordsee. Natürlich gibt es innerhalb dieses Gebiets viele regionale Unterschiede. Dennoch 10 besteht hier gegenüber dem übrigen Deutschland ein gewisses Zusammengehörigkeitsgefühl, denn diese Länder sind durch viele Gemeinsamkeiten der Geografie, der Geschichte, der Kultur und nicht zuletzt der Sprache miteinander verbunden.

Der maritime Einfluss sorgt im Norden für relativ milde Winter und 15 verhältnismäßig kühle Sommer und bringt zu allen Jahreszeiten Regen. Das Land ist flach bis leicht hügelig mit Moor- und Marschgebieten, Geest° und Heide. Die Wasserwege Norddeutschlands waren und sind wichtige Handels- und Transportrouten und daher auch Zentren des internationalen Austausches von Waren und Ideen sowie der Ein- und Auswanderung von 20 Menschen. Viele Arbeitsplätze sind direkt oder indirekt von der See und der Küste abhängig. Die frische Luft und herrliche Strände machen die Küstengebiete zu beliebten Urlaubsorten der Deutschen. Es verwundert nicht, dass unter den norddeutschen kulinarischen Spezialitäten viele Fischgerichte zu finden sind, wie etwa die Aalsuppe, die Krabbensuppe oder diverse 25 Schollenvarianten°.

Fragen zum Text

1. Was bildet die Grenze Deutschlands im Norden?
2. Bremen and Hamburg sind beide im Inland. Wie kommt es, dass sie als maritime Städte bekannt sind?
3. Wie ist das Wetter in Norddeutschland?
4. Was wurde und wird immer noch über die Wasserwege Norddeutschlands transportiert?
5. Warum machen Deutsche gerne Urlaub im Norden?

Auf der Insel Darß in der Ostsee

DIALEKTTIPP: Plattdeutsch

Hören Sie ein Beispiel dieses Dialekts.

Die verschiedenen Dialekte, die im Norden gesprochen werden, wie etwa Ostfriesisch, Westfälisch und Mecklenburg-Vorpommersch sind meist Varianten des Niederdeutschen, auch Plattdeutsch genannt. Das Niederdeutsche teilt historische Wurzeln mit dem Englischen, deshalb lässt sich oft eine Nähe zum Englischen erkennen.

Im Mittelalter war Niederdeutsch die Sprache der norddeutschen Kaufleute. Es war die Sprache des Rechts, des Handels und der Diplomatie für die gesamte nordeuropäische Region rund um Ost- und Nordsee. Heute verstehen rund 10 Millionen Menschen im Norden eine Variante des Plattdeutschen und bis zu drei Millionen können nach eigenen Angaben sehr gut Plattdeutsch „snacken". Mehr oder weniger routinemäßig wird diese Sprache in der täglichen Kommunikation benutzt. Der Norddeutsche Rundfunk° sendet sogar plattdeutsche Regionalnachrichten und produziert Sendungen für Radio und Fernsehen.

Dialekttipp. The *Dialekttipp* feature introduces students to regional varieties of German. After they read the *Dialekttipp: Plattdeutsch*, ask students: *Was ist Plattdeutsch (oder Niederdeutsch)? Welche Rolle spielte Niederdeutsch im europäischen Mittelalter? Welche Rolle spielt es heute?* After they complete the activities, write these dialect phrases on the board: *dat kolt Wedder, er sniedet dat Rindfleesch in Stücke* and ask students what they mean (*das kalte Wetter, er schneidet das Rindfleisch in Stücke*).

North German Broadcasting Corporation

Zum Dialekt

1 Wie sagt man das? Wählen Sie die richtigen Erklärungen der Unterschiede zwischen Plattdeutsch und Hochdeutsch.

Hochdeutsch → Plattdeutsch

_f_ 1.	Schwein, schlafen → Swein, slapen	a. *a, au → o*
_d_ 2.	Apfel → Appel	b. *ch → k*
_b_ 3.	ich, kochen, Milch → ik, koken, Melk	c. *ei → ee*
_g_ 4.	Tag → Dag	d. *f, pf → p*
_e_ 5.	was, Salz, sitzen → wat, Salt, sitten	e. *s, z, tz → t*
_c_ 6.	mein, nein → mien, nee	f. *sch → s*
_a_ 7.	Haar, Augen, da → Hoor, Ogen, dor	g. *t → d*

2 Im Gespräch. Wie sagt man das auf Plattdeutsch?

Hochdeutsch	**Plattdeutsch**
_c_ 1. Ich spreche Plattdeutsch.	a. To foot, geiht good.
_d_ 2. Stille Wasser gründen tief.	b. Kiek mol wedder in!
_b_ 3. Schau mal wieder rein!	c. Ik snack Platt.
_a_ 4. Zu Fuß geht's gut.	d. Dat stille Water hett den deepsten Grund.

Note. The *Grammatik* located in the second portion of the chapter is best introduced in tandem with the reading and listening selections. In addition to providing opportunities to review and practice structures, most grammar activities reinforce or expand on the themes found in the chapter *Lesetexte* and *Hörtexte*.

Lese- und Hörtexte

Lesetext 1

Introduction to *Lesetext 1.*
Have students look at Hamburg on the chapter opener map and describe its location. Then ask students what they have learned about Hamburg from the introduction to the text: *Warum heißt Hamburg Deutschlands „Tor zur Welt"? Warum heißt die Stadt „Venedig des Nordens"? Wo ist Venedig? Was ist das Besondere an Venedig? Was hat Hamburg, das mit Venedig vergleichbar ist? Wie alt ist die Stadt? Wo liegt die Stadt?* Then direct their attention to the type of text they are about to encounter: *Was kann man von einer Tour-Broschüre erwarten? Für wen ist sie geschrieben? Was für Informationen enthält ein solcher Text?*

Siehe **Kulturtipps:**
Hansestadt

Stadtrundfahrt Hamburg – HafenCity und Hansestadt (Tour-Broschüre)

Hamburg nennt sich Deutschlands „Tor zur Welt" – und mit Recht, denn der Hafen dieser Metropole gehört zu den größten und wichtigsten Europas. Aber nicht nur der Hafen an der Elbe, sondern auch die Alster und die etlichen Wasserstraßen mit den fast 2.700 Brücken, die sie überqueren, machen Hamburg zum „Venedig des Nordens". Die Stadt wurde erst im 8. Jahrhundert wegen ihrer geografisch günstigen Lage mit Zugang zur Nordsee und kurzem Landweg zur Ostsee gegründet. Heute ist die Hansestadt Hamburg einer von drei Stadtstaaten und mit etwa 1,8 Millionen Einwohnern die zweitgrößte Stadt Deutschlands. In der folgenden Tour-Broschüre bekommen Sie einen weiteren Eindruck von der Großstadt im Norden.

St. Pauli Landungsbrücken im Hamburger Hafen

Vor dem Lesen

Machen Sie mit einem Partner eine Liste der Sehenswürdigkeiten, die man vielleicht in einer Hafenstadt finden kann.

Beim Lesen

Suchen Sie die folgenden Informationen aus der Touristen-Broschüre heraus:

Beginn der Tour (wo und wann?): Hauptbahnhof, 10.00 Uhr und 14.00 Uhr

Ende der Tour (wo und wann?): Hauptbahnhof, 12.00 Uhr und 16.00 Uhr

Transportmittel: Doppeldeckerbus

Preis: €17,50 für Erwachsene, €8,75 für Kinder. Wenn eine Hafenrundfahrt auch noch erwünscht ist, kostet die Fahrt €7,00 mehr und dauert 60 Minuten länger.

Note for *Lesetexte* and *Hörtexte*. The reading and listening comprehension activities in this book are designed to help students develop skills that will transfer to authentic reading and listening beyond *Mittendrin*. Students engage in global reading and listening before focusing in on the details of texts. Remind students that they do not need to know every word to extract meaning from a text. Encourage them to look up only the unknown words that seem critical to understanding important points in the texts.

Stadtrundfahrt Hamburg

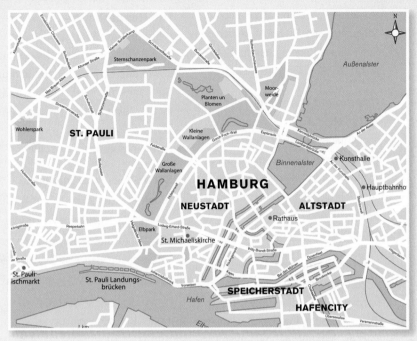

Hafenstadt, Handelsstadt, Medienstadt, Kulturstadt. Sie werden erstaunt sein, wie abwechslungsreich und spannend Deutschlands zweitgrößte Metropole ist. Nehmen Sie an einer Stadtrundfahrt im vollklimatisierten Doppeldeckerbus teil und lernen Sie die Stadt näher kennen.

Dauer: 120 Minuten

MOIN, MOIN!*

Genauer Tourenverlauf

START: Der Hauptbahnhof · Die größte deutsche Bahnhofshalle wurde Anfang des 20. Jahrhunderts im Neorenaissancestil gebaut. Mit bis zu
5 450.000 Reisenden und Besuchern pro Tag ist er der meistfrequentierte Personenbahnhof Deutschlands.

Die Kunsthalle · Das größte Kunstmuseum Deutschlands mit
10 Sammlungen aus dem Mittelalter bis ins 20. Jahrhundert. Man findet hier bedeutende Werke von Rembrandt, Rubens, Munch, Klee und Nolde sowie manchen anderen
15 europäischen Künstlern.

*Siehe **Kulturtipps**: Moin!

Die Außenalster · Heute ist der See, den Einheimische einfach Alster nennen, das beliebteste Ausflugsziel und Freizeitrevier
20 der Hamburger – Fahrrad fahren, segeln, joggen oder auf den Wiesen faulenzen: Alles mitten in der Stadt. Der Alstersee entstand im Mittelalter durch das Aufstauen eines Flusses,
25 um mit dessen Wasserkraft eine Wassermühle anzutreiben.

Die Binnenalster · Um diesen kleineren, zentral gelegenen Teil des Alstersees befinden sich Hamburgs
30 beste Hotels, nobelste Einkaufspassagen und der Jungfernstieg,

Hamburgs beliebteste Einkaufs- und Promenadenstraße.

Die Altstadt mit Rathaus · Das
35 historische Zentrum der Stadt, das Rathaus, ist bis heute Sitz der Hamburger Landesregierung. Den Marktplatz direkt vor dem Rathaus nutzt

Blick auf das Rathaus und die Alster

man für viele Veranstaltungen wie
40 Massenversammlungen, Demonstrationen oder Musikprogramme.

Die St. Michaeliskirche · 1649–1661 erbaut; dieses Wahrzeichen[a] der Stadt ist eine der schönsten Barock-
45 kirchen in Norddeutschland. Von der 82 Meter hohen Aussichtsplattform des Turmes her hat man einen herrlichen Blick über Stadt und Hafen.

Containerschiff im Hamburger Hafen

Der Hamburger Hafen · Dieser
50 größte Hafen Deutschlands und zweitgrößte Containerhafen Europas erstreckt sich über ein Achtel der Stadtfläche. Er ist das Tor zu den Märkten in Nord-, Mittel- und Osteuropa und
55 Brücke zwischen dem europäischen Kontinent und Übersee, besonders Asien. Hier wurden 2009 über sieben Millionen Container umgeschlagen[b] und jeder zehnte Arbeitsplatz der
60 Hansestadt hängt an dem Hafen.

Die Speicherstadt · Im 19. Jahrhundert lagerte[c] hier im größten Warenhauskomplex der Welt alles, was

aus fernen Ländern nach Hamburg
65 gebracht wurde. Bis heute werden die Speicher als Lagerstätten für Kaffee, Kakao, Tee und Gewürze genutzt.

Das Projekt HafenCity · Seit 1997 wird im ehemaligen Hafengebiet ein
70 neues, futuristisches Stadtgebiet hochgezogen. Hier soll über eine Bauzeit von 20 Jahren hinweg eine Mischung aus Wohngebäuden und Arbeitsplätzen, Kultur und Gastronomie, Freizeit-
75 angeboten und Parks entstehen.

Die Elbchaussee · An der berühmten Elbchaussee, die ihrem Namen nach die Elbe entlang zieht, reihen sich die großen Parks und Villen der
80 reichen Hamburger aneinander.

Der Elbstrand · An sonnigen Tagen ist der Strand an der Elbe sehr belebt. Das Ufer lädt zum Sonnen, Beobachten von vorbeifahrenden Schiffen, und zum
85 Picknick oder Spaziergang ein.

Der St. Pauli Fischmarkt · Auf dem Markt, den es bereits seit 1703 gibt, sind heute nicht nur Forelle, Steinbutt und Krabben zu kaufen.
90 Der Markt bietet fast alles, was das Herz begehrt: Neben frischem Fisch, Blumen, Bananen, lebenden Kleintieren, Schmuck und zahlreichen Souvenirs gibt es auch ein
95 Live-Musik-Programm. Allerdings findet dieser Markt nur sonntags statt und beginnt dann schon um 5.00 Uhr.

Die Reeperbahn · Die weltberühmte Vergnügungsmeile, wo viele
100 Nachtclubs, Bars und Diskotheke sowie das Operettenhaus und die Spielbank zu finden sind. Wir sagen Ihnen gleich, wo sie hingehen können und welche Fehler Sie
105 unbedingt vermeiden sollten.

STOPP: St. Pauli Landungsbrücken · Der größte Teil des Schiffsverkehrs der Elbe, sowie viele Boote für Hafenrundfahrten legen hier an.
110 Im 19. Jahrhundert verließen Millionen Menschen hier die „Alte Welt", um in der Ferne – insbesondere in Amerika – ihr Glück zu suchen.

Nach Wunsch: Übergang zur
115 **Hafenrundfahrt** (Dauer ca. 60 Minuten)
Zurück zum Hauptbahnhof.

Tour-Preise

Erwachsene	EUR 17,50
Kinder	EUR 8,75
(bis 14 Jahre)	

Hafenrundfahrt-Kombi
Zuschlag: EUR 7,00

Abfahrt täglich vom Hauptbahnhof um 10.00 Uhr und 14.00 Uhr.

Hamburg Rundfahrt GmbH
Wandsbeckerstr. 75
22179 Hamburg
Tel: 040-641 47 11
Fax: 040-641 63 32

---

[a]landmark [b]unloaded and reloaded [c]was stored

Kulturtipps. The *Kulturtipps*, which follow each reading or listening text, clarify cultural references that appear in the texts, while at the same time expanding students' knowledge of German-speaking culture. Students learn that understanding cultural contexts is often just as essential to comprehension as understanding the language used in a text.

Kulturtipps

Hansestadt

Der Beiname „Hansestadt" zeigt, dass Hamburg einmal Mitglied der mittelalterlichen Hanse war. Die Hanse war eine locker verbundene Gruppe nordeuropäischer Städte, die die gemeinsamen Handelsinteressen der Mitglieder vertreten sollte. Vom 13. bis zum 15. Jahrhundert dominierte sie den nordeuropäischen Handel. Hamburg ist eine von neun deutschen Städten, die den Beinamen Hansestadt noch heute tragen. Über die Hanse werden Sie in *Lesetext 2* noch mehr lernen.

Moin!

„Moin" oder verdoppelt „Moin, Moin!" ist ein plattdeutscher Gruß, der in ganz Norddeutschland verbreitet ist. Es kann zu jeder Tageszeit gebraucht werden, aber die Verwendung ist regional unterschiedlich. „Moin" heißt im Plattdeutschen „schön" oder „gut" und die Begrüßung ist eine Ableitung von „'n mooien Dag wünsch ik di", was im Hochdeutschen heißt: „Einen schönen Tag wünsche ich dir".

 Neue Vokabeln

Nomen

der Bahnhof, ¨e *train station*
die Brücke, -n *bridge*
die Dauer *duration, length of time*
der Fluss, ¨e *river*
das Gebiet, -e *region*
der Hafen, ¨ *harbor*
das Jahrhundert, -e *century*
das Land, ¨er *land; country; countryside*
das Mittelalter *Middle Ages*
die Regierung, -en *government*
der See, -n *lake*
die See, -n *sea*
der Sitz, -e *seat*

der Strand, ¨e *beach*
das Tor, -e *gate, gateway*
der Turm, ¨e *steeple, tower*
das Ufer, - *shore, bank*
die Veranstaltung, -en *event, activity*

Verben

nutzen *to use*
segeln *to sail*
statt·finden, fand statt, stattgefunden *to take place*
teil·nehmen (nimmt teil), nahm teil, teilgenommen *to participate, take part*

teil·nehmen an (+ *dat.*) *to take part in (something)*

Adjektive und Adverbien

beliebt *popular, favored*
berühmt *famous*
fern *distant*
ursprünglich *original(ly)*

Ausdrücke

ca. = circa *approximately*
z. B. = zum Beispiel *for example*

1-1 Textarbeit: Was passt? Bilden Sie aus den Satzteilen ganze Sätze.

_c_ 1. Das Rathaus

_f_ 2. Der Hamburger Hafen

_d_ 3. Die Kunsthalle

_b_ 4. Die St. Michaeliskirche

_e_ 5. Die Außenalster

_a_ 6. Der St. Pauli Fischmarkt

_h_ 7. Die Reeperbahn

_g_ 8. Die Elbchaussee

a. fängt sonntags um 5.00 Uhr früh an.

b. ermöglicht einen Blick auf die Stadt und den Hafen.

c. ist heute Sitz der hamburgischen Landesregierung.

d. beherbergt Meisterwerke aus vielen Jahrhunderten.

e. bietet Fußwege, Radwege und Wassersportmöglichkeiten.

f. bietet jedem zehnten Hamburger einen Arbeitsplatz.

g. ist eine noble Wohnstraße, die parallel zur Elbe verläuft.

h. ist eine Straße, wo man das berühmte Hamburger Nachtleben erleben kann.

1-2 Textarbeit: Das Beste aus Hamburg. Hamburg ist eine Stadt der Superlative. Welche Superlative nimmt die Stadt in Anspruch?

Beispiel: Hamburg hat den meistfrequentierten Personenbahnhof in Deutschland.

Possible answers for 1-2. Hamburg ist Deutschlands zweitgrößte Stadt, hat die größte Bahnhofshalle, das größte Kunstmuseum und den größten Hafen Deutschlands und den zweitgrößten Containerhafen Europas.

Teaching suggestion for 1-3. Remind students that they may have to alter vocabulary words to make them fit the syntax of a sentence, e.g. verb conjugations, adjective endings, singular vs. plural forms of nouns, etc.

1-3 Vokabelarbeit. Ergänzen Sie die Sätze mit Wörtern aus den *Neuen Vokabeln.* Achten Sie dabei auch auf die Wortform.

1. Die Alster ist ein künstlicher ___See___.

2. Die Elbe ist ein ___Fluss___.

3. Die ___Dauer___ einer Hafenrundfahrt ist 60 Minuten.

4. Der Fischmarkt ___findet___ bei jedem Wetter ___statt___.

5. Um über den Alsterkanal zu kommen, fährt man über eine ___Brücke___.

6. Die ___Regierung___ der Stadt hat ihren Sitz im Rathaus.

7. Hamburg existiert schon seit dem 9. ___Jahrhundert___.

8. Der Komponist Johannes Brahms und der Bildhauer, Grafiker und Schriftsteller Ernst Barlach waren ___berühmte___ Hamburger Künstlerpersönlichkeiten.

9. Der ___Turm___ der Michaeliskirche ist 132 m hoch.

10. Ein Zug nach Bremen verlässt den ___Bahnhof___ alle 30 Minuten.

Activity 1-4. Remind students that although activity questions are in the *Sie*-form, students should be using the *du*-form to address one another.

1-4 Zur Diskussion. Besprechen Sie die Fragen.

1. Möchten Sie diese Tour machen, wenn Sie Hamburg einmal besuchen? Warum (nicht)?

2. Welche Sehenswürdigkeit in Hamburg interessiert Sie am meisten? Welche am wenigsten? Warum?

1-5 Was machen wir in Hamburg? Sie sind mit Ihren Freunden für einen Tag in Hamburg. Besprechen Sie, welche drei Sehenswürdigkeiten Sie besuchen wollen und warum Sie diese Orte interessieren.

1-6 Ein Besuch in Hamburg. Nach der spannenden Stadtrundfahrt durch Hamburg möchten Sie einige Sehenswürdigkeiten der Stadt besser kennenlernen. Schreiben Sie eine E-Mail an Ihre deutsche Großmutter und erzählen Sie ihr, was Sie morgen alles in Hamburg machen werden. Beginnen Sie vielleicht so:

Liebe Oma,

moin, moin aus Hamburg! …

…

Dein(e) [Ihr Name]

1-7 Touristenbroschüre. Machen Sie eine Broschüre für Ihre Stadt oder für eine andere Stadt, die eine Tour für Besucher bietet. Geben Sie den Anfangs- und Endpunkt der Tour an und mindestens fünf Sehenswürdigkeiten mit einigen Informationen dazu, damit man aus der Broschüre selbst schon etwas über die Stadt herausfinden kann.

Introduction to Lesetext 2. Ask students what the introduction reveals: *Was bedeutet der Name „Hansestadt"? Wann existierte die Hanse? Wo existierte die Hanse?*

Lesetext 2

Die Hanse (Geschichte)

Achtzehn deutsche Städte tragen heute noch den Namen „Hanse-stadt" –z. B. Hansestadt Hamburg, Hansestadt Lübeck, Hansestadt Bremen und Hansestadt Stralsund. Dieser Beiname zeugt von der historischen Rolle dieser Städte als wichtige Handelszentren wäh-rend des Mittelalters in Europa. Nicht nur diese, sondern auch viele andere deutsche sowie nord-

Hansestadt Rostock

europäische Städte gehörten zum Wirtschaftsbund der Hanse. In diesem kurzen historischen Überblick erfahren Sie etwas über die Geschichte dieses Städtebundes.

Vor dem Lesen

Beschreiben Sie den Prozess des Handels. Welche Bedingungen müssen existieren, um Handel zu treiben? Was macht man, wenn man Handel treibt?

Activities 1-4 and 1-5. The *Zur Diskussion* activities present discussion topics that are a natural extension of the themes in the text. These topics can be discussed in pairs or small groups. Apart from *Zur Diskussion* activities, post-reading speaking activities include task-based and role-playing exer-cises. These involve, for instance, negotiating a compromise, finding a solution to a problem, planning an event or activity, or creating a dialog. There are also sometimes separate discussion topics for which more guidance is provided to enable and encourage students to explore topics in more depth. Wrap up collaborative work by having pairs or groups report back to the class or to each other or by having students take notes and hand in their results.

Alternative for 1-5. Have students use the information in the brochure to each write down 5 questions about Hamburg (e.g., *Warum heißt Hamburg „Venedig des Nordens"? Wo kann man in Hamburg Werke von Rembrandt und Rubens sehen?*). Then have students work in groups of 3, ask-ing each other their questions. For each question a student answers correctly, s/he earns a point. The student with the most points wins.

Activity 1-6. Clarify to students that females should use the clos-ing *Deine* and males *Dein* before their first names. Point out that this familiar form is used when writing to relatives and friends.

Suggestion for 1-7. Have students use the Hamburg tour brochure as a model. If time allows, have students present their brochures to the class, or if you have an area in the classroom or a department bulletin board, display their work publicly.

Answers for *Beim Lesen*.
1. Lübeck, Stralsund, Rostock, Wismar, Hamburg, Bremen, Kiel. Alle haben Zugang zur See.
2. Kaufleute, Handelsrechte und -privilegien, Seehandel, Luxuswaren, Nahrungsmittel, Rohstoffe, Fertigprodukte, Tuchwaren, Metallwaren, Handelsroute, Handelsmacht, wirtschaftliche Interessen.

01-07 to 01-09

Siehe **Kulturtipps**: Heiliges Römisches Reich

Beim Lesen

1. Im Text findet man die Namen einiger Hansestädte. Finden Sie die Namen dieser Städte und suchen Sie sie dann auf einer Landkarte. Was haben diese Städte gemeinsam?

2. Suchen Sie alle Wörter im Text heraus, die mit dem Thema Handel und Geschäft zu tun haben.

Die Hanse

Die Hanse war zunächst ein Zusammenschluss norddeutscher Kaufleute, der zwischen Mitte des 12. Jahrhunderts bis Mitte des 17. Jahrhunderts, zur Zeit des Heiligen Römischen Reiches existierte. Im Laufe der Zeit wurde dieser Bund der Kaufleute zu einem Bund der Städte. Die Hanse bot ihren Mitgliedern Schutz gegen Piraterie und Straßenräuberei, sicherte sich Handelsrechte und -privilegien gegenüber fremden Machthabern, und entschied Konflikte zwischen ihren Mitgliedern durch eine eigene Gerichtsbarkeit°.   5

legal jurisdiction

Der hanseatische Handel war überwiegend Seehandel. Die hanseatischen Kaufleute versorgten West- und Mitteleuropa mit Luxuswaren, Nahrungsmitteln und Rohstoffen aus dem nördlichen und östlichen Europa.   10
Hierzu gehörten z. B. Pelze°, Wachs, Getreide°, Fisch, Erze°, Flachs, Hanf, Holz und Holzbauprodukte sowie Pech, Teer und Pottasche°. Und sie brachten in diese Länder die gewerblichen° Fertigprodukte des Westens und Südens wie Tuchwaren, Metallwaren, hier insbesondere Waffen, und Gewürze.   15

furs / grain / ores
pitch, tar, and potash
commercial

extent, scope

Die wichtigste Handelsroute verlief entlang der Linie Nowgorod – Reval – Lübeck – Hamburg – London. Zum Kern der Hanse zählten 70 vorwiegend deutsche Städte, weitere 130 Städte gehörten in einem lockeren Rahmen dazu. Lübeck war 500 Jahre   20
lang Königin der Hanse. Andere norddeutsche Städte wie Stralsund, Rostock, Wismar, Hamburg, Bremen und Kiel spielten ebenfalls eine wichtige Rolle. Kein anderer   25
Städtebund des Mittelalters erreichte den Einfluss oder den Umfang° der Hanse. Die Hansestädte lagen in einem Gebiet das heute sieben europäische Staaten umfasst und ihr wirtschaftlicher Einfluss erstreckte sich auf ein Gebiet, das heute 20 europäische Staaten einschließt. Jahrhundertelang galt die   30
niederdeutsche Sprache der Hansekaufleute als Weltsprache, denn im ganzen Mittel- und Nordeuropa hat man hauptsächlich auf Plattdeutsch verhandelt und kommuniziert.

Im Laufe der Zeit entwickelte sich die Handelsmacht der Hanse auch zu einer politischen Macht. In ihrer Blütezeit, die sie gegen Ende   35 des 14. Jahrhunderts erlebte, war die Hanse so mächtig, dass sie zur Durchsetzung° ihrer wirtschaftlichen Interessen Wirtschaftsblockaden gegen Königreiche und Fürstentümer verhängte und manchmal sogar Kriege führte. In den folgenden Jahrhunderten ging der Einfluss der Hanse jedoch langsam zurück, da diese Bündnis- und Handelsform auf die Dauer nicht mit der Wirtschaftspolitik der frühneuzeitlichen Staaten konkurrieren konnte. Einerseits nahmen die einzelnen Länder den Handel selbst in die Hand und behinderten dadurch den hanseatischen Handel, andererseits erwiesen sich die kombinierten Waren- und Geldgeschäfte der großen Handelshäuser (Fugger, Welser) als viel ertragreicher° und flexibler als der Hansehandel, der hauptsächlich auf Waren beschränkt war.

    Diese Entwicklung ließ sich nicht aufhalten und führte dazu, dass der Einfluss der Hanse zurückging. Die aufkommenden nationalen und territorialen Wirtschaften ließen einer überregionalen Handelsgemeinschaft wie der Hanse keinen Raum mehr. Im Jahre 1669 fand in Lübeck das letzte Treffen der historischen Hansestädte statt.

assertion (line 36)

more lucrative (line 45)

Kulturtipps

Heiliges Römisches Reich (800–1806)

Während der Zeit der Hanse gab es in Mitteleuropa Hunderte von kleineren Territorien und freien Städten, an deren Spitze der Kaiser des Heiligen Römischen Reiches deutscher Nation stand. In diesem Reich war die politische Macht jedoch stark dezentralisiert und der Kaiser war schwach. Die Hanse wurde deshalb wichtig zum Schutz der Handelsinteressen ihrer Mitgliedstädte.

Neue Vokabeln

Nomen

der Einfluss, ⸚e *influence*

die Entwicklung, -en *development*

das Fürstentum, ⸚er *principality*

der Handel *trade*

die Macht, ⸚e *power*

das Mitglied, -er *member*

das Reich, -e *empire, realm, kingdom*

die Ware, -n *product, (pl.) goods*

die Wirtschaft, -en *economy*

Verben

bieten, bot, geboten *to offer*

entscheiden, entschied, entschieden *to decide*

sich entwickeln *to develop*

erleben *to experience*

erreichen *to reach*

führen (zu) *to lead (to)*

gelten (gilt), galt, gegolten *to be valid, apply*

gelten als *to be considered to be (something)*

konkurrieren (um) *to compete (for)*

zurück·gehen, ging zurück, ist zurückgegangen *to recede, decline*

Adjektive und Adverbien

andererseits *on the other hand*

einerseits *on the one hand*

hauptsächlich *mainly*

mächtig *powerful, influential*

wichtig *important*

Ausdrücke

auf die Dauer *in the long run*

1-8 Textarbeit: Die Hanse in Zahlen. Ergänzen Sie die Sätze mit Zahlen und Daten aus *Lesetext 2.*

1. Die Hanse existierte von der <u>Mitte des 12. Jahrhunderts</u> bis zur <u>Mitte des 17. Jahrhunderts</u>.

2. Zum Kern der Hanse gehörten _____<u>70</u>_____ Städte, obwohl noch _____<u>130</u>_____ andere Städte locker mit ihr verbunden waren.

3. _____<u>500</u>_____ Jahre lang war Lübeck Hauptstadt der Hanse.

4. Die Blütezeit der Hanse kam <u>Ende des 14. Jahrhunderts</u>.

5. Das offizielle Ende, der letzte Hansetag, fand _____<u>1669</u>_____ statt.

1-9 Textarbeit: Fragen zum Inhalt. Beantworten Sie die Fragen zum Text.

1. Was war die Hanse?
2. Wie sah Deutschland geografisch und politisch aus, als die Hanse entstand?
3. Welche Vorteile hatten ihre Mitglieder?
4. Welche Produkte importierten die Kaufleute der Hanse aus Nord- und Osteuropa?
5. Welche Produkte exportierten die hanseatischen Kaufleute nach Norden und Osten?
6. Wie viele Städte gehörten zur Hanse?
7. Warum galt das Niederdeutsche als Weltsprache?
8. Wie konnte die Hanse die Politik beeinflussen?
9. Welche Gruppen übernahmen allmählich eine führende Rolle in der Wirtschaft, als der Einfluss der Hanse zurückging?

Answers for 1-9.
1. ein Zusammenschluss norddeutscher Kaufleute/Städte; **2.** Deutschland bestand aus vielen kleinen Territorien und die Macht des Kaisers war schwach. **3.** Schutz gegen Piraterie und Straßenräuberei, Handelsrechte und -privilegien gegenüber fremden Machthabern, eine eigene Gerichtsbarkeit; **4.** Pelze, Wachs, Getreide, Fisch, Erze, Flachs, Hanf, Holz und Holzbauprodukte; **5.** Tuchwaren, Gewürze und Metallwaren wie Waffen; **6.** insgesamt etwa 200; **7.** Possible answer: Niederdeutsch war die Sprache des hanseatischen Handels im ganzen Mittel- und Nordeuropa. **8.** durch Wirtschaftsblockaden und Kriege; **9.** die frühneuzeitlichen Staaten und die großen Handelshäuser, die Warengeschäfte und Geldgeschäfte kombinierten.

1-10 Vokabelarbeit. Ergänzen Sie die Sätze mit Wörtern aus den *Neuen Vokabeln.* Achten Sie dabei auch auf die Wortform.

1. Viele nordeuropäische Städte waren _____<u>Mitglieder</u>_____ der Hanse.

2. Die Hanse _____<u>entwickelte</u>_____ _____<u>sich</u>_____ im Laufe der Jahrhunderte zu einer einflussreichen Institution in der Wirtschaft Nordeuropas.

3. Im Handel mit Hering konnte Amsterdam mit Lübeck nicht _____<u>konkurrieren</u>_____.

4. Hanseatische Kaufleute brachten _____<u>hauptsächlich</u>_____ Luxuswaren, Nahrungsmittel und Rohstoffe nach West- und Mitteleuropa.

5. Die Hanse hatte nicht nur in der Wirtschaft viel _____<u>Macht/Einfluss</u>_____, sondern auch in der Politik.

6. Die Entwicklung von Nationalstaaten und die Verbindung von Waren- und Geldgeschäften durch große Handelshäuser _____<u>führten</u>_____ allmählich zu dem Fall der Hanse.

7. Als die Macht der Hanse einen Höhepunkt erreichte, _____<u>erlebte</u>_____ auch die niederdeutsche Sprache eine Blütezeit.

8. Mit dem Verfall der Hanse _____<u>ging</u>_____ allerdings auch die Bedeutung der Sprache _____<u>zurück</u>_____.

1-11 Zur Diskussion. Besprechen Sie die Fragen.

1. Was meinen Sie: Warum entwickelte sich ein Handelsbund gerade im Norden Europas?

2. Deutschland ist heute weltweit eine der führenden Exportnationen. Welche Produkte exportiert Deutschland? Besitzen Sie selbst einige deutsche Exportprodukte?

3. Könnte man die Hanse als historischen Vorläufer der Europäischen Union beschreiben? Warum (nicht)?

1-12 Eine globale Wirtschaft. Der internationale Handel hat eine sehr lange Geschichte. Heute spricht man von der Globalisierung der Wirtschaft. Halten Sie die Globalisierung für positiv oder negativ? Denken Sie dabei an Ihr Land, andere Länder, Arbeiter und Konsumenten. Machen Sie zwei Listen: (1) Vorteile der Globalisierung und (2) Nachteile der Globalisierung.

1-13 Beruf: Kaufmann im Mittelalter. Sie leben in einer mittelalterlichen Hansestadt und sind Kaufmann bzw. Frau eines Kaufmanns. Entwerfen Sie eine Persönlichkeit für diese Person. Wie heißen Sie? Wo wohnen Sie? Was für Waren verkaufen Sie bzw. verkauft Ihr Mann? Wer gehört zu Ihrer Familie? Wie sieht Ihr Alltag aus? Stellen Sie sich in einer kurzen Biografie vor.

1-14 Recherche. Was möchten Sie noch über die Hanse wissen? Schreiben Sie fünf Fragen auf. Suchen Sie dann im Internet nach den Antworten auf Ihre Fragen und schreiben Sie sie auf. Dann stellen Sie die neuen Informationen Ihrer Klasse vor.

Hörtext 1

Urlaubsziel Mecklenburg-Vorpommern (Werbung)

Mecklenburg-Vorpommern ist mit nur 1,65 Millionen Einwohnern das am dünnsten besiedelte° deutsche Bundesland. In diesem eher ländlich geprägten Gebiet, wo die Landwirtschaft und der Schiffbau zu den bedeutendsten Wirtschaftsbranchen zählen, kann von Industrialisierung kaum die Rede sein. Die große Stärke des Landes ist eine andere – es ist die Natur selbst. Um die Schönheiten der Landschaft zu erkunden und zu genießen, kommen seit der Wiedervereinigung Deutschlands jährlich immer mehr Besucher, sodass der Tourismus hier schneller wächst als in allen anderen deutschen Bundesländern. Seit 1990 hat man mehrere Milliarden Euro in die touristische Infrastruktur investiert. Heute ist der Fremdenverkehr die größte Einnahmequelle des Landes.

In der folgenden Tourismuswerbung erfahren Sie, warum Mecklenburg-Vorpommern eines der beliebtesten Urlaubsländer in der Bundesrepublik ist.

Background info for *Hörtext 1*. The Baltic Sea coast was a popular vacation destination around the turn of the 20th century for those who could afford it. In GDR times, people were also drawn to the coast but it lacked the infrastructure—reliable transportation networks, sufficient sleeping accommodations and guest services, easy access to attractions and facilities—it possesses today. Since the later decades of the 20th century, foreign destinations, especially warmer coastal regions such as Spain, Italy, and Greece have been favored vacation destinations for (West) Germans. Recently, however, more Germans are choosing destinations within Germany. Experts attribute this new trend to a combination of factors: economic uncertainty, the accessibility of "new" destinations in formerly communist East Germany due to both reunification and a vastly improved infrastructure, and a renewed sense of national pride since Germany hosted the FIFA World Cup in 2006.

Variation for 1-12. You could also have half of the class discuss advantages while the other half discusses disadvantages of globalization. Then have them come together and compare notes.

Teaching suggestion for 1-13. Have students complete activity 1-13 as homework. Then, in class, have them each assume the role of the person they have created and stage a *Kaffeestunde* where students mingle, ask personal questions, and get to know each other. As a follow-up, ask them to report who was the most fascinating/unusual/memorable person they met and to explain why they chose this person.

Note for 1-14. Relevant web addresses for Internet research activities can be found in *MyGermanLab* and on the Companion Website.

Transcripts for all Hörtexte are located in the Instructor's Resource Manual.

Introduction to *Hörtext 1*. Have students find Mecklenburg-Vorpommern on the map of Germany on the inside front cover

populated

and describe its location. Ask: *Was bildet die Grenzen dieses Landes?* Then ask students what they learned from the introduction: *Ist das Bundesland eher städtisch oder ländlich? Hat es relativ viele oder relativ wenige Einwohner? Gibt es viel oder wenig Industrie? Nennen Sie drei wichtige Wirtschaftsbranchen dieses Bundeslandes. Seit wann kommen immer mehr Besucher nach Mecklenburg-Vorpommern?* Ask further why the year 1990 marks the beginning of this trend. *Was bringt Urlauber vor allem hierher?*

Vor dem Hören

Machen Sie eine Liste von dem, was man in so einem Land wie Mecklenburg-Vorpommern wohl unternehmen kann.

Beim Hören

Urlaubsziel Mecklenburg-Vorpommern

01-10

Answers for Beim Hören.
Mecklenburg-Vorpommern, Elbe, Müritzsee, Ostsee, Ostseeküste, Rügen, Usedom, Hiddensee, Mecklenburgische Seenplatte, Mecklenburgische Schweiz, Rostock, Wismar, Stralsund, Greifwald

Während der Werbung hören Sie folgende Vokabeln:

Kreidefelsen   *chalk cliffs*
Kaiserbäder   *seaside spas built during the Kaiserzeit, the Second Reich (1871–1918)*
leicht hügelig   *with gently rolling hills*
Bäume   *trees*
Backstein   *brick*
Binnenhäfen   *inland harbors*

Markieren Sie auf der Karte die Orte, die in der Werbung genannt werden.

Kulturtipps

Mecklenburgische Seenplatte

Die Mecklenburgische Seenplatte, im südlichen Mecklenburg ungefähr zwischen Rostock und Berlin gelegen, ist ein faszinierendes Labyrinth von über 1.000 Seen, Flüssen und Kanälen. Es ist eines der größten zusammenhängenden Seengebiete Europas. Herzstück der Landschaft ist Deutschlands zweitgrößter See, die Müritz.

Fachwerkhäuser

„Fachwerk" bezieht sich auf eine spezifische Bauweise, bei der die Wände eines Hauses ein hölzernes Gerüst (*wooden frame*) besitzen und die Räume dazwischen mit einem anderen Material ausgefüllt sind. Bei Fachwerkhäusern ist das hölzerne Gerüst meist zu sehen. Diese Bauweise war in Deutschland und anderen Teilen Nordeuropas vom Mittelalter bis ins 19. Jahrhundert vorherrschend.

Fachwerkhaus in Lüneburg

1-15 Textarbeit: Was macht man wo? Ordnen Sie jede Aktivität dem richtigen Ort in Mecklenburg-Vorpommern zu.

Kreidefelsen auf der Insel Rügen

_____f_____ Rügen

_____e_____ Usedom

_____e_____ Hiddensee

_____i_____ Mecklenburgische Seenplatte

_a, c, h_ Mecklenburgische Schweiz

_____b, g_____ Städte

a. die Gegend beim Wandern oder Radfahren erkunden
b. Fachwerkhäuser und Häfen besichtigen
c. Schlösser und Herrenhäuser sehen
d. in Kaiserbädern schwimmen
e. kein Auto fahren
f. Kreidefelsen sehen
g. Spuren der Hanse erblicken
h. 1.200 Jahre alte Bäume entdecken
i. die Landschaft per Boot, Yacht oder Kanu erkunden

 1-16 Textarbeit: Richtig oder falsch? Wenn eine Aussage falsch ist, korrigieren und ergänzen Sie sie mit Informationen aus dem Hörtext.

1. Mecklenburg-Vorpommern hat weniger Einwohner pro Quadratkilometer als jedes andere Bundesland.
2. Es gibt 25 Inseln und Halbinseln an der Küste des Landes.
3. Auf den Flüssen und Seen der Mecklenburgischen Seenplatte sind Boote aller Art verboten.
4. In der Mecklenburgischen Schweiz findet man hohe Berge.
5. In der Mecklenburgischen Schweiz findet man noch ursprüngliche Natur.
6. Das Bundesland hat fast 450 Nationalparks.
7. In den Städten sieht man Patrizierhäuser, Backsteinkirchen und Fachwerkhäuser.
8. Es kommen jährlich sechs Millionen Besucher nach Mecklenburg-Vorpommern.

Answers for 1-16. 1. R; **2.** R; **3.** F – In der Mecklenburgischen Seenplatte sind Boote erlaubt. **4.** F – In der Mecklenburgischen Schweiz findet man leichte Hügel. **5.** R; **6.** F – Das Bundesland hat fast 450 Naturschutz- und Landschutzgebiete und drei Nationalparks. **7.** R; **8.** R

 1-17 Zur Diskussion. Besprechen Sie die Fragen.

1. Was in Mecklenburg-Vorpommern interessiert Sie persönlich? Warum?
2. Warum, meinen Sie, wächst der Tourismus hier schneller als in allen anderen deutschen Bundesländern?
3. Wo machen Sie am liebsten Urlaub? Was machen Sie dort?
4. Würden Sie gerne in so einem Land wie Mecklenburg-Vorpommern leben? Warum (nicht)?

 1-18 Ein Ort in Mecklenburg-Vorpommern. Recherchieren Sie im Internet über einen Ort, der sich in Mecklenburg-Vorpommern befindet, z. B. eine Insel, einen Nationalpark, eine Stadt. Machen Sie sich beim Surfen Notizen. Dann bereiten Sie einen kurzen Vortrag vor, in dem Sie diesen Ort vorstellen.

Note for 1-18. Relevant web addresses for Internet research activities can be found in *MyGermanLab* and on the Companion Website.

Alternative for 1-18. For a less structured activity, have students look for information about Mecklenburg-Vorpommern and write down five interesting facts that they discover while surfing. Then have them share with the class what they found.

Lesetext 3

Die Zukunft der Windkraft liegt im Meer (Artikel)

trailblazer

ambitious

Introduction to *Lesetext 3.*
Introduce the text by asking students about the environmentally conscious behaviors of Germans, which students may be familiar with from their first year of German instruction and/or from news reports. *Was tun die Deutschen für die*

mainland

Umwelt? They might mention: *Müll sortieren/Recycling, Mehrweg-flaschen benutzen, öffentliche Transportmittel benutzen, Fahrrad fahren, zu Fuß gehen, eigene Tüten zum Einkaufen mitnehmen, kleinere Kühlschränke/Autos/Wohnungen haben,* etc. Some students may also know that Germany has taken a leading role internationally in promoting the reduction of greenhouse gas emissions. Ask students what the title of this article tells them about the article topic: *Schauen Sie sich den Titel des Artikels an. Was kann der Titel bedeuten?* Then ask what they have learned from the introduction to the article: *Um wie viel will Deutschland bis 2030 den CO_2-Ausstoß senken?* (The EU has committed to a 30 percent reduction by 2030. Germany achieved a 20 percent reduction by 2008.) *Wie will das Land dieses Ziel erreichen? Wo standen im Jahre 2010 die meisten deutschen Windanlagen? Wo will man Windmühlen in Zukunft noch bauen?*

Die Deutschen gelten weltweit als Vorreiter° für umweltbewusstes Verhalten. International spielt Deutschland in der Klima- und Energiepolitik eine führende Rolle und will ehrgeizige° Ziele in der Reduktion von Kohlendioxid-Emissionen realisieren. So will Deutschland den Ausstoß des klimaschädlichen Kohlendioxids bis 2020 um 40 Prozent gegenüber dem Basisjahr 1990 senken. Um dieses Ziel zu erreichen, ist neben der Steigerung der Energieeffizienz und der Energieeinsparung auch der verstärkte Ausbau der erneuerbaren Energien notwendig. Hierbei wird die Windenergie auf lange Sicht eine zentrale Rolle spielen.

Weltweit ist Deutschland gleichauf mit China und hinter den USA die Nummer zwei bei der Nutzung von Windenergie. 2010 besaß Deutschland rund 21.000 Windanlagen, die meisten davon allerdings auf dem Festland°. Der Ausbau der Windenergie auf dem Meer – also besonders im Norden Deutschlands – ist der nächste wichtige Schritt, um die Klimaschutzziele zu erreichen.

Dieser Artikel bespricht den jetzigen Stand der Windenergie in Deutschland und deren Aussichten für die Zukunft.

Vor dem Lesen

Besprechen Sie das Thema Windenergie. Ist der Wind eine wichtige Energiequelle, wo Sie wohnen? Kann der Wind eine wichtige Energiequelle werden? Was sind die Vorteile und Nachteile von Wind als Energiequelle?

Beim Lesen

1. Suchen Sie die Synonyme im Text für die Wörter „Windturbine", „Windparks" und „Windenergie".

2. Im Artikel erfährt man etwas über den jetzigen Stand der Windenergie in Deutschland sowie über die weiteren Pläne. Suchen Sie die folgenden Jahreszahlen im Text und in der Einführung zum Text, und erzählen Sie, was schon passiert ist und was noch passieren soll.

2010
2015
2020
2030

Windturbinen des Alpha Ventus

Answers for Beim Lesen.
1. Windturbine: Windkraftanlage, Anlage, Rad, Windrad, Propellerturm, Windmühle. Windparks: Offshore-Windparks, Windfelder, Offshore-Flächen. Mühlen, Anlagen, Türme. Windenergie: Windkraft. **2.** 2010 gab es rund 21.000 Windkraftanlagen. Das Offshore-Pilotprojekt Alpha Ventus ging ans Netz. Bis 2015 erhalten Windparks eine hohe Subvention pro Kilowattstunde. Bis 2020 will die Bundesregierung den Ausstoß von CO_2 um 40 Prozent reduzieren. Bis 2030 sollen Offshore-Anlagen 15 Prozent des deutschen Stroms produzieren.

Die Zukunft der Windkraft liegt im Meer

Die Energieversorgung in Deutschland steht vor einer entscheidenden Wende. Schon bald werden vor den Küsten große Offshore-Windparks entstehen, mit denen gewaltige Mengen Ökostrom produziert werden sollen.

In der Nordsee, 45 km nördlich der Insel Borkum, in 30 Meter tiefem Wasser steht Alpha Ventus, der erste deutsche Offshore-Windpark. So weit draußen und in so tiefem Wasser gibt es weltweit keinen anderen Offshore-Windpark. Die zwölf gigantischen Windkraftanlagen stehen auf einer Fläche von ungefähr 500 Fußballfeldern. Jede Anlage ist mit rund 150 Metern so hoch wie der Kölner Dom. An dem 250 Millionen Euro teuren Projekt haben sich die Energiekonzerne RWE, E.ON und Vattenfall° beteiligt. 50 Millionen davon kam als Subvention von der Bundesregierung. Im Vollbetrieb soll Alpha Ventus Strom für 50.000 Haushalte liefern – doppelt so viel wie ein Windpark an Land.

Das Pilotprojekt, das im April 2010 ans Netz ging, dient zu Testzwecken für künftige deutsche Offshore-Windfelder. Schon zehn Jahre lang hatten die Bundesregierung und Energiekonzerne riesige Windparks auf dem Meer geplant. Trotzdem drehte sich lange kein Offshore-Rad. Die wesentlichen Ursachen: Technische Schwierigkeiten, Probleme mit dem Netzanschluss°, fehlendes Geld. Offshore-Anlagen kosten dreimal so viel wie vergleichbare an Land. Um das sensible Wattenmeer zu schützen und Proteste der Tourismusbranche gegen große Propellertürme an den Stränden gar nicht erst aufkommen zu lassen, hatte die Bundesregierung bestimmt, dass die Offshore-Flächen äußerst weit vor der Küste – mindestens 30 Kilometer – liegen müssen. Aber hier hat man Windböen von 160 Kilometern pro Stunde, Wellen von 15 Metern Höhe und Schäden durch die salzhaltige Luft, die viele Unternehmen lange abschreckten. Erst die Novelle° des Erneuerbare-Energien-Gesetzes brachte mehr Sicherheit für die Investoren. Der Bundestag beschloss, die Vergütung° der Kilowattstunde von 9 auf 15 Cent zu erhöhen, wenn ein Windpark bis Ende 2015 ans Netz geht. Das ist etwa das Dreifache des derzeitigen Börsenpreises° und auch deutlich mehr, als Windkraftbetreiber pro Kilowattstunde an Land erhalten.

Die Zukunft ist offshore

Bislang sind in der Nord- und der Ostsee 29 deutsche Offshore-Projekte mit knapp 1.900 Windrädern genehmigt° worden. Mehr als 60 weitere Parks sind in Planung. Das Ziel der Bundesregierung ist klar definiert: Bis 2030 sollen Offshore-Windparks 15 Prozent des deutschen Strombedarfs decken. Windenergie werde „die zentrale Rolle im Energiemix der Zukunft spielen", so Bundesumweltminister Norbert Röttgen.

Für Kritiker der Offshore-Strategie zeigen diese großzügigen Subventionen, dass der Strom aus dem Meer nicht konkurrenzfähig werden kann.

Note: Students will learn more about the *Kölner Dom*, and the *Ruhrgebiet*, mentioned later in the article, in *Kapitel 9*.

RWE, E.ON und Vattenfall names of three large energy companies

power supply line

Siehe **Kulturtipps:** Wattenmeer

amendment

payment

Siehe **Kulturtipps:** Erneuerbare-Energien-Gesetz

stock exchange price

approved

cables	Neben den hohen Kosten der Förderung sind außerdem neue Leitungen° und
smart grids	intelligente Stromnetze° nötig, um den Strom zu transportieren. Denn der
Ruhr district of Nordrhein-Westfalen	Strom wird nicht nur in Norddeutschland genutzt, sondern auch im Ruhrgebiet° und in Süddeutschland, wo die größten Verbrauchszentren

40

Neben den hohen Kosten der Förderung sind außerdem neue Leitungen° und intelligente Stromnetze° nötig, um den Strom zu transportieren. Denn der Strom wird nicht nur in Norddeutschland genutzt, sondern auch im Ruhrgebiet° und in Süddeutschland, wo die größten Verbrauchszentren liegen. Unklar ist zudem, welche Auswirkungen der Betrieb von Windkraftanlagen auf die Umwelt hat. Kritik gab es anfangs nach Schäden im Wattenmeer bei der Legung des tonnenschweren Seekabels. Naturschützer wie der regionale Wattenrat in Ostfriesland[1] fürchten, dass die gigantischen Windmühlen den Vogelzügen im Weg stehen, mit dem Lärm ihrer Propeller Schweinswale° verscheuchen° und die Verteilung der Fischarten verändern. Allerdings haben sich die meisten Umweltorganisationen mittlerweile mit den möglichen Auswirkungen abgefunden°. „Wenn wir die Risiken der verschiedenen Technologien abwägen, ist die Windkraft als eine erneuerbare Energie klar den Atom- oder Kohlekraftwerken vorzuziehen", heißt es beispielsweise bei Greenpeace.

Bei den Großkonzernen wie E.ON, RWE oder Vattenfall glaubt man, die „steile° und teure Lernkurve" – so E.ON-Chef Frank Mastiaux – nach den Erfahrungen mit dem Forschungswindpark Alpha Ventus abgeschlossen zu haben. „Es war wie beim ersten Flug zum Mond", erklärt RWE-Manager Fritz Vahrenholt. „Fast alles musste neu konzipiert und entwickelt werden." Jetzt, da man die notwendige Technik vor sich liegen hat, sollte der Aufbau der Windparks auf Meer zur Routine werden. Von nun an werden Windparks einer nach dem anderen zügig° gebaut, versprechen die Konzernchefs.

Margin glosses:
- cables *(Leitungen)*
- smart grids *(Stromnetze)*
- Ruhr district of Nordrhein-Westfalen
- harbor porpoises / scare away
- resigned themselves to
- steep
- rapidly

Line numbers: 40, 45, 50, 55, 60

---

[1]Der Wattenrat in Ostfriesland ist ein Zusammenschluss von Naturschützern aus der Küstenregion Ostfrieslands, das der nordwestlichste Teil Niedersachsens ist.

Kulturtipps

Wattenmeer

Das Wattenmeer ist eine einzigartige Landschaft der Nordseeküste, die sich von den Niederlanden bis Dänemark erstreckt. Dieses Gebiet zwischen Land und Meer besteht aus Schlick (*mud flats*), Salzwiesen (*salt flats*) und Sanddünen und bildet einen Lebensraum für viele Tier- und Pflanzenarten. Es entsteht durch den Wechsel von Ebbe und Flut (*low and high tide*) und wird täglich

Der vom Wattenmeer umgebene Westerhever Leuchtturm

zweimal überflutet. Wegen der empfindlichen Ökologie dieser Landschaft steht der Hauptteil dieses 500 km langen Küstengebiets heute unter Naturschutz.

Erneuerbare-Energien-Gesetz (EEG)

Das EEG, das erst im Jahre 2000 verabschiedet und dann 2004 und 2009 erweitert wurde, gibt Stromproduzenten finanzielle Subventionen, um Strom aus Wind- oder Wasserkraft, Solar- oder Bioenergie sowie Erdwärme ins Stromnetz einzuspeisen. Das funktioniert über langjährig garantierte Fixpreise. Es ist das weltweit wohl erfolgreichste Gesetz zur Förderung regenerativer Energien und wird mittlerweile von über 45 Ländern kopiert.

Neue Vokabeln

Nomen

die Auswirkung, -en *effect*
die Bundesregierung *federal government*
die Erfahrung, -en *experience*
die erneuerbare Energie, die erneuerbaren Energien *renewable energy*
die Förderung, -en *support*
die Insel, -n *island*
die Küste, -n *coast*
die Luft *air*

das Meer, -e *sea*
das Risiko, Risiken *pl.* *risk*
der Schaden, ⸚ *damage*
die Schwierigkeit, -en *difficulty*
der Strom *electricity*
die Umwelt *environment*
die Zukunft *future*

Verben

sich beteiligen (an + *dat.*) *to participate (in)*
entstehen, entstand, ist entstanden *to arise, originate*

fürchten *to fear*
schützen *to protect*

Adjektive und Adverbien

allerdings *though, indeed, certainly*
deutlich *clearly*
künftig *future, in the future*
notwendig *necessary*
ungefähr *approximately*
verschieden *different, various*
wesentlich *essential, fundamental*

1-19 Textarbeit: Windenergie in Zahlen. Ergänzen Sie die Sätze mit den richtigen Zahlen aus dem Text.

1. 2010 gab es ___21.000___ Windkraftanlagen in Deutschland.

2. Der Windpark Alpha Ventus steht ___45___ Kilometer von der Küste entfernt.

3. Alpha Ventus besteht aus ___12___ Windrädern.

4. Das Projekt Alpha Ventus hat ___250 Millionen___ Euro gekostet.

5. Künftige Offshore-Windparks sollten nicht weniger als ___30___ Kilometer von der Küste entfernt gebaut werden.

6. ___29___ Offshore-Projekte wurden schon genehmigt und über ___60___ weitere Windparks im Meer stehen noch in der Planungsphase.

7. Bis 2030 soll Deutschland ___15___ Prozent seines Stroms durch Offshore-Windkraft produzieren.

Teaching suggestion for 1-20. Have students work in groups and divide up the questions so that each group member is responsible for finding the answers to at least two questions. Then have the group members share and discuss their answers with one another. Or divide the class up and have half work on the odd-numbered questions, the other half on the even-numbered questions. Then have students find a partner or pair who worked on the opposite questions and discuss their answers. Or assign the questions as homework, and then in class have students compare answers or discuss them together as a class.

Answers for 1-20. 1. Alpha Ventus ist Deutschlands erster Offshore-Windpark. Kein anderer Offshore-Park steht so weit von der Küste entfernt. Damit war er ein großes Testprojekt. **2.** Die Bundesregierung gibt Subventionen und erlässt Gesetze, die den Bau der Offshore-Windparks nicht nur fördern, sondern auch regeln. **3.** Es gab technische Schwierigkeiten, Probleme mit dem Netzanschluss und nicht genug Geld für so ein teures Projekt. **4.** Um das Wattenmeer zu schützen und sich gegen Proteste aus der Tourismusbranche zu wehren. **5.** Subventionen zeigen, dass Offshore-Windenergie nicht konkurrenzfähig ist. Deutschland braucht neue Stromnetze, um den Strom zu transportieren. Es ist noch unsicher, welche Auswirkungen die Windparks auf die Umwelt haben. **6.** Die Windkraft verursacht wohl weniger Schäden für die Umwelt als etwa Energie aus Atom- oder Kohlekraftwerken. **7.** Es war das erste solche Projekt seiner Art und man musste viele Dinge zum ersten Mal versuchen. **8.** Sie haben aus ihren Erfahrungen mit dem Bau von Alpha Ventus viel gelernt.

Follow-up for 1-20 (5). Ask students why they think the tourist industry would protest the building of wind farms near the coast.

1-20 Textarbeit: Fragen zum Inhalt. Beantworten Sie die Fragen in Bezug auf den Artikel.

1. Was ist das Besondere an Alpha Ventus?

2. Welche Rolle spielt die Bundesregierung in der Entwicklung und dem Ausbau der Windenergie?

3. Warum hat die Realisierung eines Offshore-Windparks über zehn Jahre gedauert?

4. Warum hat die Bundesregierung es verboten, Windanlagen direkt an den Nord- und Ostseeküsten zu bauen?

5. Welche Kritik gibt es an der Offshore-Windenergie?

6. Warum haben die meisten Umweltorganisationen die Windenergie akzeptiert?

7. Über den Bau von Alpha Ventus sagte der RWE-Manager Fritz Vahrenholt: „Es war wie beim ersten Flug zum Mond." Erklären Sie, was er damit meinte.

8. Warum meinen die Chefs der Energiekonzerne, dass der Bau von weiteren Windparks jetzt schneller vorangeht als bei Alpha Ventus?

1-21 Vokabelarbeit. Ergänzen Sie die Sätze mit Wörtern aus den *Neuen Vokabeln*. Achten Sie dabei auch auf die Wortform.

1. Die _____Küste_____ ist das Gebiet, wo sich Land und Meer treffen.

2. Sonne, Wind und Wasser sind alle Quellen der _____erneuerbaren_____ _____Energie_____ .

3. Diese Energiequellen will man in Zukunft immer mehr nutzen, um _____Strom_____ zu produzieren.

4. Jetzt und auch künftig _____entstehen_____ viele neue Windparks in der Nord- und der Ostsee.

5. Der Bau von Alpha Ventus sollte 180 Millionen Euro kosten. Er hat aber _____wesentlich/deutlich_____ mehr gekostet: 250 Millionen Euro.

6. Um die Natur zu _____schützen_____, hat die Bundesregierung den Bau von Windrädern direkt an der Küste verboten.

7. Man weiß nicht genau, welche _____Auswirkungen_____ solche Windparks auf die Umwelt haben.

8. Mit dem Pilotprojekt Alpha Ventus will man _____Erfahrung/Erfahrungen_____ für den Bau von weiteren Windparks sammeln.

 ## 1-22 Zur Diskussion. Besprechen Sie die Fragen.

1. Warum stehen die meisten Windräder im Norden Deutschlands?

2. Welche Unterschiede gibt es zwischen Land-Anlagen und Offshore-Windrädern?

3. Halten Sie Offshore-Windparks für eine gute Idee? Warum (nicht)? Was halten Sie von Windparks an Land?

4. Welche Schwierigkeiten könnten künftig bei dem Bau bzw. dem Betrieb von Offshore-Windparks entstehen?

5. Soll man auch in Nordamerika mehr Windenergie benutzen? Was spricht dafür? Was spricht dagegen?

6. Soll die Regierung durch Gesetze und Subventionen den Bau von Windparks und andere Arten der erneuerbaren Energie fördern? Was passiert wohl, wenn die Regierung da nichts tut?

1-23 Im Jahre 2050. Die Themen Energiekrise und Klimawandel sind heutzutage sehr aktuell. Was meinen Sie: Was wird man wohl bis 2050 erreicht haben? Welche Energiequellen und Technologien wird es geben? Wie sieht die Umwelt aus? Wie werden die Menschen leben? Sprechen Sie darüber und machen Sie sich ein Bild vom Leben im Jahre 2050.

1-24 Offshore aktuell. Recherchieren Sie im Internet weiter über das Thema Offshore-Windparks in Deutschland. Beantworten Sie die Fragen.

1. Hat man seit dem Bau von Alpha Ventus noch weitere Offshore-Windparks gebaut? Wenn ja, wie heißen sie und wo liegen sie? Wie weit sind sie von der Küste entfernt?

2. Wie viele weitere Offshore-Windparks wurden genehmigt? Wie viele weitere Parks sind noch in der Planungsphase? Gibt es mehr Parks in der Ostsee oder in der Nordsee?

1-25 Stellungnahme zur Windenergie. Es gibt Argumente für und gegen die Windenergie. Die *Ostfriesen-Zeitung* bittet um Leserbriefe zu diesem aktuellen Thema. Schreiben Sie einen Leserbrief, in dem Sie Stellung zum Thema Offshore-Windenergie nehmen und Ihre Meinung begründen.

Beginnen Sie mit dem Satz: *Meiner Meinung nach ist die Windenergie vom Meer (k)eine gute Idee, denn …*

Lesetext 4

„Meine Kindheit" von Thomas Mann (Autobiografie)

Thomas Mann (1875–1955) ist einer der bekanntesten deutschen Autoren des 20. Jahrhunderts. Seine norddeutsche Heimat prägte seine Werke. Lübeck, das er seine „Vaterstadt an der Ostsee" nannte, war nicht nur Handlungsort seines Romans *Buddenbrooks*, für den Mann 1929 den Nobelpreis für Literatur erhielt. Immer wieder bekannte er sich öffentlich zu seiner Heimatstadt und dem Einfluss, den sie auf sein ganzes Schreiben hatte. „[…] [E]s ist mein Ehrgeiz, nachzuweisen, daß[2] Lübeck als Stadt, als Stadtbild und Stadtcharakter, als Landschaft, Sprache, Architektur durchaus

Thomas Mann (1955)

---

[2]Vor der Rechtschreibreform (1996) hat man *dass* mit *ß* geschrieben (*daß*). Sprachliche Konventionen ändern sich mit der Zeit. In *Mittendrin* wird regelmäßig die Rechtschreibung des ursprünglichen Textes benutzt.

Information for 1-22 (5). The U.S. plans to produce 20 percent of its electricity via wind energy by 2030. Canada plans to achieve the same goal by 2025. Germany plans to produce enough wind energy by 2030 to replace the power generated by its nuclear plants. Students will learn more about the German commitment to end dependence on nuclear energy in *Kapitel 9*.

Teaching suggestion for 1-23. Supply vocabulary for students as needed, e. g., *der Treibhauseffekt, die globale Erwärmung, die Umweltverschmutzung, fossile Brennstoffe (Erdgas, Erdöl, Kohle), erneuerbare Energiequellen (Solarenergie, Wasserkraft, Windkraft, Biogas), Atomkraft*.

Note for 1-24. Relevant web addresses for Internet research activities can be found in *MyGermanLab* and on the Companion Website.

Introduction to *Lesetext 4.* Direct students' attention to the genre: *Was hat man von einer Autobiografie zu erwarten?* Ask students if they have heard of Thomas Mann and what they know about him. Then ask students what the introduction reveals about the author and his text: *Wer ist Thomas Mann? Lebt er noch? Wo war seine Heimat? Welche Beziehung hatte Manns Heimatort zu seinem Werk?*

nicht nur in ‚Buddenbrooks', deren unverleugneten Hintergrund es bildet, seine Rolle spielt, sondern daß es von Anfang bis zu Ende in meiner ganzen Schriftstellerei zu finden ist, sie entscheidend bestimmt und beherrscht."[3]

Im folgenden Auszug aus seinen autobiografischen Schriften erzählt Mann von seiner Herkunft und Kindheit in Lübeck.

---

[3]Aus: „Lübeck als geistige Lebensform" in: Thomas Mann, *Gesammelte Werke in dreizehn Bänden*, Bd. 11 (Frankfurt: Fischer, 1974), S. 387–388.

Vor dem Lesen

Welche Informationen erwarten Sie in einem autografischen Bericht über die Kindheit? Schreiben Sie fünf Themen auf, die Sie mit der Kindheit verbinden.

Beim Lesen

Notieren Sie während des Lesens, welche von den Themen aufkommen, die Sie im *Vor dem Lesen* genannt haben.

01-14 to 01-15

Orthography. The spelling conventions used in this book follow the rules of the most current orthographical reform as recommended by Duden. Texts written prior to the current reform, however, follow the orthography current at the time of their publication.

„Meine Kindheit"

von Thomas Mann

Ich wurde geboren im Jahre 1875 in Lübeck als zweiter Sohn des Kaufmanns und Senators der Freien Stadt Johann Heinrich Mann und seiner Frau Julia da Silva-Bruhns. Während mein Vater Enkel und Urenkel Lübecker Bürger war, hatte meine Mutter 5 in Rio de Janeiro als Tochter eines deutschen Plantagenbesitzers und einer portugiesisch-kreolischen Brasilianerin das Licht der Welt erblickt und war mit sieben Jahren nach Deutschland verpflanzt worden. Sie war von ausgesprochen romanischem Typus, in 10 ihrer Jugend eine vielbewunderte Schönheit und außerordentlich musikalisch. […]

Buddenbrook-Haus in Lübeck

cherished

Meine Kindheit war gehegt° und glücklich. Wir fünf Geschwister, drei Knaben und zwei Schwestern, wuchsen auf in einem eleganten Stadthause, das mein Vater sich und den Seinigen erbaut hatte, und erfreuten 15 uns eines zweiten Heims in dem alten Familienhause bei der Marienkirche, das meine Großmutter väterlicherseits allein bewohnte und das heute als ‚Buddenbrook-Haus' einen Gegenstand der Fremdenneugier bildet. Die lichtesten Zeiten meiner Jugend aber waren die alljährlichen Sommerferienwochen in Travemünde mit ihren Badevormittagen am Strand der 20 Ostseebucht und ihren Nachmittagen zu Füßen des fast ebenso leidenschaftlich geliebten Kurmusiktempels gegenüber der Hotelanlage. […] [W]enn die anfangs unabsehbaren vier Wochen zu Ende waren und es nach Haus in den Alltag ging, so war meine Brust von dem weichlichen Schmerz der Selbstbemitleidung zerrissen°. 25

Siehe **Kulturtipps:** Marienkirche

Siehe **Kulturtipps:** Travemünde

torn

Ich verabscheute° die Schule und tat ihren Anforderungen bis ans Ende nicht Genüge°. Ich verachtete sie als Milieu, kritisierte die Manieren ihrer Machthaber und befand mich früh in einer Art literarischer Opposition gegen ihren Geist, ihre Disziplin, ihre Abrichtungsmethoden. […] Es mag sein, daß der humanistische Lehrgang meinen geistigen Bedürfnissen angemessener 30 gewesen wäre. Zum Kaufmann bestimmt – ursprünglich wohl zum Erben der Firma –, besuchte ich die Realgymnasialklassen des Katharineums […]."

[…] Mein Vater starb an einer Blutvergiftung in verhältnismäßig jungen Jahren, als ich fünfzehn zählte. Er war dank seiner Intelligenz und seiner formalen Überlegenheit in der Stadt ein höchst angesehener, populärer und ein- 35 flußreicher Mann gewesen, hatte aber an dem Gang seiner Privatgeschäfte seit Jahren schon nicht mehr Freude gehabt, und nach einer Beerdigung°, die an Ehrenpomp und Teilnahme alles überbot, was seit langem in dieser Art gesehen worden war, liquidierte die mehr als hundertjährige Getreidefirma. […]

Wenig später verließ meine Mutter mit den jüngeren Geschwistern die 40 Stadt, um sich im Süden Deutschlands, in München, niederzulassen°. Nach notdürftigem Abschluß meiner Schulstudien folgte ich ihr nach […].

detested

tat ... nicht Genüge *ultimately didn't satisfy its demands*

Siehe **Kulturtipps**: Gymnasium

burial

to settle down

Kulturtipps

Marienkirche

Die Marienkirche im Lübecker Stadtzentrum wurde Anfang des 14. Jahrhunderts gebaut. Diese gotische Backsteinkirche diente als Vorbild für etwa 70 andere Kirchen im gesamten Ostseeraum. 1942 brannte St. Marien bei einem alliierten Bombenangriff fast völlig aus, sie wurde aber nach dem Krieg wieder aufgebaut und restauriert. Die heruntergestürzten Glocken hat man dabei auf dem Boden des Südturms als Mahnmal (*memorial*) liegen lassen.

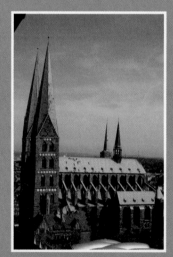
St. Marien zu Lübeck

Travemünde

Travemünde ist ein 20 km vom Zentrum entfernter Stadtteil Lübecks, der am Wasser, wo der Fluss Trave in die Ostsee mündet, liegt. Der Ort ist ein bekanntes Seebad und auch Deutschlands größter Fährhafen (*ferry port*) für den Verkehr mit Skandinavien.

Gymnasium

Das Gymnasium ist heute eine von drei Sekundarschulen im deutschen Schulsystem. Thomas Mann erwähnt das „humanistische Gymnasium", in dem die klassischen Sprachen Latein und Griechisch unterrichtet werden, und das „Realgymnasium" (heute ein „Mathematisch-naturwissenschaftliches Gymnasium" genannt), dessen Kurrikulum sich auf Mathematik und die Naturwissenschaften konzentriert.

Nomen

der Abschluss, ⁻e *conclusion,*
  completion; school degree

der Enkel, -/die Enkelin,
  -nen *grandson/granddaughter*

der Erbe, -n/die Erbin, -nen
  heir/heiress

die Heimat, -en *hometown,*
  homeland

die Jugend *youth*

der Kaufmann, Kaufleute (*pl.*)/
  die Kauffrau, -en *businessman,*
  merchant/businesswoman

die Welt, -en *world*

Verben

auf·wachsen (wächst auf), wuchs
  auf, ist aufgewachsen *to grow up*

prägen *to mold, shape*

sterben (stirbt), starb, ist
  gestorben *to die*

sterben an (+ *dat.*) *to die of*

verlassen (verlässt), verließ,
  verlassen *to leave (a person or*
  place)

Adjektive und Adverbien

außerordentlich *extraordinary;*
  extraordinarily

bekannt *known*

verhältnismäßig *relatively,*
  comparatively

Answers for 1-26. 1. 1875 in Lübeck; **2.** Sein Vater kam aus Lübeck, seine Mutter aus Rio de Janeiro. **3.** vier Geschwister, zwei Brüder und zwei Schwestern; **4.** das Haus seiner Großmutter; **5.** die Ferienwochen in Travemünde, jeden Sommer; **6.** am Strand der Ostseebucht; **7.** Er freute sich nicht und hatte Selbstmitleid. **8.** nein; **9.** Die Firma wurde liquidiert. **10.** nach München; **11.** Er musste seinen Schulabschluss machen. **12.** *Answers will vary.*

1-26 Textarbeit: Fragen zum Inhalt. Beantworten Sie die Fragen zum Text.

1. Wo und wann wurde Thomas Mann geboren?

2. Woher kamen seine Eltern?

3. Wie viele Geschwister hatte er?

4. Was ist „Buddenbrook"?

5. Wo verbrachte er die glücklichsten Zeiten seiner Jugend? Zu welcher Jahreszeit?

6. Wo konnte man ihn in dieser Zeit vormittags finden?

7. Wie fühlte er sich, wenn er nach den Ferien wieder nach Hause musste?

8. Ging er gern zur Schule?

9. Was passierte mit der Getreidefirma seines Vaters, nachdem der Vater gestorben war?

10. Wohin zog die Mutter mit der Familie nach dem Tod des Vaters?

11. Was musste er machen, bevor er zu der Familie hinziehen konnte?

12. Warum sollten die Leser von Thomas Manns Werken etwas über seine Heimat und Herkunft wissen?

1-27 Vokabelarbeit. Ergänzen Sie die Sätze mit Wörtern aus den *Neuen Vokabeln*. Achten Sie dabei auch auf die Wortform.

1. Thomas Mann _____wuchs_____ in Lübeck _____auf_____.

2. Sein Vater arbeitete als _____Kaufmann_____ in seinem eigenen Geschäft.

3. Nach dem Tod seines Vaters _____verließ_____ die Familie Mann Norddeutschland.

4. Allerdings sollte Manns norddeutsche Heimat seine Werke lebenslang _____prägen_____.

5. Nach seinem ____Abschluss____ von der Schule erschien Manns erste Novelle „Gefallen".

6. Thomas Mann ____starb____ 1955 im Alter von 80 Jahren.

7. Der ____Enkel____ von Thomas Mann heißt Frido Mann. Er ist 1940 geboren und ist ebenfalls Schriftsteller.

 1-28 Sprechen wir darüber! Besprechen Sie die Themen.

1. Beschreiben Sie Thomas Manns Familie.
2. Beschreiben Sie Ihre Familie.
3. Was machten Sie als Kind in den Sommerferien?
4. Gingen Sie damals gern zur Schule? Warum (nicht)?
5. Mussten Sie etwas machen, weil Ihre Eltern es wollten?

 1-29 Damals und heute. Thomas Mann wuchs gegen Ende des 19. Jahrhunderts auf, als das Leben ganz anders war als heute. Vergleichen Sie die Kindheit damals und die Kindheit heute. Was ist gleich geblieben und was ist heutzutage anders? Welche Vorteile und welche Nachteile hatte das Leben damals? das Leben heute? Wären Sie gerne um 1885 ein Kind gewesen? Warum (nicht)?

Note for 1-30. SAM 01-49 provides students with more guidance for this writing assignment.

 01-49 **1-30 Meine Kindheit.** Schreiben Sie einen kurzen Abriss Ihrer Kindheit, in dem Sie über Ihre Herkunft, Ihre Familie, Ihre Schulzeit, usw. erzählen. Wenn Sie einmal berühmt werden, können Ihre Fans dann diesen autobiografischen Abriss über Ihre Kindheit lesen! Benutzen Sie das Präteritum.

Transcripts for all Hörtexte are located in the Instructor's Resource Manual.

Hörtext 2

„Die Stadt" von Theodor Storm (Gedicht)

Introduction to Hörtext 2. Ask students what the introduction reveals about the poem: *Was sagt uns der Titel des Gedichts? Was für ein Text ist ein Gedicht? Welche Beziehung hat der Dichter zu dem Thema seines Gedichts? Wie beschreibt der Dichter diese Stadt?* After students have heard and read the poem, ask them to compare the images of the town in the poem to those included here from Storm's novella.

In der kleinen Stadt Husum an der Nordsee wurde der Dichter Theodor Storm 1817 geboren. In dieser Stadt lebte er die meisten Jahre seines Lebens und hier schrieb er auch viele der Novellen, die in seiner Heimat spielen. In einer dieser Novellen („In St. Jürgen") beschreibt er den Ort so: „Es ist nur ein schmuckloses Städtchen, meine Vaterstadt; sie liegt in einer baumlosen Küstenebene und ihre Häuser sind alt und finster. Dennoch habe ich sie immer für einen angenehmen Ort gehalten." Die Stadt würdigt er auch in dem folgenden Gedicht aus dem Jahre 1852.

Theodor Storm (1817–1888)

Vor dem Hören

Finden Sie die Stadt Husum auf der Landkarte zu Beginn des Kapitels. Beschreiben Sie ihre geografische Lage.

 ## Beim Hören

Hören Sie sich das Gedicht mindestens zweimal an. Ergänzen Sie die fehlenden Vokabeln im Gedicht.

„Die Stadt"

01-16

von Theodor Storm

Am grauen _____Strand_____, am grauen _____Meer_____

Und seitab liegt die Stadt;

roofs   Der _____Nebel_____ drückt die Dächer° schwer,

Und durch die _____Stille_____ braust das Meer

Eintönig um die Stadt.

rustles / flaps (its wings)   Es rauscht° kein _____Wald_____, es schlägt° im Mai

ohn' Unterlaß incessantly   Kein _____Vogel_____ ohn' Unterlaß°;

Die Wandergans mit hartem Schrei

Nur _____fliegt_____ in Herbstesnacht vorbei,

blows (in the wind)   Am Strande weht° das _____Gras_____.

Doch hängt mein ganzes _____Herz_____ an dir,

Du graue Stadt am Meer;

magic / forever   Der Jugend Zauber° für und für°

rests upon   Ruht lächelnd doch auf° dir, auf dir,

Du graue Stadt am Meer.

Answers for 1-31.
1. a b a a b; 2. Nebel hängt über der Stadt. 3. Man hört das Meer, den Schrei einer Wandergans. Man hört keinen Wald. 4. Er verbindet die Stadt mit der Zeit seiner Jugend.

1-31 Textarbeit: Fragen zum Inhalt. Beantworten Sie die Fragen zum Gedicht.

1. Wie ist das Reimschema jeder Strophe im Gedicht?
2. Warum ist die Stadt grau?
3. Welche Geräusche kann man hören? Welche kann man nicht hören?
4. Warum hängt das Herz des Sprechers an dieser Stadt?

 1-32 Zur Diskussion. Besprechen Sie die Fragen.

1. Mit welchen Adjektiven können Sie Ihre eigene Heimat beschreiben?
2. Bleibt man heutzutage in derselben Stadt, wo man geboren ist? Aus welchen Gründen zieht man aus der Heimat weg? Aus welchen Gründen bleibt man dort?
3. Würden Sie gern Ihr Leben lang in Ihrem Heimatort wohnen?

1-33 Meine Heimat. Finden Sie zwei Mitstudenten im Kurs, die aus verschiedenen Orten kommen. Dann vergleichen Sie Ihre Heimatorte. Zum Beispiel: Welcher Ort ist am größten? am kleinsten? Was kann man dort machen? Was für Leute wohnen dort? Was tun die Leute dort? Wohnt man gerne dort? Entscheiden Sie sich dann, wer die interessanteste Heimat hat und erklären Sie Ihre Wahl.

1-34 Ein Gedicht schreiben. Schreiben Sie ein Gedicht über Ihre Heimatstadt. Dann lesen Sie es in der Klasse laut vor.

Grammatik

 ## 1. Present tense (Präsens)

1-24 to 1-32 German has only one present tense. It is the equivalent of all three present tense forms in English.

$$\text{ich sage} \begin{cases} \textit{I say} \\ \textit{I am saying} \\ \textit{I do say} \end{cases}$$

The present tense is one of two verb tenses in German that consist of finite forms. This means that the verb itself is changed to provide all of the grammatical information necessary to understand its role in the sentence.

 ### Regular verbs (Regelmäßige Verben)

01-24 The present tense is usually formed by dropping the **-en** or **-n** from the infinitive and adding personal endings (**-e, -st, -t, -en, -t, -en**) to the remaining infinitive stem. Here are some examples of the present tense conjugation of regular verbs.

Infinitive	sagen	sitzen	finden	handeln
	to say	*to sit*	*to find*	*to deal, trade*
Infinitive stem	sag-	sitz-	find-	handel-
ich	sage	sitze	finde	handele
du	sagst	sitzt[a]	findest[b]	handelst
er, sie, es	sagt	sitzt	findet[b]	handelt
wir	sagen	sitzen	finden	handeln[c]
ihr	sagt	sitzt	findet[b]	handelt
Sie, sie	sagen	sitzen	finden	handeln[c]

[a] If the infinitive stem ends in **-s, -ß, -x,** or **-z,** the **-s** of the **du**-ending is omitted.
[b] If the infinitive stem ends in **-d** or **-t,** or if it ends in **-m** or **-n** preceded by a consonant other than **l** or **r** (e.g., **atmen, öffnen**), an **e** is inserted between the infinitive stem and the personal ending in the **du-, er/sie/es-,** and **ihr-** forms.
[c] If the infinitive ends in just **-n** rather than **-en,** then the personal ending of the **wir-** and **Sie/sie-** forms is simply **-n.**

Note for *Grammatik*. The *Grammatik* is best covered in tandem with the *Lesetexte* and *Hörtexte*. The activities in this section may be completed in class or assigned for homework.

Present tense. For examples of usage of the present tense, see *Lesetext 1.* All verb tenses will be reviewed again in *Kapitel 8.*

1-35 Präsens: Regelmäßige Verben. Geben Sie jeweils mindestens zwei andere Verben, die den vier Varianten der Konjugation in der Tabelle oben folgen.

Stem-changing verbs (Verben mit Stammwechsel)

01-25 to
01-27

Some strong verbs having **a, au,** or **e** in their infinitive stems undergo stem-vowel changes in the **du-** and **er/sie/es-**forms. There are four types of stem changes: **a** to **ä, au** to **äu, e** to **i,** and **e** to **ie.**

Infinitive	tragen	laufen	geben	sehen
	to wear	*to run*	*to give*	*to see*
Stem change	a → ä	au → äu	e → i	e → ie
ich	trage	laufe	gebe	sehe
du	**trägst**	**läufst**	**gibst**	**siehst**
er, sie, es	**trägt**	**läuft**	**gibt**	**sieht**
wir	tragen	laufen	geben	sehen
ihr	tragt	lauft	gebt	seht
Sie, sie	tragen	laufen	geben	sehen

- Like regular verbs, stem-changing verbs whose stems end in **-s** or **-ß** drop the **s** in the **du-**form **-st** personal ending: **wachsen → du wächst, lesen → du liest**
- Unlike regular verbs, stem-changing verbs whose stems end in **-d** or **-t** do not add an additional **e** before the **-st** or **-t** ending: **raten → du rätst, laden → er lädt, treten → er tritt**
- Some stem-changing verbs whose stems end in **-d** or **-t** do not add the **-et** ending in the **er/sie/es-**form at all: **halten → es hält, werden → es wird**

Note for 1-36. Tell students that only two verbs in German have the **au → äu** stem change: **laufen** and **saufen.**

1-36 Präsens: Verben mit Stammwechsel. Geben Sie jeweils mindestens zwei andere Verben, die den **a → ä, e → i,** und **e → ie** Varianten der Konjugation folgen.

Other irregular verbs (Andere unregelmäßige Verben)

01-25 to
01-27

A handful of very commonly used verbs have irregularities that deviate from the conjugation patterns described above. These irregularities are boldfaced in the chart below.

Infinitive	sein	haben	werden	wissen
	to be	*to have*	*to become*	*to know (a fact)*
ich	**bin**	habe	werde	**weiß**
du	**bist**	**hast**	**wirst**	**weißt**
er, sie, es	**ist**	**hat**	**wird**	**weiß**
wir	**sind**	haben	werden	wissen
ihr	**seid**	habt	werdet	wisst
Sie, sie	**sind**	haben	werden	wissen

1-37 Ein Besuch in Hamburg. Wählen Sie das passende Verb für jeden Satz, dann konjugieren Sie sie im Präsens.

besuchen	erzählen	halten	sein	verlassen

1. Heute _____besuchen_____ wir die Hansestadt Hamburg.
2. Hamburg _____ist_____ die zweitgrößte Stadt Deutschlands.
3. Der Tourbus _____verlässt_____ den Hauptbahnhof um 11.30 Uhr.
4. Die Tourleiterin _____erzählt_____ viel über Hamburgs Geschichte.
5. Der Bus _____hält_____ nur zweimal – an der Michaeliskirche und am Hafen.

dauern	empfehlen	haben	machen	sehen

6. Nach der Bustour _____mache_____ ich mit Freunden eine Hafenrundfahrt.
7. Die Hafentour _____dauert_____ ungefähr eine Stunde.
8. Vom Boot aus _____sieht_____ man, wie groß die Schiffe sind.
9. Hamburg _____hat_____ viele interessante Sehenswürdigkeiten.
10. Ich _____empfehle_____ euch allen, Hamburg mal besser kennenzulernen!

01-28

Separable prefix verbs (Verben mit trennbaren Präfixen)

In the present tense, separable prefixes are separated from the main verb and are placed at the end of the sentence.

auf·wachsen	Klaus **wächst** so schnell **auf**.	*Klaus is growing up so quickly.*
mit·nehmen	**Nehmen** Sie den Regenschirm **mit?**	*Are you taking the umbrella along?*
hin·legen	Sie **legt** den Bleistift **hin.**	*She is putting down the pencil.*

Separable prefix verbs are indicated in vocabulary lists, in the German-English Glossary in the back of the book, and in most dictionaries by a raised dot between the prefix and the verb infinitive.

1-38 In Hamburg unterwegs. Bilden Sie vollständige Sätze im Präsens.

1. der Bus / um 13.00 Uhr / am Hafen / ankommen
2. ein Tourboot / alle 30 Minuten / abfahren
3. der berühmte Fischmarkt / im Sommer / sonntags um 5.00 Uhr / stattfinden
4. die Alster / zum Radfahren oder Spazierengehen / einladen
5. wir / am Dienstag / an der Vorlesung in der Kunsthalle / teilnehmen

Answers for 1-38.
Word order may vary slightly.
1. Der Bus kommt um 13.00 Uhr am Hafen an. **2.** Ein Tourboot fährt alle 30 Minuten ab. **3.** Der berühmte Fischmarkt findet im Sommer sonntags um 5.00 Uhr statt. **4.** Die Alster lädt zum Radfahren oder Spazierengehen ein. **5.** Wir nehmen am Dienstag an der Vorlesung in der Kunsthalle teil.

Teaching suggestion for 1-39. After the students have formulated questions, have them invent answers. Alternatively, they could exchange papers or interview each other and, playing the role of Sam, answer the other student's questions.

1-39 Interviewfragen. Sie haben viele Fragen über das Leben in Norddeutschland. Ihr Freund Sam lebt jetzt für ein Jahr als Austauschstudent in Lüneburg, südlich von Hamburg. Benutzen Sie mindestens sechs der folgenden Verben und stellen Sie Sam sechs Fragen.

Beispiele: *Siehst du viele Windräder?*

Wie oft fährst du nach Hamburg?

gehen	anrufen	schwimmen
ausgehen	segeln	sprechen
regnen	haben	teilnehmen (an)
zurückkommen	besuchen	essen
fahren	hören	treffen
trinken	sein	sehen
finden	angeln	

Modal verbs (Modalverben)

01-29 to 01-30

Modal verbs express an attitude about an action. They are usually accompanied by another verb that expresses the action. German has six modal verbs. The present tense of modal verbs is irregular in the **ich-, du-,** and **er/sie/es-**forms. **Möchten** is a special form of the verb **mögen** and follows a slightly different pattern.

Infinitive	dürfen	können	mögen	müssen	sollen	wollen	möchten
	to be allowed to, may	*to be able to, can*	*to want to*	*to have to, must*	*to be supposed to*	*to want (to)*	*would like to*
ich	**darf**	**kann**	**mag**	**muss**	**soll**	**will**	**möchte**
du	**darfst**	**kannst**	**magst**	**musst**	sollst	**willst**	möchtest
er, sie, es	**darf**	**kann**	**mag**	**muss**	**soll**	**will**	**möchte**
wir	dürfen	können	mögen	müssen	sollen	wollen	möchten
ihr	dürft	könnt	mögt	müsst	sollt	wollt	möchtet
Sie, sie	dürfen	können	mögen	müssen	sollen	wollen	möchten

In the present tense, the accompanying verb occurs as an infinitive at the end of the sentence. However, the infinitive may be omitted if the meaning of the sentence is clear without it. This occurs relatively infrequently, but most typically when the infinitives are **fahren, gehen, machen, haben, sprechen,** or **tun,** but it can happen with other verbs as well.

Wir **können** Deutsch **sprechen.**

Wir **können** Deutsch. } *We can speak German.*

Willst du einen Hund **haben?**

Willst du einen Hund? } *Do you want a dog?*

Only the verb **mögen** is regularly used without an additional infinitive. The verb **mögen** is most commonly used in negative questions and in statements.

Magst du den Kuchen nicht? *Don't you like the cake?*

Ich **mag** dieses Buch. *I like this book.*

1-40 Keine Zeit für die Kieler Woche. Martin möchte Ende Juni gerne zur Kieler Woche, einem berühmten Sommerfest, das jedes Jahr in Kiel stattfindet. Kern des Festes ist eine Segelregatta, zu der Segler aus aller Welt kommen. Ergänzen Sie die Sätze mit den passenden Modalverben im Präsens.

Sven: (1) _____Willst_____ (*want*) du dieses Jahr mit uns zur Kieler Woche fahren?

Martin: Ich (2) _____möchte_____ (*would like to*) gerne einmal dabei sein. Segelboote (3) _____mag_____ (*like*) ich schon immer, und Segeln ist ein Hobby von mir. Leider (4) _____kann_____ (*can*) ich dieses Jahr nicht hingehen. Meine Frau und ich (5) _____müssen_____ (*have to*) Ende Juni nach Bremen fahren. Ihre Schwester Barbara (6) _____will_____ (*wants to*) nämlich am 27. Juni heiraten. Wir (7) _____dürfen_____ (*are allowed to*) die Hochzeit nicht verpassen.

Sven: Ach, schade. Aber dann (8) _____sollst_____ (*ought to*) du unbedingt zur „Hanse Sail" in Rostock kommen. Die findet im August statt. Sie (9) _____soll_____ (*is supposed to*) zwar kleiner sein als die Kieler Woche, sie ist aber bestimmt immer noch sehenswert.

1-41 Pläne für den Besuch in Bremen. Martins Frau, Anna, macht Pläne für die künftige Reise zur Hochzeit in Bremen. Was sagt sie? Wählen Sie ein passendes Modalverb und erklären Sie, wer was darf/muss/kann.

dürfen	müssen	können

1. wir / die Hochzeit nicht verpassen
2. wir / ein Geschenk mitbringen
3. wir / unseren Hund bei meiner Freundin lassen
4. du / nicht zu schnell fahren
5. wir / bei meiner Schwester übernachten
6. du / meine Eltern in Bremerhaven abholen
7. ich / am Hochzeitstag bei meiner Schwester bleiben
8. Barbaras Verlobter / kein Plattdeutsch

Follow-up for 1-40. Ask students some content questions about the dialog. *Was ist Kieler Woche? Warum möchte Martin gern hinfahren? Warum kann er es aber nicht? Was schlägt Sven stattdessen vor? Was ist „Hanse Sail"?*

Answers for 1-41. 1. Wir dürfen die Hochzeit nicht verpassen. **2.** Wir müssen ein Geschenk mitbringen. **3.** Wir können unseren Hund bei meiner Freundin lassen. **4.** Du darfst nicht zu schnell fahren. **5.** Wir können/dürfen bei meiner Schwester übernachten. **6.** Du musst meine Eltern in Bremerhaven abholen. **7.** Ich muss am Hochzeitstag bei meiner Schwester bleiben. **8.** Barbaras Verlobter kann kein Plattdeutsch.

01-33 to
01-35

2. Simple past tense (Präteritum)

The German simple past tense has a variety of English equivalents.

ich spielte
{
I was playing
I played
I did play
I used to play
}

The simple past tense is used primarily for narrating or describing past events or situations in written German. However, the simple past forms of **haben, sein,** and the modal auxiliaries are commonly used in conversational German as well. The same applies, though not with the same regularity, to **werden** and **wissen.**

Like the present tense, the simple past tense consists of finite verb forms. This means that the verb itself changes – either by adding suffixes or changing its stem vowel or both – to provide all the grammatical information needed to construct the tense. The simple past personal endings (**-, -st, -, -en, -t, -en**) are added to this simple past stem.

How the verb changes to mark the simple past tense depends on whether the verb is *weak, strong,* or *mixed.*

Weak verbs (Schwache Verben)

Weak verbs follow a predictable pattern. They form their simple past stem by adding a **-(e)te** suffix to the infinitive stem. An **-e** is added before the **-te** if the stem ends in **-d, -t,** or in **-m** or **-n** preceded by a consonant other than **-l** or **-r.** The simple past tense of the modal verbs **sollen** and **wollen** is identical to that of the weak verbs.

Infinitive	spielen	reden	zeichnen	wollen
	to play	*to talk*	*to draw*	*to want*
Simple past stem	spielte	redete	zeichnete	wollte
ich	spielte	redete	zeichnete	wollte
du	spieltest	redetest	zeichnetest	wolltest
er, sie, es	spielte	redete	zeichnete	wollte
wir	spielten	redeten	zeichneten	wollten
ihr	spieltet	redetet	zeichnetet	wolltet
Sie, sie	spielten	redeten	zeichneten	wollten

Strong verbs (Starke Verben)

Strong verbs create their simple past stem through an unpredictable vowel sound change (**trinken → trank, fahren → fuhr**). The stem vowel change is occasionally accompanied by a consonant change (e.g., **gehen → ging**) as well.

Infinitive	kommen	schreiben	gehen	sein	werden
	to come	*to write*	*to go*	*to be*	*to become*
Simple past stem	kam	schrieb	ging	war	wurde
ich	kam	schrieb	ging	war	wurde
du	kamst	schriebst	gingst	warst	wurdest
er, sie, es	kam	schrieb	ging	war	wurde
wir	kamen	schrieben	gingen	waren	wurden
ihr	kamt	schriebt	gingt	wart	wurdet
Sie, sie	kamen	schrieben	gingen	waren	wurden

Mixed verbs (Gemischte Verben)

Mixed verbs undergo a stem change like the strong verbs, but also use the **-te** suffix like weak verbs. The verb **haben** forms its simple past conjugations like the mixed verbs. The modal verbs with umlauts in their infinitives also form their simple past tense like the mixed verbs in that they drop the umlaut in the simple past stem.

Infinitive	wissen	können	haben
	to think	*to be able to*	*to have*
Simple past stem	wusste	konnte	hatte
ich	wusste	konnte	hatte
du	wusstest	konntest	hattest
er, sie, es	wusste	konnte	hatte
wir	wussten	konnten	hatten
ihr	wusstet	konntet	hattet
Sie, sie	wussten	konnte	hatten

Because the stem changes of strong and mixed verbs are unpredictable, their forms must be looked up or learned.

Separable prefix verbs (Verben mit trennbaren Präfixen)

As in the present tense, in the simple past tense separable prefixes are separated from the main verb and are placed at the end of the sentence. Separable prefix verbs can be weak, strong, or mixed.

auf·wachsen	Klaus **wuchs** so schnell **auf.**	*Klaus grew up so quickly.*
mit·nehmen	**Nahmen** Sie den Regenschirm **mit?**	*Did you take the umbrella along?*
hin·legen	Sie **legte** den Bleistift **hin.**	*She put down the pencil.*

1-42 Formen des Präteritums. Folgende Formen erscheinen im *Lesetext 2* zur Geschichte der Hanse. Geben Sie den Infinitiv und identifizieren Sie zu welcher Kategorie – stark, schwach oder gemischt – jedes Verb gehört.

1. war _____ *sein (stark)* _____
2. existierte _____ existieren (schwach) _____
3. bot _____ bieten (stark) _____
4. entschied _____ entscheiden (stark) _____
5. brachten _____ bringen (gemischt) _____
6. spielten _____ spielen (schwach) _____
7. erreichte _____ erreichen (schwach) _____
8. lagen _____ liegen (stark) _____

9. galt _____ gelten (stark) _____
10. entwickelte _____ entwickeln (schwach) _____
11. ging … zurück _____ zurückgehen (stark) _____
12. konnte _____ können (gemischt) _____
13. nahmen _____ nehmen (stark) _____
14. ließ _____ lassen (stark) _____
15. führte _____ führen (schwach) _____
16. fand … statt _____ stattfinden (stark) _____

1-43 Theodor Storm: Eine kurze Biografie. Ergänzen Sie den Absatz im Präteritum mit den Verben in Klammern.

Der deutsche Schriftsteller Theodor Storm (1) _____ wurde _____ (werden) 1817 in der norddeutschen Stadt Husum an der Nordseeküste geboren. Er (2) _____ studierte _____ (studieren) Jura in Kiel und Berlin. 1843 (3) _____ kam _____ er nach Husum (4) _____ zurück _____ (zurückkommen) und (5) _____ arbeitete _____ (arbeiten) dort als Rechtsanwalt. In demselben Jahr (6) _____ erschienen _____ (erscheinen) seine ersten Gedichte. 1856 (7) _____ bekam _____ (bekommen) er eine Stelle als Kreisrichter (*district court judge*). In dieser Stelle (8) _____ verdiente _____ (verdienen) er genug Geld, dass er auch nebenbei schreiben (9) _____ konnte _____ (können). Im Laufe der Jahre (10) _____ schrieb _____ (schreiben) er viele Novellen, wie z. B. „Der Schimmelreiter" und „Immensee". Storm und seine Frau Constanze (11) _____ hatten _____ (haben) zusammen sieben Kinder. Nach dem Tode von seiner Frau (12) _____ heiratete _____ (heiraten) er Dorothea Jensen. 1888 (13) _____ starb _____ (sterben) Storm an Magenkrebs (*stomach cancer*).

Die kleine Stadt Husum an der Nordseeküste

01-36 to
01-37

3. Future tense (Futur I)

The present tense is often used, frequently with specific adverbials of time, to express future time.

Morgen **zeige** ich es dir.	*I will show it to you tomorrow.*
Wir **finden** bald eine Wohnung.	*We'll find an apartment soon.*
Er **kommt** nicht.	*He's not coming. / He's not going to come.*

German also has a future tense to express future time. It is formed with the present tense of the auxiliary verb **werden** plus the infinitive of the main verb at the end of the sentence.

Ich **werde** den Mann **erkennen.**	*I will recognize the man.*
Du **wirst** den Mann **erkennen.**	*You will recognize the man.*
Er **wird** den Mann **erkennen.**	*He will recognize the man.*
Wir **werden** den Mann **erkennen.**	*We will recognize the man.*
Ihr **werdet** den Mann **erkennen.**	*You will recognize the man.*
Sie **werden** den Mann **erkennen.**	*They/You will recognize the man.*

The future tense is used less frequently in German than in English. It is used in place of the present tense, however, when the time frame would otherwise be unclear. With the addition of an adverb like **wohl** or **sicher,** the future tense also indicates probability or likelihood that something will occur.

Mein Bruder **wird wohl** an der Universität Rostock **studieren.**

My brother will probably study at the University of Rostock.

1-44 Im Jahre 2020. Schreiben Sie die Sätze ins Futur um.

1. Ein Drittel des Stromes stammt von erneuerbaren Energien.
2. Dabei spielt die Windkraft eine zentrale Rolle.
3. In Zukunft entstehen wohl mehrere Windparks in der Nordsee.
4. Offshore-Anlagen sind mehr als 30 km von der Küste entfernt.
5. Einige Naturschützer kritisieren Offshore-Anlagen.
6. Trotzdem bleibt der Wind eine relativ umweltfreundliche Energiequelle.

 1-45 In Zukunft. Besprechen Sie, wie die Zukunft wohl aussehen wird oder was Sie machen werden.

Beispiel: *Nächstes Jahr werde ich wohl in Lüneburg studieren.*

Nächstes Jahr wird Deutschland sicher einen neuen Kanzler wählen.

nächstes Semester	nächsten August	in zwei Jahren
nächstes Jahr	gleich nach dem Studium	in fünf Jahren
in den Semesterferien	im Winter	in 20 Jahren

Answers for 1-44.
1. Ein Drittel des Stromes wird von erneuerbaren Energien stammen. **2.** Dabei wird die Windkraft eine zentrale Rolle spielen. **3.** In Zukunft werden wohl mehrere Windparks in der Nordsee entstehen. **4.** Offshore-Anlagen werden mehr als 30 km von der Küste entfernt sein. **5.** Einige Naturschützer werden Offshore-Anlagen kritisieren. **6.** Trotzdem wird der Wind eine relativ umweltfreundliche Energiequelle bleiben.

4. Time, manner, place (Zeit, Art und Weise, Ort)

When a sentence contains several adverbs or adverbial expressions that appear as a group following the conjugated verb, they follow the sequence: time, manner, place. Adverbial expressions of time denote a point in time, a duration, or frequency. They answer the questions *when?*, *how long?*, or *how often?* Adverbs of manner usually answer the question *how?* Adverbial expressions of place specify location or direction and answer the questions. *where?*, *where to?* or *where from?*

	Time	Manner	Place
Ich fahre	morgen um vier Uhr	mit dem Auto	nach Flensburg.
Gehst du	später	schnell	in die Bibliothek?
Er legte das Buch		langsam	auf den Tisch.
Wir fahren	oft		zu Hans.
Sie saß		ruhig	auf dem Stuhl.

Note that general time information precedes specific time information.

heute um Viertel nach zehn	*tomorrow at four o'clock*
am Dienstag gegen Mittag	*on Tuesday around noon*

1-46 Wann? Wie? Wo? Ordnen Sie die Satzteile richtig ein.

1. Man baut __seit 1997 am Hafen__ die futuristische Hamburger Hafen-City. (seit 1997 / am Hafen)

2. Man kann __sonntags gemütlich am Elbstrand__ spazieren gehen. (gemütlich / sonntags / am Elbstrand)

3. Die Händler segelten __regelmäßig mit ihren Waren über Ost- und Nordsee__ (über Ost- und Nordsee / mit ihren Waren / regelmäßig).

4. Die Macht der Hanse ging __im 16. Jahrhundert allmählich__ zurück. (allmählich / im 16. Jahrhundert)

5. Die Festspiele Mecklenburg-Vorpommern finden __jedes Jahr zwischen Juni und September an über 60 Orten__ statt. (zwischen Juni und September / an über 60 Orten / jedes Jahr)

6. An der Küste sitzt man __bei kaltem Wetter gern im Strandkorb__. (im Strandkorb / bei kaltem Wetter / gern)

7. Es soll __bis 2030 in der Nord- und Ostsee__ mehr Windparks geben. (bis 2030 / in der Nord- und Ostsee)

8. Thomas Mann wurde __1875 in Lübeck__ geboren. (in Lübeck / 1875)

Immer weiter!

 1-47 Zur Diskussion. Besprechen Sie die Themen.

1. Auf welche Weise prägt und prägte das Meer das Leben in Norddeutschland?
2. Wählen Sie einen Ort in Norddeutschland aus und erzählen Sie, was Sie über diesen Ort wissen.

1-48 Zum Schreiben: Über Norddeutschland. In diesem Kapitel haben Sie die Landschaft, das Leben und die Kultur Norddeutschlands kennengelernt. Schreiben Sie nun für Deutschlerner im ersten Semester einen Absatz über Norddeutschland, in dem Sie Ihre Eindrücke von dieser Region mitteilen.

Weitere Themen

Wolf Biermann	Norddeutscher Rundfunk (NDR)
„Die Bremer Stadtmusikanten"	Nord-Ostsee-Kanal
Bismarckhering	die Nord- und Ostfriesischen Inseln
Günter Grass	Rügen
Heiligendamm	Hansestadt Rostock
Helgoland	Schleswig-Holstein Musik Festival
das Holstentor	Sylt
Lüneburger Heide	Helmut Schmidt
Nationalpark Jasmund	Jan Ullrich
Niederegger Marzipan	das Wattenmeer

Weitere Themen. These related topics may be used for independent or group research projects. You could have students report results of their research in a variety of ways, for example, in a written report, in an oral presentation to the class or in small groups, as a poster project, or as a blog post or web page.

Strandkörbe in Binz an der Ostsee

KAPITEL

2

Berlin

Note. Photo descriptions for chapter openers can be found on p. ii.

Warm-up. Have students look at the locator map and then the map of the Berlin metropolitan region. Ask what they know and have heard about the city and its history. *Wo liegt Berlin innerhalb Deutschlands? Wie groß ist Berlin im Vergleich zu anderen Städten in Deutschland? Was kann man in Berlin machen? Was wissen Sie über die Geschichte Berlins? Wie hat sich das Leben der Menschen seit der Wiedervereinigung wohl verändert? War jemand schon einmal in Berlin? Würden Sie gern einmal nach Berlin reisen?*

Sprachanalyse. In the *Sprachanalyse* in the *Kapitel 2* SAM, students practice distinguishing between the various uses of the verb *werden* and identifying its meaning in context. Learning to quickly recognize how this common, multifunctional verb is used will help improve students' reading proficiency.

Einführung

02-01 to 02-03

Read the *Sprachanalyse: Uses of the verb* **werden** in SAM 02-02. Then, as you read the *Einführung* and *Lesetexte*, complete the corresponding activities in the SAM (02-03, 02-06, 02-09, 02-13, 02-14, 02-17, 02-21) to practice understanding **werden** in context.

Nur ca. 80 km von der polnischen Grenze und weniger als 200 km südlich der Ostsee findet man Berlin, die Hauptstadt der Bundesrepublik Deutschland. Mit seinen 3,4 Millionen Einwohnern, wobei jeder siebte aus dem Ausland stammt, ist Berlin heute die bevölkerungsreichste° und flächengrößte° Stadt Deutschlands. Der Stadtstaat liegt wie eine Insel mitten im Bundesland Brandenburg, 5 zu dem er jahrhundertelang gehörte. Die Metropolregion der Stadt reicht heute weit in das Umland Brandenburgs hinein. Seit 1990 wird über eine politische Fusion der Länder diskutiert. Obwohl eine förmliche Fusion bisher abgelehnt° wurde, werden zunehmend viele öffentliche Einrichtungen der beiden Länder zusammengelegt. 10

most densely populated / largest in size

rejected

Die Stadt erlebte seit ihrer Gründung im Jahre 1237 eine wechselvolle Geschichte. Einst Mitglied der Hanse, war sie seit dem 15. Jahrhundert Hauptstadt Brandenburgs und Residenzstadt des Hauses Hohenzollern°, dessen Herrschaft über die Stadt 500 Jahre lang währte. In dieser Zeit entwickelte sich Berlin auch zu einem geistig-kulturellen Zentrum. Während 15 die Bedeutung der Stadt stetig stieg, gab es einen Wechsel glanzvoller° Epochen und dunkler Zeiten. Die Stadt war ab 1710 Hauptstadt Preußens°, dann des Zweiten Deutschen Reichs (1871–1918), der Weimarer Republik (1919– 1933) und des Dritten Reichs (1933–1945). Nach dem Zweiten Weltkrieg, in dem die Stadt starke Schäden erlitt, wurde Berlin – wie auch ganz Deutsch- 20 land – geteilt. Ost-Berlin wurde 1949 zur Hauptstadt der neugegründeten Deutschen Demokratischen Republik (DDR). Die Bundesrepublik Deutschland (BRD) hat dagegen ihre Hauptstadt nach Bonn verlegt. West-Berlin, das zur BRD gehörte, blieb als abgesonderte Insel mitten in der DDR. So wurde Berlin zum zentralen Schauplatz des Kalten Krieges. 1961 wurde entlang 25 der Grenze zwischen Ost- und West-Berlin eine Mauer errichtet, die zum konkreten Symbol der Trennung wurde. 1989 fiel die Berliner Mauer, und im folgenden Jahr wurden die beiden Teile Berlins und ganz Deutschland wieder vereinigt. Seit 1999 ist Berlin wieder Hauptstadt und Sitz der Regierung.

one of the most powerful royal families in German history

brilliant, splendid

Prussia

Note for *Einführung*. Remind students that the first German Empire (*das Erste Deutsche Reich*) was the Holy Roman Empire (*das Heilige Römische Reich deutscher Nation*, 800–1806), which they learned about in *Kapitel 1*.

Kaum eine andere Metropole hat so oft grundlegende Veränderungen 30 durchgemacht. Spuren dieser wechselhaften Geschichte kann man heute überall in Berlin entdecken. Die Stadt ist aber zugleich ein lebhaftes und modernes Zentrum der Kultur, Politik und Wissenschaften.

Fragen zum Text

1. Beschreiben Sie die geographische Lage Berlins.
2. Welches Verhältnis hat Berlin zu Brandenburg?
3. Für welche Territorien ist Berlin einmal Hauptstadt gewesen?
4. Was ist während des Kalten Krieges in Berlin passiert?
5. Wie lange hat die Mauer gestanden?
6. Was prägt heute das Leben in Berlin außer seiner Geschichte?

Answers to *Fragen zum Text*.
1. Es liegt mitten in dem Bundesland Brandenburg, nicht allzu weit von der polnischen Grenze. **2.** Berlin gehörte zu und war die Hauptstadt von Brandenburg über Jahrhunderte. Zur Metropolregion Berlin gehören heute weite Teile Brandenburgs. Man redet auch von einer politischen Fusion der beiden Länder, was aber noch nicht passiert ist. **3.** Brandenburg, Preußen, Zweites Deutsches Reich, Weimarer Republik, Drittes Reich, DDR (Ost-Berlin), BRD (seit 1990) **4.** Die Stadt wurde geteilt und 1961 wurde eine Mauer mitten durch die Stadt errichtet. **5.** 1961–1989 (28 Jahre) **6.** Kultur, Politik, Wissenschaften

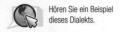

DIALEKTTIPP: Berlinerisch

Berlinerisch ist im Grunde ein mitteldeutscher Dialekt mit niederdeutschen Zügen. Im Laufe der Jahrhunderte kamen hochdeutsche, aber auch französische, jiddische und slawische Einflüsse hinzu. Das führte zu einer Sprachmischung, die für Berlin charakteristisch werden sollte. Berlinerisch kann man besonders an der Aussprache erkennen. Es gibt aber auch eine Reihe von dialektspezifischen Begriffen teils fremdsprachlichen Ursprungs wie etwa *Schrippe* (Brötchen), *Molle* (ein Glas Bier), *schnieke* (fein, elegant) oder *Bulette* (Frikadelle, französisch *Boulette*).

Diese Stadtsprache hat sich seit Mitte des 19. Jahrhunderts auch auf Brandenburg verbreitet und das brandenburgische Niederdeutsch dort fast ganz verdrängt°. Allerdings spricht man mit der Zeit in der Stadt selbst immer mehr Hochdeutsch. Im Westen Berlins wird dieser Dialekt seit jeher als Sprache der Ungebildeten° betrachtet. Berlinerisch begegnet man also eher im ehemaligen Ost-Berlin, wo es diese negativen Assoziationen nicht hatte.

suppressed

uneducated people

Dialekttipp. Ask students: Welche Sprachen haben den Dialekt beeinflusst? Woran erkennt man den Dialekt der Berliner? Welche Auswirkung hat Berlinerisch auf die Dialekte Brandenburgs gehabt? Warum spricht man den Dialekt eher im Osten als im Westen Berlins? After they complete the activities, write these two phrases on the board: „er jeht eenkoofen" and „Ick wünsch da allet Jute zum Jeburtstach". Ask students what they mean in standard German. [Er geht einkaufen; Ich wünsche dir alles Gute zum Geburtstag.]

Zum Dialekt

1 Wie sagt man das? Wählen Sie die richtigen Erklärungen der Unterschiede zwischen Berlinerisch und Hochdeutsch.

Hochdeutsch → Berlinerisch

_d_ 1.	ich, das, was → ick, det, wat	a. *g → j*
_e_ 2.	keiner, heißen → keener, heeßen	b. *au → langes o*
_b_ 3.	laufen, Augen → loofen, Oogen	c. gleiche Form im Dat. und Akk.
_a_ 4.	gut, genau → jut, jenau	d. *ch → k, s → t*
_c_ 5.	mich, mir → ma	e. *ei → ee*
_f_ 6.	Ullas Schwester → Ulla ihre Schwester	f. kein Genitiv

2 Im Gespräch. Wie sagt man das auf Berlinerisch?

	Hochdeutsch	Berlinerisch
_b_ 1.	Was macht dein Bruder?	a. Det jibs ja janich.
_d_ 2.	Er schaut sich die Augen aus dem Kopf.	b. Wat macht deen Atze?
_a_ 3.	Das gibt es ja gar nicht.	c. Wadde ma!
_c_ 4.	Warte mal!	d. Er kiekt sich die Oogen aus 'n Koop.

Lese- und Hörtexte

Lesetext 1

Freie Universität Berlin (Kurzporträt)

Die Freie Universität Berlin entstand als Folge der Entwicklungen in Deutschland nach dem Zweiten Weltkrieg. Deutschland sowie die ehemalige Hauptstadt Berlin wurden von den Siegern (Großbritannien, Frankreich, der Sowjetunion und den USA) in vier Zonen aufgeteilt. Die Sowjetunion verwaltete den östlichen Teil, und Frankreich, die USA und Großbritannien verwalteten den westlichen Teil. In den folgenden Jahren entwickelte sich die sowjetische Besatzungszone in Richtung Sozialismus, während in den drei westlichen Zonen eine demokratische Entwicklung stattfand. Da Berlins Humboldt-Universität unter kommunistischer Herrschaft stand, wurde aus Protest gegen diese Entwicklung 1948 die Freie Universität (FU) im westlichen Stadtteil gegründet.

In diesem Kurzporträt der FU Berlin aus den Internetseiten der Universität sehen Sie, wie die Geschichte Deutschlands mit der Geschichte der Universität verbunden ist.

Vor dem Lesen

Warum studieren Sie an Ihrer Universität? Hat schon jemand aus Ihrer Familie hier studiert? Was für einen Ruf hat diese Universität? Kennen Sie Universitäten, die in gewissen Bereichen einen besonders guten Ruf haben?

Beim Lesen

Welcher Satz beschreibt welchen Abschnitt des Textes?

__c__	1. Absatz	a. Die FU wird schnell weltweit bekannt und nimmt internationale Kontakte auf.
__f__	2. Absatz	b. Die FU steht in Konkurrenz mit den anderen Berliner Universitäten.
__d__	1948	
__a__	1949–1960	c. Die FU ist eine von neun Elite-Universitäten Deutschlands.
__e__	1961–1969	d. Studenten dürfen aus politischen Gründen nicht an der HU studieren.
__g__	1970–1988	
__b__	1989–heute	e. In dieser Zeit wird das Klima immer politischer.
		f. Die FU ist eine internationale Universität mit starkem Forschungsprofil.
		g. Die FU wird immer größer und bekommt finanzielle Probleme.

Introduction to *Lesetext 1.* Write the following dates on the board: 1945, 1949, 1961, 1989, 1990 and ask students what they already know about these dates in the history of Berlin and Germany (*Ende des Zweiten Weltkrieges, Gründung der BRD und der DDR, Bau der Berliner Mauer, Fall der Berliner Mauer, Wiedervereinigung*). Then have students read and discuss the introduction. *Was ist infolge des Zweiten Weltkriegs in Berlin und ganz Deutschland passiert? Wann und wo wurde die FU gegründet? Warum?*

Note for introduction. Berlin has four universities: HU, FU, Technische Universität, and Universität der Künste. Since the reunification, these universities have sought to coordinate their curricula. The city has has an additional 29 public and private institutions of higher education (*Hochschulen*). Berlin has over 130,000 post-secondary students. Around 90,000 of them study at the 3 largest of the universities: the FU, the HU, and the Technische Universität (TU).

Freie Universität Berlin

02-04 to 02-06

Heute gehört die Freie Universität (FU) zu den wissenschaftlichen Top-Adressen. Sie zählt zu den neun deutschen Hochschulen, auch Elite-Universitäten genannt, die in der Exzellenzinitiative Deutschlands erfolgreich abgeschnitten haben. Diese Auswahl fördert die Qualität der Hochschulen in Deutschland und will die internationale Wettbewerbsfähigkeit deutscher Universitäten verbessern.

Die FU zeichnet sich besonders durch ihren modernen und internationalen Charakter aus. Die 5
Universitas litterarum[a] zählt mit rund 100 Studienfächern und 33.000 Studierenden – davon 15 Prozent aus aller Welt – zu den bei Forschern und Studierenden international beliebtesten Universitäten in Deutschland. Weltweit ist die FU mit ca. 130 Hochschulen partnerschaftlich verbunden. Rund 600 auswärtige Wissenschaftler tragen jährlich zur Vielfalt in Lehre und Forschung bei. Fünfzehn Wissenschaftlerinnen und Wissenschaftler der Freien Universität erhielten bislang den 10 Gottfried-Wilhelm-Leibniz-Preis, die ranghöchste Auszeichnung[b] für Forschungsleistungen in Deutschland. Neben dem Staatszuschuss[c] von 290 Millionen Euro erhält die FU mit der Summe von jährlich ungefähr 90 Millionen Euro einen beträchtlichen Teil ihrer Einnahmen aus Drittmitteln[d].

Geschichte: 1948–heute

1948: Am 4. Dezember 1948 gründen engagierte Studenten und Professoren mit Unterstützung von Berliner Politikern und der amerikanischen Besatzungsmacht die Freie Universität. Die Gründung ist das 15 Resultat einer Protestaktion, da drei Studenten die Zulassung zum Studium an der Humboldt-Universität* aus politischen Gründen entzogen wird.

1949–1960: Die Freie Universität entwickelt sich in ihrer Ausbauphase[e] zu einer international angesehenen Universität und knüpft zahlreiche Kontakte zu ausländischen Universitäten. Es gibt Austauschprogramme, Gastvorlesungen und gemeinsame Forschungsprojekte. Besonderes Ansehen 20 erlangen die Fachbereiche Politikwissenschaft, Soziologie, Osteuropakunde und die Amerikanistik.

1961–1969: Der Mauerbau† (1961) bringt große Probleme für die Studenten aus Ost-Berlin und der DDR. Um ihr Studium an der Freien Universität fortsetzen zu können, müssen sie in den „Westen" ziehen. 1963 wird der amerikanische Präsident John F. Kennedy Ehrenbürger[f] der FU und drückt in seiner Rede die Verbundenheit der USA mit der FU aus. In den nächsten Jahren wird das Klima immer politischer. 25 Ab 1965 wird die FU zum Mittelpunkt der deutschen Studentenbewegung. Die Folge der Unruhen und Proteste ist das neue Universitätsgesetz von 1969, das Professoren und Studenten mehr Mitbestimmungsrechte[g] in der Verwaltung gibt.

---

[a]*university of letters (which unites teaching and research and promotes an all-around humanist education)* [b]*highest distinction* [c]*government subsidy* [d]*einen ... Drittmitteln a considerable part of its money from third parties* [e]*developmental phase* [f]*honorary citizen* [g]*participation rights*

*Siehe **Kulturtipps:** Humboldt-Universität (HU)
†Siehe **Kulturtipps:** Mauerbau

1970–1988: Die neuen Gesetze bleiben umstritten und 1978 gibt es ein neues Berliner Hochschulgesetz, das besonders den Professoren mehr Mitsprache in der Verwaltung der FU einräumt. Gleichzeitig [30] expandiert die Universität und baut Beziehungen nach Nord- und Südamerika sowie Asien aus. Die FU wird durch steigende Studentenzahlen zur Massenuniversität. Die Universität expandiert und viele neue Gebäude entstehen. Schon ab 1974 beginnen jedoch auch die Finanzierungsschwierigkeiten.

1989–heute: Der Fall der Mauer und die Wiedervereinigung Deutschlands mit einem vereinigten Berlin als Hauptstadt stellen die FU vor neue Herausforderungen. Trotz des Wettbewerbs mit den [35] anderen Universitäten Berlins, insbesondere der Humboldt-Universität, bewahrt die FU ihr eigenes Profil und behält mit ihrer Forschung international eine Spitzenposition[h].

———————————————

[h]*leading position*

Kulturtipps

Humboldt-Universität (HU)

Die HU Berlin ist die älteste Universität Berlins. Sie wurde 1809 auf Initiative des liberalen Bildungsreformers Wilhelm von Humboldt gegründet. Zu seinem neuen Konzept der Bildung gehörten die Verbindung von freier Forschung und Lehre sowie eine umfassende humanistische Bildung der Studierenden. Das Konzept war sehr erfolgreich und daraufhin entstanden viele Universitäten dieser Art weltweit, auch in den USA. Mit über 35.000 Studierenden ist sie eine der größten Hochschulen Berlins.

Mauerbau

Bis zum Bau der Berliner Mauer hatten 2,6 Millionen DDR-Bürger Richtung Westen ihr Land verlassen. Die 1.378 km lange Grenze zwischen der BRD und der DDR wurde seit 1952 immer stärker überwacht (*controlled*). In Berlin hingegen stand die Ost-West-Grenze noch offen. Täglich überquerten damals eine halbe Million Menschen die Sektorengrenze zur Arbeit, zum Studieren, Besuchen, Einkaufen oder zur Flucht. In der Nacht vom 12. zum 13. August 1961 ließ die DDR-Regierung die Berliner Mauer errichten. Dieser „antifaschistische Schutzwall", wie die Führungsmacht der DDR die Mauer propagandistisch bezeichnete, sollte die zunehmende Flucht der DDR-Bürger in den Westen verhindern.

Teaching Suggestion for *Kulturtipp: Mauerbau*. Have students imagine how the sudden appearance of a wall changed the lives of the residents of Berlin. *Wie fühlen sich die Menschen, die in Ost-Berlin wohnen? Die Menschen in West-Berlin? Welchen Effekt hat der Bau der Mauer auf ihren Alltag? Was hätten Sie gemacht, wenn Sie damals in Berlin gelebt hätten?*

Neue Vokabeln

Nomen

das Ansehen, - *reputation*

die Folge, -n *consequence*

der Forscher, -/die Forscherin,
-nen *researcher*

die Forschung, -en *research*

das Gesetz, -e *law*

die Grenze, -n *border*

die Herausforderung, -en *challenge*

der Krieg, -e *war*

die Mauer, -n *(freestanding) wall*

der/die Studierende, -n
(adj. noun) student

die Unterstützung *support*

die Verwaltung,
-en *administration*

die Wende *turn; here: 1990,
German reunification*

der Wettbewerb, -e *competition*

die Wiedervereinigung,
-en *reunification*

die Zulassung, -en *admission*

Verben

aus·drücken *to express*

sich aus·zeichnen *to distinguish
oneself*

bei·tragen (trägt bei), trug bei,
beigetragen (zu) *to contribute,
to add (to)*

erhalten (erhält), erhielt,
erhalten *to receive*

fördern *to foster, promote*

gründen *to found*

ziehen, zog, ist gezogen
to move

Adjektive und Adverbien

auswärtig *external, from outside*

jährlich *annually*

vereinigt *united*

Ausdrücke

mit ... verbunden sein *to be
affiliated with*

2-1 Textarbeit: Wann? Ergänzen Sie die Sätze mit Jahren aus dem Text.

1. Im Jahre _____1948_____ wird die FU gegründet.

2. Die FU wird ab _____1965_____ zum Zentrum vieler politischer Studentendemonstrationen.

3. Neue Gesetze, die den Professoren mehr Einfluss in der Verwaltung geben, entstehen im Jahre _____1978_____ .

4. Seit _____1974_____ hat die FU immer weniger Geld und es beginnt eine Zeit der finanziellen Probleme.

2-2 Textarbeit: Fragen zum Inhalt. Beantworten Sie die Fragen zum Text.

1. Welche Universität ist älter: die FU oder die HU?

2. Was soll durch die Exzellenzinitiative verbessert werden?

3. Wie viele Universitäten haben eine Partnerschaft mit der FU?

4. Welche Ehrung haben bisher 15 Forscher der FU erhalten?

5. Für welche Fachbereiche wurde die FU im Laufe der Jahrzehnte besonders bekannt?

6. Wie hat der Mauerbau das Leben der ostdeutschen Studenten verändert?

7. Welcher amerikanische Präsident hat 1963 die FU besucht?

8. Warum haben die Studenten und Professoren neue Hochschulgesetze gewollt?

Answers to 2-2. **1.** die HU; **2.** die internationale Wettbewerbsfähigkeit deutscher Universitäten; **3.** ca. 130; **4.** den Gottfried-Wilhelm-Leibniz-Preis; **5.** Politikwissenschaft, Soziologie, Osteuropakunde und Amerikanistik; **6.** Studierende aus Ost-Berlin und der DDR dürfen nicht mehr nach West-Berlin, um zu studieren. Sie müssen den Osten verlassen oder das Studium aufgeben. **7.** John F. Kennedy; **8.** Sie wollten mehr Mitbestimmungsrechte in der Verwaltung.

2-3 Vokabelarbeit. Ergänzen Sie die Sätze mit Wörtern aus den *Neuen Vokabeln.* Achten Sie dabei auch auf die Wortform.

1. Die FU Berlin hat ein gutes _____ Ansehen _____.

2. Viele _____ Forscher _____ an der FU sind weltbekannt.

3. Die neuen _____ Gesetze _____ gaben den Professoren mehr Einfluss.

4. Nach der _Wiedervereinigung / Wende_ begannen neue Herausforderungen für die FU.

5. Die FU _____ erhält _____ Geld vom Staat und aus Drittmitteln.

6. _____ Jährlich _____ arbeiten ca. 600 Wissenschaftler aus dem Ausland an der FU.

7. Die FU erhält besondere finanzielle _____ Unterstützung _____ von der Bundes-regierung, da sie eine Elite-Universität ist.

 2-4 Zur Diskussion. Besprechen Sie die Fragen.

1. Interessieren Sie sich für Geschichte? Wenn ja, was für Geschichte?

2. Wissen Sie, wann und warum Ihre Universität gegründet wurde? Hat sich die Richtung Ihrer Universität seit ihrer Gründung verändert?

3. Es wird manchmal gesagt, dass die Geschichte der FU die Geschichte Deutschlands widerspiegelt. Stimmt das? Begründen Sie Ihre Antwort.

 2-5 Ein Vergleich. Vergleichen Sie Ihre Universität mit der FU Berlin.

1. An der FU findet man viele Wissenschaftler aus aller Welt. An meiner Uni-versität …

2. Die FU hat 33.000 Studenten. Meine Uni …

3. Die FU hat finanzielle Probleme. Meine Uni …

4. …

2-6 Meine Universität. Ihre Universität interessiert sich dafür, deutschspra-chige Studierende für ein Studium an der Universität zu gewinnen. Schreiben Sie ein Profil Ihrer Uni, dem Porträt der FU ähnlich, die in einer deutschsprachigen Version der Uni-Webseite erscheinen soll.

Lesetext 2

„Wir sind ein Volk" von Willy Brandt (Rede)

Willy Brandt (1989)

Willy Brandt (1913–1992) ist einer der bekanntesten deutschen Politiker. Er war von 1957 bis 1966 Bürger-meister von West-Berlin, von 1966 bis 1969 Bundes-außenminister° und von 1969 bis 1974 Bundeskanz-ler der Bundesrepublik Deutschland. Er setzte sich in all diesen Positionen besonders für eine Ostpolitik ein, die Entspannung und Ausgleich° mit den osteu-ropäischen Staaten anstrebte. Seine Politik konzen-trierte sich auf die gemeinsamen Interessen von Ost und West und erreichte eine Annäherung der

Introduction to Lesetext 2.
Ask students what they learned from the introductory text: *Wer war Willy Brandt? Was hat er als Politiker geleistet?* Then ask them to consider the theme of his speech: *Der Titel von Willy Brandts Rede ist „Wir sind ein Volk". Was meint er wohl damit? Was will er wohl mit seiner Rede erreichen?*

Minister of Foreign Affairs

détente (easing of tension) and conciliation

beiden Länder im Namen dieser Interessen. Dafür erhielt er 1971 den Friedensnobelpreis.

Am 10. November 1989 hielt Willy Brandt seine berühmte Rede „Wir sind ein Volk" vor dem Rathaus in Berlin-Schöneberg. Der Anlass war der Fall der Berliner Mauer. In dieser symbolischen Rede spricht er von Hoffnung für ein wiedervereinigtes Deutschland und er fordert alle Deutschen auf, zusammenzuarbeiten, um dieses Ziel gemeinsam zu erreichen.

Vor dem Lesen

In der DDR und der BRD gab es vor dem Fall der Mauer Unterschiede und Gemeinsamkeiten. Ergänzen Sie die Tabelle und vergleichen Sie Ihre Antworten mit denen der anderen Studenten.

Vor dem Lesen. If students are especially interested in the differences between the two countries, you may wish to add additional categories for discussion, e.g., *Alltag der Menschen, Arbeit, Sozialhilfe, Einkaufen, Medien, Reisen.*

Bereich	BRD	DDR
Sprache	Deutsch	Deutsch
Währung	Deutsche Mark (DM)	Mark der DDR
Politisches System	parlamentarische Demokratie	diktatorisch regierter sozialistischer Staat

Beim Lesen

1. Ordnen Sie die folgenden Überschriften den sieben Textabschnitten zu.

   __3__ Gruß an alle Berliner vom Bürgermeister, der für menschliche Kontakte arbeitete

   __4__ Wir wissen nicht, wie das Zusammenrücken aussehen wird

   __6__ Was noch kommt, braucht Zeit und Solidarität

   __1__ Begrüßung der Berliner; der Mauerfall ist erst der Anfang

   __5__ Ein Stück Mauer soll zur Erinnerung erhalten bleiben

   __7__ Danke, dass Sie mir zugehört haben.

   __2__ Die Trennung von Ost und West durch menschliche Kontakte überwinden

Answers for *Beim Lesen*, **part 2.** Eine Rede ist ein gesprochener Text, der für ein Publikum bestimmt ist und meist zu einem besonderen Anlass vorgetragen wird. Charakteristische Elemente: die direkte Anrede, verkürzte Wörter, Umformulierung und Wiederholung von Konzepten

2. Das ist der Text einer Rede. Was ist eine Rede? Wie unterscheidet sich diese Form von anderen Textformen? Identifizieren Sie Elemente in der Rede, die wohl charakteristisch für eine mündliche Mitteilung sind.

02-07 to 02-09

„Wir sind ein Volk"

Rede von Willy Brandt am 10. November 1989 vor dem Rathaus Schöneberg

drüben und hüben *there and here (meaning East and West Germany)*

[1] Liebe Berlinerinnen und Berliner, liebe Landsleute von drüben und hüben°, dies ist ein schöner Tag nach einem langen Weg, aber wir befinden uns erst an einer Zwischenstation. Wir sind noch nicht am Ende des Weges angelangt. Es liegt noch 'ne ganze Menge vor uns.

[2] Die Zusammengehörigkeit° der Berliner und der Deutschen überhaupt manifestiert sich auf eine bewegende°, auf eine uns aufwühlende° Weise, und sie tut es am bewegendsten dort, wo getrennte Familien endlich wieder ganz unverhofft° und tränenvoll° zusammenfinden. Mich hat auch das Bild angerührt von dem Polizisten auf unserer Seite, der 'rübergeht zu seinem Kollegen drüben und sagt: Jetzt haben wir uns so viele Wochen, vielleicht Monate auf Abstand° gesehen, ich möchte Ihnen heute mal die Hand geben. Das ist die richtige Art, sich dem Problem zu nähern: einander die Hand zu geben, nachtragend° nur dort zu sein, wo es unbedingt sein muss. Aber wo immer es geht, Trennendes zu überwinden. Das hab' ich auch heute Mittag am Brandenburger Tor gespürt, und hier sind ja viele auf dem Platz, die auch heute Mittag am Brandenburger Tor waren.

[3] Als Bürgermeister der schwierigen Jahre von 1957 bis 1966, also auch der Zeit des Mauerbaus und danach, und als einer, der in der Bundesrepublik und für sie einiges zu tun hatte mit dem Abbau von Spannungen in Europa und mit dem jeweils erreichbaren Maß an sachlichen Verbindungen und menschlichen Kontakten°, sage ich hier heute Abend meinen ganz herzlichen Gruß an die Berlinerinnen und Berliner in allen Teilen der Stadt. Und gleichermaßen an die Landsleute drüben wie hüben, in beiden Teilen Deutschlands. Und ich füge hinzu: Es wird jetzt viel davon abhängen, ob wir uns – wir Deutschen, hüben und drüben – der geschichtlichen Situation gewachsen erweisen.

[4] Das Zusammenrücken der Deutschen, darum geht es, das Zusammenrücken der Deutschen verwirklicht sich anders, als es die meisten von uns erwartet haben. Und keiner sollte in diesem Augenblick so tun, als wüsste er ganz genau, in welcher konkreten Form die Menschen in den beiden Staaten in ein neues Verhältnis zueinander geraten werden. Dass sie in ein anderes Verhältnis zueinander geraten, dass sie in Freiheit zusammenfinden und sich entfalten können, darauf allein kommt es an.

[5] Und eines ist sicher, es wurde vorhin im Abgeordnetenhaus° gesagt: Es ist sicher, dass nichts im anderen Teil Deutschlands wieder so werden wird, wie es war. Die Winde der Veränderung, die seit einiger Zeit über Europa ziehen, haben an Deutschland nicht vorbeiziehen können. Meine Überzeugung war es immer, dass die betonierte Teilung und dass die Teilung durch Stacheldraht und Todesstreifen° gegen den Strom der Geschichte standen. Und ich habe es noch in diesem Sommer zu Papier gebracht – man kann es nachlesen, wenn man will –, ohne dass ich genau wusste, was im Herbst passieren würde: Berlin wird leben und die Mauer wird fallen. Übrigens, übrigens, liebe Freunde, ein Stück von jenem scheußlichen Bauwerk, ein Stück davon könnte man dann von mir aus sogar als ein geschichtliches Monstrum stehen lassen. So, so wie wir seinerzeit nach

togetherness

moving / stirring

unexpectedly / tearfully

at a distance

unforgiving, vengeful

Siehe **Kulturtipps:**
Brandenburger Tor

***mit ... Kontakten** with the measure of real relations and human contact that was attainable*

Berlin House of Representatives

***Stacheldraht und Todesstreifen** barbed wire fence and death strip*

Siehe **Kulturtipps:**
Gedächtniskirche

heftigen Diskussionen in unserer Stadt uns bewusst dafür entschieden haben, die Ruine der Gedächtniskirche stehen zu lassen.

[...]

[6] Ich sag' noch einmal: Nichts wird wieder so wie es einmal war. Dazu 50 gehört, dass auch wir im Westen nicht an unseren Parolen° von gestern allein gemessen werden, sondern an dem, was wir heute und morgen zu tun, zu leisten bereit und in der Lage sind, geistig und materiell. Und ich hoffe, die Schubladen° sind nicht leer, was das Geistige angeht. Ich hoffe auch, die Kassen sind nicht allzu leer. Und ich hoffe, die Terminkalender 55 lassen Raum für das, was jetzt sein muss. Die Bereitschaft nicht zum erhobenen Zeigefinger°, sondern zur Solidarität, zum Ausgleich, zum neuen Beginn, wird auf die eigentliche Probe gestellt. Es gilt jetzt, neu zusammenzurücken, den Kopf klar zu behalten, und das so gut wie möglich zu tun, was unseren deutschen Interessen ebenso entspricht wie unserer Pflicht 60 gegenüber unserem europäischen Kontinent.

[7] Ich danke für Ihre Aufmerksamkeit.

slogans

drawers (meant figuratively)

for pointing fingers

Kulturtipps

Brandenburger Tor

Das 1788–1791 erbaute Brandenburger Tor ist das bekannteste Wahrzeichen (*landmark*) der Stadt Berlin. Es befindet sich in der Stadtmitte und ist mit vielen wichtigen Ereignissen der Stadt und der Geschichte Deutschlands eng verbunden. 1945–1990 stand das Tor dicht an der östlichen Seite der Berliner Mauer, war also vom Westen aus gut sichtbar aber weder vom Osten noch vom Westen her passierbar. Amerikanische Präsidenten wie John F. Kennedy, Ronald Reagan und Bill Clinton haben hier wichtige Reden gehalten und das Tor zum Symbol für Freiheit und Einigkeit gemacht.

Gedächtniskirche

Die Kaiser-Wilhelm-Gedächtniskirche (kurz: Gedächtniskirche) ist eine evangelische Kirche, die 1895 ihre Türen öffnete. Im Zweiten Weltkrieg wurde die Kirche weitgehend zerstört. Die Berliner beschlossen in der Nachkriegszeit die Ruine der Kirche als Denkmal stehen zu lassen und mit modernen Elementen zu restaurieren. Die Gedächtniskirche ist heute ein Mahnmal (*memorial*) gegen den Krieg und ein Wahrzeichen Berlins.

Die Kaiser-Wilhelm-Gedächtniskirche

Neue Vokabeln

Nomen

der Abbau *dismantling*

die Bereitschaft *willingness*

der Bundeskanzler, -/die
Bundeskanzlerin, -nen
Federal Chancellor

der Bürgermeister, -/die
Bürgermeisterin, -nen *mayor*

die Erinnerung, -en *memory*

der Frieden *peace*

die Pflicht, -en *duty*

die Spannung, -en *tension*

die Teilung, -en *separation*

die Veränderung, -en *change*

das Verhältnis, -se *relationship*

Verben

entsprechen (entspricht),
entsprach, entsprochen
(+ *dat.*) *to correspond to*

erwarten *to expect*

leisten *to achieve*

überwinden, überwand,
überwunden *to conquer*

zusammen·rücken, ist zusammengerückt *to come together*

Adjektive und Adverbien

drüben *over there*

geistig *intellectually, spiritually*

getrennt *separated*

leer *empty*

Ausdrücke

auf die Probe stellen
to put to the test

Es hängt davon ab(, ob …)
It depends (on whether …)

Es kommt darauf an.
It depends.

den Kopf klar behalten
to keep a clear head

2-7 Textarbeit: Anders gesagt. Willy Brandt benutzt Wendungen und Metaphern, die die Zuhörer damals ohne weiteres verstanden haben. Was meint er mit diesen Wendungen? Für einige Dinge oder Ereignisse benutzt er mehr als eine Wendung oder Metapher.

Was Willy Brandt sagt:

___c___ 1. liebe Landsleute von drüben und hüben (Z. 1–2)

___e___ 2. die schwierigen Jahre von 1957 bis 1966 (Z. 18)

___d___ 3. Abbau von Spannungen in Europa (Z. 20)

___f___ 4. im anderen Teil Deutschlands (Z. 37)

___b___ 5. Winde der Veränderung (Z. 38)

___a___ 6. die betonierte Teilung (Z. 40)

___a___ 7. jenes scheußliche Bauwerk (Z. 45–46)

___a___ 8. ein geschichtliches Monstrum (Z. 47)

Was das bedeutet:

a. die Berliner Mauer

b. politische Reformen im Ostblock in den 80er-Jahren

c. Bürger der BRD und der DDR

d. Versuch ab 1969, mit Ostblockstaaten anstatt gegen sie zu arbeiten

e. die Eskalation des Kalten Kriegs, die Zeit des Mauerbaus und die politischen Spannungen, die darauf folgten

f. in der DDR

Activity 2-11. Prepare cards
or slips of paper with the names
of personalities and distribute
these to students. Possible per-
sonalities: Justin Bieber, Usain
Bolt, Steve Carrell, Walt Disney,
Albert Einstein, Sigmund Freud,
Königin Elisabeth, Lady Gaga,
Madonna, Martin Luther King,
Jr., Mahatma Gandhi, Wolfgang
Amadeus Mozart, Papst Benedikt
XVI., Michelle Obama, Michael
Phelps, Elvis Presley, William
Shakespeare, Britney Spears,
Taylor Swift, Oprah Winfrey, Tiger
Woods. You could also add fictio-
nal personalities, e.g., Elmo, Harry
Potter, Alice im Wunderland,
Rotkäppchen, Bart Simpson, etc.
If you prefer not to prepare cards
with the names on them, you can
have students choose their own
personalities. Make sure students
know they are not to reveal
their personalities to
anyone besides their dialog
partner. As students perform
the dialogs, the rest of the class
should try to guess who they are.

Alternate group activity for
2-11. Pin or tape the cards on
students' backs so that they cannot see their own identities. Have
them then circulate around the
classroom and mingle, asking
questions about themselves
that will help them guess their
own identity. To make this more
challenging, direct students to ask
yes/no questions about their own
identities and to answer only yes or
no when asked a question.

Expansion for 2-12. Have students discuss Brandt's idea. Ask
them: Was halten Sie von Brandts
Vorschlag? Ist es eine gute Idee,
einen Teil der Mauer
stehen zu lassen?
Warum (nicht)?
Welchem Zweck sollte das
dienen? Er vergleicht seinen
Vorschlag mit der Entscheidung,
die Ruine der Gedächtniskirche
stehen zu lassen. Ist das ein guter
Vergleich? Warum (nicht)?

2-8 Textarbeit: Fragen zum Inhalt. Besprechen Sie die Fragen.

1. Wie sieht Willy Brandt 1989 die Zukunft Deutschlands?

2. Was ist tatsächlich nach 1989 passiert?

3. Haben sich die Wünsche von Willy Brandt erfüllt?

4. Was meint Brandt wohl, wenn er über Deutschlands „Pflicht gegenüber unserem europäischen Kontinent" spricht?

2-9 Vokabelarbeit. Ergänzen Sie die Sätze mit Wörtern aus den *Neuen Vokabeln*. Achten Sie dabei auch auf die Wortform.

1. Willy Brandt war von 1957 bis 1966 _____Bürgermeister_____ der Stadt Berlin.

2. Die Ost- und West-Berliner waren seit 1961 durch die Mauer voneinander _____getrennt_____ .

3. Brandt _____erwartet_____ von den Berlinern, dass sie friedlich zusammenkommen.

4. Nach der Wiedervereinigung mussten die Bürger in Ost und West ein neues _____Verhältnis_____ zueinander aufbauen.

5. Willy Brandt hofft, dass sich die Menschen hüben wie _____drüben_____ Frieden wünschen.

6. Er hofft, dass alle Deutschen ihre Probleme _____überwinden_____ und einander die Hände reichen werden.

7. Heute ist ein geteiltes Deutschland nur noch eine _____Erinnerung_____ , eine Zeit, über die viele ehemalige DDR- und BRD-Bürger noch oft sprechen.

2-10 Zur Diskussion. Besprechen Sie die Fragen.

1. Wer sind für Sie wichtige politische Figuren in der Geschichte? Warum? Was haben sie erreicht oder verändert?

2. Wodurch zeichnet sich eine Person als Führungsperson aus? Welche Qualitäten braucht man, um andere Menschen positiv zu beeinflussen?

3. Waren Sie schon einmal in einer Führungsposition? Was ist an solch einer Position schwierig? Was macht dabei Spaß?

2-11 Zwei Prominente begegnen sich. Sie sind beide berühmte Personen. Schreiben Sie zusammen einen Dialog. Nennen Sie im Dialog nicht die Namen dieser Personen, aber geben Sie genug Information, dass andere raten können, wer sie sind, wenn Sie den Dialog vorspielen.

2-12 Die Mauer heute. 1989 schlug Willy Brandt vor, dass ein Teil der Berliner Mauer stehen bleibt. Suchen Sie im Internet nach Informationen über die Mauer seit 1989. Beantworten Sie die Fragen.

Note for 2-12. Relevant
web addresses for Internet
research activities can be
found in *MyGermanLab* and
on the Companion Website.

1. Hat man ein Stück der Mauer stehen lassen?

2. Wie kann man heute sehen, wo die Mauer einst stand?

3. Was macht man heute, um an die Mauer zu erinnern?

2-13 Ich als Politiker. Stellen Sie sich vor, Sie wollen Ihre Mitbürger davon überzeugen, etwas Positives zu tun. Machen Sie sich Notizen und halten Sie dann eine Rede. Benutzen Sie die Sie-Anrede.

Beispiel: Umweltfreundlicher sein

Liebe Mitbürger und Mitbürgerinnen! Sie sollen umweltfreundlicher sein, denn wir haben nur eine Erde. Sie sollen vielleicht nicht so oft mit dem Auto fahren. Fahren Sie lieber mit dem Bus oder dem Fahrrad! …

Teaching suggestion for 2-13. Possible speech topics: *umweltfreundlicher sein, langsamer fahren, Ausländer freundlicher behandeln, Geld für eine neue Schule/ein neues Museum/einen neuen Park spenden, mit Kindern/Kranken arbeiten.*

Hörtext 1

Erinnerungen an den Mauerfall: Fünf Fragen an Brunhilde Heß (Interview)

Sie werden im Folgenden ein Interview mit Brunhilde Heß hören. Frau Heß lebte, als die Mauer fiel, in der DDR. Sie spricht in dem Interview über ihre ganz persönlichen Erfahrungen zu der Zeit des Mauerfalls.

Transcripts for all Hörtexte are located in the Instructor's Resource Manual.

Introduction to Hörtext 1. Students have now learned something about the history of the Wall and German reunification. Have them tell you what they remember: *Sie haben in diesem Kapitel schon einiges über die Mauer, die Wende und die Wiedervereinigung gelernt. Nennen Sie Daten und Ereignisse.*

Vor dem Hören

Sie sind DDR-Bürger/Bürgerin und sitzen am Abend des 9. Novembers zu Hause. Ein Freund ruft Sie an und sagt, dass die Grenze zwischen Ost und West aufgemacht wurde. Wie reagieren Sie auf diese Nachricht?

Menschen auf der Berliner Mauer, November 1989

Beim Hören

Während des Interviews hören Sie folgende Vokabeln.

Erinnerungen an den Mauerfall: Fünf Fragen an Brunhilde Heß
02-10

Siehe **Kulturtipps:** Ampelmännchen

Demo *demonstration*	beibehalten *kept, retained*
Zaun *fence*	das grüne Männchen an der Ampel
sang- und klanglos *without much ado*	*the green figure in the pedestrian light*
beschimpft *insulted*	meckern und mosern *griping and*
es wäre gelogen *it would be a lie*	*complaining*

Hören Sie das Interview an und markieren Sie die Wörter, die Sie bei den jeweiligen Fragen hören.

1. Wie haben Sie den Herbst 1989 erlebt?
   <u>Fernsehen</u> • <u>Demo</u> • Radio • <u>Panik</u> • Berlin • <u>Krieg</u>
2. Was hat sich nach dem Ende der DDR für Sie verändert?
   <u>Nachbardorf</u> • Zaun • Ausland • Zeitungen • <u>Westen</u> • <u>Wende</u>
3. Wie haben Sie sich 1989 die Zukunft vorgestellt?
   <u>Grenze</u> • BRD • Sommer • <u>Bürger</u>
4. Welche Erinnerung an die DDR ist für Sie die wichtigste?
   <u>DDR</u> • 1945 • <u>Heimat</u> • Führerschein • <u>Zuhause</u> • <u>Kinderkrippen</u>
5. Was wünschen Sie sich für die Zukunft?
   <u>Kinder</u> • Theater • Krieg • <u>Frieden</u> • <u>Arbeitsplätze</u> • Region

Siehe **Kulturtipps:** Kindergärten und Kinderkrippen

Kulturtipps

Ampelmännchen

Das ostdeutsche Ampelmännchen leuchtete 1961 in Berlin als erste Fußgängerampel auf. In den folgenden Jahren wurden die roten und die grünen Leuchtfiguren sogar zu Zeichentrick-Stars (*famous cartoon characters*), die allen Kindern in der DDR bekannt waren. Nach der Wiedervereinigung wollte die BRD ihre westdeutschen Ampelmänner, die anders aussahen, im Osten einführen, doch die ehemaligen DDR-Bürger wollten ihre „alten" Ampelmänner behalten. Heute sind die alten grünen Ampelmännchen Kultfiguren und stehen für den Wunsch der ehemaligen DDR Bürger, positive Elemente aus der DDR-Kultur zu erhalten.

Der DDR-Ampelmann

Kindergärten und Kinderkrippen

Kinderkrippen (*day-care centers*) für Kinder unter drei Jahren sowie Kindergärten (*preschools*) für die Drei- bis Sechsjährigen waren selbstverständlich in der DDR. Bis 1989 hatte die DDR das dichteste Netz von Kinderkrippen in Europa. Einerseits konnten Mütter leichter eine Arbeit finden. Andererseits hatte der Staat, der das Bildungssystem kontrollierte, frühen Einfluss auf die Erziehung der Kleinkinder. In der BRD hingegen gab und gibt es heute auch nicht genug Krippen- und Kindergartenplätze für alle, ein Problem, mit dem die Regierung sich beschäftigt.

 2-14 Textarbeit: Richtig oder falsch? Wenn eine Aussage falsch ist, korrigieren und ergänzen Sie sie mit Informationen aus dem Hörtext.

Answers for 2-14. 1. R; 2. F – Vieles hat sich für die DDR-Bürger verändert. 3. F – Sie wollte bleiben, denn das war ihre Heimat. 4. F – Sie fand viele Dinge nicht gut, aber nicht alles, z. B. Kindergärten und Kinderkrippen. 5. R

1. Frau Heß bittet ihren Mann, zu Hause zu bleiben, weil sie Angst hat, dass es Krieg gibt.
2. Nach der Wende hat sich wenig für die DDR-Bürger verändert.
3. Nach der Wende wollte Frau Heß sofort die DDR verlassen.
4. Frau Heß fand alles in der DDR schlecht.
5. Frieden ist für Frau Heß das Allerwichtigste.

 2-15 Zur Diskussion. Besprechen Sie die Fragen.

1. Warum hatten die Menschen in der DDR, als die Mauer fiel, wohl Angst?
2. Das Leben in der DDR war anders als das Leben in der BRD. Warum sind dennoch die meisten Bürger in der DDR geblieben?
3. Können Sie sich vorstellen, Ihr Heimatland zu verlassen? Warum (nicht)?

2-16 Gruppenarbeit. Besprechen Sie die Fragen mit zwei Mitstudenten und schreiben Sie ihre Antworten auf.

1. Habt ihr schon einmal an einer Demonstration teilgenommen? Wenn ja, wofür?
2. Habt ihr Angst vor Krieg?
3. Wie definiert ihr das Wort „Heimat"?
4. Was ist für euch am wichtigsten: Frieden, Arbeit oder Geld? Warum?

2-17 Fragen zum Nachdenken. Ein Bürger der ehemaligen DDR betreibt einen Blog, in dem er die Fragen der **Übung 2-16** an sein Leserpublikum stellt. Wählen Sie zwei von den vier Fragen und schreiben Sie zu jeder Frage einen Absatz, der auf dem Blog erscheinen soll.

2-18 Das Leben in der DDR. Suchen Sie im Internet nach weiteren Informationen zum Leben in der DDR. Schreiben Sie sich fünf bemerkenswerte Dinge auf. Dann teilen Sie, was Sie entdeckt haben, der Klasse mit.

Note for 2-18. Relevant web addresses for Internet research activities can be found in *MyGermanLab* and on the Companion Website.

Lesetext 3

Berlin-Bärenstark! Knut tut der Wirtschaft gut (Zeitungsartikel)

Knut mit seinem Pfleger

Platz machen musste der alte Berliner Bär 2006 für einen Neuankömmling. Neben den alten Symbolbären trat der berühmte, knuddelige Knut. Knut war ein Eisbär, der im Berliner Zoo zu Hause war. Knut kam am 5. Dezember im Berliner Zoo zur Welt. Es war die erste Eisbärengeburt im Berliner Zoo seit über 30 Jahren und somit natürlich ein großes Ereignis. Knuts Mutter nahm sich des jungen Bären nicht an und so zog ihn sein Tierpfleger, Thomas Dörflein, auf. Knut war vom ersten Tag an ein Medienphänomen. Ganz Deutschland und besonders die Berliner liebten Knut.

Knut war seinerzeit so berühmt, dass es fast täglich Berichte über ihn und sein Leben in vielen Zeitungen in Deutschland gab. Der folgende online Artikel aus der Berliner Zeitung *Tagesspiegel* gibt Ihnen Informationen über Knuts Bedeutung für die Wirtschaft.

Vor dem Lesen

Der folgende Artikel hat den Titel „Knut tut der Wirtschaft gut". Wie kann ein Eisbär wohl gut für die Wirtschaft sein? Schreiben Sie drei Ideen auf.

Siehe **Kulturtipps:** Berliner Bär

Introduction to *Lesetext 3.* Ask students about their own experiences: *Waren Sie schon einmal im Zoo? Wenn ja, wo? Welche Tiere haben Sie dort gesehen? Welche Tiere haben den größten Eindruck auf Sie gemacht?* You may need to supply them with some animal vocabulary. Then ask them what they learned from the text introduction: *Was ist das Symbol Berlins? Wer ist Knut? Warum war seine Geburt ein großes Ereignis? Wer hat sich um ihn gekümmert? Warum?*

Note for *Lesetext 3.* In March 2011, Knut collapsed and died unexpectedly in his enclosure at the zoo. Only after his death was it determined that the four-year-old bear had encephalitis. You may choose to share the news of Knut's fate with students or let them discover it themselves in activity 1-24.

Beim Lesen

Suchen Sie im Lesetext, welches Unternehmen welche Knutprodukte herstellt. Manchmal passt mehr als ein Produkt zu einem Unternehmen.

Siehe **Kulturtipps**: Haribo

Unternehmen	Produkte
_g_ 1. Haribo	a. Anhänger für den Weihnachtsbaum
_a,e_ 2. Steiff	b. Bildschirmschoner für den Computer
_f_ 3. KPM	c. Knut-DVDs
_b,d,h_ 4. Jamba	d. Knut-Klingeltöne und -Logos für das Handy
_c_ 5. Der rbb-Sender	e. Knut-Plüschtiere
	f. Knut aus Porzellan
	g. Süßigkeiten in der Form von Knut
	h. Computerspiele

02-11 to 02-14

Berlin-Bärenstark! Knut tut der Wirtschaft gut

von Maren Martell

is going well

Knut haters

Das Geschäft mit dem Eisbären brummt und brummt°. Staatsgäste werden mit Porzellan-Knut beschenkt. Knut-Haribo macht Kinder froh und Knut-Hasser° kommen bei „Shoot Knut" auch auf ihre Kosten. Nebenbei ist der Eisbär sogar zum „Umweltschützer" geworden.

BERLIN. Knut ist zwar längst nicht mehr so süß, doch als bärenstarke Marke füllt er weiterhin die Kassen. Ob Plüschtiere, Porzellanfiguren, Silberschmuck oder Klingeltöne – alle Produkte rund um das Berliner Eisbärkind finden gut ein halbes Jahr nach seiner Geburt immer noch reißenden Absatz. Auch wenn das mittlerweile halbstarke, meist verdreckte Fellknäuel° sein knuddeliges Aussehen aus der Babyzeit verloren hat – der Hype hält an. Manche Unternehmen haben schon Knut-Produkte für das Weihnachtsgeschäft aufgelegt und als „Umweltbotschafter" wird der weltberühmte Bärenjunge wohl noch viele Jahre für den Klima- und Artenschutz° werben.

verdreckte Fellknäuel
dirty ball of fur

protection of climate and species

5

10

Haribo-Knut zum Klassiker

Allein der Berliner Zoo hat bisher mehr als 50.000 Knut-Plüschtiere verkauft. Schon im März – gleich nach dem ersten öffentlichen Auftritt des Eisbärenkinds – hatte sich die Zooleitung die Markenrechte gesichert. Mittlerweile gibt es rund 25 offizielle Lizenznehmer°, von der Königlichen Porzellanmanufaktur KPM bis zum Modeschmuckhersteller° Miss Bijou. Bis Jahresende könnte der Publikumsliebling dem Zoo Zusatzeinnahmen von rund 5 Millionen Euro bescheren.

licensees
producer of fashion jewelry

15

20

Der Süßwarenhersteller Haribo produziert täglich rund eine Million süße Schaumgummi-Eisbären. „Der Knuddel-Knut'sch hat große Chancen zum Klassiker zu werden", betont Sprecher Marco Alfter. Die Haribo-Werke in Solingen und Bonn kommen mit der Produktion kaum hinterher. Es gibt Anfragen aus Japan, der Schweiz und dem Baltikum. „Dorthin können wir noch nicht liefern, weil wir mit der Produktion für Deutschland und

25

Österreich völlig ausgelastet sind", sagt Alfter. 10 Cent pro verkaufte Knut-Dose gehen als „Kindergeld"- Spende an den Berliner Zoo. Bislang sind schon rund 40.000 Euro zusammengekommen. Sie sollen unter anderem für die Knut-Aufzucht° verwendet werden.

30   upbringing

Staatsgäste werden mit Porzellan-Knut beschenkt

Japanische Filmteams kommen nach Berlin, nicht nur, um das Eisbärkind im Zoo zu filmen. Sie drehen auch Beiträge über die Produktion des Porzellan-Knuts in der Königlichen Manufaktur KPM, berichtet Sprecherin Uta Petersen. Mehr als 2.000 Exemplare des 14 Zentimeter großen, handgefertigten Exemplars sind weltweit verkauft worden, auch nach China, Russland und in die USA. Die Lieferzeit beträgt gut drei Wochen. „Mit der Figur wurden schon viele Staatsgäste in Berlin beschenkt", betont Petersen.

35

Die Plüschtierfirma Steiff hat bereits mehr als 50.000 Plüsch-Knuts abgesetzt. „Die Erwartungen sind bei weitem erfüllt", heißt es am Firmensitz im schwäbischen Giengen°. Seitdem Knut zum Maskottchen der UN-Naturschutzkonferenz gekürt wurde, ist die Nachfrage besonders aus den USA enorm gestiegen. Bereits beim G8-Gipfel Anfang Juni in Heiligendamm waren Plüsch-Knuts an die Journalisten vergeben worden. Zu Weihnachten plant Steiff einen Plüschanhänger „Knut" für den Christbaum.

*Siehe **Kulturtipps:** Steiff*

40   Swabian town 120 km west of Stuttgart

rrb° verkaufte 40.000 Knut-DVDs

Der deutsche Handyklingelton-Marktführer Jamba bietet neben Klingeltö-nen („Alles wird Knut") auch Bildschirmschoner, Spiele und Logos an – insgesamt sind es 200 Knut-Produkte. „Sie sind im Moment die Topseller unseres Sortiments, die auch in Italien, Österreich, Schweden, Spanien, Portugal, Großbritannien und in den USA erfolgreich sind", betont Sprecher Niels Genzmer. Knutgegner kommen ebenso auf ihre Kosten: Für sie sind spezielle Internet-Spiele wie „Shoot Knut – Schieß Knut" oder Anti-Knut-Songs im Angebot. Auch übers Internet wird allerhand Kitsch rund um Knut vertrieben, von der Baby-Krabbeldecke bis zur Steinfigur für den Vorgarten. Der rbb-Sender verkaufte mittlerweile mehr als 40.000 seiner Knut-DVDs.

*= **Rundfunk Berlin-Brandenburg** Radio Berlin-Brandenburg*

45

50

„Weil er einfach wie Knut aussah"

„Mit so einem Riesenerfolg hatten wir nicht gerechnet", berichtet Zoo-Vorstand Gerald Uhlich. Dazu beigetragen hat auch, dass fast zeitgleich die Klimadiskussion hochkochte. „Außerdem war jeder froh, mal eine positive Nachricht zu hören", betont Uhlich. Zu seinem Erfolgsnamen ist der kleine Eisbär wohl eher zufällig gekommen: Sein Tierpfleger Thomas Dörflein soll ihn nach seiner Geburt aus einer Laune heraus so genannt haben, „weil er einfach wie Knut aussah".

55

60

Für den Berliner Zoo ist der Arten- und Klimaschutzgedanke auch wichtiger als der kommerzielle Effekt. „Mit Knuts Hilfe wollen wir verstärkt für einen respektvollen Umgang mit der Natur werben", betont Uhlich. Dafür ist die Marke „Respect Habitats. Knut" aufgelegt worden, die alle Gesellschaftsschichten° ansprechen soll: „Das ist ein sehr langfristiges Projekt und völlig unabhängig von Knuts Alter."

65

social classes

Kulturtipps

Berliner Bär

Seit über 700 Jahren ist der Bär das Symbol der Stadt. Im Jahre 1280 sieht man zum ersten Mal eine Bärenfigur auf einem Siegel (*seal*). 1709 erhielt Berlin ein neues Wappen (*coat of arms*), auf dem man zwei Adler und einen Bären sieht. Das Wappen, das wir heute mit Berlin identifizieren, ist noch relativ neu, es wurde 1990 entworfen und wird seitdem weltweit in dieser Form als Symbol der Stadt benutzt. Auch findet man an verschiedenen Orten in Berlin den Bären als Kunstobjekt.

Das Wappen Berlins

Haribo

„Haribo macht Kinder froh!" So klingt es in der Werbemusik (*ad jingle*) für den Süßwarenhersteller Haribo, den es seit 1920 gibt. Das berühmteste Produkt der Firma sind die Haribo Goldbären. Das sind Gummibären mit Fruchtgeschmack. Heute stellt Haribo in seinen 18 Betrieben über 50 verschiedene Gummiprodukte her, darunter auch Knut als weißen Gummibären mit Himbeergeschmack (*raspberry flavor*).

Steiff

Steiff ist der Markenname für einen internationalen Hersteller von Spielzeugen, vor allem bekannt durch seine Teddy- und Plüschtiere. Man erkennt ein Steiffplüschtier an der kleinen gelben Fahne (*flag*), die am Ohr eines jeden Steifftieres ist. Die Firma Steiff behauptet, den Teddybären im Jahre 1902 erfunden zu haben.

*Follow-up for **Kulturtipp: Berliner Bär**. Ask students: Hat Ihre Stadt ein Stadtsymbol oder -wappen? Kennen Sie andere Stadtsymbole?*

 Neue Vokabeln

Nomen

der Absatz, ¨e   *sales, turnover*
der Auftritt, -e   *appearance*
der Eisbär, -en   *polar bear*
die Erwartung, -en   *expectation*
der Hersteller, -   *producer*
der Klingelton, ¨e   *ringtone*
die Marke, -n   *brand*
die Nachfrage, -n   *demand*
das Plüschtier, -e   *stuffed animal*
der Umweltschützer, -/die Umweltschützerin, -nen   *protector of the environment*

das Unternehmen, -   *company, enterprise*

Verben

berichten   *to report*
liefern   *to deliver*
steigen, stieg, ist gestiegen   *to climb, rise*
verwenden   *to use*
werben (wirbt), warb, geworben   *to advertise*
werben für   *to promote*

Adjektive und Adverbien

erfolgreich   *successful*

kaum   *hardly*
knuddelig   *cuddly*
langfristig   *long-term*
mittlerweile   *meanwhile; in the meantime*
öffentlich   *public*
unabhängig (von)   *independent (from)*

Ausdrücke

Sie kommen auf ihre Kosten.   *They get their money's worth.*
unter anderem   *among other things*

2-19 Textarbeit: Richtig oder falsch? Wenn eine Aussage falsch ist, korrigieren und ergänzen Sie sie mit Informationen aus dem Text.

1. Knutprodukte wurden nicht mehr gekauft, als Knut nicht mehr klein und süß war.
2. Der Zoo verdiente durch Knutprodukte viel Geld.
3. Es gab wenig Nachfrage nach Haribos Schaumgummieisbären.
4. Ein Teil der Einnahmen von Haribo ging an den Zoo, um bei der Aufzucht von Knut zu helfen.
5. Der Porzellan-Knut war ein beliebtes Geschenk für ausländische Staatsgäste.
6. Zu Weihnachten war die Nachfrage nach Knut-Plüschtieren aus den USA enorm gestiegen.
7. Für Knutgegner gab es keine Produkte.
8. Der rbb-Sender hat Knut seinen Namen gegeben.
9. Knut half auch bei der Werbung für den Umweltschutz.

Answers for 2-19. 1. F – Der Hype hielt an. Knutprodukte wurden immer noch gekauft. **2.** R; **3.** F – Es gab große Nachfrage. **4.** R; **5.** R; **6.** F – Seitdem Knut zum Maskottchen der UN-Naturschutzkonferenz gemacht wurde, war die Nachfrage aus den USA enorm gestiegen. **7.** F – Es gab „Shoot Knut" und Anti-Knut-Lieder. **8.** F – Knuts Tierpfleger Thomas Dörflein hat ihm seinen Namen gegeben. **9.** R

2-20 Vokabelarbeit. Ergänzen Sie die Sätze mit Wörtern aus den *Neuen Vokabeln*. Achten Sie dabei auch auf die Wortform.

1. Mehr ___Absatz___ von Knutplüschbären bedeutet mehr Geld für den Zoo.
2. Der erste ___Auftritt___ von Knut kam im März, einige Monate nach seiner Geburt.
3. Die Firma Steiff stellte Knut schon bald nach seiner Geburt als ___Plüschtier___ her.
4. Der Haribo-Knut war ein ___erfolgreiches___ Produkt – die Haribo-Werke konnten diese Schaumgummibären nicht schnell genug produzieren.
5. Der rrb, Haribo, Steiff und viele andere Unternehmen ___verwenden___ Knut für ihre Werbung.
6. Kein anderer Eisbär sieht so weich und ___knuddelig___ aus wie Knut.
7. ___Umweltschützer___ sehen Knuts Erfolg teilweise kritisch – einerseits ist es gut, dass mehr Menschen an den Naturschutz denken, andererseits ist ein Zoo ein unnatürliches Habitat für einen Eisbären.

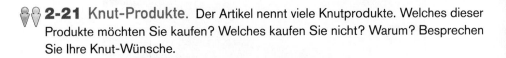

2-21 Knut-Produkte. Der Artikel nennt viele Knutprodukte. Welches dieser Produkte möchten Sie kaufen? Welches kaufen Sie nicht? Warum? Besprechen Sie Ihre Knut-Wünsche.

2-22 Zur Diskussion. Besprechen Sie die Fragen.

1. Warum, glauben Sie, waren die Deutschen von Knut so begeistert?
2. Was halten Sie davon, wie Knut für die Wirtschaft und den Zoo benutzt wurde?
3. Glauben Sie, man sollte bedrohte Tiere in Zoos halten? Warum (nicht)?

Der Berliner Bär als Kunstobjekt

2-23 Noch ein Knut-Produkt? Entwerfen Sie Ihr eigenes Knut-Produkt. Machen Sie eine Zeichnung von Ihrem Produkt und fügen Sie eine Beschreibung hinzu. Sagen Sie auch, wen dieses Produkt ansprechen soll.

Note for 2-24. Relevant web addresses for Internet research activities can be found in *MyGermanLab* and on the Companion Website.

2-24 Knuts Leben. Was ist Knut seit der Erscheinung dieses Artikels noch passiert? Schauen Sie im Internet nach Informationen über den weltberühmten Eisbären. Stellen Sie dann eine Chronik seines weiteren Lebens zusammen. Geben Sie an, in welchem Jahr was passiert ist.

Lesetext 4

Ein Wochenende in Berlin (Broschüre)

Introduction to *Lesetext 4*. To set the stage, ask students: *Machen Sie gern mal einen Kurzurlaub? Wohin reisen Sie dann? Welche Städte würden Sie gern einmal für ein langes Wochenende besuchen? Wo übernachten Sie, wenn Sie reisen?* Then ask them what they learned from the introductory text: *Wie viele Touristen besuchen Berlin jedes Jahr? Wie oft übernachten Touristen jedes Jahr in Berliner Hotels und Pensionen?*

Berlin ist immer eine Reise wert! So lautet ein bekannter Werbespruch für Berlin. Dieser Spruch scheint auch zu wirken, denn jährlich kommen Millionen von Besuchern nach Berlin. Mehr als die Hälfte von ihnen sind Deutsche. Viele von ihnen verbringen nicht nur einen Tag, sondern ein langes Wochenende in Berlin, um möglichst viele Attraktionen zu sehen und am Nachtleben der Stadt teilnehmen zu können. Jährlich zählt Berlin fast 19 Millionen Übernachtungen. Da viele Menschen gern Wochenendreisen machen, gibt es viele gute Angebote. Diese Broschüre ist ein typisches Beispiel für so ein Angebot.

Vor dem Lesen

Suggestion for *Lesetext 4*. This text can be read in tandem with reviewing the imperative mood, which is covered in the *Grammatik* of this chapter. Have students see how many examples of the imperative mood they can locate in the text. Then have them identify the form of address used. Ask them why they think the *Sie*-form is used here and how the tone would be different if the *du*-form of address were used.

Stellen Sie sich vor, Sie reisen für ein paar Tage nach Berlin. Wie kommen Sie nach Berlin? Wo übernachten Sie? Was machen Sie während des Tages und was am Abend?

Beim Lesen

Der folgende Text hat fünf Abschnitte. Jeder Abschnitt enthält Informationen über die Wochenendreise. Machen Sie sich Stichpunkte zu diesen Informationen.

Berlin   Wunschleistungen

Inklusivleistung   Hotel

Urlaubsort

Blick auf Berlin und die Spree

Ein Wochenende in Berlin

3-tägige Städtereise, Übernachtung im 5-Sterne-Hotel Kempinski, inkl. Frühstück ab € 149,-

Berlin - eine Stadt mit vielen Gesichtern! ▪ In der Hauptstadt treffen Geschichte und das neue Moderne aufeinander. Entdecken Sie

5 **Ihr** Berlin! Interessieren Sie sich für Kunst? Besuchen Sie die Museumsinsel!* Liegt Ihnen mehr am Nachtleben? Gehen Sie in eine der unzähligen Kabarettvorstellungen! Ist die Geschichte

10 der Stadt Ihre Motivation für den Besuch? Besichtigen Sie das Brandenburger Tor! Egal was Sie nach Berlin bringt, die Stadt hat für jeden etwas zu bieten und wird nie langweilig. Erkun-

15 den Sie die facettenreiche Hauptstadt und nehmen Sie eine Vielzahl neuer Eindrücke mit nach Hause!

Urlaubsort ▪ Es lohnt sich immer wieder, Berlin neu zu entdecken.

20 Keine andere Stadt hat ein so großes Freizeit- und Unterhaltungsangebot. Diese Metropole bietet ihren Gästen neben ihren berühmten Museen, dem Nachtleben oder den Shoppingmöglich-

25 keiten eine wunderschöne Nähe zur Natur. Sollten Sie nach Kultur und Shopping Lust auf Natur und Entspannung bekommen, besuchen Sie einfach eine der grünen Oasen, wie z. B. den

30 Großen Tiergarten, den größten Park Berlins. Besonders zu empfehlen ist der Natur-Park Schöneberger Südgelände.

Hier auf dem Gebiet des ehemaligen Rangierbahnhofs Tempelhof werden

35 Sie eine einmalige Naturlandschaft finden. Ein moderner Urwald inmitten der Stadt, in dem die Natur die Technik überwachsen hat. Genießen Sie echte Wildnis inmitten der Metropole!

40 **Hotel** ▪ Ihr 5-Sterne-Hotel: „Kempinski Hotel Bristol"

Das traditionsreiche Hotel bietet eine großartige Empfangshalle, Beauty-Center, Café-Bistro, Restaurant,

45 Fahrstuhl, Garage im Hotel (gegen Aufpreis), Schwimmbad, Fitnessraum, Bar, Kinder-/Babybett (verfügbar auf Anfrage), Klimaanlage in den öffentlichen Räumen, Tagungsräume und

50 drahtlose Internetverbindung im ganzen Haus. Die komfortablen Zimmer sind mit Bad oder Dusche/WC, Haartrockner, individuellen ISDN-Anschluss, Telefon, Minibar, internationale Auswahl an

55 TV-Programmen in mehreren Sprachen, Radio, Schreibtisch, Kosmetikspiegel sowie Voicemail ausgestattet. Nutzen Sie diese Gelegenheit sich verwöhnen und umsorgen zu lassen! Hier wird

60 Ihnen an NICHTS fehlen.

Das Kempinski Hotel Bristol in Berlin, das Stammhaus[a] der internationalen Kette, ist direkt am Kurfürstendamm[†]

im Herzen Berlins gelegen. Gäste aus aller Welt schätzen den Komfort

65 und den Service. Hier finden Sie alle Leistungen unter einem Dach. Nicht einmal zum Essen brauchen Sie das Hotel zu verlassen! Wenn Sie das Restaurant besuchen wollen, hat es

70 im gastronomischen Bereich einiges zu bieten. „Reinhards Restaurant" im Hotel Kempinski bietet Blick auf den Kurfürstendamm, während Sie sich

75 mit Brandenburger Kohlrouladen[b] oder Königsberger Klopsen[‡] verwöhnen lassen. Hier wurde an alles gedacht, was den Gast zum König macht.

Inklusivleistungen

- 2 Übernachtungen im gebuchten 5-Sterne-Hotel „Kempinski Hotel Bristol"
- Unterbringung im Doppelzimmer
- 2 × reichhaltiges Frühstücksbuffet
- Obst und Wasser bei Anreise auf dem Zimmer
- 10 % Ermäßigung in der Hotelbar
- Reisepreissicherungsschein

Wunschleistungen

- Einzelzimmerzuschlag: Saison A + B € 119,–, Saison C € 139,– (pro Person)
- Verlängerungsnächte auf Anfrage

[a]*company headquarters*   [b]*stuffed cabbage*

*Siehe **Kulturtipps:** Museumsinsel   †Siehe **Kulturtipps:** Kurfürstendamm   ‡Siehe **Kulturtipps:** Königsberger Klopse

Kulturtipps

Museumsinsel

Mitten durch Berlin fließt die Spree, in der im Zentrum der Stadt die Spreeinsel liegt. An der nördlichsten Spitze (*tip*) der Spreeinsel findet man viele berühmte Museen, denen diese Insel den Namen verdankt. Hier befindet sich unter anderem auch das weltberühmte Pergamonmuseum, in dem man antike, islamische und asiatische Kunst sehen kann. Seit 1999 gehört die Museumsinsel als einzigartiges und kulturelles Ensemble dem Weltkulturerbe der UNESCO (*United Nations Educational, Scientific and Cultural Organization*) an.

Das Bode-Museum an der Spitze der Museumsinsel

Kurfürstendamm

Der berühmte Kurfürstendamm, auch Ku'damm genannt, ist eine 3,5 km lange Prachtstrasse (*boulevard*) in Berlin. Der Ku'damm mit der Gedächtniskirche war am Ende des 19. Jahrhunderts eine vornehme Wohnstraße und bis zum Ersten Weltkrieg das Zentrum für Vergnügen und Einkauf. Nach dem Zweiten Weltkrieg wurde er zum Geschäftszentrum West-Berlins. Mit dem Fall der Mauer verlor er etwas an Bedeutung. Heute entwickelt sich der Ku'damm immer mehr zu einer exklusiven Einkaufsstraße.

Königsberger Klopse

Dieses Gericht findet man in ganz Deutschland. Es ist ursprünglich eine ostpreußische (*East Prussian*) Spezialität aus der einst deutschen Stadt Königsberg (heute Kaliningrad, einem Teil Russlands). Es besteht aus gekochten Fleischbällchen in weißer Sauce mit Kapern (*capers*).

Königsberger Klopse mit Kartoffel

Note for *Kulturtipp: Königsberger Klopse.* The recipe can be found in SAM activity 02-44.

 ## Neue Vokabeln

Nomen

das Angebot, -e   *offer, offering*
der Eindruck, ¨e   *impression*
die Entspannung   *relaxation*
der Höhepunkt, -e   *highlight*
der König, -e/die Königin, -nen   *king/queen*

die Leistung, -en   *service, offerings; achievement*
die Nähe   *closeness, vicinity*
der Ort, -e   *place*
der Zuschlag, ¨e   *surcharge*

Verben

empfehlen (empfiehlt), empfahl, empfohlen   *to recommend*

Adjektive and Adverbien

ausgestattet (mit)   *equipped (with)*
reichhaltig   *substantial, extensive*

Ausdrücke

auf Anfrage   *by request, on demand*
Es lohnt sich.   *It's worth it.*

2-25 Textarbeit: Richtig oder falsch? Wenn eine Aussage falsch ist, korrigieren und ergänzen Sie sie mit Informationen aus dem Lesetext.

1. Eine der berühmten Sehenswürdigkeiten ist das Brandenburger Tor.
2. Für Naturliebhaber gibt es nichts in Berlin.
3. Berlin ist die Stadt mit dem größten Freizeitangebot in Deutschland.
4. Das Hotel Kempinski ist einfach ausgestattet.
5. Im Hotel Kempinski gibt es keine Klimaanlage.
6. Alle Zimmer haben Internetanschluss.
7. Frühstück ist nicht im Hotelpreis enthalten.
8. Das Wochenendangebot ist für zwei Übernachtungen.

Answers for 2-25.1. R; **2.** F – Es gibt Parks. **3.** R; **4.** F – Das Hotel ist nicht einfach, sondern sehr gut ausgestattet. **5.** F – Es gibt eine Klimaanlage, aber nur in den öffentlichen Räumen. **6.** R; **7.** F – Das Frühstück ist im Preis enthalten. **8.** R

2-26 Vokabelarbeit. Ergänzen Sie die Sätze mit Wörtern aus den *Neuen Vokabeln.* Achten Sie dabei auch auf die Wortform.

1. Im Hotel kann man Ihnen __empfehlen__ , wo man essen kann, wohin man abends ausgehen sollte und was man unbedingt sehen muss.
2. Oft ist im Hotelpreis ein __reichhaltiges__ Frühstück enthalten.
3. Viele gute Hotels sind heute mit Internetanschluss __ausgestattet__ .
4. Berlin bietet viele Möglichkeiten zur __Entspannung__ , falls man Ruhe sucht oder sich erholen will.
5. Der __Höhepunkt__ einer Berlinreise ist für viele der Besuch des Zoos.
6. Jede Berlinreise, ob kurz oder lang, macht einen tiefen __Eindruck__ auf die Besucher.

2-27 Zur Diskussion. Besprechen Sie die Fragen.

1. Was in Berlin interessiert Sie am meisten?
2. Würden Sie im Hotel Kempinski übernachten? Warum (nicht)?
3. Interessiert Sie dieses Wochenendangebot? Warum (nicht)?
4. Haben Sie schon einmal einen Kurzurlaub gemacht? Wohin sind Sie gereist und was haben Sie dort gemacht?

2-28 Mein Traumhotel. Sie haben in einem Wettbewerb des Fernsehsenders rbb einen Kurzurlaub nach Berlin gewonnen! Sie dürfen drei Nächte übernachten, wo auch immer Sie wollen. Beschreiben Sie in einem Absatz für den Reiseagenten Ihre Traumübernachtung.

Additional speaking activity. *Sie haben die Reise nach Berlin gebucht. Sie fliegen schon morgen ab und bleiben drei Tage. Besprechen Sie, was Sie für die Reise packen und warum Sie diese Sachen mitnehmen.*

Das Brandenburger Tor bei Nacht

Note for 2-29. Relevant web addresses for Internet research activities can be found in *MyGermanLab* and on the Companion Website.

2-29 **Mein Wochenende in Berlin.** Sie kommen am Freitag um 11.00 Uhr in Berlin an und reisen am Sonntag um 17.30 Uhr ab. Was möchten Sie unbedingt sehen und erleben? Recherchieren Sie im Internet, was man in Berlin alles machen kann, und tragen Sie einen Plan für Ihren Kurzurlaub in Ihrem Kalender ein.

	Zeit	Aktivität
Freitag	11.00 Uhr	Ankunft
Samstag		
Sonntag		
	17.30 Uhr	Abfahrt

Transcripts for all Hörtexte are located in the Instructor's Resource Manual.

Hörtext 2

Ausflugsziel Brandenburg? (Gespräch)

Frank, Clara und Bernd sind schon seit zwei Jahren Studenten an der FU in Berlin. Sie treffen sich in der Mensa und sprechen über das vergangene Wochenende. Hören Sie sich das Gespräch an.

Vor dem Hören

Sehen Sie sich eine Karte von Deutschland an. Beschreiben Sie die geografische Beziehung zwischen Brandenburg und Berlin. Wissen Sie auch etwas über die historische Beziehung zwischen beiden?

Beim Hören

Hören Sie sich das Gespräch an. Markieren Sie die Wörter, die Sie hören.

Ausflugsziel Brandenburg?

02-18

Theologieseminar	Konzerte	Til Schweiger
Universität	Bibliothek	Potsdam
Tanzclub	Neuruppin	Spreewald
Salsa	Radtour	Cottbus
Restaurant	Wanderung	Vögel
Museen	Picknick	Kahnfahrt

Information for *Beim Hören.* Ask students if they have ever heard of Til Schweiger. The actor, director, writer, and producer is one of Germany's most successful filmmakers. Students may know him for his role in the Quentin Tarantino film *Inglourious Basterds.*

2-30 Textarbeit: Was hören Sie? Wählen Sie die passenden Antworten.
Manchmal treffen mehrere Antworten zu.

1. Bernd muss am Mittwoch _____ .

   ein Referat halten   arbeiten
   in die Bibliothek gehen   in eine Vorlesung gehen

2. Bernd und Clara sind am Wochenende _____ gegangen.

   ins Museum   ins Konzert   in einen Tanzclub   nach Potsdam

3. Frank und seine Freundin waren am Wochenende _____ .

   in Neuruppin   auf einer Radtour   im Schloss   beim Picknick

4. Sie haben Theodor Fontanes _____ besucht.

   Grab   Geburtshaus   Museum   Enkel

5. Am Abend sind Frank und seine Freundin _____ gegangen.

   ins Konzert   ins Museum   ins Kino   ins Restaurant

6. Bernd und Clara haben einmal _____ besucht.

   Potsdam   das Schloss Sanssouci
   das Pergamonmuseum   den Filmpark Babelsberg

7. Clara möchte _____ .

   den Spreewald besuchen   eine Kahnfahrt machen
   die Stadt Cottbus kennenlernen   öfter ins Brandenburger Land fahren

Theodor Fontane (1882)

Kulturtipps

Theodor Fontane (1819–1898)

Der deutsche Schriftsteller Theodor Fontane, ein Hauptvertreter des deutschen Realismus, wurde 1819 im brandenburgischen Neuruppin geboren. Er verbrachte die meisten Jahre seines Lebens an verschiedenen Orten in Brandenburg und in Berlin. Seine „Wanderung durch die Mark Brandenburg" ist eine literarische Hommage an seine Heimat, die auch den Hintergrund für seine großen Romane bilden, die ein kritisches Bild der preußischen Gesellschaft liefern.

Spreewald

Der Spreewald ist eine einzigartige Flusslandschaft 100 km südöstlich von Berlin. Das einmalige Wasserlabyrinth windet sich durch Wiesen, Wälder und Dörfer. Viele Ackerflächen und Bauernhöfe sind nur auf dem Wasser erreichbar. So ist es nicht ungewöhnlich, wenn eine Kuh im Kahn (*small boat*) zur Weide gebracht wird oder wenn der Postbote mit dem Kahn kommt.

Der Spreewald südöstlich von Berlin

2-31 Textarbeit: Richtig oder falsch? Wenn eine Aussage falsch ist, korrigieren und ergänzen Sie sie mit Informationen aus dem Hörtext.

Answers for 2-31. 1. F – Frank ist mit seiner Freundin in Neuruppin gewesen. Bernd und Clara sind in Berlin geblieben. **2.** R; **3.** F – Frank ist mit seiner Freundin nach Neuruppin gefahren. **4.** R; **5.** F – Frank fand sein Wochenende auf dem Land entspannend. **6.** F – Sie haben einen Film mit Til Schweiger gesehen. **7.** F – Sie sind einmal in Potsdam gewesen. **8.** R

1. Clara, Frank und Bernd haben das Wochenende zusammen verbracht.
2. Es gab am Samstag im Tanzclub Bailamor einen karibischen Salsa-Abend.
3. Frank ist mit seiner Freundin nach Frankfurt an der Oder gefahren.
4. Bernd findet die Idee, ein Wochenende auf dem Land zu verbringen, sehr langweilig.
5. Auch Frank fand sein Wochenende auf dem Land langweilig.
6. Frank und seine Freundin haben einen Film über Theodor Fontane gesehen.
7. Clara und Bernd sind schon dreimal in Potsdam gewesen.
8. Frank möchte gern einen Ausflug in den Spreewald machen.

 2-32 Zur Diskussion. Besprechen Sie die Fragen.

1. Denken Sie an Frank, Bernd und Clara. Wer ist eher ein Stadtmensch? Wer ist ein Landmensch? Erklären Sie Ihre Antworten.
2. Sind Sie eher ein Stadtmensch oder ein Landmensch? Warum?
3. Haben Sie jemals ein Museum oder die Geburtsstätte von einem Autor oder einem Künstler besucht? Was kann man dort sehen? Was lernt oder erfährt man an solchen Orten?
4. Was haben Sie am Wochenende gemacht? Was machen Sie normalerweise am Wochenende? Was möchten Sie am liebsten machen?

 2-33 Ein Ausflug aufs Land. Planen Sie einen gemeinsamen Ausflug für nächstes Wochenende. Das Ausflugsziel sollen Sie innerhalb von zwei Stunden erreichen können. Wann fahren Sie los? Wie kommen Sie hin? Was machen Sie dort? Was müssen Sie mitbringen? Machen Sie einen Plan.

Follow-up for 2-33. Have a person in each group describe their plan to the class.

Schloss Sanssouci in Potsdam

2-34 Berlin-Brandenburg. Berlin und Brandenburg sind schon seit Jahrhunderten eng miteinander verbunden. Suchen Sie im Internet nach Institutionen, die den Namen „Berlin-Brandenburg" tragen. Machen Sie eine Liste von mindestens fünf solchen Einrichtungen und beschreiben Sie ihre Funktion.

Note for 2-34. Relevant web addresses for Internet research activities can be found in *MyGermanLab* and on the Companion Website.

Additional information for 2-34. In a 1996 vote, the residents of Berlin and Brandenburg rejected a proposed fusion of the two states. Nonetheless, the governments of both states continue to work closely together and have merged several of their official functions. Share this information with the students and then ask: *Was sind die Vorteile einer solchen Fusion? Die Nachteile? Was meinen Sie: Warum haben das Volk und einige Politiker eine solche Fusion nicht gewollt?*

Grammatik

02-26 to 02-32

1. Present perfect tense (Perfekt)

In *Kapitel 1*, you learned about the simple past tense (**Präteritum**). The meanings of the present perfect tense and the simple past tense largely overlap. The difference is in usage. While the simple past tense is used mainly in writing, the present perfect tense is commonly used in everyday conversation. For this reason, the present perfect tense is also called the conversational past tense.

The present perfect tense is formed with an auxiliary verb and a past participle. It has a variety of possible English equivalents:

ich habe gekocht {
    I cooked
    I have cooked
    I was cooking
    I did cook
    I used to cook

02-26

Auxiliary verbs (Hilfsverben)

The German present perfect tense uses **haben** and **sein** as auxiliary verbs. The auxiliary verb is conjugated to agree with the sentence subject and appears in statements in the second position.

> Meine Freunde und ich **sind** in den Tiergarten **gegangen.**
>
> Dort **haben** wir einige interessante Vögel **gesehen.**

To review the present tense conjugations of *haben* and *sein*, see *Kapitel 1, Grammatik:* Present Tense: Other Irregular Verbs.

Most verbs use **haben** as their auxiliary. The verb **sein** is used with intransitive verbs (i.e., verbs that cannot take a direct object) that express a change of location or condition (e.g., **fahren, fliegen, werden, sterben**), as well as such verbs as **bleiben, passieren,** and **sein.** If you are uncertain which auxiliary to use, look it up in a dictionary.

2-35 Hilfsverben. Entscheiden Sie, ob die folgenden Verben **haben** oder **sein** als Hilfsverb verwenden. Wo es Ihnen unklar ist, suchen Sie die Informationen in einem Wörterbuch.

schreiben: _____haben_____

dauern: _____haben_____

fallen: _____sein_____

vergessen: _____haben_____

wandern: _____sein_____

essen: _____haben_____

aufstehen: _____sein_____

sagen: _____haben_____

sinken: _____sein_____

lachen: _____haben_____

2-36 Gespräch mit Batu. Jonathan ist ein amerikanischer Austauschstudent an der FU. Er lernt Batu, einen Deutschen türkischer Herkunft, kennen. Setzen sie die richtigen Formen der Hilfsverben ein.

| bin | bist | habe | haben (2x) | habt | hast | hat (2x) | ist | sind (2x) |

Jonathan: Wie lange bist du schon in Berlin, Batu?

Batu: Mein ganzes Leben.

Jonathan: Wie bitte? Du kommst nicht aus der Türkei?

Batu: Nein, ich (1) _____bin_____ eigentlich noch nie in der Türkei gewesen. Meine Großeltern (2) _____sind_____ in den 1950er-Jahren aus Istanbul ausgewandert. Sie hatten vor, irgendwann in die Türkei zurückzukehren, aber sie (3) _____sind_____ einfach hier geblieben.

Jonathan: (4) _____Haben_____ deine Großeltern in Berlin gelebt?

Batu: Nein, mein Großvater (5) _____hat_____ in der Nähe von Hamburg gelebt und gearbeitet. Da ist mein Vater geboren. Als mein Vater 19 war, (6) _____ist_____ er nach Berlin gekommen und hier (7) _____hat_____ er meine Mutter kennengelernt.

Jonathan: Ihr (8) _____habt_____ also die ganze Zeit in Berlin gelebt? Und du (9) _____bist_____ hier aufgewachsen? Erinnerst du dich noch an den Fall der Mauer? (10) _____Hast_____ du die Feierlichkeiten mitgemacht?

Batu: Kaum. Ich war erst drei Jahre alt und (11) _____habe_____ nicht viel davon verstanden. Aber mein Vater und mein älterer Bruder (12) _____haben_____ sich mit Hammer und Meißel am Abbau der Mauer beteiligt. Ich habe sogar noch ein paar Mauerstücke bei mir zu Hause.

Jonathan: Das sind aber tolle Andenken!

Past participles (Partizip II)

How a verb forms its past participle depends on whether it the verb is *weak,* *strong,* or *mixed.*

Weak		Strong		Mixed	
infinitive	*past participle*	*infinitive*	*past participle*	*infinitive*	*past participle*
fragen	gefragt	kommen	gekommen	kennen	gekannt
kosten	gekostet	schreiben	geschrieben	bringen	gebracht
regnen	geregnet	liegen	gelegen	denken	gedacht
wollen	gewollt	werden	geworden	nennen	genannt
interessieren	interessiert	sein	gewesen	müssen	gemusst
einkaufen	eingekauft	mitnehmen	mitgenommen	nachdenken	nachgedacht
überleben	überlebt	verstehen	verstanden	bekennen	bekannt

- *Weak verbs* (**Schwache Verben**). The past participle of a weak verb always consists of the infinitive stem plus the prefix **ge-** and the suffix **-(t)**. The past participles of the modal verbs **sollen** and **wollen** follow the weak verb pattern. Verbs ending in **-ieren** also belong to this category, but they omit the **ge-** prefix in their participles.

  Weak verb past participles. An *-e* is inserted before the *-t* suffix if the stem ends in *-d, -t,* or in *-m* or *-n* preceded by a consonant other than *-l* or *-r.*

- *Strong verbs* (**Starke Verben**). The past participle of a strong verb consists of the perfect stem, which may be identical to the infinitive stem or may contain a vowel change, plus the prefix **ge-** and the suffix **-en.**

  A comprehensive list of irregular verbs and their principle parts can be found in the Appendix.

- *Mixed verbs* (**Gemischte Verben**). The past participle of a mixed verb consists of the perfect stem, which contains a vowel change, plus the prefix **ge-** and the suffix **-t.** The modal verbs with umlauts follow the mixed verb pattern.

While weak verbs are predictable, both strong verbs and mixed verbs have unpredictable stem changes in their past participles and must therefore be looked up or learned.

- *Verbs with prefixes* (**Verben mit Präfixen**). When verbs have *separable prefixes*, the **ge-** prefix is inserted between the prefix and the verb stem. When verbs have *inseparable prefixes* (**be-, emp-, ent-, er-, ge-, miss-, ver-, zer-**), the **ge-** prefix is omitted. These variations can occur in the participles of all verb types: weak, strong, or mixed.

  Past participles of inseparable prefix verbs. Note that a small number of inseparable prefix verbs have the **ge-** prefix in their infinitive forms (e.g., **gehören, gefallen**) and thus retain the prefix in their past participles.

Follow-up comprehension questions for 2-37. **1.** *Wer hat damals die vier Sektoren Berlins kontrolliert?* **2.** *Warum gab es Konflikte zwischen den Alliierten?* **3.** *Wie hat West-Berlin 1948/49 die Blockade überstanden?* **4.** *Warum haben viele DDR-Bürger ihre Heimat verlassen?* **5.** *Warum brachte das Schwierigkeiten für die DDR mit sich?* **6.** *Wie viele Menschen sind bei Fluchtversuchen in den Westen gestorben?* **7.** *Wie hat die DDR die wirtschaftlichen Probleme der 80er-Jahre überstanden?* **8.** *Seit wann steht die Mauer nicht mehr als Grenze?* **9.** *Seit wann ist Berlin wieder Hauptstadt der BRD?*

Follow-up activity for 2-37. Have students identify five more past participles in the text. Have them give the infinitive form of each and state whether it is a weak, strong, or mixed verb. Possible answers:
Schwach: besetzt (besetzen), kontrolliert (kontrollieren), versorgt (versorgen), riskiert (riskieren), geströmt (strömen); Stark: gegangen (gehen), gekommen (kommen), geraten (geraten), bestanden (bestehen), abgerissen (abreißen), verloren (verlieren); Gemischt: hervorgebracht (hervorbringen), anerkannt (anerkennen)

2-37 Berlin im Kalten Krieg. Letztes Jahr hat Jonathan in seinem Deutsch-kurs an der University of Maryland ein Referat über Berlin zur Zeit des Kalten Krieges gehalten. Ergänzen Sie den Text mit den Partizipien der jeweils passenden Verben.

blockieren	erleben	führen	gründen	~~teilen~~
verlassen	werden	wollen	ziehen	

Nach dem Zweiten Weltkrieg haben die Alliierten Berlin in vier Sektoren (1) _geteilt_. Großbritannien, Frankreich und die USA haben je einen Sektor im Westteil der Stadt besetzt, während die Sowjetunion den östlichen Sektor kontrolliert hat. Schon bald darauf haben ideologische Differenzen die ersten politischen Konflikte hervorgebracht. Im Juni 1948 haben sowjetische Truppen alle Verkehrswege nach West-Berlin (2) _blockiert_. Während der elfmonatigen Blockade haben die Westalliierten die Stadt mittels Flugzeuge – der sogenannten Luftbrücke – versorgt. Kurz danach hat man die BRD und die DDR offiziell (3) _gegründet_.

In den 50er-Jahren hat die BRD einen großen wirtschaftlichen Aufstieg (4) _erlebt_. In der kommunistischen DDR ist die wirtschaftliche Situation schlechter (5) _geworden_. Außerdem haben viele Menschen mehr individuelle Freiheiten (6) _gewollt_. Viele DDR-Bürger haben ihre Heimat (7) _verlassen_ und sind in den Westen gegangen. Mehr als 2,6 Millionen Menschen sind bis 1961 in den Westen (8) _gezogen_. Das hat in der DDR zu einem dramatischen Mangel an Arbeitskräften (9) _geführt_.

anfangen	machen	öffnen	sterben	teilnehmen

Am 13. August 1961 hat die DDR-Regierung mit dem Bau der Mauer (10) _angefangen_. Trotz der Mauer haben viele Menchen bei Fluchtversuchen dennoch ihr Leben riskiert. Zwischen 1961 und 1989 sind über 130 Menschen an der Berliner Mauer (11) _gestorben_. An der innerdeutschen Grenze sind fast 1.000 Menschen ums Leben gekommen.

Im Laufe der 80er-Jahre ist die DDR wie alle Ostblockstaaten in eine finanzielle Notlage geraten, obwohl sie es nicht öffentlich anerkannt hat. Die DDR hat ökonomisch nur noch mit Hilfe von Krediten aus der BRD weiter bestanden. Immer mehr DDR-Bürger haben an Protestaktionen (12) _teilgenommen_. Am 9. November 1989 haben ostdeutsche Grenztruppen die Grenze zwischen Ost- und West-Berlin (13) _geöffnet_. Allein in der ersten Stunde sind ca. 20.000 Menschen durch die offene Grenze geströmt.

In den Monaten danach hat man die Mauer abgerissen. Nach mehr als 28 Jahren hatte sie endlich ihren Schrecken verloren. Am 3. Oktober 1990 hat man das wiedervereinigte Berlin noch einmal zur Hauptstadt Deutschlands (14) _gemacht_.

2-38 Berlin und Brandenburg. In seinem ersten Austauschsemester belegt Jonathan ein Seminar über die Geschichte Berlins. Heute diskutiert man über das historische Verhältnis zwischen Berlin und Brandenburg. Wählen Sie jeweils das passende Verb und setzen Sie es ins Perfekt.

1. Berlin _____ist_____ im 12. Jahrhundert am rechten Ufer der Spree _____entstanden_____ . (entstehen, ausdrücken)

2. Die Stadt _____hat_____ schon seit ihrer Gründung zu Brandenburg _____gehört_____ . (berichten, gehören)

3. 1451 _____haben_____ die Hohenzollern in Brandenburg Berlin als ihre Residenzstadt _____gewählt_____ . (schützen, wählen)

4. Bis zum 14. Jahrhundert _____hat_____ sich Brandenburg zum größten Fürstentum (*principality*) Deutschlands _____entwickelt_____ . (entwickeln, erreichen)

5. 1701 _____hat_____ König Friedrich I. das Königreich Preußen _____gegründet_____ . (gründen, beitragen)

6. Berlin _____ist_____ die offizielle Haupt- und Residenzstadt Preußens _____gewesen_____ . (sein, prägen)

7. Unter Friedrich dem Großen (1740–1786) _____ist_____ Preußen zu einer europäischen Großmacht _____aufgestiegen_____ . (erhalten, aufsteigen)

8. Mit der Gründung des deutschen Reichs 1871 _____sind_____ der preußische König Wilhelm I. Kaiser und Berlin Hauptstadt Deutschlands _____geworden_____ . (werden, bieten)

02-33 to 02-34

2. Past perfect tense (Plusquamperfekt)

As in English, the past perfect tense is used when already talking about the past to refer to an earlier time in the past.

Karl wollte das Schloss Charlottenburg besuchen, aber ich **hatte** es schon einmal **besucht.**	*Karl wanted to visit Charlottenburg Palace, but I* ***had*** *already* ***visited*** *it.*

The past perfect tense is formed from the simple past tense of the auxiliary verb **haben** or **sein** plus the past participle of the main verb.

Infinitive	lernen	gehen
Past participle	gelernt	gegangen
ich	hatte gelernt	war gegangen
du	hattest gelernt	warst gegangen
er, sie, es	hatte gelernt	war gegangen
wir	hatten gelernt	waren gegangen
ihr	hattet gelernt	wart gegangen
Sie, sie	hatten gelernt	waren gegangen

2-39 Berlin, Wende, Mauerfall. Unterstreichen Sie alle Formen des Plusquamperfekts. Dann verbinden Sie die Satzteile sinnvoll miteinander.

<u>d</u> 1. Als Willy Brandt Kanzler der BRD wurde,

<u>a</u> 2. Nachdem die Mauer <u>entstanden war</u>,

<u>b</u> 3. Bevor die Mauer in Berlin fiel,

<u>c</u> 4. Nachdem die Deutschen aus Ost und West sich wieder besser <u>kennengelernt hatten</u>,

<u>e</u> 5. Als die Mauer in Berlin abgerissen wurde,

a. wurden Familien voneinander getrennt.

b. <u>hatte</u> es in der DDR viele Demonstrationen <u>gegeben</u>.

c. erkannten sie viele Gemeinsamkeiten.

d. <u>hatte</u> er schon viele Erfahrungen in der Politik <u>gesammelt</u>.

e. <u>hatten</u> sich bereits viele Menschen ein Mauerstück zur Erinnerung <u>geholt</u>.

2-40 Mehr über Berlin. Schreiben Sie jeden Satz in die angegebene Zeitform um.

1. Die Stadt **benennt** man vermutlich nach dem slawischen Wort *berl* (*swamp*). → Plusquamperfekt

2. Im Laufe der Jahrhunderte **wird** die Stadt immer größer und immer wichtiger. → Perfekt

3. 1945 **zerstören** Bombenangriffe die Innenstadt und **töten** viele Tausende von Menschen. → Perfekt

4. Nach der Wende **kommen** Familienmitglieder nach vielen Jahren wieder **zusammen**. → Perfekt

5. Die Mauer **trennt** den Osten und den Westen Berlins völlig voneinander. → Plusquamperfekt

6. Verwandte **sehen** sich jahrelang nicht. → Plusquamperfekt

7. Die Wende **bringt** für viele Bürger beider Staaten Schwierigkeiten **mit sich**. → Perfekt

8. Man **redet** in der Zeit danach von der „Mauer im Kopf". → Perfekt

Answers for 2-40. **1.** Die Stadt hatte man vermutlich nach dem slawischen Wort *berl* benannt. **2.** Im Laufe der Jahrhunderte ist die Stadt immer größer und immer wichtiger geworden. **3.** 1945 haben Bombenangriffe die Innenstadt zerstört und (haben) viele Tausende von Menschen getötet. **4.** Nach der Wende sind Familienmitglieder nach vielen Jahren wieder zusammengekommen **5.** Die Mauer hatte den Osten und den Westen Berlins völlig voneinander getrennt. **6.** Verwandte hatten sich jahrelang nicht gesehen. **7.** Die Wende hat für viele Bürger beider Staaten Schwierigkeiten mit sich gebracht. **8.** Man hat in der Zeit danach von der „Mauer im Kopf" geredet.

02-37 to 02-40

3. Gender of nouns (Nomen: Geschlecht)

Every German noun has a gender. Gender is indicated by the definite articles **der** (masculine), **die** (feminine), and **das** (neuter), all of which mean *the*. While grammatical gender and natural gender are usually the same when the noun designates a person (**die Frau, der Junge**), grammatical gender has little to do with the qualities of the objects that nouns refer to. For this reason, a car can be called **das Auto** or **der Wagen** with no difference in meaning.

Grammatical gender is unpredictable. However, a limited number of nouns have features that make their gender more predictable, either due to the noun's meaning or specific linguistic features.

Masculine
• Days of the week, months, seasons, some weather features: **der Montag, der Januar, der Sommer, der Schnee, der Regen**
• Nouns ending in **-er** when derived from the verb's infinitive stem: **der Verbraucher, der Träger**
• Nouns ending in **-ant, -ast, -ich, -ig, -ismus, -ling, -or, -us: der Käfig, der Sozialismus**

Feminine
• Nouns ending in **-ei, -heit, -ie, -keit, -schaft, -tät, -ung: die Einheit, die Freundschaft, die Erinnerung**
• Nouns derived from foreign words ending in **-anz, -enz, -ik, -ion, -ur: die Dekadenz, die Reaktion**
• Most nouns ending in **-e: die Blume, die Schere, die Stelle**

Neuter
• Young persons and young animals: **das Kind, das Baby, das Lamm, das Kalb**
• Verb infinitives used as nouns: **das Schlafen, das Denken, das Wohnen**
• Names of continents, countries, towns: **das Afrika, das Deutschland, das Berlin** (Note that **die USA** is plural.)
• Nouns ending in the diminutives **-chen, -lein: das Mädchen, das Brötchen, das Büchlein**
• Nouns ending in **-ment, -tel, -tum, -um: das Element, das Mittel, das Datum**
• Nouns ending in **-ar, -är, -ent, -ier,** and **-o** when they refer to things: **das Formular, das Video**

It is important to learn the gender with each noun. Although the patterns above do not account for all German nouns and there are some exceptions, these guidelines can facilitate the task of learning of German noun genders.

2-41 Was für ein Geschlecht? Benutzen Sie die Kriterien oben und nennen Sie für jedes der folgenden Nomen, die Sie in diesem Kapitel gesehen haben, das Geschlecht.

die Sprecherin	_die_ Freiheit	_die_ Wissenschaft
das Einkaufen	_der_ Wind	_das_ Ampelmännchen
der König	_die_ Kultur	
die Politik	_die_ Metropole	

Der Reichstag, Sitz des Deutschen Bundestags

02-41 to 02-43

4. Nouns: Plural forms (Nomen: Pluralformen)

German has a number of different plural forms. The plural definite article is **die** regardless of a noun's gender in its singular form.

In the vocabulary lists and many dictionaries, plural forms directly follow the noun entry: **die Regierung, -en; das Ufer, -; der Fluss, ¨e.** Note that in some dictionaries, you will see two sets of suffixes following a noun: **die Bedeutung, -, -en** or **das Ufer, -s, -** or **der Fluss, -es, ¨e.** In this case, the second suffix is the plural form. (The first is the genitive singular ending.) The most common plural patterns are given in the chart below.

no change or ¨	Most masculine and neuter nouns ending in **-el, -en, -er**			
	der Kuchen	→ die Kuchen	das Viertel	→ die Viertel
	der Vater	→ die Väter	das Zimmer	→ die Zimmer
	Neuter nouns ending in **-chen, -lein** (no change)			
	das Männlein	→ die Männlein	das Brötchen	→ die Brötchen
-e or **¨e**	Most other masculine and neuter nouns.			
	der Tag	→ die Tag**e**	das Bein	→ die Bein**e**
	A number of one-syllable feminine nouns mostly ending in **-t.** (**¨e**)			
	die Macht	→ die Mächte	die Hand	→ die Hände
-n, -en, or **-nen**	Most feminine nouns.			
	die Frage	→ die Frage**n**	die Wohnung	→ die Wohnung**en**
	die Art	→ die Art**en**	die Schülerin	→ die Schülerin**nen**
	All masculine weak nouns.[1]			
	der Name	→ die Name**n**	der Aktivist	→ die Aktiviste**n**
-er or **¨er**	Many monosyllabic neuter nouns. No feminine nouns have plurals in this category.			
	das Blatt	→ die Bl**ätter**	das Haus	→ die H**äuser**
-s	Some words borrowed from English or French, abbreviations, and surnames.			
	das Baby	→ die Baby**s**	das Souvenir	→ die Souvenir**s**
	die CD	→ die CD**s**	Schmidt	→ die Schmidt**s**

[1]Masculine weak nouns include nearly all masculine nouns ending in **-e** and a large number of foreign nouns ending in, e.g., **-ant, -ast, -ent, -ist, -oph, -om.** You will learn more about weak nouns in *Kapitel 4.*

The plural form for each noun must be memorized along with its gender. While such categorizations can be helpful, there are exceptions for nearly every rule. If you familiarize yourself with these general tendencies, you can take special note of the exceptions when you encounter them. This approach can make knowing—and remembering—plural forms easier.

2-42 Mehr Pluralformen. Geben Sie mit Hilfe der Kategorien oben die Pluralform der folgenden Nomen aus *Kapitel 2*. Wenn Sie weitere Hilfe brauchen, schlagen Sie die Wörter im Wörterbuch nach.

die Zeitung: _die Zeitungen_   das Dorf: _die Dörfer_

der Computer: _die Computer_   der Berliner: _die Berliner_

die DVD: _die DVDs_   das Spiel: _die Spiele_

die Kunst: _die Künste_   die Figur: _die Figuren_

die Kinderkrippe: _die Kinderkrippen_   das Wahrzeichen: _die Wahrzeichen_

5. Imperative mood (Imperativ)

02-44 to 02-48

The imperative mood is used to give commands or make suggestions. The German imperative has four different forms. The form depends on who is being addressed in the command. However, all forms are based on present tense verb conjugations, use verb-first word order, and are often punctuated with an exclamation point.

Infinitive	**Sie**-*form*	**ihr**-*form*	**du**-*form*		**wir**-*form*	
gehen	Gehen Sie!	Geht!	Geh(e)!	*Go!*	Gehen wir!	*Let's go!*
an·rufen	Rufen Sie an!	Ruft an!	Ruf(e) an!	*Call!*	Rufen wir an!	*Let's call!*
fahren	Fahren Sie!	Fahrt!	Fahr(e)	*Drive!*	Fahren wir!	*Let's drive!*
lesen	Lesen Sie!	Lest!	Lies!	*Read!*	Lesen wir!	*Let's read!*
sein	Seien Sie ruhig!	Seid ruhig!	Sei ruhig!	*Be quiet!*	Seien wir ruhig!	*Let's be quiet!*

The polite particle **bitte,** as well as the particles **mal** and **doch,** are sometimes used to soften the tone of a command.

Rufen Sie **doch mal** an!   *Go ahead and call!*

Fahr **doch** schneller!   *Drive faster, will you!*

Seid **bitte** ruhig!   *Please be quiet!*

Note these variations:

- *Sie and wir.* The imperative for the polite form **Sie** and the first person plural **wir** both use their regular present tense conjugation, but with verb-first word order.

- *ihr.* The second person plural **ihr** is identical to its present tense conjugation, but the personal pronoun **ihr** is omitted.

- *du.* The imperative for the second person singular **du** is usually identical to the infinitive stem. An optional **-e** may be added to this stem. However, the **-e** is required if the stem ends in **-t, -d, -ig,** or **-m** or **-n** preceded by a consonant other than l or r.

warten → Wart**e!**   zeichnen → Zeichn**e!**

Verbs with the present tense stem change **a** → **ä** or **au** → **äu** use the unchanged infinitive stem in the **du**-imperative. However, verbs with the present tense stem change **e** → **i** or **e** → **ie** retain the stem change in the imperative. Verbs with the **e** → **i** or **e** → **ie** stem change do not add the suffix **-e**.

> fahren → Fahr(**e**)!
>
> laufen → Lauf(**e**)!
>
> lesen → L**ie**s!
>
> vergessen → Verg**i**ss!

- *The verb **sein**.* The imperative forms of **sein** are irregular in the **Sie**- and **wir**-forms.

Answers for 2-43.
A. 1. Nehmen Sie an der Orientierung teil! **2.** Lernen Sie andere Studierende kennen!
3. Belegen Sie einen Deutschkurs! **4.** Erwarten Sie, in den ersten Wochen sehr müde zu sein!
5. Ruhen Sie sich im Botanischen Garten der Universität aus!
B. 1. Kauf(e) doch keine Bücher im Buchladen! **2.** Such(e) die Bücher erst mal in der Universitätsbibliothek! **3.** Iss doch in der Mensa. Da ist es billig! **4.** Fahr(e) mit der U-Bahn oder mit dem Bus in die Stadtmitte! **5.** Benutz(e) die U-Bahn-Halteselle Dahlem-Dorf.
C. 1. Ruft mich mal an, wenn ihr heute Abend ausgeht! **2.** Sagt mir mal, welche Professoren gut sind! **3.** Empfehlt mir bitte ein gutes Internetcafé! **4.** Kommt doch mal dieses Wochenende mit mir an die Ostsee! **5.** Seid bitte nicht so laut!

2-43 Rat für das Studium.

A. Im Akademischen Auslandsamt der FU gibt die Studienberaterin Jonathan Rat für sein Studium und sein Leben an der Uni. Was rät sie ihm? Bilden Sie sinnvolle Sätze in der **Sie**-Form des Imperativs.

1. teilnehmen	einen Deutschkurs
2. kennenlernen	im Botanischen Garten der Universität
3. belegen	in den ersten Wochen sehr müde sein
4. erwarten	an der Orientierung
5. sich ausruhen	andere Studierende

B. Im Studentenwohnheim geben ihm andere Studenten weitere Tipps. Bilden Sie sinnvolle Sätze in der **du**-Form des Imperativs.

1. kaufen	die Bücher erst mal in der Universitätsbibliothek
2. suchen	doch keine Bücher im Buchladen
3. essen	die U-Bahn-Haltestelle Dahlem-Dorf
4. fahren	doch in der Mensa. Da ist es billig!
5. benutzen	mit der U-Bahn oder mit dem Bus in die Stadtmitte

C. Jetzt fordert Jonathan einige der Studenten in seinem Wohnheim auf, einiges zu tun. Bilden Sie sinnvolle Sätze in der **ihr**-Form des Imperativs.

1. anrufen	bitte nicht so laut
2. sagen	doch mal dieses Wochenende mit mir an den Ostsee
3. empfehlen	mir bitte ein gutes Internetcafé
4. mitkommen	mich mal, wenn ihr heute Abend ausgeht
5. sein	mir mal, welche Professoren gut sind

Immer weiter!

 2-44 Zur Diskussion. Besprechen Sie die Themen.

1. Die Menschen aus der DDR und der BRD waren für lange Zeit voneinander getrennt. Was für Probleme gibt es wohl, wenn diese Menschen wieder eine Nation werden möchten? Wissen Sie von Problemen, die es seit dem Fall der Mauer bei der Wiedervereinigung gegeben hat?

 2. In diesem Kapitel haben Sie von vielen Berliner Sehenswürdigkeiten gehört. Suchen Sie aus der folgenden Liste eine heraus. Suchen Sie dann im Internet weitere Informationen zu dieser Attraktion und machen Sie sich Notizen. Dann tauschen Sie Informationen mit einem Mitstudenten/einer Mitstudentin aus.

Berliner Zoo	Berliner Fernsehturm Alex
Haus am Checkpoint Charlie	Reichstagsgebäude
Deutsches Technikmuseum	Museumsinsel
Brandenburger Tor	Natur-Park Schöneberger Südgelände
Kaiser-Wilhelm-Gedächtniskirche	Pergamonmuseum
Siegessäule	Olympiastadion
Kurfürstendamm	Schloss Charlottenburg

2-45 Zum Schreiben: Über Berlin. In diesem Kapitel haben Sie einen Einblick in die Geschichte und Kultur Berlins erhalten. Schreiben Sie einen Brief an eine Freundin und berichten Sie von Ihrem Studium in Berlin. Erzählen Sie auch, was Sie in Ihrer Freizeit machen und warum Ihnen Berlin (nicht) gefällt.

Weitere Themen

die Berlinale	„Der Himmel über Berlin" (Film)
Berliner Philharmonie	Wilhelm und Alexander von Humboldt
die Berliner Mauer	
Checkpoint Charlie	Kabarett
Currywurst	die Olympischen Sommerspiele 1936
Theodor Fontane	Potsdamer Platz
Friedrich der Große	Reichstagsgebäude
Die goldenen Zwanziger	die SPD
„Good bye, Lenin!" (Film)	Unter den Linden
Hackesche Höfe	Christa Wolf
Nina Hagen	

Nordsee
Ostsee

Thüringen

Deutschland

Österreich

Schweiz
Liechtenstein

KAPITEL

3

Thüringen

NIEDERSACHSEN

SACHSEN-ANHALT

THÜRINGEN

Unstrut

Mühlhausen

Eisenach

Erfurt ★

Weimar

Jena

Saale

Ilm

Holzhausen

Arnstadt

Ohrdruf

Oberhof

Rudolstadt

Ilmenau

Thüringer Wald

Suhl

Werra

Sonneberg

SACHSEN

BAYERN

50 km

50 mi

Warm-up. To set the scene, have students look at the locator map or, for more detail, the map of Germany on the inside front cover, and ask them to describe the geographical position of Thüringen. *Wo liegt Thüringen? Was kann diese zentrale Lage für ein Bundesland bedeuten? Wo hat die Grenze zwischen 1949 und 1990 gelegen?* Then have them look at the detail map and photos of Thüringen and describe what these reveal about the region.

03-01 to 03-02

Einführung

Read the *Sprachanalyse: **der**-words and their uses* in SAM 03-02, which explains the multiple ways in which **der**-words are used in the *Einführung*. As you read the *Lesetexte* in this chapter, do the *Sprachanalyse* activities in the SAM (03-05, 03-08, 03-13, 03-17, 03-21) to practice understanding how *der*-words are used in context.

„Herrlich, herrlich!" So beschrieb einst der Dichter Johann Wolfgang von Goethe seine Thüringer Umgebung. „Wo finden Sie auf einem so engen Fleck noch so viel Gutes?", bemerkte er. Weite Waldlandschaften, bunte Wiesen, idyllische Täler und liebliche Berge machen das Land, das in der geografischen Mitte Deutschlands liegt, zum „grünen Herzen" Deutschlands. Weniger als 5 drei Prozent der deutschen Bundesbürger – 2,3 Millionen Einwohner – leben in Thüringen. Die Hauptstadt und gleichzeitig auch größte Stadt Erfurt hat nur 200.000 Einwohner.

Thüringen existiert in unterschiedlichen Konfigurationen mindestens seit dem 6. Jahrhundert. Im Spätmittelalter begann die Zerteilung des 10 Gebiets in mehrere kleinere Territorien. Die kleinen Fürsten und Herzöge° konnten sich keine Kriege leisten und erwarben stattdessen Ansehen durch die Förderung der Künste und Wissenschaften. Hier lebten und wirkten ab dem 16. Jahrhundert einige der renommiertesten Autoren, Künstler, Musiker und Philosophen der deutschen Kulturgeschichte. Thüringen wurde 15 somit zu einem wichtigen Schauplatz der protestantischen Reformation, Geburtsort der ersten deutschen Demokratie und Gründungsort der revolutionären Kunstbewegung Bauhaus. In den Städten Weimar und Jena entwickelten sich die Klassik und die Romantik, zwei bedeutende literarische Strömungen°, die einen unbestrittenen Höhepunkt in der deutschen Literatur- 20 geschichte darstellen.

Heute wollen die Thüringer ihre lange geistige Tradition fortsetzen. Mit vier Universitäten und fünf weiteren Hochschulen, rund 50 Forschungsinstituten und 20 Technologiezentren will man hier die Wirtschaft mit Wissenschaft unterstützen. Enge Kooperation zwischen 25 Wissens-institutionen und Unternehmen ermöglichen technische Innovation. Das ist die Antwort Thüringens auf die Herausforderung, sich wirtschaftlich umzustrukturieren – eine Aufgabe, vor der alle neuen Länder seit der Wiedervereinigung 1990 mit dem Übergang von einer sozialistischen Planwirtschaft zu einer Marktwirtschaft standen und noch stehen. 30 Erfolge sieht man in Thüringen in der Neugestaltung alter Industrien wie Optik, Automobilbau und Maschinenbau wie in der Entwicklung neuer Branchen wie Solarindustrie, Kunststoffindustrie° und Luftfahrttechnik°.

Die Wirtschaft des Landes wächst damit schneller als die fast aller anderen Länder im Ostteil der Bundesrepublik. Dennoch haben die meis- 35 ten Unternehmen des Landes weniger als 100 Angestellte. In Thüringen hat man immer wieder erlebt, dass große Leistungen auf kleinem Raum durchaus möglich sind.

Es ist gerade diese Verbindung von Tradition und Zukunft, von Geschichte und Moderne, von Natur und Kultur, die die Eigenart von 40 Thüringen ausmacht.

Sprachanalyse. The *Sprachanalyse* in the *Kapitel 3* SAM draws students' attention to the use of *der*-words as demonstrative and relative pronouns. Students learn how to identify and decipher these pronouns within

Fürsten und Herzöge
princes and dukes

their larger context and thus develop strategies for making vital connections between bits of information in increasingly complex constructions.

trends

plastics industry / aviation

Possible answers to *Fragen zum Text.* **1.** Es hat viel Natur – Wälder, Wiesen, Täler, Berge und liegt in der geografischen Mitte Deutschlands. **2.** 2,3 Millionen; **3.** über 1.400 Jahre alt; **4.** Die Fürsten und Herzöge haben die Künste gefördert. **5.** protestantische Reformation, Gründung der ersten deutschen Demokratie, die Kunstbewegung Bauhaus, literarische Strömungen von Klassik und Romantik; **6.** In der DDR gab es eine Planwirtschaft, seit der Wiedervereinigung gibt es eine Marktwirtschaft. **7.** durch die Verbindung von Wirtschaft und Wissenschaft; **8.** Optik, Automobilbau, Maschinenbau, Solarindustrie, Kunststoffindustrie, Luftfahrttechnik, Landwirtschaft, Tourismus

Fragen zum Text

1. Warum nennt man Thüringen „das grüne Herz" Deutschlands?
2. Wie viele Einwohner hat das Land?
3. Wie alt ist Thüringen?
4. Warum kamen ab dem 16. Jahrhundert so viele Künstler und Wissenschaftler nach Thüringen?
5. Welche wichtigen geschichtlichen Ereignisse fanden hier statt?
6. Warum musste Thüringen seine Wirtschaft neu aufbauen?
7. Wie wollte und will das Land seine Wirtschaft erneuern?
8. Was sind einige der wichtigsten Wirtschaftsbranchen?

Hören Sie ein Beispiel dieses Dialekts.

DIALEKTTIPP: Thüringisch

roots Thüringisch ist ein mitteldeutscher Dialekt. Es teilt seine Wurzeln° mit dem Sächsischen, das im benachbarten Sachsen gesprochen wird. Die politische Fragmentierung sowie auch natürliche Grenzen wie die Flüsse Saale und Unstrut und das Gebirge Thüringer Wald ließen hier mit der Zeit ein sehr diverses Dialektgebiet entstehen, sodass Forscher heute sieben Varianten des Thüringischen identifizieren können. Die Unterschiede zwischen den thüringischen Dialekten stammen teilweise von verschiedenen Einflüssen aus den angrenzenden Regionen.

Südlich des Thüringer Waldes spricht man nicht thüringische, sondern fränkische Dialekte, die der Sprache Nordbayerns ähnlicher sind als der Thüringens.

Zum Dialekt

Dialekttipp. After they have read the text, ask students: *Warum ist die Dialektlandschaft Thüringens so vielfältig?* In northeastern Thüringen, the influence of the Berlin dialect (*Berlinerisch*) can be heard. Hessian (*Hessisch*) influences can be heard in eastern Thüringen. Students will learn more about *Sächsisch*, which shares its roots with *Thüringisch*, in the *Kapitel 6 Dialekttipp.*

Wie sagt man das? Wählen Sie die richtigen Erklärungen der Unterschiede zwischen Thüringisch und Hochdeutsch.

Hochdeutsch → Thüringisch

<u>e</u> 1. essen, gehen → asse, gehe
<u>g</u> 2. Bett, still → Bette, stelle
<u>f</u> 3. aber, Leben → awer, Laawen
<u>b</u> 4. finden, Kinder → finge, Kinger
<u>a</u> 5. ich, Luft → ech, Loft
<u>d</u> 6. Bein, laufen → Been, loofe
<u>c</u> 7. schlägt, Nagel → schleet, Nööl

a. $i \rightarrow e, u \rightarrow o$
b. $nd, nt \rightarrow ng$
c. Kontraktion von -ag(e)
d. $ei \rightarrow ee, au \rightarrow oo$
e. -n-Endung an Infinitiven fehlt
f. $b \rightarrow w$
g. -e am Ende von Nomen, Adjektiven, Adverbien

Lese- und Hörtexte

Lesetext 1

Auf den Spuren Johann Sebastian Bachs in Thüringen (Biografie)

Über sechs Generationen lebte die Familie Bach in Thüringen und schrieb damit musikalische Geschichte. In dieser Zeit weist die Familie über 70 Berufsmusiker auf, darunter 20 Komponisten. Der weitaus bekannteste unter ihnen war Johann Sebastian

Ein Konzert in Weimar anlässlich der Thüringer Bachwochen.

Bach. Der gilt heute als bedeutendster Musiker des Barocks und als einer der größten Komponisten aller Zeiten. Schon zu seinen Lebzeiten wurde Bach vor allem als hervorragender Organist und Cembalospieler° berühmt. Die erste Hälfte seines Lebens verbrachte er an verschiedenen Orten in Thüringen. Ab 1717 nahm er dann eine Stelle außerhalb Thüringens – erst in Köthen, dann in Leipzig – an.

Es gibt jedes Jahr zu Ehren des Thüringer Sohnes das Musikfest Thüringer Bachwochen, das größte Musikfestival Thüringens. Die Veranstaltungen finden jedes Frühjahr drei Wochen lang in neun verschiedenen Städten statt. Neben traditionellen Aufführungen durch große Ensembles gibt es z. B. auch Konzerte junger Künstler und moderne Bach-Interpretationen im Tanztheater und Jazz. Es werden außerdem Vorträge° gehalten und Kinofilme über Bach gezeigt. Mit diesem Fest ehren Thüringer „ihren" großen Komponisten und zeigen gleichzeitig seine Relevanz für die Gegenwart.

In diesem Text aus dem Programm des Festivals lesen Sie, was der junge Bach während seiner Thüringer Zeit schon alles erlebt und geleistet hat.

Vor dem Lesen

Was wissen Sie schon über Johann Sebastian Bach? Woher kennen Sie den Namen? Welche Assoziationen haben Sie mit seinem Namen?

Beim Lesen

Der Text behandelt die folgenden Stationen im Leben Bachs:

Die Weimarer Zeit	Die frühe Meisterschaft
Der Beginn der Komponistenlaufbahn	Bei seinem Bruder in Ohrdruf
Die Kindheit in Eisenach	

Lesen Sie den Text und schreiben Sie die passenden Überschriften über die Textabschnitte.

Introduction to *Lesetext 1*.
Introduce the topic by asking students about their own experiences: *Kommen irgendwelche berühmten Persönlichkeiten aus Ihrer Heimat? Wenn ja, welche Bedeutung hat er/sie für den Ort? Gibt es z. B. Gebäude, Denkmäler, Feste zu Ehren dieser Person?* After students have read the introduction, ask them what they learned about Bach and his connection to the region. *Wie kommt es, dass Johann Sebastian Bach mit Thüringen verbunden ist? Was meinen Sie: Welche Bedeutung hat er für Thüringen? Was macht man in Thüringen, um den Komponisten zu feiern? Wann ist das Bachfest und wie lange dauert es? Was kann man auf dem Fest machen?*

Siehe **Kulturtipps**: Barock

harpsichord player

lectures

Answers for *Beim Lesen*.
Die Kindheit in Eisenach (1685–1695); Bei seinem Bruder in Ohrdruf (1695–1700); Der Beginn der Komponistenlaufbahn (1703–1707); Die frühe Meisterschaft (1707–1708); Die Weimarer Zeit (1708–1717)

Auf den Spuren Johann Sebastian Bachs in Thüringen

_____ **(1685–1695)**

Johann Sebastian Bach wurde am 21. März 1685 in Eisenach geboren und wuchs hier bis zu seinem zehnten Lebensjahr auf. Er wurde in der *baptized* Georgenkirche getauft° und besuchte wie Martin Luther die Lateinschule im alten Dominikanerkloster. Seinem Vater Ambrosius, der in Eisenach Instrumentalunterricht gab, verdankte der junge Johann Sebastian sein bemerkenswertes *skill* Geschick° als Geiger.

Johann Sebastian Bach (1748)

_____ **(1695–1700)**

Von seinem älteren Bruder Johann Christoph wurde Johann Sebastian in Ohrdruf aufgenommen, als er mit zehn Jahren die Eltern verlor. Dort wurde er lutherisch erzogen und war, wie seine Lehrer berichteten, bald bekannt für seine außergewöhnliche Intelligenz. Schon im ersten Jahr dort war er Klassenbester. Er lernte Latein, Griechisch, Religion und erhielt fünf Stunden Musikunterricht pro Woche. Sein Bruder, Organist an der St. Michaeliskirche und selbst Schüler des sehr bekannten Organisten *Johann Pachelbel (1653– 1706) German Baroque composer and organist* Pachelbel°, wurde sein erster Klavierlehrer, der ihn auch an Orgel und Cembalo sowie in der Komposition von Stücken ausbildete. Diese Zeit nimmt in Johann Sebastians Entwicklung eine ganz besondere Stellung ein: Hier trennt ihn sein Leben und Lernen von der *ancestors* Tradition seiner Vorfahren°, die sich der weltlichen Seite des Berufes zuwendeten.

_____ **(1703–1707)**

Arnstadt, Thüringens ältester Ort, ist sehr eng mit der Musikerfamilie Bach verbunden. Allein in Arnstadt wurden 17 „Bachs" geboren *married* und acht getraut°. Im Sommer 1703 wurde der Bau der neuen Orgel in *completed* der Neukirche vollendet°. Die Stadt lud den damals 18-jährigen Johann Sebastian Bach zur Prüfung der Orgel ein. Es war sein erster derarti- *authority on the subject* ger Auftrag, und seine Wahl als Sachverständiger° zeugt von seinem bereits erworbenen großen Ruf. Auf die Prüfung folgte die öffentliche *dedication* Einweihung°, zu der Bach die Orgel spielte. Sein Probespiel muss über- *must have been convincing* zeugt haben°, denn man bot ihm die Stelle als Organist an, ohne dass weitere Bewerber eingeladen wurden. Zum ersten Mal stand jetzt eine Orgel zu seiner freien Verfügung. Hier begann wahrscheinlich seine Laufbahn als Komponist.

_____ (1707–1708)

Sein zweites Organistenamt° hatte der 22-jährige Bach in Mühlhausen an der Divi-Blasii-Kirche. Dank der gut bezahlten Stelle konnte Bach hier eine Familie gründen; 1707 heiratete er Maria Barbara. Zugleich begann ein Jahr lebhafter Tätigkeit. Er schuf die Kantate „Gott ist mein König", die am 4. Februar 1708 unter großer Beteiligung der Mühlhäuser uraufgeführt wurde°. Diese ist die einzige Kantate Bachs, die schon zu seinen Lebzeiten gedruckt wurde. Seine Mühlhäuser Zeit wird heute wegen der Vielzahl an Kompositionen als die der „frühen Meisterschaft" bezeichnet. Hier konnte Bach sich musikalisch ausleben und eifrig komponieren.

position as an organist

uraufgeführt wurde was performed for the first time

_____ (1708–1717)

Neun Jahre lang hatte Bach in Weimar seine Wirkungsstätte°. In der „Himmelsburg", der heute nicht mehr erhaltenen Kapelle des Stadtschlosses, erklangen erstmals seine Kirchenkantaten dieser Jahre. In Weimar galt Bach als Organist von unerreichter Technik und als Komponist von einer Kraft und Kühnheit° des melodischen Ausdrucks, an die vorher niemand heranreichte. Aus allen Landesteilen Deutschlands erhielt er Rufe, um neue Orgeln auszuprobieren, Organistenstellen zu prüfen oder selbst als Organist zu arbeiten. In Weimar wurde ihm der Titel „Konzertmeister" verliehen und ein professionelles Orchester und Sänger zur Seite gestellt. Bach verdiente gut in Weimar; sieben Kinder wurden geboren, unter ihnen Wilhelm Friedemann und Carl Philipp Emanuel, die selbst später Komponisten werden sollten. Sein Auftrag in Weimar verpflichtete Bach, monatlich Kantaten zu schreiben. Als erste erklang 1714 die Kantate „Himmelkönig sei willkommen". Auch sein berühmtes „Orgelbüchlein" stammt aus der Weimarer Zeit.

place of activity

boldness

Kulturtipps

▬ Barock

Der Barock ist die europäische Kulturepoche von etwa 1600 bis 1750. Der Begriff bezieht sich auf Entwicklungen in der Literatur, Kunst, Architektur und Musik. Der Barockstil ist hauptsächlich der Stil des Absolutismus und der katholischen Gegenreformation, kam aber auch später in protestantischen Gebieten auf. Monteverdi, Vivaldi und Händel gehören auch in diese Epoche. Bach bildet zugleich den Höhepunkt und das Ende dieser Bewegung.

Neue Vokabeln

Nomen

der Auftrag, ¨-e *job, order*

der Ausdruck, ¨-e *expression*

der Bau, Bauten *pl.* *building, construction*

der Geiger, -die Geigerin, -nen *violinist*

die Kraft, ¨-e *strength, power*

die Orgel, ¨-n *organ*

die Prüfung, -en *test, inspection*

der Ruf, -e *reputation, call*

die Stunde, -n *hour*

der Unterricht *instruction*

die Wahl, -en *choice, selection*

Pronomen

niemand *nobody*

Verben

an·bieten, bot an, angeboten *to offer*

aus·bilden *to train, educate*

bezeichnen (als) *to label (as)*

drucken *to publish, print*

ein·laden (lädt ein), lud ein, eingeladen *to invite*

folgen (+ *dat.*), ist gefolgt *to follow*

komponieren *to compose*

schaffen, schuf, geschaffen *to create*

zeugen (von) *to be evidence (of), to bear witness (to)*

Adjektive und Adverbien

außergewöhnlich *exceptional, extraordinary*

einzig *only, sole*

wahrscheinlich *probable; probably*

weltlich *worldly, secular*

Ausdrücke

zur Verfügung stehen *to be at one's disposal*

Teaching suggestion for 3-1. Have students look at the map of Thüringen at the beginning of the chapter and locate each of the "Bach-Orte" mentioned in the program.

3-1 Textarbeit: Wo hat Bach was gemacht? Ordnen Sie die Episoden aus Bachs Leben den Orten zu, wo er diese Erfahrungen gemacht hat: Arnstadt, Eisenach, Mühlhausen, Ohrdruf oder Weimar.

1. Hier wurde Johann Sebastian geboren. _____Eisenach_____

2. Hier wurden sieben seiner Kinder geboren. _____Weimar_____

3. Hier hat er Maria Barbara geheiratet. _____Mühlhausen_____

4. In diesem Dorf erhielt er musikalische Ausbildung von seinem Bruder. _____Ohrdruf_____

5. Hier wurde er zum Konzertmeister. _____Weimar_____

6. An diesem Ort hatte er seine erste Stelle als Organist. _____Arnstadt_____

7. Hier lernte er Orgelmusik zum ersten Mal kennen. _____Ohrdruf_____

8. Hier komponierte er die Werke für sein „Orgelbüchlein". _____Weimar_____

9. Hier besuchte er die gleiche Schule wie Martin Luther. _____Eisenach_____

10. Hier hat er viele seiner frühen Werke komponiert. _____Mühlhausen_____

Possible answers for 3-2.
1. Sein Vater und sein Bruder Johann Christoph **2.** In der Schule war er Klassenbester. Er wurde mit 18 Jahren zur Prüfung der neuen Orgel in Arnstadt eingeladen. Er erhielt die Organistenstelle, ohne dass andere Bewerber eingeladen wurden. **3.** Er spielte Geige, Orgel, Cembalo und komponierte. **4.** Hier komponierte er viele Stücke. **5.** Er wurde von überall in Deutschland eingeladen, um neue Orgeln auszuprobieren, Organistenstellen zu prüfen oder als Organist zu arbeiten.

3-2 Textarbeit: Fragen zum Inhalt. Beantworten Sie die Fragen in Bezug auf den Text.

1. Wer hatte einen großen Einfluss auf Bachs Entwicklung zum großen Musiker?

2. Welche Erfahrungen in seinem frühen Leben zeugen von seinem besonderen Talent?

3. Welche musikalischen Talente hatte Bach?

4. Warum nennt man seine Zeit in Mühlhausen die Zeit der „frühen Meisterschaft"?

5. Welche Erfahrungen aus der Weimarer Zeit zeugen schon von dem großen Ruf des jungen Bachs?

3-3 Vokabelarbeit. Ergänzen Sie die Sätze mit Wörtern aus den *Neuen Vokabeln.* Achten Sie dabei auch auf die Wortform.

1. Johann Sebastians Bruder Johann Christoph spielte _____Orgel_____ an der St. Michaeliskirche in Ohrdruf.

2. Bach ___schuf/komponierte___ sein ganzes Leben lang Kantaten.

3. Johann Sebastian ist nicht der _____einzige_____ Bach, der Komponist wurde.

4. Die Aufführung der Matthäuspassion, Bachs längstes Werk, dauert drei _____Stunden_____.

5. Von dem Herzog in Weimar erhielt er den _____Auftrag_____, Kantaten zu komponieren.

6. Bach hat meist religiöse Stücke komponiert, aber auch einige _____weltliche_____ Werke geschaffen.

7. Schloss Belvedere und die Jakobskirche in Weimar sind zwei _____Bauten_____ aus der Barockzeit.

8. Heute _____bezeichnet_____ man Bach als einen der bedeutendsten Komponisten aller Zeiten.

3-4 Zur Diskussion. Besprechen Sie die Fragen.

1. Hören Sie gern klassische Musik? Wenn ja, welche Komponisten hören Sie gern? Was für Musik hören Sie sonst gern?

2. Spielen Sie ein Musikinstrument? Wenn ja, wie lange spielen Sie das Instrument schon? Wie haben Sie es gelernt? Spielen auch andere Mitglieder Ihrer Familie dieses Instrument? Gibt es ein Instrument, das Sie lernen möchten?

3. Über Generationen interessierten sich viele Mitglieder der Familie Bach für Musik. Teilen mehrere Mitglieder Ihrer Familie ein ähnliches Talent oder Interesse?

4. Wer hat in Ihrem Leben schon einen großen Einfluss auf Sie gehabt? Wie hat diese Person Ihr Leben beeinflusst?

3-5 Wer bin ich? Sie und Ihre Mitstudenten sind bekannte Musiker, Künstler oder Schriftsteller. Stellen Sie Fragen an einander und versuchen Sie zu raten, wer die anderen sind.

3-6 Und wie geht's weiter? Bach verbrachte die erste Hälfte seines Lebens in Thüringen. Wo hat er die zweite Hälfte seines Lebens verbracht und was hat er alles gemacht? Schreiben Sie für eine Broschüre des Bach-Festes seine Biografie zu Ende.

3-7 Die Stationen meines Lebens. Schreiben Sie eine kurze Autobiografie für Ihre Kinder und Enkelkinder. Organisieren Sie Ihren Bericht wie die Bach-Biografie in Abschnitten, die entweder chronologisch oder geografisch geordnet sind.

Teaching suggestion for 3-5. You may wish to have students prepare this activity or part of it as homework. Students can research a musician, artist, or author ahead of time so that they are better informed when asked questions. You might also have them write down 10 interview questions in advance so that they are more prepared to ask relevant questions.

Activity 3-6. This activity may be assigned as a library activity, an Internet activity, or a combination of both. Relevant web addresses can be found in MyGermanLab and at the Companion Website. Encourage students to use at least three sources of information. Have them take notes while researching and remind them to write their texts in their own words.

Teaching suggestion for 3-7. Have students write about their lives up to now or incorporate a creative element and have them write a retrospective about their lives from a future point in time. They may write in the first person or the third person.

Introduction to *Lesetext 2*.
Ask students what the text introduction reveals about the topic of the text: *Was ist die Wartburg? Warum hat sie die UNESCO-Kommission in ihre Welterbeliste aufgenommen? Wo in Thüringen ist diese Burg? Warum ist ihre geografische Lage etwas Besonderes?* Then direct students' attention to the text type: *Was für Informationen findet man in einem Buchtipp? Welche Informationen über die Wartburg erwarten Sie vielleicht in diesem Text?*

Lesetext 2

Welterbe Wartburg (Buchtipp)

Die kleine Stadt Eisenach am nordwestlichen Ende des Thüringer Waldes ist nicht nur als Geburtsort von Johann Sebastian Bach bekannt, sondern auch für die Wartburg, die aus 220 Meter Höhe auf die Stadt blickt. Die über 900 Jahre alte Burg wurde 2000 als „hervorragendes Denkmal der feudalen Epoche in Mitteleuropa" von der UNESCO-Kommission ernannt. Aber diese mittelalterliche Burg ist mehr als nur ein historisches Bauwerk. Mit ihr ist eine Reihe von hervorragenden Persönlichkeiten und wichtigen Ereignissen in der deutschen Geschichte verbunden. Sie gilt deswegen oft als „die deutscheste aller Burgen" und ist sehr eng mit „kulturellen Werten von universeller Bedeutung" verknüpft.

Wartburg

In der neueren Geschichte hat die Wartburg auch zusätzlich an Bedeutung gewonnen. Obwohl Eisenach und die Wartburg sehr nah an der ehemaligen Ost-West-Grenze lagen, blieb dieses Denkmal der deutschen Geschichte während der DDR-Zeit für den Westen weitgehend verschlossen. Und manche ostdeutsche Bürger erstiegen damals den Turm der Wartburg, um nur einen Blick nach Westen zu werfen. Mit der Wiedervereinigung fand sich die Wartburg in der Mitte Deutschlands und erneuerte damit ihre Bedeutung in der deutschen Kulturgeschichte.

Im Jahre 2000 ist ein Buch erschienen, das die Kulturgeschichte der Burg würdigt. Der folgende Buchtipp berichtet, warum dieses Buch über das Welterbe Wartburg lesenswert ist.

Vor dem Lesen

1. Welche Assoziationen haben Sie mit einer mittelalterlichen Burg? Wo findet man solche Burgen? Wie war das Leben auf einer Burg im Mittelalter? Was macht man heute auf einer solchen Burg?
2. Finden Sie die Stadt Eisenach auf einer Karte. Beschreiben Sie ihre geografische Lage.

Beim Lesen

Ordnen Sie während des Lesens die Begriffe den richtigen Namen zu.

Personen	**Begriffe**
_c_ 1. Richard Wagner	a. Demonstrationen
_f_ 2. Elisabeth von Thüringen	b. Leiterin der Wartburgstiftung
_e, g_ 3. Martin Luther	c. „Tannhäuser"
_a_ 4. die studentischen Burschenschaften	d. Fotograf
_b, i_ 5. Jutta Krauß	e. Bibelübersetzung
_d_ 6. Ulrich Kneise	f. Heilige
_h_ 7. Moritz von Schwind	g. Schriften zur Reform des Katholizismus
	h. Maler von Fresken über die Geschichte der Wartburg
	i. Autorin von „Welterbe Wartburg"

03-06 to 03-08

Welterbe Wartburg

von Klaus Krämer

Sie gilt als *die* mittelalterliche Burganlage überhaupt und ist somit die Lieblingsburg der Deutschen – die Wartburg bei Eisenach in Thüringen. 934 Jahre nach ihrer Gründung lässt sich feststellen, dass sich mit ihr 5 nahezu ausschließlich positive geschichtliche Ereignisse verbinden.

Da ist die Burg als geistig-künstlerisches Zentrum der höfischen° Kultur im 12. Jahrhundert. Dem Sängerkrieg auf 10 der Wartburg setzte Richard Wagner[1] später ein Denkmal mit seiner romantischen Oper „Tannhäuser". Da ist das beispielhafte karitative° Wirken der Landgrafengemahlin° Elisabeth von Thü- 15 ringen, die zu einer der beliebtesten Heiligen° wurde.

Jutta Krauß / Ulrich Kneise:
Welterbe Wartburg
Verlag: Schnell und Steiner, 2000
Preis: € 15,00 / DM 29,00

Aufnahme in die UNESCO-Liste des Weltkulturerbes°

Dann ein Geschehen von Weltbedeutung – der Aufenthalt des Reformators Martin Luther auf der Wartburg. Dort übersetzte er im 16. Jahrhundert erstmals das Neue Testament der Bibel ins Deutsche und verfasste zahlreiche bedeutende reformatorische Schriften. Zu Beginn des 19. 20 Jahrhunderts waren es die studentischen Burschenschaften, die bei ihrem Wartburgtreffen für demokratische Rechte und ein einiges Vaterland demonstrierten.

---

[1]Richard Wagner (1813–1883) war deutscher Komponist, Dirigent und Dramatiker, der das Musikleben des 19. Jahrhunderts dominierte und die Oper revolutionierte. Sie lernen mehr über Wagner in *Kapitel 5*.

Information for *Lesetext 2.*
Tell students that the *Deutsche Mark* (*DM*) was the currency of the Federal Republic of Germany from 1948 to 2001. In 2002, it was replaced by the euro (€). During the period of transition, prices were usually given in both currencies. *Deutsche Mark* may be mentioned in texts written before 2002 or in texts that refer to Germany before that time.

courtly
Siehe **Kulturtipps**:
Sängerkrieg und Elisabeth von Thüringen

*charitable / wife of a landgrave (a title of nobility; **Graf** = count, earl)*
saint

UNESCO World Heritage List

Siehe **Kulturtipps**:
Martin Luther und Burschenschaften

fortress / cradle

Die Festung° als Wiege° einer progressiven, bürgerlichen Oppositions-
bewegung in Deutschland. Wegen ihrer Lage an der innerdeutschen Grenze 25
galt die Wartburg seit 1949 als Symbol für deutsche Integration und Einheit.
Die Belohnung: Im Jahr 2000 wurde die Anlage in die UNESCO-Liste des
Weltkulturerbes aufgenommen.

Die Highlights der Burggeschichte sowie zahlreiche weniger bekannte –
aber dennoch interessante Ereignisse werden in dem Band mit außeror- 30

expertise

Wartburg Foundation

dentlich großer Sachkenntnis° geschildert. Jutta Krauß, die Autorin, ist
wissenschaftliche Leiterin der Wartburgstiftung°. Und obwohl sie vermutlich von jedem Stein eine eigene Geschichte erzählen könnte, gelingt ihr

dazzling

Zitaten ... Gemälden quotes,
drawings, and paintings

eine kompakte und sprachlich schillernde° Zusammenstellung, garniert
mit Zitaten, Zeichnungen und Gemälden°. 35

Gedankliche Zeitreise durch die Jahrhunderte

Was für die Historie gilt, trifft auch zu auf die Darstellung der bauge-
schichtlichen und künstlerischen Würdigung der Wartburg. Sie geschieht vor
allem durch die rund 125 zum Teil grandiosen Fotos von Ulrich Kneise.

Außenansichten der Burg zu verschiedenen Tages- und Jahreszeiten,
Motive vom spätromanischen Regierungsgebäude, dem sogenannten 40

defensive corridors

*Detailaufnahmen ...
Moritz von Schwinds*
close-ups of columns,
capitals, tapestries, and
the frescoes of Moritz von
Schwind (19th-century
German painter)

international standing

Palas, von Wehrgängen° und den geschichtsträchtigen Räumen. Ins rechte
Licht gerückt, gibt es daneben Detailaufnahmen von Säulen, Kapitellen,
Bildteppichen, den Fresken Moritz von Schwinds° zur Wartburggeschichte,
von Skulpturen und wertvollen Exponaten des Museums.

Alles in allem ist dieser prächtige Band dazu angetan, sich auf eine 45
gedankliche Zeitreise durch die Jahrhunderte zu machen. Danach ist es fast
so, als wäre man dort gewesen – auf der beliebtesten Burg der Deutschen
mit Weltgeltung°. Und das für ganze 29 DM.

🔊 Neue Vokabeln

Nomen

der Aufenthalt, -e *stay, residence*
der Band, ¨e *volume (book)*
die Burg, -en *castle, fortress*
die Darstellung, -en *depiction*
das Denkmal, ¨er *monument*
die Einheit *unity*
das Ereignis, -se *event, occurrence*
die Geschichte, -n *history; story*
die Lage, -n *position*

der Leiter, - / die Leiterin,
   -nen *leader, director*
die Oper, -n *opera*
das Recht, -e *right*
die Schrift, -en *writing*
der Wald, ¨er *forest*

Verben

gelingen (+ *dat.*), gelang, ist
   gelungen *to succeed*
geschehen (+ *dat.*) (geschieht),
   geschah, ist geschehen *to
   happen, occur*

übersetzen *to translate*
verfassen *to write*

Adjektive und Adverbien

bürgerlich *middle-class, bourgeois*
geschichtlich *historical*
mittelalterlich *medieval*
prächtig *magnificent, grand*
überhaupt *in general, at all*
vermutlich *presumably*
zahlreich *numerous*

Kulturtipps

Sängerkrieg

Einer alten Legende nach trafen sich im Jahre 1206 sechs berühmte Sänger auf der Wartburg. Zu diesem Anlass soll der Landgraf Hermann I. einen Wettbewerb organisiert haben, bei dem der beste Sänger gefunden werden sollte. Diese Legende wurde weit verbreitet und in den nächsten Jahrhunderten wurden viele Lieder und Gedichte – und in der Neuzeit auch andere Literatur – über den vermutlichen Sängerkrieg geschrieben.

Elisabeth von Thüringen (1207–1231)

Die ungarische Königstochter kam schon mit vier Jahren als Verlobte des künftigen Landgrafen Ludwig IV. nach Thüringen. Als Landgräfin kümmerte sich Elisabeth um Arme und Kranke. Sie verteilte Essen an Hungernde und gründete ein Hospital am Fuße der Wartburg. Nach dem Tod ihres Mannes verließ sie Thüringen, entsagte allem weltlichen Luxus, führte ein Leben in Armut und half den Armen. Sie ist auch heute noch wegen ihrer Hilfsbereitschaft für Arme und Kranke sehr populär.

Die Heilige Elisabeth von Thüringen

Martin Luther (1483–1546)

Der deutsche Theologe Martin Luther ist von großer Bedeutung für die deutsche und europäische Kultur und Politik. Er wurde zum Vater der protestantischen Reformation und seine Schriften trugen außerdem zur Entwicklung der deutschen Sprache bei. 1521 wurde er wegen seiner Kritik an Missständen in der katholischen Kirche exkommuniziert, seine Schriften wurden verboten und seine Haft angeordnet (*his arrest was ordered*). Er flüchtete ins Exil auf die Wartburg, wo er sich zehn Monate lang versteckte und die Zeit zu weiterer theologischer Arbeit nutzte.

Burschenschaften (*Fraternities*)

Die erste Burschenschaft war eine 1815 gegründete, politisch orientierte Studentenverbindung an der Universität Jena. Daraufhin entstanden Burschenschaften schnell im ganzen deutschen Raum. 1817 kamen Burschen von fast allen deutschen Universitäten zum Wartburgfest. Unter dem Motto „Ehre, Freiheit, Vaterland" forderten sie demokratische Reformen und nationale Einheit aller Deutschen. Heute gibt es etwa 300 Burschenschaften an deutschen Hochschulen, die sich in dieser Tradition stehend immer noch als politische Organisationen sehen.

Orthography. Before the spelling reform of 1996, triple consonants were routinely reduced to double consonants. These are no longer reduced, e.g., *Missstände, Schifffahrt.*

Answers for 3-8. **1.** R; **2.** F –
über 900 Jahre alt; **3.** R; **4.** F – das
Neue Testament; **5.** F – Studenten
demonstrierten im 19. Jahrhundert
auf der Burg. **6.** F – seit 2000;
7. R; **8.** R

3-8 Textarbeit: Richtig oder falsch? Wenn eine Aussage falsch ist, korrigieren Sie und ergänzen Sie sie mit Informationen aus dem Text.

1. Die Wartburg ist die beliebteste Burg der Deutschen.
2. Die Wartburg ist über 1.000 Jahre alt.
3. Die Heilige Elisabeth war für ihre guten Werke für die Menschen bekannt.
4. Auf der Wartburg übersetzte Martin Luther „Tannhäuser".
5. Studenten schrieben im 19. Jahrhundert reformatorische Schriften auf der Burg.
6. Die Burg gehört seit 1949 zur UNESCO-Liste des Weltkulturerbes.
7. Das Buch zur Wartburg enthält Highlights aus ihrer Geschichte.
8. Der Band enthält Fotos von dem Äußeren und dem Inneren der Burg.

Possible answers for 3-9.
1. Weil so viele positive
Ereignisse der deutschen
Geschichte mit ihr verbunden
sind. **2.** Die Wartburg lag zu
DDR-Zeiten nicht weit von der
innerdeutschen Grenze. **3.** Positiv;
interessante Ereignisse,
mit außerordentlich großer
Sachkenntnis, eine kompakte
und sprachlich schillernde
Zusammenstellung, grandiose
Fotos, dieser prächtige Band

3-9 Textarbeit: Fragen zum Inhalt. Beantworten Sie die Fragen zum Text.

1. Warum ist die Wartburg beides „die deutscheste" und „die beliebteste" aller deutschen Burgen?
2. Warum „galt die Burg seit 1949 als Symbol für deutsche Integration und Einheit"? Denken Sie auch an das, was Sie in *Kapitel 2* über die deutsche Geschichte gelernt haben.
3. Bewertet der Autor von diesem Buchtipp das Buch eher positiv oder negativ? Welche Wörter und Ausdrücke im Text zeigen, dass es eine positive oder negative Bewertung ist?

3-10 Vokabelarbeit. Ergänzen Sie die Sätze mit Wörtern aus den *Neuen Vokabeln.* Achten Sie dabei auch auf die Wortform.

1. Die Wartburg wurde ___vermutlich___ im Jahre 1067 gebaut, aber erst 1080 wird von der Burg in Büchern berichtet.
2. Ob 1067 oder 1080 gebaut, sie ist auf alle Fälle eine _mittelalterliche_ Burg.
3. Der ___Aufenthalt___ von Martin Luther auf der Wartburg dauerte zehn Monate.
4. Es ___gelang___ Luther, in nur elf Wochen das Neue Testament ins Deutsche zu übersetzen.
5. Das Wartburgtreffen war ein wichtiges ___Ereignis___ in der politischen Geschichte Deutschlands.
6. Die Autorin des Bandes weiß so viel über die Wartburg, weil sie ___Leiterin___ der Wartburgstiftung ist.
7. Wegen der ___Lage___ Eisenachs nahe der alten innerdeutschen Grenze wuchs die Stadt zu DDR-Zeiten nicht mehr.
8. Wagner schuf „Tannhäuser", „Der Fliegende Holländer", „Der Ring der Nibelungen" und auch andere beliebte ___Opern___.

3-11 Zur Diskussion. Besprechen Sie die Fragen.

1. Haben Sie schon einmal eine mittelalterliche Burg besucht? Wenn ja, wo ist die Burg und was haben Sie dort gemacht und gesehen? Welche Burgen möchten Sie noch besuchen?

2. Gibt es Denkmäler oder Bauten in Ihrer Stadt oder Ihrem Bundesstaat, die mit wichtigen geschichtlichen Ereignissen verbunden sind?

3. Lesen Sie gern Bücher über Geschichte? Was gehört zu einem guten Geschichtsbuch? Was für Bücher lesen Sie am liebsten?

3-12 Ein Wartburg-Besuch. Sie sind in Erfurt und wollen am Samstag nach Eisenach, um die Wartburg zu besichtigen. Suchen Sie im Internet nach Informationen für den Besuch: Weg vom Hauptbahnhof Eisenach zur Wartburg, Öffnungszeiten, Eintrittskosten, Touren, andere Sehenswürdigkeiten in Eisenach usw. Dann schreiben Sie Ihren Tagesplan auf.

03-47

3-13 Mein Buchtipp. Sie schreiben für die nächste Ausgabe eines Magazins einen Buchtipp über ein Non-Fiction-Buch, das Sie einmal gelesen haben. Geben Sie den Autor, den Verlag, das Publikationsdatum und den Preis des Bandes an. Beschreiben Sie den Inhalt und dann sagen Sie, warum Sie anderen Lesern das Buch empfehlen.

Hörtext 1

Tourismus im Thüringer Wald in Zeiten des Klimawandels (Radiobericht)

Der Thüringer Wald ist ein 120 km langes, bis zu 35 km breites Gebirge, das sich von Eisenach südöstlich bis hin zur bayrischen Grenze zieht. Die Landschaft ist geprägt von mittelhohen Bergen, dichten Wäldern, blumenreichen Wiesen und Dörfern, die auf den Höhen und in den Tälern liegen. Das Klima ist kühl und es regnet bzw. schneit relativ viel, sodass dieses Gebiet im Winter mehr Schnee hat als andere Teile Mitteldeutschlands. Hier befindet sich auch der älteste und beliebteste Wanderweg Deutschlands, der Rennsteig.

Schon seit dem Mittelalter gibt es hier handwerkliche Kleinindustrie, die z. B. für die Herstellung von Spielwaren, Glas, Porzellan und Produkten aus Holz und Metall bekannt ist. Aber die

Thüringer Wald bei Steinach

Oberhof im Winter

Note for 3-12. Relevant web addresses for Internet research activities can be found in *MyGermanLab* and on the Companion Website.

Alternative for 3-12. A more challenging activity would be to have students conduct further research on the themes mentioned in the text: *Burschenschaften, Eisenach, Elisabeth von Thüringen, Martin Luther, Richard Wagner, Sängerkrieg, Tannhäuser, Wartburgfest.* You could also assign peripheral themes, e.g., *das Wartburg-Auto der DDR, Bachhaus Eisenach, Lutherhaus Eisenach,* etc. Students could write up the results of their research and/or present their findings to the class.

Introduction to *Hörtext 1.* Have students examine the image and introductory text as well as the location of the *Thüringer Wald* as labeled on the map at the beginning of the chapter, and discuss their initial impressions of the region: *Wo liegt der Thüringer Wald? Beschreiben Sie die Landschaft und das Klima. Was meinen Sie: Womit verdienen die Menschen dieser Gegend ihr Geld?*

Siehe **Kulturtipps**: Rennsteig

Wirtschaft lebt hauptsächlich von den Urlaubern – Naturliebhabern, Sportlern, Kulturinteressierten und Entspannungssuchenden, die in die Region kommen. Im folgenden Bericht hören Sie, was für Auswirkungen der Klimawandel auf den Tourismus dieser Gegend hat, insbesondere für die Stadt Oberhof, der meistbesuchte Ferienort im Thüringer Wald.

Vor dem Hören

1. Welche Sportarten kann man im Winter betreiben? Machen Sie gern Wintersport?

2. Es wird in dem Text über den Wintersportort Oberhof berichtet. Was findet man wohl an einem solchen Ort, der sich auf Wintersport spezialisiert?

Beim Hören

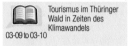
Tourismus im Thüringer Wald in Zeiten des Klimawandels
03-09 to 03-10

Während des Interviews hören Sie folgende Vokabeln.

Pension   *bed-and-breakfast*
Geschäft   *business*
Mittelgebirge   *low mountain ranges*
druckende Hitze   *oppressive heat*
im Vorteil   *at an advantage*
Alleinstellungsmerkmale   *unique selling points*

überleben   *to survive*
nimmt … Geld in die Hand   *earns money*
sich breit aufstellen   *diversify*
gerüstet für   *equipped for*

Im Bericht kommen viele Zahlen vor. Wozu passt jede Zahl?

__b__ Zimmer in der Pension	a.	2
__d__ Betten in der Pension	b.	10
__e__ Tage Schnee in den Wintermonaten	c.	20
__c__ Tage Schnee weniger als normal	d.	21
__h__ Einwohner im Dorf Oberhof	e.	35
__i__ Touristen, die nach Oberhof kommen	f.	400
__g__ Meter Höhe des Dorfes Oberhof	g.	800
__f__ Zimmer im Panorama-Hotel	h.	1.600
__a__ Kilometer langer Skitunnel	i.	60.000
__j__ Euro für den Bau des Skitunnels	j.	12 Millionen

Skilanglauf

Kulturtipps

Rennsteig

Der Rennsteig ist ein knapp 170 Kilometer langer Fernwanderweg, der sich durch den Thüringer Wald zieht. Da er auf dem Kamm (*ridge*) eines Gebirges entlang führt, bietet der Weg traumhafte Blicke. Natur, Geschichte und Tradition sind hier eng miteinander verbunden, denn im Laufe der Jahrhunderte haben Soldaten, Kaufleute, Postboten (*messengers*), Handwerker, Hirten (*shepherds*), Studenten, Dichter, Touristen und viele andere den Höhenweg zu verschiedenen Zwecken benutzt.

Wellness

Seit einigen Jahren ist Wellness der große Trend in Deutschland. In der modernen Gesellschaft möchte der Mensch sich von dem Stress und der Hektik des Alltags entspannen. Zu Wellness gehören zum Beispiel gesundes Essen, Massagen, Ruhe, Erholung, Meditation, Fitness, neue Therapien und vor allem Reisen an Orte, wo man Körper und Geist pflegen lässt. Mehr als die Hälfte der Deutschen geben an, wenigstens schon einmal einen Wellnessurlaub gemacht zu haben.

Information for *Kulturtipp: Wellness*. Tell students that it is common for such a wellness vacation to be paid for by health insurance in Germany.

 3-14 Textarbeit: Richtig oder falsch? Wenn eine Aussage falsch ist, korrigieren Sie und ergänzen Sie sie mit Informationen aus dem Hörtext.

Answers for 3-14. 1. R; 2. R; 3. F – weniger Schnee; 4. F – vom Tourismus; 5. R; 6. F – durch seine Wellness-Angebote; 7. R

1. Weniger Touristen übernachteten im letzten Winter in Frau Meiers Pension.
2. Wintersportler aus Thüringen, Sachsen, Berlin und Brandenburg machen Urlaub in Oberhof.
3. Bis zum Jahre 2025 soll Oberhof im Winter mehr Schnee haben.
4. Die Wirtschaft in Oberhof hängt hauptsächlich vom Exporthandel ab.
5. Frau Weigel meint, dass Touristen im Sommer nach Oberhof kommen, um im Thüringer Wald zu wandern.
6. Das Panorama-Hotel gewinnt Kunden durch seine neuen Skikurse.
7. Die Unternehmen der Region müssen neue Angebote entwickeln, um in Zeiten des Klimawandels zu überleben.

 3-15 Textarbeit: Klimawandel – Strategienwandel. Wie will man sich in Oberhof auf den Klimawandel vorbereiten, damit die Touristen dennoch kommen? Markieren Sie was man in dem Bericht vorschlägt.

einen Freizeitpark	einen größeren Bahnhof	eine Tanzschule
gut gepflegte Wanderwege	eine neue Sporthalle	mehr Hotels
Kletterwände	einen Streichelzoo	Wellness-Angebote
einen Skitunnel		

Activity 3-17. (1) You may need to supply students with some vocabulary words that are relevant to the local effects of climate change, e.g., *das Hochwasser, die Dürre, die Hitzewelle*, etc. **(2)** You may want to give students some ideas to get started: *Recyceln Sie? Sparen Sie Energie, indem Sie das Licht ausmachen, wenn Sie ein Zimmer verlassen? Was können Sie z. B. tun, um weniger Auto zu fahren? Wie können Sie im Winter warm bleiben bzw. im Sommer kühl bleiben und dabei weniger Energie gebrauchen? Wie können Sie anders leben? anders einkaufen?*

Follow-up for 3-17 (2). Have students create posters or PowerPoint presentations with climate protection tips. Have each student present one such tip (*Klimaschutztipp*) or his/her own climate-friendly behaviors (*Mein Beitrag zum Klimaschutz*). Or have each student create a promotional poster demonstrating 3 (or 4 or 5) *Tipps zur Reduktion des Kohlendioxids in der Atmosphäre*.

Alternative for 3-18. You could assign a specific *Thüringer Wald* location to each student to research and then have each one report back to the class, or share on a class website what makes their chosen location distinct. Relevant places: *Biosphärenreservat-Vessertal, der Rennsteig, Brotterode, Eisenach, Friedrichroda, Ilmenau, Lauscha, Masserberg, Neuhaus am Rennweg, Oberhof, Oberweißbach, Ruhla, Schmalkalden, Schmiedefeld am Rennsteig, Suhl, Steinach, Stützerbach, Tabarz, Tambach-Dietharz, Zella-Mehlis.*

3-16 **Kommen Sie doch mal nach Oberhof!** Sie arbeiten bei der Tourist-Information Oberhof. Ein/e Tourist/in ruft an, um Informationen über Oberhof zu bekommen. Er/Sie steht Oberhof als gutem Wintersportort etwas skeptisch gegenüber. Überzeugen Sie diese Person, dass Oberhof doch das richtige Ziel für einen Winterurlaub ist. Spielen Sie den Dialog.

Beispiel: **Angestellte/r:** *Tourist-Information Oberhof, guten Tag. Frau/Herr Niemeyer.*

Tourist/in: *Guten Tag, ich möchte gern Informationen über Wintersportmöglichkeiten in Oberhof.*

Angestellte/r: *Ja, was machen Sie denn gern?*

…

3-17 **Der Klimawandel bei mir zu Hause.** Besprechen Sie die Fragen.

1. Erleben Sie Auswirkungen des Klimawandels, wo Sie wohnen?

2. Der Klimawandel ist eine Folge der schnell steigenden Kohlendioxidemissionen. Was kann man als Individuum zur Reduktion des CO_2-Ausstoßes und zum Klimaschutz beitragen? Was machen Sie persönlich? Was können Sie noch machen?

3-18 **Urlaub im Thüringer Wald.** Besuchen Sie die Internetseite des Regionalverbunds Thüringer Wald. Was bietet die Gegend für Urlauber? Was kann man jetzt dort tun? Suchen Sie sich mindestens drei Aktivitäten und Veranstaltungen aus und erklären Sie, warum sie Sie interessieren.

Beispiel: *Wenn ich dieses Wochenende in den Thüringer Wald reisen würde, möchte ich erstens …, zweitens …, drittens …*

Lesetext 3

Deutschlands erstes Bratwurstmuseum (Interview)

Wenn man an deutsche Esskultur denkt, kommen einem wahrscheinlich Kartoffeln, Brot, Sauerkraut, Bier und natürlich auch Wurst in den Sinn. Solche Verallgemeinerungen lassen aber vergessen, dass die deutsche Küche regional sehr unterschiedlich ist. Im deutschen Sprachraum gibt es zum Beispiel mehr als 1.500 verschiedene Wurstsorten, und jede

Thüringer Rostbratwurst

Gegend scheint ihre eigene Lieblingsvariante zu haben, ob bayrische Weißwurst, Frankfurter Würstchen, Berliner Currywurst oder Thüringer Rostbratwurst. Seit 2006 gibt es sogar ein Museum zu Ehren des Thüringer Lieblings, der seit Jahrhunderten zur Kulturgeschichte der Region gehört. Dieser ist laut EU-Verordnung mindestens 15–20 cm lang und besteht hauptsächlich aus Schweinefleisch. Serviert wird die Rostwurst traditionell in einem aufgeschnittenen Brötchen mit original Thüringer Senf.

Im folgenden Interview mit Thomas Mäuer, Mitbegründer des Bratwurstmuseums, lesen Sie über den Ursprung des Museums in dem kleinen Dorf Holzhausen und erfahren, warum die Thüringer so stolz sind auf ihre lokale Spezialität.

Vor dem Lesen

1. Was halten Sie für typisch deutsches Essen? Welche deutschen Spezialitäten oder Produkte haben Sie schon mal probiert?
2. Was findet man wohl in einem Bratwurstmuseum?

Beim Lesen

1. Bevor Sie den Text lesen, schauen Sie sich die Interviewfragen an. Was für Antworten erwarten Sie zu diesen Fragen? Unterstreichen Sie Stichwörter im Text, die die Fragen beantworten.
2. Finden Sie sechs Wörter oder Ausdrücke, die der Interviewpartner Herr Mäuer als Synonyme für die Thüringer Bratwurst verwendet.

Introduction to *Lesetext 3*. Ask students to think about the text type and title: *Was kann man vielleicht aus einem Interview über ein Bratwurstmuseum erfahren? Wer gibt ein solches Interview?* After students have read the introduction, ask them what they have learned: *Wie viele verschiedene Wurstsorten gibt es im deutschen Sprachgebiet? Was lernen Sie aus dem Text über die Thüringer Bratwurst?* Personalize the topic by asking students about their own experiences: *Haben Sie schon mal eine Bratwurst (oder eine andere Wurstsorte) probiert? Wenn ja, wo und wann? Hat sie so ausgesehen wie auf dem Foto? Wie hat sie Ihnen geschmeckt?*

Answers for *Beim Lesen (2)*. ein hochwertiges Lebensmittel, ein erfolgreiches Wirtschaftsgut, ein Stück Lebensart, das leckerste Kulturgut unseres Landes, eine weltbekannte Spezialität, dieses Lebensmittel, die bekannteste Thüringerin, die Bratwurst, Original Thüringer Bratwürste.

03-11 to 03-13

Deutschlands erstes Bratwurstmuseum

Ein Interview mit Herrn Thomas Mäuer, Mitbegründer des Museums

Interviewer: Herr Mäuer, wie sind Sie auf die Idee gekommen, ein Bratwurstmuseum zu gründen?

Herr Mäuer: Die Idee zur Eröffnung des Bratwurstmuseums basiert auf der urkundlichen Ersterwähnung der Thüringer Bratwurst aus dem Jahre 1404. Der Eintrag aus dem Arnstädter Benediktiner Jungfrauenkloster wurde von unserem Freund und Vereinsmitglied, dem Archivar Peter Unger, im Jahr 2000 gefunden. Diese ist wohl die älteste Bratwurstrechnung der Welt. Der sensationelle Fund sorgte auch für Aufsehen bei den Medien. „Das muss ins Museum", dachten wir. Aus dem Freundeskreis ging schließlich der Verein „Freunde der Thüringer Bratwurst" hervor, der ist auch Träger° des Museums.

Interviewer: Ist Ihr Museum tatsächlich das erste Bratwurstmuseum Deutschlands?

Thomas Mäuer, Mitbegründer des Bratwurstmuseums

sponsor

5

10

15

Offizielles Logo für die echte
Thüringer Rostbratwurst

Herr Mäuer: Ja, unser Museum ist das erste und einzige Bratwurstmuseum in Deutschland. Und vielleicht auch in der ganzen Welt!

Interviewer: In Deutschland ist jede Region stolz auf ihre eigene Bratwurst. Was ist das Besondere an der Thüringer Bratwurst?

Herr Mäuer: Die Thüringer sind sehr stolz auf ihre Bratwurst. Die ist 20 für uns nicht nur ein hochwertiges Lebensmittel und ein erfolgreiches Wirtschaftsgut. Die ist ein Stück Lebensart, eben das leckerste Kulturgut unseres Landes. Das Besondere ist der hervorragende und einzigartige Geschmack. Nicht umsonst ist die Thüringer Bratwurst eine weltbekannte *trademarked* Spezialität, welche europaweit markenrechtlich geschützt° ist. Trotzdem ist 25 Geschmack natürlich subjektiv. Das wirklich Besondere ist: In Thüringen verbindet sich mit diesem Lebensmittel eine über sechshundertjährige Kulturgeschichte, welche bis heute in lebendigen Traditionen fortbesteht.

Interviewer: Was kann man in Ihrem Museum alles sehen und tun?

Herr Mäuer: Im Museum kann man sich über Geschichte, Kunst, Kultur 30 und Kult rund um die Bratwurst informieren: Herstellung, Bratwursthistorie, Bratwurstregionen, Bratwurstfeste, Bratwurstlokale, Bratwurst in aller Welt. *bratwurst-related* Neben Maschinen, Geräten, Modellen, Bratwurstdevotionalien° aus aller *devotional objects / with a* Welt, und vieles anderes mehr, werden, stets mit einem Augenzwinkern°, *wink* Geschichte und Geschichten über die bekannteste Thüringerin erzählt. Und 35 was zu essen gibt es natürlich auch. Bei uns wird ständig gegrillt, so dass jeder Besucher die Thüringer Bratwurst probieren kann.

Interviewer: Besucher aus aller Welt kommen in Ihr Museum. Haben Sie gewusst, dass man sich auch im Ausland so sehr für die Bratwurst interessiert?

Herr Mäuer: Unser Museum wird, nach unserem Verständnis, sehr gut 40 besucht. Wir befinden uns mit dem Museumsgebäude im ländlichen Raum, trotzdem – oder deshalb? – finden gerade in den Sommermonaten bis zu 1.000 Besucher monatlich zu uns. Dass darunter ca. 30 Prozent ausländische Besucher sind, freut uns natürlich sehr. Das haben wir nicht erwartet. Wir wussten nicht, dass es so viele Bratwurstfans auf der Welt gibt. Gerade aus 45 den USA haben wir regelmäßig Gäste und Anfragen. Wir hatten auch schon einen Bericht in der *Washington Post*.

Interviewer: Wie ist Ihre persönliche Beziehung zur Bratwurst? Sind Sie Metzger von Beruf?

Herr Mäuer: Wie die meisten aus unserem Verein bin ich kein Metzger. Ich bin 50 *co-owner of a company* Mitinhaber eines kleinen Dienstleistungsunternehmens° und betreibe nebenbei *in the service sector* mit einem Partner eine Gaststätte. Da ich auf dem Lande aufgewachsen bin, ist mir das Thema Hausschlachtung seit frühester Jugend bekannt. Auch heute *slaughter* noch schlachten° wir viermal im Jahr. Unser Verein veranstaltet jährlich sein eigenes Schlachtfest. Dabei werden natürlich auch Original Thüringer Brat- 55 würste von uns selbst hergestellt.

Nomen

der Bericht, -e *report*

die Gaststätte, -n *restaurant*

das Gerät, -e *tool, equipment*

der Geschmack, ¨er *taste*

das Gut, ¨er *good(s)*

die Herstellung *production*

die Kunst, ¨e *art*

das Lebensmittel, - *food; groceries (pl.)*

der Ursprung, ¨e *origin*

der Verein, -e *association, club*

Verben

sich befinden, befand, befunden *to be located*

her·stellen *to produce*

probieren *to try; to have a taste*

veranstalten *to organize (an event)*

Adjektive und Adverbien

hervorragend *outstanding, eminent*

regelmäßig *regular(ly)*

stolz auf (+ acc.) *proud of*

trotzdem *nevertheless*

3-19 Textarbeit: Fragen zum Inhalt. Beantworten Sie die Fragen zum Lesetext.

1. Welches Ereignis hat die Thüringer Freunde motiviert, ein Museum zu gründen?
2. Wie unterscheidet sich die Thüringer Bratwurst nach der Meinung von Herrn Mäuer von anderen Wurstsorten?
3. Wie viele Bratwurstmuseen gibt es in Deutschland?
4. Was bietet das Museum für Besucher?
5. Wie viele Gäste besuchen das Museum? Woher kommen sie?
6. Warum interessiert sich Herr Mäuer für die Bratwurst? Wie zeigt sich sein Interesse daran?

3-20 Vokabelarbeit. Ergänzen Sie die Sätze mit Wörtern aus den *Neuen Vokabeln*. Achten Sie dabei auch auf die Wortform.

1. Das Museum ____befindet____ ____sich____ in Holzhausen, ein Ort mit weniger als 700 Einwohnern.
2. Das Museum wurde von einem ____Verein____ gegründet.
3. Der Verein „Freunde der Thüringer Bratwurst" ____veranstaltet____ jedes Jahr zwei große Bratwurstfeste.
4. In der ____Gaststätte____ von Herrn Mäuer steht Bratwurst bestimmt auf der Speisekarte.
5. Wenn man ein Rezept hat, kann man auch zu Hause eigene Bratwürste ____herstellen____.
6. Ein Grill ist ein ____Gerät____, mit dem man Bratwürste grillen kann.
7. Bratwurst, Brötchen und Senf sind alle ____Lebensmittel____.

Possible answers for 3-19. **1.** die Entdeckung einer Bratwurstrechnung aus dem Jahr 1404; **2.** Sie hat eine 600 Jahre alte Kulturgeschichte, ist markenrechtlich geschützt und wirtschaftlich erfolgreich. Er hält sie auch für das leckerste Kulturgut des Landes. Man merkt, er ist stolz darauf. **3.** nur eins; **4.** Man lernt über die Geschichte und Herstellung der Bratwurst, sieht Geräte und Modelle und kann eine Bratwurst probieren. **5.** bis zu 1.000 Besucher pro Monat aus aller Welt und regelmäßig Gäste aus den USA; **6.** Er ist mit dem Schlachten aufgewachsen. Er nimmt am jährlichen Schlachtfest teil und stellt mit dem Verein zusammen eigene Bratwürste her.

Teaching suggestion for 3-21. Have students write down interview questions as homework and then work together in class to invent answers to their questions as they prepare the dialog.

3-21 Interview. Sie besuchen das Bratwurstmuseum zu seinem jährlichen Museumsfest. Ein/e Journalist/in (ein/e Mitstudent/in) möchte Sie spontan interviewen, als Sie das Museum verlassen. Spielen Sie einen Dialog.

Beispiel:

Journalist/in: *Entschuldigen Sie, bitte. Darf ich Ihnen ein paar Fragen stellen?*

Museums-besucher/in: *Selbstverständlich. / Gerne. / Zu welchem Zweck?*

Journalist/in: ...

3-22 Zur Diskussion. Besprechen Sie die Fragen.

1. Hat Ihre Heimat eine regionale Spezialität? Was für Essen isst man gern, wo Sie herkommen?
2. Was essen Sie gern? nicht gern? Gibt es ein Lebensmittel oder ein Gericht, das Sie regelmäßig essen oder ein Getränk, das Sie täglich trinken?
3. Probieren Sie gern neue Gerichte? Was würden Sie nicht essen?

3-23 Mein eigenes Museum. Sie wollen ein Museum zu Ehren Ihres Lieblingsessens eröffnen. Entwickeln Sie einen Plan für Ihr Museum, um Investoren dafür zu gewinnen. Wo befindet es sich? Was ist in Ihrem Museum? Warum werden Besucher kommen wollen?

3-24 Noch ein Interview. Sie sind Journalist/in für die *Thüringer Allgemeine Zeitung*. Für die Sonntagsausgabe führen Sie ein (fiktives) Interview mit einer Person Ihrer Wahl (real oder fiktiv, lebendig oder tot). Denken Sie sich interessante Fragen aus und erfinden Sie dann plausible Antworten aus der Perspektive des Interviewpartners.

Introduction to *Lesetext 4*. Ask students what they already know or have learned about Weimar: *Was wissen Sie schon über Weimar? Wo in Thüringen liegt Weimar?* After they have read the introduction, ask them what further information they can share. *Warum nennt man die Stadt „Universitätsstadt Weimar"? Welche Hochschulen hat die Stadt? Woran denkt man, wenn man den Namen „Weimar" hört?*

Lesetext 4

Universitätsstadt Weimar (Stadtporträt)

Weimar ist der Standort von zwei Hochschulen: der Bauhaus-Universität und der Hochschule für Musik Franz Liszt. Wenn man an Weimar denkt, denkt man nicht gerade als erstes an ihre zwei Hochschulen, sondern an die Geschichte Weimars und die Traditionen, denen beide Institutionen ihre Namen verdanken. Neben Bauhaus und Liszt lässt sich eine Reihe von namhaften Personen und wichtigen Ereignissen in Verbindung mit Weimar nennen. Die Geschichte Weimars – besonders die vom 16. bis ins 21. Jahrhundert – liest sich in mancher Hinsicht wie ein Abriss der deutschen Kulturgeschichte mit all ihren Höhepunkten und Tiefpunkten.

Hauptgebäude der Bauhaus-Universität Weimar, einer der Kunstschulbauten Henry van de Veldes

Sie lesen in dem folgenden Stadtporträt über das umfangreiche kulturelle Erbe Weimars, das diese Stadt zu einem geeigneten Studienort macht.

Vor dem Lesen

1. Beschreiben Sie die Stadt, in der sich Ihre Universität befindet. Ist sie eine typische Universitätsstadt? Was gehört zu einer typischen Universitätsstadt?

2. Weimar verbindet man mit den Namen vieler bedeutenden Persönlichkeiten. Von wem haben Sie schon etwas gehört? Versuchen Sie die Berufe den richtigen Personen zuzuordnen.

Siehe **Kulturtipps**: Bauhaus

__f__	1.	Lucas Cranach der Ältere (1472–1553)
__i__	2.	Johann Sebastian Bach (1685–1750)
__h__	3.	Christoph Martin Wieland (1733–1813)
__e__	4.	Johann Gottfried Herder (1744–1803)
__c__	5.	Johann Wolfgang von Goethe (1749–1832)
__d__	6.	Friedrich Schiller (1759–1804)
__j__	7.	Franz Liszt (1811–1886)
__b__	8.	Henry van de Velde (1853–1957)
__a__	9.	Walter Gropius (1883–1969)
__g__	10.	Friedrich Nietzsche (1844–1900)

a. Architekt und Begründer des Bauhauses

b. belgischer Architekt, Begründer einer Kunstschule in Weimar

c. Dichter der Deutschen Klassik, Autor des Dramas *Faust*

d. Dichter der Deutschen Klassik, Dramatiker, Theoretiker

e. Kultur- und Geschichtsphilosoph, Theologe, Dichter der Deutschen Klassik

f. Maler und Grafiker der Reformation, Freund von Martin Luther

g. Philosoph des Nihilismus und klassischer Philologe

h. Schriftsteller der Aufklärung, Wegbereiter der Deutschen Klassik

i. Orgelvirtuose und Komponist des Barocks

j. österreichisch-ungarischer Klaviervirtuose, Komponist des 19. Jahrhunderts

Beim Lesen

Finden Sie das passende Datum im Lesetext für jedes der Ereignisse.

__1800__ Zeit der Deutschen Klassik

__1919__ Ausrufung der Weimarer Republik

__1933__ Machtübernahme der Nazis in Deutschland

__1937__ Bau des Konzentrationslagers Buchenwald

__2004__ Ernennung Weimars zur Universitätsstadt

__1999__ Ernennung Weimars zur europäischen Kulturstadt

__13. April 2005__ Investitur des Rektors an der Bauhaus-Universität

Universitätsstadt Weimar

„…Weimar ist eigentlich ein Park, in dem eine Stadt liegt – man kann es wie ein Historiker sehen oder als Museum, als auratischen° Ort der großen Geister der deutschen Klassik, als Wahlheimat großer Europäer wie Franz Liszt, als Gründungsort des staatlichen Bauhauses mit Weltgeltung, als Ausgangs- und Endpunkt der Weimarer Republik. Weimar ist eigentlich eine Universität, in der eine Stadt liegt. …"

Prof. Dr.-Ing. Gerd Zimmermann,
Rektor der Bauhaus-Universität bei seiner
Antrittsrede am 13. April 2005

03-14 to 03-17

aura-filled

10 Blick auf Weimar

Weimar ist nicht irgendeine Kleinstadt. Die historische Stadt mit ihren weiten Parklandschaften war einst Heimat von Wissenschaftlern, Schriftstellern, Künstlern und Architekten wie Johann Wolfgang von Goethe und Friedrich Schiller, Johann Sebastian Bach und Franz Liszt, Lucas Cranach und Walter Gropius u. v. a. 15

„Hier ist jedes Haus ein Museum oder ein Gedenkhaus – sind nur die Pavillons des großen Museums, das Weimar heißt." So beschreibt Egon Erwin Kisch° die Stadt, doch in den vergangenen zehn Jahren ist in Weimar eine ganze Reihe von weit beachteten Neubauten entstanden, die zum Ziel von Architekturinteressierten aus aller Welt geworden sind. Professoren und Mitarbeiter der Bauhaus-Universität haben viele dieser Gebäude selbst geplant und gefördert. 20

Egon Erwin Kisch (1885–1948) Czech-Austrian journalist and author

Von den ca. 65.000 Einwohnern der Stadt sind 6.500 Studierende der beiden Hochschulen – der Bauhaus-Universität Weimar und der Musikhochschule Franz Liszt. Zusammen mit den etwa 1.000 Angestellten stellen diese Hochschulen einen wichtigen Teil des öffentlichen Lebens dar. So trägt die Stadt seit 2004 den Titel „Universitätsstadt".

Seit der sogenannten Weimarer Klassik* um 1800 war die Stadt ein führendes Zentrum des 25 deutschen Geisteslebens. Hier wirkten neben Wieland, Herder, Goethe, Schiller und Nietzsche

Weimarer Markt

einige der bedeutendsten deutschen Dichter und Denker. Im Jahre 1919 wurde im Nationaltheater die Weimarer Republik† ausgerufen. Sie war ein erster, wenn auch nur kurzlebiger Versuch, eine Demokratie in 30 Deutschland zu gründen.

1933 übernahmen die Nationalsozialisten die Macht in Deutschland. So begann für Weimar eines der dunkelsten Kapitel seiner Geschichte: 1937 wurde das Konzentrationslager° Buchenwald vor den Toren 35 der Stadt eingerichtet. Politische Häftlinge und später

concentration camp

*Siehe **Kulturtipps**: Deutsche Klassik
†Siehe **Kulturtipps**: Weimarer Republik

weiter >>>

persecuted

Park an der Ilm mit Goethes
Gartenhaus

Kriegsgefangene und auch Juden und andere Volksgruppen, die auf
Grund der Rassenlehre der Nazis verfolgt° wurden, waren dort inhaftiert.
Mehr als 56.000 Menschen wurden ermordet.

Das neue Weimar präsentiert sich in der renovierten Weimarhalle, 40
einem der modernsten Kultur- und Kongresszentren Deutschlands,
im Goethe-Nationalmuseum mit seiner neuen Ausstellung zum Leben
und Werk des Dichters und im Neuen Museum, dem ersten Museum
für moderne Kunst in den neuen Bundesländern. Beim alljährlichen
„Kunstfest" lernt man die neusten Entwicklungen im internationalen 45
Tanz, Theater und in der zeitgenössischen Literatur kennen. Zum
alten Weimar gehören seine einzigartigen historischen Zeugnisse und
Sammlungen der Deutschen Klassik und der Bauhaus-Bewegung.
In der Welterbeliste der UNESCO sind elf Stätten des klassischen
Weimars wie z. B. das ehemalige Residenzschloss in der Innenstadt und Goethes Gartenhaus im 50
Park an der Ilm verzeichnet, sowie auch die zwei Kunstschulbauten Henry van de Veldes und das
Haus am Horn, die zur Bauhaus-Universität gehören. Weimar sieht sich selbst als Ort der Kultur
und ist stolz auf den Titel „Kulturstadt Europas", den es im Jahre 1999 erhielt.

 Neue Vokabeln

Nomen

der/die Angestellte, -n (*adj.
noun*) *employee*

der Dichter, -/die Dichterin,
-nen *poet*

das Gebäude, - *building*

der Geist, -er *intellectual (person);
mind, spirit*

die Hochschule, -n *institution of
higher education*

der Künstler, -/die Künstlerin,
-nen *artist*

die Sammlung, -en *collection*

der Schriftsteller, -/die
Schriftstellerin, -nen *author*

der Versuch, -e *attempt*

der Wissenschaftler, -/die
Wissenschaftlerin, -nen *scholar,
scientist*

das Ziel, -e *destination, goal*

Verben

ermorden *to murder*

übernehmen (übernimmt), übernahm, übernommen *to take over*

wirken *to have an effect, to work*

Adjektive und Adverbien

eigentlich *actually*

einst *once, at one time (in the past)*

inhaftiert *imprisoned*

vergangen *past*

zeitgenössisch *contemporary*

Ausdrücke

eine ganze Reihe *a whole series*

u. v. a. = und viele(s) andere
and many others

Kulturtipps

Bauhaus

Das „Staatliche Bauhaus" wurde 1919 in Weimar vom Architekten Walter Gropius gegründet. Ziel dieser neuen Kunsthochschule war es, alle Künste unter ein Konzept zu bringen und die Einheit von Kunst und Technik, von Form und Funktion zu fördern. Das bis 1933 bestehende Bauhaus sieht man heute als Kunstlaboratorium der Moderne. Die revolutionären Ideen haben die moderne Architektur und modernes Design langfristig geprägt und beeinflussen heute noch die Kunsttheorie und -praxis auf internationaler Ebene.

Deutsche Klassik

Die Deutsche Klassik (1786–1805) ist eine literarische Epoche, in der die zwei Hauptvertreter – Goethe und Schiller – einen bisher unerreichten Höhepunkt in der deutschen Literatur erlangt haben. Der Ort Weimar war zu einer solchen kulturellen Blüte geeignet, auch in Musik, Theater, Kunst und Wissenschaft, weil die Herzogin (*Duchess*) Anna Amalia und nachher ihr Sohn Großherzog (*Grand Duke*) Carl August das geistig-kulturelle Leben bewusst gefördert haben. Deswegen wird diese Epoche auch als „Weimarer Klassik" bezeichnet.

Goethe-Schiller-Denkmal vor dem Nationaltheater in Weimar

Weimarer Republik

Die Weimarer Republik (1918–1933) war die Staatsform Deutschlands in der Epoche zwischen Ende des Ersten Weltkrieges und der Machtübernahme der Nazis. Im Deutschen Nationaltheater Weimars traf sich die Nationalversammlung (*National Assembly*), wo sie sich auf eine Verfassung (*constitution*) für diesen neuen demokratischen Staat einigte. Nach dem Ort dieser Versammlung wurde die neue Republik benannt.

Answers for 3-25. **1.** R; **2.** F – viele historische und moderne Gebäude; **3.** R; **4.** F – erst seit 2004; **5.** R; **6.** R; **7.** F – über die neusten Entwicklungen in Tanz, Theater und Literatur; **8.** F – Die Kunstschulbauten Henry van de Veldes und das Haus am Horn gehören der Bauhaus-Universität.

3-25 Textarbeit: Richtig oder falsch? Wenn eine Aussage falsch ist, korrigieren Sie und ergänzen Sie sie mit Informationen aus dem Lesetext.

1. In Weimar wohnten einst Johann Sebastian Bach und Walter Gropius.
2. Die Stadt hat viele historische und nur sehr wenige moderne Gebäude.
3. Einige Professoren an der Universität arbeiten im Bereich der Architektur.
4. Weimar gilt schon seit Jahrhunderten als „Universitätsstadt".
5. Die Weimarer Republik war die erste deutsche Demokratie.
6. Im Konzentrationslager Buchenwald starben Tausende von Menschen.
7. Auf dem jährlichen Kunstfest erfährt man hauptsächlich über die Geschichte der Kunst.
8. Das Residenzschloss und Goethes Gartenhaus gehören der Bauhaus-Universität.

3-26 Textarbeit: Weimar für alle. Was bietet die Stadt für Besucher und Einwohner, die sich für folgende Bereiche interessieren?

Kunst	Architektur	Studium
Musik	politische Geschichte	Kulturgeschichte

3-27 Vokabelarbeit. Ergänzen Sie die Sätze mit Wörtern aus den *Neuen Vokabeln*. Achten Sie dabei auch auf die Wortform.

1. Die Bauhaus-Universität ist eine von zwei _____Hochschulen_____ in Weimar.

2. 2005 _____übernahm_____ Gerd Zimmermann die Rektorstelle an der Bauhaus-Universität.

3. Goethe und Schiller waren _____Dichter/Schriftsteller_____, die 1799 bis 1805 zusammen am Weimarer Theater _____wirkten_____.

4. Lucas Cranach war der _____Künstler_____, der Porträts von Martin Luther und seiner Frau gemalt und die Bibel und viele protestantische Schriften illustriert hat.

5. Das Neue Museum beherbergt nicht historische, sondern _____zeitgenössische_____ Kunst.

6. Das Bauhaus-Museum besitzt eine der größten _____Sammlungen_____ der Bauhauskunst in der Welt.

7. Im KZ Buchenwald waren über 250.000 Menschen _____inhaftiert_____ und mehr als 50.000 wurden _____ermordet_____.

3-28 Zur Diskussion. Besprechen Sie die Fragen.

1. Was meinte der Journalist Egon Erwin Kisch, als er Weimar als ein großes Museum bezeichnete?
2. Rektor Zimmermann sagte: „Weimar ist eigentlich eine Universität, in der eine Stadt liegt." Erklären Sie diese Charakterisierung.
3. Vergleichen Sie Ihre Universitätsstadt mit Weimar. Wie alt ist Weimar? Wie alt sind die Hochschulen Weimars? Wie alt ist Ihre Universität? Ihre Stadt? Wie hoch ist der Anteil der Studierenden unter den Einwohnern in Weimar? in Ihrer Stadt? Spielt Ihre Universität eine wichtige Rolle in der Stadt? Wie ist es in Weimar?

3-29 Meine Stadt. Weimar bezeichnet man als „eine Universität, in der eine Stadt liegt". Schreiben Sie ein Stadtporträt für Studienanfänger an Ihrer Universität, damit sie den besonderen Charakter der Stadt kennenlernen. Wodurch zeichnet sich Ihre Stadt aus? Beginnen Sie mit einem Satz wie unten, dann erklären Sie, warum Sie die Stadt so bezeichnen.

_____ *ist eine Stadt, wo …*

_____ *ist eine Stadt, die …*

_____ *ist eine Stadt, in der …*

Information for 3-30. A list of people named in the text can be found in the *Beim Lesen* section above. Other personalities associated with Weimar include: *Herzogin Anna Amalia, Herzog Carl August, Max Beckmann, Paul Klee, August von Kotzebue, Jean Paul, Oskar Schlemmer, Charlotte von Stein, Richard Strauss, Christiane Vulpius, Richard Wagner.*

Activity 3-30. Having students write in the first person discourages the verbatim use of language from third person accounts.

Note for 3-30. Relevant web addresses for Internet research activities can be found in *MyGermanLab* and on the Companion Website.

Introduction to *Hörtext 2.* Ask students what they learned from *Lesetext 4* about Weimar's institutions of higher education: *Wie heißen Weimars Hochschulen? Was wissen Sie schon darüber?* After students have read the introduction to the *Hörtext,* ask them what else they have learned: *Warum wählen Studenten Weimar als Studienort? Welche Vorteile haben Studenten hier, die man an größeren Orten und Universitäten wohl nicht hat?*

3-30 Wer ist wer in Weimar? Sie bewerben sich um ein Sommerpraktikum in Weimar, in dem Sie in einem Museum die Rolle einer historischen Persönlichkeit spielen. Dafür müssen Sie die Biografie dieser Person gut kennen. Wählen Sie eine Person und sammeln Sie Informationen. Dann schreiben Sie eine Autobiografie (in der **ich-**Form!) in eigenen Worten.

Hörtext 2

Zwei Studentinnen in Weimar (Gespräch)

Studierenden in der Stadt Weimar steht unbestritten viel an Kultur zur Verfügung. Aber nicht nur deswegen kommen Studienbewerber in die kleine Stadt an der Ilm. Während an Massenuniversitäten oft von überfüllten Vorlesungen und einer unpersönlichen Atmosphäre die Rede ist, hat man an beiden Weimarer Hochschulen engen persönlichen Kontakt zu

Deutsches Nationaltheater in Weimar

den Professoren sowie modern ausgestattete Hörsäle und Seminarräume. Im Vergleich zu den großen Universitätsstädten sind die Lebenskosten in Weimar auch relativ niedrig. Und hier redet man nicht von Studiengebühren, wie in manchen anderen Bundesländern – das Studium bleibt vorläufig kostenlos.

Diese Vorteile scheinen die Thüringer Landsleute selbst am meisten zu schätzen, denn etwa ein Drittel der 6.500 Studierenden in Weimar kommen aus Thüringen.

Im folgenden Gespräch hören Sie zwei Studentinnen, Gisela Braun und Nadia Schweigert, über das Leben in Weimar reden.

Vor dem Hören

Was machen Sie gern mit Freunden in Ihrer Freizeit? Was bietet Ihre Stadt für Studenten? Was meinen Sie: Was machen Studierende in Weimar gern in ihrer Freizeit?

Zwei Studentinnen unterhalten sich im Café.

Zwei Studentinnen in Weimar

03-18

Beim Hören

Während des Geprächs hören Sie folgende Vokabeln.

Quadratmeter	*square meters*	Umzug	*move*
WG (Wohngemeinschaft)	*people sharing an apartment*	zerstört	*destroyed*
		Rede	*public speech*
Bahn	*train*	Ermäßigung	*price reduction*

Hören Sie sich das Gespräch an und ordnen Sie die Opern und Theaterstücken ihren Autoren zu.

_f_ 1. William Shakespeare

_a_ 2. Jean Racine

_d, e_ 3. Johann Wolfgang von Goethe

_b_ 4. Georges Bizet

_i_ 5. Gioacchino Rossini

_c, g, h_ 6. Richard Wagner

a. „Bérénice"

b. „Carmen"

c. „Die Walküre"

d. „Faust. Erster Teil"

e. „Faust. Zweiter Teil"

f. „Othello"

g. „Ring des Nibelungen"

h. „Siegfried"

i. „Wilhelm Tell"

Alternative to 3-30.
Have students choose a place or event from the text and prepare an oral or written report on the subject. Relevant topics include: *Bauhaus-Universität, Musikhochschule Franz Liszt, Deutsches Nationaltheater, Konzentrationslager Buchenwald, Landes-museum (Neues Museum), Goethemuseum/Goethehaus, Weimarhalle, Residenzschloss, Goethes Gartenhaus, Park an der Ilm, Haus am Horn, Bauhaus, Kunstfest, die Weimarer Republik.* You could also have students choose a related topic that is not mentioned in the text. Numerous other places and events can be located on Weimar's official tourist site. Have students report results in a class presentation or a research/writing assignment. If you have a course website, students could post their research in a public forum.

Kulturtipps

Semesterticket

An deutschen Hochschulen zahlen alle Studierende als Teil ihrer Studienbeiträge (*student fees*) eine Gebühr zur Nutzung von öffentlichen Verkehrsmitteln. Der Studentenausweis gilt dann in der Region von der jeweiligen Hochschule als Fahrkarte für bestimmte Transportmittel. Manchmal gilt das Ticket in allen Verkehrsmitteln – Bahnen, Busse, S-Bahnen und U-Bahnen – im ganzen Bundesland, an anderen Orten gilt es nur für die Bahn innerhalb eines begrenzten Gebiets.

3-31 Textarbeit: Gisela oder Nadia? Wer macht was?

1. ___Gisela___ kommt aus Rudolstadt.

2. ___Gisela___ studiert an der Bauhaus-Universität.

3. ___Nadia___ ist vor einer Woche nach Weimar umgezogen.

4. ___Nadia___ hat drei Mitbewohner.

5. ___Nadia___ hat eine Klassenfahrt nach Weimar gemacht.

6. ___Gisela___ war vor kurzer Zeit im Nationaltheater.

7. ___Nadia___ möchte in ein Konzert gehen.

8. ___Gisela___ hat die Filmversion einer Wagner-Oper gesehen.

9. ___Gisela___ schlägt vor, dass sie die Karten sofort kaufen sollten.

10. ___Nadia___ will heute noch spazieren gehen.

Possible answers for 3-32.
1. Sie sind Kusinen. **2.** Sie wohnt in einer zentral gelegenen WG mit drei Mitbewohnern. Ihr Zimmer ist 27 Quadratmeter groß. **3.** auspacken, das Zimmer einrichten, Unterlagen für die Hochschule ausfüllen, einkaufen **4.** ins Kino oder in Clubs gehen, Parks genießen, Museen, Veranstaltungen und Konzerte besuchen, auf Märkte und Volksfeste gehen; **5.** Theaterstücke, Opern, Konzerte, Reden **6.** das Sinfoniekonzert am Sonntag um 19.30, die Vorstellung von Wagners „Walküre" morgen Abend.

3-32 Textarbeit: Fragen zum Inhalt. Beantworten Sie die Fragen in Bezug auf das Gespräch.

1. Wie kennen sich Nadia und Gisela?

2. Beschreiben Sie Nadias Wohnsituation.

3. Was macht Nadia, seitdem sie in Weimar ist?

4. Was können Studenten in Weimar in ihrer Freizeit machen?

5. Was für Veranstaltungen finden im Theatergebäude statt?

6. Für welche Veranstaltungen entscheiden sich die beiden?

3-33 Zur Diskussion. Besprechen Sie die Fragen.

1. Beschreiben Sie die Geschichte Ihrer Universität. Wann wurde sie gegründet? Von wem? Warum? Ist sie eine öffentliche Hochschule oder eine private Hochschule? Was ist der Unterschied?

2. Wie weit wohnen Sie von der Universität? Wie kommen Sie zur Uni? Benutzen Sie ein Transportmittel, wenn Sie einkaufen gehen? wenn Sie mit Freunden ausgehen? Ist alles zentral gelegen oder liegt alles weit auseinander?

3. Gibt es ein Theater in Ihrer Universitätsstadt? Sind Sie schon mal ins Theater oder ins Konzert gegangen? Wenn ja, was haben Sie gesehen/ gehört?

3-34 Dialog. Ein guter Freund aus Ihrer Schulzeit zieht jetzt in Ihre Stadt, weil er nächstes Semester hier studieren wird. Sie treffen sich heute zum Mittagessen. Schreiben Sie zusammen einen Dialog. Sprechen Sie über das Leben in Ihrer Stadt und planen Sie zusammen etwas für heute Abend.

3-35 Liebes Tagebuch! Sie haben sich heute mit einem alten Schulfreund getroffen, der vor ein paar Tagen in Ihre Stadt gezogen ist. Schreiben Sie in Ihrem Tagebuch über den Tag. Was haben Sie zusammen gemacht? Worüber haben Sie gesprochen?

Grammatik

1. Noun Cases (Kasus der Nomen)

03-26 to 03-28

Cases are used in German to convey what function nouns and pronouns have in sentences. German has four cases: nominative, accusative, dative, and genitive. Each case has multiple functions.

Nominative case (Nominativ)

Subject (*Subjekt*): *The person, thing, idea, or entity that does the action or carries out the meaning of the verb.*

| Unsere Großeltern wohnen in Sonneberg. | Our grandparents live in Sonneberg. |
| Am Wochenende fahre **ich** zu ihnen. | On the weekend I am going to drive to their house. |

Predicate nominative (*Prädikatsnomen*): *A noun that restates the subject; the subject and the predicate nominative both refer to the same person or thing. It occurs primarily with the verbs **sein, heißen, werden**, and occasionally **bleiben.***

| Die Stadt heißt **Erfurt.** | The city is called Erfurt. |
| Er wird eines Tages **Bürgermeister.** | He will become mayor someday. |

Accusative case (Akkusativ)

Direct object (*Direktes Objekt*): *The person, thing, entity, or idea that is acted upon by the subject.*

| Bach komponierte **viele Orgelwerke.** | Bach composed many works for the organ. |
| Kennst du **den neuen Professor?** | Do you know the new professor? |

Expression of definite time or duration (*Akkusativ der Zeit*): *Noun phrase that expresses specific time or length of time without the use of a preposition.*

| Die Kinder haben **den ganzen Tag** gespielt. | The children played all day. |
| **Nächstes Jahr** reisen wir an die Nordsee. | Next year we'll travel to the North Sea. |

3-36 Die Kindheit Johann Sebastian Bachs. Geben Sie für jeden unterstrichenen Satzteil die grammatikalische Funktion an: Subjekt, Prädikatsnomen, direktes Objekt oder Akkusativ der Zeit.

1. Seit 1520 lebte <u>die Familie Bach</u> in Thüringen.
2. <u>Johann Sebastian</u> war <u>das jüngste</u> von acht Kindern.
3. <u>Er</u> erhielt <u>die erste musikalische Ausbildung</u> durch seinen Vater.
4. <u>Der junge Bach</u> besuchte <u>zwei Jahre lang</u> <u>die Lateinschule</u> in Eisenach.
5. <u>Sein Bruder</u> wurde <u>sein erster Klavierlehrer</u>.
6. In Ohrdruf hatte <u>er</u> <u>jede Woche</u> fünf Stunden <u>Musikunterricht</u>.

Answers for 3-36. 1. die Familie Bach (Subjekt); 2. Johann Sebastian (Subjekt), das jüngste (Prädikatsnomen); 3. Er (Subjekt), die erste musikalische Ausbildung (direktes Objekt); 4. Der junge Bach (Subjekt), zwei Jahre lang (Akkusativ der Zeit), die Lateinschule (direktes Objekt); 5. Sein Bruder (Subjekt), sein erster Klavierlehrer (Prädikatsnomen); 6. er (Subjekt), jede Woche (Akkusativ der Zeit), Musikunterricht (direktes Objekt)

Activities 3-36 and 3-37. In these activities students will rely on context to determine case function. In later activities they will focus on article endings to aid them in determining case.

Dative case (Dativ)

Indirect object (*Indirektes Objekt*): *To or for whom the action is being done.* The indirect object is typically a living being (a person, an animal) or a group of beings (a club, a nation) and requires the presence of a direct object.

Jakob bot **mir** einen Kaffee an.	*Jakob offered me a coffee.*
Zeig **deiner Lehrerin** das Buch!	*Show the book to your teacher!*

Object of a dative verb (*Objekt eines Dativverbs*). The object of a verb that requires a dative object. These are marked in your vocabulary lists with (+ dat.). These verbs have only a dative object and no accusative object.

Rauchen schadet **der Gesundheit**.	*Smoking damages one's health.*
Was ist **dir** passiert?	*What happened to you?*

Here are some of the more common dative verbs:

antworten *to answer*	**gehören** *to belong to*	**reichen** *to be enough for*
begegnen *to encounter*	**gelingen** *to be successful*	**schaden** *to damage*
danken *to thank*	**geschehen** *to happen*	**schmecken** *to taste (good)*
dienen *to serve*	**glauben** *to believe (a person)*	**schwer·fallen** *to be difficult for*
drohen *to threaten*	**gratulieren** *to congratulate*	**vertrauen** *to trust*
ein·fallen *to occur to*	**helfen** *to help*	**verzeihen** *to forgive*
entsprechen *to correspond to*	**leid·tun** *to be sorry*	**weh·tun** *to hurt*
fehlen *to be missing/lacking*	**nutzen** *to be useful to*	**widersprechen** *to contradict*
folgen *to follow*	**passen** *to suit*	**zu·hören** *to listen to*
gefallen *to be pleasing to*	**passieren** *to happen to*	

Object in a fixed idiomatic expression (*Dativobjekt in einem idiomatischen Ausdruck*): The object of any number of adjectives or idiomatic expressions that require a dative object.

Wie geht es **deinen Eltern?**	*How are your parents? (Literally: How is it going for your parents?)*
Ist es **dir** kalt?	*Are you cold? (Literally: Is it cold to you?)*
Diese Jacke ist **ihm** zu teuer.	*This jacket is too expensive for him.*
Er war **seinem Professor** dankbar.	*He was thankful to his professor.*

A number of adjectives are used with a dative object, as in the last three examples above. Here are some of the more common ones:

ähnlich *similar*	**dankbar** *thankful*	**klar** *clear*	**schädlich** *damaging*
bekannt *known*	**egal** *of no matter*	**leicht** *easy*	**schwer** *difficult*
bequem *comfortable*	**fremd** *foreign*	**möglich** *possible*	**teuer** *expensive*
bewusst *known*	**interessant** *interesting*	**nützlich** *useful*	**wichtig** *important*

Genitive case (Genitiv)

Possession and relationships (*Genitivattribut*): Shows possession or a close relationship between nouns, often equivalent to the English possessive 's or the use of the preposition of.

> Der Geburtsort **meines Opas** liegt heute in Polen.
>
> *Today my grandfather's birthplace lies in Poland.*

> Die Kosten **der Wiedervereinigung** sind höher als erwartet.
>
> *The costs of the reunification are higher than expected.*

Expression of indefinite time (*Genitiv der Zeit*): Noun phrase that expresses non-specific time and that does not use a preposition.

> **Eines Tages** sehen sie sich wieder.   *One day they will see each other again.*

3-37 Auf den Thüringer Bachwochen. Michael Krenz erzählt von den letzten Thüringer Bachwochen. Geben Sie für jeden unterstrichenen Satzteil die grammatikalische Funktion an: indirektes Objekt, Objekt eines Dativverbs, Genitivattribut oder Genitiv der Zeit.

1. Die Bachwochen sind das größte Musikfestival <u>Thüringens</u>.

2. Das Fest bietet <u>Musikfreunden</u> drei Wochen lang mehr als 30 Veranstaltungen.

3. <u>Eines Abends</u> lasen wir das Programm durch und suchten <u>uns</u> einige interessante Konzerte aus.

4. Ich habe <u>meinen Eltern</u> Karten für das Eröffnungskonzert in Weimar geschenkt.

5. Die Musik <u>des amerikanischen Bach Ensembles</u> hat <u>ihnen</u> sehr gut gefallen.

6. Die modernen Interpretationen <u>der Jazzkünstler</u> entsprachen auch ganz <u>meinem Geschmack</u>.

Die Traukirche St. Bartholomäus Dornheim, wo Bach seine erste Frau, Maria Barbara, geheiratet hat.

Expansion for 3-37. Once students have named the functions of the underlined dative and genitive items, have them reexamine the sentences to identify subjects, predicate nominatives, direct objects, and accusative expressions of time: *1. Bachwochen (Subjekt), das größte Musikfestival (Prädikatsnomen); 2. das Fest (Subjekt), drei Wochen lang (Akkusativ der Zeit), mehr als 30 Veranstaltungen (direktes Objekt); 3. wir (Subjekt), das Programm (direktes Objekt), einige interessante Konzerte (direktes Objekt); 4. Ich (Subjekt), Karten (direktes Objekt); 5. Die Musik (Subjekt); 6. Die modernen Interpretationen (Subjekt)*

Answers for 3-37. 1. Thüringens (Genitivattribut); **2.** Musikfreunden (indirektes Objekt); **3.** Eines Abends (Genitiv der Zeit), uns (indirektes Objekt); **4.** meinen Eltern (indirektes Objekt); **5.** des amerikanischen Bach Ensembles (Genitivattribut), ihnen (Objekt des Dativverbs *gefallen*) **6.** der Jazzkünstler (Genitivattribut), meinem Geschmack (Objekt des Dativverbs *entsprechen*)

03-29 to 03-33

2. Articles: der-words and ein-words (Artikel: *der*-Wörter und *ein*-Wörter)

Articles (*the, a, an*) and determiners (*every, this,* etc.) are words that precede and modify nouns. In German sentences, such words are declined to show the cases of their accompanying nouns.

There are two basic categories of articles: the definite articles, or **der**-words, and the indefinite articles, also called **ein**-words. Each category has a distinctive pattern of declination for each gender as well as for the plural form.

03-29

Definite articles / *der*-words (Bestimmte Artikel / *der*-Wörter)

	Masculine	Feminine	Neuter	Plural
Nominative	**der** Mann	**die** Frau	**das** Kind	**die** Leute
Accusative	**den** Mann	**die** Frau	**das** Kind	**die** Leute
Dative	**dem** Mann	**der** Frau	**dem** Kind	**den** Leuten
Genitive	**des** Mannes	**der** Frau	**des** Kindes	**der** Leute

Several other determiners, which are referred to as **der**-words, have the same declension as the definite article.

dieser, diese, dieses *this, the latter, these (pl.)*	**mancher, manche, manches** *many a (sing.),*	
welcher, welche, welches *which*	*some, several*	
jeder, jede, jedes *each, every*	**solcher, solche, solches** *such a (sing.), such*	
jener, jene, jenes *that, the former, those (pl.)*		

Note that these **der**-words use an **-es** ending (**dieses, jedes,** etc.), rather than **-as** (like **das**) in the neuter nominative and accusative.

	Masculine	Feminine	Neuter	Plural
Nominative	**dieser** Mann	**diese** Frau	**dieses** Kind	**diese** Leute
Accusative	**diesen** Mann	**diese** Frau	**dieses** Kind	**diese** Leute
Dative	**diesem** Mann	**dieser** Frau	**diesem** Kind	**diesen** Leuten
Genitive	**dieses** Mannes	**dieser** Frau	**dieses** Kindes	**dieser** Leute

Note that in three instances, the noun also takes an ending. Nouns in the dative plural add **-n** where the plural form does not already end in **-n** or **-s: den** Künstler**n, den** Ereignisse**n.** And masculine and neuter nouns in the genitive case have the suffix **-s** (if the noun has two or more syllables) or sometimes **-es** (if the noun has one syllable): die Werke **des** Schriftsteller**s,** die Lage **des** Wald**es.**

The genitive suffix **-s** can also be used with proper names to show possession: die Opern Richard Wagner**s** = Richard Wagner**s** Opern; die Geschichte Thüringen**s** = Thüringen**s** Geschichte.

3-38 Die Heilige Elisabeth auf der Wartburg. Ergänzen sie die Sätze mit den passenden Formen des **der**-Wortes (**der, die, das** und ihre Variationen).

1. Elisabeth war __die__ Tochter __des__ ungarischen Königs Andreas II.

2. __Die__ Eltern haben sie __den__ ältesten Sohn __des__ Landgrafen von Thüringen versprochen, als sie noch ein Baby war.

3. __Die__ Königstocher hat mit vierzehn Jahren __den__ Landgrafen geheiratet.

4. __Die__ armen Menschen taten __der__ Landgräfin Elisabeth leid.

5. Sie brachte __den__ Armen Lebensmittel und pflegte __die__ Kranken persönlich.

6. Sie gründete __das__ Krankenhaus am Fuße __der__ Burg.

7. Sie verkaufte alle ihre extravaganten Sachen und schenkte __dem__ armen Volk __das__ Geld.

8. __Der__ Landgraf unterstützte __die__ selbstlosen Werke seiner Frau.

9. Landgräfin Elisabeth wurde zur Heiligen __der__ katholischen Kirche.

03-30

Indefinite articles / *ein*-words (Unbestimmte Artikel / *ein*-Wörter)

The article **ein** (*a, an*) has no forms in the plural. However, all of the other **ein**-words do have plural forms and therefore follow the pattern for **kein**.

	Masculine	Feminine	Neuter	Plural
Nominative	**ein** Mann	**eine** Frau	**ein** Kind	— Leute
	kein Mann	**keine** Frau	**kein** Kind	**keine** Leute
Accusative	**einen** Mann	**eine** Frau	**ein** Kind	— Leute
	keinen Mann	**keine** Frau	**kein** Kind	**keine** Leute
Dative	**einem** Mann	**einer** Frau	**einem** Kind	— Leuten
	keinem Mann	**keiner** Frau	**keinem** Kind	**keinen** Leuten
Genitive	**eines** Mann**es**	**einer** Frau	**eines** Kind**es**	— Leute
	keines Mann**es**	**keiner** Frau	**keines** Kind**es**	**keiner** Leute

The negative *kein*   The article **kein** (*not a, no, not any*) is used to negate nouns preceded by an **ein**-word or by no article at all.

Hinter dem Haus ist **ein Garten,** oder?	*There's a garden behind the house, isn't there?*
Nein, hinter dem Haus ist **kein Garten.**	*No, there is not a garden behind the house.*
Hast du **neue Schuhe?**	*Do you have new shoes?*
Nein, ich habe **keine neuen Schuhe.**	*I don't have any new shoes.*

Teaching suggestion for *kein*. Remind students that *nicht* is used instead of *kein* to negate nouns preceded by a ***der*-**word or a possessive adjective or to negate any other part of speech or entire sentences.

Possessive adjectives *(Possessive Adjektive)*   The possessive adjectives are also **ein**-words in that they have the same declension as the indefinite article.

mein *my*	**unser** *our*
dein *your (informal, sing.)*	**euer, eur-** *your (informal, pl.)*
sein *his, its*	**Ihr** *your (formal, sing. and pl.)*
ihr *her, its*	**ihr** *their*

When **euer** adds endings, the final **-e-** of the root is dropped, e.g., **eure, euren, eurem.**

	Masculine	Feminine	Neuter	Plural
Nominative	**unser** Hund	**unsere** Katze	**unser** Pferd	**unsere** Tiere
Accusative	**unseren** Hund	**unsere** Katze	**unser** Pferd	**unsere** Tiere
Dative	**unserem** Hund	**unserer** Katze	**unserem** Pferd	**unseren** Tieren
Genitive	**unseres** Hund**es**	**unserer** Katze	**unseres** Pferd**es**	**unserer** Tiere

3-39 Wartburg-Ausflug. Thomas wohnt mit seinen Eltern und seiner Schwester in Würzburg in Bayern. Er erzählt von ihrem Ausflug auf die Wartburg. Ergänzen Sie die Endungen. Wenn keine Endung notwendig ist, schreiben Sie – in die Lücke.

Letzten Sommer hat (1) mein_e_ Familie (2) ein_en_ Tagesausflug nach Eisenach gemacht, um die Wartburg zu besuchen. Wir sind angekommen, haben den Eintritt bezahlt und gleich (3) ein_e_ Burgführung gemacht. Der Tourleiter hat (4) unser_er_ Gruppe viele Anekdoten aus der Geschichte der Burg erzählt, besonders viel über Martin Luther. (5) Sein_–_ Arbeitszimmer haben wir auch gesehen. (6) Ein_–_ nettes Café ist auf dem Burghof und dort haben (7) mein_e_ Eltern (8) ein_en_ Kaffee getrunken und (9) mein_e_ Schwester und ich (10) ein_e_ Cola. Als mein Vater zahlen wollte, konnte er sein Geld nicht finden. Und (11) mein_e_ Mutter hatte auch (12) kein_–_ Geld dabei, weil sie (13) ihr_e_ Handtasche zu Hause vergessen hatte. Plötzlich kam (14) ein_–_ Mann an unseren Tisch und sagte (15) zu mein_em_ Vater: „Gehört Ihnen dieses Portemonnaie?" Das war tatsächlich das Portemonnaie (16) mein_es_ Vaters! Wir haben bezahlt und sind noch eine Zeit lang oben auf der Burg geblieben. Der Blick von oben hat (17) mein_er_ Mutter besonders gut gefallen. Mit der Kamera (18) mein_er_ Schwester haben wir einige sehr schöne Fotos gemacht. Am späten Nachmittag machten wir uns dann endlich auf den Weg nach Hause.

3-40 Die Thüringer Küche. Ergänzen Sie die Sätze zum Thema Thüringer Küche mit den passenden Artikeln. Wenn Sie das Geschlecht eines Wortes nicht kennen, schlagen Sie es im Wörterbuch nach. Achten Sie auf die Endungen.

1. Die Thüringer Rostbratwurst ist (*a*) ____ein____ bekanntes Gericht und auch (*a*) ____eine____ geschützte Marke.

2. (*The*) ____Das____ Museum erlaubt (*the*) ____dem____ Besucher (*a*) ____einen____ Blick in die Geschichte (*this*) ____dieses____ Lebensmittel**s**.

3. Sind die Nürnberger Rostbratwurst und (*your, informal pl.*) ____eure____ Thüringer Bratwurst ähnlich?

4. Nein. (*The former*) ____Jene____ Wurst ist viel kleiner und Majoran gibt ihr (*its,* Achtung! **Wurst** ist feminin.) ____ihren____ besonderen Geschmack.

5. (*Which*) ____Welche____ anderen Spezialitäten gibt es in Thüringen?

6. Auf der Speisekarte (*every*) ____jeder____ thüringischen Gaststätte findet man Thüringer Klöße.

7. (*This*) ____Dieses____ Kartoffelgericht isst (*the*) ____die____ Familie (*my*) ____meines____ Freund**es** (*every*) ____jeden____ Sonntag.

8. Karls Großmutter hat (*his*) ____seiner____ Mutter schon als Kind gezeigt, wie man die Klöße macht.

03-36 to 03-38

3. Personal pronouns (Personalpronomen)

A pronoun substitutes for or refers to a noun or noun phrase. Personal pronouns, like articles, have distinct forms for case and number (singular or plural). They also have distinct forms for person. Personal pronouns refer to the speaker (first person), the person(s) being addressed (second person), and other person(s) or things (third person).

		Nominative	**Accusative**	**Dative**	
Singular	1st person	ich	mich	mir	(*I, me*)
	2nd person	du	dich	dir	(*you—informal, sing.*)
	3rd person	er	ihn	ihm	(*he, him, it*)
		sie	sie	ihr	(*she, her, it*)
		es	es	ihm	(*it*)
Plural	1st person	wir	uns	uns	(*we, us*)
	2nd person	ihr	euch	euch	(*you—informal, pl.*)
		Sie	Sie	Ihnen	(*you—formal, sing. and pl.*)
	3rd person	sie	sie	ihnen	(*they, them*)

Note that 3rd-person pronouns also have distinct forms for gender. A pronoun must have the same gender as the noun it replaces. The pronoun may have a different case than the noun, however, depending on how it is used in a sentence.

> 1860 wurde **die Kunstschule** gegründet. Heute heißt **sie** Bauhaus-Universität.
>
> *The art school was founded in 1860. Today it is called Bauhaus University.*
>
> **Dieser Wald** ist sehr beliebt. **Er** liegt im Süden Thüringens. Wir besuchen **ihn** bald.
>
> *This forest is very popular. It is in the south of Thüringia. We'll visit it soon.*

Answers for 3-41. Die Stadt (Sie), das Klavier (es), der Geigenunterricht (er), meine Eltern (ihnen), Das Orchester (Es), diesem Freund (ihm), Das Orchester und die Band (Sie)

3-41 Julia macht Musik in Weimar. Die 18-jährige Julia Becker erzählt von ihrer musikalischen Ausbildung. Ersetzen Sie jeden fett gedruckten Ausdruck mit dem passenden Personalpronomen.

Ich wohne schon mein ganzes Leben in Weimar. **Die Stadt** ist eine schöne Stadt und hat vieles von Interesse für Musikliebhaber.

Mit drei Jahren bekam ich mein erstes Musikinstrument: ein kleines Klavier. Ich habe **das Klavier** sehr gern gespielt. Ab der 4. Klasse fing ich dann mit dem Geigenunterricht an. **Der Geigenunterricht** hat mir so viel Spaß gemacht, dass meine Eltern mir eine Geige gekauft haben. Aber ich musste **meinen Eltern** erst mal versprechen, dass ich mit dem Unterricht noch weiter mache. Na, klar!

Schon seit drei Jahren spiele ich in einem Orchester hier in Weimar. **Das Orchester** ist recht gut und über die Stadtgrenzen hinaus bekannt. Ein guter Freund von mir spielt auch im Orchester mit. Mit **diesem Freund** und ein paar anderen Bekannten habe ich Ende letzten Jahres eine Ska-Band gegründet, in der ich jetzt singe.

Nach dem Gymnasium möchte ich an der Bauhaus-Uni studieren. Somit kann ich hier bleiben und weiterhin mit dem Orchester und der Band musizieren. **Das Orchester und die Band** würden mir fehlen, wenn ich nicht in Weimar bleiben dürfte!

Suggestion for 3-42. You may need to remind students that at the secondary level pupils use *Sie* with their teachers and teachers use *du* with pupils.

3-42 Nach dem Abschluss. Julia Becker ist Schülerin der 12. Klasse auf dem Goethegymnasium in Weimar. Sie redet mit einem Lehrer und zwei Schulfreunden über ihre Pläne für die Zukunft. Ergänzen Sie den Dialog mit den passenden Personalpronomen.

Herr Winkler: So, was wollt (1) __ihr__ alle nach dem Abschluss machen?

Julia: (2) __Ich__ bleibe hier in Weimar und mache ein Studium in Visueller Kommunikation an der Bauhaus-Uni.

Herr Winkler:	Nicht in Musik an der Musikhochschule? Das überrascht (3) _mich_ ! .
Markus und Jens:	Ja, das hat (4) _uns_ auch überrascht.
Julia:	Musik als Hobby zu betreiben, das gefällt (5) _mir_ sehr gut. Wenn eine Arbeit daraus wird, habe (6) _ich_ Angst, dass es (7) _mir_ keinen Spaß mehr macht. Verstehen (8) _Sie_?
Herr Winkler:	Allerdings. Und Jens, was hast (9) _du_ vor?
Jens:	(10) _Ich_ ziehe im September nach Berlin und werde dann Arabistik an der FU studieren.
Herr Winkler:	An der Freien Universität? Ich gratuliere (11) _dir_, Jens! Eine tolle Universität! Da habe ich nämlich auch studiert.
Jens:	Tatsächlich? Hat es (12) _Ihnen_ gefallen?
Herr Winkler:	Ja, sehr! Berlin ist eine herrliche Stadt, das Leben ist spannend, man trifft Leute aus aller Welt. Es ist nie langweilig.
Markus:	(13) _Du_ ziehst zu weit weg und wirst uns vergessen!
Jens:	Berlin ist doch nicht so weit. Ich komme ab und zu am Wochenende nach Hause, dann besuche ich (14) _euch_ beide. Und (15) _ihr_ könnt (16) _mich_ in Berlin besuchen.

03-39 to 03-40

4. Word order: Accusative and dative objects (Wortstellung: Akkusativ- und Dativobjekte)

When a sentence has both a direct and an indirect object and these objects both follow the conjugated verb, specific word order rules apply:

If both objects are nouns, then the indirect object precedes the direct object.

	Indirect object	**Direct object**	
Ich kann	**den Gästen**	**die Bratwurst**	empfehlen.

If both objects are pronouns, then the direct object precedes the indirect object.

	Direct object	**Indirect object**	
Ich kann	**sie**	**ihnen**	empfehlen.

If the objects consist of one noun and one pronoun, then the pronoun precedes the noun.

	Pronoun	**Noun**	
Ich kann	**sie**	**den Gästen**	empfehlen.
Ich kann	**ihnen**	**die Bratwurst**	empfehlen.

Answers for 3-43. 1. Goethe legte ihr sein neues Theaterstück vor. **2.** Schiller zeigte sie Goethe. **3.** Die Lehrerin hat es ihnen vorgelesen. **4.** Goethe schickte ihm den Roman „Wilhelm Meisters Lehrjahre". **5.** Andere Autoren schickten sie ihnen. **6.** Ich kann sie Ihnen sehr empfehlen. **7.** Kannst du es mir leihen? **8.** Ich schenke ihn dir.

3-43 Wem? Was? Ersetzen Sie jedes unterstrichene Nomen mit dem entsprechenden Personalpronomen. Wenn nötig, ändern Sie auch die Wortstellung.

1. Goethe legte <u>der Herzogin</u> sein neues Theaterstück vor.
2. Schiller zeigte Goethe <u>seine Ballade</u>.
3. Die Lehrerin hat <u>den Schülern</u> <u>das Gedicht</u> vorgelesen.
4. Goethe schickte <u>seinem Freund</u> den Roman „Wilhelm Meisters Lehrjahre".
5. Andere Autoren schickten <u>Goethe und Schiller</u> ihre Werke.
6. Ich kann Ihnen <u>die anderen Gedichte Schillers</u> sehr empfehlen.
7. Kannst du mir <u>das Schiller-Buch</u> leihen?
8. Ich schenke dir <u>den Band</u>.

03-41 to 03-47

Immer weiter!

3-44 Zur Diskussion. Besprechen Sie die Themen.

1. In *Kapitel 1* haben Sie gelernt, dass das Leben in Norddeutschland von seiner Nähe zum Meer stark geprägt wird. Ganz anders ist es in Thüringen, denn dieses Bundesland liegt weit entfernt vom Meer. Was prägt das Leben in Thüringen? Geben Sie Beispiele.

2. In der Einführung zu diesem Kapitel liest man, dass „große Leistungen auf kleinem Raum durchaus möglich sind". Welche Beispiele davon hat man in Thüringen erlebt?

3-45 Zum Schreiben: Eine Einladung nach Erfurt. Ein Freund, der gerade in Erfurt studiert, hat Sie zu Besuch eingeladen. Schreiben Sie ihm eine E-Mail, in der Sie seine Einladung akzeptieren. Erzählen Sie ihm, wann Sie kommen und wie lange Sie bleiben möchten und was Sie während Ihrer Zeit in Thüringen unbedingt sehen und machen wollen.

Weitere Themen

Ernst Abbe	Open-Air-Festival „Kulturarena"
Erfurter Dom	Franz Liszt
Fachhochschule Jena	der Rennsteig
Friedrich-Schiller-Universität	Spielzeugmuseum
die Glasbläserstadt Lauscha	der Skitunnel in Oberhof
Johann Wolfgang von Goethe	der Thüringen Grammy
Walter Gropius	Thüringer Klöße
Jenoptik Jena	die Thüringer Rose
JenTower	das DDR-Auto Wartburg
die Krämerbrücke	Weimarer Zwiebelmarkt

Nordsee

Ostsee

Deutschland

Wien

Österreich

Schweiz

Liechtenstein

KAPITEL

4

NIEDERÖSTERREICH

Wien

Warm-up. Ask students what they already know about Austria. *Was wissen Sie über Österreich? Wissen Sie, was die Hauptstadt Österreichs ist?* Have them look at the map of Austria on the inside front cover and the map of Europe on the inside back cover. *An welche anderen Länder grenzt Österreich? Ist das Land größer oder kleiner als Deutschland / die Schweiz / Liechtenstein? Wo liegt Wien?* Then have students examine the detail map and photos of Vienna and describe the layout of the city-state and what they expect to find there.

Donau

Ringstraße

Sigmund-Freud-Museum

Stephansdom

Donauturm

Burgtheater

Mozarthaus

Hundertwasserhaus

Wiener Volksoper

Prater

Rathaus

Donauinsel

Parlament

Linz

Donau

WIEN

Wien

Donaukanal

Salzburg
Innsbruck

Schloss Schönbrunn

Wiener Musikverein

Naturhistorisches Museum

Wiener Staatsoper

Kunsthistorisches Museum

Zentralfriedhof

Liesing

NIEDERÖSTERREICH

5 km

5 mi

Einführung

04-01 to 04-02

Read the *Sprachanalyse: Various uses of **zu*** in SAM 04-02, which explains the multiple ways in which **zu** is used in the *Einführung*. As you read the *Lesetexte* in this chapter, do the *Sprachanalyse* activities in the SAM (04-05, 04-11, 04-14, 04-18, 04-21) to practice understanding how **zu** is used in context.

Im Nordosten der Republik Österreich liegt ihre Hauptstadt – Wien. Jeder vierte Österreicher lebt in der Hauptstadt, die mit beinah 1,7 Millionen Einwohnern die größte Stadt des Landes ist. Insgesamt leben ungefähr 8,5 Millionen Menschen in Österreich. Es besteht aus neun Bundesländern und Wien ist, ebenso wie Berlin, gleichzeitig Hauptstadt und Bundesland. 5

Die günstige Lage an der Donau sowie am Landverkehrsweg zwischen Ostsee und Mittelmeer machte Wien schon früh zum Mittelpunkt eines weiten Wirtschaftsraums. Im Laufe der Jahrhunderte hinterließen Zu- und Durchwanderer aus vielen Regionen Mitteleuropas ihre Einflüsse auf die Sprache und Kultur Wiens. Kulinarisch zeigt sich dies an der traditionellen 10 Wiener Küche, z. B. am Apfelstrudel und Gulasch, die beide aus Ungarn nach Österreich kamen, und am Kaffee, den die Türken in die Stadt brachten.

Als Residenzstadt (1278–1918) und ab 1558 kaiserliche Hauptstadt der Habsburger[1] (im Heiligen Römischen Reich, im Kaisertum Österreich und in der Doppelmonarchie Österreich-Ungarn) wurde Wien im Laufe der Jahr- 15 hunderte zum bedeutenden Kulturzentrum. Besonders unter Kaiserin Maria Theresia (1740–1780) setzte eine Blütezeit° in der Kunst, der Kultur und besonders der Musik ein, die bis in das 20. Jahrhundert hineinreichte. Hier lebten und wirkten sowohl Joseph Haydn und Wolfgang Amadeus Mozart als auch andere weltberühmte Komponisten wie Ludwig van Beethoven, 20 Johann Strauss und Arnold Schönberg. Ihre Werke führten zu neuen Entwicklungen in der Musik und machten Wien zur Weltmetropole der klassischen Musik – ein Titel, den die Stadt mit Recht immer noch trägt. Heutzutage genießen der Wiener Walzer, die Wiener Sängerknaben°, die Wiener Staatsoper und die Wiener Philharmoniker weltweit großes Ansehen. 25

Nicht nur Musik, sondern auch Theater, Kunst und Architektur gehören zum Kulturleben der Stadt. Zu den prächtigen historischen Gebäuden, die das Stadtbild prägen, zählen die Hofburg, das Wiener Rathaus, die Karlskirche, das Burgtheater, der Stephansdom und die Schlösser Belvedere und Schönbrunn. Diese Bauten sind heute noch als Kirchen, Theater, Regierungs- 30 gebäude und Museen mit Kunstsammlungen von Weltrang zu besuchen. Architekturinteressierte finden in der Stadt ein fast schon zu großes Angebot, denn es gibt neben den verschiedenen historischen Bauten aus allen Epochen auch moderne architektonische Denkmäler. Keiner kann heute in Wien leben, ohne die kulturellen Traditionen der Stadt täglich zu spüren°. 35

golden age (marginal gloss)

Vienna Boys' Choir (marginal gloss)

sense (marginal gloss)

Fragen zum Text

1. Beschreiben Sie mit Hilfe der Karte die geografische Lage Wiens.
2. Welche kulinarischen Spezialitäten sind mit Wien verbunden?
3. Warum konnte Wien zu einem kulturellen Zentrum werden?
4. Warum hat Wien einen besonderen Ruf als Musikstadt?
5. Welche Funktion haben heute viele der historischen Bauten der Stadt?

Answers for *Fragen zum Text*. 1. Wien liegt an der Donau und am Rand des Wienerwalds und ist vom Bundesland Niederösterreich umgeben. **2.** Apfelstrudel, Gulasch, Kaffee. **3.** Wien war über Jahrhunderte Haupt- und Residenzstadt der Habsburger. **4.** Viele namhafte Komponisten lebten und wirkten hier und trugen zu neuen Entwicklungen in der Musik bei. Der Wiener Walzer ist hier entstanden und hier haben die Wiener Sängerknaben, die Wiener Staatsoper und die Wiener Philharmoniker ihr Zuhause. **5.** Sie dienen noch als Kirchen, Theater oder als Regierungsgebäude oder Museen.

[1]Die Habsburger waren einst eine der mächtigsten Königsfamilien Europas, von der über mehrere Jahrhunderte viele deutsche Kaiser und Könige abstammten.

DIALEKTTIPP: Wienerisch

 Hören Sie ein Beispiel dieses Dialekts.

Das Wienerische ordnet man den oberdeutschen Dialekten zu. Im Mittelalter haben sich die Bayern nach Osten verbreitet und auch ihre Kultur und Sprache mitgebracht. Da vermischte sich das oberdeutsche Bairische° mit slawischen Sprachelementen. Dazu kamen mit der Zeit auch andere Einflüsse aus dem Französischen, Jiddischen (*Etsses* „gute Ratschläge"), Tschechischen (*pomali,* „langsam") und Ungarischen u. a.° hinzu. Vor allem im Wortschatz liegt die Eigenart° des Wienerischen, z. B. *oewäu* (allweil, immer), *Maknschlecka* (Postbeamte).

Bavarian

= unter anderem among others / unique character

Der Einfluss des Wienerischen lässt sich jetzt auch in anderen Städten Österreichs finden. Neben den Dialekten Österreichs existiert auch eine österreichische Standardsprache, die sich von der Deutschlands unterscheidet, aber für Deutsche leicht verständlich ist. Der Wiener Dialekt wird dieser Standardsprache mit der Zeit immer ähnlicher, ohne seine charakteristische Aussprache und Vokabeln zu verlieren.

Zum Dialekt

Note for *Dialekttipp.* Like the Berlin dialect, the Viennese dialect has traditionally been viewed as a language of the working class. As a result, fewer and fewer people speak pure Viennese dialect. The Viennese dialect is gradually becoming a regional colloquial language that retains many of the words and the pronunciation of Viennese but that is closer to Austrian Standard German.

1 Wie sagt man das? Wählen Sie die richtigen Erklärungen der Unterschiede zwischen Wienerisch und Hochdeutsch.

Hochdeutsch → Wienerisch

b 1.	also, fehlen, schnell → oeso, föhn, schnöö	a. *ei → a*
e 2.	Pech, Tag, Knech → Bech, Dag, Gnechd	b. *l* nach einem Vokal fällt weg
f 3.	Kindlein/Kindchen → Kindel/Kinderl	c. *ü → i, ö → e*
d 4.	hart, Gefahr → hoat, Gfoa	d. *a → oa*
a 5.	heiß, eins, kleine → has, ans, glana	e. *p, t, k → b, d, g*
c 6.	Glück, schön → Gligg, schee	f. Verkleinerungsform *-chen / -lein → -(e)l* oder *-erl*[2]

2 Im Gespräch. Wie sagt man das auf Wienerisch?

	Hochdeutsch		Wienerisch
b 1.	Hallo. / Tschüss.	a.	Loss mi in Kraut!
c 2.	Das Fest war super!	b.	Hawe d'Ehre. [Ich habe die Ehre.]
d 3.	Hier liegt der Fehler.	c.	Des Festl woa leiwand!
a 4.	Lass mich in Ruhe!	d.	Do ist da Hund begrobn. [Da ist der Hund begraben.]

---

[2]Die Diminutive vieler Wörter werden nicht nur als Verkleinerungsformen gebraucht, sondern sind auch die üblichsten (*most common*) Formen der Wörter (z. B., Sackerl = *Tüte;* Zuckerl = *Bonbon;* Leiberl = *T-Shirt*).

Lese- und Hörtexte

Siehe **Kulturtipps**:
Donauinsel

Lesetext 1

Introduction to *Lesetext 1*.
Ask students about their own
experiences with festivals: *Haben
Sie schon einmal ein Musikfest
besucht? Was für Musik gab es
da? Gehen Sie gern in Konzerte?
Was kann man bei einem Musikfest machen? Gibt es in Ihrer Stadt
Themenfeste, zum Beispiel ein
Pfirsichfest?* Then ask students
what they learned about the
Donauinselfest from the introductory text. *Wie lange existiert das
Fest schon? Was macht man auf
dem Fest? Wer geht dahin?*

*representative of the Social
Democratic Party of
Austria*

**Teaching suggestion for
Lesetext 1.** Ask students how
they think alcohol consumption,
especially among young people,
can be controlled at such a large
festival. *Was meinen Sie: Kann
man den Alkoholkonsum auf so
einem großen Festival kontrollieren? Wenn ja, wie kann man
das machen?* Alcoholic drinks can
usually be purchased at festivals
in German-speaking countries,
while this is not always the case in
the U.S. Anyone of legal drinking
age can buy and consume alcoholic beverages, and ID checks
and enforcement of the legal age
tend to be very lax.

Das 24. Donauinselfest: Eine rauschende Party – ganz ohne Promille (Artikel)

Seit 1984 findet das Donauinselfest, ein Freiluftmusikfestival, meist Ende Juni in Wien statt. Es ist ein kulturelles Fest, bei dem die Österreicher nicht nur die unterschiedliche einheimische Musik, sondern auch internationale Musik genießen können. Auf etwa 27 Bühnen kann man internationale Musiker der verschiedensten Musikrichtungen erleben. Die Idee dazu kam von dem Wiener SPÖ-Abgeordneten° Harry Kopietz, der bis 2008 noch aktiv an dem Fest mitgearbeitet hat. Es ist das größte Festival dieser Art in Europa und es kommen jährlich über drei Millionen Besucher, um daran teilzunehmen. Allerdings

Eine Bühne mit Publikum auf dem Donauinselfest

kommt die Mehrheit der Besucher aus Österreich. Die vielen Besucher kommen nicht nur wegen der Musik, sondern auch um hier gut zu essen und zu trinken.

Ganz anders als bei vielen großen Stadt- und Musikfesten, wie zum Beispiel dem Oktoberfest in München, hoffen die Veranstalter, den Alkoholkonsum auf diesem Fest zu senken. Im folgenden Artikel, der auf der Internetseite des Donauinselfests erschien, erfährt man, wie die Organisatoren versuchen, den Alkoholkonsum zu kontrollieren.

Vor dem Lesen

Was kann man wohl bei einem Freiluftmusikfestival sehen, tun und erleben?

Beim Lesen

Verbinden Sie die Satzteile, die zusammenpassen.

_f_	1. Das Security-Team	a. ärgert sich über die Kontrollen.
_a_	2. Michael Seiser	b. hat nichts gegen Kontrollen.
_d_	3. 48er	c. hängt ein Schild mit den Regeln auf.
_b_	4. Hildegard Wabrik	d. reinigen die Insel.
_c_	5. Edgar Hartenstein	e. bieten Trinkbrunnen an.
_e_	6. Die Wasserwerke	f. kontrolliert Taschen.

04-03 to 04-05

Das 24. Donauinselfest: Eine rauschende Party – ganz ohne Promille°

Erstmals werden heuer° Alkoholkontrollen durchgeführt

Über 600 Stunden Programm mit über 2.000 KünstlerInnen am 24. Wiener Donauinselfest: Eine rauschende Party ist wohl garantiert – und das auch ohne Promille. Damit das größte und friedlichste Open-Air-Festival Europas auch weiterhin das sicherste bleibt, werden heuer erstmals Alkoholkontrollen durchgeführt.   5

„Gem. § 11 WrJSCHG° 2002 ist es Personen bis zur Vollendung des 16. Lebensjahres generell untersagt°, alkoholische Getränke an allgemein zugänglichen Orten und/oder bei öffentlichen Veranstaltungen zu erwerben und/oder zu konsumieren. Der Veranstalter behält sich in diesem Zusammenhang die Kontrolle vor Ort durch Mitarbeiter und   10 Behörden ausdrücklich vor°", heißt es in der Haus- und Platzordnung, die heuer erstmals flächendeckend ausgehängt° wurde. Und tatsächlich: Um 15.30 Uhr war eine erste Kontrolle beim Abgang der U6-Brücke in vollem Gange. Alex Kaiser vom Security-Team und einige seiner Kollegen haben sich postiert, um Rücksäcke und Taschen der Festgäste stich-   15 probenartig° zu kontrollieren. Insgesamt werden an den Inselfesttagen etwa 30 Personen unterwegs sein, um diese Auflagen zu überprüfen. Patrik und Alex – sie mussten gerade ihre Rucksäcke öffnen – finden die Kontrolle „schon in Ordnung". Schließlich sei das, „damit sich die kleinen Kinder nicht ansaufen°", sagt Patrik, der gerade schlanke 19   20 Jahre auf die Waage bringt.

„Bei den Jungen ist das ja OK", ärgert sich Michael Seiser über die Kontrolle. „Die sollten aber schon selektieren. Ich bin 58 Jahre alt und kann mitnehmen, was ich will!" Dass das so nicht stimmt, versucht ihm Alex Kaiser zu erklären. Schließlich ist auch das Mit-   25 bringen von Glasflaschen nicht erlaubt, und zwar aus Sicherheitsgründen. „Es gibt genug kleine Kinder, die barfuß herumlaufen. Auch die Standler° dürfen keine Getränke in Glasflaschen verkaufen." Wirklich einsichtig zeigt sich Herr Seiser zwar nicht, Lob hat er wenigstens für die „48er"°: „Die sind schon super. Wie die das   30 jeden Tag schaffen, die Insel wieder sauber zu bekommen." Ebenfalls über 16 ist auch Hildegard Wabrik. Sie ist 56 Jahre alt und hat bereitwillig ihre Tasche zur Kontrolle geöffnet. Denn das mit dem Komatrinken findet sie „wirklich schrecklich!": „Ich hab das erste Mal ein Glas Rotwein getrunken, als ich 21 wurde. Da hab ich quasi   35 die Volljährigkeit° gefeiert."

Ein Beitrag zur aktuellen Diskussion ums „Komatrinken"

„Niemand hat etwas dagegen, wenn jemand einen Weißen Spritzer zu seinem Steckerlfisch trinkt, oder ein Glas Bier zum Gulasch – sofern er oder

Margin notes:

ganz ohne Promille without consuming alcohol this year (Austrian German)

Siehe **Kulturtipps**: KünstlerInnen

= Gemäß dem Artikel 11 des Wiener Jugendschutzgesetzes according to article 11 of the Viennese youth protection law / prohibited

behält sich vor retains the right
posted all over the area

randomly

get drunk

vendors (Austrian German)

city workers responsible for garbage collection

legal age

Siehe **Kulturtipps**: Steckerlfisch und Gulasch

= *Landtagsabgeordneter*
member of parliament

sie über 16 Jahre alt ist", garantiert LAbg.° Harry Kopietz, Mastermind des Donauinselfestes. „Uns geht es darum, einen Beitrag zur aktuellen Diskussion ums ‚Komatrinken' zu leisten und etwaige Alkoholexzesse erst gar nicht entstehen zu lassen. Wir werden sanften Druck auf jene ausüben, die fälschlicherweise glauben, dass man sich ohne Alkohol nicht auch hervorragend amüsieren kann", so Kopietz. Und auch die Wiener Nationalrätin Laura Rudas – sie unterstützt die Aktion „fit statt fett" einer überparteilichen Plattform – will Jungen über 16 nicht den Alkohol verbieten. „Aber alles in Maßen! Das Donauinselfest soll ja in erster Linie Spaß machen!" Und es wäre schade, wäre dieses vorzeitig vorbei. Denn: „Der Veranstalter behält sich vor, stark alkoholisierte Personen, die für sich selbst und/oder Dritte eine Gefährdung darstellen, des Veranstaltungsareals zu verweisen°", heißt es weiter in der Hausordnung.

banish

Alkoholfreie Getränke – ein halber Liter um 1,50 Euro

Um es vor allem jungen Gästen mit kleinem Budget leichter zu machen, wurde dieses Jahr eigens ein günstiger Drink ohne Alkohol kreiert; sämtliche Standler haben die Auflage°, zumindest ein alkoholfreies Getränk in der Menge von einem halben Liter zum Preis von 1,50 Euro anzubieten. Im Angebot sind etwa Soda Himbeer-Zitron, Soda Orange oder Eistee. Auch sind hochprozentige und billige Lockangebote° untersagt, Alkohol an Personen unter 16 Jahre darf generell nicht ausgeschenkt werden. Die Einhaltung dieser Auflagen° wird ebenfalls streng kontrolliert. „An Jugendliche wird kein Alkohol ausgeschenkt" – Edgar Hartenstein hat ein großes Schild an seinem Stand angebracht. „Ich hab ja selbst drei Kinder im Alter von 8 bis 21 Jahren", sagt der Wirt, der sich auch zutraut, das Alter der Kids richtig einzuschätzen. „Und im Zweifelsfall° brauchen sie eben einen Ausweis."

obligation

teasers

Die ... Auflagen compliance
with the rules

in case of doubt

22 Trinkbrunnen auf der Donauinsel – Wasserbar der Wiener Wasserwerke

Als weitere Alternative zur Löschung akuter Durstanfälle° bietet sich natürlich das bewährte Wiener Hochquellwasser an: Dieses steht an insgesamt 59 Trinkbrunnen gratis zur Verfügung – 22 Trinkbrunnen befinden sich direkt auf der Donauinsel, 20 am linken Donaudamm°, wo sich die Wiener Städtische Versicherung-Country & Western-Insel° befindet, 17 weitere Trinkbrunnen stehen am rechten Donaudamm. Außerdem betreiben die Wiener Wasserwerke auf der „Sicheres-Wien-Insel" eine Wasserbar. Diese hat zwar heute Freitag aufgrund der aufrechten Sturmwarnung noch geschlossen, ab morgen soll aber kräftig ausgeschenkt werden.

attacks of thirst

dam of the Danube

Wiener ... Western-Insel
the part of the island where
the Vienna Insurance
Company sponsors the
performance of country-
and-western music

Kulturtipps

Donauinsel

Die Donauinsel ist eine künstliche Insel in der Donau, deren Bau von 1972 bis 1988 dauerte. Die ca. 20 km lange und nur 200 m breite Insel soll die Stadt gegen Hochwasser schützen. Inzwischen ist sie auch zu einem beliebten Ausflugsziel der Wiener geworden. Die Donauinsel bietet Wanderwege, Bademöglichkeiten und ist außerdem ein Naturrevier, in dem man seltene Vögel, Fische, aber auch Rehe (*deer*), Hasen und Biber (*beavers*) findet.

Blick auf die Donauinsel

KünstlerInnen

Das Wort Künstler bezieht sich auf männliche Künstler, die weibliche (*feminine*) Form im Plural ist Künstlerinnen. Um zu zeigen, dass man beide Künstler und Künstlerinnen meint, ohne beide Wörter gebrauchen zu müssen, gibt es die Wortkombination *KünstlerInnen*. Bis vor etwa 20 Jahren benutzte man oft nur die männlichen Formen und besonders im Plural (z. B. Studenten, Mitarbeiter), auch wenn Frauen gemeint waren. Heutzutage benutzt man manchmal die Pluralform, die auf -*Innen* mit großem *I* endet, als Alternative zu den geschlechtsspezifischen Formen.

Steckerlfisch und Gulasch

Steckerlfisch und Gulasch sind zwei Spezialitäten, die man auf vielen Festen und in Biergärten in Österreich aber auch in Bayern finden kann. Der Steckerlfisch ist ein Fisch, oft eine Forelle (*trout*) oder Makrele (*mackerel*), der erst mariniert, dann auf einen Stock – auch Stöckerl oder Steckerl genannt – aufgespießt und schließlich gegrillt wird. Das Wiener Gulasch gilt heute als das eigentliche Gulasch und ist ein Ragout aus verschiedenen Fleischsorten, meistens Rind (*beef*) und Schwein mit Paprika und Zwiebeln.

Steckerlfisch

Gulasch mit Knödeln

Nomen

der Ausweis, -e *identification card, ID*

der Brunnen, - *fountain, well*

der/die Jugendliche, -n *(adj. noun) young person, adolescent*

die Kontrolle, -n *inspection*

das Lob, -e *praise*

das Schild, -er *sign*

die Tasche, -n *bag; pocket*

Verben

aus·schenken *to pour, to serve (a drink)*

betreiben, betrieb, betrieben *to operate*

durch·führen *to carry out*

ein·schätzen *to estimate, to assess*

erklären *to explain*

schaffen *to manage (to do something)*

überprüfen *to check*

Adjektive und Adverbien

barfuß *barefoot*

gratis *for free*

günstig *inexpensive*

sämtlich *all*

schließlich *after all, finally*

sicher *safe, secure*

vorzeitig *before its time, prematurely*

zumindest *at least*

Ausdrücke

Alles in Maßen! *Everything in moderation!*

Das stimmt (nicht). *That is (not) correct/right.*

Druck aus·üben auf (+ *acc.*) *to put pressure on (someone)*

etwas dagegen haben *to object to something*

Answers for 4-1. 1. F – Es werden auf dem 25. Donauinselfest zum ersten Mal Kontrollen durchgeführt. **2.** F – Das Security-Team kontrolliert Taschen stichprobenartig. **3.** R; **4.** R; **5.** F – Sie will den Menschen, die über 16 sind, den Alkoholkonsum nicht verbieten. **6.** R

4-1 Textarbeit: Richtig oder falsch? Wenn eine Aussage falsch ist, korrigieren und ergänzen Sie sie mit Informationen aus dem Lesetext.

1. Auf dem Donauinselfest werden seit drei Jahren Alkoholkontrollen durchgeführt.

2. Das Security-Team kontrolliert alle Taschen.

3. Das Security-Team besteht aus 30 Personen.

4. Auf dem Fest werden keine Getränke in Glasflaschen verkauft.

5. Laura Rudas will, dass niemand auf dem Fest Alkohol trinkt.

6. Auf dem Fest kann man an einem der vielen Trinkbrunnen gratis Wasser trinken.

Answers for 4-2. 1. Sie wollen ein friedliches Fest. Sie wollen nicht, dass die Jugendlichen trinken. **2.** 16; **3.** Das Team kontrolliert Taschen und Rucksäcke. **4.** Glasflaschen können zerbrechen und Kinder aber auch Erwachsene können sich an den Glasscherben verletzten. **5.** Sie müssen das Festgelände verlassen. **6.** Man kann Wasser, Soda oder Eistee trinken.

4-2 Textarbeit: Fragen zum Inhalt. Beantworten Sie die Fragen in Bezug auf den Text.

1. Warum wollen die Veranstalter des Donauinselfests Alkoholkontrollen durchführen?

2. Wie alt muss man sein, um in Wien Alkohol kaufen bzw. trinken zu können?

3. Was ist die Aufgabe des Security-Teams auf dem Festival?

4. Welche Gefahr gibt es mit Glasflaschen?

5. Was passiert auf dem Festival mit Personen, die zu viel getrunken haben?

6. Welche Alternativen gibt es für alkoholische Getränke auf dem Fest?

4-3 Vokabelarbeit. Ergänzen Sie die Sätze mit Wörtern aus den *Neuen Vokabeln.* Achten Sie dabei auch auf die Wortform.

1. Personen, die jung aussehen, müssen ihren ____Ausweis____ vorzeigen, damit man ihr Alter kontrollieren kann.

2. Auf dem Fest gibt es ____Schilder____, auf denen die Regeln zum Alkohol- verkauf stehen.

3. Da nicht alle Besucher des Festes kontrolliert werden können, ____führt____ man Kontrollen stichprobenartig ____durch____.

4. Kinder aber auch Erwachsene, die ____barfuß____ herumlaufen, können auf Glasscherben treten und sich dabei verletzen.

5. Die Ständler müssen neben alkoholischen Getränken auch Getränke ____ausschenken____, die keinen Alkohol enthalten.

6. Die Veranstalter wollen mit den neuen Regeln ____Druck____ ____auf____ die Besucher ____ausüben____, damit alle ein sicheres Fest erleben können.

4-4 Zur Diskussion. Besprechen Sie die Fragen.

1. Auf dem Donauinselfest werden Taschen kontrolliert und die Jugendlichen müssen ihre Ausweise vorzeigen, um Alkohol kaufen zu können. Warum mögen einige Festivalbesucher diese neuen Regeln nicht? Was halten Sie von den neuen Regeln?

   Hilfreiche Ausdrücke:
   Ich glaube/denke/meine, …   *Ich halte die Regeln für gut/schlecht/(un)fair.*
   Ich bin der Meinung, dass …   *Meiner Meinung nach sind die Regeln …*

2. Was ist für die Organisatoren das Wichtige an dem Festival?

3. Denken Sie, dass es wegen der neuen Regeln weniger Besucher auf dem Festival geben wird?

4. Wie würden Sie reagieren, wenn ein Mitglied des Security-Teams Ihre Tasche überprüfen wollte?

4-5 Alkoholkontrollen: Ja oder nein? Sie sind Mitglied von dem Komitee, das das Donauinselfest organisiert. Besprechen Sie, ob die Alkoholkontrollen auch im nächsten Jahr wieder stattfinden sollen. Was spricht dafür? Was spricht dage- gen? Machen Sie zwei Listen, dann treffen Sie eine gemeinsame Entscheidung.

4-6 Meine Meinung zum alkoholfreien Donauinselfest. Sie haben gerade auf der Internetseite des Donauinselfests den Artikel „Eine rauschende Party – ganz ohne Promille" gelesen. Schreiben Sie einen online Kommentar zum Artikel, in dem Sie Ihre Meinung geben und begründen.

Beginnen Sie so: *Ich finde es (gut/schlecht/ prima/ungewöhnlich/?), dass man auf dem Donauinselfest den Konsum von Alkohol kontrolliert.*

Teaching suggestion for 4-4. If you deem it an appropriate topic for your group of students, you could personalize the discussion about alcohol consumption. *Wie alt muss man sein, um alko- holische Getränke zu sich nehmen zu dürfen? Wie ist das hier bei uns? Was meinen Sie: Warum gibt es diesen Unterschied? Ist das „Komatrinken" hier ebenfalls ein Problem? Wenn ja, wo und bei wem? Was macht man, um das Komatrinken zu bekämpfen? Was könnte man noch dagegen tun?*

Note for 4-7. Relevant web addresses for Internet research activities can be found in *MyGermanLab* and on the Companion Website.

4-7 Infos zum Donauinselfest. Sie möchten das Donauinselfest besuchen. Finden Sie auf der Internetseite des Fests die folgenden Informationen und schreiben Sie sie auf.

1. Wann findet das Festival statt?
2. Nennen Sie zwei Veranstaltungen für jeden Festtag.
3. Wie viel kostet der Eintritt?
4. Finden Sie eine Veranstaltung, die Sie besonders interessiert.

Introduction to *Hörtext 1*. Ask students: *Warum ist Wien als Welthauptstadt der Musik bekannt?* Ask students what they learned about Mozart from the introduction. *Was erfahren wir über seine Familie? Wann und wo ist er geboren? gestorben? Wo lebte Mozart während seines Lebens?*

Hörtext 1

Ein Anruf beim Vienna Ticket Office (Telefongespräch)

Mit Recht nennt man Wien Welthauptstadt der Musik. Neben dem jüngeren Donauinselfest gibt es traditionsreiche und international bekannte Einrichtungen wie die Wiener Staatsoper, die Wiener Volksoper, die Wiener Philharmoniker und die Wiener Sängerknaben. Hier haben auch mehr berühmte Komponisten gelebt als in irgendeiner anderen Stadt der Welt. Der bekannteste unter ihnen ist wohl Mozart, dessen Kompositionen immer noch häufig gespielt werden.

Wolfgang Amadeus Mozart

Wolfgang Amadeus Mozart wurde 1756 in Salzburg geboren. Sein Vater war Musiker und so erhielt Wolfgang als kleiner Junge Unterricht in Klavier, Geige und Komposition. Schon mit sechs Jahren machte das „Wunderkind" Konzertreisen. Im Laufe der Jahre reiste er nach München, Paris, London, Italien und natürlich auch nach Wien, wo er zeitweise arbeitete und nach 1781 auch lebte. 1791 starb er im Alter von nur 36 Jahren in Wien. Heute kann man sein Ehrengrab° auf dem Zentralfriedhof in Wien besuchen. Da Mozart erst in Salzburg und später in Wien lebte, teilen die beiden Städte den Anspruch auf den weltberühmten Musiker. So findet man in beiden Städten Mozartdenkmäler und Mozartmuseen.

honorary grave financed by cities for residents with extraordinary service or achievements
Siehe **Kulturtipps**: Zentralfriedhof

Im folgenden Telefongespräch hören Sie einen Herrn beim Vienna Ticket Office anrufen, um sich über das aktuelle Angebot an Mozartaufführungen zu informieren.

Vor dem Hören

Haben Sie schon mal die Musik von Mozart gehört? Wenn ja, wo? Welche Kompositionen kennen Sie?

Beim Hören

Hören Sie sich das Telefongespräch an. Setzen Sie die Daten in den Zeitplan. Einige Daten benutzen Sie mehr als einmal.

Ein Anruf beim Vienna Ticket Office

04-06 to 04-08

Austrian Dinner Show	*Così fan tutte*	*Don Giovanni*
Wiener Rathauskeller	Wiener Mozart Orchester	Wiener Musikverein
Wiener Volksoper	*Die Zauberflöte*	

Wiener Musikverein

Datum	Veranstaltung	Veranstaltungsort
8. März	*Die Zauberflöte*	Wiener Volksoper
9. März	*Don Giovanni*	Wiener Volksoper
	Wiener Mozart Orchester	Wiener Musikverein
13. März	*Così fan tutte*	Wiener Volksoper
19. März	*Die Zauberflöte*	Wiener Volksoper
kein Datum	Austrian Dinner Show	Wiener Rathauskeller

Kulturtipps

Zentralfriedhof

Der Zentralfriedhof wurde 1874 eröffnet und ist der zweitgrößte Friedhof (*cemetery*) in Europa. Er ist Friedhof für Menschen aller Glaubensrichtungen (*denominations*) und auch eine Touristenattraktion, da es hier viele Gräber und Ehrengräber von bekannten Österreichern wie den Komponisten Ludwig van Beethoven (1770–1827) und Johannes Brahms (1833–1897), den Schriftstellern Franz Grillparzer (1791–1872) und Ernst Jandl (1925–2000) und dem Popstar Falco (1957–1998) gibt.

4-8 Textarbeit: Stichwörter. Machen Sie Stichwörter zu den folgenden Punkten.

1. die Oper, die Herr Bündig sehen will _____ Mozarts *Zauberflöte* _____

2. wann er die Oper sehen möchte _____ den 9. März _____

3. für wie viele Personen er Karten will _____ zwei _____

4. der Anlass, aus dem er Karten kaufen will _____ der Geburtstag seiner Frau _____

5. die Vorstellung, die er wählt _____ das Konzert im Wiener Musikverein am 9. März _____

6. wie viel er für die Karten bezahlt _____ 105 Euro pro Person _____

7. was im Preis der Karten mit inbegriffen ist _____ das Konzert, ein dreigängiges Abendessen, ein Glas Sekt _____

Answers for 4-9.
1. Herr Bündig meint, Wien ist die Mozartstadt, aber Frau Bündig hält Salzburg für die echte Mozartstadt. **2.** Sie sagt, Mozart hat seine besten Werke in Wien verfasst, hat seine wichtigsten Jahre hier verbracht und hat auch sein Grab in dieser Stadt. **3.** Die Opern sind auf Italienisch und seine Frau mag lieber Opern auf Deutsch. **4.** Er meint, sie ist eher für Touristen. **5.** Man kann nach dem Konzert die Musiker kennenlernen und Autogramme bekommen.

4-9 Textarbeit: Noch mehr Details. Beantworten Sie die Fragen.

1. Worüber können sich Herr und Frau Bündig nicht einigen?
2. Warum sieht Frau Kramer Wien als die richtige Mozartstadt?
3. Warum will er keine Karten für die Oper *Don Giovanni* oder *Così fan tutte*?
4. Warum möchte er nicht in die Austrian Dinner Show?
5. Was ist sonst noch im Preis der teuersten Karten für das Konzert im Musikverein mit inbegriffen?

4-10 Mein Musikgeschmack. Welche zwei Musikrichtungen gefallen Ihnen am besten? Welche zwei am wenigsten? Vergleichen Sie Ihre Wahl mit der Ihrer Mitstudenten. Finden Sie jemanden, der denselben Geschmack in der Musik hat wie Sie?

einige Musikrichtungen:

Alternative	Heavy Metal	klassische Musik	Rockmusik
Blues	Hip-Hop	Popmusik	Techno
Countrymusik	Jazz	Reggae	Volksmusik

Note for 4-11 and 4-12. Relevant web addresses for Internet research activities can be found in MyGermanLab and on the Companion Website.

4-11 Mehr zur Biografie Mozarts. Suchen Sie nach weiterer Information zum Leben Mozarts. Schreiben Sie zu jedem der folgenden Stichwörter ein paar Sätze in Ihren eigenen Worten: Kindheit, Geschwister, Frau und Kinder, Kompositionen, Lebensverhältnisse.

4-12 Mozart aktuell. Der Name Mozart ist heute noch sehr aktuell und lässt sich in vielen Lebensbereichen wiederfinden. Wo kann man seinen Namen außer im Zusammenhang mit seiner Musik sonst noch finden? Suchen Sie im Internet nach mindestens fünf Bezügen zu ihm und listen Sie sie auf.

Beispiel: *Mozartkugeln: Die weltbekannten Schokoladenpralinen sind nach ihm benannt.*

die österreichische 1-Euro-Münze: Mozarts Porträt findet man darauf.

Lesetext 2

Stephansdom (Internetseite)

Introduction to *Lesetext 2.* Ask students what they learned from the text introduction. *Wie nennt man in Wien den Stephansdom? Wie alt ist der Dom? Warum besteht er aus verschiedenen Stilen der Architektur? Welche Teile des Doms sind am bekanntesten? Wer zahlt die Kosten der Renovierung?*

Siehe **Kulturtipps**
Gotische und romanische
Architektur
cast

federal coat of arms

Der Stephansdom, offiziell die Domkirche St. Stephan zu Wien und von den Wienern auch „Steffl" genannt, liegt im Zentrum der Stadt. Der Bau des Doms begann im 12. Jahrhundert und über die nächsten Jahrhunderte wurden die verschiedenen Türme und Teile des Doms hinzugefügt. So hat der Dom gotische und romanische Architektur, aber auch modernere Teile. Die zwei bekanntesten Teile sind die Pummerin – eine große Glocke, die 1877 aus über 200 Kanonenkugeln, die die Türken gelassen hatten, gegossen° wurde – und das Dach. Auf dem Dach sieht man zwei Adler. Einer trägt das österreichische Bundeswappen°, der andere das Wiener Wappen.

DaderDomsehraltist,musserständigrenoviert werden. Da die Kosten für die Renovierung zu hoch sind, um nur von der Stadt bezahlt zu werden, wendet man sich an die Besucher des Doms. Sie kommen gern in den Dom und geben auch Spenden für seine Erhaltung, aber auch das reicht nicht aus. Seit 1987 gibt es den Verein „Unser Stephansdom", der versucht, Menschen in aller Welt anzuregen, Geld für die Restaurierung zu geben. Der folgende Text ist aus dem Informationsmaterial dieser Organisation und gibt einen kurzen Überblick über die Funktion des Doms.

Stephansdom

Vor dem Lesen

Besichtigen Sie Kirchen, wenn Sie reisen? Warum (nicht)? Welche ist die schönste oder beeindruckendste Kirche, die Sie je besucht haben?

Dach des Stephansdoms mit Wiener Wappen

Beim Lesen

Suchen Sie beim Lesen die Zahlen, die zu diesen Informationen passen.

_____7_____ Gottesdienste, die während der Woche gefeiert werden

_____10_____ Gottesdienste am Sonntag

_____7_____ Anzahl der Jahre, die notwendig waren, den Dom nach dem Zweiten Weltkrieg wieder aufzubauen

2 Millionen Touristen, die Wien jährlich besuchen

Lesetext 2. This reading from the Internet was written prior to the spelling reform and therefore uses pre-reform orthography.

Stephansdom

Der Wiener Stephansdom wird wegen seiner wichtigen Stellung im kulturellen und gesellschaftlichen Leben Wiens unterschiedlich beschrieben:

04-09 to 04-11

- er ist bewegendes Gotteshaus
- er ist weltberühmtes Kulturgut und ein Bauwerk, das international keine Vergleiche zu scheuen braucht[a]

5

- er ist das nationale Wahrzeichen[b] Österreichs und Symbol der österreichischen Identität
- er ist Touristenmagnet ersten Ranges

---

[a]*das ... braucht that needn't fear international comparisons* [b]*emblem*

weiter >>>

Der Wiener Stephansdom ist – neben seiner kulturellen Bedeutung – natürlich auch Kirche:
An jedem Wochentag werden sieben, an jedem Sonntag zehn Gottesdienste[c] gefeiert. Besonders zu den
hohen Feiertagen (Ostern, Pfingsten[d], Weihnachten, etc.) wird die stets wunderschön geschmückte Kirche   10
„Stephansdom" von vielen Kirchgängern besucht. Gottesdienste von allgemeinem Interesse (Hochzeiten,
Requien bedeutender Persönlichkeiten, etc.) werden oft live im Fernsehen übertragen. Zu solchen beson-
deren Anlässen und zu den hohen Feiertagen läutet die Pummerin diese Festgottesdienste ein[e].

Das Bauwerk und das Kulturgut „Stephansdom" ist Gegenstand zahlreicher Bücher, Bildbände,
Untersuchungen, etc. Die Einzigkeit dieses Domes und die zigtausenden Details, aus denen er   15
zusammengesetzt ist, machen ihn zu einer kunsthistorischen und architektonischen Schatzkiste[f].
Jedes Detail hat seine Bestimmung[g], Hintergrund und Geschichte: Altäre, Tore, Türme, Pfeiler-
figuren, Bilder …

In den letzten Kriegstagen wurde der Stephansdom bei einem Brand schwer beschädigt. Schutt
und Asche prägten den zerstörten Dom. In nur sieben Jahren konnte unter Einsatz aller der Dom   20
wieder aufgebaut werden. Das Wahrzeichen Österreichs und das Identifikationszeichen Österreichs war wieder erstanden.

Um dieses Kulturerbe für die nächsten Generationen zu bewahren und um einen Verfall zu verhindern, muß der Stephansdom weiterhin sorgfältig restauriert werden.

Mit über zwei Millionen Wienbesuchern pro Jahr steht der Stephansdom ganz oben auf der   25
Liste der Sehenswürdigkeiten: Rundgänge im und um den Dom bieten viel Sehenswertes und
Interessantes. Man kann den Stephansdom aber auch besteigen (Südturm, Türmer Stube) bzw.
mit dem Lift zur Pummerin hinauffahren (Nordturm) oder in die Katakomben hinabsteigen. Detail-
informationen zum Dom erfährt man in den angebotenen Führungen.

Ein besonderes Erlebnis ist ein Konzert im Stephansdom. „Unser Stephansdom" organisiert   30
auch Konzerte im Dom.

---

[c]*church services*   [d]*Pentecost*   [e]**läutet ein** *rings in*   [f]*treasure chest*   [g]*designation*

Kulturtipps

Gotische und romanische Architektur

Typisch für die romanische Architektur sind runde Bögen (*arches*), dicke Mauern und kleine Fenster.
Diese Merkmale kennzeichnen die Burgen, Kirchen und Klöster, die bis ins 13. Jahrhundert in Europa
gebaut wurden. Ab dem 12. Jahrhundert entwickelt sich gleichzeitig der neue Baustil der Gotik, in
der man spitze (*pointed*) Bögen, dünnere Wände und große Fenster findet. So konnte viel mehr Licht
und Sonne das Innere dieser Gebäude erhellen, und sie wirken dadurch leichter und freundlicher.

Nomen

der Anlass, ⸚e   *occasion*

die Bedeutung, -en   *importance, relevance*

der Brand, ⸚e   *fire*

der Dom, -e   *cathedral*

der Feiertag, -e   *holiday*

der Gegenstand, ⸚e   *object, thing*

die Glocke, -n   *bell*

der Hintergrund, ⸚e   *background*

(das) Ostern   *Easter*

die Spende, -n   *donation*

die Untersuchung, -en   *study, investigation*

der Verfall   *decay*

der Vergleich, -e   *comparison*

(das) Weihnachten   *Christmas*

Verben

auf·bauen   *to build (up)*

beschädigen   *to damage*

bewahren   *to conserve*

feiern   *to celebrate*

verhindern   *to prevent*

Adjektive und Adverbien

allgemein   *general*

stets   *always*

Ausdrücke

bzw. (beziehungsweise)   *and/or*

Schutt und Asche   *rubble and ashes*

4-13 Textarbeit: Fragen zum Inhalt. Beantworten Sie die Fragen in Bezug auf den Text.

1. Wann kommen besonders viele Besucher in den Dom?
2. Was ist die Pummerin und wann wird sie benutzt?
3. Warum gibt es so viele Bücher über den Dom?
4. Wann und wie wurde der Dom schwer beschädigt?
5. Warum ist es den Österreichern wichtig, den Dom zu erhalten?
6. Was können Besucher im Dom machen?
7. Was bietet der Verein „Unser Stephansdom" Besuchern?

Answers for 4-13. **1.** zu den hohen Feiertagen; **2.** zu hohen Feiertagen und zu Gottesdiensten von allgemeinem Interesse; **3.** weil der Dom so einzigartig ist und zigtausend Details hat und eine Schatzkiste ist; **4.** während des Zweiten Weltkrieges durch einen Brand; **5.** Der Dom ist Kulturerbe, Symbol der österreichischen Identität und nationales Wahrzeichen Österreichs. **6.** Rundgänge und Führungen machen, die Türme des Doms besteigen, die Katakomben besichtigen; **7.** Konzerte

4-14 Vokabelarbeit. Ergänzen Sie die Sätze mit Wörtern aus den *Neuen Vokabeln*. Achten Sie dabei auch auf die Wortform.

1. Alte, große und wichtige Kirchen werden oft Kathedralen oder _____Dome_____ genannt.

2. An den ____Feiertagen____ wird die Kirche festlich geschmückt.

3. Türkische Soldaten ___beschädigten___ während der Belagerung Wiens den Dom.

4. Der ____Verfall____ von alten Gebäuden ist nur schwer zu verhindern.

5. Die Spenden sollen ____verhindern____, dass der Dom langsam kaputtgeht.

6. Die Konzerte im Dom ____feiern____ unter anderem große Musiker wie Mozart und Bach.

7. Der Stephansdom ist im ____Vergleich____ zur Votivkirche viel älter, denn letztere wurde erst im 19. Jahrhundert erbaut.

4-15 Zur Diskussion. Besprechen Sie die Fragen.

1. Wer sollte die Restaurationskosten des Doms bezahlen? Würden Sie Geld dafür spenden?

2. Ist es wichtig, Kulturdenkmäler zu erhalten? Warum (nicht)?

3. Helfen Sie in Organisationen, die anderen Menschen helfen? Was machen Sie da? Warum helfen Sie?

4. Wem würden Sie finanziell helfen, wenn Sie viel Geld hätten? Warum?

4-16 In eigenen Worten. Der Text berichtet über den Dom als Gotteshaus, Kulturgut, Wahrzeichen Österreichs, Symbol der österreichischen Identität und Touristenmagnet. Erzählen Sie einem Freund, der nichts über den Stephansdom weiß, über drei dieser Aspekte.

Beispiel: *Der Stephansdom ist ein Gotteshaus, weil man dort …*

4-17 Leserbrief: Weg mit den alten Gebäuden! Sie wohnen in einer kleinen Stadt mit vielen alten Gebäuden. Doch viele der Bürger wollen die alten Gebäude abreißen, um Platz für neue Wohnhäuser zu machen. Schreiben Sie einen kurzen Leserbrief an Ihre Zeitung, in dem Sie für die Erhaltung der alten Bauwerke plädieren.

Beginnen Sie so: *Ich bin gegen den Abriss der alten Gebäude unserer Stadt. …*

4-18 Bewerbung. Der Verein „Unser Stephansdom" sucht nach einer Person, die in den Sommermonaten die Gäste durch den Dom führen kann. Schreiben Sie eine E-Mail an den Verein, in der Sie Ihr Interesse an der Stelle ausdrücken, Ihre Erfahrungen beschreiben und nach weiteren Informationen über die Stelle fragen.

Introduction to *Lesetext 3*. Ask students what they associate with the term *Kaffeehaus*. Then ask them what they learned about Viennese coffeehouses from the text introduction. *Was macht man in einem Wiener Kaffeehaus? Was ist anders in einem Kaffeehaus bei Ihnen? Was ist ähnlich?*

Lesetext 3

Kaffee. Wien – Mit Leib und Seele (Reiseführer-Auszug)

Die Wiener lieben sie und Besucher verlieben sich oft in sie: die Wiener Kaffeehäuser. Man besucht sie, um hier ebenso wie schon vor langer Zeit stundenlang bei einem Kaffee zu sitzen, Zeitung zu lesen und sich zu entspannen. Der Kaffee wird hier traditionell mit einem Glas Wasser serviert und viele Kaffeehäuser bieten neben den verschiedenen Kaffeesorten auch Kuchen, Torten und warmes Essen an. Die Einrichtungen der Kaffeehäuser sind von gemütlich bis modern kühl und viele haben auch draußen Plätze, die man als „Schani-gärten" bezeichnet.

Im Café Sacher, berühmt für seine Sachertorte

Der folgende Auszug aus dem Wien City Guide stellt Ihnen eine Legende vor und gibt Ihnen einen Einblick in die Ent-wicklung der Wiener Kaffeehäuser.

Café Central   Kuchen im Café Central

Vor dem Lesen

1. Trinken Sie Kaffee? Wann trinken Sie Kaffee? Was verbinden Sie mit dem Kaffeetrinken?
2. Kennen Sie das Wort „Kaffeeklatsch"? Was bedeutet es?

Beim Lesen

Welche Daten gehören zu welchem Ereignis?

| 1683 | 1685 | 18. Jahrhundert | 19. Jahrhundert | 1900 | heute |

_____1900_____ Die Blütezeit des Kaffeehauses fängt an.

_____1683_____ Kaffeebohnen werden in der Stadt zurückgelassen.

_____1685_____ Das erste Kaffeehaus wird eröffnet.

__19. Jahrhundert__ Kaffeehäuser werden beliebt als Schauplätze für Konzerte.

_____heute_____ Es gibt rund 500 Kaffeehäuser in Wien.

__18. Jahrhundert__ In Kaffeehäusern werden erstmals Gesellschaftsspiele gespielt.

04-12 to 04-14

Kaffee. Wien – Mit Leib und Seele

Lesetext 3. This text was written prior to the spelling reform and therefore uses pre-reform orthography.

Mehr als 300 Jahre ist es alt und seit fast 100 Jahren ein Mythos: das Kaffeehaus, eine Wiener Institution ersten Ranges, um die sich Anekdoten und Gerüchte° en masse ranken. Gleich am Anfang steht eine Legende: Nach der Belagerung° Wiens anno 1683 hätten die Türken Säcke voll unscheinbarer° graugrüner Bohnen zurückgelassen, deren sich ein gewisser Kolschitzky 5 annahm; er sei damit – zum Dank für seine hilfreichen Kundschafterdienste° – der erste Wiener Cafetier geworden. Soweit eines der Lieblingsgerüchte der Wiener. Indes, nicht der polnische Spion Kolschitzky, sondern ein armenischer Kaufmann namens Deodato hat erwiesenermaßen das erste Kaffeeschankprivileg erhalten, und zwar 1685. Und noch lange blieben 10 armenische Kaufleute führend in der Kaffeesiederbranche° der Stadt. Kein Gerücht ist ferner, daß sich dieses Gewerbe rasch der (vorerst ausschließlich männlichen) Publikumsgunst erfreute.

rumors

siege / nondescript

spy services

coffee brewing business

Der Kaffeegenuß wird im 18. Jh. mit weiteren Vergnügungen ergänzt: Man spielte jetzt Billard und Schach oder las Zeitungen. Im 19. Jh. wird das Kaffeehaus vollends zu einem Mittelpunkt des gesellschaftlichen Lebens, luxuriös eingerichtet in der Stadt, billiger, wenngleich nicht weniger pompös, in der Vorstadt. Hier trank der Stammgast „seinen" Kaffee, las „seine" Zeitung, spielte, dachte nach oder konversierte. Auch speisen konnte (und kann) man im Kaffeehaus. Und in den Konzertcafés spielten im Biedermeier die Walzerkönige auf. Zur Jahrhundertwende brach schließlich die eigentliche Blütezeit° der Wiener Kaffeehauskultur an. Dicht an dicht, so wird es zumindest kolportiert, saßen die brillanten Geister um die Marmortische, vor sich einen Mocca oder Einspänner, über den Köpfen die dicken Schwaden der Zigarren, dazu stets griffbereit ein Notizheft, die Zeitung, dazwischen das Staccato ihres geistreichen Wortwitzes. Daheim hatten sie womöglich bloß ein kaltes Zimmer, wenn überhaupt, weil das Geld fehlte. So will es die Legende, so erzählen es die zahlreichen Anekdoten, und so oder ähnlich mag es auch gewesen sein im Café Griensteidl, Central oder Herrenhof. „Im Kaffeehaus sitzen die Talente so dicht an einem Tisch, daß sie einander gegenseitig an der Entfaltung° hindern", spottete Karl Kraus°, der es wissen mußte, denn er saß auch dort, ebenso wie Schnitzler, Freud oder Hofmannsthal, Loos, Klimt oder Schiele[3], der noch unbekannte Operettenkomponist Franz Lehár und ein noch unbekannterer Herr Bronstein alias Leo Trotzki. Und der Literat Peter Altenberg gab überhaupt gleich als Adresse „Wien 1, Café Central" an. Damals wurde das Kaffeehaus endgültig zur Institution, für manche gar zur „Weltanschauung"°. Und für viele ist das, trotz Kaffeehausschwund und verringerter Muße, bis heute so. Immerhin gibt es in ganz Wien noch an die 500 Kaffeehäuser, und für sie alle gilt, was Alfred Polgar° einst über das Café Central gemeint hat: „Teilhaftig der eigentlichen Reize dieses wunderlichen Caféhauses wird allein der, der dort nichts will als dort sein. Zwecklosigkeit heiligt den Aufenthalt."

Margin notes:

Siehe **Kulturtipps**: Stammgast und Stammtisch

Siehe **Kulturtipps**: Biedermeier

heyday

Siehe **Kulturtipps**: Mocca und Einspänner

development / (1874–1936) österreichischer Schriftsteller und Publizist

Siehe **Kulturtipps**: Sigmund Freud

philosophy of life

(1873–1955) österreichischer Schriftsteller und Kritiker

Neue Vokabeln

Nomen

das Gerücht, -e *rumor*
der Leib, -er *body*
die Seele, -n *soul*
der Witz, -e *joke*
der Zweck, -e *purpose*

Verben

ergänzen *to complete, to add*
fehlen (+ *dat.*) *to lack, be absent*
nach·denken (über), dachte nach, nachgedacht *to reflect (about), to ponder*
spotten *to joke*

Adjektive und Adverbien

dicht *close together*
eingerichtet *furnished*
endgültig *finally*
gegenseitig *mutually*
geistreich *witty*
gesellschaftlich *social*

---

[3]Wie Freud waren die Schriftsteller Karl Kraus (1874–1936), Arthur Schnitzler (1862–1931) und Hugo von Hofmannsthal (1874–1929), der Architekt Adolf Loos (1870–1933) und die Maler Gustav Klimt (1862–1918) und Egon Schiele (1890–1918) österreichische Intellektuelle und zentrale Gestalten der Wiener Moderne, einer geistigen Bewegung, die 1890 bis 1910 das Kulturleben Wiens prägte.

Kulturtipps

Stammgast und Stammtisch

In den deutschsprachigen Ländern findet man in Lokalen (*pubs, restaurants*) oft einen Tisch, auf dem ein Schild mit der Aufschrift „Stammtisch" steht. Das bedeutet, dass dieser Tisch für Stammgäste reserviert ist. Ein Stammgast ist ein Gast, der zu regelmäßigen Tagen und Zeiten in dieses Lokal kommt und sich hier mit Freunden trifft, die auch Stammgäste sind.

Biedermeier

Das Biedermeier ist die Zeit zwischen 1815 und 1848. Der Begriff bezeichnet die Kunst, Kultur, Literatur und Musik jener Zeit. Besonders betont wird dabei die Idylle, die Resignation über alles Politische und der Rückzug (*retreat*) ins private Leben. Es entwickelte sich eine Biedermeiertradition, die man sogar in der Mode und den Möbeln der Zeit findet. Das Biedermeier ist nur in Deutschland, Österreich und den skandinavischen Ländern zu finden, wobei Wien die Hochburg (*stronghold*) für Musik und Kultur dieser Bewegung war.

Mocca und Einspänner

In den Kaffeehäusern Wiens stehen viele verschiedene Kaffeegetränke auf der Karte. Zwei der beliebtesten Getränke sind der Mocca und der Einspänner. Ein Mocca ist ein starker schwarzer Kaffee. Ein Einspänner ist ein großer Mocca mit Schlagsahne (*whipped cream*).

Sigmund Freud

Sigmund Freud (1856–1939) ist wohl der bekannteste Psychologe aller Zeiten. Von 1860 bis 1938 lebte, studierte und arbeitete Freud in Wien. Hier entwickelte er seine weltbekannten psychoanalytischen Methoden. Seine Forschungsarbeit konzentrierte sich auf die Traumanalyse, um zu erkunden, wie er seine Patienten behandeln sollte. Das Sigmund-Freud-Museum in Wien wurde 1971 in seiner langjährigen Wohnung und Praxis in der Berggasse 19 eröffnet. Dort steht auch die bekannte Couch des Psychoanalytikers

Answers for 4-19. 1. Seit 1685, da wurde das erste Kaffeehaus eröffnet. **2.** mit einem Sack Bohnen; **3.** Sie tranken Kaffee, spielten Billard und Schach, lasen Zeitungen, dachten nach, diskutieren, aßen und genossen Walzermusik. **4.** um die Jahrhundertwende; **5.** oft sehr einfach; **6.** Man kann ihn nur erfahren, wenn man ohne Absicht und Zweck dort ist.

4-19 Textarbeit: Fragen zum Inhalt. Beantworten Sie die Fragen mit Informationen aus dem Text.

1. Wie lange schon gibt es Kaffeehäuser in Wien?
2. Womit wurde der Spion Kolschitzky angeblich für seine Dienste bezahlt?
3. Was machten im 19. Jahrhundert die Stammgäste in den Kaffeehäusern?
4. Wann war die Blütezeit der Kaffeehäuser?
5. Wie lebten die Künstler zu Hause?
6. Was sagt Alfred Polgar über den Charakter der Kaffeehäuser?

4-20 Vokabelarbeit. Ergänzen Sie die Sätze mit Wörtern aus den *Neuen Vokabeln.* Achten Sie dabei auch auf die Wortform.

1. Die Kaffeehäuser sind oft gemütlich ___eingerichtet___ und laden dazu ein, etwas länger zu bleiben.

2. Viele Dichter kamen in die Kaffeehäuser, hier sprachen sie über ihre Werke, ___dachten___ ___nach___ und diskutierten.

3. Die ___Witze___ der Dichter bestanden oft aus lustigen Wortspielen und brachten die anderen Künstler zum Lachen.

4. Im Kaffeehaus gibt es etwas sowohl für den ___Leib___ als auch für die Seele.

5. Die Kaffeehäuser dienten und dienen keinem echten ___Zweck___, man soll sich hier entspannen und erholen.

6. Kaffeehäuser sind auch heute Orte für ___gesellschaftliche___ Treffen.

 4-21 Komm doch mit ins Café! Sie sind mit zwei Freunden in Wien und wollen sich hinsetzen und etwas trinken. Gehen Sie zu Starbucks oder in ein Kaffeehaus? Besprechen Sie, wohin Sie gehen sollten.

Hilfreiche Ausdrücke: *Das ist eine hervorragende Idee / Das ist keine gute Idee.*

Ich möchte gern … / Ich würde lieber …

Alternative for 4-22. *Sie machen Kurzzeitarbeit für ein Marketingunternehmen mit der Aufgabe, das Tun und Verhalten der Kunden in den Cafés Ihrer Stadt zu beschreiben. Besuchen Sie ein Café und beobachten Sie dessen Gäste. Machen Sie sich während des Cafébesuchs Notizen. Dann schreiben Sie Ihren Bericht.*

Alternative for 4-23. *Schreiben Sie für eine Wiener Lokalzeitung einen Artikel über ein Kaffeehaus in der Stadt. In Ihrem Artikel beschreiben Sie das Kaffeehaus und erzählen Sie, wer es besucht und was die Menschen dort beim Kaffeetrinken alles machen.*

4-22 Mein Besuch im Café Central. Sie haben während Ihres Wienbesuchs einen Nachmittag in einem der berühmten Kaffeehäuser verbracht. Sie haben stundenlang dort gesessen und gelesen und Leute beobachtet. Schreiben Sie einen kurzen Bericht in Ihr Reisetagebuch über diesen Kaffeehausbesuch.

4-23 Reisetipp „Kaffeehaus"! Während Ihrer Kurzarbeit bei der *Neuen Kronen Zeitung* in Wien schreiben Sie einen Reisetipp für Ausländer. In diesem Tipp empfehlen Sie Touristen den Besuch eines Kaffeehauses.

Beginnen Sie so: *Wenn Ihre nächste Reise Sie nach Wien führt, dann müssen Sie unbedingt eines der vielen traditionellen Kaffeehäuser besuchen. …*

Hörtext 2

Margarete Schachermeier: Eine Wienerin stellt sich vor (Interview)

Introduction to *Hörtext 2*. Introduce students to the theme before they read the text introduction. *Sind Sie gern in einer Großstadt? Warum (nicht)? Was gibt es in einer typischen Großstadt zu tun?*

Wenn man in Wien lebt und arbeitet, ist man ständig von Kultur und Kunst umgeben. Geht man durch die Stadt, so kommt man an alten Kirchen und Museen vorbei, und möchte man ins Theater oder Konzert gehen, so ist es oft schwierig zu entscheiden, was man sehen will, denn das Angebot ist immer groß. Doch wie sehen die Wiener selbst ihre Stadt und das reichhaltige Angebot? Nimmt der durchschnittliche Wiener an den Angeboten teil? Und was kann ein echter Wiener Besuchern empfehlen? Im folgenden Interview erzählt die Wienerin Margarete Schachermeier von ihrer Heimatstadt.

Margarete Schachermeier

Vor dem Hören

Welche Sehenswürdigkeiten, meinen Sie, schlägt Margarete Schachermeier dem Besucher vor? Glauben Sie, dass Frau Schachermeier die vielen kulturellen Angebote nutzt?

Beim Hören

In diesem Interview hören Sie die folgenden Vokabeln:

04-15 — Margarete Schachermeier: Eine Wienerin stellt sich vor.

>   Aufführungen   *performances*
>   drehend(en)   *rotating*
>   Währung   *currency*

Hören Sie sich das Interview an. Markieren Sie alles, was von Margarete Schachermeier genannt wird.

die österreichische Kulturgeschichte	die Ringstraße
der Zentralfriedhof	das Freudmuseum
die Universität Wien	der Stephansdom
das Burgtheater	der Prater
Mozart	das Riesenrad
das Donauinselfest	der Donauturm
der Heurige	

Kulturtipps

Heuriger

Der Begriff „Heuriger" hat gleich zwei Bedeutungen. Das Wort „heuer" heißt, dass etwas aus diesem Jahr stammt. So beschreibt Heuriger einerseits einen jungen Wein. Die andere Bedeutung des Wortes beschreibt ein Lokal oder eine Gaststätte. Man kann also einen Heurigen in einem Heurigen trinken. Man findet die Wörter „heuer" und „Heuriger" hauptsächlich in Österreich und Südwestdeutschland, da es sich bei diesen Worten um regionale Varianten handelt.

Ringstraße

Seit Mitte des 19. Jahrhunderts verläuft die Ringstraße, auch der Ring genannt, ringartig um die Wiener Altstadt herum. Um Platz für diese wichtige Repräsentationsstraße zu machen, wurden damals auf Befehl des Kaisers die seit 600 Jahren bestehenden Stadtmauern abgerissen. An dieser Straße stehen heute die Staatsoper, das Parlamentsgebäude, das Rathaus, das Museum für Völkerkunde (*ethnology*) und etliche andere beeindruckende Gebäude.

Prater

Der Wiener Prater ist ein Vergnügungspark, den es seit 1766 gibt. 1896/97 wurde das Riesenrad gebaut, mit dem man auch heute noch hoch über die Stadt fahren kann. Das Riesenrad ist eines der Wahrzeichen der Stadt. Der Eintritt in den Prater ist gratis, aber man muss natürlich für die Achterbahnen (*rollercoasters*) sowie Essen und Trinken an den Ständen bezahlen.

Das Riesenrad im Prater

 4-24 Textarbeit: Wer ist Frau Schachermeier? Hören Sie während des Interviews gut zu, und markieren Sie, ob jede Aussage richtig oder falsch ist.

Answers for 4-24. 1. R;
2. F – Sie reist manchmal.
3. F – Sie unterrichtet Deutsch und österreichische Kulturgeschichte. 4. R; 5. F – Sie möchte am liebsten jeden Tag in Konzerte, Opern und ins Theater gehen. 6. R

1. Margarete Schachermeier ist in Wien geboren.
2. Sie reist nie.
3. Sie unterrichtet Englisch.
4. Sie ist verheiratet.
5. Sie geht am liebsten nur an Wochenenden in Konzerte, Opern und ins Theater.
6. Sie sieht sich als Österreicherin und Wienerin.

Answers for 4-25. 1. amerikanische Studenten; 2. drei;
3. das Burgtheater; 4. die Ringstraße; 5. ein Riesenrad; 6. den Donauturm; 7. wegen der Sprache und der Kultur

4-25 Textarbeit: Fragen zum Inhalt. Beantworten Sie die Fragen in Bezug auf das Interview.

1. Wer studiert am Institut für Europäische Studien?
2. Wie viele Opernhäuser gibt es in Wien?
3. Wie heißt das berühmteste Theater der Stadt?
4. Welche Straße umgibt Wien?

5. Was bietet der Prater für Besucher?

6. Welche Attraktion kann man nach Frau Schachermeier auslassen?

7. Warum sieht sich Frau Schachermeier als Wienerin und Österreicherin?

 4-26 Was sollen wir besichtigen? Sie machen eine Bahnreise nach Italien. Auf dem Weg haben Sie zwei Stunden Aufenthalt in Wien. Es gibt also Zeit, eine Sehenswürdigkeit hier zu besuchen. Diskutieren Sie, was Sie besuchen wollen.

 4-27 Zur Diskussion. Besprechen Sie die Fragen.

1. Was für Sehenswürdigkeiten gibt es in Ihrer Stadt? Welche würden Sie einem Touristen empfehlen und welche nicht?

2. Nehmen Sie die kulturellen Angebote Ihrer Universität und Ihrer Stadt wahr? Warum (nicht)?

3. Margarete Schachermeier sagt, sie ist Wienerin und Österreicherin. Wie sehen Sie sich? Als Amerikaner/in? Als Einwohner/in eines Staates oder einer Stadt? Warum definieren Sie sich so?

4-28 Kultur – ganz umsonst! Sie sind Student/in an der Uni Wien. Schreiben Sie für die Unizeitung einen kurzen Artikel, in dem Sie für mehr kostenlose kulturelle Angebote für Studenten plädieren. Geben Sie an, welche Angebote es geben sollte und warum sie möglichst kostenlos sein sollten.

Lesetext 4

„Das Fenster-Theater" von Ilse Aichinger (Kurzgeschichte)

Introduction to *Lesetext 4*. Ask students what they learned about the author from the text introduction. *Was erfahren Sie über Ilse Aichingers Familie? Hat sie einen Universitätsabschluss? Was für Texte hat sie geschrieben?*

Ilse Aichinger (1999)

Ilse Aichinger zählt heute zu den bekanntesten und wichtigsten Schriftstellern Österreichs. Ihr Werk ist international bekannt und gehört in der gesamten deutschsprachigen Welt zum Lesestoff in Schulen und Universitäten.

Ilse Aichinger wurde 1921 als Zwilling in Wien geboren und sie und ihre Zwillingsschwester wuchsen bei der Mutter in Wien auf. Ihre Mutter war jüdisch und so bekam Ilse als Halbjüdin nach ihrer Matura keinen Studienplatz. Nach Kriegsende 1945 begann sie ein Medizinstudium, das sie aber nicht beendete. 1948 wurde ihr einziger Roman „Die größere Hoffnung" veröffentlicht. Der Roman ist ein autobiografischer Bericht über Aichingers Leben in der Kriegszeit in Wien. In den folgenden Jahren veröffentlichte sie Hörspiele und Erzählungen, für die sie viele Auszeichnungen und Preise erhielt. 1995 erhielt Aichinger für ihr Lebenswerk den Großen Österreichischen Staatspreis für Literatur.

Siehe **Kulturtipps**: Matura

Die folgende Kurzgeschichte aus dem Jahre 1949 beschäftigt sich mit dem Thema der Perspektive, und wie das unser Verstehen und die Interpretation von Ereignissen beeinflusst, allerdings auch mit den Lebensverhältnissen älterer Menschen in den Großstädten, insbesondere wenn sie allein leben.

Lesetext 4. This short story was written prior to the spelling reform and therefore uses pre-reform orthography.

Vor dem Lesen

Raten Sie, wovon die Geschichte handelt. Was ist wohl ein Fenster-Theater?

Beim Lesen

Machen Sie beim Lesen zwei Listen mit Informationen zu den beiden Charakteren:

Frau	alter Mann
starrer Blick	lächelt

Das Fenster-Theater

04-16 to 04-18

von Ilse Aichinger

blew Die Frau lehnte am Fenster und sah hinüber. Der Wind trieb° in leichten Stößen vom Fluß herauf und brachte nichts Neues. Die Frau hatte den star- *insatiable* ren Blick neugieriger Leute, die unersättlich° sind. Es hatte ihr noch niemand *run over by a car* den Gefallen getan, vor ihrem Haus niedergefahren° zu werden. Außerdem wohnte sie im vorletzten Stock, die Straße lag zu tief unten. Der Lärm rauschte 5 nur mehr leicht herauf. Alles lag zu tief unten. Als sie sich eben vom Fenster *turned on* abwenden wollte, bemerkte sie, dass der Alte gegenüber Licht angedreht° hatte. Da es noch ganz hell war, blieb dieses Licht für sich und machte den *blazing* merkwürdigen Eindruck, den aufflammende° Straßenlaternen unter der *lit* Sonne machen. Als hätte einer an seinen Fenstern die Kerzen angesteckt°, 10 noch ehe die Prozession die Kirche verlassen hat. Die Frau blieb am Fenster.

Der Alte öffnete und nickte herüber. Meint er mich? dachte die Frau. Die Wohnung über ihr stand leer und unterhalb lag eine Werkstatt, die um diese Zeit schon geschlossen war. Sie bewegte leicht den Kopf. Der Alte nickte wieder. Er griff sich an die Stirne, entdeckte, daß er keinen Hut auf- 15 hatte, und verschwand im Inneren des Zimmers.

Gleich darauf kam er in Hut und Mantel wieder. Er zog den Hut und lächelte. Dann nahm er ein weißes Tuch aus der Tasche und begann zu win- *immer eifriger more and* ken. Erst leicht und dann immer eifriger°. Er hing über die Brüstung°, daß man *more fervently / railing* Angst bekam, er würde vornüberfallen. Die Frau trat einen Schritt zurück, 20 aber das schien ihn nur zu bestärken. Er ließ das Tuch fallen, löste seinen Schal vom Hals – einen großen bunten Schal – und ließ ihn aus dem Fenster wehen. Dazu lächelte er. Und als sie noch einen weiteren Schritt zurücktrat, warf er den Hut mit einer heftigen Bewegung ab und wand den Schal wie einen Tur- *took a bow / **kniff zu** shut* ban um seinen Kopf. Dann kreuzte er die Arme über der Brust und verneigte 25 *tightly* sich°. Sooft er aufsah, kniff er das linke Auge zu°, als herrsche zwischen ihnen *agreement* ein geheimes Einverständnis°. Das bereitete ihr so lange Vergnügen, bis sie *velvet pants* plötzlich nur mehr seine Beine in dünnen, geflickten Samthosen° in die Luft ragen sah. Er stand auf dem Kopf. Als sein Gesicht gerötet, erhitzt und freund- *informed* lich wieder auftauchte, hatte sie schon die Polizei verständigt°. 30

Und während er, in ein Leintuch gehüllt, abwechselnd an beiden Fenstern erschien, unterschied sie schon drei Gassen° weiter über dem Geklingel der Straßenbahnen und dem gedämpften Lärm der Stadt das Hupen des Überfallautos°. Denn ihre Erklärung hatte nicht sehr klar und ihre Stimme erregt geklungen. Der alte Mann lachte jetzt, so daß sich sein Gesicht in tiefe Falten legte°, streifte dann mit einer vagen Gebärde° darüber, wurde ernst, schien das Lachen eine Sekunde lang in der hohlen Hand zu halten und warf es dann hinüber. Erst als der Wagen schon um die Ecke bog, gelang es der Frau, sich von seinem Anblick loszureißen.

Sie kam atemlos unten an. Eine Menschenmenge hatte sich um den Polizeiwagen gesammelt. Die Polizisten waren abgesprungen, und die Menge kam hinter ihnen und der Frau her. Sobald man die Leute zu verscheuchen° suchte, erklärten sie einstimmig, in diesem Hause zu wohnen. Einige davon kamen bis zum letzten Stock mit. Von den Stufen beobachteten sie, wie die Männer, nachdem ihr Klopfen vergeblich blieb und die Glocke allem Anschein nach nicht funktionierte, die Tür aufbrachen. Sie arbeiteten schnell und mit einer Sicherheit, von der jeder Einbrecher° lernen konnte. Auch in dem Vorraum, dessen Fenster auf den Hof sahen, zögerten sie nicht eine Sekunde. Zwei von ihnen zogen die Stiefel aus und schlichen° um die Ecke. Es war inzwischen finster° geworden. Sie stießen an einen Kleiderständer, gewahrten den Lichtschein am Ende des schmalen Ganges und gingen ihm nach. Die Frau schlich hinter ihnen her.

Als die Tür aufflog, stand der alte Mann mit dem Rücken zu ihnen gewandt noch immer am Fenster. Er hielt ein großes weißes Kissen auf dem Kopf, das er immer wieder abnahm, als bedeutete er jemandem, daß er schlafen wolle. Den Teppich, den er vom Boden genommen hatte, trug er um die Schultern. Da er schwerhörig war, wandte er sich auch nicht um, als die Männer auch schon knapp hinter ihm standen und die Frau über ihn hinweg in ihr eigenes finsteres Fenster sah.

Die Werkstatt unterhalb war, wie sie angenommen hatte, geschlossen. Aber in die Wohnung oberhalb mußte eine neue Partei eingezogen sein. An eines der erleuchteten Zimmer war ein Gitterbett° geschoben, in dem aufrecht ein kleiner Knabe stand. Auch er trug sein Kissen auf dem Kopf und die Bettdecke um die Schultern. Er sprang und winkte herüber und krähte vor Jubel°. Er lachte, strich mit der Hand über das Gesicht, wurde ernst und schien das Lachen eine Sekunde lang in der hohlen Hand zu halten. Dann warf er es mit aller Kraft den Wachleuten ins Gesicht.

streets

of a police car

so dass ... legte *so that his face was deeply wrinkled* / *gesture*

shoo away

burglar

crept / dark

crib

krähte vor Jubel *screeched with joy*

Kulturtipps

Matura

Die Matura ist in Österreich, Liechtenstein, der Schweiz, Tschechien und Polen die Abschlussprüfung an den Oberschulen (*secondary schools*). Sie ist das, was in Deutschland das Abitur ist. Besteht man die Matura, kann man an einer Hochschule oder Universität studieren.

Nomen

der Anblick, -e *sight*

die Bewegung, -en *movement*

der Blick, -e *glance, look*

die Kerze, -n *candle*

das Kissen, - *pillow*

der Lärm *noise*

der Schritt, -e *step, stride*

die Stirn, -en *forehead*

die Stufe, -n *stair, step*

der Stock, Stockwerke[4] (*pl.*) *floor, story (of a building)*

das Tuch, ¨er *cloth*

die Werkstatt, ¨en *workshop, garage*

das Vergnügen, - *pleasure*

Verben

erscheinen, erschien, ist erschienen *to appear*

lachen *to laugh*

nicken *to nod*

verschwinden, verschwand, ist verschwunden *to disappear*

wenden, wandte, gewandt *to turn*

werfen (wirft), warf, geworfen *to throw*

winken *to wave*

zögern *to hesitate*

Adjektive und Adverbien

atemlos *breathless*

erregt *excited, agitated*

merkwürdig *strange*

neugierig *curious*

schwerhörig *hard of hearing*

Answers for 4-29. 1. F – Die Frau wohnt im vorletzten Stock. **2.** R; **3.** R; **4.** F – Der alte Mann kreuzt die Arme, lächelt, steht auf dem Kopf, benimmt sich verrückt. **5.** F – Die Frau ruft die Polizei. **6.** R; **7.** R; **8.** F – Er hat Theater für das kleine Kind im Haus gegenüber gespielt.

4-29 Textarbeit: Richtig oder falsch? Wenn eine Aussage falsch ist, korrigieren und ergänzen Sie sie mit Informationen aus dem Lesetext.

1. Die Frau wohnt in dem letzten Stock.
2. Der alte Mann wohnt im Haus gegenüber von der Frau.
3. Der alte Mann setzt einen Hut auf.
4. Der alte Mann spielt auf einer Geige und singt.
5. Die Frau ruft laut um Hilfe.
6. Die Frau ist neugierig, was der alte Mann da tut.
7. Die Polizei bricht in die Wohnung des Mannes ein.
8. Der alte Mann hat Theater für die Frau im Haus gegenüber gespielt.

Answers for 4-30. 1. Sie lehnt aus dem Fenster. **2.** Niemand wohnt dort. **3.** eine Werkstatt; **4.** Sie glaubt, er macht es für sie. **5.** als er auf dem Kopf steht; **6.** Eine Menschenmenge folgt den Polizisten, unter ihnen die Frau von gegenüber. **7.** Er ist schwerhörig. **8.** dass über ihr neue Nachbarn eingezogen sind und dort ein Kind am Fenster steht

4-30 Textarbeit: Fragen zum Inhalt. Beantworten Sie die Fragen in Bezug auf den Text.

1. Was macht die Frau, als sie den Mann gegenüber bemerkt?
2. Wer wohnt in der Wohnung über der Frau?
3. Was befindet sich in der Wohnung unter der Frau?
4. Für wen, glaubt die Frau, macht der Mann sein Theater?
5. Wann wird der Frau das Theater des Mannes merkwürdig?
6. Wer folgt der Polizei in das Haus des Mannes?
7. Warum hört der Mann die Polizisten nicht?
8. Was realisiert die Frau, als sie in das Haus gegenüber schaut?

---

[4]Merken Sie sich: *das Erdgeschoss* = *ground floor*; *der erste Stock* = *the second floor*; z. B. **Ich wohne im dritten Stock.** = *I live on the fourth floor.*

4-31 Vokabelarbeit. Ergänzen Sie die Sätze mit Wörtern aus den *Neuen Vokabeln*. Achten Sie dabei auch auf die Wortform.

1. Die Frau ist ___neugierig___ und möchte wissen, was auf der Straße passiert, deshalb lehnt sie sich aus dem Fenster.

2. Sie wohnt im ___Stock___ über der Werkstatt.

3. Die Frau beobachtet, wie ein Mann im Haus gegenüber sich ___merkwürdig___ verhält.

4. Der Mann legt sich ein ___Kissen___ auf den Kopf.

5. Der alte Mann kann das Polizeiauto nicht hören, weil er ___schwerhörig___ ist.

6. Die Frau wird durch das Verhalten des Mannes sehr ___erregt___.

7. Nach dem Anruf der Frau ___erschien___ die Polizei innerhalb von wenigen Minuten.

 4-32 Zur Diskussion und Interpretation. Besprechen Sie die Fragen.

1. Aus welcher Perspektive wird erzählt? (Frau? Mann? Kind? allwissender Erzähler?)

2. Wie verhält sich die Frau? Warum ruft sie die Polizei an?

3. Wie verhält sich der Mann? Was macht er und warum?

4. Was, glauben Sie, wird die Polizei jetzt mit dem Mann tun?

5. Würden Sie in dieser Situation auch die Polizei anrufen?

6. Warum heißt die Geschichte „Das Fenster-Theater"?

7. Was will Aichinger wohl mit ihrer Geschichte sagen?

8. Wie unterscheidet sich Theater von Kino? Welches mögen Sie lieber und warum?

9. Kann ein Film, ein Theaterstück oder ein Buch einen Menschen in seinem Denken beeinflussen? Erklären Sie!

 4-33 Rollenspiel. Spielen Sie die Rollen der Frau und eines Polizisten. Machen Sie ein kurzes Rollenspiel, in dem die Frau und der Polizist auf der Straße zusammentreffen.

Beispiel: **Frau:** *Da sind Sie ja endlich! Ich habe sie doch schon vor einer halben Stunde gerufen.*

  Polizist: *Ja, hier sind wir. Wo wohnt der Mann, der sich so merkwürdig verhält?*

  Frau: …

4-34 Meine Perspektive. Stellen Sie sich vor, Sie sind das Kind im Haus gegenüber von dem Mann. Schreiben Sie einen Bericht über das Geschehen aus der Perspektive des Kindes.

 4-35 Mehr über Ilse Aichinger und ihre Werke. Erfahren Sie noch mehr über die Werke der Autorin, indem Sie im Internet recherchieren. Machen Sie sich Notizen und berichten Sie der Klasse, was Sie herausgefunden haben.

Note for 4-35. Relevant web addresses for Internet research activities can be found in MyGermanLab and on the Companion Website.

Grammatik

1. Prepositions (Präpositionen)

04-26 to 04-35

Prepositions are words that are used in combination with a noun or pronoun object to form prepositional phrases. These phrases are used to modify other parts of speech in a sentence.

In *Kapitel 3* you reviewed the German cases. The objects of prepositions must be declined in the correct case. Each preposition requires that its objects be in a certain case. Prepositions are thus grouped according to the case of their objects.

Accusative prepositions (Präpositionen mit Akkusativ)

04-26 to 04-27

There are five commonly used accusative prepositions: **durch, für, gegen, ohne, um.**

durch [durchs = durch das] *through; by, by means of*

> Unsere Wanderung führte **durch den Wienerwald.**
> *Our hike led through the Vienesse Woods.*

> **Durch ihre Forschung** haben die Wissenschaftler neue Erkenntnisse gewonnen.
> *The scientists have gained new insights through their research.*

für [fürs = für das] *for*

> Ich backe einen Kuchen **für meinen Sohn**[5].
> *I'm baking a cake for my son.*

> International ist die österreichische Küche **für das Wiener Schnitzel** bekannt.
> *Austrian cuisine is known internationally for Wiener Schnitzel.*

gegen *against, contrary to; around, approximately (with times)*

> Studenten protestieren **gegen den Krieg.**
> *Students are protesting against the war.*

> Das Konzert fängt **gegen 20.00 Uhr** an.
> *The concert starts around 8 p.m.*

ohne *without*

> **Ohne mein Handy** kann ich nicht leben.
> *I can't live without my cell phone.*

---

[5]Someone doing something for somebody can sometimes also be expressed using an indirect object (dative case) rather than a prepositional phrase (**für** + accusative case). Accordingly, this sentence could also be conveyed with: **Ich backe** *meinem Sohn* **einen Kuchen.**

um [ums = um das] *around; at (with times)*

Wir fuhren mit dem Auto rund **um den See.**
We drove by car around the lake.

Der Zug soll **um 9.20 Uhr** ankommen.
The train is supposed to arrive at 9:20 am.

4-36 Das Donauinselfest. Anna hat den Tag auf dem Donauinselfest verbracht. Setzen Sie die richtigen Akkusativpräpositionen (**durch, für, gegen, ohne, um**) in ihren Bericht ein

1. Ich kam mit dem Auto zum Donauinselfest und musste _____durch_____ die ganze Stadt fahren.

2. Ich hatte leider meinen Ausweis vergessen und _____ohne_____ ihn konnte ich keinen Alkohol kaufen, da ich sehr jung aussehe.

3. Ich habe nichts _____gegen_____ die neuen Regeln und finde es gut, dass man sie beachtet.

4. Das Feuerwerk sollte _____um/gegen_____ 10.00 Uhr beginnen, aber es gab Probleme und so begann es erst eine halbe Stunde später.

5. Da gibt es Interessantes rund _____um_____ die Uhr.

6. Bevor ich dann nach Hause fuhr, habe ich noch schnell ein T-Shirt _____für_____ meinen Bruder gekauft.

Dative prepositions (Präpositionen mit Dativ)

04-28 to 04-29 There are ten commonly used dative prepositions: **ab, aus, außer, bei, gegen-über, mit, nach, seit, von, zu.**

ab *(starting) from (a certain point on)*

Kinder lernen Englisch **ab der ersten Klasse.**
Children learn English beginning in the first grade.

Unser Café ist **ab dem 1. April** geöffnet.
Our café is open from April 1 on.

aus *out of (a point of origin or a bounded space), from*

Der Schriftsteller Arthur Schnitzler kam **aus Wien.**
The author Arthur Schnitzler was from Vienna.

Leutnant Gustl ist eine Figur **aus einer berühmten Novelle** Schnitzlers.
Lieutenant Gustl is a character from a famous novella of Schnitzler's.

Die beiden Touristen kommen gerade **aus dem Schloss.**
The two tourists are just coming out of the palace.

außer	*except (for), besides, apart from*

Außer mir hat keiner den Donauturm besucht.
Nobody but me visited the Danube Tower.

Außer Wien wollen wir Graz und Salzburg besuchen.
Besides Vienna, we also want to visit Graz and Salzburg.

bei	[**beim** = **bei dem**] *by, near, at (a place of residence or employment); with, on, among (people); while (doing something), on the occasion of (an event)*

Beim Musikfest hört man Musik unterschiedlicher Art.
At the music festival one hears different types of music.

Ihr könnt **bei uns** übernachten.
You can sleep at our place.

Dieses Kaffeehaus ist seit Jahrzehnten **bei den Wienern** beliebt.
This coffeehouse has been popular with the Viennese (people) for decades.

Mozart starb 1791 **beim Komponieren** seines „Requiems".
Mozart died in 1791 while composing his "Requiem."

gegenüber	*opposite; vis-à-vis, toward; with respect to;* follows a personal pronoun object, but precedes other objects

Ein Künstler wohnt **mir gegenüber**.
An artist lives opposite me.

Der katholische Kaiser Joseph I war **gegenüber Protestanten** sehr tolerant.
The Catholic Emperor Joseph I was very tolerant toward Protestants.

gegenüber is also sometimes combined with **von** to mean *opposite, across from* and can mean the same thing as **gegenüber**.

Das moderne Haas-Haus steht direkt **gegenüber vom** Stephansdom.
The modern Haas House is directly across from St. Stephen's Cathedral.

mit	*with; by (means of transportation)*

Mit sechs Jahren machte Mozart **mit seinen Eltern** seine erste Konzertreise.
At the age of 6, Mozart went with his parents on his first concert tour.

Ich fahre täglich **mit dem Fahrrad** zur Arbeit.
I travel to work by bike every day.

nach   *to, toward (a city, country, continent, etc.); after; according to*

Wir kamen mit dem Boot von Wien **nach Budapest.**
We came by boat from Vienna to Budapest.

Nach dem Ersten Weltkrieg zerfiel die Doppelmonarchie
Österreich-Ungarn.
After World War I the dual monarchy of Austria-Hungary disintegrated.

Nach der letzten Volkszählung sind 75 Prozent der Österreicher
katholischen Glaubens.
According to the last census, 75 percent of Austrians are Catholic.

seit   *since; for (a period of time; used with the present tense to refer
to a state or activity begun in the past that continues in the
present).*

Seit 1995 ist Österreich Mitglied der Europäischen Union.
Since 1995 Austria has been a member of the European Union.

Wien ist schon **seit Jahrhunderten** eine Stadt der Musik.
Vienna has been a music city for centuries.

von   [**vom = von dem**] *from; by (what or whom something is done); of*
(in place of the genitive)

Innsbruck ist ungefähr 480 km **von Wien** entfernt.
Innsbruck is approximately 480 km away from Vienna.

„Die Zauberflöte" ist eine Oper **von Mozart.**
"The Magic Flute" is an opera by Mozart.

Das ist die Lieblingsoper **von meinem Onkel.**[6]
That is my mother's favorite opera (the favorite opera of my mother).

zu   [**zum = zu dem, zur = zu der**] *to, toward (a building, a place of work
or residence); at (a time or place); about (a topic); for (a purpose); on
(a date or an occasion)*

Wie komme ich am besten **zum Bahnhof?**
What is the best way to get to the train station?

Zu Silvester finden in Wien mehrere Bälle statt.
On New Year's Eve in Vienna there are several balls.

Das Museum verteilt eine Broschüre **zum Klimawandel.**
The museum distributes a brochure about climate change.

Ich lese gern **zur Entspannung.**
I like to read for relaxation.

---

[6]Alternatively, with genitive (instead of **von** + dative): **Das ist die Lieblingsoper** *meines Onkels.*

4-37 Aus dem Leben von Sigmund Freud. Der weltbekannte Psychoanalytiker Sigmund Freud lebte in Wien. Ergänzen Sie die Sätze über sein Leben mit passenden Dativpräpositionen (**ab, aus, außer, bei, gegenüber, mit, nach, seit, von, zu**).

1. Das Leben von Sigmund Freud ist ____nach____ den Berichten sehr bescheiden gewesen.

2. Jeden Tag ____außer____ Sonntag stand er um 7.00 Uhr auf.

3. Er aß jeden Tag um 13.00 Uhr ____mit____ seiner Familie zu Mittag und machte dann einen Spaziergang.

4. Seine Spaziergänge führten meist durch den Votivpark, der ____gegenüber____ seinem Haus lag.

5. Oft kam Freud abends sehr spät ____von____ der Arbeit wieder nach Hause.

6. Freud gefielen aber auch die Kaffeehäuser. Seine Lieblingscafés waren Café Landtmann und das Altwiener Café Korb. ____Zu____ diesen Cafés ging er am Wochenende besonders oft.

7. Die Künstler und Philosophen, mit denen er sich dort traf und unterhielt, waren auch fast alle ____aus____ Wien.

8. ____Nach____ 78 Jahren in Wien musste er 1938 vor den Nazis fliehen. ____Ab____ diesem Zeitpunkt lebte er in London.

Genitive prepositions (Präpositionen mit Genitiv)

04-30 to 04-31

Six of the most commonly used genitive prepositions are: **(an)statt, außerhalb, innerhalb, trotz, während, wegen.**[7]

(an)statt   *instead of*; **statt** and **anstatt** can be used interchangeably

Im täglichen Leben wird **anstatt der Hochsprache** das Wienerische gesprochen.
In daily life the Viennese dialect is spoken instead of the standard language.

außerhalb   *outside*

Außerhalb Österreichs heißen die Frankfurter Würstel meist „Wiener".
Outside of Austria frankfurters are usually called wieners.

innerhalb   *within, inside of*

Innerhalb der EU gehört Wien zu den wohlhabendsten Städten.
Vienna is among the most prosperous cities within the EU.

---

[7]Although **(an)statt, trotz, während,** and **wegen** are genitive prepositions and they are used with the genitive in formal and written German, they are often used with the dative case in colloquial speech.

trotz   *despite, in spite of*

> **Trotz der vielen Spenden** kommt das Projekt nicht weiter.
> *Despite the many donations the project is not progressing.*

während   *during*

> **Während meines Besuchs** im Kaffeehaus habe ich stundenlang Zeitung gelesen.
> *During my coffee house visit I read the newspaper for hours.*

wegen   *because of; with regard to*

> **Wegen des Unwetters** gab es Schäden in Millionenhöhe.
> *Because of severe weather there were damages in the millions.*

4-38 Österreich im Winter. Viele Touristen verbringen ihren Winterurlaub in Österreich. Setzen Sie die fehlenden Genitivpräpositionen (**anstatt, außerhalb, innerhalb, trotz, während, wegen**) ein.

Eislaufen am Rathausplatz in Wien

1. Touristen kommen auch im Winter nach Österreich. Dann natürlich nicht, um hier zu wandern, sondern ____wegen____ der vielen Angebote zum Wintersport.

2. In den meisten Wintersportorten kann man ____innerhalb____ kurzer Zeit viele Sportarten ausprobieren.

3. Die günstigsten Angebote für Winterurlaub findet man ____außerhalb____ der Hochsaison, wenn nicht so viele Leute reisen.

4. ____Trotz____ vieler Winterurlaubsangebote in Bayern, Thüringen und im Schwarzwald, fahren eine große Anzahl Deutscher lieber nach Österreich.

5. ____Statt/Anstatt____ eines Wochenendurlaubs in Wien machen viele Touristen lieber einen längeren Urlaub in einem der schönen Gebirgsorte.

6. Oft besuchen die Touristen ____während____ ihrer Reise dann aber auch noch Wien oder Salzburg.

04-32 to 04-34

Two-way prepositions (Wechselpräpositionen)

Each of the nine two-way prepositions—**an, auf, hinter, in, neben, über, unter, vor, zwischen**—is used with the dative case or the accusative case depending on context. They take a dative object when they denote a location and an accusative object when they indicate a direction of movement or movement toward a destination. German also uses these prepositions with the dative or the accusative in several idiomatic expressions.

Two-way prepositions. Students will learn more about verb + preposition idioms in *Kapitel 7.*

an Dat.: [am = an dem] *on (a vertical surface), on (a day or date), at, at the edge of (an object)*
Acc.: [ans = an das] *onto, to, (directed) toward*

Wien liegt **an der Donau.** (DATIV)
Vienna lies on (at the edge of) the Danube River.

Der österreichische Nationalfeiertag ist **am 26. Oktober.** (DATIV)
The Austrian national holiday is on October 26.

Fahren wir heute Nachmittag **an die Donau!** (AKKUSATIV)
Let's go to the Danube this afternoon!

2004 ging der Literatur-Nobelpreis **an die österreichische Schriftstellerin** Elfriede Jelinek. (AKKUSATIV)
In 2004, the Nobel Prize for Literature went to the Austrian author Elfriede Jelinek.

auf Dat.: *on (a horizontal surface), at, in (a place, an open space)*
Acc.: [aufs = auf das] *onto (a horizontal surface), to, toward (a destination, an open space), into*

1983 fand das erste Musikfestival **auf der Donauinsel** statt. (DATIV)
The first music festival on the Danube Island took place in 1983.

Meine Klasse macht in der letzten Schulwoche einen Ausflug **auf die Donauinsel.** (AKKUSATIV)
During the last week of school, my class is taking a field trip to the Danube Island.

1944 begannen die Luftangriffe **auf Wien.** (AKKUSATIV)
In 1944 the air attacks on Vienna began.

hinter Dat.: *behind*
Acc.: *behind*

Die berühmte Wissenschaftlerin saß **hinter mir.** (DATIV)
The famous scientist was sitting behind me.

Die berühmte Wissenschaftlerin setzte sich **hinter mich.** (AKKUSATIV)
The famous scientist sat down behind me.

in Dat.: [im = in dem] *in, within (a bounded space), at (a location); in (a month or season)*
Acc.: [ins = in das] *in, to (a country whose name contains an article), toward (a location), into (a bounded space)*

Um 1900 wohnten viele Künstler und Wissenschaftler **in dieser Stadt.** (DATIV)
Around 1900 many artists and scientists lived in this city.

Im Frühjahr findet das Maifest statt. (DATIV)
In spring, the May Festival takes place.

Das rege Kulturleben zog viele Künstler und Wissenschaftler **in die Stadt.** (AKKUSATIV)
The lively cultural atmosphere drew many artists and scientists to the city.

neben Dat.: *beside, next to, alongside*
Acc.: *beside, next to*

Ein begabter Künstler wohnt im Haus **neben uns.** (DATIV)
A talented artist lives in the house next to us.

Der Mann legte die Zeitung **neben seine Kaffeetasse.** (AKKUSATIV)
The man laid the newspaper down beside his coffee cup.

über Dat.: *above, over*
Acc.: *above, over; across, via; about*

Die Festung Hohensalzburg liegt hoch **über der Stadt** Salzburg. (DATIV)
Hohensalzburg Castle lies high above the city of Salzburg.

Hier führt eine Brücke **über den Fluss.** (AKKUSATIV)
Here a bridge leads across the river.

Der Zug fuhr **über Wien** nach Prag. (AKKUSATIV)
The train went to Prague via Wien.

Der Schriftsteller schrieb **über seine Wanderungen** in den Alpen. (AKKUSATIV)
The author wrote about his hikes in the Alps.

unter Dat.: *under, below, beneath; among*
Acc.: *under, underneath*

Unter den Habsburgern wurde Wien zur kaiserlichen Hauptstadt und Residenzstadt. (DATIV)
Under the Habsburgs, Vienna became the imperial capital and seat of power.

Unter den Besuchern waren viele Eltern mit Kindern. (DATIV)
Among the visitors there were many parents with children.

Der Zahn kommt **unter das Kopfkissen.** (AKKUSATIV)
The tooth goes under the pillow.

vor Dat.: *in front of, before; ago*
Acc.: *in front of*

Der Autofahrer **vor mir** fährt viel zu langsam. (DATIV)
The driver in front of me is driving much too slowly.

Die Geschichte Wiens beginnt **vor 4.000 Jahren.** (DATIV)
The history of Vienna begins 4,000 years ago.

Am Nikolausabend stellen Kinder ihre Schuhe **vor die Tür.** (AKKUSATIV)
On the night before St. Nicholas's Day, children put their shoes in front of the door.

| zwischen | Dat: *between* |
| | Acc.: *between* |

Der Deutsche Krieg von 1866 war hauptsächlich ein Konflikt **zwischen Preußen und Österreich.** (DATIV)
The Austro-Prussian War of 1866 was primarily a conflict between Prussia and Austria.

Er setzte sich **zwischen Peter und seinen Bruder.** (AKKUSATIV)
He sat down between Peter and his brother.

Im Inneren des Stephansdoms

4-39 Was ist wo im Stephansdom? Unterstreichen Sie die Wechselpräpositionen (**an, auf, hinter, in, neben, über, unter, vor, zwischen**) und geben Sie an, ob das Objekt der Präposition im Dativ oder im Akkusativ steht.

1. Die Pummerin hängt <u>in</u> dem Nordturm. __Dativ__

2. <u>Auf</u> dem Dach sind zwei Adler abgebildet. __Dativ__

3. Viele Besucher gehen <u>unter</u> die Kirche, um hier die Katakomben zu besichtigen. __Akkusativ__

4. Es gibt einige Marienstatuen <u>zwischen</u> den Säulen. __Dativ__

5. Die große Orgel ist hoch oben <u>über</u> dem Eingang. __Dativ__

6. <u>An</u> den Seiten der Kirche findet man kleine Kapellen. __Dativ__

7. Wenn man durch den Dom geht, geht man hier und da <u>über</u> die Gräber von Kardinälen und Bischöfen. __Akkusativ__

4-40 Ein Abend in der Stadt. Elisabeth und ihr Freund Jochen verbringen den Abend zusammen in der Stadt. Ergänzen Sie die Sätze mit den passenden Kombinationen von Präposition und Artikel.

an den	auf die	neben meinem
an der	ins	über der
an diesem	in einen	vor der

1. ___Vor der___ Vorstellung trafen wir uns im Kaffeehaus.

2. Nach einer schönen Melange und einer Kleinigkeit zu essen gingen wir ___ins___ Burgtheater.

Das Burgtheater

3. Beim Eingang sahen wir _____an der_____ Decke _____über der_____ Treppe die berühmten Gemälde von Gustav Klimt.

4. Im Zuschauerraum saß links _____neben meinem_____ Freund ein Mann, der sehr laut sprach.

5. Aber als die Schauspieler _____auf die_____ Bühne kamen, wurde das Publikum endlich ruhig.

6. Das Theaterstück _____an diesem_____ Abend – Schnitzlers „Professor Bernhardi" – war hervorragend.

7. Nach der Aufführung gingen wir _____in einen_____ Heurigen.

8. Als die Kellnerin unser Essen _____an den_____ Tisch brachte, war ich mehr als glücklich. Ich hatte einen Bärenhunger!

2. Da- and wo-compounds (*Da- und wo-Verbindungen*)

The object of a preposition can be either a noun or a pronoun. However, in German only pronouns that refer to persons can be used as prepositional objects. When pronouns refer to things or ideas, a **da**-compound or a **wo**-compound is used instead of the prepositional phrase.

Da-compounds (*Da-Verbindungen*)

04-36 to 04-37 A **da**-compound replaces a prepositional phrase when the object of a prepositional phrase (1) is a pronoun and (2) refers to an inanimate object. **Da**-compounds are formed with the prefix **da-** plus the preposition: **dadurch, davor.** If the preposition begins with a vowel, then **da-** becomes **dar-: daraus, darin.** Compare the following pairs of sentences:

Hast du schon mal **von Sandra** gehört?	Ja, ich habe neulich **von ihr** gehört.
Have you heard from Sandra yet?	*Yes, I've heard from her lately.*
Hast du schon mal **von dieser Marke** gehört?	Ja, ich habe schon mal **davon** gehört.
Have you ever heard of this brand?	*Yes, I've heard of it.*

The **da**-compound expresses the meaning of the preposition plus *it* (singular) or *them* (plural). Note that **da** cannot be combined with the prepositions **ab, außer, bis, gegenüber, ohne, seit,** or with the genitive prepositions.

Answers for 4-41. 1. darüber; 2. Dadurch; 3. Davon; 4. Über ihn; 5. Dafür; 6. Damit

4-41 Linz, die zweitgrößte Stadt Österreichs. Ersetzen Sie die fett gedruckten Satzteile mit der richtigen **da-**Verbindung oder mit der Präposition und dem passenden Pronomen.

1. Die Stadt Linz ist die zweitgrößte Stadt Österreichs. Man kann im Internet leicht Information **über die Stadt Linz** finden.

2. Die Donau fließt durch Österreich. **Durch die Donau** ist Linz im Westen begrenzt.

3. Jedes Jahr gibt es hier Musik- und Kunstfeste. **Von den jährlichen Musik- und Kunstfesten** sind die Linzer begeistert.

4. In Linz lebte und arbeitete der berühmte romantische Komponist Anton Bruckner von 1855 bis 1868. **Über den Komponisten** und seine Musik lernen heutzutage Musikstudenten sehr viel, da er ein innovativer Komponist seiner Zeit war.

5. Die Stadt hat eine lange Geschichte. **Für diese Geschichte** ist die Stadt besonders bekannt.

6. Die Stadt Linz erhielt 2009 eine Auszeichnung. **Mit dieser Auszeichnung** wurde sie eine europäische Kulturhauptstadt.

04-38 to 04-39

Wo-compounds (*Wo-Verbindungen*)

Wo-compounds replace prepositional phrases whose object would otherwise be the interrogative pronoun **was.** The prefix **wo-** is combined with the preposition: **wovon, wofür.** If the preposition begins with a vowel, then **wo-** becomes **wor-: worauf, worüber.** When the interrogative pronoun refers to a person, however, the preposition plus the correct interrogative pronoun is used: **wen** (*acc.*), **wem** (*dat.*). Note that the genitive pronoun **wessen** is generally not used as a prepositional object. Compare the following pairs of sentences:

Von wem hast du schon gehört?
From whom have you heard already?

Ich habe schon mal **von Sandra** gehört.
I've already heard from Sandra.

Wovon hast du nicht gehört?
What have you not heard of?
(*Of what have you not heard?*)

Ich habe **von dieser Marke** noch nicht gehört.
I haven't ever heard of this brand.

The **wo-**compound contains the meaning of the preposition plus *what.* The restrictions on combinations with **wo** are the same as for those with **da.**

4-42 Wie war denn dein Urlaub in Wien? Sie sind gerade von einem Urlaub in Wien zurückgekommen und ein Freund hat viele Fragen. Beantworten Sie die Fragen.

1. Womit bist du nach Wien gefahren?

2. Mit wem hast du dort gesprochen?

3. Wofür ist die Stadt so berühmt?

4. Für wen hast du Postkarten gekauft?

5. Wovon hast du in Wien Fotos gemacht?

04-40 to 04-41

3. Weak nouns (Schwache Nomen)

Weak nouns, also called *masculine n-nouns,* are a special group of masculine nouns that add the ending **-n** (usually when the noun ends in **-e**[8]) or **-en** to every form of the noun except the nominative singular. You already know two such weak nouns: **der Eisbär, der Erbe.** A very small subgroup of weak nouns (e.g., **der Name, der Gedanke**) also adds an **-s** in the genitive singular (**des Namens, des Gedankens**).

	singular	plural	singular	plural	singular	plural
Nominative	der Bär	die Bären	der Erbe	die Erben	der Name	die Namen
Accusative	den Bären	die Bären	den Erben	die Erben	den Namen	die Namen
Dative	dem Bären	den Bären	dem Erben	den Erben	dem Namen	den Namen
Genitive	des Bären	der Bären	des Erben	der Erben	des Namens	der Namen

Weak nouns include most masculine nouns that end in **-e** (e.g., **der Türke, der Name**) and many masculine nouns of foreign origin ending in **-and, -ant, -ast, -ent, -et, -ist, -nom, -oph, -ot,** etc. (e.g., **der Philosoph, der Patient**). Some weak nouns have no particular identifying features at all (e.g., **der Herr, der Mensch, der Student**).

You can determine if a noun is a masculine weak noun by looking it up. In many dictionaries, two suffixes are listed following a noun entry. For example: **Frau, -, -en; Bär, -en, -en.** The first suffix is the genitive singular ending, the second is the noun plural form. When the genitive ending is **-(e)n** or **-(e)ns**, then the noun is weak. Read the preface of your dictionary to determine if it uses this system of notation or an alternative one.

4-43 Mozarts Leben. Setzen die passenden Nomen ein. Benutzen Sie die Endungen für schwache Nomen bzw. die Pluralform, wo nötig.

Fürst	Junge	Mensch	Name	Hoforganist	Komponist

1. Der __Name/Komponist__ Wolfgang Amadeus Mozart ist heute weltweit bekannt.

2. Der Vater machte über die Jahre viele Konzertreisen mit dem ____Jungen____ .

3. Mit 16 Jahren wurde er vom _____Fürsten_____ in Salzburg zum Konzertmeister der Salzburger Hofkapelle ernannt.

4. Später nahm er die vakante Stelle des ____Hoforganisten____ an.

5. In Wien war er Musiklehrer und unabhängiger ____Komponist____ , der auf Auftrag arbeitete.

6. Die Musik von Mozart gefällt auch heute noch vielen ____Menschen____ weltweit.

---

[8]In addition, the weak noun **Herr** adds only an **-n** in its singular forms (**der Herr, den Herrn, dem Herrn, des Herrn**).

Immer weiter!

4-44 Zur Diskussion. Besprechen Sie die Themen.

1. Das Leben in Wien ist von Musik, Kunst und Kultur bestimmt. Sie studieren Musikgeschichte und wollen unbedingt einen Sommer in Wien verbringen. Denken Sie sich Gründe aus, um Ihre Eltern zu überzeugen, dass Sie einfach nach Wien müssen.

2. Machen Sie eine Liste aller Sehenswürdigkeiten in Wien, die Sie kennen. Dann fragen Sie einander, ob Sie bei einem Wienbesuch diese Sehenswürdigkeiten besuchen würden und warum (nicht).

4-45 Zum Schreiben: Wien. Sie nehmen an einem Wettbewerb einer norddeutschen Zeitung teil, bei dem man einen Kurzurlaub nach Wien gewinnen kann. Schreiben Sie einen Aufsatz darüber, warum Wien ein guter Ort für einen Wochenendurlaub ist und was Sie dort machen möchten.

Weitere Themen

Ausstellungshaus der Wiener Secession	Gustav Klimt	Sisi
Burgtheater	Konzerthaus	Spanische Reitschule
Sigmund Freud	Wolfgang Amadeus Mozart	Urania
die Habsburgermonarchie	Leopold-Museum	Wiener Sängerknaben
Hofburg	Neujahrskonzert des Wiener Musikvereins	Wiener Staatsoper
Elfriede Jelinek		Wiener Werkstätte
Friedensreich Hundertwasser	Römermuseum	
	Sachertorte	

Wiener Staatsoper bei Nacht

KAPITEL

5

Nordsee · Ostsee

Deutschland

Bayern

Österreich

Schweiz

Liechtenstein

Warm-up. To set the scene, have students look at the maps of Bavaria and ask them to describe its geographic location. *Wo liegt Bayern innerhalb Deutschlands? An welche anderen Länder und Bundesländer grenzt es?* Have them examine the detail map and describe the geography of Bavaria. Then ask them if they know anything about the region. *Was verbinden Sie mit Bayern? Was wissen Sie schon über dieses Bundesland?* Have them look at the photos and describe what they reveal about the state. You might want to point out that the stereotypical image of Bavaria, including Lederhosen, beer, and sausage, is what many non-Germans have in mind when they think about Germany. Bavaria in fact has more in common culturally—e.g., cuisine, traditions, dialect features—with neighboring Austria than with the rest of Germany.

Bayern

THÜRINGEN · SACHSEN

HESSEN

TSCHECHIEN

BADEN-WÜRTTEMBERG

Aschaffenburg

Main

Bamberg · Bayreuth

Würzburg

Main-Donau-Kanal

Erlangen

Fürth · Nürnberg

Rothenburg

BAYERISCHER WALD

FRÄNKISCHE ALB

Regensburg

Ingolstadt

Donau

Deggendorf

Passau · Donau

BAYERN

Lech · Landshut

Isar

Augsburg

ÖSTERREICH

Wörishofen

★ München

Stephansried

Starnberger See

Bodensee

BAYERISCHE ALPEN

Lindau

SCHWEIZ

Garmisch-Partenkirchen · Inn

50 km

50 mi

Read the *Sprachanalyse: Alternatives to the passive voice* in SAM 05-02, which explains how certain structures in the *Einführung* mimic the effects of the passive voice. As you read the *Lesetexte* in this chapter, do the *Sprachanalyse* activities in the SAM (05-05, 05-08, 05-12, 05-17) to practice identifying passive alternatives and understanding their effects.

05-01 to 05-02

📖 Einführung

Bayern mit seiner Hauptstadt München liegt im Südosten und ist das größte Bundesland Deutschlands. Die Donau teilt das Land in zwei Groß-landschaften: das Mittelgebirge im Norden, zu dem die Fränkische Alb und der Bayerische Wald gehören, und die Alpen mit dem Alpenvor-land im Süden. Nicht nur seine Landschaft trägt zur Anziehungskraft des Landes bei, sondern auch die entspannte Lebensart der Bayern und der ungezwungene° Umgang der Menschen miteinander. Dies lässt sich auf den Einfluss der mediterranen Kultur auf das bayerische Leben zurückführen.

easy, informal

Von 1180 bis 1918 wurde Bayern von der Familie Wittelsbach regiert. In kaum einer anderen Region findet man eine so lange und konstante Geschichte, wie die Bayern sie unter den Wittelsbachern erleben durften. Daraus hat sich die auch heute noch zu findende „bayerische Identität" entwickelt, die sich besonders im Stolz der Bayern auf ihren Freistaat° und dem Pflegen von Traditionen – Trachten, Küche, Dialekte – ausdrückt. Bay-ern, so wie es sich heute geografisch präsentiert, gibt es allerdings erst seit 1805, als man ihm die Gebiete Franken und Schwaben zusprach. So sehen wir heute zwar ein Land mit bayerischer Identität, aber unter den drei Regionen Bayerns – Franken, Schwaben und Altbayern (dem ursprünglichen Bayern) – sind auch deutliche Variationen in Sprache, Kultur und Küche zu erkennen.

Free State

Nach dem Zweiten Weltkrieg verwandelte sich der Agrarstaat Bayern in ein modernes Industrieland. Heute gehört das Land mit seinen 12,5 Millionen Einwohnern zu den wirtschaftsstärksten Regionen Europas. Über 1.200 ausländische Unternehmen haben einen Sitz in Bayern. Zu den wichtigsten Branchen zählen der Maschinen- und Automobilbau (BMW, Audi), die Informationstechnologie (Siemens, Microsoft) und die Medien (ProSiebenSat.1, Bayerischer Rundfunk, Bavaria Film). Mit seinen 155 Verlagen ist München hinter New York die zweitbedeutendste Buch-verlagstadt der Welt. Die Hauptstadt ist ebenfalls zweitgrößtes Bankenzen-trum und zweitgrößter Versicherungsstandort° Deutschlands. Nürnberg, die nächstgrößte Stadt des Bundeslandes ist besonders bedeutend in der Kommunikationstechnik. In Augsburg, der drittgrößten Stadt, findet man die Maschinenfabrik Augsburg-Nürnberg (MAN).

location for insurance companies

Bei allem Wandel in einen modernen Staat hat Bayern sein traditionel-les Gesicht bewahrt. Über 50 Prozent des Landes werden immer noch für Landwirtschaft und gut ein Drittel wird für Forstwirtschaft genutzt. Tradi-tion und Fortschritt°, das ist die Maxime des Freistaats.

progress

Answers for *Fragen zum Text*. **1.** Bayern ist das größte Bundesland. Es hat Mittelgebirge im Norden und Alpen im Süden. **2.** Die Regierungszeit der Wittelsbacher dauerte fast 750 Jahre. Daraus entwickelte sich die bayerische Identität. **3.** in der Sprache, der Kultur und der Küche; **4.** nach dem Zweiten Weltkrieg; **5.** Maschinen- und Automobilbau, Medien, Bankwesen, Versicherung, Kommunikationstechnik.

Fragen zum Text

1. Beschreiben Sie die Geografie Bayerns.
2. Wie lange regierte in Bayern die Familie Wittelsbach? Was war das Resultat der langen Regierungszeit von derselben Familie?
3. Worin sieht man Unterschiede in den drei bayerischen Regionen?
4. Wann beginnt in Bayern die Verwandlung in einen modernen Industriestaat?
5. Welche Bereiche sind wichtig für die Wirtschaft Bayerns?

DIALEKTTIPP: Bairisch

Hören Sie ein Beispiel dieses Dialekts.

Wegen schwankender Grenzen seit dem Mittelalter gibt es in Bayern sehr unterschiedliche Dialektgruppen. Neben dem Bairischen im Südosten herrschen im nordwestlichen Bayern fränkische und im südwestlichen Bayern schwäbische Dialekte vor. Bairische Varianten spricht man auch im größten Teil Österreichs und in Südtirol (in Norditalien), so muss man zwischen *Bairisch* (der Dialektgruppe) und *Bayerisch* (all dem, was mit dem Freistaat verbunden ist) unterscheiden.

Bairisch ist ein oberdeutscher Dialekt, der ein relativ hohes Ansehen genießt und in Umfragen immer wieder der beliebteste Dialekt in Deutschland ist.

Dialekttipp. Ask students what they have discovered about the Bavarian dialect. *Warum ist das bairische Dialektgebiet nicht dem Bundesland Bayern gleichzusetzen? Wo spricht man außer Bayern bairische Varianten?*

Zum Dialekt

Wie sagt man das? Wählen Sie die richtigen Erklärungen der Unterschiede zwischen Bairisch und Hochdeutsch.

Hochdeutsch → Bairisch

_h_ 1.	Kindchen, Hähnchen → Kindl, Hendl	a. kein Genitiv
_f_ 2.	Nase, Straße → Nosn, Strass	b. *p, t, k → b, d, g*
_e_ 3.	müde, können → miad, kenna	c. *l* nach einem Vokal fällt weg
_d_ 4.	eins, zwei, ich heiße → oans, zwoa, i hoas	d. *ei → oa*
_c_ 5.	kalt, Schule, Milch → koit, Schui, Muich	e. Umlaute fehlen
_b_ 6.	putzen, Tisch, Kreuz → butzn, Disch, Greiz	f. kein *-e* am Wortende
_a_ 7.	das Auto des Vaters → am Vadda sei Audo	g. Perfekt statt Präteritums
_g_ 8.	ich dachte, er ging → i hob denkt, er ist ganga	h. Verkleinerungsform *-chen/-lein → -l*

Introduction to *Lesetext 1.*
Ask students what associations they have with the name Richard Wagner. *Kennen Sie den Namen Richard Wagner? Kennen Sie einige seiner Werke?* Then ask them what they learned from the text. *Wofür ist er berühmt? Woher hatte er die Stoffe für seine Opern? Warum ist er umstritten? Was sind die Richard-Wagner-Festspiele? Wer leitet die Festspiele?*

Information for *Lesetext 1.*
At the time of the interview, it was not clear whether the interviewee or her half sister, both great-granddaughters of Richard Wagner, would take over directorship of the festival. Shortly after the interview, it was decided that both women would share the role.

Lese- und Hörtexte

Lesetext 1

„Public Viewing macht die Festspiele nicht kaputt" (Interview)

Richard Wagner (um 1850)

Richard Wagner (1813–1883), dessen Namen Sie schon in *Kapitel 3* gehört haben, war ein bekannter deutscher Komponist, Schriftsteller, Dramatiker, Theaterregisseur und Dirigent. Er benutzte Stoffe aus Heldensagen und der germanischen Mythologie und komponierte dazu Musik, die heute als der Anfang der modernen Musik gilt. Zu seinen berühmten Werken zählen unter anderem *Der fliegende Holländer, Tannhäuser, Lohengrin, Tristan und Isolde,* und die Tetralogie *Der Ring der Nibelungen.* Doch Wagner ist nicht nur ein berühmter, sondern auch ein umstrittener° Künstler wegen seiner antisemitischen Haltung und weil er von Hitler immer wieder als deutscher Komponist par excellence hervorgehoben wurde. Wagner lebte und arbeitete in Dresden, Zürich, Venedig, Paris, Wien und Moskau und zog 1872 nach Bayreuth, wo ein Festspielhaus auf dem Grünen Hügel eigens für seine Werke gebaut wurde.

controversial

Jedes Jahr im August finden hier seit 1876 die Richard-Wagner-Festspiele in Bayreuth statt. Jährlich gibt es nur 30 Vorstellungen und die Karten sind schon auf Jahre im Voraus ausverkauft, sodass Wagnerfreunde oft bis sieben Jahre darauf warten müssen. Seit Beginn hat immer ein Mitglied der Familie Wagner die Leitung der Festspiele übernommen. Katharina Wagner, die Urenkelin von Richard Wagner, sprach in einem Interview mit der Wochenzeitung *Die Zeit* über ihren Plan, die traditionellen Festspiele zum ersten Mal live im Internet zu übertragen.

Vor dem Lesen

1. Hören Sie gern klassische Musik? Welche Komponisten mögen Sie?
2. Haben Sie schon Musik von Wagner gehört? Wenn ja, wie würden Sie sie beschreiben?
3. Würden Sie jahrelang auf eine Karte für ein Konzert warten? Warum (nicht)?

Beim Lesen

Machen Sie beim Lesen eine Liste mit den genannten Operntiteln. Schreiben Sie dann, ob jede dieser Opern im Internet übertragen wird.

	Titel der Oper	Wurde sie im Internet übertragen?
1.	*Die Meistersinger von Nürnberg*	*ja*
2.	*Tristan und Isolde*	*nein*
3.	*Der Ring des Nibelungen*	*nein*
4.	*Parsifal*	*nein*

„Public Viewing macht die Festspiele nicht kaputt"

Wagners Festspielhaus in Bayreuth

Katharina Wagner will Bayreuth in die Zukunft führen. Deshalb lässt sie nun die Opern per Internet in alle Welt übertragen. Im Interview erklärt sie ihr Konzept.

ZEIT ONLINE: Noch vor einem Jahr sagten Sie, Live-Übertragungen aus Bayreuth seien kein Thema. Wie kommt es, dass Sie Ihre Meinung geändert haben?

Katharina Wagner: Aufwendige Live-Schaltungen aus dem Festspielhaus wären im vergangenen Jahr noch gar nicht möglich gewesen. Wir mussten unter anderem sicherstellen°, dass durch die Kameraaufnahmen keine Plätze im Zuschauerraum wegfallen. Inzwischen sind aber alle nötigen technischen Voraussetzungen erfüllt.

ZEIT ONLINE: Sie hatten damals aber auch gesagt, dass Oper live nur im Opernhaus erlebt werden könne. Alles andere wäre eine Illusion.

Wagner: Natürlich ist die Akustik im Festspielhaus durch nichts zu ersetzen. Andererseits können Übertragungen auf Großleinwände und im Internet Menschen neugierig machen, die nicht ohne Weiteres eine Opernkarte kaufen würden. In Bayreuth kommt noch hinzu, dass man erst nach mehreren Jahren Wartezeit an Karten kommt°.

ZEIT ONLINE: Glauben Sie, dass Sie mit den neuen Angeboten ein jüngeres Publikum für Bayreuth gewinnen können?

Wagner: Das hoffe ich zumindest. Wer sich am 27. Juli *Die Meistersinger von Nürnberg* auf der Leinwand oder zu Hause am Computer anschauen möchte, muss sich nicht unbedingt schick anziehen. Ein solches Erlebnis in einem zwanglosen Rahmen° kann also Hemmschwellen° abbauen. Mit Live-Streaming im Internet können wir überdies auch viele Menschen im Ausland erreichen.

ZEIT ONLINE: Wie groß ist das Interesse an Tickets für die Online-Übertragung?

Wagner: Bei uns sind bereits zahlreiche Buchungen aus aller Welt eingegangen, sogar aus dem Südseestaat Tuvalu. Selbst Bayreuther, die die Aufführung eigentlich auf der Großleinwand sehen könnten, haben sich für die Internet-Option entschieden. Ich freue mich, dass unser Konzept so gut angenommen wird.

ZEIT ONLINE: Was halten Sie von Live-Schaltungen in Kinos?

Wagner: Das Internet ist attraktiver, da es leichter zugänglich ist. Die Leute müssen dafür nicht an einen bestimmten Ort kommen.

ZEIT ONLINE: Mit den *Meistersingern* sind Sie 2007 erstmals als Regisseurin auf dem Grünen Hügel aufgetreten. Was macht diese Oper so geeignet für Bayreuths Online-Premiere?

guarantee

an Karten kommt comes by tickets

in ... Rahmen in a relaxed setting / inhibitions

Wagner: Das *Meistersinger*-Team ist extrem stressresistent, da die Produk- ₄₀ tion im vergangenen Jahr unter starker Beobachtung° stand. Das ist eine gute Voraussetzung für eine internationale Live-Übertragung. Die Oper ist überdies leichter verständlich als etwa *Tristan und Isolde*. *Der Ring des Nibelungen* wiederum hätte mehrere Tage in Anspruch genommen°. Da fiel uns die Entscheidung relativ leicht. ₄₅

observation

in Anspruch genommen
lasted

ZEIT ONLINE: Am 25. Juli, dem Eröffnungsabend der diesjährigen Festspiele, steht ein neuer *Parsifal* in der Regie von Stefan Herheim auf dem Programm. Wäre das nicht auch eine Option gewesen?

Wagner: Nein. Ich bin dagegen, Neuinszenierungen sofort live in alle Welt zu übertragen. Das würde zusätzlichen Druck schaffen. Die Spannung vor ₅₀ einer Premiere in Bayreuth ist auch so schon groß genug, die muss man nicht noch weiter erhöhen.

ZEIT ONLINE: In Kürze soll die neue Homepage der Bayreuther Festspiele online gehen. Was können wir dort erwarten?

Wagner: Wir planen einen täglichen Podcast zur Festspielzeit mit interes- ₅₅ santen Einblicken in das Festspielgeschehen. Hinzu kommen Interviews von Regisseuren und Dramaturgen. Trailer von Vorstellungen werden aber nicht gezeigt. Wir wollen den Besuchern der Website vor allem Einblicke in den Probenalltag gewähren. Vorgesehen ist außerdem ein virtueller Rundgang° durch das Festspielhaus. Insgesamt soll die Homepage ₆₀ übersichtlicher° werden und mehr Informationen bieten.

tour
clearer

ZEIT ONLINE: Sie wollen Bayreuth auch den Kindern öffnen. Was genau haben Sie vor?

Wagner: Wir stecken noch mitten in den Vorbereitungen. Fest steht bereits, dass wir Schulwettbewerbe ausschreiben und die Gewinner zu Proben ein- ₆₅ laden werden. Angedacht sind auch spezielle Führungen für Kinder durch das Festspielhaus. Wir wollen künftig gezielt mit Schulen zusammenarbeiten, um Kindern das Werk von Richard Wagner näherzubringen.

ZEIT ONLINE: Ob Sie und Ihre Halbschwester Eva Wagner-Pasquier die Nachfolge Ihres Vaters Wolfgang Wagner antreten° werden, ist noch ₇₀ nicht entschieden. Hoffen Sie, dass Ihre neue Vermarktungsstrategie Ihre Chancen erhöhen kann?

Nachfolge antreten
succeed

Wagner: Für mich sind das zwei voneinander getrennte Bereiche. Im Moment bin ich bei den Festspielen angestellt. Da gehört es zu meinem Job, mich um die Vermarktung zu kümmern. Welche Entscheidung der ₇₅ Stiftungsrat° letztlich treffen wird, kann ich nicht absehen. Theoretisch kann auch jemand anders für die Festspielleitung bestimmt werden.

board of trustees

ZEIT ONLINE: Über die Zukunft der Festspiele wird viel diskutiert. Was sollte sich in Bayreuth noch ändern, was sollte so bleiben wie bisher?

Wagner: Bayreuth funktioniert an sich so, wie es ist, sehr gut. Eine Neuerung wie Public Viewing macht den Charakter der Festspiele nicht kaputt. Anders verhielte es sich, wenn plötzlich auch Beethoven und Stockhausen gespielt würden. Das braucht Bayreuth nicht. Überhaupt ist in der Stiftungsurkunde° genau festgelegt, welches Repertoire aufgeführt werden kann. Von außen kommen häufig Verbesserungsvorschläge von Leuten, die unsere Strukturen gar nicht kennen. Ich käme überhaupt nicht auf die Idee, anderen zu sagen, wie sie ihre Häuser führen sollen, wenn ich diese im Grunde gar nicht kenne.

80

deed of foundation

85

ZEIT ONLINE: Wie steht es um Ihr gemeinsames Opernprojekt mit der Bombast-Rockgruppe Rammstein im Teutoburger Wald?

Siehe **Kulturtipp:**
Rammstein

Wagner: Das ist bisher nur lose angedacht. Es gibt weder einen konkreten Termin noch einen Vertrag. Da steht eine Idee im Raum, die Sache ist also nicht vom Tisch. Mehr dazu würde ich aber erst dann sagen, wenn alles unter Dach und Fach° wäre.

90

unter Dach und Fach
finalized

Das Gespräch führte Corina Kolbe.

Kulturtipps

Rammstein

Die heute weltweit bekannte Rockgruppe Rammstein wurde 1994 in Berlin gegründet. Die Musik der Band reicht von Hardrock über Metal bis zum Industrial Rock und die Texte ihrer oft kontroversen Lieder sind auf Deutsch. Nach den Billboard Charts ist Rammstein die international erfolgreichste Musikgruppe mit deutschen Texten.

 ## Neue Vokabeln

Nomen

die Aufführung, -en
  performance
der Bereich, -e   *area, region*
der Einblick, -e   *insight*
die Entscheidung, -en   *decision*
die Führung, -en   *guided tour*
der Hügel, -   *hill*
die Leinwand, ⁻e   *projection screen*
der Regisseur, -e / die
  Regisseurin, -nen   *director*
die Sendung, -en   *show, broadcast*
der Vertrag, ⁻e   *contract, agreement*

die Voraussetzung,
  -en   *condition, requirement*
die Vorbereitung, -en   *preparation*

Verben

an·stellen   *to hire*
erhöhen   *to increase*
übertragen (überträgt), übertrug,
  übertragen   *to transmit,*
  broadcast
vor·haben   *to plan, intend (to do*
  something)

Adjektive und Adverbien

aufwendig   *extravagant, costly*

bereits   *already*
geeignet (für)   *suitable, fitting*
  (for)
gemeinsam   *common, mutual*
häufig   *frequently*
unbedingt   *at all costs, neces-*
  sarily, absolutely
verständlich   *comprehensible*
zugänglich   *accessible*
zusätzlich   *additionally*

Ausdrücke

in Kürze   *shortly, soon*
Was halten Sie von ... ?   *What*
  do you think of . . . ?

Answers for 5-1. 1. R; 2. F –
Die Opern klingen bei der Übertragung im Internet nicht so gut wie
im Opernhaus. 3. R; 4. F – Eine
Aufführung dauert mehrere Tage.
5. F – Auf der Homepage kann
man keine Trailer sehen. 6. F – Es
hat noch keine Schulwettbewerbe
gegeben. 7. R; 8. F – Die Idee für
ein Opernprojekt mit der Rockgruppe Rammstein ist erst in der
Planung.

5-1 Textarbeit: Richtig oder falsch? Wenn eine Aussage falsch ist, korrigieren und ergänzen Sie sie mit Informationen aus dem Text.

1. Erst in diesem Jahr ist es aus technischen Gründen möglich, live aus
   Bayreuth zu übertragen.

2. Die Opern klingen bei der Übertragung im Internet ebenso gut wie im
   Opernhaus.

3. Frau Wagner glaubt, dass besonders junge Leute die Oper im Internet
   sehen werden.

4. Eine Aufführung von *Der Ring der Nibelungen* dauert vier Stunden.

5. Auf der Homepage der Bayreuther Festspiele kann man Trailer für die
   verschiedenen Opern sehen.

6. Bei einem Schulwettbewerb haben Kinder einen Probenbesuch in Bayreuth
   gewonnen.

7. Frau Wagner meint, dass in Bayreuth auch weiterhin nur die Werke von
   Wagner aufgeführt werden sollen.

8. Die Rockgruppe Rammstein wird nächstes Jahr an der Opernaufführung
   teilnehmen.

5-2 Textarbeit: Was gehört zusammen? Machen Sie aus den Satzteilen
sinnvolle Sätze.

_g_	1. Im vergangenen Jahr	a. leidet nicht leicht unter Stress.
_f_	2. Musikfreunde, die nicht auf eine Opernkarte warten wollen,	b. gibt es einen neuen *Parsifal*.
		c. beträgt oft mehrere Jahre.
_c_	3. Die Wartezeit für Karten	d. ist zur Zeit des Interviews noch nicht entschieden.
_e_	4. Live Konzerte in Kinos	e. findet Frau Wagner nicht so gut wie Übertragungen im Internet.
_a_	5. Das *Meistersinger*-Team	
_b_	6. Am Eröffnungsabend in diesem Jahr	f. zeigen oft Interesse, wenn sie Sendungen im Internet sehen können.
_d_	7. Ob Eva Wagner-Pasquier oder Katharina Wagner in Zukunft die Bayreuther Festspiele leitet,	g. gab es keine live Internet-Übertragung der Festspiele.

5-3 Vokabelarbeit. Ergänzen Sie die Sätze mit Wörtern aus den *Neuen
Vokabeln*. Achten Sie dabei auch auf die Wortform.

1. Da es jedes Jahr nur eine begrenzte Anzahl von ___Aufführungen___ der
   Wagner-Opern gibt, ist es schwierig Tickets zu bekommen.

2. Wagner Liebhaber, die ___unbedingt___ eine Oper live in Bayreuth sehen
   wollen, müssen auf ein Ticket warten.

3. Nicht alle Wagner-Opern sind nach Meinung von Katharina Wagner für
   das Internet ___geeignet___.

4. Es war für Katharina Wagner eine leichte ___Entscheidung___, die *Meistersinger*
   im Internet zu zeigen.

5. Wenn die Sendung über das Internet ein Erfolg ist, werden auch künftig Wagner-Opern im Internet ___übertragen___ .

6. Auf der Homepage der Festspiele bekommt man einen ___Einblick___ in die Vorbereitungen für die Aufführungen.

7. Die Bayreuther Festspiele haben einen ___Vertrag___ mit United Motion für die Übertragung der Oper auf der Leinwand und im Internet.

8. In der Nähe von Bayreuth findet man keine hohen Berge, sondern eher ___Hügel___ .

 5-4 Zur Diskussion. Besprechen Sie die Fragen.

1. Sehen Sie manchmal Fernsehsendungen oder Filme im Internet? Warum sieht man solche Sendungen im Internet anstatt im Fernsehen?

2. Würden Sie für ein Konzert / eine Oper / ein Theaterstück als Internetübertragung bezahlen? Warum (nicht)?

3. Glauben Sie, dass diese Wagner-Übertragung ein Erfolg sein wird? Warum (nicht)?

 5-5 Live oder im Internet? Sie sind ein Fan von Wagners Opern und wollen die Festspiele in Bayreuth erleben. Besprechen Sie, ob Sie eine Oper im Internet sehen werden oder ob Sie noch ein paar Jahre auf Karten warten wollen. Begründen Sie Ihre Entscheidung.

5-6 Bayreuther Festspiele aktuell. Besuchen Sie die Internetseite der Bayreuther Festspiele und beantworten Sie die Fragen.

Note for 5-6. Relevant web addresses for Internet research activities can be found in *MyGermanLab* and on the Companion Website.

1. Wann beginnen die nächsten (bzw. begannen die letzten) Bayreuther Festspiele? Wie lange dauern (bzw. dauerten) sie?

2. Welche Opern werden aufgeführt?

3. Wie kann man Tickets bestellen?

4. Wie viel kostet das billigste Ticket? Das teuerste?

5. Stöbern Sie noch weiter und finden Sie noch drei bemerkenswerte Informationen zu den Festspielen und dem Festspielhaus.

5-7 Ausgehen mit einem Freund. Schreiben Sie eine E-Mail an einen Freund, mit dem Sie am Wochenende ins Theater oder ins Konzert gehen wollen. Sagen Sie ihm, für welches Theaterstück oder Konzert Sie sich interessieren, wann und wo es stattfindet und warum Sie sich auf diese Veranstaltung freuen.

Introduction to *Lesetext 2.* Ask students to explain what a *Geheimtipp* is and if they would participate in such a competition. *Wie ist ein Geheimtipp anders als nur ein Tipp? Würden Sie an so einem Wettbewerb über Ihre Stadt teilnehmen? Was für generelle Informationen kann man in diesen kurzen Texten wohl erwarten?*

Lesetext 2

Vier Geheimtipps von Bayern für Bayern! (Ortsbeschreibungen)

In einem bayerischen Reisemagazin gab es vor kurzem einen Wettbewerb, in dem Menschen aus Bayern in einer kurzen Beschreibung darstellen konnten, warum ihre Stadt einen Besuch wert ist. Als Preis gab es Gutscheine° und

gift certificates

Wochenendreisen zu gewinnen. Viele Bürger aus den verschiedenen Regionen des Bundeslandes nahmen an dem Wettbewerb teil. Hier lesen Sie vier Ortbeschreibungen von Bayern für Bayern.

Vor dem Lesen

Machen Sie eine Liste mit Personen, Dingen, Orten und Speisen, die Ihnen zu dem Wort Bayern einfallen.

Beim Lesen

Ergänzen Sie die Tabelle mit den gegebenen Informationen, wo vorhanden.

Name	Alter	Stadt	Beruf	besondere Tipps
1. Karin	24	Bamberg	Studentin	Blues- und Jazzfest, Kaiserdom, alte Gebäude
2. Miriam Mayer	43	Landshut	—	Landshuter Hochzeit
3. Markus	33	Garmisch-Partenkirchen	Skischulbesitzer	Zugspitze, Gebiet um Garmisch, Sport
4. Herr Krumm	—	Lindau	—	Bodensee, Lindau, Landgasthaus Thalegg

📖 Vier Geheimtipps von Bayern für Bayern!
05-06 to 05-08

Geheimtipp 1: Bamberg (Region Franken)

Kaiserdom in Bamberg

Grüß Gott,* ich heiße Karin, bin 24 Jahre alt und lebe und studiere in Bamberg. Mein Geheimtipp ist der Besuch unseres ganz tollen Blues- und Jazzfestivals, das hier im Sommer stattfindet. Das Beste daran ist, dass es kostenlos ist. Dieses Jahr sind wieder über 40 Bands aus aller Welt zu hören. Diese spielen ihre Musik auf verschiedenen Bühnen in der Innenstadt. Aber auch 5
zu anderen Jahreszeiten ist die Stadt einen Besuch wert, denn sie hat viel Geschichte und Tradition. Es gibt hier circa 2.400 denkmalgeschützte Häuser, die reich verziert[a] sind und oft ganz faszinierende Details in den Fassaden[b] haben. Wie Rom ist Bamberg auf sieben Hügeln erbaut worden und hier befindet sich außer der unveränderten Altstadt auch der Kaiserdom, ein sehenswertes Bauwerk für alle Geschichtsinteressierten. 10

Wer allerdings die Natur lieber hat als unser schönes Städtlein, der kann zu jeder Jahreszeit Wanderungen durch das Weingebiet zwischen Bamberg und Würzburg unternehmen. Auf dem Weg kann man natürlich auch den fruchtigen Frankenwein probieren, für den unsere Region so berühmt ist.

---

[a]*decorated*   [b]*fronts of buildings*

*Siehe **Kulturtipps**: Grüß Gott!

Geheimtipp 2: Landshut (Region Altbayern)

Frauen in mittelalterlichen Kostümen auf der Landshuter Hochzeit

Meine Name ist Miriam Mayer, ich bin 43 Jahre alt und lebe in Landshut. In meiner Stadt gibt es ein ganz besonderes Erlebnis, das sehr zu empfehlen ist: Die Landshuter Hochzeit. Dies ist natürlich keine richtige Hochzeit, sondern es ist ein Fest, bei dem über 2.000 Bürger der Stadt die Hochzeit der polnischen Königstochter Hedwig mit dem Wittels- 5
bacher Herzog Georg von Bayern-Landshut nachspielen. Die Hochzeit fand 1475 statt, aber heute ist es ein großes Spektakel, das leider nur alle vier Jahre stattfindet, und es kommen Besucher aus aller Welt. Mir gefällt dieses Fest so gut, weil es unsere Geschichte feiert und mir die Chance gibt für ein paar Tage eine wunderschöne Tracht* zu tragen, 10
denn ich spiele auch bei diesem Fest mit. Am aufregendsten finde ich dabei immer wieder das Ritterturnier und den Festumzug[a]. Die Wittelsbacher Hochzeit wird oft mit dem Oktoberfest[†] verglichen, das ebenfalls auf einer historischen Hochzeit basiert. Doch meines Erachtens lassen sich die beiden Feste nicht vergleichen, denn unser Landshuter Fest ist viel älter und ich finde es schöner. Zu unserem Fest kommt man nicht nur um Bier zu trinken, bei uns wollen 15
die Bürger zeigen, dass sie stolz sind auf ihre Geschichte und Tradition. Das Fest ist eben mehr für uns als für Touristen.

[a]*jousting competition and festival parade*

*Siehe **Kulturtipps**: Tracht
†Siehe **Kulturtipps**: Oktoberfest

Geheimtipp 3: Garmisch-Partenkirchen (Region Altbayern)

Blick auf die Zugspitze

Ich heiße Markus, bin 33 Jahre alt und lebe in Garmisch-Partenkirchen, wo ich im Winter eine Skischule betreibe und im Sommer Bergfüh- rungen leite. Mein Geheimtipp ist deshalb das Gebiet um Garmisch- Partenkirchen, da man hier im Sommer wie im Winter tolle Landschaften und ein reiches Angebot an Sportarten finden kann. Ganz in der Nähe 5
ist auch die Zugspitze mit ihren 2.962 Metern Höhe, wo man das ganze Jahr über Ski fahren kann. Die Zugspitze ist der höchste Berg Deutsch- lands und man kann mit einer Seilbahn[a] hinauffahren oder natürlich auch hinaufwandern. Ich halte meine Stadt für besonders interessant, denn hier sind viele Angebote für die Gesundheit zu finden. Die meisten Besucher und Einwohner treiben das ganze Jahr lang Sport und 10
lassen sich oft mit Massagen, Yoga und Entspannungstraining verwöhnen[b]. Das entspricht meinem Lebensgefühl[c], und ich glaube, dass ich noch lange in dieser Stadt bleiben werde.

[a]*cable car*   [b]*spoil*   [c]*attitude toward life*

Geheimtipp 4: Lindau (Region Schwaben)

Der Hafen in Lindau

Ich bin Herr Krumm und lebe seit über 30 Jahren in Lindau am Bodensee. Diese Stadt ist mein Geheimtipp für alle, die die Kombination von Bergen, Wasser, Tradition, Kultur und hervorragenden kulinarischen Köstlichkeiten suchen. Der Bodensee ist umgeben von wunderschönen Bergen und so hat man das 5 ganze Jahr einen unvergleichlichen Ausblick. Vom besonderen Interesse ist natürlich auch ein Besuch der Insel Lindau. Auf der Insel sind wunderschöne alte Gebäude und eine Fußgängerzone zu entdecken und immer wieder gibt es einen herrlichen Blick auf den See und die Berge. Kulinarisch gefällt es mir hier so gut, da es hier neben den bayerischen 10 auch Spezialitäten aus dem nahen Italien, Österreich und der Schweiz gibt. Mein Lieblingsrestaurant ist der Landgasthof Thalegg, da die Atmosphäre hier so gemütlich ist und man bei schönem Wetter auch draußen essen kann. Hier gibt es meiner Meinung nach das beste Schnitzel* in ganz Bayern.

*Siehe **Kulturtipps**: Schnitzel

Kulturtipps

Grüß Gott!

Dies ist die typische Begrüßungsform in Bayern und Österreich und hört sich in der bairischen Aussprache eher an wie „Griaß God!" Der Gruß kann wörtlich übersetzt werden als „Gruß an Gott", was auf die Religiosität der Bayern, die vorwiegend katholisch sind, zurückgeht. Doch es ist historisch nicht klar, ob es sich hier am Anfang um das Wort „Gott" oder die bairische Aussprache von „gut" handelt.

Tracht

Die Tracht ist die traditionelle Kleidung der ländlichen Bevölkerung. Jede Region hat ihre eigene in Form, Farbe und Tragweise einheitliche Tracht, wobei die bekanntesten Trachten der Bayern Lederhosen und Dirndl sind. An den meisten Orten wird traditionelle Kleidung jedoch nur noch zu besonderen Anlässen wie Hochzeiten und Volksfesten getragen. Es gibt in Deutschland ungefähr 2.000 Trachtenvereine mit rund 2 Millionen Mitgliedern, die es sich zum Ziel setzen, ihre jeweiligen heimischen Trachtentraditionen zu pflegen.

Lederhosen und Dirndl bei einer Parade zum Oktoberfest in München

Oktoberfest

Das Oktoberfest ist es eines der größten und bekanntesten Volksfeste der Welt. Es wurde im Jahre 1810 auf der Theresienwiese (*Therese's Green*) – daher auch „die Wiesn" genannt – zum ersten Mal gefeiert. Hier findet es noch heute statt. Der Anlass war die Heirat der Prinzessin Therese mit dem bayerischen Kronprinzen Ludwig.

Schnitzel

Bei einem Schnitzel wird ein dünnes Stück Schweinefleisch paniert (*breaded*) und dann knusprig gebraten. Beliebte Variationen sind das Jägerschitzel, bei dem Pilze (*mushrooms*) dazu kommen, und das Zigeunerschnitzel, das eine scharfe (*spicy*) Soße mit Paprika hat. Besonders bekannt ist das sogenannte Wiener Schnitzel, das statt Schweinefleisch aus Kalbfleisch besteht und das im 19. Jahrhundert in Österreich viel zubereitet und bald in allen deutschsprachigen Ländern beliebt wurde.

Wiener Schnitzel mit Pommes

 Neue Vokabeln

Nomen

der Ausblick, -e *view*
der Bürger, -/die Bürgerin, -nen *citizen*
die Fußgängerzone, -n *pedestrian area*
der Herzog, ̈-e/die Herzogin, -nen *duke/duchess*
die Hochzeit, -en *wedding*
die Köstlichkeit, -en *delicacy*

Verben

halten (hält), hielt, gehalten *to hold, stop*
halten für *to deem, regard as*
vergleichen, verglich, verglichen *to compare*

Adjektive und Adverbien

aufregend *exciting*
draußen *outside*

gemütlich *comfortable, cozy*
kostenlos *(for) free*
unverändert *unchanged*
umgeben *surrounded*

Ausdrücke

meiner Meinung nach *in my opinion*

5-8 **Textarbeit: Fragen zum Inhalt.** Beantworten Sie die Fragen in Bezug auf den Text.

1. Was macht Karin in Bamberg?
2. Inwiefern ist Bamberg Rom ähnlich?
3. Wann fand die richtige Landshuter Hochzeit statt?
4. Wer spielt bei der Hochzeit heute die verschiedenen Rollen?
5. Wie kann man den Gipfel der Zugspitze erreichen?
6. Warum entspricht das Leben in Garmisch-Partenkirchen dem Lebensgefühl von Markus?
7. Was macht die Landschaft am Bodensee so besonders?
8. Warum empfiehlt Herr Krumm den Landgasthof Thalegg?

Answers for 5-8. **1.** Sie lebt und studiert dort. **2.** Es ist auf sieben Hügeln erbaut. **3.** Sie fand 1475 statt. **4.** Die Bürger der Stadt Landshut spielen bei dem Fest mit. **5.** Mit der Seilbahn oder zu Fuß. **6.** Es gibt viel Sport und Entspannungsangebote/viele Angebote für ein gesundes Leben. **7.** Die Kombination von Bergen und Seen. **8.** Hier kann man draußen sitzen und es gibt das beste Schnitzel in ganz Bayern.

5-9 Textarbeit: Wo macht man was? Ergänzen Sie die Sätze mit den Namen von Städten, Regionen oder Veranstaltungen aus dem Lesetext. Es gibt manchmal mehr als eine Möglichkeit.

1. Wenn man viele Menschen in Trachten sehen will, geht man zu
   der Landshuter Hochzeit / dem Oktoberfest .

2. Wenn man hohe Berge mag, besucht man
   Garmisch-Partenkirchen / die Alpen / die Zugspitze .

3. Leute, die sich für Geschichte interessieren, besuchen gern
   Bamberg / den Kaiserdom / die Landshuter Hochzeit / Lindau .

4. Wenn man immer wieder gern auf Berge und Seen schaut, fährt man am besten nach _Lindau_ .

5. Wenn man sich mit Yoga entspannen will, fährt man nach
   Garmisch-Partenkirchen .

6. Wer im Sommer gern Musik an der frischen Luft hört, geht zum
   Blues- und Jazzfestival in Bamberg .

7. Wer den berühmten Frankenwein probieren möchte, sollte
   Franken / das Weingebiet zwischen Bamberg und Würzburg besuchen.

5-10 Vokabelarbeit. Ergänzen Sie die Sätze mit Wörtern aus den *Neuen Vokabeln*. Achten Sie dabei auch auf die Wortform.

1. Schnitzel, Knödel und Weißbier sind nur ein paar der bayerischen
   Köstlichkeiten , die in Biergärten und Restaurants in Bayern beliebt sind.

2. Den Festumzug bei der Landshuter Hochzeit kann man _kostenlos_ von der Straße aus sehen, reservierte Plätze kosten aber viel Geld.

3. Bei der Landshuter Hochzeit spielen die _Bürger_ der Stadt die verschiedenen Rollen.

4. Im Süden von Bayern sind die kleinen Dörfer oft von hohen Bergen
   umgeben .

5. Eine Fahrt auf die Zugspitze mit der Seilbahn ist ein _aufregendes_ Erlebnis, da man hoch in der Luft durch die Berge gleitet.

6. Von der Zugspitze hat man bei klarem Wetter einen _Ausblick_ über viele Kilometer.

7. Zu einem _gemütlichen_ Fest gehören gute Freunde, gutes Essen und gute Stimmung.

5-11 Was schlägst du vor? Sprechen Sie darüber, was man in Ihrer Universitätsstadt alles in der Freizeit machen kann. Was ist Ihr persönlicher Geheimtipp? Fragen Sie dann ein anderes Paar, was sie für Geheimtipps haben.

5-12 Zur Diskussion. Besprechen Sie die Fragen.

1. Besuchen Sie gern alte Gebäude? Warum sind alte Gebäude beliebte Attraktionen?

2. Würden Sie als Schauspieler an der Landshuter Hochzeit teilnehmen? Warum (nicht)?

3. Gibt es Feste oder Veranstaltungen, die in Ihrem Land vergangene Zeiten feiern? Haben Sie schon einmal an so etwas teilgenommen? Wenn ja, hat es Ihnen gefallen? Können Sie beschreiben, was Sie hier gesehen oder gemacht haben?

4. Haben Sie schon auf den Rat eines Freundes etwas gemacht, was dann nicht so gut war? Erzählen Sie davon.

5-13 Ich wähle Geheimtipp X. Sie sind in dem Komitee, das den Gewinner des Wettbewerbs wählen soll. Welchen der vier Geheimtipps halten Sie für den besten? Warum? Schreiben Sie eine kurze Notiz für die anderen Mitglieder des Komitees, um Ihre Wahl zu erklären.

5-14 Mein Geheimtipp. Schreiben Sie einen Geheimtipp für einen Wettbewerb in einem deutschen Reisemagazin. Wählen Sie dafür einen Ort oder ein Ereignis aus Ihrer Heimat. Folgen Sie dabei den Beispielen der vier Bayern.

Alternative for 5-14. This could also be an online research activity. Have students write their *Geheimtipp* on a different town or region in Bavaria.

Hörtext 1

Praktikum bei BMW (Interview)

Neben Finanzdienstleistungen, Tourismus und Informations- und Elektrotechnik ist der Fahrzeug- und Maschinenbau eine der wichtigsten Wirtschaftsbranchen in Bayern. Aus diesem Bundesland kommen 25 Prozent aller in Deutschland produzierten Automobile. Zu den Firmen dieser Industrie mit Sitz in Bayern zählen BMW, Audi, MAN und Continental Automotive.

Hauptsitz und Museum von BMW in München

BMW (Bayerische Motoren Werke AG) ist weltweit der drittgrößte Autohersteller und heute einer der großen Arbeitgeber Münchens. Das Unternehmen, das heute seinen Hauptsitz und auch ein Museum in München hat, zählt in Deutschland fast 80.000 und weltweit über 100.000 Mitarbeiter. Es stellt seit 1913 Motoren, seit 1923 Motorräder und seit 1929 Autos her. Zu der BMW Group gehören auch die Marken MINI und Rolls-Royce. Die Autos von BMW sind weltweit für ihre hohe Qualität und ihr innovatives Design bekannt.

In den verschiedenen Autowerken BMW gibt es jedes Jahr viele Angebote für Praktika für Schüler und Studenten. Im folgenden Interview hören Sie von der Studentin Nikole Cappato über ihr Praktikum bei der BMW Group.

Introduction to *Hörtext 1.* Ask students about any internship plans they might have. *Müssen Sie für Ihr Studium ein Praktikum machen? Wollen Sie ein Praktikum machen? Warum (nicht)?* Then ask them what they already know about BMW. *Was haben Sie schon über die deutsche Automarke BMW gehört? Wofür ist sie bekannt?*

Vor dem Hören

Haben Sie schon mal ein Praktikum gemacht? Wenn ja, wo und was waren Ihre Aufgaben? Warum macht man ein Praktikum?

Beim Hören

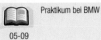

Praktikum bei BMW
05-09

Während des Interviews hören Sie die folgenden Vokabeln.

Abteilung *branch*	betreut *is in charge of*
zukunftsträchtig(e) *with a promising future*	Ansprechpartner *contact person*
Maßnahmen *measures*	Ausbeutung *exploitation*
arbeite vor *do preliminary work*	sich zu trauen *to dare*
Werbeagentur *advertising agency*	Werkstudententätigkeiten *student trainee work*
Vortragsreihe *lecture series*	
Bewerbungsgespräch *job interview*	herausragend(e) *outstanding*
eingebunden *integrated*	sich zu beweisen *to prove oneself*

Hören Sie sich das Interview an. Markieren Sie, was Frau Cappato bei ihrem Praktikum tut.

kocht Kaffee	betreut ein Projekt
unterstützt Kollegen	übersetzt Projekte ins Englische
schreibt Briefe	teilt Post aus
macht Recherchen	macht Kopien
beantwortet Telefonanfragen	reist nach Italien

5-15 Textarbeit: Richtig oder falsch? Wenn eine Aussage falsch ist, korrigieren und ergänzen Sie sie mit Informationen aus dem Hörtext.

Answers for 5-15. **1.** R; **2.** R; **3.** F – Sie ist in der Abteilung Marketing (Innovationen). **4.** F – Es ist ein sechsmonatiges Praktikum. **5.** R; **6.** R; **7.** R

Answers for 5-16. **1.** Sie nimmt 5.000 auf. **2.** Es ist mit der Firma MINI. **3.** Sie studiert an der Fachhochschule München. **4.** Sie haben sie gut und herzlich aufgenommen. **5.** Sie sieht es als gute Erfahrung. **6.** Sie verdient 880 Euro im Monat. **7.** sich trauen, sich qualifizieren, sich differenzieren, Praktika machen (Werkstudent sein), besondere Kurse belegen, Sprachen kennen, herausragende Qualifikationen erwerben

1. Bei einem Praktikum sieht man, ob man in eine bestimmte Branche passt.
2. Frau Cappato macht ihr Praktikum in München.
3. Sie ist in der Abteilung Forschung.
4. Das Praktikum von Frau Cappato dauert einen Monat.
5. Es ist ihr erstes Praktikum bei BMW.
6. Es war relativ einfach für Frau Cappato, dieses Praktikum zu bekommen.
7. Frau Cappato kann sich mit Fragen und Problemen an ihren Ansprechpartner wenden.

5-16 Textarbeit: Fragen zum Inhalt. Beantworten Sie die Fragen in Bezug auf das Gespräch.

1. Wie viele Praktikanten nimmt die BMW Group jedes Jahr auf?
2. Mit welcher anderen Autofirma ist das Projekt, an dem Frau Cappato arbeitet?
3. Wo studiert Frau Cappato?
4. Wie haben die Kollegen Frau Cappato aufgenommen?

5. Sieht Frau Cappato das Praktikum als eine gute Erfahrung oder als Ausbeutung?

6. Wie viel verdient Frau Cappato als Praktikantin pro Monat?

7. Nennen Sie mindestens zwei Dinge, die Frau Cappato anderen Interessenten rät.

5-17 Zur Diskussion. Besprechen Sie die Fragen.

1. Wie sieht Ihrer Meinung nach ein gutes Praktikum aus? Wie sieht ein nicht erfolgreiches Praktikum aus?

2. Sollten alle Studenten ein Praktikum machen, bevor sie sich für einen Beruf entscheiden? Warum (nicht)? Wann und für wie lange sollte man am besten ein Praktikum machen? Würden Sie auch bei einem unbezahlten Praktikum mitmachen?

3. Warum bietet eine große Firma wie BMW jedes Jahr so viele Praktika?

5-18 Ein Praktikum in München. Sie suchen nach einem Praktikum in München. Finden Sie ein Praktikum, das Sie interessiert, und beantworten Sie die Fragen.

Note for 5-18. Relevant web addresses for Internet research activities can be found in *MyGermanLab* and on the Companion Website.

1. In welcher Branche oder welchem Bereich ist das Praktikum?

2. Welches Unternehmen bietet das Praktikum an?

3. Wann beginnt das Praktikum und wie lang dauert es?

4. Welche Qualifikationen braucht man dazu?

5. Welche Aufgaben hat ein/e Praktikant/in in dieser Stelle?

5-19 Meine Bewerbung als Praktikant/in. Sie haben das ideale Praktikum gefunden. Jetzt müssen Sie sich bewerben. Füllen Sie das Bewerbungsformular aus.

Bewerbungsformular

Vor- und Nachname: _____ Geburtsdatum: _____

Geburtsort: _____ Postanschrift: _____

Studienfach und Semester: _____

Gewünschte Dauer des Praktikums: _____

Beantworten Sie bitte die folgenden Fragen, damit wir Ihnen einen passenden Praktikumsplatz finden können:

Was wollen Sie während Ihres Praktikums lernen? _____

Warum wollen Sie in unserer Firma ein Praktikum machen? _____

Introduction to *Lesetext 3*.
Ask students if they are familiar
with the concept of vacationing
on a farm and what they think this
might be like. *Können Sie sich
vorstellen, auf einem Bauernhof
Ferien zu machen? Was macht
man bei so einem Urlaub? Warum,
glauben Sie, ist diese Urlaubsform
in Deutschland so populär?*

Lesetext 3

Urlaub auf dem Bauernhof (Blog)

Urlaub auf dem Bauernhof ist eine beliebte Urlaubsform für viele Deutsche und wird immer beliebter. In Deutschland gibt es etwa 5.000 Höfe, auf denen man diese Art von Urlaub machen kann. Viele Höfe bieten Fitness, Wellness oder spezielle Kurse, etwa im Kochen, an. Für viele liegt der große Unterschied einfach darin, dass man nicht in einem anonymen Hotel übernachtet, sondern bei Privatvermietern auf dem Land. Besonders Familien mit Kindern finden diese Urlaubsform attraktiv, da man hier über das Landleben, Tierhaltung und Natur durch Erfahrungen lernen kann.

Der 16-jährige Gymnasiast Felix zu Hause in Halle

Der folgende Ferienblog wurde von dem Teenager Felix, der mit seiner Familie in Halle lebt, erstellt, als er mit seinen Eltern und seiner Schwester Clara zum ersten Mal Ferien auf einem Bauernhof in Bayern machte.

Vor dem Lesen

Welche Assoziationen haben Sie mit den folgenden Begriffen: Bauernhof? Tiere? Arbeit? Landschaft?

Beim Lesen

Die folgenden Sätze beschreiben jeweils einen der Ferientage. Bringen Sie beim Lesen die Sätze in die richtige Reihenfolge.

10. Juli	11. Juli	12. Juli	13. Juli	14. Juli	15. Juli

13. Juli	Arbeit auf dem Hof macht müde und hungrig.
11. Juli	Wir erkunden den Hof und Deggendorf.
15. Juli	Auch der schönste Urlaub muss einmal zu Ende gehen.
14. Juli	München hat für alle Besucher etwas zu bieten.
12. Juli	Museen können gerade bei Regenwetter unterhaltsam sein.
10. Juli	Der Hof ist überraschend modern.

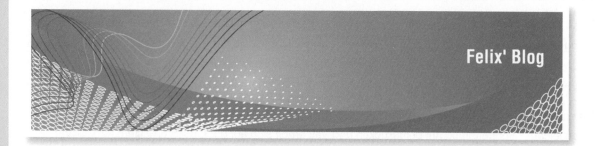

Urlaub auf dem Bauernhof

05-10 to
05-12

10. Juli

Heute ist schon unser 3. Ferientag und endlich sind wir nach Bayern gefahren, wo wir dieses Jahr unseren Urlaub verbringen. Die Familie hatte gemeinsam beschlossen, dass wir Ferien auf einem Bauernhof machen wollen. Das ist mal was ganz anderes für uns. Sonst sind wir immer an die Ostsee, nach Grömitz, gefahren. Aber dieses Jahr wollen wir mal Berge und Bayern erkunden. Noch bin ich ein bisschen skeptisch, wie der Urlaub wohl wird, denn ich weiß nicht, was man auf dem Hof machen kann, um Spaß zu haben. 5

Wir sind heute gegen Mittag angekommen. Der Hof und unsere Ferienwohnung sind anders, als ich erwartet habe! Die Wohnung hat drei Schlafzimmer, eine Küche, ein Bad und einen Balkon. Alles ist total modern und auch ein neuer Fernseher ist da. Besonders froh bin ich, dass es hier sogar einen Pool gibt. Das war kaum zu erwarten! Ansonsten habe ich bis jetzt ein paar kleine Pferde, viele bunte Hühner, etliche graue Katzen und zwei Hunde gesehen. Morgen wird uns Herr Hackel, der Hofbesitzer, den 10 ganzen Hof zeigen.

Das ist für unseren ersten Tag hier erstmal alles. Mutti hat mich schon zweimal zum Essen gerufen. Wir haben im Dorf frische Semmeln* gekauft und die werden wir uns jetzt schmecken lassen.

---

11. Juli

Unser erster ganzer Tag begann hier tatsächlich mit Hahnenge-schrei! Ganz früh und ganz laut! Aber Mutti meinte, man soll ruhig öfter mal früh aufstehen, denn dann kann man den ganzen Tag genießen. Heute haben wir zuerst mit Herrn Hackel den Hof erkun-det. Das Bauernhaus ist ein ganz typisches, genau das, was einem in den Sinn kommt, wenn man an einen bayerischen Bauernhof denkt. 15

20

Der Hof ist schon recht groß, aber er ist lange nicht der größte im Dorf. Herr Hackel hat viele Klein-tiere und nur 40 Milchkühe. Wir dürfen auch jederzeit bei der Hofarbeit helfen. Clara fand das prima und durfte dann auch gleich die jungen Hühner füttern.

---

*Siehe **Kulturtipps**: Semmeln

weiter >>>

Nach dem Mittagessen sind wir dann nach Deggendorf gefahren. Und es ist nicht zu glauben, aber Deggendorf hat ein ganz tolles, großes Freibad und Hallenbad. Es hat eine Wasserrutsche, riesige ₂₅ Schwimmbecken, eine Eisdiele und ein Erlebnisbecken mit Brunnen und Wasserfall. Wenn das mit diesen tollen Überraschungen so weiter geht, dann werde ich noch ein totaler Bayernfan!

Da es heute so schön sonnig war, haben wir den ganzen Nachmittag dort verbracht. Mutti hat jetzt einen leichten Sonnenbrand auf dem Rücken und Vati erholt sich auf der Couch und sieht fern. Clara hat das auch sehr viel Spaß gemacht und sie war so erschöpft, dass sie schon auf der Heimfahrt im ₃₀ Auto eingeschlafen ist. Ich werde auch gleich ins Bett gehen, denn Landluft macht ja doch recht müde.

12. Juli

Es ist erst unser zweiter Tag hier und schon muss es regnen. Beim Frühstück haben wir entschieden, dass man bei so einem Wetter ins Museum gehen muss. So sind wir wieder nach Deggendorf gefahren, wo es doch tatsächlich drei Museen gibt, und das in einer Stadt mit nur 32.000 Einwohnern!

Unsere Wahl ist dann auf das Handwerksmuseum gefallen. Es war richtig interessant. Wir haben ₃₅ viele alte Werkzeuge gesehen und Vati hat uns immer erst raten lassen, was man damit machen kann, bevor wir uns die Beschreibungen angesehen haben. Mir hat besonders die Ausstellung zum modernen Kunsthandwerk mit den coolen Plastiken[a] am besten gefallen. Clara fand alles, was mit Weben und Stricken[b] zu tun hatte, am interessantesten und Vati war besonders von den großen, gefährlich aussehenden Mähmaschinen[c] fasziniert. ₄₀

Nach dem Museumsbesuch haben wir in Deggendorf im Gasthaus *Blaue Donau* gegessen. Das Essen war so lecker!! Ich habe Reindl gegessen, das ist Schweinebraten in Biersoße und dazu Semmelknödel* und Sauerkraut, Mutti und Vati haben jeder einen Grillteller gegessen, auf dem knackige Wurst und ein bunter Salat waren, und Clara hatte das Schweizer Pfandl, ein Nudelgericht mit Schinken und Käse. Danach waren wir so satt, dass wir nur noch in unsere Ferienwohnung ₄₅ wollten. Nach einem kurzen Mittagsschlaf haben wir dann einen langen Spaziergang über Weiden und Felder gemacht. Inzwischen hat auch der Regen aufgehört und Herr Hackel meint, dass das Wetter morgen wieder sonnig und warm wird.

13. Juli

Heute war ein anstrengender Tag und das, obwohl wir Ferien haben! Clara und ich haben fast den ganzen Tag bei der Hofarbeit geholfen. Erst haben wir die jungen Hühner gefüttert, dann die ₅₀ kleinen Hasen und als letztes die Kühe. Als nächstes haben wir die Ställe sauber gemacht. Das hat nicht gut gerochen und Clara hat ständig gesagt „Mein Gott, wie das stinkt!" Als Belohnung für die viele Arbeit am Morgen hat Bauer Hackel uns zum Mittagessen mit seiner Familie eingeladen. Das war eine echt bayerische Erfahrung. Der bairische Dialekt lässt sich nicht leicht verstehen und

[a]*sculptures*   [b]*weaving and knitting*   [c]*mowers*

*Siehe **Kulturtipps**: Semmelknödel

weiter >>>

vieles klingt schon lustig. Aber wir haben uns alle gut verstanden. Das Essen war auch prima. Es 55
gab Wurst und Semmelknödel und frisches Gemüse aus dem Garten. Zum Nachtisch hat Frau
Hackel Pudding mit wilden Erdbeeren gemacht. So etwas Leckeres habe ich noch nie gegessen.

Am Nachmittag haben wir dann noch ein wenig mit dem Heuwenden[d] geholfen, aber wir waren doch
recht müde und sind dann so gegen 15.00 Uhr an den Pool im Garten gegangen. Hier haben wir dann
Vati und Mutti gefunden, die faul in der Sonne gelegen haben. Wir haben dann geschwommen und uns 60
von der Arbeit erholt. Ich glaube, ich weiß jetzt, dass ich nicht Bauer werden möchte. Jeden Tag früh
aufstehen, auch am Wochenende, immer schwere körperliche Arbeit – ich glaube, dazu bin ich zu faul.

Morgen wollen wir nach München fahren. Darauf freuen wir uns schon. Ich habe die Stadt noch nie
besucht, aber Mutti und Vati waren schon öfter dort und kennen sich gut aus.

14. Juli

München! Eine tolle Stadt. Gleich morgens sind wir los gefahren. Von Deggendorf bis in die Stadt 65
sind es nur 140 km, aber da es viel Verkehr gab, hat es doch zwei Stunden gedauert.

Wir sind dann als erstes in das Karl-Valentin-Museum gegangen. Das war Muttis Wunsch. Wir
durften uns jeder eine Attraktion aussuchen, damit wir alle Spaß haben. Also, der Karl Valentin war
ein Komiker, der von 1882 bis 1948 hauptsächlich in München lebte und als Komiker, Schauspieler
und Sänger bekannt war. Das Museum hatte viele lustige Bilder und Auszüge aus seinen Filmen. 70

Dann war Claras Wunsch an der Reihe. Sie wollte das Neue Rathaus
sehen, dass das Glockenspiel mit den Rittern und Tänzern hat.
Anschließend sind wir dann mit dem Fahrstuhl auf den Rathausturm
gefahren und haben die Stadt von oben sehen können. Heute hatten
wir auch Glück, dass das Wetter ganz klar war und wir konnten sogar
die Alpen sehen. Dann sind wir noch über den Viktualienmarkt gebummelt, wo man die appetitlichsten Lebensmittel sehen und kaufen kann.
Vati hätte am liebsten an jedem Stand halt gemacht und probiert –
besonders an den Käseständen blieb er immer wieder stehen.

Dann war Vati dran und man soll es doch kaum glauben, aber er wollte unbedingt ins Hofbräuhaus.* 80
Mutti fand das doof, denn sie sagt, da gehen nur echte Touristen hin, aber Vati sagte, er ist ja auch
ein Tourist. Mir war das Ganze nur peinlich. Aber nach einiger Diskussion sind wir tatsächlich zum
Mittagessen ins berühmte Hofbräuhaus gegangen. Es ist fast nicht zu fassen, aber es war dann
doch richtig lustig. Es gab bayerische Volksmusik und Touristen aus Japan und den USA kannten
die Texte zu den Liedern und haben laut mitgesungen. Das Essen war auch ganz gut und ich habe 85
wieder Knödel gegessen, aber diesmal mit Schnitzel. Vati hat sich köstlich amüsiert und auch Clara,
Mutti und ich mussten zugeben, dass es ganz lustig war. Dann war endlich ich dran – na ja, ihr

[d]*turning of the hay*

*Siehe **Kulturtipps**: Hofbräuhaus

weiter >>>

wisst ja, wo ich hin wollte: In den Olympiapark. Wir sind mit der U-Bahn hingefahren und es war dann einfach toll. Hier haben die Olympischen Spiele 1972 stattgefunden und seitdem viele 90 Fußballspiele und irgendwann werde ich es auch schaffen, hier eins zu sehen. Vielleicht kann ich hier auch irgendwann einmal ein Konzert besuchen. Wir sind auch auf den Olympiaturm gefahren, von dort aus ist nicht nur der ganze Olympiapark, sondern auch die Stadt zu sehen. Es war echt super! 95

15. Juli

Jetzt sind wir schon wieder zu Hause.

Heute gegen Mittag sind wir aus Deggendorf abgefahren. Es war ein kurzer aber doch echt schöner Urlaub. Mutti und Vati haben uns versprochen, dass wir nächstes Jahr wieder nach Deggendorf auf den Hof der Familie Hackel fahren, dann aber für mindestens zwei Wochen, denn es gibt dort noch so viel zu erkunden. Es ist kaum glauben, dass ich seit unserer Abfahrt nicht ferngesehen habe und nur am Computer war, um meinen Blog zu schreiben! 100

Kulturtipps

■ Semmeln

Variationen in den Dialekten Bayerns finden sich nicht nur in der Aussprache, sondern auch im Lexikon in den verschiedenen Regionen. So ist das hochdeutsche „Brötchen" in Altbayern als „Semmel" oder „Semme" bekannt, in Franken als „Wecke" und in Schwaben oft als „Weck" zu finden.

■ Semmelknödel

Diese Spezialität ist vor allem in Süddeutschland, Österreich und im tschechischen Böhmen zu finden. Semmelknödel werden aus alten Brötchen, Milch, Zwiebeln, Eiern und Petersilie (*parsley*) gemacht. Sie sind eine beliebte Beilage zu allen Fleischgerichten.

Bayerischer Schweinebraten mit Semmelknödel und Blaukraut

■ Hofbräuhaus

Das Hofbräuhaus war ursprünglich eine Brauerei in München, die seit dem 16. Jahrhundert Bier für die Familie Wittelsbach herstellte. Heute ist das ehemalige Brauhaus ein weltbekanntes Restaurant, in dem man bei bayerischen Spezialitäten von bayerischer Musik unterhalten wird. Obwohl es ein beliebtes Touristenziel ist, sind von den 30.000 täglichen Besuchern die Hälfte Stammgäste. Es gibt sogar eine Nachbildung des Hofbräuhauses in Las Vegas.

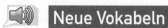

Neue Vokabeln

Nomen

der Bauer, -n, -n/die Bäuerin,
  -nen *farmer*
der Bauernhof, ¨-e *farm*
das Feld, -er *field*
das Pferd, -e *horse*
der Ritter, - *knight*
der Schauspieler, -/die Schauspielerin, - nen *actor/actress*
der Verkehr *traffic*
die Weide, -n *meadow*
das Werkzeug, -e *tool*

Verben

sich amüsieren *to have fun*
bummeln, ist gebummelt
  to stroll

sich erholen *to recuperate*
erkunden *to explore*
füttern *to feed (an animal)*
raten (rät), riet, geraten *to guess*
riechen, roch, gerochen *to smell*
unterhalten (unterhält), unterhielt, unterhalten *to entertain,*
  amuse
verbringen, verbrachte, verbracht *to spend (time)*

Adjektive und Adverbien

anstrengend *exhausting*
doof (*colloq.*) *dumb, stupid*
erschöpft *exhausted*
etliche *several*
faul *lazy*

lustig *funny, amusing*
peinlich *embarrassing*

Ausdrücke

an der Reihe sein *to have one's*
  turn
dran sein *to have a turn*
Ich bin dran. *It's my turn.*
na ja *oh well*

5-20 Textarbeit: Was macht die Familie? Schreiben Sie auf, was für Aktivitäten die Familie macht.

5-21 Textarbeit: Fragen zum Inhalt. Beantworten Sie die Fragen in Bezug auf den Text.

1. Wo hat die Familie sonst immer Urlaub gemacht?
2. Was überrascht Felix bei der Ankunft auf dem Hof?
3. Was macht die Familie bei Regen?
4. Was bekommen Clara und Felix als Belohnung für ihre Arbeit auf dem Hof?
5. Warum ist die Sprache der Familie Hackel für Felix und Clara schwer zu verstehen?
6. Was isst die Familie Hackel zu Mittag?
7. Warum möchte Felix von Beruf nicht Bauer werden?
8. Welche Attraktionen besucht die Familie in München?
9. Hat Felix der Urlaub auf dem Bauernhof gefallen? Glauben Sie der Urlaub hat auch der Mutter, dem Vater und Clara gefallen? Begründen Sie Ihre Antwort.

Possible Answers for 5-20.
den Bauernhof erkunden, Hühner füttern, das Freibad besuchen, das Museum besuchen, einen Spaziergang machen, bei der Hofarbeit helfen, Ställe sauber machen, Heu wenden, Hasen und Kühe füttern, am Pool liegen, München besichtigen

Additional comprehension questions for 5-21. *Welche Überraschung erwartet Felix am zweiten Tag in Deggendorf? Wie groß ist Deggendorf? Was hat den Familienmitgliedern im Museum besonders gefallen? Was haben sie im Gasthaus gegessen? Was haben sie an den verschiedenen Orten in München gesehen und erlebt?*

Answers for 5-21. 1. In Grömitz an der Ostsee. **2.** Die Wohnung ist modern, es gibt sogar Fernsehen und einen Pool. **3.** Sie gehen ins Handwerkmusem, essen danach im Gasthaus und machen dann einen kurzen Mittagsschlaf. **4.** Als Belohnung bekommen sie eine Einladung zum Mittagessen mit der Familie Hackel. **5.** Sie sprechen bairischen Dialekt. **6.** Wurst, Knödel und frisches Gemüse und zum Nachtisch Pudding mit wilden Erdbeeren. **7.** Weil man schwer arbeiten muss und jeden Tag früh aufstehen muss. **8.** Sie besucht das Karl-Valentin-Museum, das Rathaus, das Hofbräuhaus und den Olympiapark. **9.** Ja, denn die Familie wird im nächsten Jahr wieder nach Deggendorf fahren.

5-22 Vokabelarbeit. Ergänzen Sie die Sätze mit Wörtern aus den *Neuen Vokabeln*. Achten Sie dabei auch auf die Wortform.

1. Auf einem _____Bauernhof_____ findet man Kühe, Hühner und viele andere Tiere.

2. Die Tiere leben in Ställen, in denen es meist nicht gut _____riecht_____.

3. Bauern müssen jeden Tag früh aufstehen und die Arbeit mit den Tieren und auf den Feldern ist sehr _____anstrengend_____.

4. Kühe und Schafe verbringen im Sommer die meiste Zeit draußen auf einer _____Weide_____.

5. Im Sommer fressen die Tiere das Gras, aber im Winter muss man sie _____füttern_____.

6. Felix war von der Arbeit auf dem Hof _____erschöpft_____ und musste sich ausruhen.

7. Die Eltern von Felix und Clara liegen gern _____faul_____ am Pool.

8. Nächstes Jahr will die Familie ihren Urlaub auch wieder auf dem Hof der Familie Hackel _____verbringen_____.

5-23 Zur Diskussion. Besprechen Sie die Fragen.

1. Warum bieten einige Bauern in Deutschland Ferien auf ihren Bauernhöfen an?

2. Warum ist es besonders für Kinder wichtig und interessant, Zeit auf einem Bauernhof zu verbringen?

3. Würden Sie gern einmal so einen Urlaub machen? Warum (nicht)?

5-24 Urlaub auf dem Bauernhof ist prima! Oder nicht? Sie sind Felix. Ihr Freund Martin und seine Familie planen ebenfalls einen Urlaub auf einem Bauernhof. Martin möchte seine Ferien aber lieber in einer Großstadt im Ausland verbringen. Diskutieren Sie mit Ihrem Freund über die Vor- und Nachteile von einem Urlaub auf dem Bauernhof.

5-25 Kommentar auf Felix' Blog. Sie sind ein/e Freund/in von Felix und haben auch schon einmal Ferien auf einem Bauernhof gemacht. Kommentieren Sie jetzt Felix' Blog.

Introduction to *Hörtext 2*. Ask students if they have ever been to a market of any sort or a Christmas market. *Gibt es in Ihrer Stadt einen Markt? Waren Sie einmal auf einem Weihnachtsmarkt? Was haben Sie dort gemacht?*

Christmas tree decorations

Hörtext 2

Weihnachtsmarkt mit langer Tradition (Radioreportage)

In der Weihnachts- und Vorweihnachtszeit gibt es in vielen deutschen Städten große und kleine Weihnachtsmärkte. Auf ihnen findet man nicht nur Geschenke und traditionellen Christbaumschmuck° sondern auch Essen, Getränke und oftmals Musik und Unterhaltung. Der Besuch eines Weihnachtsmarkts gehört für viele Deutsche zu der Festzeit ebenso wie ein Adventskranz mit seinen vier

Kerzen oder ein Adventskalender, mit dem die Kinder die 24 Tage bis zum Fest abzählen.

Der Nürnberger Christkindlesmarkt ist einer der beliebtesten und meistbesuchten Weihnachtsmärkte Deutschlands. Er wird jedes Jahr am Freitag vor dem ersten Advent auf dem Hauptmarkt eröffnet und ist am 24. Dezember zu Ende.

Die folgende Radioreportage vom Nürnberger Christkindlesmarkt gibt Ihnen Informationen über die Geschichte des Marktes. Sie werden auch hören, was die Leute an dem Markt anzieht.

Christkindlesmarkt in Nürnberg

Vor dem Hören

1. Was kann man auf einem typischen Markt kaufen? Gehen Sie gern auf Märkte? Warum (nicht)?

2. Machen Sie eine Liste mit Dingen, die man wohl auf einem Weihnachtsmarkt finden kann.

 ## Beim Hören

Während des Interviews hören Sie folgende Vokabeln.

Weihnachtsmarkt mit langer Tradition
05-13

Weihnachten *Christmas*	in Trümmern *in ruins*
Passanten *passers-by*	ausgefallen *unusual*
Nachweis *evidence*	Glühwein *hot mulled wine*
Schachtel *box*	Gewürze *spices*
Händler *merchants*	Geschicklichkeitsspiele *games of skill*
Handwerker *craftsmen*	Christbaumkugeln *Christmas tree ornaments*
Budenstadt *booth city*	Rauschgoldengel *gold foil angels used as tree toppers*
fanden Gefallen an *took delight in*	deftiger Imbiss *hearty snack*
verkleidet(e) *dressed up*	

Im Bericht hören Sie verschiedene Daten. Welches Ereignis passt zu der entsprechenden Jahreszahl?

1628	1737	1933	1948

___1933___ Eröffnung des Marktes mit großer Feier

___1948___ Das erste Christkind eröffnet den Markt

___1628___ Erster Nachweis des Marktes

___1737___ Fast alle Handwerker haben Buden auf dem Markt

Kulturtipps

Christkind

In den katholischen Regionen Deutschlands sowie in der Schweiz und in Österreich findet man diese Symbolfigur für das Weihnachtsfest. Wie der Weihnachtsmann der Symbolfigur der protestantischen Regionen ist, bringt das Christkind die Geschenke für die Kinder in den katholischen Regionen. Das Nürnberger Christkind spielt immer eine junge Frau, die lange blonde Locken, eine Krone und ein weiß-goldenes Kleid trägt und einem Engel gleichen soll.

5-26 Textarbeit: Wer macht was? Ordnen Sie zu, was zusammenpasst.

Das Nürnberger Christkind

f	1. Passanten	a. verkleiden sich als Christkind.
c	2. Händler	b. isst besonders gern die originalen Nürnberger Rostbratwürste.
e	3. Nationalsozialisten	c. bieten Waren in ihren Buden an.
a	4. Schauspielerinnen	d. mag den Weihnachtsgeruch auf dem Markt.
d	5. Die Passantin	e. mögen den Markt und seine Traditionen.
b	6. Der Passant	f. machen Weihnachtseinkäufe.

5-27 Textarbeit: Richtig oder falsch? Wenn eine Aussage falsch ist, korrigieren und ergänzen Sie sie mit Informationen aus dem Hörtext.

Answers for 5-27. **1.** R; **2.** F – Im 18. Jahrhundert waren fast alle Handwerker auf dem Markt vertreten. **3.** R; **4.** F – Während des Krieges fand kein Christkindlesmarkt statt. **5.** F – Sie hat schon einen Rauschgoldengel auf ihrem Baum. **6.** R

1. Der Nürnberger Christkindlesmarkt ist einer der ältesten Weihnachtsmärkte.

2. Im 18. Jahrhundert waren nur wenige Nürnberger Handwerker auf dem Markt vertreten.

3. Das Christkind tritt mit zwei Engeln auf.

4. Während des Zweiten Weltkrieges war der Markt sehr klein und nicht gut besucht.

5. Die Frau, die der Reporter befragt, will auf dem Markt einen Rauschgoldengel kaufen.

6. Der Mann, den der Reporter befragt, ist mit seiner Familie auf dem Christkindlesmarkt.

5-28 Geschenke vom Weihnachtsmarkt? Sie suchen auf dem Weihnachtsmarkt nach Geschenken für ihre Freunde und Familie. Besprechen Sie, was Sie diesen Personen kaufen wollen.

1. Ihren Eltern, die gern kochen

2. Ihrem kleinen Bruder, der erst vier Jahre alt ist

3. Ihrer Tante, die gern reist

4. Ihrem Lieblingsprofessor/Ihrer Lieblingsprofessorin

5. Ihrer Oma, die gern spazieren geht

6. …

5-29 Zur Diskussion. Besprechen Sie die Fragen.

1. Was würden Sie für sich auf einem Weihnachtsmarkt kaufen?

2. Was macht Weihnachtsmärkte in Deutschland so beliebt?

3. Was für Traditionen haben Sie in der Weihnachtszeit oder zu anderen Festtagen in Ihrer Familie? Ist es wichtig, Traditionen an Kinder weiterzugeben? Warum?

4. Beschreiben Sie Ihre Lieblingstradition und sagen Sie auch, warum sie für Sie wichtig ist.

5-30 Viele Grüße vom Christkindlesmarkt. Sie haben mit Ihrer Familie den Christkindlesmarkt in Nürnberg besucht und schreiben jetzt eine Postkarte an Ihre Tante in Hamburg. Schreiben Sie auf der Karte auch, was Ihnen am besten gefallen hat.

*Introduction to **Lesetext 4**. Ask students if they have heard of the author Erich Kästner and if they have ever come across a children's story with a theme similar to that of "Das doppelte Lottchen." Kennen Sie den Schriftsteller Erich Kästner? Kennen Sie Geschichten, in denen Zwillinge oder Personen, die sich sehr ähnlich sehen, einander finden und dann die Plätze tauschen ("The Prince and the Pauper," "Charlie und Louise," "The Parent Trap")? Was passiert am Ende in diesen Geschichten?*

Lesetext 4

„Das doppelte Lottchen" von Erich Kästner (Romanauszug)

Erich Kästner wurde 1899 in Dresden geboren und starb 1974 in München. Er ist bekannt als Schriftsteller, Drehbuchautor° und Kabarettist. Er war auch politisch aktiv und setzte sich gegen Krieg und Gewalt° ein. Besonders beliebt und bekannt ist er aber für seine Kinderbücher, die auch heute noch viel gelesen werden. Erich Kästners erstes und bis heute berühmtestes Kinderbuch *Emil und die Detektive* erschien 1929, als er noch in Berlin lebte und arbeitete. Nach dem Zweiten Weltkrieg zog er nach München. Hier entstanden viele seiner bekannten Werke wie *Das doppelte Lottchen* (1949) und *Die Konferenz der Tiere* (1949).

Erich Kästner

screenplay writer

violence

Der folgende Text ist ein kurzer Auszug aus dem Kinderroman *Das doppelte Lottchen*. Die Geschichte handelt von den neunjährigen Zwillingen Luise und Lotte, deren Eltern sich getrennt haben, als die Kinder noch klein waren. Die Mädchen wissen nichts voneinander, bis sie sich in den Ferien in einem Feriencamp in den Alpen treffen und feststellen, dass sie Zwillinge sind. Da sie den jeweils anderen Elternteil kennenlernen wollen, machen sie einen Plan. Der folgende Auszug beschreibt den Plan der beiden Mädchen.

Vor dem Lesen

1. Kennen Sie Zwillinge oder sind sie selber ein Zwilling? Hätten Sie gern einen Zwilling? Warum (nicht)?

2. Wenn Sie mit einer anderen Person Ihr Leben tauschen könnten, würden Sie das tun? Mit wem würden Sie tauschen und warum?

Beim Lesen

Aus welcher Erzählperspektive ist die Erzählung geschrieben? Was für einen Einfluss hat das auf den Inhalt?

*Answers for **Beim Lesen**. Allwissender Erzähler – Man erfährt von dem Geschehen wie auch den Gedanken und Gefühlen der Charaktere, ohne das die Charaktere sich direkt darüber äußern müssen.*

Lesetext 4. Students may notice that the spelling in Kästner's novel differs somewhat from the current orthographical standard. 05-14

„Das doppelte Lottchen"

von Erich Kästner

Merkt ihr, was sich anspinnt? Die Zwillinge wollen den Eltern noch immer nicht erzählen, daß sie Bescheid wissen. Sie wollen Vater und Mutter nicht vor Entscheidungen stellen. Sie ahnen, dass sie kein Recht dazu haben. Und sie fürchten, die Entschlüsse° der Eltern könnten das junge Geschwisterglück sofort und endgültig wieder zerstören. Aber das andere brächten sie 5 erst recht nicht übers Herz°: als wäre nichts geschehen, zurückzufahren, woher sie gekommen sind! Weiterzuleben in der ihren von den Eltern ungefragt zugewiesenen° Hälfte! Nein! Kurz und gut, es ist eine Verschwörung° im Gange! Der von Sehnsucht und Abenteuerlust geweckte, phantastische Plan sieht so aus: Die beiden wollen die Kleider, Frisuren, Koffer, Schürzen° 10 und Existenzen tauschen! Luise will, mit braven Zöpfen° (und auch sonst ums Bravsein bemüht°), als sei sie Lotte, zur Mutter, von der sie nichts als eine Fotografie kennt, „heimkehren"°! Und Lotte wird, mit offenem Haar und so lustig und lebhaft, wie sie's nur vermag, zum Vater nach Wien fahren!

Die Vorbereitungen auf die zukünftigen Abenteuer waren gründ- 15 lich. Die Oktavhefte° sind randvoll° von Notizen. Man wird einander postlagernd° schreiben, wenn Not am Mann ist° oder wenn wichtige unvorhergesehene Ereignisse eintreten sollten.

Vielleicht wird es ihrer gemeinsamen Aufmerksamkeit am Ende sogar gelingen zu enträtseln, warum die Eltern getrennt leben? Und vielleicht wer- 20 den sie dann eines schönen, eines wunderschönen Tages miteinander und mit beiden Eltern – doch soweit wagen sie kaum zu denken, geschweige denn, darüber zu sprechen.

Das Gartenfest am Vorabend der Abreise ist als Generalprobe vorgesehen. Lotte kommt als lockige, quirlige° Luise. Luise erscheint als brave, 25 bezopfte Lotte. Und beide spielen ihre Rollen ausgezeichnet. Niemand merkt etwas! Nicht einmal Trude, Luises Schulkameradin aus Wien! Es macht beiden einen Mordsspaß°, einander laut beim eigenen verschenkten Vornamen zu rufen. Lotte schlägt vor Übermut Purzelbäume°. Und Luise tut so sanft und still, als könne sie kein Härchen trüben und kein Wässerchen krümmen°. 30

Die Lampions° schimmern in den Sommerbäumen. Die Girlanden schaukeln im Abendwind. Das Fest und die Ferien gehen zu Ende. An der Tombola° werden die Gewinne verteilt. Steffie, das arme Hascherl°, gewinnt den ersten Preis, die Rollschuhe mit Kugellager°. (Besser ein schwacher Trost° als gar keiner!) 35

Die Schwestern schlafen schließlich, ihren Rollen getreu, in den vertauschten Betten und träumen vor Aufregung wilde Dinge. Lotte beispielsweise wird in Wien am Bahnsteig abgeholt, und daneben steht ein weißbemützter° Hotelkoch mit einem Schubkarren° voll gefüllter dampfender Palatschinken – brrr! 40

decisions

brächten ... Herz really could not get themselves to do
assigned without consent / conspiracy

aprons

braids

trying to be good

to return home

*composition notebooks / full to the brim / via general delivery / **wenn ... ist** if worst comes to worst*

lively

devilishly good time

*schlägt ... Purzelbäume does somersaults because she is so high-spirited / **als ... krümmen** cool as a cucumber / Chinese lanterns*

raffle
poor thing (Bavarian German) / roller skates with ball bearings / consolation

wearing a white cap / wheelbarrow
Siehe **Kulturtipps:** *Palatschinken*

Am nächsten Morgen, in aller Herrgottsfrühe°, fahren in der Bahnstation Egern, bei Seebühl am Bühlsee, zwei aus entgegengesetzten Richtungen kommende Züge ein. Dutzende kleiner Mädchen klettern schnatternd in die Abteile°.

Lotte beugt sich° weit aus dem Fenster. Aus einem Fenster des anderen Zuges winkt Luise. Sie lächeln einander Mut zu. Die Herzen klopfen. Das Lampenfieber° wächst. Wenn jetzt nicht die Lokomotiven zischten und spuckten, – die kleinen Mädchen würden vielleicht im letzten Moment doch noch –

Aber nein, der Fahrplan hat das Wort. Der Stationsvorsteher hebt sein Szepter. Die Züge setzen sich in Bewegung. Kinderhände winken.

Lotte fährt nach Wien.

Luise fährt nach München.

at the crack of dawn

train compartments

45 *leans*

stage fright

50

55

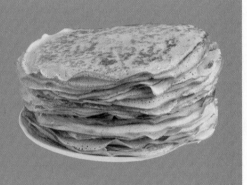

Kulturtipps

Palatschinken

Dieses Gericht aus Ei, Milch und Mehl hat in den verschiedenen deutschsprachigen Regionen viele verschiedene Namen. Man findet sie als Pfannkuchen, Eierkuchen, Flädle oder auch als Crêpes. Palatschinken wird dies oft im Südosten Deutschlands, in Österreich und in Ungarn genannt. Hier bäckt man sie ganz dünn und füllt sie süß oder salzig.

 ## Neue Vokabeln

Nomen

das Abenteuer, - *adventure*
die Aufmerksamkeit *attention*
die Aufregung, -en *excitement*
die Sehnsucht, ¨e (nach) *desire, longing (for)*
der Zwilling, -e *twin*

Verben

ahnen *to suspect*
klettern, ist geklettert *to climb*
tauschen *to exchange*
vermögen (vermag), vermochte, vermocht *to be capable*
verschenken *to give something away*
verteilen *to distribute, spread*
wagen *to dare*
zerstören *to destroy*

Adjektive und Adverbien

lockig *curly*
brav *well-behaved*
sanft *gentle, mild*
unvorhergesehen *unexpected*

Ausdrücke

Bescheid wissen *to be in the know*
geschweige denn *let alone, much less*

Answers for 5-31. 1. F – Die Zwillinge wollen den Eltern nichts davon erzählen. 2. R; 3. R; 4. F – Niemand merkt, dass sie die Rollen getauscht haben. 5. F – Sie haben Lampenfieber und Herzklopfen.

5-31 Textarbeit: Richtig oder falsch? Wenn eine Aussage falsch ist, korrigieren und ergänzen Sie sie mit Informationen aus dem Text.

1. Luise und Lotte wollen den Eltern erzählen, dass sie ihren Zwilling gefunden haben.
2. Die Mädchen schmieden einen Plan.
3. Die Mädchen schreiben auf, wie sie sich bei dem anderen Elternteil verhalten müssen.
4. Bei der Abschlussparty erkennen die Freunde sofort, dass Luise und Lotte ihre Rollen getauscht haben.
5. Die Mädchen haben keine Angst davor, die Rollen zu tauschen, als sie abfahren.

5-32 Textarbeit: Fragen zum Inhalt. Beantworten Sie die Fragen zum Text.

Answers for 5-32. 1. Luise ist wild, lustig und lebhaft. Sie trägt ihre Haare offen. Lotte ist brav, sie ist auch still und sanft. Sie hat Zöpfe. 2. Sie wollen die Eltern nicht vor Entscheidungen stellen und sie haben Angst, dass die Eltern sie vielleicht wieder trennen. 3. Luise und Lotte wollen ihre Plätze tauschen. 4. Sie wollen herausfinden, warum die Eltern getrennt leben. 5. Lotte träumt, dass sie in Wien am Bahnhof von einem Hotelkoch mit einer Schubkarre voll Palatschinken abgeholt wird. 6. Luise fährt nach München zur Mutter und Lotte fährt nach Wien zum Vater.

1. Lotte und Luise sind Zwillinge, die sich in manchen Dingen sehr ähnlich sind, aber es gibt auch viele Unterschiede zwischen ihnen. Beschreiben Sie beide Mädchen. Worin unterscheiden sie sich?
2. Warum haben die Mädchen den Eltern nicht berichtet, dass sie ihren Zwilling gefunden haben?
3. Was ist der Plan der Mädchen?
4. Was hoffen Sie durch den Tausch herauszufinden?
5. Wovon träumt Lotte in der letzten Nacht?
6. Wohin und zu wem fahren Luise und Lotte jetzt?

5-33 Vokabelarbeit. Ergänzen Sie die Sätze mit Wörtern aus den *Neuen Vokabeln*. Achten Sie dabei auch auf die Wortform.

1. _____Zwillinge_____ sehen sich oft so ähnlich, dass man sie leicht verwechseln kann.
2. Die Mädchen _____ahnen_____, dass sie nicht zufällig so gleich aussehen.
3. Die Zwillinge wollen ihre Rollen _____tauschen_____, da sie hoffen, mehr über ihre Eltern zu erfahren.
4. Sie wissen, dass der Tausch ein großes _____Abenteuer_____ sein wird.
5. Beide Zwillinge haben _____Sehnsucht_____ nach dem Elternteil, mit dem sie nicht leben.
6. Die lustige und lebhafte Luise muss lernen _____brav_____ und _____sanft_____ zu sein.
7. Die Mädchen werden einander per Post benachrichtigen, wenn ein _____unvorhergesehenes_____ Ereignis eintritt oder es Probleme gibt.
8. Als die Mädchen am letzten Tag in den Zug _____klettern_____, sind sie sehr nervös.

5-34 Zur Diskussion. Besprechen Sie die Fragen.

1. Was würden Sie machen, wenn Sie in der Situation von Lotte und Luise wären?
2. Glauben Sie, dass Zwillinge anders sind als einfache Geschwister? Warum (nicht)?
3. Wie kann die Geschichte enden? Besprechen Sie verschiedene Alternativen.

 5-35 Ein guter Plan? Besprechen Sie den Plan der beiden Mädchen. Ist es ein guter Plan? Welche Probleme kann es dabei geben? Was sollen die Mädchen vielleicht anders machen?

5-36 Das Leben tauschen. Stellen Sie sich vor, Sie könnten Ihr Leben mit dem einer anderen Person tauschen. Schreiben Sie einen Tagebucheintrag darüber, wie ein Tag in diesem anderen Leben wohl aussieht.

Beispiel: *Ich stelle mir vor, ich bin X für einen ganzen Tag. Da ich Schauspieler bin, muss ich nicht mehr früh aufstehen, sondern ich schlafe lange, denn ich muss erst abends arbeiten. ...*

Grammatik

1. Adjective endings (Adjektivendungen)

Adjectives are used in one of two ways in German. A predicate adjective is linked to a noun through the use of a verb—usually the verb **sein** or **bleiben,** a verb of sense (**aussehen, klingen, riechen**), or a verb that expresses appearance or becoming (**werden, scheinen**).

Der Garten sieht **schön** aus.	*The garden looks beautiful.*
Der Krieg war **lang**.	*The war was long.*

An attributive adjective, on the other hand, appears directly before the noun it describes and following any determiners that accompany the noun.

Der **schöne** Garten ist hinter dem Haus.	*The beautiful garden is behind the house.*
In einem **langen** Krieg gewinnt keiner.	*In a long war nobody wins.*

Unlike a predicate adjective, an attributive adjective takes an ending that is determined by the gender, number, and case of the noun it modifies and by any determiner that precedes it.

Unpreceded adjectives: Strong endings (Starke Flexion)

When no article is present to carry the case, gender, and number information of the noun, the adjective assumes this function. The strong adjective endings are identical to the endings of the **der**-words, with the exception of the masculine and neuter genitive.

	Masculine	Feminine	Neuter	Plural
Nominative	frischer Fisch	frische Milch	frisches Brot	frische Äpfel
Accusative	frischen Fisch	frische Milch	frisches Brot	frische Äpfel
Dative	frischem Fisch	frischer Milch	frischem Brot	frischen Äpfeln
Genitive	frischen Fisches	frischer Milch	frischen Brotes	frischer Äpfel

Note these additional points regarding adjective endings:

- All attributive adjectives in a series describing the same noun will have the same endings: **günstige, gesunde Lebensmittel** (*inexpensive, healthy groceries*); **mit zartem, geräuchertem Schinken** (*with tender smoked ham*).

- A few common adjectives of foreign origin never take endings, e.g., **rosa, lila, orange, beige, super, prima.**

- Adjectives ending in **-el** and those ending in **-er** that are preceded by a vowel drop the final **-e-** of the root before an adjective ending: **komfortabel: komfortable Möbel** (*comfortable furniture*); **sauer: saurer Wein** (*sour wine*).

- Adjectives derived from city names are created by adding **-er** and take no additional endings. These are always capitalized: der **Augsburger** Puppenkisten (*Augsburg Puppet Theater*); die **Berliner** Mauer (*the Berlin Wall*).

5-37 Bayerische Spezialitäten. In den verschiedenen Regionen Bayerns gibt es unterschiedliche Spezialitäten. Ergänzen Sie die Adjektivendungen.

1. In Oberfranken findet man wilden_____ Honig (*m.*).

2. Unterfranken ist für trockene_____ Weißweine mit würzigem_____ Geschmack bekannt.

3. In Franken findet man viel gesundes_____ Obst, z. B. Erdbeeren, Pflaumen, süße_____ Kirschen und Äpfel.

4. Nürnberger_____ Lebkuchen ist ab September erhältlich. Das Weihnachtsgebäck gibt es in rechteckiger_____ oder runder_____ Form (*f.*).

5. Frischer_____ Fisch ist seit fast tausend Jahren eine Spezialität der Oberpfalz.

6. Klares_____ , qualitativ hochwertiges_____ Mineralwasser entspringt der Bissinger Auerquelle in Schwaben.

7. In München stehen warme_____ Weißwürste mit süßem_____ Senf fast immer auf dem Frühstückstisch.

8. In ganz Bayern isst man hausgemachte_____ Knödel (*pl.*) zu vielen_____ verschiedenen_____ Gerichten.

Adjective endings with der-words: Weak endings (Schwache Flexion)

05-25 to 05-26

Adjectives take so-called weak endings when they are preceded by **der**-words: **der/die/das, dies-, welch-, jed-, jen-, manch-, solch-.** Because these articles carry case, number, and gender markers (strong endings), the adjective takes a weak ending, either **-e** or **-en.**

To review **der**-words, see the *Kapitel 3 Grammatik.*

	Masculine	Feminine	Neuter	Plural
Nominative	der alte Hund	die alte Katze	das alte Pferd	die alten Tiere
Accusative	den alten Hund	die alte Katze	das alte Pferd	die alten Tiere
Dative	dem alten Hund	der alten Katze	dem alten Pferd	den alten Tieren
Genitive	des alten Hundes	der alten Katze	des alten Pferdes	der alten Tiere

5-38 Ritterspiele in Pappenheim. Martina schreibt ihrer Tante eine E-Mail über die Ritterspiele, die jedes Jahr in ihrer Heimatstadt Pappenheim im Altmühltal stattfinden. Setzen Sie die richtigen Adjektivendungen ein.

Liebe Tante Marianne,

auch dieses Jahr gab es hier (1) die unterhaltsam___ Ritterspiele. Wieder waren (2) die alt___ Burgruine (*f.*) und (3) die zwei schön___ Schlösser die Kulisse (4) für die zweitägig___Veranstaltung. Der Turnierplatz war am Fuße (5) der alt___ Festungsmauern (*fortress walls*) (*pl.*) und (6) bei dem aufregend___ Reitturnier konnte man über zwanzig Reiter bewundern. (7) Trotz des schlecht___ Wetters am ersten Turniertag kamen viele Touristen. Auf der Burg konnte man (8) an den beid___ Tagen (9) die gruselig___Folterkammer (*torture chamber*) (*f.*) besichtigen oder sich (10) den groß___Kräutergarten anschauen. Ein verliebtes Paar hatte dieses Jahr (11) den mittelalterlich___ Rittersaal (*m.*) am zweiten Abend gemietet und sie haben dort ihre Hochzeit gefeiert. (12) Statt des normal___ Brautkleids trug (13) diese zauberhafte___ Braut (*bride*) (*f.*) ein mittelalterliches Kostüm. Es war schon ein wenig kitschig (*cheesy*), aber irgendwie auch schön.

Ich hoffe, dass du uns nächstes Jahr (14) zum jährlich___ Ritterfest besuchen kannst, denn dann ist immer richtig viel los hier.

Mit ganz lieben Grüßen

Deine Martina

Adjective endings with ein-words (Flexion mit unbestimmten Artikeln)

05-27

To review **ein**-words, see the *Kapitel 3 Grammatik.*

Adjectives following **ein**-words—**ein, kein,** and the possessive adjectives—have the same weak endings as those following the **der**-words, with three exceptions: the masculine nominative and the neuter nominative and accusative. In these three instances, the **ein**-words (unlike the **der**-words) have no endings to indicate case, gender, and number. Here, the adjective carries the strong ending.

	Masculine	**Feminine**	**Neuter**	**Plural**
Nominative	mein alter Hund	meine alte Katze	mein altes Pferd	meine alten Tiere
Accusative	meinen alten Hund	meine alte Katze	mein altes Pferd	meine alten Tiere
Dative	meinem alten Hund	meiner alten Katze	meinem alten Pferd	meinen alten Tieren
Genitive	meines alten Hundes	meiner alten Katze	meines alten Pferdes	meiner alten Tiere

5-39 Mein Geheimtipp: Rothenburg ob der Tauber. Lesen Sie Sonjas Geheimtipp und setzten Sie die passenden Adjektive aus der Liste ein. Achten Sie auf die Adjektivendungen. Jedes Adjektiv wird einmal benutzt.

außergewöhnliches	erholsamen	kühles	langsamer
bayerischen	große	lange	leicht
bekannt	gutes	langjährigen	mittelalterlichen

Mein Name ist Sonja und ich lebe (1) mit meinem ___langjährigen___ Freund in Rothenburg. Diese Stadt ist (2) ___bekannt___ als die romantischste Stadt (3) unseres ___bayerischen___ Landes. Hier findet man (4) eine ___große___ Anzahl alter Gebäude und (5) einen ___mittelalterlichen___ Markt. Rothenburg hat (6) eine ___lange___ Geschichte und (7) ein ___außergewöhnliches___ Museum, das Mittelalterliche Kriminalmuseum. (8) Ein ___langsamer___ Spaziergang durch die mittelalterliche Stadt ist meiner Meinung nach besonders zu empfehlen. Außerdem kann man in den guten Restaurants auch leicht (9) ein ___gutes___ Schnitzel und (10) ein ___kühles___ Bier finden. (11) Bei so einem ___erholsamen___ Gasthausbesuch kann man dann den Alltag leicht vergessen und einfach das Leben genießen. Deshalb gefällt es uns hier und wir hoffen noch lange hier bleiben zu können.

5-40 Wer bin ich? Bilden Sie Sätze, indem Sie die gewünschten Satzteile wählen und mindestens ein passendes Adjektiv einsetzen.

alt	entspannend	groß	klein	kurz	rustikal
anstrengend	erfolgreich	grün	lang	neu	schneereich
bayerisch	faul	gut	langsam	neugierig	schwierig
deutsch	gemütlich	hektisch	laut	prächtig	spannend
einsam	golden	italienisch	lustig	ruhig	voll

Beispiele: (Ein Haus / Eine Wohnung / Ein Bauernhof / Ein Garten / Ein Nachbar) gefällt mir (nicht).

> *Eine **große**, **helle** Wohnung gefällt mir.*
> *Ein **neugieriger** Nachbar gefällt mir nicht.*

1. Ich wohne (nicht) gern (auf dem Land / in einer Stadt / in einem Dorf).
2. Ich mag (Wälder / die Natur / Musik / Essen / keine Großstädte / unseren Hund).
3. (Ein Haus / Eine Wohnung / Ein Bauernhof / Ein Garten / Ein Nachbar) gefällt mir (nicht).
4. Ich freue mich auf den Anfang (des Jahres / meiner Arbeit / des Semesters / des Urlaubs).
5. Ich verbringe meinen Urlaub gern (am Strand / in den Bergen / auf einer Insel / mit Freunden).
6. Ich bringe (meinen Rucksack / ein Buch / eine Freundin / keine Arbeit) mit.
7. (Ein Film / Ein Konzert / Eine Oper / Ein Museum) steht öfters auf dem Plan (für das Wochenende / für den Abend / für den Urlaub).

05-31 to 05-35

2. Degrees of adjectives and adverbs: Positive, comparative, superlative (Steigerung der Adjektive und Adverbien: Positiv, Komparativ, Superlativ)

In both English and German, adjectives and adverbs have three degrees: positive, comparative, and superlative. The positive form is the basic form of the adjective or adverb. While English has two ways of forming comparatives and superlatives (*higher, more interesting; highest, most interesting*), German uses only a one-word form with suffixes. The comparative of most adjectives and adverbs is created by adding **-er** to the positive form. The superlative form is created by adding **-(e)st**. Examine the following examples.

Positive	Comparative	Superlative	English adjective forms
billig	billiger	billigst- / am billigsten	*cheap, cheaper, cheapest*
jung	jünger	jüngst- / am jüngsten	*young, younger, youngest*
sauer	saurer	sauerst- / am sauersten	*sour, sourer, sourest*
laut	lauter	lautest- / am lautesten	*loud, louder, loudest*
neu	neuer	neu(e)st- / am neu(e)sten	*new, newer, newest*

Note these variations:

- A number of common one-syllable words take an umlaut in addition to the **-er** and **-(e)st** suffixes:

alt	*old*	kalt	*cold*	lang	*long*	schwach	*weak*
arm	*poor*	klug	*clever*	oft	*often*	schwarz	*black*
dumm	*dumb*	krank	*sick*	rot	*red*	stark	*strong*
jung	*young*	kurz	*short*	scharf	*sharp*	warm	*warm*

- Comparative: Adjectives ending in **-er** preceded by a vowel and in **-el** omit that final **e** in their root when adding the comparative ending (**plausibler, saurer**).
- Superlative: Adjectives ending in **-s, -ß,** or **-z,** and most ending in **-d, -t,** or **-sch,** insert an **-e-** before the superlative **-st** suffix (**am heißesten, am lautesten**). Words ending in a long vowel may optionally add the **e** before **-st** (**am neu[e]sten**).
- Like English, German has a few very common adjectives and adverbs that are irregular in the comparative and/or the superlative.

Positive	Comparative	Superlative	English adjective forms
groß	größer	größt- / am größten	*big, bigger, biggest*
gut	besser	best- / am besten	*good, better, best*
hoch	höher	höchst- / am höchsten	*high, higher, highest*
nah	näher	nächst- / am nächsten	*near, nearer, nearest/next*
viel	mehr	meist- / am meisten	*much, more, most*
gern(e)	lieber	liebst- / am liebsten	*gladly, preferably, most preferably*

Usage of the comparative and superlative

The positive and comparative forms are used to make comparisons between two items:

		Adjective	Adverb
(nicht) so [POSITIV] **wie**	**so hoch wie**	*as high as*	*as highly as*
	nicht so eng wie	*not as narrow as*	*not as narrowly as*
[KOMPARATIV] **als**	**kälter als**	*colder than*	*more coldly than*
	besser als	*better than*	*better than*

The comparative can be used to express a progressive development with **immer:**

immer [KOMPARATIV]	**immer tiefer**	deeper and deeper	more and more deeply
	immer langsamer	slower and slower	more and more slowly

Remember that an attributive adjective requires an adjective ending.

Der Hase ist ein schnell**es** Tier.	*The hare is a fast animal.*
Der Löwe ist ein noch schnell**eres** Tier.	*The lion is an even faster animal.*
Der Gepard ist das schnell**ste** Tier.	*The leopard is the fastest animal.*

Unlike the positive and comparative forms, the superlative has an ending when used as a predicate adjective or an adverb. Here, German uses a prepositional phrase consisting of the contraction **am** plus the superlative form with the adjective ending **-en.**

| Dieses Ziel ist <u>**am**</u> wichtig**sten.** | *This goal is the most important.* |
| Hier ist der See <u>**am**</u> tief**sten.** | *Here the lake is the deepest.* |

Note that **mehr, gern,** and **lieber** never have adjective endings.

Bayern hat **mehr** Einwohner als Thüringen. | *Bavaria has more inhabitants than Thuringia.*

Wir wandern **gern** im Bayerischen Wald. | *We like to go hiking in the Bavarian Forest.*

5-41 Im Vergleich dazu. Vergleichen Sie die Dinge mit dem Komparativ + **als** oder **(nicht) so … wie.**

Beispiele: die Donau – der Inn → *Die Donau ist **länger als** der Inn.*
*Der Inn ist **nicht so lang wie** die Donau.*

1. eine Oper – ein Film
2. Winter – Sommer
3. Wasser – Bier
4. Wurst – Schnitzel
5. fernsehen – Musik hören
6. ein Urlaub am Strand – ein Urlaub auf dem Bauernhof
7. München – Deggendorf
8. die Zugspitze – der Olympiaturm
9. Gemüse vom Bauernhof – Gemüse vom Supermarkt
10. Bayern – Berlin

5-42 Immer weiter! Wie werden diese Dinge? Benutzen Sie **immer** + den Komparativ. Hier sind einige Adjektive, die Sie benutzen können: **anstrengend, billig, bitter, groß, gut, heiß, kalt, klein, kompliziert, schnell, schmutzig, schön, schwierig, süß, teuer, trocken, warm, wichtig.**

Beispiel: Kaffee → *Kaffee wird **immer bitterer.***

| das Wetter | Wein | die Welt | Computer |
| die Stadt | Handys | die Universität | die Umwelt |

5-43 Gut, besser, am besten. Geben Sie jeweils erst die Komparativform und im letzten Satz die Superlativform an.

1. Das Leben auf dem Land ist schön. Das Leben in den Bergen ist
   _____schöner_____. Das Leben in München ist ___am schönsten___.

2. Die Berge im Harz sind hoch. Die Berge im Schwarzwald sind
   _____höher_____. Die Berge in den Alpen sind ___am höchsten___.

3. Ein japanisches Auto ist teuer. Ein italienisches Auto ist _____teurer_____.
   Ein deutsches Auto ist ___am teuersten___.

4. Das Wetter ist im Mai warm. Das Wetter ist im Juni _____wärmer_____.
   Das Wetter ist im Juli ___am wärmsten___.

5. Die Bayern trinken gern Mineralwasser. Die Rheinländer trinken
   _____lieber_____ Wein. Viele Menschen trinken ___am liebsten___ Bier.

6. Ein Fahrrad fährt schnell. Ein Motorrad fährt _____schneller_____. Ein
   Rennwagen fährt ___am schnellsten___.

3. Cardinal numbers (Kardinalzahlen)

05-36 to 05-38

0	null	12	zwölf	24	vierundzwanzig	90	neunzig
1	eins	13	dreizehn	25	fünfundzwanzig	100	(**ein**)hundert
2	zwei	14	vierzehn	26	sechsundzwanzig	101	(**ein**)hunderteins
3	drei	15	fünfzehn	27	siebenundzwanzig	200	zweihundert
4	vier	16	**sech**zehn	28	achtundzwanzig	1.000	(**ein**)tausend
5	fünf	17	**sieb**zehn	29	neunundzwanzig	2.000	zweitausend
6	sechs	18	achtzehn	30	dreißig	1.000.000	eine Million
7	sieben	19	neunzehn	40	vierzig	2.000.000	zwei Millionen
8	acht	20	zwanzig	50	fünfzig	1.000.000.000	eine Milliarde
9	neun	21	**ein**undzwanzig	60	**sech**zig	2.000.000.000	zwei Milliarden
10	zehn	22	zweiundzwanzig	70	**sieb**zig	1.000.000.000.000	eine Billion
11	elf	23	dreiundzwanzig	80	achtzig	2.000.000.000.000	zwei Billionen

Note:
- When followed by the suffixes **-zehn** or **-zig, sechs** drops the final **-s** (**sechzehn, sechzig**) and **sieben** drops the final **-en** (**siebzehn, siebzig**).
- When **eins** is used in combinations where it does not appear at the end of the word, it drops the final **-s** (**einundachtzig, eintausend**).
- All numbers below a million are written as a single word. **Million, Milliarde,** and **Billion** are separate words (82.100.650 = **zweiundachtzig Millionen einhunderttausendsechshundertfünfzig**). The German **Milliarde** is equivalent to the English *billion*. The German **Billion** is equal to the English *trillion*.
- Where English uses a comma to separate hundreds from thousands, thousands from millions, etc., German uses a period or just a space (e.g., **10.000** or **10 000**). Where English uses a decimal point, German uses a comma: **2,5** (**zwei Komma fünf**). With amounts of money, the currency is named where the comma appears: **€12,75** (**zwölf Euro fünfundsiebzig**).

5-44 Bayern in Zahlen. Beantworten Sie die Fragen.

4,90 Euro	1.150 Museen	70.551 Quadratkilometer	7,1 Millionen Besucher
12 bis 15 Zentimeter	2.705 Kilometer	1.331.000 Einwohner	12.540.000 Einwohner
20 Prozent	2.962 Meter		

Information for 5-44. (10)
The record number of visitors at Oktoberfest was at the 175th anniversary celebration in 1985.

Answers for 5-44. 1. 70.551 Quadratkilometer; **2.** 12.540.000 Einwohner; **3.** 1.331.000 Einwohner; **4.** 20 Prozent; **5.** 2.705 Kilometer; **6.** 1.150 Museen; **7.** 2.962 Meter; **8.** 12 bis 15 Zentimeter; **9.** 4,90 Euro; **10.** 7,1 Millionen Besucher

1. Wie groß ist Bayern?
2. Wie viele Menschen wohnen im Freistaat?
3. Wie viele Menschen wohnen in München?
4. Welcher Anteil der Einwohner lebt in Großstädten?
5. Wie lang sind die Landesgrenzen?
6. Wie viele Museen befinden sich in Bayern?
7. Wie hoch ist die Zugspitze?
8. Wie lang ist eine Münchner Weißwurst?
9. Wie viel kostet der Apfelstrudel im Hofbräuhaus?
10. Was ist der Rekord für Anzahl der Gäste beim Oktoberfest?

Activity 5-44. By now, students are familiar with cardinal numbers and have some proficiency at counting. However, naming the larger quantities and saying numbers aloud when they encounter numerals is more challenging. Have students alternate reading and answering questions aloud. Alternately, if this is completed as a written activity, have the students write the numbers in words.

05-39 to 05-40

4. Ordinal numbers (Ordinalzahlen)

Ordinal numbers are adjectives that express a position in a series or order (*first, second, third,* etc.). Ordinal numbers are created by adding **-t** to cardinal numbers under 20, and **-st** to cardinal numbers 20 and above. For numbers above 100, the suffix is determined by the last two digits according to the same rule.

5.	fünf**t**-	20.	zwanzig**st**-
13.	dreizehn**t**-	67.	siebenundsechzig**st**-
116.	hundertsechzehn**t**-	138.	hundertachtunddreißig**st**-

Only four ordinal numbers deviate from the above pattern.

1.	erst-	7.	siebt-
3.	dritt-	8.	acht-

Ordinal numbers take adjective endings because they are adjectives and are always used attributively.

Heute ist der elft**e** Februar.	*Today is the eleventh of February.*
Bald feiert er seinen achtzig**sten** Geburtstag.	*Soon he will celebrate his eightieth birthday.*

In writing, ordinal numbers can also be expressed by adding a period after the numeral. When reading these numbers aloud, however, the correct ordinal suffix and adjective ending must be included. The following sentences are therefore read aloud exactly like the previous examples.

Heute ist der 11. Februar.

Bald feiert er seinen 80. Geburtstag.

5-45 Zahlen. Ergänzen Sie die Sätze zuerst mündlich und dann schreiben Sie die Zahlen in Worten aus. Achten Sie auf die Adjektivendungen.

1.	2.	3.	6.	21.	60.	100.	200.

1. Bayern existiert seit dem _____sechsten_____ Jahrhundert, das ist schon über 1.500 Jahre her.

2. Der _____Erste_____ Weltkrieg dauerte von 1914 bis 1918.

3. Während des _____Dritten_____ Reiches verlor Bayern seinen Status als Freistaat.

4. 1939 begann der _____Zweite_____ Weltkrieg.

5. Wir leben jetzt im _____einundzwanzigsten_____ Jahrhundert.

6. 2009 feierte der Freistaat seinen _____sechzigsten_____ Geburtstag.

7. 2010 fand das _____zweihundertste_____ Jubiläum des Oktoberfestes statt.

8. 2016 feiert BMW in München seinen _____einhundertsten/hundertsten_____ Geburtstag.

Activity 5-45. Students should be able to infer several of the answers based on what they have read and learned in this and previous chapters.

5. Dates (Kalenderdaten)

As in English, the day of the month in a date is given using ordinal numbers.

Heute ist der 3. [dritte] Juni. *Today is the third of June.*

Sie hat am 14. [vierzehnten] August *Her birthday is on August fourteenth.*
Geburtstag.

In German, sometimes an ordinal number is used for the month as well as the day. Thus, the sentences above may be written or stated as follows.

Heute ist der 3.6. [dritte sechste]

Sie hat am 14.8. [vierzehnten achten] Geburtstag.

To ask for a date, German uses the word **wievielt-.**

Den Wievielten haben wir heute?
Der Wievielte ist heute? } *What is today's date?*

Years are stated using hundreds. Unlike in English, the word *hundred* may not be omitted.

1991 neunzehnhunderteinundneunzig

1648 sechzehnhundertachtundvierzig

Years whose second digit is a zero are stated using thousands.

2015 zweitausendfünfzehn

1066 tausendsechsundsechzig

Years are never preceded by *in* as they are in English. Years may be optionally preceded by the phrase **im Jahr(e)**.

Ich bin 1994 geboren.
Ich bin im Jahr(e) 1994 geboren. } *I was born in 1994.*

 5-46 Wann passiert was? Beantworten Sie die Fragen.

1. Der Wievielte ist heute?
2. Wann bist du geboren?
3. Wann beginnt das neue Jahr?
4. In welchem Jahr ist die nächste Präsidentenwahl in den USA?
5. An welchem Tag feiert man in den USA den Unabhängigkeitstag?
6. Wann ist der Tag der Deutschen Einheit?
7. In welchem Jahr war der Zweite Weltkrieg zu Ende?
8. Wann ist die Berliner Mauer gefallen?

Immer weiter!

05-42 to 05-48

 5-47 Zur Diskussion. Besprechen Sie die Themen.

1. In diesem Kapitel haben Sie gelernt, dass in Bayern Tradition und Moderne nebeneinander existieren. Suchen Sie sich einen bayerischen Ort aus und besprechen Sie, wie dieser Ort sowohl traditionell als auch modern ist.

2. Welchen Eindruck hatten Sie von Bayern, bevor Sie diesen Kapitel gelesen haben? Wie sehen Sie das Land jetzt?

5-48 Zum Schreiben: Land der Gegensätze. Sie studieren für ein Jahr in München. Eine norddeutsche Freundin fragt, welche Eindrücke Sie von Bayern haben. Erklären Sie ihr in einer E-Mail, warum Sie Bayern als Land der Gegensätze empfinden und wie Sie das im täglichen Leben hier sehen.

Weitere Themen

Bavaria Film	Nürnberger Prozesse
Franz Anton Beckenbauer	Oberammergauer Passionsspiele
Dampfnudel	Olympische Sommerspiele 1972
Dirndl und Lederhose	Carl Orff
Albrecht Dürer	Pinakothek
Michael Ende	Regensburg
FC Bayern München	Sophie und Hans Scholl
Die Fuggers in Augsburg	Schuhplattler
König Ludwig II.	Würzburg
Löwenbräu	
Ludwig-Maximilians-Universität München	

KAPITEL

6

Sachsen

Warm-up. To set the scene, have students look at the locator map and detail map of Sachsen, or the map of Germany on the inside front cover, and ask them to describe its geographic position. *Wo liegt Sachsen innerhalb Deutschlands? Beschreiben Sie die Grenzen des Bundeslandes. Inwiefern ist die geografische und politische Lage Sachsens heute anders als vor 50 Jahren? Von welchen Städten haben Sie schon mal gehört?* Then have them examine the detail map and photos and describe what these reveal about Sachsen.

Nordsee

Ostsee

Sachsen

Deutschland

Österreich

Schweiz

Liechtenstein

BRANDENBURG

SACHEN-ANHALT

Mulde

Elbe

Leipzig

Hoyerswerda

Spree

Neiße

POLEN

Meißen

Bautzen

SACHSEN

Bischofswerda

Görlitz

Dresden ★

Pirna

Zittau

Freiberg

SÄCHSISCHE SCHWEIZ

Chemnitz

THÜRINGEN

Zwickau

Ehrenfriedersdorf

E R Z G E B I R G E

TSCHECHIEN

BAYERN

Einführung

06-01 to 06-03

Read the *Sprachanalyse: Participles as adjectives and adverbs* in SAM 06-02, which explains the use of present and past participles in the *Einführung*. As you read the *Lesetexte* activities in this chapter, do the *Sprachanalyse* activities in the SAM (06-02, 06-03, 06-06, 06-09, 06-13, 06-15, 6-20) to practice identifying participles and predicting their meanings.

Mit seinen 4,2 Millionen Einwohnern ist Sachsen das bevölkerungsreichste der Länder im Ostteil Deutschlands. Obwohl es zu den „neuen" Bundesländern zählt, ist Sachsen in der Tat über tausend Jahre alt. Im Jahre 929 ließ Heinrich I. hier eine Burg bauen, um die beginnende deutsche Besiedlung° inmitten des damals slawischen Gebiets zu sichern. Seitdem besteht Sachsen fast durch- 5   *settlement* gehend, wenn auch in sich wandelnder politischer Gestalt.

Vom Mittelalter bis in die Neuzeit war der Reichtum an Bodenschätzen°   *mineral deposits* im Erzgebirge eine entscheidende Grundlage für den andauernden Erfolg Sachsens. Es gehörte einst zu den reichsten deutschen Gebieten. In der Entwicklung Sachsens spielten seit jeher die heute vier größten Städte – 10 Dresden, Leipzig, Chemnitz und Zwickau – unterschiedliche Rollen, die diese Städte noch wesentlich prägen. Die Industriemetropole Chemnitz am Fuße des Erzgebirges und das kleinere, westlicher gelegene Industriezen- trum Zwickau lagen an günstigen Orten für die Verarbeitung° der Rohstoffe   *processing* aus dem Bergbau°. Ins Handels- und Wissenschaftszentrum Leipzig flossen 15   *mining* seit dem Mittelalter progressive Ideen. Auch hier begannen 1989 die Pro- teste und Demonstrationen, die zum Sturz der DDR-Regierung führten. Die heutige Landeshauptstadt Dresden, die an der Elbe gelegen ist, war seit dem 15. Jahrhundert Residenzstadt der sächsischen Kurfürsten° und Könige. Die   *electoral princes* vielen Meisterwerke der barocken Baukunst und die staatlichen Museen 20 erinnern an den früheren Wohlstand° Sachsens.   *prosperity*

Rund ein Drittel der Bevölkerung Sachsens lebt heute in diesen vier tra- ditionsreichen Städten. Das Städtedreieck bildete von Beginn des 19. Jahr- hunderts bis zum Zweiten Weltkrieg das industrielle Herz Deutschlands. Jede dieser Städte wurde durch Bombenangriffe schwer beschädigt. Beson- 25 ders Dresden war mit einer fast völlig zerstörten Innenstadt und etwa 25.000 Toten hart getroffen. Nach dem Krieg konnte Sachsen trotzdem wieder zu einem bedeutenden Industriezentrum werden, sodass hier 40 Prozent der gesamten Industrieproduktion der DDR erwirtschaftet wurde. Wo einst Bergbau, Textilherstellung und Schwerindustrie vorherrschten, entstanden 30 Maschinen- und Automobilbau und Metallverarbeitung. Nach der Wende musste sich Sachsen noch einmal neu orientieren. Zu den industriellen Schwerpunkten sind heute zukunftsorientierte Hochtechnologien wie Solar- energie, Biotechnologie und Mikrotechnologie hinzugekommen. Sachsen ist neben Thüringen das einzige Bundesland im Osten, das gleichrangig mit 35 den westdeutschen Ländern in Bezug auf Wohlstand und Entwicklung ist.

Trotz der wechselvollen Geschichte Sachsens sieht man Kontinuitäten in den vielen über Jahrhunderte bestehenden Institutionen und Traditionen, in der gemeinsamen Kulturgeschichte und in den gemeinsamen Erfahrun- gen der dort lebenden Menschen. Kontinuität aber auch tiefgreifende Verän- derungen sind bezeichnend für die Entwicklung Sachsens und die Erfah- 40 rungen seiner Bewohner.

Answers for *Fragen zum Text*. **1.** Es liegt im Osten und grenzt an zwei nicht deutschsprachige Staaten. Es hat die meisten Einwohner im Ostteil Deutschlands. Wirtschaftlich ist es erfolgreicher als die meisten neuen Länder. **2.** Im Jahre 929, um die neue deutsche Besiedlung auf slawischem Gebiet zu sichern. **3.** Der Reichtum basierte auf den Bodenschätzen im Erzgebirge. **4.** Chemnitz und Zwickau sind Industriestädte. Leipzig ist Handelsstadt und Wissenschaftszentrum. Dresden ist kulturelles Zentrum und Sitz der Landesregierung Sachsens. **5.** Vom Beginn des 19. Jahrhunderts bis zum Zweiten Weltkrieg, dann wieder in der DDR, und auch heute ist es ein wichtiges wirtschaftliches Zentrum. **6.** 19. Jahrhundert: Bergbau, Textilherstellung und Schwerindustrie; 20. Jahrhundert: Maschinenbau, Automobilbau, Metallverarbeitung; 21. Jahrhundert: Solarenergie, Biotechnologie, Mikrotechnologie

Hören Sie ein Beispiel dieses Dialekts.

Nuscheln oder Mund-faulheit mumbling or having a lazy mouth

Dialekttipp. After they have read the text, ask students: *Wie ist die Aussprache des Sächsischen? Warum gibt es viele Ähnlichkeiten zwischen Hochdeutsch und Sächsisch? Warum hat der Dialekt an Prestige verloren? Mit welchem anderen Dialekt ist Sächsisch verwandt?* After students have completed the activities, write the following words on the board: „misch" (mich), „Garden" (Karten or Garten), „heeflisch" (höflich) and ask: *Wie könnte wohl ein Sachse meinen, wenn er diese Wörter sagt?*

Fragen zum Text

1. Wo und wie steht Sachsen im Vergleich zu den anderen Bundesländern?
2. Wann und warum wurde Sachsen erst gegründet?
3. Wie konnte Sachsen zu einem der reichsten deutschen Länder werden?
4. Beschreiben Sie die Unterschiede zwischen den vier größten Städten Sachsens.
5. Wann spielte Sachsen eine wichtige Rolle in der deutschen Wirtschaft?
6. Welche Wirtschaftsbranchen machten Sachsen zum industriellen Herzen Deutschlands im 19. Jahrhundert? im 20. Jahrhundert? im 21. Jahrhundert?

DIALEKTTIPP: Sächsisch

Sächsisch ist ein mitteldeutscher Dialekt, der mit dem Thüringischen verwandt ist. Das Sächsische erkennt man vor allem an seiner Aussprache, die von Nicht-Sachsen oft als Nuscheln oder Mundfaulheit° beschrieben wird. Die Vokabeln und Grammatik sind jedoch dem Hochdeutschen relativ ähnlich, denn Sächsisch war ursprünglich eine Grundlage der heutigen deutschen Standardsprache. Als das einst mächtige Sachsen dann im 18. Jahrhundert an politischer Macht verlor, hat die Sprache der Sachsen ihre Prominenz verloren. Heute wird Sächsisch in Umfragen manchmal als ein unattraktiver deutscher Dialekt bewertet. Umfragen zeigen aber, dass trotz aller Stigmatisierung die Sachsen ihren Dialekt unbedingt bewahren wollen.

Zum Dialekt

1 Wie sagt man das? Wählen Sie die richtigen Erklärungen der Unterschiede zwischen Sächsisch und Hochdeutsch.

Hochdeutsch → Sächsisch

<u>c</u> 1. süß, müssen → sieß, missn

<u>b</u> 2. schön, zwei → scheen, zwee

<u>a</u> 3. Arbeit, Ofen → Orbeit, Oufen

<u>g</u> 4. haben wir, sind wir → hammer, simmer

<u>h</u> 5. Sachsen, Künstler → Sachs'n, Ginstl'r

<u>f</u> 6. Tisch, dich, fettig → disch, disch, feddsch

<u>d</u> 7. prima, dort, kaputt → brima, dord, gabudd

<u>e</u> 8. deswegen, genügend → desweechen, genieschend

a. *a → o, o → u*

b. *ö, ei → langes e*

c. *ü → i(e)*

d. *p, t, k → b, d, g*

e. *g → (s)ch*

f. *-ich, -isch* und *-ig* klingen alle wie *isch*

g. Wörter werden zusammengezogen

h. Vokale verschwinden

2 Im Gespräch. Wie sagt man das auf Sächsisch?

Hochdeutsch	Sächsisch
_d_ 1. Wir trinken unseren Kaffee heiß und süß.	a. Da geht doch werglisch nischt.
_c_ 2. Das müssen wir noch ein bisschen üben.	b. Mir brummd dr Nischl. [Mir tut der Kopf weh.]
_e_ 3. Schau mal dahin.	c. Das miss' mir noch ä biss'l üb'm.
_a_ 4. Das geht doch wirklich nicht.	d. Mir drink'n unsern Gaffee hejs und sieße.
_b_ 5. Ich habe Kopfschmerzen.	e. Gugge ma dord drüb'm. [Gucke mal dort drüben.]

Lese- und Hörtexte

Lesetext 1

Stollen nach Dresdner Tradition (Erinnerung)

Der Dresdner Stollen, wohl das weltweit bekannteste Erzeugnis der sächsischen Küche, hat eine lange Tradition. Stollen oder Striezel, wie man ihn in Dresden nennt, hat man schon im 15. Jahrhundert gebacken und auf dem Weihnachtsmarkt dort verkauft. Zunächst lediglich aus Mehl, Hefe° und Wasser als Fastengebäck° herge-stellt, kamen im Laufe der Zeit auch Butter,

Dresdner Christstollen

yeast / baked goods for Lenten fasting

Früchte und andere Zutaten hinzu, um das reichhaltige Festgebäck zu erschaf-fen, das man heute kennt. Die traditionelle Form des Stollens, ein in Tüchern gewickeltes und in der Krippe liegendes Christkind, hat sich bis heute erhalten.

Dresdner Originale kann man heute in der Weihnachtszeit bei einem von ca. 150 Bäckern und Konditoren erhalten. Oder natürlich kann man sie selber ba-cken. Obwohl man sich heutzutage nur noch selten auf die aufwendige Arbeit des Stollenbackens einlässt, gehörte das einst zu den Weihnachtstraditionen vieler sächsischer Familien. Im folgenden Beitrag, der im Internet-Forum einer Webseite über Weihnachtstraditionen erschien, erzählt Annaliese Krause von ihren Erinnerungen an das Stollenbacken in ihrer Familie in der DDR.

Vor dem Lesen

Pflegt Ihre Familie irgendwelche Traditionen? Gibt es eine Tradition aus Ihrer Kindheit, die Ihre Familie nicht mehr pflegt? Wenn ja, warum hat man diese

Introduction to *Lesetext 1.* Introduce the topic. *Haben Sie Stollen schon mal probiert? Wie war der Stollen? Wie schmeckte er? Haben Sie Stollen schon mal gebacken?* Then ask students about the text introduction. *Wie alt ist die Tradition des Stollen-backens in Sachsen? Welche Zutaten hat ein Stollen? Wie sieht der Stollen traditionell aus?*

Tradition aufgegeben? Oder wenn diese Tradition in Ihrer Familie noch besteht, von wem wird sie besonders gepflegt?

Answers for *Beim Lesen*. die Tante, die Erzählerin Annaliese, der Vater, der Bruder, die Mutter, die Oma, der Bäcker

Beim Lesen

Achten Sie beim Lesen darauf, welche Personen am Stollenbacken teilnehmen.

Stollen nach Dresdner Tradition

06-04 to 06-06

Ich bin jetzt 55, wohne seit 12 Jahren der Liebe wegen in Niedersachsen, stamme aber aus der ehemaligen DDR, aus Dresden nämlich. Es ist es also vielleicht nicht wunderlich, dass zu meinen schönsten Erinnerungen das alljährliche Stollenbacken gehört.

Natürlich wurde bei uns zu Hause echter Christstollen (der Striezel – deshalb heißt der Dresdner Weihnachtsmarkt auch Striezelmarkt) gebacken. Ende November, also vor dem ersten Advent, 5
begannen die Vorbereitungen dazu. Die Zutaten mussten besorgt werden – Butterschmalz, Zucker, süße und bittere Mandeln, Hefe. Rosinen und Zitronat[a] kamen meist von der Tante im Westpaket.*
Mein Bruder und ich waren immer verurteilt zum Mandeln schälen[b]. Sie wurden mit heißem Wasser übergossen, so lösten sich die Schalen[c] leichter. Diese wurden dann teilweise gehackt und teils grob gemahlen, was die Aufgabe meines Vaters war. Meine Lieblingsarbeit war immer, Rosinen 10
auszulesen[d]. Obwohl ich es nicht durfte, gelang es mir mit einiger Übung, einzelne Rosinen unter der Zunge zu verstecken. Der süße Geschmack breitete sich allmählich in meinem Mund aus und ich stellte mir vor, wie ich am Weihnachtsabend das erste Stück Stollen essen würde.

Wir haben jedes Jahr rund zehn Stollen gebacken, jeder so um 1–1,5 kg Gewicht, und das konnte man natürlich nicht im heimischen Ofen bewältigen. Deshalb machte man Anfang Dezember mit 15
dem Lieblingsbäcker einen Termin zum Backen aus. Schon am Vorabend ging es los. Meine Mutter holte das bewährte Familienrezept aus seinem Versteck im Schrank und las es vor, während meine Oma die Backvorräte dann auf den Küchentisch stapelte. Früh am Morgen des Backtages wurden alle Zutaten – außer dem Mehl, das kam vom Bäcker – in einen Korb geladen und man fuhr mit dem Handwagen in die Backstube. Dort waren dann schon mehrere Frauen, die auch ihre Stollen 20
gebacken haben wollten. Der Bäcker bereitete jede Menge Teig gesondert in der Teigmaschine zu, damit die Zutaten jeder Familie getrennt blieben, denn so manche Hausfrau machte aus ihrem Rezept und den Zutaten ein Geheimnis. Bevor der Bäcker unter strenger Aufsicht der Frauen die Stollen in den Ofen schob, wurde von jeder Familie ein Aluminiumschild mit Namen in jeden unge-
backenen Laib[e] hineingesteckt, um Verwechslungen auszuschließen. Dann konnte man für ein paar 25
Stunden wieder nach Hause gehen. Am späten Nachmittag waren dann die Stollen fertig gebacken und man fand sich wieder beim Bäcker ein, um sie abzuholen und ein kleines Backgeld zu zahlen. Die fertigen Stollen wurden sorgfältig in einen Korb oder auf ein mitgebrachtes Küchenbrett[f] gelegt.

---

[a]*candied lemon peel*   [b]*remove the skin from*   [c]*skins*   [d]*to sort out*   [e]*loaf*   [f]*cutting board*

*Siehe **Kulturtipps**: Westpaket

Für den Heimtransport musste mein Vater die Verantwortung tragen und den ganzen Heimweg lang war meine Mutter in Sorge, mein Vater könnte irgendwo stolpern oder anstoßen. Es war schließlich Winter und die Straßen waren glatt. Falls ein Stollen auf dem Transport brach oder sogar vom Brett fiel, mahnte[g] die Oma, sollte im neuen Jahr jemand in der Familie sterben. 30

Zu Hause stand schon die Großmutter bereit, um die Stollen mit flüssiger Butter zu bestreichen und mit Puderzucker[h] zu bestreuen. Dieser wichtige Vorgang wurde drei- bis viermal wiederholt, um eine schöne Zuckerkruste zu bilden. Dann wurden die Stollen sorgfältig in Leinentücher gewickelt 35 und drei Wochen lang im Keller zum Ziehen gelassen, denn – wie meine Mutter sagte – lag das Geheimnis, aus einem guten Stollen einen besseren zu machen, in der Reife[i]. Der erste Christstollen wurde an Heiligabend nach der Messe[j] und keinen Moment früher angeschnitten. Aber damit das Warten nicht zu lang wurde, buk[k] der Bäcker aus ein wenig Stollenteig einen Stollenkuchen, der dann in Vorfreude[l] auf die richtigen Stollen schon probiert werden durfte. 40

Noch heute kann ich mich lebhaft an die herrlichen Gerüche, die Vorfreude auf den Genuss[m] und die spannenden Tage beim Bäcker erinnern. Das war eine Sache der ganzen Familie und eher ein Fest als wirkliche Arbeit. Schade, dass diese vorweihnachtliche Freude so aus der Mode gekommen ist. Der Stollen im Handel ist ja nicht schlecht, aber an den selber gebackenen reicht er nicht heran. 45

Eine schöne Adventszeit wünscht euch Annaliese.

---

[g]*warned* [h]*powdered sugar* [i]*maturity* [j]*mass* [k]*alternate form for* **backte** [l]*anticipation* [m]*enjoyment*

Kulturtipps

Westpaket

„Westpakete" nannte man in der DDR die Päckchen, die von westdeutschen Verwandten gesandt wurden. Die Pakete, die man besonders zu Weihnachten erwarten konnte, enthielten das, was in der DDR knapp war oder fehlte, z. B. Kleidung, Kaffee, Schokolade und Backzutaten. Da Familien beiderseits der Grenze sonst wenig persönlichen Kontakt haben durften, wurden neben Briefen diese Pakete wohl zu der intensivsten Form der Kommunikation zwischen Ost und West während der deutschen Teilung.

Teaching suggestion for Kulturtipp: Westpaket. Ask students if they can remember exactly when Germany existed as two states (1949–1989). Then ask: *Welche Kommunikationsmittel existieren heute, die vor 1989 nicht existierten? (z. B., Internet, E-Mail, Handys, Kabel- und Satellitenfernsehen). Warum waren in der DDR einige Waren nicht leicht zu finden? (Planwirtschaft vs. Marktwirtschaft, beschränkter Handel mit anderen Ländern.)* You might also tell them there were strict rules pertaining to mail and packages from the West and that it was not uncommon for goods to be confiscated by customs officials.

Neue Vokabeln

Nomen

das Geheimnis, -se *secret*

der Korb, ⁻e *basket*

die Mandel, -n *almond*

das Mehl *flour*

die Rosine, -n *raisin*

der Teig *dough*

der Termin, -e *appointment, fixed date*

die Verantwortung, -en *responsibility*

der Vorgang, ⁻e *process, occurrence*

die Zutat, -en *ingredient*

Verben

besorgen *to obtain*

sich erinnern an (+ *acc.*) *to remember*

stammen aus *to originate from*

verstecken *to hide*

wiederholen *to repeat*

Adjektive und Adverbien

allmählich *gradually*

bewährt *tried and true*

ehemalig *former*

fertig *finished*

sorgfältig *carefully*

Ausdrücke

aus der Mode kommen *to go out of style*

Schade! *What a pity!*

Answers for 6-1. 1. die Tante in Westdeutschland; 2. Annaliese und ihr Bruder; 3. der Vater; 4. Annaliese; 5. die Mutter; 6. die Oma; 7. der Bäcker; 8. die Familie; 9. der Vater; 10. die Oma

6-1 Textarbeit: Wer macht was? Wer macht die folgenden Aufgaben beim Stollenbacken in Annalieses Familie?

1. die Familie mit Rosinen versorgen
2. Mandeln schälen
3. Mandeln hacken oder mahlen
4. Rosinen auslesen
5. das Rezept vorlesen
6. die Zutaten auf den Tisch stellen
7. den Teig zubereiten
8. kleine Schilder in den Teig stecken
9. die fertigen Stollen nach Hause tragen
10. die Zuckerkruste am Stollen zubereiten

Additional comprehension questions for 6-2. *Warum wohnt die Erzählerin nicht mehr in Dresden? Wie hat man sichergestellt, dass beim Bäcker die Stollen der Familien getrennt blieben?*

Answers for 6-2. 1. Schon Ende November begannen die Vorbereitungen. 2. Stollen macht man aus Butterschmalz, Mandeln, Hefe, Rosinen, Zitronat und Mehl. 3. In der DDR waren sie knapp und man musste sie aus dem Westen bekommen. 4. Der Ofen zu Hause war nicht groß genug

6-2 Textarbeit: Fragen zum Inhalt. Beantworten Sie die Fragen in Bezug auf den Text.

1. Wann fing die Familie jedes Jahr an, sich auf das Stollenbacken vorzubereiten?
2. Woraus macht man Stollen?
3. Warum durfte die Erzählerin die Rosinen nicht essen?
4. Warum hat man die Stollen nicht zu Hause gebacken?
5. Wie sind die Zutaten zum Bäcker gekommen?
6. Wie hat diese Familie ihre Stollen nach Hause gebracht?
7. Welcher Aberglaube ist mit der Stollentradition verbunden?
8. Wann hat man die Stollen gegessen? Warum musste man warten?

für so viele Stollen. 5. Man fuhr sie mit dem Handwagen zur Bäckerei. 6. Der Vater trug sie in einem Korb oder auf einem Küchenbrett. 7. Man sagt, wenn ein Stollen während des Transports von der Bäckerei nach Hause bricht oder hinfällt, stirbt im nächsten Jahr jemand in der Familie. 8. Erst an Heiligabend nach der Messe hat man den ersten Christstollen gegessen, denn Stollen muss man nach dem Backen liegen lassen, damit sie reif werden.

6-3 Vokabelarbeit. Ergänzen Sie die Sätze mit Wörtern aus den *Neuen Vokabeln*. Achten Sie dabei auch auf die Wortform.

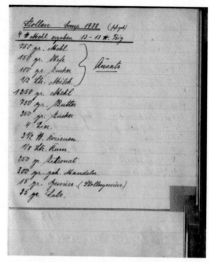

Ein altbewährtes Rezept für Stollen

1. Damals trug der Bäcker die ___Verantwortung___ für die Zubereitung und das Backen der Stollen.

2. Den ___Teig___ für einen Stollen macht man aus Mehl, Zucker, Hefe, Butter, Mandeln und trockenen Früchten.

3. Auch wenn jeder Dresdner Bäcker sein ___Geheimnis___ hat, bleiben Grundzutaten und Herstellungsweise für einen echten Dresdner Stollen gleich.

4. Nach dem Backen soll man die Stollen ___verstecken___, damit man sie nicht isst, bevor sie reif werden.

5. Der älteste Nachweis für Stollen ___stammt___ ___aus___ Naumburg, einer Stadt, die heute im Bundesland Sachsen-Anhalt liegt.

6. Das Fastengebäck aus dem 15. Jahrhundert wurde ___allmählich___ zu dem köstlichen Weihnachtskuchen, den man heute kennt.

7. Wenn man eine Handlung regelmäßig ___wiederholt___, wird sie zur Tradition.

6-4 Zur Diskussion. Besprechen Sie die Fragen.

1. Warum ist das Stollenbacken eine besonders schöne Erinnerung für Annaliese? Erinnern Sie sich gern an besondere Feiertage oder Traditionen aus Ihrer Kindheit?

2. Was meinen Sie: Warum ist die Tradition des Stollenbackens aus der Mode gekommen? Sollte man versuchen, solche Traditionen wieder ins Leben zu rufen? Warum (nicht)?

3. Annaliese erzählt vom Aberglauben, dass ein gebrochener Stollen einen Tod in der Familie prophezeit. Welche anderen Aberglauben kennen Sie?

4. Feiern Sie Weihnachten, Hanukkah, Kwanzza oder einen anderen besonderen Tag? Vergleichen Sie die Traditionen in Ihren Familien.

Information for Activity 6-4 (2). Ask students to think about the role of regional traditions in the context of globalization. Experts have observed, perhaps contrary to what one might expect, that globalization has brought an upswing in the propagation and revival of local traditions.

6-5 Frau Krause. Erinnerungen an dieselben Ereignisse sind nicht immer gleich. Berichten Sie über das Stollenbacken aus der Sicht von Annalieses Mutter für eine Internetseite über Weihnachtstraditionen.

6-6 Eine Erinnerung. Ein Newsletter über Traditionen, die in der Familie gefeiert werden, bittet um Beiträge. Erzählen Sie für die nächste Ausgabe dieses Newsletters von einer Familientradition, an die Sie sich aus Ihrer Kindheit erinnern.

Introduction to *Lesetext 2*.
Acquaint students with the topic
and ask what they learned from
the text introduction. *Kennen Sie
den Namen Gerhard Richter?
Wer ist er? Welchen Bezug hat er
zu Sachsen? Welche Bedeutung
könnte eine solche Ausstellung
mit Richters Werken für ein
Museum wie die Galerie Neue
Meister haben?*

ließ sich nieder settled

continued

examination, analysis

= die tageszeitung
Name einer überregionalen
Tageszeitung

Lesetext 2

Zwei Farben Grau (Kunstkritik)

Gerhard Richter, einer der weltweit bedeutendsten, einflussreichsten und teuersten zeitgenössischen Künstler, wurde 1932 in Dresden geboren. 1951 bis 1956 studierte er an der traditionsreichen Kunstakademie in Dresden. 1961 floh er aus der DDR und ließ sich in Düsseldorf nieder°, wo er an der Kunstakademie sein Studium fortsetzte° und später auch als Professor für Malerei tätig war. Heute lebt und arbeitet er in Köln. Charakteristisch für sein vielfältiges Werk ist, dass es sich einem einzigen künstlerischen Stil nicht zuordnen lässt. An seinem Schaffen erkennt man vielmehr eine experimentierende Auseinandersetzung° mit der Wirklichkeit, bei der der Künstler viele verschiedene Techniken und Stilrichtungen benutzt.

Gerhard Richter (2008)

Der folgende Zeitungsartikel aus der *taz*° berichtet von einer Ausstellung 2004/2005 in der Galerie Neue Meister, bei der zahlreiche Werke von Gerhard Richter hier zum ersten Mal ausgestellt wurden. Die Galerie Neue Meister ist eines von elf Museen, die die Staatlichen Kunstsammlungen Dresden ausmachen, und gehört zu den wichtigsten Museen der Moderne in Deutschland.

Vor dem Lesen

Waren Sie schon einmal in einem Kunstmuseum? Wenn ja, wo und wann? Was haben Sie dort gesehen?

Beim Lesen

Ordnen Sie die Zusammenfassungen den Absätzen des Lesetextes zu.

____4____ Kunstwerke aus seiner Dresdner Zeit gehören nicht zur Ausstellung.

____2____ Die ausgestellten Werke Richters bringen frischen Wind in das Museum.

____5____ Im ersten Richter-Raum sind vor allem seine fotorealistischen Werke zu sehen.

____6____ Der zweite Raum enthält unterschiedliche Bilder, der dritte nur seine abstrakten Werke.

____3____ Richters Werke ergänzen die traditionellen Schwerpunkte des Museums.

____1____ Gerhard Richter besucht das Albertinum in Dresden.

Zwei Farben Grau

von Robert Hodonyi

Note for *Sprachanalyse*. A few of the participle-derived modifiers in *Lesetext 2 (avancierten, entstandenen, angelehnte)* are part of longer extended adjective modifiers. Extended adjective constructions will be treated extensively in the *Sprachanalyse* in the *Kapitel 7* SAM and are thus excluded from analysis in the *Sprachanalyse* activity in SAM 06-09.

Gerhard Richter hat der Gemäldegalerie Neue Meister in Dresden 41 seiner Werke als Dauerleihgabe° überlassen.

Nein, als ein geschichtsträchtiger° Tag sei die Ankunft in seiner Geburtsstadt nicht zu werten. In den letzten Monaten hätte er Dresden ja schon öfters besucht. Für Gerhard Richter (72), der am vergangenen Freitag im Rahmen einer Pressekonferenz drei neue Räume mit seinen Bildern, Glas- und Spiegelarbeiten in der Galerie Neue Meister im Albertinum einweihte°, sei 5 Bedingung der Kooperation mit den Staatlichen Kunstsammlungen Dresden gewesen, so der Künstler mit einem Augenzwinkern°, dass der „graue Kasten°" erst einmal renoviert werde. Richter, der sonst eigentlich nichts gegen die Farbe Grau einzuwenden hat, meinte damit die leicht heruntergekommenen Räume im zweiten Obergeschoss des Albertinums. 10

Hier sind jetzt an frisch geweißten Wänden 41 Werke ausgestellt, die einen Querschnitt° der letzten 40 Jahre seines Schaffens zeigen. Damit besitzt Dresden eine der weltweit größten Richter-Sammlungen überhaupt und kann selbst mit dem MoMa°-Bestand konkurrieren. Die Dauerleihgaben aus dem Besitz des Künstlers und privater Sammler führten dementsprechend zu einer veränderten Konzeption der Galerie Neue Meister. Seltsam selbstkritisch heißt es dazu 15 im Katalog: „Er gibt den ins Schwimmen geratenen° Staatlichen Kunstsammlungen Dresden Halt°, indem er die für ein Museum der modernen Kunst existenzbedrohende Lücke im Bereich der Gegenwartskunst mit einem Block von herausragenden Werken exemplarisch schließt. [...] Dieser Vorgang ist für das 20 Albertinum mehr als nur ein Glücksfall, es eröffnet nach mehr als 70 Jahren Perspektiven für eine veränderte Zukunft, weil mit Gerhard Richter die Gegenwart auf einem ganz neuen Niveau in den Dresdener Museen Einzug hält°."

Hatte man es bisher versäumt°, Gegenwartskunst repräsentativ und breit auszustellen, unter anderem, weil man konsequent an den traditionellen Schwerpunkten der Galerie – der romantischen Malerei des 19. 25 Jahrhunderts sowie der klassischen Moderne – festhielt, bedeuten die drei Richter-Räume zugleich eine stärkere Orientierung auf das späte 20. Jahrhundert, wie bereits im neuen Titel der Dauerpräsentation deutlich wird: „Von Caspar David Friedrich bis Gerhard Richter". 30

Richter, der sich als Betriebsmaler für Agitprop-Transparente° durchschlug, bevor er 1952 an der Dresdener Kunstakademie angenommen wurde, hat die Hängung und Auswahl der Werke in Eigenregie ausgeführt. Das älteste Bild in der Ausstellung stammt von 1963, aus demselben Jahr, in dem der Künstler zusammen mit Konrad Lueg in einem Düsseldorfer 35 Möbelhaus die berühmte Ausstellung „Leben mit Pop – Eine Demonstration für den Kapitalistischen Realismus" in Szene setzte.

Arbeiten aus seiner Dresdner Zeit, die 1961 mit der Übersiedlung in die Bundesrepublik endete, sind nicht zu sehen. Die meisten dieser Arbeiten

permanent loan

steeped in history

inaugurated

wink
box

cross section

Museum of Modern Art in New York City

***ins Schwimmen geratenen** floundering /* ***gibt Halt** stabilizes*

***Einzug hält** finds its way into / neglected*

Siehe **Kulturtipps**: Caspar David Friedrich

banners
Siehe **Kulturtipps**: Agitprop

Siehe **Kulturtipps**: Kapitalistischer Realismus

missing gelten allerdings als verschollen°. Über Jahre wollte der Künstler auch   40
nichts von seiner Dresdner Vergangenheit wissen.

Die Konzeption der neuen Richter-Räume in Dresden bestimmt keine line-
are Erzählstruktur oder chronologische Anordnung. Im ersten Raum dominie-
ren die auf Grundlage des inzwischen selbst zum Kunstwerk avancierten „Atlas
der Fotos, Collagen und Skizzen" entstandenen fotorealistischen Arbeiten der   45
Sechzigerjahre wie „Tote" (1963), „Sekretärin" (1964) oder „Motorboot" (1965).
Das für Richter wichtige Prinzip der Serie, die Anordnung von Werkgruppen zu
Reihen, kann man ebenfalls im ersten Raum beobachten: Die Porträts der „Acht
Lernschwestern" (1971) korrespondieren etwa mit
den unmittelbar darunter angeordneten gleichforma-   50
tigen abstrakten Arbeiten, die Ende der Neunziger-
jahre entstanden sind. Eines der neuesten Bilder, die
Arbeit „14. Februar 1945" (2002), stellt einen Bezug zu
Dresden her: Die Stadtansicht aus der Luftperspek-
tive nach dem Angriff der Alliierten in der Nacht vom   55
13. auf den 14. Februar 1945. Das Bild könnte leicht
mit einer der vielen herkömmlichen Stadtansichten
Richters verwechselt werden, wären da nicht die
zahlreichen Bombenkrater. Man kann darüber nachdenken, ob es eventuell sinnvoll gewesen wäre, ein   60
Bild aus dem zweiten Raum, nämlich „Onkel Rudi"

„Onkel Rudi" (1965)
von Gerhard Richter

Unschärfe und
Verwischung fuzziness and
blurring / military uniform

hidden

(1965/2000), das in typisch grauer Unschärfe und
Verwischung° einen lächelnden Deutschen in Wehr-
machtsuniform° zeigt, in unmittelbare Nachbarschaft
des „14. Februar 1945" zu hängen. Damit wäre ein Zusammenhang von Ursa-   65
che und Wirkung hergestellt, der in Dresden ab und zu ausgeblendet° wird.

Neben „Onkel Rudi", den bekannten „Zwei Kerzen" (1982), der Farbfeld-
malerei aus den Siebzigerjahren, der etwas verloren wirkenden „Wolkenstu-
die" (1970) und dem an die Vanitasmotivik°

vanity motif (in art,
symbolizing the brevity of
life and the transience of
all earthly pleasures and
achievements) / damaged by
flood / donated

angelehnte „Schädel" (1983) befindet sich im   70
zweiten Raum unter anderem auch das Bild
„Fels" (1989), welches Richter im November
2002 für die Auktion anlässlich der flutgeschä-
digten° Staatlichen Kunstsammlungen gestif-   75
tet°. hatte. Für 2,6 Millionen Euro wurde das
Gemälde damals in der Neuen Nationalgale-
rie neben Werken von Baselitz, Immendorff
und Lüpertz[1] versteigert° Der dritte neue

auctioned

Siehe **Kulturtipps**:
Sommerflut des Jahres 2002

„Fels" (1989) von Gerhard
Richter

Richter-Raum ist ganz den abstrakten Bildern   80
vorbehalten, die größtenteils in den Neunzi-
gerjahren entstanden sind und die jüngste
Schaffensperiode des Künstlers markieren.

---

[1]Georg Baselitz (geb. 1938 in Sachsen), Jörg Immendorff (1945–2007) und Markus Lüpertz
(geb. 1941) sind einige der bekanntesten Künstler der deutschen Moderne.

Kulturtipps

Caspar David Friedrich (1774–1840)

Der aus Greifswald an der Ostsee stammende Maler und Zeichner wurde zu einem der bedeutendsten Vertreter der deutschen Romantik. Mit seinen religiös-symbolhaften, subjektiven Landschafts- und Natur-gemälden bildete sein Werk einen starken Kontrast zum Realismus der vorangehenden Kunstepoche. Ab 1798 lebte er durch viele Reisen unterbrochen in Dresden, wo er an der Kunstakademie studierte und später auch unterrichtete.

Agitprop

Das aus den Wörtern „Agitation" und „Propaganda" gebildete Kurzwort Agitprop bezeichnete in der DDR die Beeinflussung der öffentlichen Meinung im Sinne der kommunistischen Doktrin. In der DDR war der Begriff positiv geprägt, im Westen hingegen wurde und wird das Wort häufig abwertend (*pejoratively*) gebraucht.

Caspar David Friedrichs „Felsen-landschaft im Elbsandsteingebirge" (1822–1823) hängt heute in der Österreichischen Galerie in Wien.

Kapitalistischer Realismus

Richter und Lueg starteten diese Kunstrichtung, mit der sie Kritik an den Konsum- und Lebens-gewohnheiten im Westen der 60er-Jahre geübt haben. Gewählt wurde der Name als Gegenpol zum „Sozialistischen Realismus". Nach dieser offiziellen Kunstdoktrin der DDR sollte die Kunst partei-politischen Zielen folgen und beispielsweise mit heroisierten Darstellungen aus dem Leben der Arbeiter und Bauern das Volk ideologisch manipulieren.

Sommerflut des Jahres 2002

Im August 2002 führte anhaltender Regen zu einer Hochwasserkatastrophe, bei der die Elbe in Sachsen einen Rekordhöchststand erreichte und die historische Altstadt Dresdens überflutet wurde. Innerhalb kurzer Zeit mussten 23.000 Kunstobjekte der Staatlichen Kunstsammlungen – darunter 700 Gemälde im Albertinum – aus unterirdischen Depots evakuiert werden. Fast alle Kunstwerke wurden gerettet, das Museumsgebäude hingegen erlitt schwere Schäden und benötigte Sanierung (*restoration*).

Neue Vokabeln

Nomen

der Angriff, -e *attack*

die Ausstellung, -en *exhibit*

die Bedingung, -en *condition*

der Bezug, ˸e *connection*

die Gegenwart *present (time)*

das Gemälde, - *painting, picture*

die Lücke, -n *gap, hole*

der Maler, -/die Malerin, -nen *painter*

die Malerei, -en *painting*

der Schwerpunkt, -e *main emphasis, focus*

die Vergangenheit *past*

der Zusammenhang, ˸e *connection, context*

Verben

an·nehmen (nimmt an), nahm an, angenommen *to accept*

beobachten *to observe*

bestimmen *to decide, determine*

fest·halten an (+ *dat.*) (hält fest), hielt fest, festgehalten *to hold fast to*

Adjektive und Adverbien

ab und zu *from time to time*

in Bezug auf (+ *acc.*) *in relation to*

damals *back then, at that time*

eventuell *perhaps*

herkömmlich *conventional*

unmittelbar *immediate(ly)*

Answers for 6-7. 1. F – In den letzten Monaten hat Gerhard Richter Dresden öfters besucht. **2.** R; **3.** F – Die Richter-Werke im Museum stammen aus dem Besitz Richters und privater Sammler. **4.** F – Das Museum spezialisiert sich auf Werke vom 19. bis ins späte 20. Jahrhundert / bis in die Gegenwart. **5.** F – Die Ausstellung zeigt Werke, die in den letzten 40 Jahren entstanden sind. **6.** R; **7.** R; **8.** F – Das Bild „Fels" hat er 2002 für die Auktion der Galerie gestiftet.

6-7 Textarbeit: Richtig oder falsch? Wenn eine Aussage falsch ist, korrigieren und ergänzen Sie sie mit Informationen aus dem Text.

1. Zur Eröffnung der Ausstellung besuchte Gerhard Richter Dresden zum ersten Mal seit Jahren.
2. Kaum ein anderes Museum stellt so viele seiner Werke aus.
3. Alle Richter Werke im Museum stammen aus dem Besitz von Richter selbst.
4. Das Museum spezialisiert sich ausschließlich auf Werke aus dem 20. Jahrhundert.
5. Die Ausstellung zeigt Werke, die das ganze Arbeitsleben von Richter umspannen.
6. Im ersten Richter-Raum befinden sich fotorealistische wie auch abstrakte Bilder.
7. Dresden erscheint als eine Thematik in seinen Arbeiten.
8. Das Bild „Fels" hat er 2002 für die Galerie Neue Meister gemalt.

Follow-up for 6-8. Have students surmise why Richter wanted little to do with his hometown for so many years. *Was hatte er wohl gegen Dresden? Warum hat er 1961 die Stadt verlassen? Warum hat er der Stadt bis 2002 den Rücken gekehrt?* It might be helpful to tell them that he has refused to allow his thesis project from the Dresdener Kunstakademie, a five-by-fifteen-meter wall painting in the style of social realism located in the Dresdner Hygienemuseum that has been whitewashed for years, to be shown. *Warum hat er wohl jetzt nach so vielen Jahren wieder Kontakt mit seiner Heimat aufgenommen?*

6-8 Textarbeit: Fragen zum Inhalt. Beantworten Sie die Fragen in Bezug auf den Text.

1. Welche Bedingung sollte das Museum für Richters Kooperation erfüllen?
2. Worauf bezieht sich der Titel des Artikels „Zwei Farben Grau"?
3. Warum sind die neuen Kunstwerke Richters für die Galerie Neue Meister besonders wichtig?
4. Aus welchem Zeitraum stammen die Werke in der Richter-Ausstellung des Museums?
5. Warum ist keines seiner Werke aus der Zeit vor 1961 in der Ausstellung zu sehen?
6. Welchen Vorschlag hat der Autor des Artikels für das Bild „Onkel Rudi"? Warum?
7. Wodurch hat die Galerie Geld für Renovierungen nach der Flut des Jahres 2002 verdient?

6-9 Vokabelarbeit. Ergänzen Sie die Sätze mit Wörtern aus den *Neuen Vokabeln.* Achten Sie dabei auch auf die Wortform.

1. Zur Galerie Neue Meister gehören rund 2.500 ___Gemälde___ aus dem 19. bis 21. Jahrhundert.

2. Heute liegt der ___Schwerpunkt___ der Sammlungsaktivitäten auf der zeitgenössischen Dresdner und deutschen Malerei.

3. Es kommen in Zukunft ___eventuell___ noch zusätzliche Werke von Richter in den Besitz der Galerie.

4. Einige Kunstkenner nennen Gerhard Richter den „Picasso des 21. Jahrhunderts" und halten ihn für den erfolgreichsten Maler der ___Gegenwart___.

5. Richter selbst ___bestimmte___, welche Werke in der Ausstellung gezeigt und wie sie ausgestellt wurden.

6. In der Ausstellung war keine ___herkömmliche___ Anordnung seiner Werke – weder eine chronologische noch eine thematische – zu beobachten.

7. ___Unmittelbar___ nach dieser Ausstellung wurde das Gerhard-Richter-Archiv als ein Institut der Staatlichen Kunstsammlungen Dresden gegründet.

8. Obwohl der Maler seit langem nicht mehr in Dresden lebt, besucht er seine Heimatstadt immer noch ___ab___ ___und___ ___zu___.

6-10 Ein Besuch in der Galerie Neue Meister. Schauen Sie sich zwei Gemälde aus der Galerie Neue Meister an und besprechen Sie sie. Benutzen Sie die folgenden Fragen als Ausgangspunkt Ihrer Diskussion.

1. Beschreiben Sie, was Sie auf jedem Bild sehen. Welche Farben und Themen haben die Bilder?

2. Wie heißen die Gemälde? Finden Sie beide Titel passend? Erfinden Sie einen alternativen Titel für jedes Bild.

3. Vergleichen Sie beide Gemälde. Welches Bild ist älter? größer? Sind sie Bilder von demselben Künstler oder von unterschiedlichen Künstlern? Welches Bild gefällt Ihnen besser? Warum?

6-11 Zur Diskussion. Besprechen Sie die Fragen.

1. Interessieren Sie sich für Kunst? Was für Kunst mögen Sie am liebsten? Welche Künstler mögen Sie besonders gern? Was für Kunst gefällt Ihnen nicht so sehr? Möchten Sie gerne die Ausstellung „Von Caspar David Friedrich bis Gerhard Richter" sehen? Warum (nicht)?

2. Haben Sie künstlerisches Talent? Was können Sie besonders gut machen: zeichnen, malen, basteln oder vielleicht etwas anderes? Haben Sie schon einmal an einem Kunstkurs teilgenommen? Wenn ja, was haben Sie in dem Kurs gemacht oder gelernt?

3. Gibt es ein Kunstmuseum in Ihrer Stadt? Wo kann man in Ihrer Stadt sonst noch Kunst sehen? Welche Rolle spielt die Kunst in Ihrem Leben? in der Gesellschaft?

Answers for 6-8. 1. Das Museum sollte die Räume, die für seine Werke zur Verfügung gestellt wurden, renovieren. **2.** Er bezieht sich einerseits auf die graue Farbe des unrenovierten Museums und andererseits auf die Farbe Grau, die Richter häufig in seinen Gemälden gebraucht. **3.** Sie schließen eine Lücke in der Sammlung der Gegenwartskunst und bringen eine stärkere Orientierung auf die Kunst des späten 20. Jahrhunderts. **4.** Das älteste Bild stammt vom Jahr 1963, das neueste ist 2002 entstanden. **5.** Die meisten Arbeiten aus seiner Dresdner Zeit gelten als verschollen. Außerdem wollte der Künstler jahrelang nichts von seiner Dresdner Vergangenheit wissen. **6.** Er schlägt vor, dass man das Bild neben das Bild „14. Februar 1945" hängt, um einen Zusammenhang von Ursache (Militär, NS-Zeit) und Wirkung (Zerstörung) herzustellen. **7.** Sie haben gestiftete Werke renommierter Künstler versteigert.

Note for 6-10. You will need to bring images to class, have students access the images online during class, or assign students to bring two images to class. You could assign specific images or have students choose their own. You will find relevant web links in MyGermanLab and at the Companion Website.

Alternative for 6-10. Have students visit Gerhard Richter's official web page and choose two images by the artist to complete the assignment. You could have them choose paintings mentioned in the article or let them choose freely from among all of his works.

Introduction to *Hörtext 1*. Ask students if they've ever heard of Dresden and if so, in what context. Then ask them what they learned from the text introduction. *Wofür ist Dresden bekannt? Was hat August I. zu der Stadt beigetragen? Was ist während des Krieges mit den Kulturgütern Dresdens passiert? Wissen Sie etwas über die italienische Stadt Florenz? Warum nennt man Dresden wohl „Elbflorenz"?* If students are not familiar with Florence, you can tell them that the city, also situated on a river, is known for its world-class art collections and its architecture.

6-12 Ein Besuch im Museum. Beschreiben Sie einen Besuch in einem Museum für eine Internetseite, die Erfahrungsberichte über Reiseziele und Sehenswürdigkeiten sammelt. Erzählen Sie, warum Sie das Museum besucht haben, was Sie gesehen haben, was Ihnen besonders gefallen hat, für wen das Museum besonders interessant sein könnte, usw.

Hörtext 1

Many buildings in Dresden were influenced by or modeled after Italian and Florentian architecture.

Dresden-Touren (Werbung)

Die ehemalige sächsische Residenz- und heutige Landeshauptstadt ist ein Kunst- und Kulturzentrum von europäischem Rang°. Den Weltruf Dresdens begründete vor allem Kurfürst° August I., der im frühen 18. Jahrhundert Dresden zur modernsten Residenzstadt Europas machen wollte. Sein Hofstaat° war damals sogar glanzvoller° als der des Kaisers. August I. ließ prächtige Bauten in und außerhalb der Stadt entstehen, lud namhafte° Künstler, Komponisten und Dichter nach Dresden ein, um an seinem Hof zu arbeiten, und sammelte Kunstgegenstände, die heute zu den Staatlichen Kunstsammlungen Dresden gehören.

importance

electoral prince

royal court
more splendid

renowned

Dresden nach den Bombenangriffen Februar 1945

Obwohl die Stadt 1945 durch Luftangriffe bis zu 80 Prozent zerstört und der Wiederaufbau zu DDR-Zeiten nur langsam – wenn überhaupt – voranging, sind die historischen Baudenkmäler heute größtenteils wieder aufgebaut und restauriert. Kunstwerke, die während des Krieges verschwanden, befinden sich auch mittlerweile größtenteils wieder in Dresden. Die Meisterwerke der Architektur, die wertvollen Kunstschätze und die malerische Lage beiderseits der Elbe locken Touristen aus aller Welt an. Diese „Elbflorenz" – so genannt wegen Ähnlichkeiten mit der italienischen Kunstmetropole – hat pro Kopf mehr Besucher als jede andere Stadt Deutschlands.

Blick auf die Dresdner Altstadt heute

Eine Reihe von Reiseveranstaltern organisiert Führungen in und um Dresden, damit man die Stadt und ihre Geschichte kennenlernen kann. In der folgenden Radiowerbung erfahren Sie von einem dieser Tourenangebote.

Vor dem Hören

Was machen Sie, um eine Stadt kennenzulernen, wenn Sie die Stadt zum ersten Mal besuchen?

Beim Hören

Während der Werbung hören Sie folgende Vokabeln.

Dresden-Touren
06-10

Molkerei *dairy*
Gewölbe *vault*
Schatzkammer *treasure room*
Gewand(e) *garb, clothing*

Einheimischer *local inhabitant*
Jagdschloss *hunting chateau, hunting lodge*
Fürsten *rulers*

Hören Sie sich die Werbung an und markieren Sie, was Sie hören.

Stadtrundfahrt	Milchladen	historische Touren
Villengebiete	Augustusbrücke	Fahrradtouren
Blaues Wunder	Kathedrale	Porzellan
Elbtal	Residenzschloss	Nationalpark
Elbtunnel	Martin-Luther-Kirche	Landschaften
Elbschlösser	Rundgänge	Gärten

Kulturtipps

Dresdner Elbtal

Dresden liegt in einem etwa 20 km breiten und 40 km langen Tal der Elbe, das sich von Pirna bis Meißen erstreckt. Ein Teil des Tals wurde 2004 wegen der natürlichen Flusslandschaft und der prächtigen Architektur und hochwertigen Kunstschätze aus dem 18. und 19. Jahrhundert in die UNESCO-Liste des Welterbes (*World Heritage Sites*) aufgenommen. Seinen Welterbe-Titel verlor das Elbtal allerdings 2009 wegen des Baus einer umstrittenen vierspurigen (*four-lane*) Autobrücke durch die einzigartige Kulturlandschaft.

Semperoper

Das Opernhaus, das von 1838 bis 1841 vom Baumeister Gottfried Semper errichtet wurde, ist eines der bekanntesten Bauwerke der Stadt. Zweimal wurde das Gebäude zerstört – 1869 durch einen Brand und 1945 während der Luftangriffe auf Dresden – und nach den Plänen Sempers wieder aufgebaut.

Dresdner Frauenkirche

Die 1726 bis 1743 errichtete Frauenkirche, ein Meisterwerk des Barocks und der bedeutendste protestantische Kirchenbau Sachsens, wurde 1945 während der Bombenangriffe auf Dresden zerstört. Etwa fünfzig Jahre lang lag der Trümmerhaufen (*heap of rubble*) als Mahnmal (*memorial*) gegen den Krieg mitten in der Dresdner Altstadt. Nach der Wende wollte man die Kirche als Symbol der Versöhnung (*reconciliation*) wieder aufbauen. Von 1994 bis 2005 dauerte die Arbeit, die durch Stadt und Staat sowie von Spendern aus aller Welt unterstützt wurde.

Sächsische Schweiz

Der Teil des im deutsch-tschechischen Grenzgebiet liegenden Elbsandsteingebirges, der zu Deutschland gehört, heißt die Sächsische Schweiz. Diesen Namen soll das Gebiet von zwei im 18. Jahrhundert durchwandernden schweizerischen Malern erhalten haben. Charakteristisch für die Landschaft sind bizarre Sandsteintürme (*towers of sandstone*) und Tafelberge (*high plateaus*), die sich über dem Tal der Elbe erheben. Das Gebiet wurde 1990 zum Nationalpark erklärt.

Blick auf die Basteibrücke, das tief unten liegende Elbtal und die Tafelberge der Sächsischen Schweiz

6-13 Textarbeit: Richtig oder falsch? Wenn eine Aussage falsch ist, korrigieren und ergänzen Sie sie mit Informationen aus dem Text.

Answers for 6-13. 1. F – Die Rundfahrt erfolgt in einem Doppeldeckerbus. **2.** R; **3.** R; **4.** F – Das Grüne Gewölbe befindet sich im Residenzschloss. **5.** F – Rundfahrten starten täglich zwischen 10.00 und 17.00 Uhr alle 20 Minuten. **6.** R; **7.** F – Rundgänge gibt es zweimal täglich. **8.** R; **9.** F – Moritzburg war das Jagdschloss der sächsischen Fürsten.

1. Die Rundfahrt erfolgt in einer historischen Straßenbahn.
2. Im Elbtal kann man einige historische Schlösser besichtigen.
3. Um die Königstraße ist Architektur aus der Barockzeit zu sehen.
4. Das Grüne Gewölbe befindet sich in der Semperoper.
5. Rundfahrten starten täglich zwischen 10.00 und 17.00 Uhr alle 30 Minuten.
6. Die Tourleiter der Rundgänge tragen historische Kostüme.
7. Rundgänge gibt es dreimal täglich.
8. Die Stadt Meißen ist mehr als 1.000 Jahre alt.
9. Moritzburg war die Residenz der sächsischen Fürsten.

Hörbücher live vorgetragen

Viel junges Publikum war auch bei den Hörbüchern zu finden. Das ist im Zeitalter der Technik wohl keine Überraschung. Besonders große Menschentrauben° sammelten sich, wenn das Hörbuch nicht aus den großen Lautsprechern kam, sondern vom Autor persönlich vorgelesen wurde. Dabei wurden natürlich allerlei Fragen rund um die Schreiberei beantwortet. – Wer spontan eines der vielen Bücher nicht mehr loslassen wollte, konnte vor Ort gleich zuschlagen.° „Um das triste Aprilwetter zu überbrücken, habe ich mir einige Krimis zugelegt", sagt Nadine. Dazu hat die 15-jährige Leipzigerin bei zahlreichem Bonusmaterial, wie CDs mit Hörproben, Katalogen, Zeitungen und Magazinen, zugeschlagen. „So habe ich auch in den nächsten Wochen genügend Lesestoff ", sagt sie.

clusters of people

(colloq.) buy

25

30

Prominente Autoren getroffen

Aufmerksame Besucher wurden auf ihrem Gang durch die Hallen mit einem Blick auf den einen oder anderen Prominenten, wie Jung-Schriftsteller Benjamin Lebert oder Nobelpreisträger Günter Grass, belohnt. Auch Kolumnistin Sarah Kuttner mischte sich unters Volk und präsentierte ihren ersten Roman *Mängelexemplar*. Friedrich aus Freital ist begeistert. „Ich war schon mehrmals auf der Messe", sagt er, „und finde sie immer wieder interessant. Auch im nächsten Jahr habe ich den Termin fest eingeplant." Da wird Friedrich sicher nicht der einzige sein.

Siehe **Kulturtipps**: Benjamin Lebert, Günter Grass und Sarah Kuttner

35

Fazit: Die Leipziger Buchmesse ist auch bei Jugendlichen angesagt: Ob populäre Comics, das Treffen mit bekannten Autoren oder neue Bestseller, die zum Schmökern° einladen. Den Termin sollte sich jeder im Kalender vormerken.

40

browsing

 Neue Vokabeln

Nomen

der Anhänger, -/die Anhängerin, -nen *supporter, fan*

die Belletristik *literary fiction*

der Gang, ⸚e *path*

der Held, -en, -en/die Heldin, -nen *hero/heroine*

der Krimi, -s *mystery novel, crime thriller*

die Messe, -n *trade fair, exhibition*

das Sachbuch, ⸚er *non-fiction book*

der Treffpunkt, -e *meeting place*

die Überraschung, -en *surprise*

der Verlag, -e *publishing house*

Verben

belohnen *to reward*

gleichen (+ *dat.*), glich, geglichen *to resemble*

sich verwandeln in (+ *acc.*) *to transform oneself into*

vor·lesen (liest vor), las vor, vorgelesen *to read (something) to (somebody)*

Adjektive und Adverbien

eigen *one's own*

begeistert (von) *enthusiastic (about)*

bunt *colorful*

genügend *sufficient*

spannend *exciting*

verkleidet *dressed up, disguised*

Ausdrücke

vor Ort *on site, on the spot*

Kulturtipps

Benjamin Lebert, Günter Grass und Sarah Kuttner

Der 1982 geborene Benjamin Lebert ist ein Schriftsteller, der mit seinem Roman *Crazy* schon mit 17 einen internationalen Bestseller hatte. Der Schriftsteller Günter Grass (geb. 1927) gehört zu den bedeutendsten deutschsprachigen Autoren der Gegenwart. Er erhielt 1999 den Literatur-Nobelpreis für seinen 1959 erschienenen Roman *Die Blechtrommel*. Die Fernseh- und Radiomoderatorin und Kolumnistin Sarah Kuttner (geb. 1979) schaffte es mit ihrem Roman *Mängelexemplar* auf die Bestsellerliste.

Günter Grass stellt sein neustes Werk vor.

Answers for 6-18. 1. Sie findet einmal im Jahr für vier Tage statt. **2.** 40 Verlage; **3.** 40 Länder; **4.** Sie haben sich als Helden aus den Comics verkleidet. **5.** Sie hat Lesestoff gesammelt. **6.** Benjamin Lebert, Günter Grass und Sarah Kuttner. **7.** Sie meint, für junge Menschen sind die populären Comics, das Treffen mit bekannten Autoren und die neuen Bestseller von Interesse.

6-18 Textarbeit: Fragen zum Inhalt. Beantworten Sie die Fragen in Bezug auf den Text.

1. Wie oft findet die Messe statt und wie lange dauert sie?
2. Wie viele Verlage nehmen an der Messe teil?
3. Wie viele Länder sind auf der Messe vertreten?
4. Wie haben sich einige Messebesucher verkleidet?
5. Was hat die 15-jährige Nadine aus Leipzig auf der Messe gemacht?
6. Welche bekannten Schriftsteller kann man beispielweise auf der Messe erblicken?
7. Was macht die Messe nach der Ansicht der Autorin zu einem attraktiven Ziel für jungen Menschen?

Possible answers for 6-19. Man kann sich ältere und neu erschienene Bücher anschauen, sich wie ein Comicheld verkleiden oder die verkleideten Anhänger sehen, andere Comicfans treffen, Comics von Autoren signieren lassen, Hörbücher vom Lautsprecher hören, Autorenlesungen live erleben, neue Bücher kaufen. Autoren Fragen stellen, Zeitungen oder Magazine kaufen, Prominente erblicken.

Small group follow-up for 6-19. Have students discuss where and when they might do each of the activities they named in activity **6-19** besides at a book fair.

6-19 Textarbeit: Messebesuch. Beschreiben Sie mindestens sechs Aktivitäten, die man auf der Messe machen oder erleben kann. Sagen Sie auch, welche Sie am liebsten und welche Sie am wenigsten mögen.

6-20 Vokabelarbeit. Ergänzen Sie die Sätze mit Wörtern aus den *Neuen Vokabeln*. Achten Sie dabei auch auf die Wortform.

1. Würdige Neuerscheinungen werden mit dem Preis der Leipziger Buchmesse _____belohnt_____.

2. Ich bin ein großer _____Anhänger_____ von Günter Grass. Ich habe alle seine Romane gelesen.

3. Der ____Held/Jugendliche____ in seinem bekanntesten Werk *Die Blechtrommel* heißt Oskar Matzerath.

4. Mein Freund hat ein _____Sachbuch_____ über die Geschichte des Flugzeugs gekauft.

5. Das Buch wurde von einem kleinen Leipziger _____Verlag_____ gedruckt.

6. Mein Freund und ich waren von der Buchmesse sehr _____begeistert_____ und werden sie auf jeden Fall auch nächstes Jahr besuchen.

6-21 Bestseller! Sie haben eine großartige Idee für den nächsten Bestseller! Entwerfen Sie einen Abriss für dieses Buch.

1. Erfinden Sie einen Titel.
2. Nennen Sie das Genre (z.B. Krimi, Manga, Biografie, Lexikon).
3. Bei Belletristik beschreiben Sie die Charaktere und fassen Sie die Handlung kurz zusammen. Bei einem Sachbuch beschreiben Sie das Thema.
4. Beschreiben Sie, welche Leser Sie mit dem Buch erreichen wollen. Vergessen Sie nicht: das Buch muss ein großes Publikum ansprechen, wenn es erfolgreich sein soll!

Besucher auf der Leipziger Buchmesse

 6-22 Zur Diskussion. Besprechen Sie die Fragen.

1. Lesen Sie gern? Was lesen Sie? Welche von den Genres, die auf der Messe vertreten sind, interessieren Sie am meisten?
2. Haben Sie schon Erfahrung mit Hörbüchern? Wie unterscheidet sich ein Hörbuch von einem gedruckten Buch? Was für Bücher eignen sich besonders gut für Hörbücher und welche nicht?
3. Lesen Sie manchmal E-Bücher? Welche Vorteile hat ein E-Buch gegenüber einem gedruckten Buch? Welche Nachteile hat es?
4. Welche Rolle spielen Bibliotheken im technologischen Zeitalter? Gehen Sie manchmal in eine Bibliothek? Warum (nicht)?

6-23 Ein Buch. Denken Sie an ein gutes Buch, das Sie neulich gelesen haben, und schreiben Sie für einen Buchkatalog eine Zusammenfassung des Inhalts.

Lesetext 4

„Das Hochzeitsfoto" von Dieter Zimmer (Romanauszug)

Introduction to Lesetext 4.
Ask students what they learned about the author and his work. *Unter welchen politischen Verhältnissen hat Dieter Zimmer während seines Lebens bisher gelebt? Was hat er als Autor bisher geschrieben? Welche andere Tätigkeit außer Schriftsteller hat er ausgeübt? Welche autobiografischen Züge sind in der Handlung von „Das Hochzeitsfoto" zu erkennen? Welche Bedeutung hat das Hochzeitsfoto in dem Roman?*

Dieter Zimmer wurde 1939 in Leipzig geboren und flüchtete 1953 mit seiner Mutter nach West-Berlin. Nach dem Studium arbeitete er als Fernsehjournalist und später auch als Schriftsteller. Er ist der Autor von zahlreichen Reportagen und Dokumentationen, vor allem über deutsch-deutsche und zeitgeschichtliche Themen. Seit 1980 hat er eine Reihe von meist autobiografisch geprägten Romanen und auch viele Sachbücher verfasst. Heute lebt der Schriftsteller mit seiner Familie in Wiesbaden.

Dieter Zimmer

Der folgende Auszug stammt aus Zimmers 1992 erschienenem Roman *Das Hochzeitsfoto*, in dem der Autor sich wohl an seine letzten Tage in Leipzig erinnert. In diesem Roman, der im Frühjahr 1953 spielt, erfährt der dreizehnjährige

Thomas aus Leipzig, dass er in knapp zwei Wochen mit seiner Mutter in den Westen flüchten wird. Als die Mutter beim Packen auf ein Hochzeitsfoto stößt, hat Thomas plötzlich das Gefühl, dass er in seinen nur noch wenigen Tagen in Leipzig möglichst viel über die Menschen, die er in Leipzig zurücklassen wird, herausfinden muss.

Vor dem Lesen

1. Beschreiben Sie die politische Situation Deutschlands zur Zeit der Handlung 1953. Was hatten die Menschen alles in den zehn Jahren davor erlebt?
2. Was wissen Sie über den Kommunismus? über den Marxismus? Wer regiert in einem marxistisch-sozialistischen Staat?

Beim Lesen

Was wird im Romanauszug über die folgenden Leipziger Orte gesagt? Ordnen Sie die Beschreibungen den Orten zu.

Information for _Vor dem Lesen_. 1. _1953 bestand Deutschland aus zwei Ländern, der BRD und der DDR. Die DDR wurde als sozialistischer Staat mit Planwirtschaft gegründet, die BRD als föderale Demokratie mit sozialer Marktwirtschaft. 1945 ging der Krieg zu Ende. Über vier Millionen Einwohner Deutschlands kamen im Krieg um. Alle großen und viele mittelgroße Städte lagen in Schutt und Asche und der Wiederaufbau zog sich über viele Jahre hin._ **2.** _Kommunismus ist der Theorie nach eine klassenlose Wirtschafts- und Gesellschaftsform. Es gibt demnach keinen Privatbesitz, alle Menschen sind sozial gleich gestellt und jeder kann nach seinen Bedürfnissen leben. Nach der marxistischen Lehre ist die Geschichte seit jeher eine Abfolge von Klassenkämpfen zwischen den arbeitenden Klassen und den Klassen, die Grund und Boden, Industrieanlagen und Maschinen besitzen. Der Kommunismus ist das Endstadium dieser Entwicklung. Dabei ist der Sozialismus, bei dem die Arbeiter die politische Macht tragen, die Vorstufe des Kommunismus._

__d__ Fleischerplatz	a.	wo Thomas' Eltern heirateten
__b__ Augustusplatz	b.	Stadtplatz, der zu DDR-Zeiten Karl-Marx-Platz hieß
__a__ Universitätskirche	c.	Gebäude, an dem man 1953 noch gebaut hat
__k__ Bildermuseum	d.	Stadtplatz, der 1953 Friedrich-Engels-Platz hieß
__h__ Reichsgericht	e.	ein zerstörtes Haus, in dem sich die Kommunisten vor dem Ersten Weltkrieg versammelten
__c__ Opernhaus	f.	Fabrik, in der die Oma einst gearbeitet hat
__g__ Krochhochhaus	g.	Gebäude mit einer eigenartigen Uhr oben auf dem Dach
__j__ Gohlis	h.	Gebäude, das zu DDR-Zeiten als Kunstmuseum benutzt wurde
____ Baumwollspinnerei	i.	die älteste Kirche der Stadt
__i__ Nikolaikirche	j.	Vorort Leipzigs, wo Thomas wohnt
__e__ Max Klingers Atelier	k.	Gebäude, das einst eine Gemäldegalerie war

Augustusplatz mit Blick auf Krochhochhaus links und Opernhaus rechts

06-14 to 06-15

„Das Hochzeitsfoto"

von Dieter Zimmer

Vom Waldplatz fuhr Thomas, seine Klaviernoten unter dem Arm, mit der
Linie 6, links neben dem Fahrer stehend wie immer, über den Friedrich-
Engels-Platz, den die meisten noch Fleischerplatz nannten, durch den
Brühl, wo also Leo gearbeitet hatte, zum Karl-Marx-Platz, den die meisten
noch Augustusplatz nannten. Die Schaffner° riefen allerdings auf gut Sächsisch aus: Gormorgsblotz°! Thomas kam zu früh, die Oma war noch nicht
eingetroffen.

Er sah sich auf dem Platz um, dessen Größe die Leipziger selbst-
bewußt anführten, wenn die Dresdner mit ihrem Altmarkt protzten°. Dem
Altmarkt natürlich, wie er vor dem 13. Februar 1945 gewesen war. In der
Universitätskirche, wußte Thomas nun, hatten 1936 seine Eltern geheiratet. Vielleicht konnte er vor der Flucht noch einmal mit der Mutter die
Kirche anschauen. Nebenan die ausgebrannte Universität, in der Onkel
Wolfgang, wie er sagte, studiert hätte, wenn er nicht mit achtzehn in den
Krieg gezogen wäre, um mit dreißig aus der Gefangenschaft heimzukeh-
ren. Schräg gegenüber die Ruine der Gemäldegalerie, die die Leipziger einfach Bildermuseum nannten. Die Gemälde hingen nun im Reichsgericht°,
das jetzt Georgii-Dimitroff-Museum hieß. Auf der anderen Seite des Platzes
war das neue Opernhaus im Bau. Alle, die Thomas kannte, schworen, es
könne kein richtiges Opernhaus werden in diesen Zeiten. Am meisten am
Augustus-Morgs-Platz mochte Thomas das Krochhochhaus mit den beiden
Glockenmännern auf dem Dach. Jede Viertelstunde schlugen sie mit ihren
Hämmern bedächtig die Zeit. Jetzt war es genau eine Minute vor halb, Thomas schaute nach oben.

Die Großmutter tippte ihm auf die Schulter. Sie war pünktlich, wie
jeden Dienstagnachmittag, wenn sie sich nach Thomas' Klavierstunde hier
trafen. Sie hatte, wie immer, ihr dunkelgraues Kostüm an, das an immer
mehr Stellen zu glänzen anfing. Sie trug keinen Mantel mehr, da der Frühling angebrochen war. Sie hatte, wie immer, das Einkaufsnetz am Arm, falls
irgendein Geschäft etwas hereinbekommen° hatte. Sie trug, da ihre Augen
immer schlechter wurden, eine Brille mit sehr dicken Gläsern. Thomas gab
seiner Großmutter einen Kuß. „Na, mein Junge!", sagte sie, wie immer.

„Alles in Ordnung!" sagte Thomas.

„Was machen wir heute?" fragte sie, auch wie immer. Die Großmutter
hatte stets einen fertigen Plan. Was Thomas von seiner Stadt kannte, außer
seinem Vorort° Gohlis und ein paar Fußballplätzen, kannte er durch die
Nachmittage mit seiner Großmutter.

Siehe **Kulturtipps**: Karl
Marx und Friedrich Engels

5 *conductors*

*"Karl-Marx-Platz" in
Saxon dialect*

showed off

10 **Teaching suggestion and
information for *Lesetext 4.***
After reading the text, ask students
to identify passages that under-
score the historical setting of the
story. *Wo im Lesetext erkennt man,
dass hier von 1953 in Leipzig die*
15 *Rede ist, d. h. dass es die Nachkriegszeit in der jungen DDR ist?*

*Supreme Court of the
German Empire*

Among other things they might
20 mention that the grandmother
brings a shopping bag along with
her in case some store gets some
goods in stock (the shortage of
goods was an ongoing problem in
East Germany), that most people
still remember how things used
25 to be pre-war and pre-GDR (e.g.,
the reference to the *Dresdner
Altmarkt* before it was bombed, the
reference to the recent renaming
of places in honor of socialist
heroes, e.g., *Fleischerplatz* was

30 *got something in*

now *Friedrich-Engels-Platz*;
Augustusplatz became *Karl-
Marx-Platz*, the *Reichsgericht*
was refunctioned and renamed
Georgii-Dimitroff-Museum).
35 Georgi Dimitrov was a

suburb

Bulgarian Communist leader who later became a Soviet citizen. Arrested in Berlin as an alleged co-
conspirator in the Reichstag fire in 1933, he was put on trial in the Reichsgericht in Leipzig. During
the trail he gained world renown for accusing the Nazi regime of staging both the fire and the trial for
political ends.

for a change

Ausnahmsweise° hatte Thomas heute selbst einen Vorschlag: „Ich möchte in die Baumwollspinnerei².“

Die Großmutter sah ihn überrascht an: „Die Baumwolle? Da war ich seit fünfundvierzig nicht mehr.“

„Eben“, antwortete Thomas.

Siehe **Kulturtipps**: Nikolaikirche

„Ich wollte heute mit dir in die Nikolaikirche, die kennst du noch nicht. Die älteste Kirche in Leipzig. Eine ganz ungewöhnliche Kirche. Die

pillars

Säulen° sind wie Palmen. Es wirkt auf den ersten Blick ganz modern, aber in Wahrheit…“

„Die Baumwolle“, bat Thomas.

„Ich habe mir geschworen, nie wieder hinzugehen.“

„Aber ich muß das nochmal sehen“, sagte Thomas. „Ich war ja damals erst fünf.“

Die Großmutter schüttelte den Kopf, dann hob sie die Schultern.

Sie stiegen in die Linie 2. Die Straßenbahn, morgens und abends stets überfüllt, war um diese Zeit fast leer. Thomas setzte sich neben die Großmutter auf eine Holzbank, obwohl er sonst immer neben dem Fahrer stand und der Ansicht war, die Bänke seien nur für Kleinkinder, Greise

old people and invalids

und Versehrte°. Er kannte fast alle Straßenbahnlinien von Endstelle zu Endstelle, aber mit der 2 nach Plagwitz war er nie mehr gefahren, seitdem die Großeltern, kurz nach dem Krieg, aus ihrer Werkswohnung in der Leipziger Baumwollspinnerei hinausgeworfen worden waren. Bis zur Karl-Heine-Straße schwieg die Großmutter. Dort endlich siegte ihr

urge to tell others
studio
Siehe **Kulturtipps**: Max Klinger

Mitteilungsdrang°, und sie wies Thomas auf das zerstörte Haus hin, das einmal Max Klingers Atelier° gewesen sei: „Der Beethoven, weißt du?“ Am „Felsenkeller“ sprach sie wieder: „Da war ich zweimal. Kurz vor dem Krieg. Vor dem ersten. Da hatten die Kommunisten ihre Versammlungen. Ich wollte einfach mal wissen, was die wollten.“ Sie schaute sich um und dämpfte in der leeren Straßenbahn die Stimme: „Wenn der Großvater das gewußt hätte! Für den waren das alles Umstürzler und Staatsfeinde°.

Umstürzler und Staatsfeinde revolutionists and enemies of the state / riffraff

Rotes Gesindel°. Mich haben sie aber auch nicht überzeugt. Ich kannte ja unsere Arbeiter. Die Vorstellung, die würden nun über alles bestimmen? Na, ich weiß nicht.“ Sie sprach wieder etwas lauter: „Beim zweitenmal

Siehe **Kulturtipps**: Rosa Luxemburg

hat Rosa Luxemburg gesprochen. Die hat mir gefallen. Ich war richtig traurig, als sie später ermordet wurde. Aber dem Großvater erzählst du nichts davon, nicht wahr?“

---

²Die 1884 gegründete Leipziger Baumwollspinnerei (*cotton spinning mill*) war bis 1907 die größte ihrer Art in Kontinentaleuropa. Zur Fabrikanlage gehörten Arbeiterwohnungen, ein eigener Kindergarten und eine Gartensiedlung.

Kulturtipps

Karl Marx und Friedrich Engels

Karl Marx (1818–1883) und Friedrich Engels (1820–1895) sind die Väter des Marxismus und des Kommunismus. Die Emanzipation der Arbeiterklasse, die am Kapitalismus litt, war für sie die Voraussetzung für eine egalitäre kommunistische Gesellschaft. Ihre Schriften bestimmten die Programme vieler sozialistischer und kommunistischer Parteien, beeinflussten die Theorie, aber weniger die politische Praxis, in der DDR und anderen kommunistisch regierten Ländern und hatten somit enormen Einfluss auf das politische Geschehen des 20. Jahrhunderts.

Marx war auf dem 100-Mark-Schein der DDR, Engels auf dem 50-Mark-Schein abgebildet.

Nikolaikirche

Die evangelisch-lutherische Nikolaikirche, deren Bau bereits 1165 begann, ist sowohl die größte Kirche als auch ein Wahrzeichen von Leipzig. Aus den Friedensgebeten (*prayers for peace*), die hier seit 1981 immer montags stattfanden, entstanden die Montagsdemonstrationen, die 1989 zum Ausgangspunkt der friedlichen Revolution in der DDR wurden.

Nikolaikirche und im Vordergrund das Denkmal für die friedliche Revolution

Max Klinger (1857–1920)

Der in Leipzig geborene Maler, Grafiker und Bildhauer (*sculptor*) ist in seiner Kunst dem Stil des Symbolismus zuzuordnen. Sein bildhauerisches Hauptwerk ist das 1902 vollendete Denkmal des sitzenden Beethoven in farbigem Marmor (*marble*), das damals viel diskutiert wurde und heute im Leipziger Museum der Bildenden Künste zu sehen ist.

Rosa Luxemburg (1871–1919)

Rosa Luxemburg war eine Politikerin, die eine bedeutende Rolle in der internationalen sozialistischen Bewegung zu Beginn des 20. Jahrhunderts spielte. Sie schrieb Zeitungsartikel und hielt Reden, agitierte gegen den Krieg und sah im Kommunismus die Möglichkeit einer humaneren Welt. Sie war Gründungsmitglied der Kommunistischen Partei Deutschlands und hat einen großen Teil des Parteiprogramms selbst verfasst. 1919 wurde sie von Rechtsradikalen in Berlin ermordet.

Neue Vokabeln

Nomen

die Bank, ⁻e *bench*

die Flucht, -en *escape*

die Größe, -n *size*

die Stimme, -n *voice*

die Versammlung, -en *meeting, gathering*

der Vorschlag, ⁻e *suggestion*

die Vorstellung, -en *idea*

Verben

ein·treffen (trifft ein), traf ein, ist eingetroffen *to arrive*

hin·weisen auf, wies hin, hingewiesen *to point out, make aware of*

schweigen, schwieg, geschwiegen *to remain silent*

schwören, schwor, geschworen *to swear, pledge*

überzeugen *to convince*

Adjektive und Adverbien

ungewöhnlich *unusual*

Ausdrücke

Alles in Ordnung! *All's well!*

der Ansicht sein *to be of the opinion*

Suggestion for 6-24. Explain to students that a chronology is a sequence in time and not necessarily the order in which information appears in the story. You might have them first order the information in the order it is revealed in the narrative and then have them resequence the information chronologically as a second step.

6-24 Textarbeit: Chronologie. Tragen Sie die Zahlen 1 bis 8 unten ein, um das Geschehen in chronologische Reihenfolge zu bringen.

__8__ Thomas und seine Großmutter fahren mit der Straßenbahnlinie 2 Richtung Baumwollspinnerei.

__2__ Thomas' Eltern heiraten.

__5__ Thomas fährt mit Straßenbahnlinie 6 zum Karl-Marx-Platz.

__4__ Thomas hat Klavierstunde.

__1__ Die Oma geht zu Versammlungen der Kommunisten.

__7__ Thomas küsst seine Großmutter.

__3__ Die Großeltern werden aus der Werkswohnung hinausgeworfen.

__6__ Er sieht sich um, während er auf seine Großmutter wartet.

Answers for 6-25. 1. Er betrachtet die Gebäude und den Marktplatz. Er muss dabei an den Krieg denken, an seine Familie und wie alles in jüngster Zeit umbenannt worden ist. **2.** Sie treffen sich jeden Dienstagnachmittag und besuchen jedes Mal einen Ort in oder um Leipzig.
3. Er schlägt ein Ausflugsziel vor. Die Oma ist überrascht und weigert sich zunächst, lässt sich aber schließlich darauf ein. Sie hatte mit ihm in die Nikolaikirche gehen wollen. **4.** *Answers will vary.*
5. Dort hatten die Kommunisten ihre Versammlungen und sie wollte wissen, welche politischen Vorstellungen sie hatten. **6.** Sie ist in der DDR und hat Angst, dass jemand hört, dass sie sich gegenüber dem Kommunismus kritisch äußert.
7. *Answers will vary.*

6-25 Textarbeit: Fragen zum Inhalt. Beantworten Sie die Fragen in Bezug auf den Text.

1. Was sieht Thomas, während er auf seine Großmutter wartet? Was für Assoziationen fallen ihm ein?

2. Wie oft trifft sich Thomas mit seiner Großmutter? Was machen sie bei diesen Treffen zusammen?

3. Was macht Thomas an diesem Tag, was er normalerweise nicht macht? Wie reagiert die Oma darauf? Was hatte die Oma für einen Plan gehabt?

4. Warum hatte sich die Oma wohl geschworen, nie wieder in die Baumwollspinnerei zu gehen? Warum, meinen Sie, will Thomas das unbedingt sehen?

5. Warum war die Oma mal in dem Haus, das Max Klingers Atelier gewesen ist?

6. Warum spricht die Oma plötzlich leise und dann wieder normal?

7. Warum, meinen Sie, will die Großmutter nicht, dass der Großvater über ihre Besuche bei den Versammlungen der Kommunisten vor über 30 Jahren weiß?

6-26 Vokabelarbeit. Ergänzen Sie die Sätze mit Wörtern aus den *Neuen Vokabeln*. Achten Sie dabei auch auf die Wortform.

1. Vor der _____Flucht_____ möchte Thomas so viel wie möglich über seine Heimat herausfinden.

2. Thomas _____überzeugt_____ seine Oma, ihm ihren früheren Arbeitsplatz und Wohnort zu zeigen.

3. Zunächst hatte seine Oma einen anderen _____Vorschlag_____.

4. Es ist _____ungewöhnlich_____, dass Thomas selber ein Ausflugsziel für Dienstagnachmittag wählt.

5. In der Straßenbahn setzt sich Thomas ausnahmsweise auf die _____Bank_____. Normalerweise bleibt er stehen.

6. Die Oma _____ist_____ _____der_____ _____Ansicht_____, dass Fabrikarbeiter keine guten Politiker machen.

 6-27 Flucht aus der Heimat. Heute hat man Ihnen gesagt, Sie müssen in zwei Wochen Ihr Heimatland auf immer verlassen und dürfen nur einen Koffer mitnehmen. Besprechen Sie die Situation mit Hilfe der Fragen.

1. Was wollen Sie unbedingt machen, bevor Sie Ihre Heimat verlassen?

2. Was nehmen Sie mit? Machen Sie eine Liste und erklären Sie, warum Sie gerade diese Gegenstände als wichtig und wertvoll betrachten.

3. Was werden Sie an Ihrer Heimat am meisten vermissen?

4. Wohin flüchten Sie?

6-28 Assoziationen. Während der Straßenbahnfahrt durch Leipzig sehen Thomas und seine Oma Gebäude und Orte, die für sie persönliche Erinnerungen und Assoziationen mit sich tragen. Sie meinen, das ist ein hervorragendes Konzept für einen autobiografischen Roman! Stellen Sie sich vor, Sie besuchen einen Ort aus Ihrer Vergangenheit und verbinden damit alle möglichen Assoziationen.

Beispiel: *Ich bin zum ersten Mal seit fünfzehn Jahren wieder in der kleinen Stadt, wo ich die ersten fünf Jahre meiner Kindheit verbrachte. Wir fahren am Kaufhaus vorbei, wo ich so oft mit meiner Mutter einkaufen ging. Dort langweilte ich mich manchmal und erfand kleine Spiele. ... Nach dem Einkaufen aßen wir manchmal ein Eis in dem Café nebenan. Ich bestellte immer Pistazieneis, denn ich mochte die grüne Farbe. Das Café gibt es nicht mehr. An seiner Stelle steht heute ein Friseursalon, der zufälligerweise eine pistaziengrüne Farbe hat. ...*

Introduction to *Hörtext 2*. Ask students to locate the Erzgebirge on the map at the beginning of the chapter and describe its location. Then ask them what else they learned from the introduction. *Warum heißt das Erzgebirge so? Wie hat der Bergbau wohl die Region geprägt?*

Hörtext 2

Ehrenfriedersdorf – Typisch Erzgebirge (Reisejournal)

Blick ins Erzgebirge

Das Erzgebirge ist ein etwa 130 km langes Mittelgebirge, das sich entlang der Grenze zwischen Sachsen und der Region Böhmen in der Tschechischen Republik erstreckt. Das Gebirge bekam seinen Namen auf Grund seiner reichen Erz-vorräte°, die erst im Mittelalter entdeckt wurden. Zinn°, Eisenerz°, Zink, Blei°, Kupfer und besonders Silber führten zu einem regen Bergbau°, der vielen Menschen Arbeit und den sächsischen Landesfürsten großen Reichtum brachte. Mittlerweile sind die Vorkommen an Bodenschätzen fast vollständig erschöpft. Der Bergbau hat im Laufe der Jahrhunderte seine Einflüsse auf die Kultur und das Bewusstsein° der Region hinterlassen. Auch das Kunsthandwerk, das dem Erzgebirge den Ruf als „Weihnachtsland" über seine Grenzen hinaus einbringt, verdankt seine Entstehung dem Rückgang° des Bergbaus und hat jedoch den Bergbau oft zum Motiv.

ore deposits
tin / iron ore / lead

mining

consciousness

decline

Über die Kleinstadt Ehrenfriedersdorf, die mitten im Erzgebirge liegt, informiert das folgende Reisejournal aus dem Kulturprogramm eines Radiosenders. Bei der auditiven° Reise durch die Entwicklung der Stadt, deren Geschichte und Kultur für das Erzgebirge beispielhaft sind, lernen Sie die beliebteste Urlaubsregion Sachsens näher kennen.

auditory

Vor dem Hören

Welche Auswirkungen hat der Bergbau wohl auf die Kultur und die Wirtschaft eines Ortes?

Beim Hören

Während der Sendung hören Sie folgende Vokabeln:

Ehrenfriedersdorf –
Typisch Erzgebirge

06-16

> Harz   *a mountain range in southeast Niedersachsen and southwest Sachsen-Anhalt*
> zweischiffiger   *double nave (bay)*
> Posamentiergewerbe   *making trimmings or edgings for clothing and furniture*
> Bandweberei   *ribbon weaving*
> Nachwuchs   *younger generation*
> eingestellt   *discontinued*
> aus Rentabilitätsgründen   *for reasons of profitability*
> Berggrabebrüderschaft   *miners' society*
> Edelsteinschleiferei   *gemstone polishing shop*
> Turnhallen   *gymnasiums*
> Kegelbahnen   *bowling alleys*
> Rodelhänge   *sledding runs*
> Abstecher   *side trip*

Hören Sie sich die Sendung an. Ordnen Sie die Daten den passenden historischen Ereignissen zu.

__e__ 12. Jahrhundert
__a__ 13. Jahrhundert
__g__ 15. Jahrhundert
__d__ 16. Jahrhundert
__f__ 17. bis 18. Jahrhundert
__b__ 1990
__c__ 1338

a. Bergleute ziehen in die Gegend.
b. Zinn wird nicht mehr abgebaut.
c. Bergmänner gründen einen Verein zur gegenseitigen Unterstützung.
d. Der Bergbau verliert an Bedeutung und andere Produktionszweige blühen auf.
e. Ehrenfriedersdorf wird gegründet.
f. Das Klöppeln erlebt seine Blütezeit.
g. Ehrenfriedersdorf gehört zu den reichsten Städten des Erzgebirges.

Kulturtipps

▪ Klöppeln und Schnitzen

Diese Handwerke entstanden im 17. Jahrhundert, als der Niedergang des Bergbaus wirtschaftliche Not und Armut (*poverty*) in das einst reiche Erzgebirge brachte. Um überleben zu können, fingen die Bergleute und deren Familien an, handwerklich Gebrauchsgegenstände (*basic commodities*) zu fertigen. Die Frauen klöppelten (*made lace by braiding and twisting threads wound on bobbins*) und die Männer beschäftigten sich mit Schnitz- und Drechselarbeiten (*carving and turning*). Das Erzgebirge ist heute für seine Handklöppelspitzen (*hand-made bobbin lace*) und handgefertigten, hölzernen Nussknacker, Räuchermännchen und Weihnachtspyramiden weltbekannt.

Traditionelle Holzschnitzkunst aus dem Erzgebirge

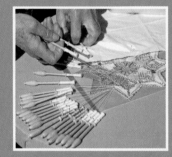
Eine Frau beim Klöppeln

▪ „Glück auf!"

Das Glückauf ist eine Begrüßungs- bzw. Abschiedsformel, die vor Jahrhunderten unter sächsischen Bergmännern entstanden ist, um sich eine glückliche Rückkehr aus der Grube (*mine*) „herauf" zu wünschen. In früheren Zeiten kamen tödliche Grubenunfälle (*mining accidents*) nicht selten vor und auch das Herausklettern nach langer Schichtarbeit (*shift work*) war gefährlich. Im Erzgebirge wird heute der Gruß, der im Dialekt der Region sich wie „Gliggauf" anhört, nicht nur unter Bergleuten verwendet, sondern ist allgemein gebräuchlich.

6-29 Textarbeit: Ehrenfriedersdorf. Wählen Sie alle Antworten, die richtig sind.

1. Wer hat die Stadt gegründet?
    a. <u>Bauern aus dem Raum Rheinhessen</u>
    b. Bergleute aus Franken und aus dem Harz
    c. Handwerker und Kaufleute

2. Was wurde hier abgebaut?
    a. Eisen   b. Gold   c. Kupfer   d. <u>Silber</u>   e. <u>Zinn</u>

3. In welcher Epoche wurde die Kirche gebaut?
    a. Renaissance   b. <u>Gotik</u>   c. Barock   d. Rokoko   e. Romantik

4. Was kann man heute in Ehrenfriedersdorf machen?
    a. <u>beim Klöppeln und Schnitzen zuschauen</u>
    b. das Schloss besichtigen
    c. <u>an einer Führung durch ein Bergwerk teilnehmen</u>
    d. Mineralien vom Berg selber abbauen
    e. <u>im Gras Ski fahren</u>
    f. den Zoo besuchen
    g. <u>wandern</u>

6-30 Textarbeit: Mehr über Ehrenfriedersdorf. Ergänzen Sie die Sätze mit Informationen aus der Radiosendung.

1. Ehrenfriedersdorf liegt etwas südlich von _____Chemnitz_____.

2. Die Geschichte des Bergbaus in der Stadt reicht _____750_____ Jahre zurück.

3. In der Stadt leben heute _etwas mehr als 5.000_ Einwohner.

4. Im 15. Jahrhundert wurde die _____Kirche_____ gebaut, in der ein Altar von Hans Witten zu besichtigen ist.

5. Kinder können Kurse im _____Klöppeln_____ oder _____Schnitzen_____ machen.

6. Ehrenfriedersdorf hat eines der ältesten _____Bergwerke_____ Europas.

7. Im _____Mineralogischen_____ _____Museum_____ kann man abgebaute Mineralien besichtigen.

8. Von Ehrenfriedersdorf aus kann man alle Ausflugsziele im _____Erzgebirge_____ leicht erreichen oder sogar eine kurze Reise über die Grenze nach _____Tschechien_____ machen.

6-31 Tagesausflug. Sie sind zufällig in Chemnitz. Sie hören diesen Beitrag im Radio und entscheiden sich, einen Tagesausflug nach Ehrenfriedersdorf zu machen. Besprechen Sie, was Sie dort machen wollen.

6-32 Spuren der Geschichte. Besprechen Sie die Themen.

1. Zeugnisse der jahrhundertelangen Geschichte Ehrenfriedersdorfs kann man heute überall in der Stadt finden. Geben Sie Beispiele.

2. Wo kann man in Ihrer Universitätsstadt noch Spuren der Geschichte erleben? Machen Sie eine Liste von fünf historischen Zeugnissen. Erklären Sie, wie jedes Zeugnis die Geschichte der Stadt zeigt. Dann vergleichen Sie Ihre Liste mit der Liste eines anderen Paars.

6-33 Reisetipp für Sachsen. Sie sind Radiojournalist/in von Beruf. Wählen Sie einen Ort in Sachsen und schreiben Sie einen Reisetipp für das Kulturmagazin in Radio Sachsen. Der Reisetipp soll einen Blick auf die Geschichte des Ortes werfen und berichten, wo und wie man dessen Kulturgeschichte heute noch spüren und erleben kann.

06-17

6-34 Stadtgeschichte. Eine Gruppe sächsischer Schüler macht eine drei Wochen lange Klassenreise in Ihre Heimatstadt. Bevor sie ankommen, sollten die Schüler etwas über die Stadt wissen. Schreiben Sie eine kurze Geschichte Ihrer Heimatstadt für diese Schüler, indem Sie auch angeben, wo man Zeugnisse dieser Geschichte heute noch erleben kann.

Activity 6-33. Students will have to choose and research a place before they begin writing. Relevant Internet resources are provided at MyGermanLab and the Companion Website.

Teaching suggestion for 6-33. Have students record their *Reisetipps* in MyGermanLab as if for a radio broadcast.

Grammatik

06-25 to 06-26

1. Word order: Independent clauses (Wortstellung: Hauptsätze)

An independent clause, or main clause, is a simple sentence. It contains a subject and a verb, expresses a complete thought, and can be a statement, question or command. German independent clauses can be divided into two groups: clauses that use verb-second word order and clauses that use verb-first word order.

Verb-second word order (Verb an zweiter Stelle)

The conjugated verb is in the second position in statements and in questions that employ question words (**wo?, was?, wie viel?,** etc.). Note that the first element in the sentence can consist of one word, a phrase, or an entire clause; however, it must form one grammatical unit. That grammatical unit can be the subject, an object, an adverb, or prepositional phrase, or a dependent clause.

	First element	Conjugated verb	
Subject:	Dieses alte Haus	gehört	meinen Großeltern.
	Wer	möchte	noch ein Stück Kuchen?
Object:	Einen schönen Garten	haben	Sie, Herr Müller!
	Wem	zeigst	du das Buch
Adverb:	Hoffentlich	kommen	sie bald zu Besuch.
	Wie lange	wohnt	ihr schon hier?
Prepositional phrase:	Im Sommer	gab	es wärmeres Wetter.
Dependent clause:	Ob er heute kommt,	wissen	wir nicht.

Note that the first sentence element may include additional modifiers that logically belong with that grammatical unit.

	First element	Conjugated verb	
Adverb + prepositional phrase:	Heute um acht Uhr	**frühstücke**	ich.
Subject + adverb:	Der neue Schüler dort	**stammt**	aus Polen.
Object + genitive modifier:	Die Frau meines Lehrers	**treffen**	wir heute.

Verb-first word order (Verb an erster Stelle)

Two types of independent clauses use verb-first word order: yes-no questions and commands.

	Conjugated verb	
Yes-no questions:	**Erinnerst**	du dich an die alte Lehrerin?
	Hat	Michael alle Zutaten besorgt?
Commands:	**Wiederholen**	Sie bitte Ihren Namen!
	Stell	dir mal die Möglichkeiten vor!

Verbal bracketing (Satzklammer)

In independent clauses, the conjugated verb must appear in the first or second position. If the clause contains any other verbs or verb parts, i.e., infinitives, past participles, or separable prefixes, then these appear at the end of the sentence. This principle is known as *verbal bracketing*.

	Conjugated verb		Additional verb element(s)
Mein Kollege	**lädt**	uns zum Abendessen	**ein.**
	Fangen	wir nun	**an!**
Silvia	**kann**	vier Sprachen	**sprechen.**
	Wolltet	ihr mit uns nach Köln	**fahren?**
Deswegen	**wird**	er wohl	**ausziehen.**
Solche Denkmäler	**sind**	überall in der Stadt	zu **sehen.**
Wie lange	**hat**	dein Bruder am Meer	**gelebt?**
Morgen	**wollen**	wir	**spazieren gehen.**

6-35 Zu Besuch in Dresden. Kurt und Elke telefonieren mit ihrer Tochter und erzählen ihr von ihrem ersten Tag in Dresden. Bilden Sie aus den Satzteilen ganze Sätze, indem Sie das Subjekt nicht an den Satzanfang stellen.

1. wir / heute / eine Schiffrundfahrt durch das Elbtal / haben / gemacht / .
2. wir / unsere Tourleiterin / wegen ihrer sächsischen Aussprache / nicht gut / verstehen / konnten / .
3. ihr / die Tafelberge und die Festung Königstein / habt / gesehen / ?
4. Elke / die Weinhänge und Schlösser im schönen Elbtal / viel / hat / fotografiert / .
5. wir / heute Abend / zu einer Ausstellung im Albertinum / gehen / wollen / ?
6. ein Kunstprofessor / aus seinem neuen Werk über Gerhard Richter / vor / liest / .
7. die Lesung / um wie viel Uhr / an / fängt / ?
8. morgen / an einem Rundgang durch die Altstadt / teil / nehmt / !

Possible answers for 6-35.
1. Heute haben wir eine Schiffrundfahrt durch das Elbtal gemacht. **2.** Wegen ihrer sächsischen Aussprache konnten wir unsere Tourleiterin nicht gut verstehen. **3.** Habt ihr die Tafelberge und die Festung Königstein gesehen? **4.** Die Weinhänge und Schlösser im schönen Elbtal hat Elke viel fotografiert. **5.** Wollen wir heute Abend zu einer Ausstellung im Albertinum gehen? **6.** Ein Kunstprofessor liest aus seinem neuen Werk über Gerhard Richter vor. **7.** Um wie viel Uhr fängt die Lesung an? **8.** Nehmt morgen an einem Rundgang durch die Altstadt teil!

06-27 to 06-28

2. Coordinating conjunctions (Koordinierende Konjunktionen)

A coordinating conjunction is a word that joins independent clauses or words and phrases. The conjunction itself does not count as a sentence element; it acts as a junction between clauses and other sentence elements. German has five commonly used coordinating conjunctions: **aber** (*but*), **denn** (*because, for*), **oder** (*or*), **sondern** (*but, on the contrary*), **und** (*and*). A comma is required before **aber, denn,** and **sondern.** It is optional before **oder** and **und.**

Er möchte einen Hund, **aber** er ist nicht oft zu Hause.	*He would like a dog, but he isn't home often.*
Redest du mit ihm(,) **oder** soll ich mit ihm reden?	*Are you going to speak with him or should I speak with him?*
Sie verkaufen Bücher für Kinder **und** Jugendliche.	*They sell books for children and adolescents.*

Although **aber** and **sondern** both mean *but*, they are not interchangeable. **Sondern** follows a negation and offers an alternative to what is being negated.

Das Buch ist schwer, **aber** interessant.	*The book is difficult, but interesting.*
Das Buch ist nicht schwer, **sondern** leicht.	*The book is not difficult, but (on the contrary) easy.*

Answers for 6-36. 1. Der traditionelle Stollen wiegt vier Pfund, **aber** man kann ihn größer oder kleiner machen. **2.** Man soll keineswegs Margarine, **sondern** immer nur Butter gebrauchen. **3.** Zur Abwechslung kann man Marzipan hinzugeben **oder/und** die Rosinen in Rum einweichen. **4.** Vor dem Mischen muss man die Mandeln klein hacken **und** das Zitronat fein schneiden. **5.** Man kann den Stollen selbst formen **oder** in einer Stollenbackform backen. **6.** Nach dem Backen soll man den Stollen mit Butter bestreichen, **denn** das Fett konserviert das Aroma. **7.** Schon nach zwei Tagen kann man den Stollen essen, **aber** am besten lässt man den Kuchen mindestens eine Woche lang liegen. **8.** Der Stollen soll drei Monate lang halten, **aber** meistens wird er schon lange davor aufgegessen.

6-36 Tipps zum Stollenbacken. Kombinieren Sie die Satzpaare mit der passenden koordinierenden Konjunktion: **aber, denn, oder, sondern, und.** Sie können die Sätze auch kürzen, wenn beide Satzteile die gleichen Informationen enthalten.

1. Der traditionelle Stollen wiegt vier Pfund. Man kann ihn größer oder kleiner machen.

2. Man soll keineswegs Margarine gebrauchen. Man soll immer nur Butter gebrauchen.

3. Zur Abwechslung kann man Marzipan hinzugeben. Man kann die Rosinen in Rum einweichen.

4. Vor dem Mischen muss man die Mandeln klein hacken. Vor dem Mischen muss man das Zitronat fein schneiden.

5. Man kann den Stollen selbst formen. Man kann den Stollen in einer Stollenbackform backen.

6. Nach dem Backen soll man den Stollen mit Butter bestreichen. Das Fett konserviert das Aroma.

7. Schon nach zwei Tagen kann man den Stollen essen. Am besten lässt man den Kuchen mindestens eine Woche lang liegen.

8. Der Stollen soll drei Monate lang halten. Meistens wird er schon lange davor aufgegessen.

Note on Word order: Dependent clauses.

Double infinitives and their word order in dependent clauses are discussed in *Kapitel 8 Grammatik.*

06-29 to 06-35

3. Word order: Dependent clauses (Wortstellung: Nebensätze)

Dependent clauses are clauses whose meanings do not alone express a complete thought. To make sense, dependent clauses must be combined with at least one independent clause. Compare the following sentence pairs:

Independent:	Mein Kollege **lädt** uns zum Abendessen **ein.**
	My colleague is inviting us to dinner.
Independent and dependent:	Habe ich gesagt, dass mein Kollege uns zum Abendessen **einlädt?**
	Have I mentioned that my colleague is inviting us to dinner?

Independent:	Warum **wird** er **ausziehen?**
	Why is he moving out?
Dependent and independent:	Warum er **ausziehen wird,** verstehe ich nicht.
	Why he is moving out, I do not understand.

Note that the conjugated verb—the verb that appears in the second or first position in an independent clause—appears at the very *end* of the dependent clause. With a separable prefix verb, the main verb reunites with its prefix at the end of the clause, as in the first example above.

Note also that when the dependent clause begins the sentence, the entire clause, as a cohesive unit of meaning, serves as the first element in the sentence. The dependent clause, which is separated from the rest of the sentence by a comma, is therefore immediately followed by the conjugated verb of the independent clause. Notice that the verbal bracket of the independent clause remains intact.

Dependent clause	Independent clause
Obwohl ich wenig Zeit habe,	**muss** ich mit meinem Bruder **telefonieren**.
Although I have little time	*I have to phone my brother.*
Bevor der Zug abgefahren ist,	**haben** wir uns **verabschiedet**.
Before the train departed	*we said good-bye.*

The two most common types of dependent clauses in German are clauses that begin with a subordinating conjunction and relative clauses. In this chapter, we will focus on subordinate clauses.

You will learn more about relative clauses in *Kapitel 9*.

06-29 to 06-35

4. Subordinating conjunctions (Subordinierende Konjunktionen)

Subordinating conjunctions turn an independent clause into a dependent clause, also called a subordinate clause, and connect a dependent clause to a main clause. German has several subordinating conjunctions[3]:

als *when*	**ehe** *before*	**sobald** *as soon as*
als ob *as if*	**falls** *in case*	**solange** *as long as*
bevor *before*	**indem** *by (doing sth.)*	**sooft** *as often as*
(an)statt dass *instead of (sth. occurring)*	**nachdem** *after*	**während** *while*
	ob *whether*	**weil**[4] *because*
bis *until, by the time*	**obwohl** *although*	**wenn** *when, if, whenever*
da[4,5] *since, because*	**ohne dass** *without (sth. occurring)*	
damit *so that*	**seitdem**[5] *since*	**wenn auch** *even though*
dass *that*		

---

[3]In spoken language, there is an increasing trend toward using the subordinating conjunctions **weil, obwohl,** and **während** with verb-second word order, e.g.: **Ich gehe heute nicht zur Arbeit, weil ich <u>bin</u> krank.** This verb-second position is still considered improper usage in written form, however.

[4]**Da** and **weil** (*because*) are sometimes interchangable, but there is a difference in meaning. The **da**-clause usually comes before the independent clause and typically states a reason that is already known, e.g.: <u>**Da**</u> **seine Eltern geschieden waren, sah er seinen Vater kaum.** By contrast, the **weil**-clause usually follows the independent clause and expresses a cause that is relatively important or that wasn't known before, e.g.: **Sie machten Urlaub in Spanien, <u>weil</u> ihre Freunde dort leben. Weil** is the only conjunction that can answer *why*-questions.

[5]**Da** means *since* in the causal sense (*because*), while **seitdem** means *since* with reference to time. **Seitdem** is used with the present tense to relate an action that began in the past and continues into the present. The English equivalent is typically in the present tense: **Seitdem wir einen neuen Wagen haben, fahren wir öfter ans Meer.** *Since we have had a new car, we drive to the sea more often.*

Note on *da*, *weil* and *denn*. Ask students if they recall what other conjunction means *because* besides *weil* and *da*. You might point out that *denn* is more often used in formal contexts than in informal spoken communication. In addition, as a coordinating conjunction, it can only be used between independent clauses and never begins a sentence.

Interrogative words such as **wann, warum, wie, wie viel, wo, wohin,** etc. can also function like subordinating conjunctions when used in indirect questions.

Question	Indirect question
Wie lange **dauert** die Fahrt?	→ Wir wissen nicht, wie lange die Fahrt **dauert.**
How long will the trip take?	*We don't know how long the trip will take.*
Woher **kommt** er?	→ Sie hat ihn gefragt, woher er **kommt.**
Where is he from?	*She asked him where he is from.*

Conjunctions *als, wenn,* and *wann*

Although **als, wenn,** and **wann** can all mean *when,* they are not interchangeable. The conjunction **als** refers to a one-time event in the past.

> **Als** ich nach Prag fuhr, habe ich meinen Koffer verloren.
> *When I was traveling to Prague, I lost my suitcase.*

> Er wohnte in Bautzen, **als** er ein Kind war.
> *He lived in Bautzen when he was a child.*

The conjunction **wenn** can mean *when, whenever,* or *if.* It can refer to events in the past, present, or future, but when used with a past tense indicates habitual or repeated action.

> Wir kaufen uns ein Segelboot, **wenn** wir genug Geld haben.
> *We'll buy ourselves a sailboat when we have enough money.*

> **Wenn** ich müde war, habe ich Kaffee getrunken.
> *Whenever I was tired, I drank coffee.*

The interrogative adverb **wann** is used as a subordinating conjunction only in indirect questions.

> Wisst ihr, **wann** die Post geöffnet hat?
> *Do you know when the post office is open?*

Blick auf die kleine Stadt Bautzen in Ostsachsen

6-37 August der Starke. Ergänzen Sie die Sätze mit den jeweils passenden subordinierenden Konjunktionen. Benutzen Sie jede Konjunktion nur einmal.

als	da	indem	obwohl	solange
bevor	dass	nachdem	ohne dass	weil

1. _____Als_____ sein älterer Bruder starb, wurde Friedrich August I. unerwartet der neue Kurfürst Sachsens.

2. Er hieß „der Starke", _____weil_____ er immer wieder seine große körperliche Kraft bewies.

3. _____Da_____ er gleichzeitig König von Polen werden wollte, konvertierte der protestantische Kurfürst zum Katholizismus.

4. _____Obwohl_____ er Katholik wurde, versprach er jedem Sachsen die Religionsfreiheit.

5. Er veranstaltete jährlich zahlreiche exorbitante Feste und Feiern, _____ohne dass_____ er sich um die Kosten kümmerte.

6. _____Bevor_____ er Kurfürst wurde, führte er ein freieres Leben und konnte Europa bereisen und lernte dabei barocke Kunst und Architektur kennen.

7. Er hat seine Spuren in und um Dresden hinterlassen, _____indem_____ er viele barocke Meisterwerke bauen ließ.

8. _____Solange_____ er an der Macht war, sammelte er wertvolle Stücke für die kurfürstliche Kunstsammlung.

9. _____Nachdem_____ er gestorben war, hat sein Sohn August III. die Sammlertätigkeit des Vaters fortgesetzt.

10. Man kann nicht bestreiten, _____dass_____ die beiden Augusts Dresden zu einer der prächtigsten Städte Europas machten.

6-38 Leipzig liest. Kombinieren Sie die Sätze, indem Sie jeweils gegebene subordinierende Konjunktionen an die gegebene Stelle einsetzen.

1. (als) Ich war auf der Leipziger Buchmesse. Ich habe am Lesefestival „Leipzig liest" teilgenommen.

2. Ich habe gelesen. (dass) Es ist das größte Festival seiner Art in Europa.

3. Über 1.500 Autoren machen mit. (indem) Sie halten überall an teilweise ungewöhnlichen Veranstaltungsorten Lesungen.

4. Ich war zum Beispiel in der Bahnhofsbuchhandlung. (wo) Ein Autor las aus seinem Sachbuch über Züge vor.

5. (da) Christian Führer stellte sein Buch über die Montagsdemonstrationen vor. Er hielt seine Lesung in der Nikolaikirche.

6. (nachdem) Die Lesung war zu Ende. Ich konnte mit dem Autor über seine Erfahrungen sprechen.

7. (obwohl) Die Buchmesse selbst hat viel zu bieten. Man sollte auf jeden Fall bei einigen Lesungen dabei sein.

8. Ein Programmheft kann man im Internet finden. (damit) Man kann sich schon vorher Interessantes aussuchen.

Answers for 6-38. 1. Als ich auf der Leipziger Buchmesse war, habe ich am Lesefestival „Leipzig liest" teilgenommen. **2.** Ich habe gelesen, dass es das größte Festival seiner Art in Europa ist. **3.** Über 1.500 Autoren machen mit, indem sie überall an teilweise ungewöhnlichen Veranstaltungsorten Lesungen halten. **4.** Ich war zum Beispiel in der Bahnhofsbuchhandlung, wo ein Autor aus seinem Sachbuch über Züge vorlas. **5.** Da Christian Führer sein Buch über die Montagsdemonstrationen vorstellte, hielt er seine Lesung in der Nikolaikirche. **6.** Nachdem die Lesung zu Ende war, konnte ich mit dem Autor über seine Erfahrungen sprechen. **7.** Obwohl die Buchmesse selbst viel zu bieten hat, sollte man auf jeden Fall bei einigen Lesungen dabei sein. **8.** Ein Programmheft kann man im Internet finden, damit man sich schon vorher Interessantes aussuchen kann.

6-39 Jasmin und Ulrike. Am Wochenende besucht Ulrike ihre Freundin Jasmin, die in Meißen lebt. Ergänzen Sie die Sätze und achten Sie dabei auf die Wortstellung.

1. Ulrike besucht ihre Freundin Jasmin in Meißen, weil …
2. Seitdem Jasmin in Meißen lebt, …
3. Statt dass sie das ganze Wochenende in Meißen bleiben, …
4. Ulrike war einmal im Erzgebirge, als …
5. Während die beiden Frauen im Zug saßen, …
6. Wenn Ulrike sich dafür interessiert, …
7. Ulrike hat ihr Handy mitgebracht, falls …
8. Jasmin weiß nicht, ob …

06-37 to 06-38

To review the use of **kein**, see *Kapitel 3 Grammatik*.

5. Position of nicht (Wortstellung von *nicht*)

The article **kein** is used to negate nouns without an accompanying article or nouns preceded by **ein**. The adverb **nicht** can be used to negate all other elements of a sentence, as well as to negate an entire clause.

When **nicht** is used to negate a sentence, it usually follows the subject, conjugated verb, any time expressions, and accusative and dative objects. **Nicht** precedes predicate nouns and adjectives, prepositional phrases, other adverbs, and additional verbs or verb parts.

Subject	Verb	Indirect obj./ Direct obj.	Time expression	nicht	Non-time adverb	Predicate adj. or noun	Prep. phrase	Verb 2
Ich	kenne	deinen Freund		nicht.				
Er	hat	es dir		nicht	gern			gesagt.
Wir	kommen		heute Abend	nicht.				
Elke	fährt			nicht	schnell		nach Hause.	
Er	ist		jetzt	nicht		krank.		
Sie	heißt			nicht		Renate.		
Max	machte	das Licht		nicht				an.
Wir	können	euch	am Wochen-ende	nicht				besuchen.

Note that a prepositional phrase can function as a modifier of a different sentence element, in which case it is grouped along with that element.

Prepositional phrase modifes direct object

Sie haben das Hotel in Passau **nicht** reserviert.

They did not reserve the hotel in Passau.

Prepositional phrase modifies subject

Mir gehört die Brille auf dem Tisch **nicht**.

The glasses on the table do not belong to me.

The general word order of **nicht** can also vary to negate particular sentence elements rather than entire clauses. Compare:

Negates clause	**Negates element**
Wir haben alles **nicht** verstanden.	Wir haben **nicht** alles verstanden.
We didn't understand anything.	*We didn't understand everything.*
Er hat es mir **nicht** gesagt.	Er hat es **nicht** mir gesagt.
He didn't tell me.	*He didn't tell me (but maybe someone else).*

When a particular sentence element is negated, sometimes an alternative to the negated element is offered using the coordinating conjunction **sondern**.

> **Nicht** meine Mutter, **sondern** meine Großmutter kommt aus Salzburg.
>
> *Not my mother, but my grandmother comes from Salzburg.*

6-40 Montagsdemonstrationen. Rolf redet mit Katja, Ursula und Wolff über ihre Erfahrungen in Leipzig zur Zeit der Montagsdemonstrationen. Aber das Gespräch ist verkehrt. Setzen Sie das Adverb **nicht** ein, um alle Sätze zu negieren.

Rolf: Habt ihr 1989 in Leipzig gewohnt?

Katja: Ich habe in Leipzig gewohnt.

Rolf: Erinnerst du dich an die Montagsdemonstrationen?

Katja: Ich kann mich gut daran erinnern. Ich durfte alleine hingehen.

Ursula: Meine Eltern waren begeistert. Ihrer Meinung nach konnten die Folgen positiv sein.

Rolf: Wolltet ihr ausreisen?

Wolff: Wir wollten unsere Heimat verlassen. Aber eine Reform der DDR war in Sicht.

Ursula: Zum Glück griff die Polizei während der Demonstrationen ein. Sonst wären sie friedlich ausgegangen.

Answers for 6-40. Rolf: Habt ihr 1989 *nicht* in Leipzig gewohnt? Katja: Ich habe *nicht* in Leipzig gewohnt. Rolf: Erinnerst du dich *nicht* an die Montagsdemonstrationen? Katja: Ich kann mich *nicht* gut daran erinnern. Ich durfte *nicht* alleine hingehen. Ursula: Meine Eltern waren *nicht* begeistert. Ihrer Meinung nach konnten die Folgen *nicht* positiv sein. Rolf: Wolltet ihr *nicht* ausreisen? Wolff: Wir wollten unsere Heimat *nicht* verlassen. Aber eine Reform der DDR war *nicht* in Sicht. Ursula: Zum Glück griff die Polizei während der Demonstrationen *nicht* ein. Sonst wären sie *nicht* friedlich ausgegangen.

6-41 Was ich gestern (nicht) alles gemacht habe! Sagen Sie, ob Sie folgende Aktivitäten gemacht oder nicht gemacht haben, indem Sie **nicht** an die richtige Stelle einsetzen.

Beispiel: S1: *Bist du spät aufgestanden?*

S2: *Nein, ich bin nicht spät aufgestanden.*

spät aufgestanden	im Restaurant gegessen	in die Kneipe gegangen
gefrühstückt	am Abend gelernt	deine Eltern besucht
krank geworden	ferngesehen	gearbeitet
dein Zimmer aufgeräumt	für Freunde gekocht	früh ins Bett gegangen
in den Bergen gewandert	drei Filme gesehen	?

Teaching suggestion for 6-42 (2). Have students think about the concepts of continuity and change first mentioned in the chapter *Einführung*. Ask them to consider what changes have taken place in Saxony over time and to identify the cultural practices, traditions, and institutions that have endured through those changes. Have them specifically consider what each of the *Lesetexte* and *Hörtexte* contributed to their knowledge of Saxony in the areas mentioned in the activity.

06-39 to 06-45

Immer weiter!

 6-42 Zur Diskussion. Besprechen Sie die Themen.

1. Wählen Sie einen Ort Sachsens aus und erzählen Sie, was Sie über diesen Ort wissen.

2. Sachsen existiert schon seit über tausend Jahren. Was ist „Sachsen"? Denken Sie dabei nicht nur an seine geografische und politische Lage, sondern auch an Traditionen, Institutionen und Erfahrungen, die die Einwohner Sachsens miteinander teilen. Denken Sie auch an die Veränderungen, die die Einwohner erlebt haben bzw. immer noch erleben.

6-43 Zum Schreiben: Ein Wochenende in Sachsen. Sie studieren ein Semester an der Universität Bayreuth in Bayern, nicht sehr weit von der sächsischen Grenze entfernt. Sie wollen am Wochenende mit einer Freundin das Land Sachsen erkunden. Schreiben Sie ihr eine E-Mail und beschreiben Sie ihr, was Sie am liebsten machen und sehen wollen.

Weitere Themen

Autostadt Zwickau	Die Prinzen
Die Brücke (Künstlergruppe)	Sächsisches Industriemuseum
Chemnitz	Clara Schumann
Stephan Heym	Silberstraße
Leipzig liest	Silicon Saxony
Luftangriffe auf Dresden	Sorben
Karl May	Tag der Sachsen
Meißner Porzellan	Thomanerchor Leipzig
Montagsdemonstrationen	Waldschlösschenbrücke
Plauener Spitze	Weihnachtspyramide

KAPITEL

7

Nordsee   Ostsee

Deutschland

Zürich

Österreich

Schweiz   Liechtenstein

Zürich

DEUTSCHLAND

KANTON SCHAFFHAUSEN

Rhein

Warm-up. Ask students about their prior knowledge and views of Switzerland: *Was wissen Sie schon über die Schweiz? Was verbinden Sie mit diesem Land oder was haben Sie schon davon gehört? Waren Sie schon mal in der Schweiz?* Have them look at the map of Europe inside the back cover and ask: *Wo ist die Schweiz? Wo liegt Zürich innerhalb der Schweiz? Innerhalb Europas?* Then have them look at the map of Zürich and describe its geography. *Wo liegt die Stadt innerhalb des Kantons? Was findet man in oder in der Nähe der Stadt?* Ask them what the map and the photos reveal about Zürich.

Rhein

Thur

Andelfingen

KANTON THURGAU

Bülach

Töss

Dielsdorf

Glatt ✈

KANTON ZÜRICH

Kempt

Spielzeugmuseum   ETH   Zoo

Uni Zürich

Bahnhofstrasse

Züricher Schauspielhaus

Paradeplatz

Kunsthaus Zürich

Pfäffikon

Uetliburg

Uster

Pfäffikersee

Landiwiese

Greifensee

Hinwil

Grossmünster

Zürichsee

Meilen

Affoltern

Sihl

Horgen

Stäfa

KANTON ZUG

KANTON SCHWYZ

↓ *die Alpen*

07-01 to 07-02

Read the *Sprachanalyse: Extended modifiers* in SAM 07-02, which demonstrates how extended adjective constructions are used in the *Einführung*. As you read the *Lesetexte* in this chapter, do the *Sprachanalyse* activities in the SAM (07-06, 07-09, 07-10, 07-16, 07-21) to practice recognizing and deciphering extended modifiers.

incomes

Note for *Einführung*. In 2008, Zürich took first place for the 7th year running in the Quality of Living Survey conducted annually by Mercer Human Resource Consulting of London. In 2009, 2010, and 2011, Vienna took the top spot and Zürich fell to second place, due in large part to the global financial crisis. The survey ranks cities based on an analysis of 39 social, economic, environmental, and political criteria.

Language map. The map shows where each language is the primary language of a majority of residents. The percentages indicate the proportion of the total population that speaks each of the national languages as a native language. Not shown are the 8,9 % of Swiss citizens whose native

Confederation

language is something other than one of the national languages.

characters

official language

Answers for *Fragen zum Text*.
1. Zürich ist die größte Stadt der Schweiz, zählt zu den teuersten Städten der Welt, ist unter den Städten mit der höchsten Lebensqualität. **2.** Zürich ist eine Großstadt mit der Atmosphäre einer kleineren Stadt. **3.** Man kann z. B. Museen besuchen, nachts ausgehen, einkaufen, am See spazieren gehen, eine Bootfahrt machen oder baden. **5.** Zürich existiert schon seit der Römerzeit. **6.** Sie bestanden jahrhundertelang als autonome Republiken. **7.** Fast zwei Drittel der 7,7 Millionen Einwohner. Andere Amtssprachen sind Französisch, Italienisch und Rätoromanisch.

Einführung

Zürich – „Tor zu den Alpen" und „kleine große Stadt" – ist mit seinen 374.000 Einwohnern die mit Abstand größte Stadt der Schweiz. Die am nördlichen Ende des Zürichsees gelegene Stadt ist im Herzen Europas zu finden. Zürich zählt zu den teuersten Städten der Welt, aber die Einkommen° sind ebenfalls unter den welthöchsten. Die Stadt ist am bekanntesten als Banken- und Finanzmetropole, und in der Tat ist die Stadt schon seit dem 19. Jahrhundert das wichtigste Wirtschaftszentrum der Schweiz. 5

Wegen seiner für eine Großstadt eher kleinen Einwohnerzahl besitzt Zürich die Vorteile einer großen Metropole mit der gemütlichen Atmosphäre einer kleineren Stadt. Keine Wolkenkratzer, keine U-Bahn findet man hier, sondern eine mittelalterliche Altstadt, die man leicht zu Fuß erkunden kann, und nostalgische, blau-weiße Trams, die jährlich 200 Millionen Fahrgäste befördern. Die Ufer des Sees und des Flusses Limmat eignen sich zu Spaziergängen, Bootfahrten und zum Baden. Außerdem sorgen die bewaldeten Berge, die die Stadt umgeben, ebenso wie die nur 60 km entfernten Alpen für schöne Panoramaansichten oder Tagesausflüge. Das vielfältige Kultur- und Freizeitangebot macht die kleine Großstadt am Wasser zur Weltstadt, die in Umfragen immer wieder unter den Städten mit der welthöchsten Lebensqualität ausgezeichnet wird. 10

„Züri" – wie die Stadt auf Zürichdeutsch heißt – ist auch die Hauptstadt des gleichnamigen Kantons, der 1,3 Millionen Einwohner hat. Das Leben im Kanton wird weithin von der Hauptstadt dominiert. Die Stadt Zürich, die schon seit der Römerzeit existiert, wurde 1351 Teil der Schweizer Eidgenossenschaft°, um sich vor dem Expansionsdrang der Habsburger zu schützen. Jahrhundertelang bestand der Kanton Zürich wie alle Mitglieder des schweizerischen Staatenbunds als autonome Republik. So entwickelten sich die Kantone der Schweiz mit der Zeit sehr unterschiedliche Eigenarten°. Es gibt vier offizielle Sprachen – Deutsch, Französisch, Italienisch und Rätoromanisch – und jeder Kanton bestimmt seine Amtssprache° selbst. Die Amtssprache Zürichs ist Deutsch. Knapp zwei Drittel der 7,8 Millionen Schweizer sprechen Deutsch als erste Sprache, und Deutsch ist die Amtssprache in 17 der 26 Schweizer Kantone. 20 25 30

- Deutsch (63,7%)
- Französisch (20,4%)
- Italienisch (6,5%)
- Rätoromanisch (0,5%)

Sprachen in der Schweiz

Fragen zum Text

1. Welche Superlative nimmt Zürich in Anspruch?
2. Warum heißt Zürich die „kleine große Stadt"?
3. Was kann ein Besucher in Zürich machen?
4. Wie alt ist die Stadt Zürich?
5. Warum unterscheiden sich die Kantone der Schweiz so stark voneinander?
6. Wie viele Schweizer sprechen Deutsch als erste Sprache? Welche anderen Amtssprachen hat die Schweiz?

Dialekttipp. Ask students what they have learned from the text. *Welche Unterschiede gibt es zwischen Schweizerdeutsch und der Standardsprache in Deutschland? Warum ist Zürichdeutsch der Schweizer Dialekt, der am häufigsten benutzt wird?* After they have completed the activity, write the following Swiss dialect words on the board: *Tüechli, Café crème,*

DIALEKTTIPP: Schweizerdeutsch und Zürichdeutsch

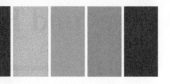

Hören Sie ein Beispiel dieses Dialekts.

Schriiber, Frankeländer, Chueh. Ask them to guess what each of the words means. Answers: *Tüechli* = Tuch; *Café crème* = Kaffee mit Sahne; *Schriiber* = Schreiber, Stift; *Frankeländer* = Franzose; *Chueh* = Kuh.

Schweizerdeutsch unterscheidet sich vom Hochdeutschen, das man in Deutschland kennt. In der Schweizer Schriftsprache schreibt man zum Beispiel das Esszett (*ß*) immer als *ss*. Im Wortschatz sind oft andere Wörter gebräuchlich° (*Serviertochter* = Kellnerin; *zügeln* = umziehen). Auch der Anteil von Wörtern französischen oder englischen Ursprungs, die nicht eingedeutscht° worden sind, ist größer als in Deutschland (*Glacé* = Eis; *Goal* = Tor [im Fußball]).

common

Germanized

Orthography. Because the texts in this chapter are of Swiss German origin, they use Swiss spelling conventions. Most notably, the *ß* is absent, except in *Lesetext 4.*

Zürichdeutsch – oder *Züritüütsch* – wird hauptsächlich im Kanton Zürich gesprochen. Es klingt weniger melodisch als die anderen Dialekte der Schweiz. Aber gerade wegen seiner relativen Einfachheit und Verständlichkeit ist Zürichdeutsch der am weitesten verbreitete alemannische° Dialekt in der Schweiz und ist häufig im Fernsehen und Radio zu hören.

Alemannic (group of dialects in the southwestern part of German-speaking Europe)

Charakteristisch für Zürichdeutsch und für Schweizerdeutsch überhaupt ist die Aussprache des *ch*, das immer wie *ch* in *ach* und nicht wie *ch* in *ich* klingt. So sagt man *ich* mit gutteralem *ch*. Die Grammatik ist relativ einfach. Verben kennen beispielsweise nur das Präsens, das Perfekt und den Konjunktiv.

All activities surrounding the texts, except where direct quotes and proper names are used, and the words appearing in the vocabulary lists will retain Standard German orthography.

Zum Dialekt

Wie sagt man das? Wählen Sie die richtigen Erklärungen der Unterschiede zwischen Zürichdeutsch und Hochdeutsch.

Hochdeutsch → Zürichdeutsch

c 1. Fest, gestern → Fäscht, geschter

d 2. Haus, Weißwein, Leute → Huus, Wiiswii, Lüüt

a 3. Stück, Karotten → Stückli, Rübeli

e 4. gut, müde, Brüder → guet, müed, Brüeder

b 5. Schokolade → Schoggi

f 6. klein, Küche, danke → chlii, chuchi, danche

g 7. trinken, Fenster → trinch, Feischter

a. Verkleinerungsform *–li*[1]

b. *e* am Wortende → *i*

c. *s* vor einem Konsonanten → *sch*

d. Diphthonge *au, ei, eu* → langes *u, i, ü*

e. einige Monophthonge → Diphthonge

f. *k* → *ch* (wie in *ach*, nicht wie in *ich*)

g. *-n* fehlt am Ende und im Innern des Wortes

---

[1]Im Schweizerdeutschen benutzt man Verkleinerungsformen viel häufiger als in der deutschen Standardsprache.

Lese- und Hörtexte

Lesetext 1

Kreative Gastroszene (Restaurantführer)

Die Schweiz ist bekannt für ihre Schokolade und ihren Käse, doch hinter diesem klischeehaften Bild steckt eine kaum vorstellbare kulinarische Vielfalt, die die etwa 450 Käsesorten und die ebenso riesige Auswahl an Schokoladenprodukten widerspiegeln. Einflüsse aus Deutschland, Frankreich und Norditalien haben ihre Spuren in der Küche der verschiedenen Regionen hinterlassen. So trägt jede Region mit ihren eigenen kulinarischen Spezialitäten zur nationalen Vielfalt bei. Dabei stellt auch Zürich mit dem Zürcher Geschnetzelten, Rösti und dem Tirggel, einem Weihnachtsgebäck, keine Ausnahme dar.

Nicht nur in den Gerichten, sondern auch in der Gastronomie tritt der Charakter von Zürich zu Tage. Bis 1998 galt im Kanton ein gastronomisches Gesetz, das nur ein Restaurant pro 300 Einwohner zuließ. Seit der Aufhebung° dieses Gesetzes hat sich die Anzahl der Gaststätten in der Zürcher Innenstadt verdoppelt. Damit hat Zürich neben Paris die höchste Restaurantdichte° pro Einwohner in ganz Europa und ein entsprechend abwechslungsreiches° kulinarisches Angebot. Denn bei solcher Konkurrenz muss sich ein Restaurant durch etwas Besonderes – ob gutes Essen, günstige Preise, einmalige Atmosphäre oder ein unvergessliches Erlebnis – auszeichnen.

Im Restaurantführer lernen Sie einige der bewährten und beliebtesten Gaststätten der Stadt kennen.

Vor dem Lesen

Gehen Sie gerne in Restaurants? Nach welchen Kriterien wählen Sie ein Restaurant, wenn Sie essen gehen wollen?

Beim Lesen

Der Autor des Restaurantführers charakterisiert jeden Betrieb mit einem passenden Motto. Welches Motto passt zu welchem Restaurant?

	Restaurant	**Motto**
_f_	1. Café und Confiserie Sprüngli	a. Essen im Dunkeln
_d_	2. Kronenhalle	b. etwas Besonderes für Käse-Liebhaber
_a_	3. blindekuh	c. Gesunder Genuss
_c_	4. Hiltl	d. kein Restaurant, sondern ein Mythos
_e_	5. Zeughaus	e. rustikaler Bier- und Wursttempel
_b_	6. Fonduetram	f. Süsse Träume

Introduction to *Lesetext 1.* Introduce students to the topic by asking about their perceptions of Swiss food. *Wofür ist die Schweiz bekannt? Haben Sie etwas Kulinarisches aus der Schweiz schon mal probiert?* After they have read the introduction, ask what they have learned. *Welche kulinarischen Spezialitäten hat die Schweiz? Welche Einflüsse sind in der Schweizer Küche zu erkennen? Warum ist die Anzahl von Restaurants in der Zürcher Innenstadt seit 1998 deutlich gestiegen? Was bedeutet eine hohe Anzahl an*

Siehe **Kulturtipps**: Zürcher Geschnetzeltes mit Rösti

Gaststätten für die Stadt? Für die Gaststätten selbst?

repeal

density of restaurants

varied

Kreative Gastroszene

Café und Confiserie Sprüngli

Bahnhofstr. 21
Am Paradeplatz 8001 Zürich
http://www.spruengli.ch/

Information for *Lesetext 1*.
The Swiss Franc (*Schweizer Franken*) (abbreviated CHF or SFr.) is the currency of Switzerland and Liechtenstein. A *Franken* has 100 *Rappen*.

Luxemburgerli in diversen Geschmackssorten

In der Café-Bar der berühmten Confiserie trifft man sich vor oder nach dem Shopping in der Bahnhofstrasse*. Seine günstige Lage am Paradeplatz, aber auch seine 170 Jahre lange Tradition als Hersteller von exquisiten Süsswaren machen das Sprüngli zum würdigen Treffpunkt für eine kleine Pause. Vom Boulevardcafé aus kann man bei jedem Wetter dem Leben und Treiben an Zürichs schönster Einkaufsstrasse zuschauen.   5

Sprüngli ist renommierter Hersteller von Trüffeln, Pralinen und Tafelschokolade von feinster Qualität, aber der beliebteste und bekannteste Artikel aus dem Sprüngli-Sortiment sind „Luxemburgerli"[a], von denen die Confiserie etwa 650 kg pro Tag herstellt. Allerdings steht hier nicht nur Süsses zur Auswahl. Morgens kann man ein kleines Frühstück von Gipfeli[b], Brioche oder Birchermüesli† geniessen. Zu Mittag bieten sich nach Saison wechselnde und regionale Spezialitäten und am frühen Abend wird frisch   10 gebackenes, pikantes Gebäck zu einem Apéritif oder einem Glas Champagner gereicht. Den ganzen Tag hindurch werden heisse Kaffee- und Schokoladengetränke im edlen Porzellan serviert. Öffnungszeiten des Cafés: Mo. bis Fr. 7.00 bis 19.00 Uhr, Sa 7.30 bis 18.00 Uhr.

Kronenhalle

Rämistr. 4
Am Bellevue-Platz
8001 Zürich
http://www.kronenhalle.com/

Das legendäre Restaurant ist berühmt für seine Gäste und seine Kunstsammlung. Hier sitzt man unter einem echten Chagall, Matisse oder Warhol und teilt das traditionsreiche Lokal mit Prominenten aus Kultur, Wirtschaft, Politik und Mode. Zu den bekannten Gästen des 20. Jahrhunderts gehörten James Joyce, der hier einen Großteil seines Romans *Ulysses* verfasste,   5 Max Frisch, Richard Strauss, Pablo Picasso und Modegrößen wie Yves Saint Laurent. Trotz der eleganten Ausstattung von Mahagoni, Marmor, Kristall, Leder und Bronze wirkt das Ambiente eher entspannt als formell. Der Mix des Publikums trägt ebenfalls zur einmaligen Atmosphäre bei.

Brasserie mit Gemälde von Marc Chagall

Im Angebot stehen Schweizer Klassiker wie Zürcher Geschnetzeltes mit Rösti aber auch internationale   10 Gerichte wie z. B. Heringe in Sahnesauce, rotes Thunfisch-Sashimi und Risotto mit Scampi. Die Mousse au chocolat soll die beste in ganz Zürich sein. Obwohl etwas teuer – Hauptgerichte liegen zwischen CHF 28,– und 64,–, Desserts zwischen CHF 14,– und 18,– – ist dieses ebenso beliebte wie bekannte Etablissement eine Zürcher Institution, die man besucht haben muss. Täglich von 12.00 bis 24.00 Uhr geöffnet.

---

[a]*sweet, light almond wafers with a rich cream filling, produced in a variety of flavors*   [b]*Swiss German variant of* Hörnchen *or* Croissant

*Siehe **Kulturtipps**: Bahnhofstrasse und Paradeplatz
†Siehe **Kulturtipps**: Birchermüesli

blindekuh

Mühlebachstrasse 148
8008 Zürich
www.blindekuh.ch

Ein Erlebnis der ganz besonderen Art bietet seit 1999 das Restaurant blindekuh in Zürich, das weltweit erste Dunkelrestaurant. Hier findet die Mahlzeit völlig im Dunkeln statt. Blinde Menschen servieren
das Essen und führen die hilflosen Sehenden sicher an die Tische. Dieses seitdem in vielen anderen
Städten nachgeahmte Projekt bietet Sehenden die Möglichkeit, sich einmal in die Welt der Blinden zu
versetzen und schafft gleichzeitig Arbeitsmöglichkeiten für Blinde und Sehbehinderte. Die Mehrheit der   5
Mitarbeitenden ist blind oder sehbehindert, was grundlegend zum Erfolg des Konzepts beiträgt.

Das kulinarische Angebot wechselt wöchentlich und hängt von der Saison ab. Verschiedene Vor-
speisen, drei Hauptgänge jeweils mit Fleisch, mit Fisch, oder vegetarisch und mehrere Desserts
stehen stets zur Auswahl. Die Speisen enthalten frische und einheimische Produkte sowie Fleisch aus
tiergerechter Haltung[c].   10

Das Restaurant bietet Platz für 70 Gäste. Da hier jährlich Zehntausende von Gästen einkehren, ist
die rechtzeitige Reservierung empfehlenswert. Öffnungszeiten: Di. bis Fr. 11.30 bis 14.00 Uhr, Mo.
bis Sa. 18.30 Uhr bis 23.00 Uhr, So 18.00 bis 23.00 Uhr

Hiltl

Sihlstr. 28
8001 Zürich
http://www.hiltl.ch/

Das 1898 eröffnete Haus Hiltl gilt als das älteste vegetarische
Restaurant Europas. Seit der Neueröffnung gibt es doppelt so
viel Platz und mehr Licht, aber für die Stammgäste ist viel Altes und   Das Buffet enthält mehr als nur Salate.
Vertrautes noch geblieben. Die Sitzplätze für mehr als 400 Gäste
sind gemütlich auf verschiedene Räume verteilt. Außerdem stehen regionale und internationale Zei-   5
tungen zur Verfügung. Die angenehme Atmosphäre des Interieurs bildet einen deutlichen Kontrast zur
neonbeleuchteten, asphaltgrauen Sihlstrasse draussen.

Täglich gibt es im Hiltl zahlreiche fleischlose Angebote für jeden Geschmack. Neben reichhaltigen
Pastagerichten und Salaten stehen beispielsweise Gemüse-Paella, Pilz-Stroganoff und verschiedene
Currygerichte auf dem regelmässig wechselnden Tagesmenü. Bestellen kann man sogar ein vege-   10
tarisches Züri Geschnetzeltes oder fleischloses Cordon bleu. Legendär ist im Hiltl jedoch das größte,
von 10.30 bis 23.00 Uhr durchgehend geöffnete Salatbuffet Zürichs mit einer Unzahl von Delikates-
sen. Zu trinken gibt es frisch gepresste Fruchtsäfte, Bio-Biere und erlesene Weine. Die Nachspeisen
sind ebenfalls zu empfehlen.

Vom frühen Morgen bis spät in die Nacht können die Gäste am gesunden Genuss teilnehmen, ob im   15
Lokal oder zu Hause, denn das gesamte Angebot gibt es auch als Take-Away. Geöffnet So. bis Mi. 6
bis 2 Uhr, Do bis Sa. 6 bis 4 Uhr.

---

[c]humane meat

Zeughauskeller

Bahnhofstr. 28a (beim Paradeplatz)
8001 Zürich
http://www.zeughauskeller.ch/

Wer gutes Essen zu günstigen Preisen in einer geselligen [d] Atmosphäre sucht, befindet sich im Zeughauskeller am richtigen Ort. Diese volkstümliche Bierhalle, die trotz des Namens eigentlich kein Keller ist, gilt unter Einheimischen als eine der besten Adressen in der Stadt für traditionelle Zürcher Küche. Der erstmals 1497 als Büchsenhaus [e] errichtete Bau wurde erst 1927 zum Restaurant umgebaut. Das Dekor, zu dem mittelalterliche und neuere Waffen und Porträts von Rittern gehören, zeugt   5
von der Geschichte des Gebäudes. Der lebhafte Betrieb mit Holzmöbeln und rustikalem Interieur erinnert an den Charme des Münchner Hofbräuhauses.

Neben klassischen Gerichten wie Zürcher Geschnetzeltem serviert das Restaurant auch über zwölf verschiedene Wurstsorten aus allen Regionen der Schweiz. Zu diesen Wurstspezialitäten werden auch pro Jahr über 36 Tonnen des hausgemachten Kartoffelsalats serviert. Für die internationalen Gäste stehen Speisekarten in neun Sprachen zur Verfügung. Allerdings speisen noch viele Zürcher hier, Banker   10
wie einfache Angestellte, Seite an Seite. An den großen Tischen ergeben sich oft Gespräche zwischen Fremden. Täglich von 11.30 bis 23.00 Uhr geöffnet.

Fonduetram

Abfahrt ab Bellevue
Kontakt: Verkehrsbetriebe Zürich
http://www.vbz.ch/

Ein besonderes Erlebnis ist es, in einem Zürcher Tram Fondue* zu essen. Das eigenartige, auf Schienen fahrende Restaurant bietet 42 Gästen Platz und fährt von November bis Ende Februar quer durch die beleuchtete Stadt. Im neu renovierten Tram können Gäste ihre kulinarische Rundfahrt in einer frischen, moderneren Atmosphäre geniessen, ohne dass sie auf den nostalgischen Charme verzichten müssen. Das vom *Zunfthaus zur Zimmerleuten* [f] gecaterte Essen wird Gäste bestimmt auch nicht   5
enttäuschen. Im Pauschalpreis von CHF 89,– pro Person sind die zweistündige Stadtrundfahrt, ein Welcome Drink, eine Vorspeise, Fondue à discrétion [g], Dessert und Kaffee inbegriffen. Kinder bis 10 Jahre fahren 50 Prozent günstiger mit. Alkoholische Getränke werden separat verrechnet.

Das Tram verkehrt mittwochs und samstags, und im Dezember ausserdem noch montags, freitags und sonntags, jeweils zwei Fahrten pro Tag. Tischreservationen unter 044 434 44 34 oder fonduetram@   10
vbz.ch.

---

[d]*genial*   [e]*=* **Zeughaus** *armory, building for storing weapons and supplies*   [f]*Guild Hall of Carpenters (name of a restaurant)*   [g]*unlimited, all you can eat*

*Siehe **Kulturtipps**: Fondue

Kulturtipps

Zürcher Geschnetzeltes mit Rösti

Die regionale Spezialität Zürcher Geschnetzeltes besteht gewöhnlich aus einer Mischung von Kalbfleisch, Kalbsnieren (*calf livers*) und Champignons (*mushrooms*) in einer Sauce aus Rahm (*cream*) und Weißwein. Traditonell wird das Gericht mit einer knusprigen Rösti serviert – einer einfachen Beilage aus geriebenen (*grated*) und in der Pfanne gebratenen Kartoffeln.

Bahnhofstrasse und Paradeplatz

Die am Hauptbahnhof beginnende, 1,5 km lange Bahnhofstrasse, die am Ufer des Zürichsees endet, zählt zu den elegantesten Einkaufsstraßen Europas. Hier finden sich z. B. zahlreiche Juweliere, Modegeschäfte und Uhrenläden.

Einkaufen in der Bahnhofstrasse

Hauptsitz der Crédit Suisse am Paradeplatz

Mittelpunkt der Luxusgeschäfte und auch Drehscheibe des Zürcher Tramverkehrs ist der Paradeplatz. Hier haben auch Schweizer Großbanken wie Crédit Suisse ihren Hauptsitz. Den Luxus zeigt man in Zürich aber nicht nach außen. Man versteckt ihn, wie auch das viele Geld und Gold in den Banktresoren (*bank vaults*) direkt unter dem Paradeplatz.

Birchermüesli

Birchermüesli, auch weltweit einfach als Müesli oder Müsli bekannt, wurde um 1900 von dem Schweizer Arzt Maximilian Oskar Bircher-Benner erfunden. Das Originalrezept enthält Haferflocken (*rolled oats*), Wasser, Zitronensaft, Milch, frische Äpfel und Nüsse; heute sind die Rezepte für Müesli aber sehr unterschiedlich. Das Müesli wird in der Schweiz zum Frühstück oder als leichtes Abendessen gegessen oder auch stark gesüßt und mit viel Sahne als Nachspeise.

Fondue

Das Fondue stammt ursprünglich aus der französischen Schweiz. Verschiedene Käsesorten werden mit Wein und Gewürzen in einem speziellen Topf geschmolzen (*melted*). Bei Tisch wird der Käse warm gehalten, und mit einer langen, dünnen Gabel taucht man Brot- oder Gemüsestückchen in den Käse. Obwohl ursprünglich ein Käsegericht, wird in anderen Fonduevariationen z. B. Fleisch in Fett frittiert und mit Saucen serviert oder Obst- und Gebäckstücke werden in geschmolzene Schokolade getaucht.

Neue Vokabeln

Nomen

die Auswahl, -en   *selection*

der Betrieb, -e   *business, operation*

das Erlebnis, -se   *experience*

das Gericht, -e   *dish (food)*

die Küche, -n   *cuisine; kitchen*

das Lokal, -e   *restaurant, bar, venue*

der Mitarbeiter, -/die Mitarbeiterin, -nen   *co-worker, colleague*

die Vielfalt   *diversity*

Verben

enthalten (enthält), enthielt, enthalten   *to contain*

enttäuschen   *to disappoint*

erinnern (an + *acc.*)   *to remind (of)*

gehören (+ *dat.*)   *to belong (to)*

gehören zu   *to be part of, to rank among*

genießen, genoss, genossen   *to enjoy*

(sich) treffen (trifft), traf, getroffen   *to meet (each other)*

reichen   *to reach, to hand*

(sich) unterscheiden, unterschied, unterschieden   *to differentiate (oneself)*

verzichten auf (+ *acc.*)   *to do without*

wechseln   *to change, alternate*

zu·schauen (+ *dat.*)   *to observe, watch*

Adjektive und Adverbien

ebenfalls   *likewise*

echt   *genuine*

einheimisch   *local, native*

einmalig   *unique*

völlig   *completely*

7-1 Textarbeit: Welches Restaurant? Zu welchem Restaurant passt jede der folgenden Aussagen? Manchmal gibt es mehr als eine Möglichkeit.

1. Dieser Betrieb wurde neulich renoviert.
2. Hier kann man Zürcher Geschnetzeltes probieren.
3. Zur Auswahl gibt es hier immer drei Hauptgerichte.
4. Hier kann man sich beim Essen die Gemälde weltberühmter Künstler ansehen.
5. Hier kann man um 8.00 Uhr morgens einen Kaffee und ein kleines Frühstück einnehmen.
6. In diesem Betrieb kann man verschiedene Schweizer Würste probieren.
7. Dieses Lokal befindet sich auf der beliebtesten Einkaufsstraße der Stadt.
8. Berühmte Gäste haben hier gegessen.
9. In diesem Restaurant kann man das Essen, das man bestellt und isst, nicht sehen.
10. Dieser Betrieb hat nur vier Monate im Jahre geöffnet.

Answers for 7-1. 1. Hiltl und Fonduetram; 2. Kronenhalle, Hiltl (vegetarisch) und Zeughauskeller; 3. blindekuh; 4. Kronenhalle; 5. Sprüngli und Hiltl; 6. Zeughauskeller; 7. Sprüngli und Zeughauskeller; 8. Kronenhalle; 9. blindekuh; 10. Fonduetram

7-2 Textarbeit: Fragen zum Inhalt. Beantworten Sie die Fragen in Bezug auf den Text.

1. Was macht das *Café Sprüngli* zu einem idealen Treffpunkt in der Stadt?
2. Warum besuchen viele Gäste das Restaurant *Kronenhalle*, obwohl das Essen dort so teuer ist?
3. Was meinen Sie: Wie kann man im Restaurant *blindekuh* wissen, was auf der Speisekarte steht?

Possible answers for 7-2. 1. Es ist zentral gelegen und genießt einen guten Ruf. 2. Um berühmte Leute zu sehen, um sich die Kunst anzuschauen, oder weil das Essen gut ist. 3. Die Kellner sagen den Gästen, was im Angebot steht. (Deswegen gibt es eine eher kleine Auswahl.)

4. Es ist gesellig, lebhaft und rustikal. **5.** Das Tram hat wohl keine richtige Küche. **6.** Man kann den Leuten zuschauen (Sprüngli), sich die Kunstwerke ansehen oder berühmte Leute sehen (Kronenhalle), ausländische Zeitungen lesen (Hiltl), mit Fremden sprechen (Zeughauskeller), eine Stadtrundfahrt genießen (Fonduetram).

4. Beschreiben Sie die Atmosphäre des *Zeughauskellers*.

5. Was meinen Sie: Warum wird das Essen im *Fonduetram* gecatert und nicht direkt dort vorbereitet?

6. Was kann man in den verschiedenen Restaurants tun außer essen und trinken?

7-3 Vokabelarbeit. Ergänzen Sie die Sätze mit Wörtern aus den *Neuen Vokabeln*. Achten Sie dabei auch auf die Wortform.

1. Alle Restaurants bieten gastronomische Qualität, aber sie ____unterscheiden____ ____sich____ stark nach Preis, Atmosphäre und Auswahl an Gerichten.

2. In den Restaurants *Hiltl* und *blindekuh* ____wechselt____ die Speisekarte regelmäßig.

3. Im Haus *Hiltl* ____enthalten____ alle Gerichte nur vegetarische Zutaten.

4. Die Waffen und Porträts des *Zeughauskellers* ____erinnern____ ____an____ die Geschichte des Gebäudes.

5. Das Restaurant *Kronenhalle* bietet klassische schweizerische wie auch internationale ____Küche/Gerichte____.

6. Ein Zürcher Geschnetzeltes bekommt man im *Zeughauskeller* und ____ebenfalls____ im Restaurant *Kronenhalle*.

7. Im Restaurant *blindekuh* zu essen ist ein einmaliges ____Erlebnis____.

8. Ein Luxemburgerli von *Sprüngli* zu probieren: das ____gehört____ einfach zu einem Besuch in Zürich.

 7-4 Zur Diskussion. Besprechen Sie die Fragen.

1. Der Restaurantführer behauptet, dass in Zürcher Restaurants kreative Ideen zu finden sind. Welche Konzepte aus diesen sechs Betrieben finden Sie am kreativsten?

2. Beschreiben Sie Ihr Lieblingsrestaurant. Was für Essen steht im Angebot? Ist das Essen eher günstig oder teuer? Wie oft essen Sie dort? Was essen Sie dort am liebsten?

3. Haben Sie schon mal in einem außergewöhnlichen Restaurant gegessen? Was war das Außergewöhnliche daran?

4. Wann sind Sie das letzte Mal essen gegangen? Beschreiben Sie das Erlebnis.

 7-5 Mittagessen! Sie und zwei Mitstudenten sind für einen Tag in Zürich. Besprechen Sie, in welchem der Restaurants aus dem Restaurantführer Sie zu Mittag essen wollen. Dann erklären Sie Ihre Entscheidung vor der Klasse.

Activity 7-6. Suggested restaurants and search instructions are located in MyGermanLab and at the Companion Website.

7-6 Essen in Zürich. Zürich besitzt rund 2.000 Lokale. Lernen Sie ein anderes Restaurant der Stadt kennen. Finden Sie die Adresse und Öffnungszeiten, sehen Sie sich die Speisekarte und die Bilder des Lokals an. Dann schreiben Sie einen Absatz über das Restaurant. Sagen Sie dabei auch, was das Besondere an diesem Restaurant ist.

7-7 Mein Lieblingsrestaurant. Ein Schweizer Reisemagazin gibt eine Sonderausgabe über Ihre Stadt heraus, in der ein kleiner Restaurantführer stehen soll. Beschreiben Sie für den Restaurantführer Ihr Lieblingsrestaurant. Benutzen Sie die Beschreibungen aus dem Text als Modell.

Lesetext 2

„Wir nennen uns Zoogler!" (Interview)

Zürich gehört zu den wichtigsten Finanzplätzen weltweit und ist das wirtschaftliche Zentrum der Schweiz. Und das bezieht sich nicht nur auf die Stadt Zürich. Die *Greater Zurich Area* umfasst die Region, die innerhalb von 60 Minuten vom internationalen Flughafen Zürich aus erreichbar ist. Innerhalb von diesem Wirtschaftsraum lebt fast die Hälfte der Schweizer Bevölkerung und haben rund 140.000 internationale und Schweizer Unternehmen einen Sitz. Darunter befinden sich bekannte Namen wie Cisco Systems, John Deere, Dow, Kraft Foods and Google. 90 Prozent der Beschäftigten in der *Greater Zurich Area* sind im Dienstleistungssektor° tätig, d. h. vor allem in Finanz, Versicherung, Rechts- und Unternehmensberatung°, Informatik oder Immobilienverwaltung°. An zunehmender Bedeutung gewinnen aber auch Wirtschaftszweige, die auf Forschung und Wissen ausgerichtet sind, z. B. Präzisionstechnologien wie Biotechnologie, Robotik und Informations- und Kommunikationstechnologie.

In dem Interview, das *Insight-Magazin* mit Randy Knaflic von Google führte, erfahren Sie mehr über Zürich als wirtschaftlichen Standort.

Vor dem Lesen

1. Was meinen Sie: Welche Vorteile bietet Zürich für außereuropäische Unternehmen, die eine Branche in Europa eröffnen wollen?
2. Was ist Google? Benutzen Sie manchmal Google Produkte?

Beim Lesen

Der Interviewpartner Randy Knaflic erwähnt während des Interviews verschiedene Menschengruppen. Was sagt er über sie?

_e_	1.	Europäische Ingenieure	a. machen Praktika bei Google.
_c_	2.	Die Schweizer	b. fahren manchmal mit dem Fahrrad auf den Uetliberg.
_a_	3.	ETH-Absolventen	c. haben eine gute Bildung und Interesse an Technologie.
_b_	4.	Google-Ingenieure	d. sind begeistert von dem Schweizer Essen.
_d_	5.	Amerikaner	e. wollen in Europa bleiben.

Introduction to *Lesetext 2*. Ask students what they learned from the introduction and interpret some of the information based on what they already know. *Wie unterscheidet sich Zürich von* der Greater Zurich Area? *Warum bezeichnet man die Region wohl auf Englisch? Wie viele Schweizer leben in* der Greater Zurich Area? *Warum haben hier wohl so viele Unternehmen einen Sitz? Können Sie sich vorstellen, in dieser Region zu leben? Was für eine Arbeit würden Sie vielleicht finden?*

service sector

legal services and consulting / real estate management

Randy Knaflic von Google
Zürich

„Wir nennen uns Zoogler!"

Google hat im Frühling 2004 ihr europäisches Entwicklungszentrum in Zürich eröffnet. Dieses ist seither äusserst schnell gewachsen und beschäftigt heute über 700 Mitarbeiter. Google forscht in Zürich an sprachspezifischen Verbesserungen ihrer Suchmaschinen-Technologie, Internet-Werbung, Kartographie, Youtube, dem Google-Kalender und anderem 5 mehr. Wir hatten die Gelegenheit, uns mit Randy Knaflic zu unterhalten, dem „Director Staffing & Programs, EMEA" bei Google in Zürich.

Insight: Herr Knaflic, wie viele Personen arbeiten im Moment in Googles europäischem Forschungszentrum in Zürich?

Randy Knaflic: Wir haben bei der Eröffnung im Jahr 2004 mit einem 10 Software-Entwickler und einer Verkaufsperson angefangen. Heute beschäftigen wir über 700 Leute in Zürich und wachsen immer noch. Wir werden bis zu 600 Mitarbeiter beschäftigen. Zürich war das erste und ist das grösste europäische Entwicklungszentrum neben unseren Standorten in London, Trondheim, Aarhus, Moskau und Tel Aviv – und das drittgrösste weltweit. 15

Insight: Weshalb haben Sie in Zürich das grösste Entwicklungszentrum Europas?

Randy Knaflic: Zürich liegt sehr zentral, verfügt über viele hoch qualifizierte Arbeitskräfte und bietet eine exzellente Lebensqualität. Es ist viel einfacher, Mitarbeiter aus ganz Europa nach Zürich zu bringen als 20 anderswohin. Viele begabte Ingenieure wollen in Europa bleiben, in der Nähe ihrer Familien. Trotzdem möchten sie an gleichen Themen forschen wie Google in den USA. Die Schweiz hat ausserdem ein ähnliches Arbeitsrecht wie die USA.

Insight: Müssen Sie die Bewerber überzeugen, nach Zürich zu kommen? 25

Randy Knaflic: Nein, Zürich selbst ist bereits ein genügend gutes Argument! Ingenieure möchten aus alten und neuen EU-Mitgliedsländern und von überall aus der Welt nach Zürich kommen. Heute sind in unserem Zürcher Entwicklungszentrum 70 verschiedene Nationalitäten vertreten.

Insight: Welche Fähigkeiten schätzen Sie bei den Mitarbeitern, die Sie in der 30 Schweiz rekrutieren?

Randy Knaflic: Die Schweizer passen gut zur Google-Kultur, da sie sehr gut ausgebildet sind und sich stark für Technologie interessieren. Google bietet ihnen die Chance, an äusserst spannenden Projekten mitzuarbeiten. Ausserdem pflegen wir mit der Eidgenössischen Technischen Hochschule ETH 35 Zürich engen Kontakt.

Siehe **Kulturtipps**: Eidgenössische Technische Hochschule (ETH)

Insight: Welche Art von Kontakt ist das?

Randy Knaflic: Wir organisieren und unterstützen Anlässe, um gegenseitig Wissen auszutauschen. Die ETH-Studenten und -Absolventen sind grossartige Softwareingenieure und wir bieten ihnen Praktikumsstellen an.

Insight: Wie beurteilen Sie Zürichs Zukunft als ICT°-Forschungsstandort?

information and communication technology

Randy Knaflic: Es gibt gute Gründe, weshalb Firmen wie IBM und Google in Zürich Forschung und Entwicklung betreiben. Wir können hier die richtigen Leute rekrutieren!

Insight: Google ist bekannt für ihre spezielle Unternehmenskultur. Gibt es eine Zürcher Kultur bei Google?

Randy Knaflic: Ja, wir nennen uns sogar „Zoogler" und haben viel Swissness zu unserer US-Kultur hinzugefügt. So laden wir zum Beispiel mit einem „Heidi"-Lied die Zoogler zu unserem Freitagstreffen ein. Manchmal radeln° einige Ingenieure nachmittags auf den Uetliberg und im Winter gehen wir Ski fahren.

Siehe **Kulturtipps:** Heidi-Lied und Uetliberg

bike

Insight: Das hört sich sehr attraktiv an!

Randy Knaflic: Oh, und natürlich mein Lieblingsvergnügen: Schwimmen im Zürichsee in der Mittagspause! Dieser ist sehr schnell zu Fuss erreichbar. Hervorragend ist auch das Schweizer Essen. Viele Besucher aus den USA sind beeindruckt von unserem Frühstücksangebot (Müesli und Gipfeli), dem Mittagessen (zum Beispiel „Spätzli" mit Steak) oder dem Abendessen (wie in den grossartigen Restaurants Lily's oder Hiltl). Aber das Wichtigste ist und bleibt die Schweizer Schokolade, die überall in unserem Büro herumliegt!

Note on *Spätzli*. *Spätzli* is a pasta dish common in the southern German-speaking regions. Students will learn about the Swabian variant *Spätzle* in *Kapitel 8.*

Insight: Herzlichen Dank für das Interview! Wir freuen uns auf ein noch dynamischeres Forschungszentrum von Google in Zürich!

Die Greater Zurich Area ist der erweiterte Wirtschaftsraum Zürich. Hier leben und arbeiten 3 Millionen Menschen in 150'000 Unternehmen. http://www. greaterzuricharea.ch

Kulturtipps

Eidgenössische Technische Hochschule (ETH) Zürich

Die 1855 gegründete ETH ist eine nationale technisch-naturwissenschaftliche Universität, die neben Bachelor- und Master-Studiengängen in Ingenieur- und Naturwissenschaften, Bauwesen und Architektur auch zahlreiche Doktorprogramme anbietet. Die Hochschule genießt weltweit einen Ruf für ihre hervorragende Forschung und Lehre. Bis heute wurden 21 Nobelpreise an Forscher vergeben, die ETH-Professoren oder -Absolventen sind oder waren. Unter ihnen war Albert Einstein, der an der ETH studierte und dort auch später als Professor tätig war.

Heidi-Lied

Heidi ist die weltbekannte Titelfigur eines Romans der Zürcher Autorin Johanna Spyri. Die 1880/81 erschienene Heidi-Geschichte, die vom Leben eines Waisenkindes (*orphan*) in der idyllischen Bergwelt handelt, ist seitdem in über 50 Sprachen übersetzt, über 50 Millionen Mal verkauft und mehrmals verfilmt worden. Mit ihren Erzählungen über das einfache Leben in den Schweizer Alpen trug Spyri erheblich zu dem noch heute weit verbreiteten, romantischen Bild der Schweiz bei. Aus der beliebten Heidi-Zeichentrickserie (*cartoon series*) aus den 70er-Jahren, die auf Spyris Erzählungen basiert, stammt das sogenannte Heidi-Lied, das unter Deutschsprachigen weit und breit bekannt ist.

Uetliberg

Der 869 m hohe Uetliberg ist der bekannteste Berg Zürichs und ein beliebtes Ausflugsziel für Stadtbewohner wie auch Touristen. Von den Wanderwegen und der Mountain-Bike-Strecke aus hat man eine großartige Aussicht über die ganze Stadt und den Zürichsee bis hin zu den Alpen.

Blick vom Uetliberg

 Neue Vokabeln

Nomen

der Absolvent, -en, -en / die
  Absolventin, -nen   *graduate*
die Fähigkeit, -en   *ability*
die Gelegenheit, -en   *opportunity, occasion*
der Standort, -e   *site, location*
das Wissen   *knowledge*

Verben

aus·tauschen   *to exchange*
beschäftigen   *to employ, engage*

beurteilen   *to assess, judge*
eröffnen   *to open, start*
sich freuen auf (+ *acc.*)   *to look forward to*
sich interessieren für   *to be interested in*
passen (+ *dat.*)   *to fit*
passen zu   *to be suited to*
pflegen   *to maintain, care for*
schätzen   *to value, estimate*
sich unterhalten (unterhält),
  unterhielt, unterhalten   *to chat*

unterstützen   *to support*
verfügen über (+ *acc.*)   *to have at one's disposal or command*
wachsen (wächst), wuchs, ist gewachsen   *to grow*

Adjektive und Adverbien

äußerst   *extremely*
außerdem   *besides, in addition*
beeindruckt (von)   *impressed (by/with)*
großartig   *splendid, superb*

Answers for 7-8. 1. Angestellte des Google Entwicklungszentrums in Zürich **2.** Zürich liegt sehr zentral, verfügt über qualifizierte Menschen, bietet eine großartige Lebensqualität. **3.** Sie wollen in der Nähe ihrer Familien in Europa bleiben. **4.** Sie tauschen gegenseitig Wissen aus und Google bietet ETH-Absolventen Praktika als Softwareingenieure an.

7-8 Textarbeit: Fragen zum Inhalt. Beantworten Sie die Fragen zum Text.

1. Was sind „Zoogler"?
2. Warum ist Zürich laut Randy Knaflic ein guter Standort für ein Unternehmen wie Google?
3. Warum, sagt Herr Knaflic, wollen viele Mitarbeiter lieber in der Zürcher Niederlassung von Google anstatt an dem Hauptsitz in den USA arbeiten?
4. Welche Kontakte hat Google mit der ETH Zürich?

5. Warum haben laut Herrn Knaflic Google und IBM gerade in Zürich Niederlassungen?

6. Was machen die Google-Mitarbeiter in ihrer Freizeit?

7. Wofür interessieren sich amerikanische Besucher?

7-9 Vokabelarbeit. Ergänzen Sie die Sätze mit Wörtern aus den *Neuen Vokabeln.* Achten Sie dabei auch auf die Wortform.

1. Google ___beschäftigt___ 700 Mitarbeiter im Zürcher Entwicklungszentrum und will diese Zahl noch erhöhen.

2. Google schätzt das ___Wissen___ und die ___Fähigkeiten___ der ETH-Absolventen. Sie sind gut ausgebildet und hochqualifiziert.

3. Die ETH und Google ___unterstützen___ sich gegenseitig: Google profitiert von den Talenten der Studenten, die ETH-Studenten und -Absolventen sammeln Erfahrung bei ihrer Arbeit für Google.

4. Wer ___über___ eine Ausbildung als Softwareingenieur ___verfügt___, kann sich um die offene Stelle bewerben.

5. Außer dem Sitz in Zürich hat Google beispielsweise auch ___Standorte___ in Kalifornien, London und Tel Aviv.

6. Herr Knaflic ___freut___ ___sich___ an warmen Sommertagen ___auf___ seine Mittagspause.

7. Bewerber bei Google Zürich sind von der Unternehmenskultur sehr ___beeindruckt___.

 7-10 Zur Diskussion. Besprechen Sie die Fragen.

1. Möchten Sie bei Google Zürich arbeiten? Warum (nicht)? Wenn ja, was würden Sie für Google machen? Was würden Sie in Ihrer Freizeit machen?

2. Können Sie sich vorstellen, auf längere Zeit im Ausland zu leben? Was würden Sie dann besonders schön finden? Worauf müssten Sie verzichten? Was würden Sie von zu Hause vermissen?

3. Was möchten Sie von Beruf werden? Was für Fähigkeiten und was für eine Ausbildung braucht man für diese Arbeit?

 7-11 Ein neuer Standort. Sie sind Geschäftsführer in einem internationalen Unternehmen im Bereich Technologie. Der Betrieb wächst äußerst schnell und braucht neue Niederlassungen. Besprechen Sie, ob Ihre Universitätsstadt der richtige Standort für das Unternehmen wäre. Geben Sie mindestens drei Gründe für Ihre Entscheidung.

7-12 Wirtschaftszentrum Zürich. Viele Schweizer und internationale Betriebe haben ihren Hauptsitz im Kanton Zürich. Sammeln Sie Informationen zu dem Zürcher Hauptsitz eines Unternehmens. Dann stellen Sie die Firma in der Klasse vor.

5. In Zürich kann man die richtigen Leute für anspruchsvolle Stellen finden. 6. Sie fahren mit dem Fahrrad auf den Uetliberg, fahren im Winter Ski, gehen in der Mittagspause im Zürichsee schwimmen. 7. Sie interessieren sich für das Schweizer Essen.

Teaching suggestion for 7-12. Have students visit the official website of the *Greater Zurich Area,* which features companies that have headquarters in the region and provides information on the companies and their reasons for choosing this region for their businesses. Alternatively, they could gather their information directly from the company websites. Links to relevant websites can be found at MyGermanLab or the Companion Website.

Introduction to *Hörtext 1.*
Ask students what they learned
from the introduction. *Welchen
Anteil der Schweizer Bevölkerung
machen Ausländer aus? Meinen
Sie, dass der Ausländeranteil in
Zürich größer, kleiner oder der
gleiche ist wie in der gesamten
Schweiz?* As an urban center, the
percentage of foreigners in the city
is, not surprisingly, even greater, at
over 30 percent. *Warum kommen
so viele Ausländer in die Schweiz?
Nach Zürich? Warum sind in
der Schweiz lebende Ausländer
wichtig für das Land?* The canton
of Zürich offers several programs
and services to help foreigners
become integrated in the economic, social, and cultural life of
Switzerland. These include such
things as welcome meetings, German language courses, integration
courses, individual consultation
and advising, and education and
career training programs.

indispensable

7-13 Standortmarketing. Sie arbeiten für die Handelskammer (*Chamber of Commerce*) Ihrer Stadt und arbeiten an einer Broschüre, die Unternehmen überzeugen soll, eine Niederlassung in Ihrer Stadt zu eröffnen. Schreiben Sie einen Werbetext für die Broschüre, in der Sie die Vorteile Ihrer Stadt für ein Unternehmen beschreiben.

Hörtext 1

Elizabeth Barton: Eine Ausländerin in Zürich (Personenporträt)

In der gesamten Schweiz machen ausländische Einwohner rund 22 Prozent der Bevölkerung aus. In der Stadt Zürich besitzt sogar fast ein Drittel der Bevölkerung keinen Schweizer Pass. Viele Faktoren machen die Schweiz zu einem attraktiven Migrationsziel. Der hohe Lebensstandard, die politische Neutralität und Stabilität des Landes und die schon bestehende kulturelle, politische und religiöse Vielfalt des Staates sind nur einige der Faktoren, die Ausländer in die Schweiz locken. Darüber hinaus erschafft die florierende Wirtschaft eine Nachfrage an Arbeitern, die der einheimische Arbeitsmarkt nicht decken kann. Hoch qualifizierte aber auch weniger gebildete Arbeitskräfte aus dem Ausland sind für die wirtschaftliche Stabilität der Schweiz also unentbehrlich°.

Im folgenden Personenporträt erzählt die in Zürich lebende Ausländerin Elizabeth Barton von ihren Einwanderungsgründen, Eindrücken und Erfahrungen in der Schweiz.

Vor dem Hören

Teaching suggestion for *Vor
dem Hören.* Ask students to
surmise which nations supply the
most immigrants to the Zürich
area. *Was meinen Sie? Aus
welchem Land / welchen Ländern
kommen die meisten Einwanderer? Warum?* As they might
expect, partly due to proximity and
language compatibility, Germans
are by far the largest group of immigrants year after year. In 2010,
33% of all immigrants to Zürich
came from Germany, followed
by Italy, Great Britain, Portugal,
and France (each between 5 and
5.5%). Less than 3% of immigrants to Zürich came from the
USA in 2010.

Schauen Sie sich die Grafiken zur Einwanderung in den Kanton Zürich an. Woher kommen die meisten Ausländer nach Zürich? Aus welchen Gründen wandern die meisten Ausländer ein?

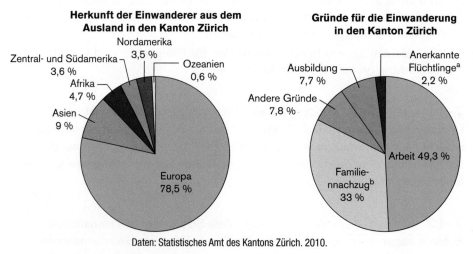

Herkunft der Einwanderer aus dem Ausland in den Kanton Zürich

Nordamerika 3,5 %
Zentral- und Südamerika 3,6 %
Ozeanien 0,6 %
Afrika 4,7 %
Asien 9 %
Europa 78,5 %

Gründe für die Einwanderung in den Kanton Zürich

Ausbildung 7,7 %
Anerkannte Flüchtlinge[a] 2,2 %
Andere Gründe 7,8 %
Arbeit 49,3 %
Familiennachzug[b] 33 %

Daten: Statistisches Amt des Kantons Zürich. 2010.

[a] *recognized refugees*   [b] *joining of family members*

Beim Hören

Während des Interviews hören Sie folgende Vokabeln.

Elizabeth Barton: Eine
Ausländerin in Zürich

07-11 to 07-12

fühlt sich … wohl   *feels comfortable*
auf Schritt und Tritt   *at every turn*
Niederlassung   *branch office*
Xaphon   *name of a company*
„Ohni Lüüt gaat nüüt." = **Ohne Leute geht nichts.**
Hüftimplantate   *hip implants*
Hauptsitz   *headquarters*
Austauschprogramm   *exchange program*
Stäfa, Rapperswil, Lachen   *names of three small towns on Lake Zurich*
Luzern   *name of a city and a canton*
Gemeinde   *community*
ein Katzensprung   *a stone's throw*
Heimweh   *homesickness*

Elizabeth Barton mit ihrem Hund

1. Hören Sie sich das Personenporträt an und schreiben Sie Stichwörter zu folgenden Punkten auf.

   a. Elizabeths Herkunft
   b. ihr Beruf (was? wo? wann?)
   c. ihre Freizeit
   d. ihre Freunde und Familie
   e. Zürich

2. Inwiefern passt Elizabeth Barton in die Statistiken zur Einwanderung, die Sie in den Grafiken oben analysiert haben?

Kulturtipps

▬Grüezi!

„Grüezi" ist eine Verkürzung des Ausdrucks „Ich grüsse Sie" und ist eine übliche Begrüßung in der Schweiz. Sie wird nur gegenüber unbekannten Personen oder als Höflichkeitsform gebraucht, aber nie bei Personen verwendet, die man duzt. Da sagt man eher „Grüessdi" (eine Verkürzung von „Ich grüsse dich"), „Hoi", „Ciao" oder „Salü."

▬Appenzeller Sennenhund

Der Appenzeller Sennenhund genießt in der Schweiz eine Art Kultstatus. Dieser Hund wird schon seit dem Mittelalter als treuer Begleiter der Schweizer Bauern geschätzt. Diese Rasse eignet sich zum Hüten und Treiben von Viehherden (*cattle herds*) im Alpengebiet und ist ein verlässlicher Wachhund für Haus und Familie.

7-14 Textarbeit: Leben in Zürich. Was sieht Elizabeth Barton als das Positive an ihrem Leben in Zürich? Kreuzen Sie an, was Sie hören.

__x__ Die Landschaft ist schön.

__x__ Die Menschen sind freundlich.

_____ Die Universität bietet gute Ausbildungsmöglichkeiten.

__x__ Man kann sich tags und nachts in der Stadt sicher fühlen.

__x__ Die Menschen genießen das Leben.

__x__ Der Zürichsee ist sauber.

_____ Sie verdient viel Geld.

_____ Die Lebenskosten sind nicht hoch.

__x__ Sie wohnt in der Nähe eines Waldes.

__x__ Das Stadtzentrum ist nicht weit entfernt.

_____ Sie muss täglich Deutsch mit ihren Mitarbeitern sprechen.

_____ Ihre Freunde aus Sydney wohnen jetzt auch in der Nähe.

Answers for 7-15. 1. 33
2. Sie musste an Meetings in der Schweiz teilnehmen. 3. Sie hat an einem 2-jährigen Austauschprogramm teilgenommen.
4. Sie sind offen und freundlich und genießen das Leben. 5. Es ist sicher und es gibt unterschiedliche Kulturen ganz in der Nähe. 6. Sie machen Tagesausflüge mit dem Auto oder dem Motorrad und verbringen auch gern Zeit mit Freunden. 7. Sie leitet ein Team bei Phonak. 8. Sie möchte besser Deutsch sprechen.

Follow-up for 7-16. Have a few pairs reenact their conversation for the class.

Alternative for 7-17. Have students play the respective roles of recruiter and potential employee. The recruiter must convince the potential employee that s/he should move to Zurich to work for this company and the potential employee will ask questions about the job and about life in Zürich.

Follow-up for 7-18. Have students deliver their speeches to the class or have them record them, as they would for a radio program, in MyGermanLab. If they do record them, you could have students work in pairs and have them each play the role of narrator for one another so that they can produce a radio program similar to the one in *Hörtext 1*.

7-15 Textarbeit: Fragen zum Inhalt. Beantworten Sie die Fragen in Bezug auf das Gespräch.

1. Wie alt ist Elizabeth Barton?
2. Warum war sie früher oft in der Schweiz?
3. Warum ist sie dann für zwei Jahre nach Zürich gezogen?
4. Welchen Eindruck hatte sie von den Menschen in Zürich?
5. Wie unterscheidet sich das Leben in Zürich von ihrem Leben in Sydney (Australien)?
6. Was machen Elizabeth und ihr Freund John gern in der Freizeit?
7. Was macht Elizabeth heute beruflich?
8. Was möchte sie an ihrem Leben in der Schweiz noch verändern?

7-16 Elizabeth und John. Elizabeth und John wollen ihr Deutsch verbessern und entscheiden sich, auch zu Hause Deutsch zu sprechen. Spielen Sie die Rollen von Elizabeth und John und inszenieren Sie ein Gespräch zwischen dem Paar beim Frühstück.

7-17 Mitarbeiter und Mitarbeiterinnen gesucht! Sie arbeiten für ein großes Unternehmen in Zürich, das behauptet, die beste Schokolade der Welt herzustellen. Sie sollen gut qualifizierte ausländische Mitarbeiter rekrutieren. Denken Sie sich Argumente aus, mit denen man Mitarbeiter werben kann. Denken Sie dabei an das Leben in Zürich und die Vorteile, die Ihr Unternehmen bietet.

7-18 Im Radio. Ein Journalist hat Sie gebeten, an einer Radiosendung über die Lebensqualität in Ihrer Stadt teilzunehmen. Bereiten Sie einen Monolog vor. Erzählen Sie, warum Sie dort wohnen, wo Sie dort beschäftigt sind, was Sie in der Freizeit machen, was Sie an Ihrem Leben dort verändern möchten und ob Sie eines Tages an einen anderen Ort ziehen wollen.

Introduction to *Lesetext 3*. Ask students about their experiences. *Sprechen Sie mehr als eine Sprache? Wenn ja, wann benutzen Sie welche Sprachen?* Then ask students what they learned from the text introduction. *Welche Sprachen sprechen Schweizer? Welche Rolle spielt die Sprache in der Identität der deutschsprachigen Schweizer? In welchen Situationen spricht man eine Mundart? Wann benutzt man Hochdeutsch? Wie lernen Kinder in der Schweiz Hochdeutsch? Welche besondere Schwierigkeit gibt es bei den Kindern von Ausländern?*

Lesetext 3

Umstrittenes Hochdeutsch im Kindergarten (Zeitungsartikel)

Während Deutsche in ihrem täglichen Umgang Hochdeutsch zu sprechen pflegen, ziehen die deutschsprachigen Schweizer – ob zu Hause, bei der Arbeit oder im öffentlichen Leben – meist den Dialekt vor°. Denn Hochdeutsch, auch Standarddeutsch genannt, ist eine Erfindung des großen deutschen Nachbarn im Norden, und die Mundart (der Dialekt) ist Teil der deutschschweizerischen Identität. Der Gebrauch der Mundart im Alltag° unterscheidet die deutschsprachigen Schweizer also von den Deutschen. In der Deutschschweiz gibt es allerdings eine Vielzahl regional unterschiedlicher Dialekte, für die es keine einheitliche Schreibweise gibt und die sich sehr vom Standarddeutschen in Aussprache sowie in Vokabeln und Grammatik unterscheiden. Hochdeutsch benutzen die Schweizer also als Schriftsprache und auch damit die Sprecher der verschiedenen schweizerdeutschen Dialekte mit Deutschsprachigen aus anderen Regionen sprechen können.

ziehen vor prefer

everyday life

Weil die meisten in der Deutschschweiz lebenden Kinder mit der Mundart zu Hause aufwachsen, lernen sie Hochdeutsch erst in der Schule. Dann gibt es auch die Kinder der in der Schweiz lebenden Ausländer, die beim Schuleintritt weder Hochdeutsch noch eine deutsche Mundart sprechen. Zur Frage, wie man diese Sprachmischung in der Schule behandeln soll, gibt es weit auseinander liegende Meinungen. Im folgenden Artikel aus der *Neuen Zürcher Zeitung*, der wichtigsten Schweizer Tageszeitung, erfahren Sie von der laufenden Debatte über Sprachen in der Schule.

Kinder mit Kindergärtnerin

Note for introduction. Unlike most regional languages of Europe, Swiss German dialect is the everyday spoken language at all social levels in German-speaking Switzerland. Standard German is primarily a written language and is spoken only in a few specific contexts, for example, in schools, in the news broadcasts of public (but generally not private) radio and TV stations, or in situations with German speakers from outside the region who do not know the local Swiss dialect. Swiss German dialects are thus the primary form of communication and Standard German is widely considered to be a foreign language, even though it is an official language of Switzerland.

Vor dem Lesen

Welche Sprache sprechen Sie im Alltag? Mit welchen Sprachen sind Sie aufgewachsen? Gab es Schüler in Ihrer Klasse, die eine andere Muttersprache hatten als Sie? Haben Sie heute Freunde oder Verwandte, die eine andere erste Sprache haben als Sie? Wie kommunizieren Sie miteinander?

Beim Lesen

Ordnen Sie die Sätze den Absätzen 1 bis 7 im Artikel zu.

___2___ Basel und Zürich haben einen hohen Anteil an fremdsprachigen Kindern in ihren Kindergärten.

___7___ Hochdeutsch und Mundart sind beide wichtig für die spätere Integration der Jugendlichen in der Schule und im Beruf.

___6___ Kindergärtner und Kindergärtnerinnen wollen hauptsächlich in Mundart unterrichten.

___4___ In Zürich sollte man teilweise Standarddeutsch, teilweise Mundart sprechen.

<u> 5 </u>   Standarddeutsch in den Kindergärten verbessert die Sprachkompetenzen der Kinder nicht.

<u> 1 </u>   Standarddeutsch soll in Zukunft in allen Kantonen der deutschsprachigen Schweiz in Kindergärten eingeführt werden.

<u> 3 </u>   Studien und Probezeiten wurden und werden in den Kindergärten gemacht.

Umstrittenes Hochdeutsch im Kindergarten

07-13 to 07-16

Die frühe Deutschförderung wird vor allem in den beiden Basler Halbkantonen° und im Kanton Zürich heiss diskutiert

von Katja Baigger

Basler Halbkantonen Basel half cantons, refers to Basel-Stadt and Basel-Landschaft

Information for *Lesetext 3*. With the implementation of a 2008 law, attending a *Kindergarten* is obligatory for children in Switzerland from the age of four. In most cantons, children attend kindergarten for two years. You might need to remind students that *Kindergarten* is the American equivalent of preschool and is not the same as "kindergarten" in the U.S.

Siehe **Kulturtipps**: Pisa

in terms of

less educated

leading role

name of a city in the metropolitan region of Zürich

teachers

[1] Ein Mädchen fällt hin und weint. Die Kindergärtnerin tröstet das 5-jährige Kind auf Hochdeutsch. Diese Vorstellung finden viele Lehrpersonen und Politiker absurd. Eine solche Szene könnte sich aber bald nicht mehr nur in Pilot-Projekten abspielen – in allen Kantonen der deutschsprachigen Schweiz soll in Kindergärten künftig teilweise Standarddeutsch gesprochen werden. Die Schweizerische Konferenz der kantonalen Erziehungsdirektoren (EDK) gab diese Empfehlung bereits im Jahr 2003 bekannt, als Reaktion auf die Pisa-Studie aus dem Jahre 2000. Damals stellte man bei Schülern punkto° Lesekompetenz unter dem europäischen Durchschnitt liegende Werte fest, insbesondere bei ausländischen Jugendlichen. Durch eine frühe Gewöhnung der Kinder an die Standardsprache erhofft sich die EDK positive Auswirkungen auf die Lesekompetenz, eine frühe Förderung von fremdsprachigen Kindern und solchen aus bildungsfernen° Schichten. 5 10

Fremdsprachige Kinder profitieren

[2] Eine Vorreiterrolle° bei der Einführung von Standarddeutsch nehmen die Kantone Basel-Stadt und Zürich ein. Beide haben einen hohen Anteil an fremdsprachigen Kindern. Im Kanton Zürich sind in den rund 1.300 Kindergärten schätzungsweise 27 Prozent der Kindergärtler nicht deutscher Muttersprache, in Basel-Stadt sind es in den 120 Kindergärten gar rund 60 Prozent. Schon im Jahr 2000 wurde im zürcherischen Schlieren° ein Pilotprojekt gestartet. Gleichzeitig wurde in einem Basler Kindergarten mit vielen ausländischen Kindern auf Initiative der Lehrkräfte° begonnen, Hochdeutsch zu unterrichten. 15 20

[3] Mathilde Gyger, Abteilungsleiterin des Instituts Primarstufe an der Fachhochschule Nordwestschweiz, hat mehrere Studien begleitet, etwa ein vierjähriges Projekt in Basel-Stadt, bei dem man zwei Hochdeutsch-Kindergärten mit zwei Mundart-Kindergärten verglich. Widerstand gebe es 25

vor allem in Quartieren° mit überwiegend deutschsprachigen Kindern, sagt
Gyger. Manche Eltern und Politiker sähen den Sinn der Umstellung° nicht
ein, die Lehrpersonen seien in ihrer Meinung gespalten°. Eine längere Erpro- 30
bungsphase° soll zu einer breiten Akzeptanz verhelfen. Für die Schuljahre
2006 bis 2008 konnten dafür 31 Kindergarten-Teams gewonnen werden.

districts
change
divided
test phase

In Zürich ab Spätsommer Realität

[4] Diesbezüglich° ist man im Kanton Zürich schneller vorangeschritten°.
Das kantonale Volksschulgesetz° sieht vor, dass als Unterrichtssprache
auf der Kindergartenstufe „teilweise" Standarddeutsch gesprochen 35
wird. In der Erprobungsfassung° des Kindergarten-Lehrplanes wurde
der Gesetzestext wie folgt ausgelegt: „Mundart- und Hochdeutsch-
Blöcke sind etwa gleichgewichtig° anzusetzen." Kindergärtnerinnen testen den Lehrplan nun freiwillig, mit klar deklarierten Hoch-
deutsch- und Mundart-Blöcken. 40

in this respect / advanced
elementary school law

draft version

equally weighted
Note. The article uses the feminine *Kindergärtnerinnen* because
the majority of preschool teachers
in Switzerland are women. In
2007/08, only 4% of teachers at
the *Kindergarten* level were men.
demand

[5] Für Gabriella Fink ist das zu viel Standardsprache im Kindergarten. Die
Präsidentin des Verbands der Kindergärtnerinnen im Kanton Zürich
kritisiert Hochdeutsch im Kindergarten als „Forderung° von oben". Die
Erfahrung in der Praxis zeige, dass mehr Unterrichtseinheiten° in Hochdeutsch nicht zu besseren Sprachkompetenzen in der Standardsprache 45
führe, aber zu einer schlechteren Sprachentwicklung der Erstsprache,
die für die meisten die Mundart sei.

teaching units

Standarddeutsch als Beziehungssprache

[6] Eine Informationsveranstaltung Ende Januar 2008 hat laut Fink gezeigt,
dass eine Mehrheit der befragten Kindergärtnerinnen für Dialekt als
Unterrichtssprache plädiere. Hochdeutsch könne durchaus einen Platz 50
erhalten, solle aber nicht so stark gewichtet° werden. Zürcher Kantons-
rat° Samuel Ramseyer unterstützt die Argumentation von Fink. Er
glaubt nicht, dass sich Standarddeutsch im Kindergarten positiv auf
die Lesekompetenz auswirke, vielmehr befürchte er einen „Sprach-
wirrwarr"°. Fremdsprachige würden zudem besser über Dialekt inte- 55
griert. Wenn ein ausländischer Jugendlicher eine Lehre mache, werde
der Lehrmeister kaum Hochdeutsch mit ihm sprechen, glaubt Ramseyer.

*weighted / state parliament
representative*

language confusion

[7] Dies könnte zwar zutreffen, erwidern die Experten Gyger und Peter
Sieber, Professor für Sprachwissenschaften an der Universität Zürich
und Prorektor der Pädagogischen Hochschule Zürich. Aber Lehrlinge 60
müssten in der Berufsschule° Standarddeutsch können. Beide sind
überzeugt, dass ein bewusster Umgang mit Hochdeutsch und Dialekt
entscheidend sei für die spätere Schullaufbahn. Für viele Zürcher Kindergärtnerinnen sei die Umstellung auf Hochdeutsch laut Sieber weniger gravierend als zunächst angenommen. Auch Gyger ist zuversicht- 65
lich°: Die Basler Kindergärtnerinnen realisierten allmählich, dass man
auch trösten und lustig sein könne auf Hochdeutsch.

vocational school

confident

Kulturtipps

Pisa-Studie

Pisa oder das „Programme for International Student Assessment" ist eine Schulleistungsstudie, an der viele Länder weltweit teilnehmen. Alle drei Jahre werden 15-jährige Schüler jeweils in einer von drei Kompetenzen geprüft: Lesen, Mathematik und Naturwissenschaften. Bei der ersten solchen Prüfung im Jahre 2000 lag der Schwerpunkt auf der Lesekompetenz. Ergebnisse (*results*) der Pisa-Studie stellten die Bildungssysteme der Länder im internationalen Vergleich dar und lösten damals heftige Debatten über Bildung aus, die heute noch weitergeführt werden.

Neue Vokabeln

Nomen

der Durchschnitt, -e   *average*

die Lehre, -n   *apprenticeship, lesson*

die Mehrheit, -en   *majority*

die Mundart, -en   *dialect*

der Sinn, -e   *sense, meaning*

die Schicht, -en   *social class; layer*

der Umgang   *contact, dealings*

der Wert, -e   *value*

der Widerstand, ¨e   *resistance, opposition*

Verben

trösten   *to comfort*

unterrichten   *to teach*

weinen   *to cry*

zu·treffen (trifft zu), traf zu, zugetroffen   *to apply to, be correct*

Adjektive und Adverbien

durchaus   *absolutely*

freiwillig   *voluntarily*

fremdsprachig   *foreign language-speaking*

gleichzeitig   *simultaneously*

teilweise   *partly*

überwiegend   *predominantly*

umstritten   *controversial*

zwar   *admittedly, to be precise*

7-19 Textarbeit: Standarddeutsch oder Mundart? Ergänzen Sie die Aussagen mit **Standarddeutsch** oder **Mundart** nach den Informationen aus dem Artikel.

1. Nach der Pisa-Studie hat man empfohlen, _Standarddeutsch_ bereits im Kindergarten zu verwenden.

2. Experten meinen, dass vor allem fremdsprachige Kinder davon profitieren, wenn der Kindergartenunterricht in _Standarddeutsch_ abläuft.

3. Die Eltern von deutschsprachigen Kindern wollen lieber, dass _Mundart_ während des Unterrichts gesprochen wird.

4. Gabriella Fink meint, dass _Standarddeutsch_ im Kindergartenunterricht die Sprachentwicklung der Kinder behindern kann.

5. Die Mehrheit der Kinder in Zürcher Kindergärten sprechen _Mundart_ als erste Sprache.

6. Die Mehrheit der Kindergärtnerinnen will in _Mundart_ unterrichten.

7. Fremdsprachige Kinder kann man am besten über _Mundart_ integrieren, meint Herr Ramseyer.

8. Mit Jugendlichen in einer Lehre wird der Lehrmeister wohl _Mundart_ sprechen.

9. In der Berufsschule werden Lehrlinge _Standarddeutsch_ sprechen müssen.

7-20 Textarbeit: Welche Sprache spricht man? Die einzigartige sprachliche Situation der Schweiz spielt eine entscheidende Rolle in der Schulpolitik wie auch im täglichen Umgang der Menschen miteinander.

1. Erklären Sie die sprachliche Situation im Kanton Zürich mit Hilfe der folgenden Begriffe aus dem Text.

   Standardsprache   Unterrichtssprache

   Mundart/Dialekt   Fremdsprachige Kinder

   Muttersprache/Erstsprache   Jugendliche

2. Beschreiben Sie nun die sprachliche Situation in Ihrer Heimat mit Hilfe derselben Begriffe.

7-21 Vokabelarbeit. Ergänzen Sie die Sätze mit Wörtern aus den *Neuen Vokabeln*. Achten Sie dabei auch auf die Wortform.

1. In Europa legt man mehr ____Wert____ auf den Fremdsprachenunterricht als in Nordamerika.

2. Die ____Mehrheit____ der Kindergärtler im Kanton Zürich spricht zu Hause eine deutsche Mundart.

3. Künftig soll man im Kanton Zürich noch früher in der Schule auf Hochdeutsch ____unterrichten____ .

4. Man kann beide Sprachen nicht ____gleichzeitig____ gebrauchen, sondern man teilt den Unterricht in Mundart- und Hochdeutsch-Blöcke.

5. Es ist anfangs ____zwar____ schwierig in Hochdeutsch zu unterrichten, aber mit der Zeit wird es leichter.

6. Kindergärtnerinnen erfahren mit der Zeit, dass es ____durchaus____ möglich ist, auf Hochdeutsch zu spielen und zu trösten.

7. Die Mundart können fremdsprachige Kinder auch im täglichen ____Umgang____ mit deutschsprachigen Kindern lernen.

7-22 Zur Diskussion. Besprechen Sie Ihre Meinungen.

1. Was meinen Sie: Sollen Kindergärtnerinnen Hochdeutsch sprechen? Welche Auswirkungen könnte es wohl auf den Unterricht haben?

2. Kann man fremdsprachige Kinder Ihrer Meinung nach besser über Mundart oder Standardsprache integrieren? Warum?

3. Können Kinder, deren Erstsprache eine deutsche Mundart ist, vom Kindergartenunterricht in der Standardsprache profitieren?

4. Wie sollte ein Schultag im Kindergarten mit „Mundart- und Hochdeutsch-Blöcken" aussehen?

5. Welche Sprachen sprechen Sie? Haben Sie als Kind in der Schule Sprachunterricht gehabt? Sollen Kinder in Ihrer Heimat in der Schule eine Fremdsprache lernen? Warum (nicht)?

Alternative for 7-22 (1–3). Have students come up with lists of the potential advantages and disadvantages of using the standardized form of the language at the kindergarten level. You could have each group of students focus on examining one side of the argument (just advantages or just disadvantages), or each group could come up with ideas for both lists.

Teaching suggestion for 7-23. Assign various roles to the students, e.g.: *Mutter/Vater eines deutschsprachigen Kindes, ein in Zürich lebender Ausländer/eine in Zürich lebende Ausländerin mit zwei Kindern, Kindergärtner/in, 4-jähriges Kind aus Serbien, 5-jähriges Schweizer Kind, Politiker/in der Stadt Zürich, Professor/in für Sprachwissenschaften, Grundschullehrer/in der 4. Klasse, Jugendliche/r in einer Lehre,* etc. Students could prepare their positions as homework to present to the class. Alternatively, you could have students defend their respective positions to one another while working in smaller groups. The groups could be mixed or the students could be grouped based on their roles—the parents in one group, the children in another group, teachers in a third group, etc. If time allows, you could organize a debate on the topic. Or alternatively, you could frame the discussion as a referendum posted on the website of the canton and have the students carry out the debate in writing in an online forum.

7-23 Forum Hochdeutsch im Kindergarten. Der Kanton Zürich will bald entscheiden, wie viel Hochdeutsch in den Kindergärten gesprochen werden soll. Die Stadt veranstaltet ein öffentliches Forum für Einwohner. Spielen Sie die Rolle eines Einwohners der Stadt Zürich und teilen Sie Ihre Meinung und Erfahrungen im Forum mit.

Information for 7-24. Students will find examples of such reader comments in SAM 07-15. They can refer to these as models for their own texts.

7-24 Leserkommentar. Schreiben Sie nun als betroffener Bürger/betroffene Bürgerin des Kantons Zürich einen Leserkommentar zum Artikel für die *Neue Zürcher Zeitung.* Identifizieren Sie Ihre Rolle, z. B. Kindergärtner/in, Lehrer/in, Elternteil, geben Sie Ihre Meinung und unterstützen Sie Ihre Meinung mit konkreten Gründen oder Beispielen.

Introduction to *Hörtext 2*. To start students thinking about the topic, ask: *Wodurch zeichnet sich eine sehr gute Universität oder Hochschule aus?* Then ask what they learned from the text introduction. *Welche Hochschulen besitzt Zürich? Wie viele Hochschulen gibt es in der Schweiz? Woran erkennt man die Qualität der beiden Hochschulen Zürichs?*

Hörtext 2

Das ungleiche Paar: Universität und ETH in Zürich (Radiosendung)

Hörtext 2. In this radio broadcast, students will have the opportunity to hear Swiss accents. Note that all of the speakers are speaking *Schweizer Standardsprache,* the Swiss variant of *Hochdeutsch,* and not their respective dialects, which would prove much more difficult even for German native speakers from other regions to understand.

In *Lesetext 2* haben Sie von der Eidgenössischen Technischen Hochschule Zürich erfahren. Zürich hat aber auch eine zweite renommierte Hochschule: die Universität Zürich. Die Uni ist die größte von zehn Universitäten in der Schweiz, die ETH die größte von zwei technischen Hochschulen. Beide zählen zu den besten 100 Hochschulen der Welt. Was bedeutet es, wenn zwei ausgezeichnete Hochschulen eine Stadt teilen müssen? Zum Anlass der 175-Jahr-Feier der Universität hat man die Beziehung zwischen den beiden Hochschulen untersucht und darüber in einer Radiosendung in Schweizer Radio DRS berichtet.

Vor dem Hören

Wie viele Hochschulen gibt es in Ihrer Stadt oder in Ihrer Gegend? Wie unterscheiden sie sich? Konkurrieren sie um Studierende oder sprechen sie unterschiedliche Bewerber an?

Beim Hören

Während des Interviews hören Sie folgende Vokabeln.

Das Ungleiche Paar: Universität und ETH in Zürich
07-17

Doppelspurigkeiten *duplicate tracks*
Ménage à deux (*French*) *household/ marriage of two*
eidgenössisch(e) *(Swiss) federal/ national*
platzte *fell through*
Bund *federal government*
Vorlesungen *lectures*

Zusammenarbeitsvereinbarung *agreement to cooperate*
steiget *increases*
Lausanne *capital city of the canton Waadt in southwest Switzerland*
Geldverschwendung *waste of money*
dotiert *endowed*

Hauptgebäude der ETH Zürich   Hauptgebäude der Universität Zürich

Hören Sie sich die Radiosendung an. Worauf beziehen sich die Zahlen?

_e_	halb so viele	a. Franken vom Kanton gespart, aber vom Bund ausgegeben
_g_	2	b. Jahre der Universität Zürich
_f_	20	c. Professoren bei der Gründung der Uni
_h_	22	d. Jahre der ETH Zürich
_c_	26	e. Studenten an der ETH als an der Uni
_d_	153	f. geteilte Professuren heute an den Hochschulen
_i_	160	g. gemeinsame Institute
_b_	175	h. Jahre nach der Gründung der Universität entsteht die ETH
_a_	50 Millionen	i. Studenten bei der Gründung der Uni

 7-25 Textarbeit: Zusammenfassung. Ergänzen Sie die Zusammenfassung des Hörtexts mit Informationen aus der Radiosendung.

Die Universität Zürich wurde im Jahre (1) ___1833___ gegründet. Die ETH entstand (2) ___22___ Jahre später. Seit (3) ___2001___ besteht ein Vertrag zur Zusammenarbeit zwischen den zwei Hochschulen.

Die Universität in Lausanne ließ die ETH Lausanne drei Fächer komplett übernehmen: Chemie, Physik und (4) ___Mathematik___. Obwohl man über eine solche Arbeitsteilung in Zürich diskutiert hat, hat man sich dagegen entschieden, denn dadurch kann man wahrscheinlich kein (6) ___Geld___ sparen.

Man meint, eine Doppelspurigkeit ist nicht schlecht an sich, denn nicht Effizienz, sondern Kapazität ist das Problem. Zürich will mehr (5) ___Studierende___, und das passiert am ehesten, wenn zwei Hochschulen zur Auswahl stehen, auch wenn beide einige derselben Fächer anbieten, weil sie dann unterschiedliche Stärken und Schwerpunkte haben.

Zum Beispiel: An der Uni Zürich steht das Studium der (6) ___Medizin___ der Praxis näher als an der ETH. Und die Universität ist stärker und besser im Fach (7) ___Biologie___. Aber in der (8) ___Chemie___ gehört die ETH zur Weltspitze.

Die ETH hat mehr (9) ___Geld___, aber die Universität Zürich hat mehr (10) ___Studierende___. Manchmal ist die Verwaltung der Universität neidisch, aber sie versucht dies durch andere Mittel auszugleichen.

Answers for 7-26. 1. R; **2.** R; **3.** R; **4.** F – Sie haben nicht immer eng zusammengearbeitet. **5.** F – Es gibt Konkurrenz zwischen den beiden Hochschulen. **6.** R; **7.** F – Einige Fächer werden von beiden Hochschulen angeboten. **8.** R

7-26 Textarbeit: Eine Stadt, zwei Hochschulen. Markieren Sie, ob jede Aussage richtig oder falsch ist. Korrigieren und ergänzen Sie die falschen Aussagen mit Informationen aus dem Hörtext.

1. Die beiden Hochschulen stehen im Wettkampf miteinander.
2. Die Universität Zürich wurde schon vor der ETH gegründet.
3. Die ETH hieß ursprünglich das Polytechnikum.
4. Die Hochschulen haben immer eng zusammengearbeitet.
5. Es gibt keine Konkurrenz zwischen den beiden Hochschulen.
6. Chemie, Physik und Mathematik kann man an der ETH Lausanne, aber nicht an der Uni Lausanne studieren.
7. Keine Fächer werden von der ETH sowie der Uni Zürich angeboten.
8. Die ETH hat nur halb so viele Studierende wie die Uni Zürich.

7-27 Zur Diskussion. Besprechen Sie die Fragen.

1. Die folgende Frage wird zu Anfang der Radiosendung gestellt: Sind die ETH und die Universität Zürich mehr Partner oder Konkurrenten? Wie wird die Frage beantwortet?
2. Warum haben Sie sich für Ihre jetzige Universität entschieden? Haben Sie sich damals auch andere Universitäten angeschaut? Was ist für Sie wichtig an einer Universität? Nennen Sie mindestens fünf Eigenschaften.
3. Was studieren Sie? Warum haben Sie dieses Hauptfach gewählt? Was müssen Sie für einen Abschluss in diesem Fach machen? Gibt es z. B. spezifische Kurse, ein Praktikum, Laborstunden, ein Auslandsstudium, eine Abschlussprüfung usw.? Wie lange dauert das Studium?

Activity 7-28. Remind students that they should use the *du*-form when speaking to other students, even if they are strangers.

7-28 Ein Studium bei uns. Sie arbeiten für Ihre Universität und haben den Auftrag, sich mit Studienbewerbern zu treffen und sie über die Vorteile Ihrer Universität zu informieren. Was können Sie sagen? Denken Sie sich eine Liste von mindestens fünf Vorteilen aus, mit denen sie für Ihre Uni werben können.

7-29 Studieren in Zürich. Sie interessieren sich für ein Studium in Zürich, entweder an der ETH oder der Universität Zürich. Schreiben Sie mindestens fünf Fragen über eine der Hochschulen auf. Besuchen Sie dann die Internetseite dieser Hochschule und suchen Sie nach den Antworten auf Ihre Fragen.

Note for 7-29. Relevant web addresses for Internet research activities can be found in *MyGermanLab* and on the Companion Website.

7-30 Deutschsprachige Studierende gesucht! Ihre Universität interessiert sich dafür, deutschsprachige Studierende für ein Studium an der Universität zu gewinnen. Schreiben Sie einen Werbetext für Ihre Uni, die in einer deutschsprachigen Version der Uni-Webseite erscheinen soll.

Lesetext 4

„Andorra" von Max Frisch (Dramenauszug)

Introduction to *Lesetext 4*. Ask students what they learned from the introduction. *Beschreiben Sie das Verhältnis Max Frischs zu Zürich. Wer ist der Held seines Dramas „Andorra"? Welche Figur weiß von Andris eigentlicher Herkunft? Welche falsche Vorstellung haben die Andorraner von Andri?*

Der Schweizer Schriftsteller Max Frisch (1911–1991) gehört zu den bedeutendsten deutschsprachigen Schriftstellern der Nachkriegszeit. In Zürich geboren und aufgewachsen, verbrachte Frisch auch viele Jahre als Erwachsener in der Großstadt. Er studierte an der Universität Zürich und später an der ETH und arbeitete in Zürich als Journalist, Architekt und dann als freier Schriftsteller. Im Zürcher Schauspielhaus wurden die meisten seiner Theaterstücke uraufgeführt°. Nach vielen Reisen und Aufenthalten in anderen Städten und Ländern kehrte er 1984 nach Zürich zurück, wo er bis zu seinem Tode lebte. Der Nachlass° seines Werkes befindet sich heute im Max-Frisch-Archiv der ETH Zürich.

Max Frisch in den 70er-Jahren

performed for the first time

estate

Zu Lebzeiten erhielt Frisch viele Preise für seine Werke. In seinem wohl bekanntesten Theaterstück *Andorra* (1961) nimmt er die von ihm beliebten Themen von Identität und Schuld wieder auf. Die Hauptfigur des Werkes ist der vermeintliche° Jude Andri. Der Lehrer soll ihn vor einem antisemitischen Nachbarvolk, den „Schwarzen", gerettet und als seinen Pflegesohn° angenommen haben. Andri ist allerdings kein Judenkind, sondern der illegitime Sohn des Lehrers, der die Wahrheit verschweigt. Selbst Andri weiß von seiner eigentlichen Herkunft nicht. Alle Andorraner betrachten und behandeln Andri ihren Vorurteilen nach als Juden, bis Andri allmählich anfängt, die Erwartungen der anderen zu erfüllen. Zum Schluss marschieren die antijüdischen Schwarzen in Andorra ein und ermorden Andri.

supposed

foster son

Der folgende Auszug aus dem Werk zeigt, wie die Andorraner mit Andri umgehen. Der Titel des Dramas bezieht sich nicht auf das reale Land Andorra, wie Frisch selbst erklärte, sondern auf ein fiktives Land, das als repräsentatives Beispiel gelten soll: „Andorra ist der Name für ein Modell." Frisch will seinen Zuschauern zeigen, was an jedem Ort zu jeder Zeit passieren könnte.

Vor dem Lesen

1. Wie unterscheidet sich ein Theaterstück von einem Prosatext? Von einem Gedicht?

2. Was ist ein Vorurteil? Haben Sie schon erlebt, dass man Vorurteile gegen Sie gehabt hat? Wenn ja, was waren die Umstände? Wie haben Sie gemerkt, dass man Vorurteile gegen Sie hatte?

Answers for *Beim Lesen*.
1. Andri; **2.** der Geselle;
3. der Geselle; **4.** der Tischler;
5. der Lehrer; **6.** der Tischler;
7. der Tischler; **8.** der Lehrer;
9. der Geselle; **10.** Andri;
11. der Tischler; **12.** Andri;
13. Andri

Beim Lesen

Wer im Stück drückt die folgenden Gedanken aus: Andri, der Lehrer, der Tischler oder der Geselle?

1. Am besten bin ich auf der rechten Seite, aber ich spiele, wo auch immer ihr mich braucht.
2. Bei deinem ersten Stuhl hast du Glück gehabt.
3. Der Meister schreit mich nie an.
4. Du sollst Verkäufer werden, das hast du im Blut.
5. Er ist mein Sohn – mein Pflegesohn, meine ich.
6. Gekauft ist gekauft, ich handle nicht.
7. Ich hätte dich nie in die Werkstatt aufnehmen sollen.
8. Ich verdiene nicht viel Geld.
9. Ich wollte mit ihm sprechen, aber später hat er mich sogar nicht mehr mal gegrüßt.
10. Nicht jenen, sondern diesen Stuhl habe ich gemacht.
11. Wie hat man wissen können, dass er eigentlich kein Jude ist?
12. Wie schön, dass wir befreundet sind!
13. Wieso wollt ihr die Wahrheit nicht akzeptieren?

07-18

„Andorra"

von Max Frisch

Erstes Bild

[…]

pub   *Man sieht den Platz von Andorra. Der Tischler und der Lehrer sitzen vor der Pinte°.*

[…]

Lehrer: Nämlich es handelt sich um meinen Sohn.

Tischler: Ich sagte: 50 Pfund.   5

Lehrer: – um meinen Pflegesohn, meine ich.

Tischler: Ich sagte: 50 Pfund.

[…]

Lehrer: Das bleibt Ihr letztes Wort?

Tischler: Ich heiße Prader.   10

Lehrer: 50 Pfund?

haggle   **Tischler:** Ich feilsche° nicht.

profiteering   **Lehrer:** Sie sind ein feiner Mann, ich weiß … Prader, das ist Wucher°, 50 Pfund für eine Tischlerlehre, das ist Wucher. Das ist ein Witz, Prader, das wissen Sie genau. Ich bin Lehrer, ich habe mein schlichtes Gehalt, ich habe   15

wealth   kein Vermögen° wie ein Tischlermeister – ich habe keine 50 Pfund, ganz rundheraus, ich habe sie nicht!

Orthography. Frisch's drama reflects the orthographic conventions used at the time of its publication.

Tischler: Dann eben nicht.

Lehrer: Prader –

Tischler: Ich sagte: 50 Pfund. 20

Der Tischler geht.

Lehrer: Sie werden sich wundern, wenn ich die Wahrheit sage. Ich werde dieses Volk vor seinen Spiegel zwingen, sein Lachen wird ihm gefrieren°. *freeze*

[…]

Zweites Bild

[…] 25

Vordergrund° *foreground*

Der Tischler tritt an die Zeugenschranke°. *witness stand*

Tischler: Ich gebe zu: Das mit den 50 Pfund für die Lehre, das war eben, weil ich ihn nicht in meiner Werkstatt wollte, und ich wußte ja, es wird nur Unannehmlichkeiten° geben. Wieso wollte er nicht Verkäufer werden? Ich dachte, 30 *trouble* das würd ihm liegen. Niemand hat wissen können, daß er keiner ist. Ich kann nur sagen, daß ich es im Grund wohlmeinte° mit ihm. Ich bin nicht schuld, daß *meant well* es so gekommen ist später.

Drittes Bild

Man hört eine Fräse°, Tischlerei, Andri und Geselle je mit einem fertigen Stuhl. *milling machine*
Andri: Ich habe auch schon Linksaußen° gespielt, wenn kein andrer wollte. 35 *left wing* Natürlich will ich, wenn eure Mannschaft mich nimmt.

Geselle: Hast du Fußballschuh?

Andri: Nein.

Geselle: Brauchst du aber.

Andri: Was kosten die? 40

Geselle: Ich hab ein altes Paar, ich verkaufe sie dir. Ferner brauchst du natürlich schwarze Shorts und ein gelbes Tschersi, das ist klar, und gelbe Strümpfe natürlich.

Andri: Rechts bin ich stärker, aber wenn ihr einen Linksaußen braucht, also einen Eckball bring ich schon herein. 45

Andri reibt° die Hände. *rubs*

Das ist toll, Fedri, wenn das klappt.

Geselle: Warum soll's nicht?

Andri: Das ist toll.

Geselle: Ich bin Käpten, und du bist mein Freund. 50

Andri: Ich werde trainieren.

Geselle: Aber reib nicht immer die Hände, sonst lacht die ganze Tribüne. *Andri steckt die Hände in die Hosentaschen.* Hast du Zigaretten? So gib schon. Mich bellt er nicht an°! Sonst erschrickt er nämlich über sein Echo. Oder hast du je gehört, daß der mich anbellt? 55

Der Geselle steckt sich eine Zigarette an.

Andri: Das ist toll, Fedri, daß du mein Freund bist.

Geselle: Dein erster Stuhl?

Andri: Wie findest du ihn?

Der Geselle nimmt den Stuhl von Andri and versucht ein Stuhlbein herauszureißen, 60 *Andri lacht.*

Die sind nicht zum Ausreißen!

Geselle: So macht er's nämlich.

Andri: Versuch's nur!

Der Geselle versucht es vergeblich. 65

Er kommt.

Geselle: Du hast Glück.

Andri: Jeder rechte Stuhl ist verzapft°. Wieso Glück? Nur was geleimt° ist, geht aus dem Leim°.

Auftritt der Tischler. 70

Tischler: … schreiben Sie diesen Herrschaften, ich heiße Prader. Ein Stuhl von Prader bricht nicht zusammen, das weiß jedes Kind, ein Stuhl von Prader ist ein Stuhl von Prader. Und überhaupt: bezahlt ist bezahlt. Mit einem Wort: Ich feilsche nicht.

Zu den beiden. 75

Habt ihr Ferien?

Der Geselle verzieht sich° flink.

Wer hat hier wieder geraucht?

Andri schweigt.

Ich riech es ja. 80

Andri schweigt.

Wenn du wenigstens den Schneid° hättest –

Andri: Heut ist Sonnabend.

Tischler: Was hat das damit zu tun?

Andri: Wegen meiner Lehrlingsprobe. Sie haben gesagt: Am letzten Sonn- 85 abend in diesem Monat. Hier ist mein erster Stuhl.

Der Tischler nimmt einen Stuhl.

Margin glosses:

bellt an barks at

mortised / glued

geht aus dem Leim (colloq.) falls apart

verzieht sich withdraws

(colloq.) the guts

Nicht dieser, Meister, der andere!

Tischler: Tischler werden ist nicht einfach, wenn's einer nicht im Blut hat. Nicht einfach. Woher sollst du's im Blut haben. Das hab ich deinem Vater aber gleich gesagt. Warum gehst du nicht in den Verkauf? Wenn einer nicht aufgewachsen ist mit dem Holz, siehst du, mit unserem Holz – lobpreiset eure Zedern vom Libanon°, aber hierzuland wird in andorranischer Eiche° gearbeitet, mein Junge.

Zedern vom Libanon
cedars of Lebanon / oak

Andri: Das ist Buche°.

beech

Tischler: Meinst du, du mußt mich belehren?

Andri: Sie wollen mich prüfen, meinte ich.

Tischler: *versucht ein Stuhlbein auszureißen.*

Andri: Meister, das ist aber nicht meiner!

Tischler: Da –

Der Tischler reißt ein erstes Stuhlbein aus.

Was hab ich gesagt?

Der Tischler reißt die andern drei Stuhlbeine aus.

– wie die Froschbeine, wie die Froschbeine. Und so ein Humbug soll in den Verkauf. Ein Stuhl von Prader, weißt du, was das heißt? – da,

Der Tischler wirft ihm die Trümmer vor die Füße. schau's dir an!

Andri: Sie irren sich°.

irren sich are mistaken

Tischler: Hier – das ist ein Stuhl!

Der Tischler setzt sich auf den andern Stuhl.

Hundert Kilo, Gott sei's geklagt, hundert Kilo hab ich am Leib, aber was ein rechter Stuhl ist, das ächzt° nicht, wenn ein rechter Mann sich draufsetzt, und das wackelt° nicht. Ächzt das?

creaks
wobbles

Andri: Nein.

Tischler: Wackelt das?

Andri: Nein.

Tischler: Also!

Andri: Das ist meiner.

Tischler: – und wer soll diesen Humbug gemacht haben?

Andri: Ich hab es Ihnen aber gleich gesagt.

Tischler: Fedri! Fedri!

Die Fräse verstummt.

Tischler: Nichts als Ärger hat man mit dir, das ist der Dank, wenn man deinesgleichen in die Bude nimmt, ich hab's ja geahnt.

Auftritt der Geselle.

Fedri, bist du ein Gesell oder was bist du?   125

Geselle: Ich –

Tischler: Wie lang arbeitest du bei Prader & Sohn?

Geselle: Fünf Jahre.

Tischler: Welchen Stuhl hast du gemacht? Schau sie dir an. Diesen oder
diesen? Und antworte.   130

Der Geselle mustert die Trümmer.

Antworte frank und blank.

Geselle: – ich …

Tischler: Hast du verzapft oder nicht?

Geselle: – jeder rechte Stuhl ist verzapft …   135

Tischler: Hörst du's?

Geselle: – nur was geleimt ist, geht aus dem Leim …

Tischler: Du kannst gehn.

Geselle: *erschrickt.*

Tischler: In die Werkstatt, meine ich.   140

Der Geselle geht rasch.

Das laß dir eine Lehre sein. Aber ich hab's ja gewußt, du gehörst nicht in eine
Werkstatt.

Der Tischler sitzt und stopft sich eine Pfeife.

Schad ums Holz.   145

Andri: *schweigt.*

°heating **Tischler:** Nimm das zum Heizen°.

Andri: Nein.

zündet … an *lights his* **Tischler:** *zündet sich die Pfeife an°.*
pipe
dirty trick **Andri:** Das ist eine Gemeinheit°!   150

Tischler: *zündet sich die Pfeife an.*

Andri: … ich nehm's nicht zurück, was ich gesagt habe. Sie sitzen auf meinem
Stuhl, ich sag es Ihnen, Sie lügen, wie's Ihnen grad paßt, und zünden sich die
tremble Pfeife an. Sie, ja, Sie! Ich hab Angst vor euch, ja, ich zittere°. Wieso hab ich kein
humble Recht vor euch? Ich bin jung, ich hab gedacht: Ich muß bescheiden° sein. Es hat 155
keinen Zweck, Sie machen sich nichts aus Beweisen. Sie sitzen auf meinem Stuhl.
Das kümmert Sie aber nicht? Ich kann tun, was ich will, ihr dreht es immer gegen
ridicule mich, und der Hohn° nimmt kein Ende. Ich kann nicht länger schweigen, es
eats away zerfrißt° mich. Hören Sie denn überhaupt zu? Sie saugen an Ihrer Pfeife herum,

und ich sag Ihnen ins Gesicht: Sie lügen. Sie wissen ganz genau, wie gemein° Sie 160   *mean*
sind. Sie sind hundsgemein. Sie sitzen auf dem Stuhl, den ich gemacht habe, und
zünden sich Ihre Pfeife an. Was hab ich Ihnen zuleid getan°? Sie wollen nicht,   ***zuleid getan*** *done to harm/*
daß ich tauge°. Warum schmähen° Sie mich? Sie sitzen auf meinem Stuhl. Alle   *am worth anything / revile*
schmähen mich und frohlocken° und hören nicht auf. Wieso seid ihr stärker als   *rejoice*
die Wahrheit? Sie wissen genau, was wahr ist. Sie sitzen drauf –   165

Der Tischler hat endlich die Pfeife angezündet.

Sie haben keine Scham –.

Tischler: Schnorr° nicht soviel.   *cadge*

Andri: Sie sehen aus wie eine Kröte°!   *toad*

Tischler: Erstens ist hier keine Klagemauer°.   170   *wailing wall*

Der Geselle und zwei andere verraten sich° durch Kichern°.   ***verraten sich*** *give them-*
selves away / snickering

Tischler: Soll ich eure ganze Fußballmannschaft entlassen°?   *dismiss*

Der Geselle und die andern verschwinden.

Erstens ist hier keine Klagemauer, zweitens habe ich kein Wort davon gesagt,
daß ich dich deswegen entlasse. Kein Wort. Ich habe eine andere Arbeit für   175
dich. Zieh deine Schürze° aus! Ich zeige dir, wie man Bestellungen° schreibt.   *apron/ orders*
Hörst du zu, wenn dein Meister spricht? Für jede Bestellung, die du herein-
bringst mit deiner Schnorrerei, verdienst du ein halbes Pfund. Sagen wir: ein
ganzes Pfund für drei Bestellungen. Ein ganzes Pfund! Das ist's, was deinesgleichen im Blut hat, glaub mir, und jedermann soll tun, was er im Blut hat. Du   180
kannst Geld verdienen, Andri, Geld, viel Geld …

Andri reglos°.   *motionless*

Abgemacht?°   *Is it a deal?*

Der Tischler erhebt sich und klopft Andri auf die Schulter.

Ich mein's gut° mit dir.   185   ***mein's gut*** *mean well*

Der Tischler geht, man hört die Fräse wieder.

Andri: Ich wollte aber Tischler werden …

Vordergrund

Der Geselle, jetzt in einer Motorradfahrerjacke, tritt an die Zeugenschranke.

Geselle: Ich geb zu: Es war mein Stuhl und nicht sein Stuhl. Damals. Ich wollte   190
ja nachher mit ihm reden, aber da war er schon so, daß man halt nicht mehr
reden konnte mit ihm. Nachher hab ich ihn auch nicht mehr leiden können°,   ***nicht … können*** *couldn't*
geb ich zu. Er hat einem nicht einmal mehr guten Tag gesagt. Ich sag ja nicht,   *stand anymore*
es sei ihm recht geschehen, aber es lag halt auch an ihm°, sonst wär's nie so   ***lag … an ihm*** *was because*
gekommen. Als wir ihn nochmals fragten wegen Fußball, da war er sich schon   195   *of him*
zu gut für uns. Ich bin nicht schuld, daß sie ihn geholt haben später.

[…]

Neue Vokabeln

Nomen

der Ärger   *trouble, annoyance*

der Beweis, -e   *evidence*

das Blut   *blood*

das Gehalt, ¨er   *salary*

der Geselle, -n, -n   *journeyman*

das Holz   *wood*

der Jude, -n, -n   *Jew*

der Tischler, -   *carpenter*

die Trümmer (*pl.*)   *debris, rubble*

der Vorurteil, -e   *prejudice*

die Wahrheit, -en   *truth*

Verben

aus·reißen, riss aus,
  ausgerissen   *to pull out*

erschrecken (erschrickt),
  erschrak, erschrocken   *to
  frighten; to be startled*

sich handeln um   *to be about
  something, to concern*

holen   *to get*

klappen   *to go as planned*

lügen, log, gelogen   *to lie; tell a lie*

sich verraten (verrät), verriet,
  verraten   *to betray (oneself),
  give (oneself) away*

zu·geben (gibt zu), gab zu,
  zugegeben   *to admit*

Adjektive und Adverbien

eben   *just, simply, precisely*

je   *ever, each*

wieso   *why*

vergeblich   *in vain, futilely*

Ausdrücke

Es hat keinen Zweck.   *It serves
  no purpose.*

Ich bin nicht schuld (daran).
  I am not to blame (for it).

Answers for 7-31. 1. R;
2. F – Der Tischler ist nicht bereit, den Preis zu reduzieren. 3. R;
4. F – Andri möchte gern Fußball
spielen. 5. F – Der Tischler zer-
bricht den Stuhl, den der Geselle
gemacht hat. 6. R; 7. F – Der
Geselle hat den schlechteren Stuhl
gemacht. 8. F – Andri erzählt
dem Tischler nicht, dass der
Geselle gelogen hat. 9. F – Der
Tischler bietet Andri eine Stelle
als Verkäufer an. 10. R

7-31 Textarbeit: Richtig oder falsch? Wenn eine Aussage falsch ist, korrigieren und ergänzen Sie sie mit Informationen aus dem Text.

1. Der Lehrer findet 50 Pfund einen zu teuren Preis für eine Lehre.
2. Der Tischer ist bereit, die Kosten der Lehre zu reduzieren.
3. Der Geselle will Andri seine alten Schuhe verkaufen.
4. Andri möchte gerne Kapitän der Fußballmanschaft werden.
5. Der Tischler reißt den Stuhl, den Andri gemacht hat, auseinander.
6. Andri hat den besseren Stuhl gemacht.
7. Der Tischler hat den schlechteren Stuhl gemacht.
8. Andri erzählt dem Tischler, dass der Geselle gelogen hat.
9. Der Tischler bietet Andri eine Stelle als Geselle an.
10. Nach dieser Episode will Andri die Freundschaft des Gesellen nicht mehr.

 7-32 Textarbeit: Zur Interpretation. Besprechen Sie die Fragen zum
Dramenauszug.

1. Warum will der Tischer Andri nicht gern als Lehrling annehmen?
2. Der Geselle sagt Andri: „Du bist mein Freund." Kurz danach sagt ihm
   Andri: „Das ist toll, Fedri, dass du mein Freund bist." Ist der Geselle
   tatsächlich Andris Freund? Was spricht dafür? Was dagegen?
3. Warum will der Tischer nicht akzeptieren, dass Andri den besseren Stuhl
   gemacht hat?
4. Welche Arbeit bietet der Tischler Andri an? Warum? Wie reagiert Andri auf
   das Angebot?
5. Man erfährt erst im Laufe des Dramas die Namen der Figuren, sonst
   heißen sie „der Lehrer", „der Tischler", „der Geselle". Warum haben hier
   die Figuren außer Andri keine Eigennamen?
6. Lesen Sie noch mal die Ausreden des Tischlers und des Gesellen an der
   Zeugenschranke. Wie erklären beide, dass sie nicht schuld an Andris
   Schicksal sind? Was halten Sie von ihren Erklärungen?

7-33 Vokabelarbeit. Ergänzen Sie die Sätze mit Wörtern aus den *Neuen Vokabeln*. Achten Sie dabei auch auf die Wortform.

1. In dem Drama ___handelt___ es ___sich___ ___um___ ein vermeintliches Judenkind namens Andri.

2. Andris Vater hat ___gelogen___, als er allen erzählte, dass Andri sein Pflegesohn sei.

3. In seinem Handwerk benutzt ein Tischler viel ___Holz___.

4. Andri wollte am liebsten Tischler werden, aber das hat nicht ___geklappt___.

5. Der Geselle will nicht ___zugeben___, dass er den stabilen Stuhl nicht gemacht hat.

6. Andri versteht nicht, ___wieso___ der Tischler ihm nicht glauben will.

7. Die Andorraner haben alle ___Vorurteile___ gegen Andri.

8. Fedris Verhalten soll für Andri ein ___Beweis___ sein, dass er kein echter Freund ist.

7-34 Zur Diskussion. Besprechen Sie die Fragen.

1. Woher kommen Vorurteile? Welche Stereotypen gibt es von Deutschen? von Amerikanern bzw. Kanadiern? von Studenten? von Professoren? Ist es möglich, ohne Vorurteile zu leben?

2. Woraus bildet sich die Identität eines Menschen? Was gehört zu Ihrer Identität (z. B. Student/in, Tochter/Sohn, Musikfan usw.)?

3. Sind Sie schon mal ins Theater gegangen? Wenn ja, was haben Sie gesehen? Beschreiben Sie die Erfahrung.

4. Haben Sie schon mal als Schauspieler in einem Theaterstück gespielt? Wenn ja, beschreiben Sie das Stück und Ihre Rolle in dem Stück. Werden Sie nervös, wenn Sie vor einem Publikum auftreten müssen?

7-35 Vater-Sohn-Gespräch. Andri selbst weiß nicht, dass er eigentlich kein Judenkind ist. Später im Theaterstück wird der Vater versuchen, Andri die Wahrheit zu sagen. Stellen Sie sich vor, was der Lehrer sagt und wie Andri auf die Nachricht reagiert. Spielen Sie dann eine Szene vor, in der der Lehrer seinem Sohn Andri von seiner Herkunft erzählt.

7-36 Mein Theaterstück. Erfinden Sie eine kurze dramatische Szene, in der zwei Figuren im Konflikt miteinander stehen. Benutzen Sie direkte Rede, wie in einem Drama üblich ist, und Bühnenanweisungen (*stage directions*), um den Ort des Geschehens und das Verhalten der Figuren zu beschreiben. Geben Sie Ihrer Szene auch einen passenden Titel.

07-50

Information for 7-35. In Scene 6 (*Sechstes Bild*) of the drama, the teacher attempts to tell Andri the truth about his birth, but Andri rebuffs his attempts. When the *Pater* later attempts to tell Andri who he really is, Andri has fully assimilated the identity that the Andorrans ascribe to him and is unable to accept the truth. Since students have only basic information about the characters, however, they will be able to employ more creativity in their dramatic scenarios.

Teaching suggestion for 7-35. This activity could alternatively be used as a writing assignment.

Teaching suggestions for 7-36. You may wish to give students additional instructions for the assignment, if you think they need more guidance. You can provide them with possible scenarios, for example: *ein Streit zwischen Geschwistern; ein Gespräch zwischen Eltern und einem Kind, das gelogen hat; ein Dialog zwischen zwei Kindern, die um das gleiche Spielzeug kämpfen*, etc. Alternatively, you could suggest possible titles. e.g.: *Die Wahrheit, Der Wettkampf, Zwei Brüder, Zwei Generationen*. More guidance is also provided in the SAM assignment 7-50. If time allows, you could also have the students put on performances of their scenes for the class.

Grammatik

07-26 to 07-29

1. Reflexive pronouns and reflexive verbs (Reflexivpronomen und –verben)

Certain verbs in German, called reflexive verbs, require a reflexive object pronoun. Many verbs with similar meanings in English do not always use a reflexive object. Compare, for instance: **Sie erkältete <u>sich</u>**. (*She caught a cold.*) **Er interessiert <u>sich</u> dafür.** (*He is interested in that.*)

In addition to the so-called reflexive verbs, nearly any transitive verb (that is, a verb that can take an object) can be used reflexively. A reflexive pronoun refers to the same thing or person as the sentence subject. A non-reflexive object pronoun refers to a different person or thing than the subject. Often the reflexive meaning of a verb is slightly different from its meaning when used non-reflexively.

Non-reflexive object	Reflexive object
Ich wasche **das Auto.**	Ich wasche **mich.**
I'm washing the car.	*I'm washing up. (I am washing myself.)*
Du erinnerst **mich** an meinen Bruder.	Erinnerst du **dich** an meinen Bruder?
You remind me of my brother.	*Do you remember my brother?*

The German reflexive pronouns are the same as the personal non-reflexive pronouns with the exception of the third person forms. The case forms are distinct only in the first and second person singular. The English equivalents use *-self* or *-selves*.

		Accusative	Dative	
Singular	1st person	mich	mir	(*myself*)
	2nd person	dich	dir	(*yourself* – informal, sing.)
	3rd person	sich		(*himself, herself, itself*)
Plural	1st person	uns		(*ourselves*)
	2nd person	euch		(*yourselves* – informal, pl.)
		sich		(*yourselves* – formal, sing. & pl.)
	3rd person	sich		(*themselves*)

Some verbs require a reflexive direct object in the accusative case.

| sich beeilen | Ich beeile **mich.** | *I'm hurrying.* |
| sich freuen | Freust du **dich?** | *Are you pleased?* |

A smaller number of verbs require a dative reflexive object.

| sich etwas an·sehen | Ich sehe **mir** den Film an. | *I'm watching the film.* |
| sich etwas ein·bilden | Das bildest du **dir** nur ein. | *You're just imagining that.* |

Some verbs can take a reflexive object in either case, depending on the context of the sentence. In general, if the sentence already contains a direct object, then the reflexive pronoun will be in the dative case.

Ich wasche **mich.**   *I'm washing (myself) up.*
Ich wasche **mir** die Haare.   *I'm washing my hair.*

In vocabulary lists and glossaries, reflexive verbs are marked by including the reflexive pronoun **sich** along with the infinitive. Reflexive verbs or reflexive usages of verbs are normally marked in dictionaries with a notation such as *vr.* Check the preface of your dictionary to see what notation it uses to indicate reflexive verbs.

In your vocabulary lists through *Kapitel 6*, you have learned the following reflexive verbs
sich amüsieren
sich auszeichnen
sich befinden
sich beteiligen (an)
sich entwickeln
sich erholen
sich erinnern (an)
sich lohnen
sich verwandeln (in).

7-37 Gut essen in Zürich. Lisa, Sara und Michael studieren an der Universität Konstanz in Süddeutschland und machen einen Tagesausflug nach Zürich. Ergänzen Sie die Sätze mit den passenden Reflexivverben und -objekten. Konjugieren Sie die Verben und achten Sie auf die Formen der Reflexivpronomen.

Teaching suggestion for 7-37. Students form the present tense of verbs in sentences 1–5, but sentences 6–9 use compound verb structures (helping verb + past participle, modal verb + infinitive). You may wish to tell students to pay particular attention to verb forms and word order in these last four sentences.

sich amüsieren	sich entscheiden	sich setzen
sich befinden	sich erinnern	sich treffen
sich bestellen	sich kaufen	sich unterhalten

1. _____Treffen_____ wir _____uns_____ um 13.00 Uhr in Café Sprüngli?

2. Nach stundenlangem Einkaufen _____setze_____ ich _____mich_____ nämlich gerne und genieße einen Kaffee und ein Stück Kuchen.

3. Das Café _____befindet_____ _____sich_____ in der Bahnhofstrasse.

4. _____Kaufst_____ du _____dir_____ ein paar Luxemburgerli für die Fahrt nach Hause, Sara?

5. _____Erinnert_____ ihr _____euch_____ an unseren letzten Besuch in Zürich?

6. Michael konnte _____sich_____ nicht _____entscheiden_____, ob er lieber im Haus Hiltl oder im Zeughauskeller essen wollte.

7. Wir haben im Zeughauskeller gegessen und haben _____uns_____ lange mit einem Zürcher Ehepaar _____unterhalten_____.

8. Ich habe _____mir_____ eine große Wurst _____bestellt_____ und konnte nicht mal die Hälfte davon essen.

9. In Zürich können wir _____uns_____ immer schön _____amüsieren_____.

Answers for 7-38. **1.** sich; **2.** dich; **3.** uns; **4.** mich; **5.** dir; **6.** euch; **7.** sich; **8.** mir

7-38 Google Zürich. Jeder Satz enthält ein Objekt, das nicht reflexiv ist. Ersetzen Sie das fett gedruckte Objekt mit dem passenden Reflexivpronomen. Achten Sie dabei auf den Kasus.

Beispiel: Ich informierte **meinen Chef** über die neuen Gesetze.
*Ich informierte **mich** über die neuen Gesetze.*

1. Herr Knaflic stellt **das neue Forschungszentrum von Google** vor.
2. Erinnerst du **mich** an das Freitagtreffen?
3. Wir unterscheiden **diese Firma** von allen anderen Unternehmen.
4. Ich beschäftige **unsere Mitarbeiter** mit neuen Forschungsprojekten.
5. Kannst du **den Ingenieuren** diese Resultate erklären?
6. Ihr müsst **den Chef** von euren Fähigkeiten überzeugen.
7. Die Mitarbeiter nennen **die Angestellten am Standort in Zürich** „Zoogler".
8. Ich hole **unserem Gast** einen Kaffee. Möchten Sie auch etwas trinken?

07-30 to 07-33

2. Verb + preposition idioms (Idiome mit Verb + Präposition)

In English, some verbs are almost always used with certain prepositions (*to participate in, to rely on, to consist of*). German also has such phrasal verbs. These verb-preposition combinations differ from separable prefix verbs in that the prepositions never function as prefixes; they are prepositions with their own objects.

In your vocabulary lists through *Kapitel 6*, you have learned the following combinations
bei·tragen zu
sich beteiligen an (+ *dat.*)
sich erinnern an (+ *acc.*)
fest·halten an (+ *dat.*)
führen zu
halten für
hin·weisen auf (+ *acc.*)
konkurrieren um
nach·denken über (+ *acc.*)
sterben an (+ *dat.*)
teil·nehmen an (+ *dat.*)
sich verwandeln in (+ *acc.*)
zeugen von.

schmecken nach	*to taste like (something)*
Diese Soße **schmeckt nach** Fisch.	*This sauce tastes like fish.*
reagieren auf (+ *acc.*)	*to react to (something)*
Er **reagierte auf** die Frage nicht.	*He didn't react to the question.*

As in English, the verb-preposition pairs are idiomatic and the choice of preposition is quite unpredictable. It makes sense to memorize such pairings as you encounter them. If you don't know which preposition should be used with a given verb or you're uncertain which case to use with a two-way preposition, you should look up the verb in a dictionary.

Verb + preposition idioms. Remind students that accusative prepositions always have objects in a the accusative, dative prepositions objects in the dative case. Cases used with two-way prepositions in idioms vary. As a general guide, combinations with *auf, in,* and *über* tend to use the accusative case more often than the dative. Idioms using *an* and *vor* more frequently use the dative. Other two-way prepositions appear less commonly in verb-preposition idioms.

7-39 Die Schweizer Wirtschaft. Ergänzen Sie die Sätze mit den passenden Idiomen mit Verb + Präposition.

Teaching suggestion for 7-39. Remind students of the difference between prepositions used in verb + preposition idioms and those in separable prefix verbs. In the former, the preposition takes an object, while in the latter the preposition is used as part of the verb and takes no object.

| ab·hängen von | gehören zu | konkurrieren um | verfügen über |
| sich beteiligen an | halten für | sorgen für | |

1. Viele Unternehmen ____halten____ Zürich ____für____ einen geeigneten Standort.

2. Nestlé und Novartis ____gehören____ ____zu____ den größten Schweizer Unternehmen.

3. Die Wirtschaft der Schweiz ____hängt____ sehr ____von____ ausländischen Angestellten ____ab____ .

4. Immer mehr Ausländer, die im Kanton Zürich arbeiten, ____verfügen____ ____über____ einen Hochschulabschluss.

5. Die ETH und IBM ____beteiligen____ ____sich____ ____an____ dem Bau eines Forschungszentrums für Nanotechnologie.

6. Die Schweizer selbst ____sorgen____ ____für____ über 50 Prozent des Verkaufs von Schweizer Schokolade.

7. Die vielen Restaurants in Zürich ____konkurrieren____ ____um____ Gäste.

7-40 Birgit Wentz: ETH-Studierende. Bilden Sie aus den Satzteilen vollständige Sätze. Wenn Sie nicht wissen, welchen Kasus eine Präposition in einem Idiom braucht, schlagen Sie das Verb im Wörterbuch nach.

1. ich / schon immer / Informatik / sich interessieren für / . (Perfekt)

2. warum / du / ein Studium an der ETH / sich entscheiden für / ? (Perfekt)

3. die ETH / in Informatik / die renommiertesten Hochschulen der Welt / zählen zu / . (Präsens)

4. ich / nächstes Semester / ein Praktikum bei Microsoft / teil·nehmen an / . (Futur)

5. Studierende / Berufe in vielen Bereichen / sich vor·bereiten auf / . (Präsens)

6. hoffentlich / mein Abschluss / ein Beruf in der Computerspielindustrie / führen zu / . (Präsens)

7. wir / die guten Berufschancen / sich freuen über / . (Präsens)

Answers for 7-40. 1. Ich habe mich schon immer für Informatik interessiert. 2. Warum hast du dich für ein Studium an der ETH entschieden? 3. Die ETH zählt zu den renommiertesten Hochschulen der Welt in Informatik. 4. Ich werde nächstes Semester an einem Praktikum bei Microsoft teilnehmen. 5. Studierende bereiten sich auf Berufe in vielen Bereichen vor. 6. Hoffentlich führt mein Abschluss zu einem Beruf in der Computerspielindustrie. 7. Wir freuen uns über die guten Berufschancen.

07-34 to 07-40

3. Review: Cases (Wiederholung: Kasus)

When used in sentences, nouns and pronouns take cases. German has four cases: nominative, accusative, dative, and genitive.

For more information on case functions and forms, see the Grammatik sections of Kapitel 3 and Kapitel 4.

1. Case functions

The case of a noun or pronoun signifies its function in a sentence. Each case has multiple functions.

Nominative case:

1. Subject (**Subjekt**)
2. Predicate nominative (**Prädikatsnomen**)

Accusative case:

1. Direct object (**Direktes Objekt**)
2. Expression of definite time or duration (**Akkusativ der Zeit**)
3. Object of one of the accusative prepositions: **durch, für, gegen, ohne, um** (**Objekt einer Präposition mit Akkusativ**)
4. Object of a two-way preposition denoting direction and in idiomatic expressions: **an, auf, hinter, in, neben, über, unter, vor, zwischen** (**Objekt einer Wechselpräposition**)

Dative case:

1. Indirect object (**Indirektes Objekt**)
2. Object of a dative verb (**Objekt eines Dativverbs**)
3. Object in a fixed idiomatic expression (**Dativobjekt in einem idiomatischen Ausdruck**)
4. Object one of the dative prepositions: **ab, aus, außer, bei, gegenüber, mit, nach, seit, von, zu** (**Objekt einer Dativpräposition**)
5. Object of a two-way preposition denoting location and in idiomatic expressions (**Objekt einer Wechselpräposition**)

Genitive case:

1. Possession and relationships (**Genitivattribut**)
2. Expression of indefinite time (**Genitiv der Zeit**)
3. Object of one of the genitive prepositions: **[an]statt, außerhalb, innerhalb, trotz, während, wegen** (**Objekt einer Präposition mit Genitiv**)

---

2. Patterns of noun declension

There are two basic patterns of inflection for the determiners that mark case in German, that of the definite articles (**der**-words) and that of the indefinite articles (**ein**-words).

A. Definite articles / der-words. These include the forms **der, die, das,** but also **dies-** *this, these,* **jed-** *each, every,* **jen-** *that, those,* **welch-** *which,* **manch-** *many a, several,* **solch-** *such,* **all-** *all,* **beid-** *both.* Note that the neuter forms of the **der**-words other than **das** have an **-es** ending (**dieses, jedes**), rather than **-as,** in the neuter nominative and accusative.

B. Indefinite articles / *ein*-words. The **ein**-words include the indefinite article **ein**, its negation **kein,** and all of the possessive adjectives: **mein** *my,* **dein** *your* (*informal, sing.*), **sein** *his, its,* **ihr** *her, its, their,* **unser** *our,* **euer, eur-** *your* (*informal, pl.*), **Ihr** *your* (*formal, sing. and pl.*).

	Masculine	**Feminine**	**Neuter**	**Plural**
Nominative	**der** Mann	**die** Frau	**das** Kind	**die** Leute
	ein Mann	**eine** Frau	**ein** Kind	**keine** Leute
Accusative	**den** Mann	**die** Frau	**das** Kind	**die** Leute
	einen Mann	**eine** Frau	**ein** Kind	**keine** Leute
Dative	**dem** Mann	**der** Frau	**dem** Kind	**den** Leuten
	einem Mann	**einer** Frau	**einem** Kind	**keinen** Leuten
Genitive	**des** Mannes	**der** Frau	**des** Kindes	**der** Leute
	eines Mannes	**einer** Frau	**eines** Kindes	**keiner** Leute

Patterns of noun declension. Remind students that the two declension patterns differ only in the masculine nominative and the neuter nominative and accusative. In those three instances, the *ein*-word omits the case ending that the corresponding *der*-word takes.

3. Personal pronoun forms

All pronouns have forms that reflect their case.

	1st person		**2nd person**		**3rd person**	
	Sing. *I, me*	*Pl.* *we, us*	*Sing.* *you*	*Pl.* *you*	*Sing.* *he, she, it,* *him, her*	*Pl.* *they, them*
Nominative	ich	wir	du Sie	ihr Sie	er, sie, es	sie
Accusative	mich	uns	dich Sie	euch Sie	ihn, sie, es	sie
Dative	mir	uns	dir Ihnen	euch Ihnen	ihm, ihr, ihm	ihnen

Schifffahrt auf dem Zürichsee

7-41 *Homo faber.* Ergänzen Sie die Zusammenfassung von Max Frischs Roman *Homo faber* mit den passenden Artikeln und Personalpronomen.

1957 ist (1. *the*) __der__ Roman *Homo faber* von Max Frisch erschienen. Die Hauptfigur heißt Walter Faber. (2. *He*) __Er__ ist (3. *an*) __ein__ erfolgreicher Maschinenbauingenieur. Als Assistent an der ETH lernt er (4. *the*) __die__ Kunststudentin Hanna kennen. (5. *one*) __Eines__ Tages erzählt sie (6. *him*) __ihm__, dass sie schwanger ist. Zuerst will Walter (7. *her*) __sie__ heiraten, aber dann nimmt er (8. *a*) __eine__ Stelle in Bagdad an und trennt sich von Hanna.

Über 20 Jahre später lernt Walter (9. *a*) __eine__ junge Frau, Sabeth, kennen. Er verliebt sich in sie und folgt (10. *her*) __ihr__ von Frankreich über Italien nach Griechenland. Dort wird Sabeth eines Morgens am Strand von einer Schlange gebissen. Walter bringt (11. *her*) __sie__ ins Krankenhaus, aber bald darauf stirbt (12. *she*) __sie__. Als Sabeths Mutter im Krankenhaus erscheint, erfährt er (13. *the*) __die__ Wahrheit: Hanna ist Sabeths Mutter und er ist (14. *her*) __ihr__ Vater.

Walter gibt (15. *his*) __seine__ Stelle auf und will bei Hanna in Athen bleiben. Es stellt sich aber heraus, dass er an Magenkrebs leidet. Der Bericht endet vor (16. *his*) __seiner__ Magenoperation. Aber die Handlung lässt vermuten, dass er die Operation nicht überlebt.

Homo faber ist heute eines (17. *the*) __der__ meistgelesenen Bücher von Frisch. Man liest (18. *it*) __es__ in der Schule, aber nicht nur dort. (19. *The*) __Das__ Werk wurde in über 40 Sprachen übersetzt und hat sich 3 Millionen Mal verkauft. 1991 hat der deutsche Filmregisseur Volker Schlöndorff (20. *the*) __den__ Roman auch verfilmt.

07-41 to 07-43

4. Expansion: Adjectival nouns (Erweiterung: Adjektivnomen)

Almost any German adjective—including comparatives and superlatives and present and past participles—can be used as a noun. When an adjective becomes a noun, it is capitalized and takes the same adjective endings it would take if the missing noun were still present.

Die Blonde (Frau) drüben ist Elkes Schwester.

The blonde (woman) over there is Elke's sister.

Ein Fremder (Mann) saß neben mir im Zug.

A stranger (strange man) sat next to me on the train.

Some adjectival nouns that refer to people have been adopted into common usage.

der/die Angestellte	*employee*	der/die Gefangene	*prisoner*
der/die Arbeitslose	*unemployed person*	der/die Jugendliche	*young person*
der Beamte[1]	*civil servant*	der/die Reisende	*traveler*
der/die Bekannte	*acquaintance*	der/die Studierende	*student*
der/die Deutsche	*German person*	der/die Verwandte	*relative*
der/die Erwachsene	*adult*	der/die Vorsitzende	*chairperson*
der/die Fremde	*foreigner*		

Neuter adjectival nouns refer to abstract qualities. They frequently follow the neuter definite article or indefinite pronouns such as **alles, etwas, nichts, viel, wenig,** etc.

Das ist **das Beste,** was ich je gehört habe!   *That's the best thing I've ever heard!*
Heute ist **nichts Interessantes** passiert.   *Nothing interesting happened today.*

7-42 Zürcher Eindrücke. Ergänzen Sie die Sätze mit den passenden Adjektivnomen. Achten Sie dabei auf Großschreibung und Adjektivendungen.

angestellt	erwachsen	reisend	verwandt
deutschsprachig	kunstinteressiert	studierend	wichtig

1. Wir reisten nach Zürich, um einen _____Verwandten_____ meiner Frau zu besuchen.

2. _____Deutschsprachige_____ aus anderen Regionen verstehen die Schweizer Mundarten oft nicht.

3. Ein _____Angestellter_____ vom Tourismusbüro hat unsere Fragen beantwortet.

4. Das Kunsthaus bietet allen _____Kunstinteressierten_____ eine achtstündige Audioführung durch das Museum.

5. Das Spielzeugmuseum ist nicht nur für Kinder, sondern auch für _____Erwachsene_____.

6. Jeder _____Reisende_____, der länger als drei Monate in der Schweiz bleiben möchte, braucht ein Visum.

7. 90 Prozent der _____Studierenden_____ aus dem Kanton Zürich wählen eine Hochschule in Zürich.

8. Wenn man wenig Zeit hat, lernt man alles _____Wichtige_____ über die Stadt in einer Stadtführung kennen.

---

[1]The word for female civil servant, **Beamtin,** is not an adjectival noun.

Immer weiter!

 7-43 Zur Diskussion. Besprechen Sie die Themen.

1. Sie haben sich entschieden, ein Jahr in Zürich zu verbringen. Was machen Sie während dieses Jahres? Arbeiten Sie? Studieren Sie? Was möchten Sie während dieser Zeit in der Stadt und der Umgebung unbedingt machen und erleben?

2. Sie werden nun das Jahr in Zürich verbringen, das Sie oben in #1 beschrieben haben. Welche Erfahrungen mit der Sprache erwarten Sie? Welche Sprache(n) müssen Sie in verschiedenen Situationen wohl verstehen und sprechen? Was machen Sie schon vor der Abreise, um sich auf die sprachliche Situation vorzubereiten?

7-44 Zum Schreiben: Zürich. Jahraus, jahrein wird Zürich immer wieder zu einer der Städte mit der weltbesten Lebensqualität gekürt. Was ist Lebensqualität und welche Aspekte des Lebens in Zürich tragen zu dieser Lebensqualität bei? Schreiben Sie für ein Wirtschaftsmagazin einen kurzen Artikel über die Lebensqualität Zürichs und warum diese Stadt immer unter den besten ist.

Weitere Themen

Crédit Suisse	Tirggel
Dadaismus	Victorinox
Gottfried Keller	Winterthur
Knabenschiessen	Zoo Zürich
das Limmatquai	Zünfte
Lindt & Sprüngli	Zürcher Schauspielhaus
Johann Heinrich Pestalozzi	Zürich West
der Rheinfall	„Züri rollt"
Sihlcity	Züritüütsch
Johanna Spyri	Huldrych Zwingli

KAPITEL 8

Nordsee Ostsee

Deutschland

Baden-Württemberg

Österreich

Schweiz Liechtenstein

Baden-Württemberg

RHEINLAND-PFALZ HESSEN

FRANKREICH

Rhein

Mannheim

Heidelberg

Karlsruhe Maulbronn Heilbronn

Pforzheim

⭐ Stuttgart

Baden-Baden Calw

BADEN-WÜRTTEMBERG

Neckar

Tübingen

SCHWARZWALD

Rhein

Donau

Furtwangen

Freiburg

N

Ulm

SCHWÄBISCHE ALB

Donau

Ravensburg

50 km

50 mi

Gaienhofen Friedrichshafen

Konstanz

Bodensee

SCHWEIZ

Warm-up. To set the scene, have students look at the maps of Germany and Europe on the inside covers and ask them to describe the geographical position of Baden-Württemberg. Wo liegt Baden-Württemberg innerhalb Deutschlands? Woran grenzt das Bundesland? Wo liegt das Land innerhalb der EU? Was kann diese Lage für ein Bundesland wohl bedeuten? Von welchen Orten haben Sie schon einmal gehört? Then have them look more closely at the region map and describe what the map and photos reveal about the state.

Einführung

08-01 to 08-03

Read the *Sprachanalyse: Word order* in SAM 08-02, which explains some variations on basic German word order that appear in the *Einführung*. As you read the *Lesetexte* in this chapter, do the *Sprachanalyse* activities in the SAM (08-03, 08-06, 08-09, 08-15, 08-19, 08-22) to practice deciphering a wide variety of sentence configurations.

natural resources

inventors

matchstick
most prosperous

affiliations

tribe

Baden-Württemberg liegt im Südwesten Deutschlands. Es ist mit 10,7 Millionen Einwohnern das drittgrößte Bundesland der Republik. Die Landschaft ist überwiegend hügelig und bis zu 40 Prozent bewaldet. An den Flüssen, zu denen der Rhein, die Donau und der Neckar zählen, befinden sich die größten Städte des Südweststaats. Die Landeshauptstadt Stuttgart ist mit 600.000 5 Einwohnern die größte Stadt.

Obwohl hier kaum Bodenschätze° vorkommen, konnte sich das Land zum führenden Industriestandort und Exportland entwickeln. Das liegt nach Meinung der Baden-Württemberger an dem legendären Erfindergeist der Menschen hier. In diesem „Land der Tüftler° und Denker" wurden bei- 10 spielsweise Einstein, Kepler, Hegel und Heidegger geboren und das Automobil, der Zeppelin, das Fahrrad und das Streichholz° erfunden. Heute ist der Staat eine der wohlhabendsten° Regionen der EU und ein wichtiger wirtschaftlicher Motor Deutschlands. Wichtige Branchen sind Maschinen- und Fahrzeugbau sowie Elektrotechnik, und in Hochtechnologie – beson- 15 ders Informations- und Biotechnologie, Energie- und Umwelttechnik – ist der Südwesten eine der wichtigsten Regionen Europas. In Forschung investiert das Bundesland mehr Geld als fast jede andere Region der EU. Die zahlreichen Forschungsinstitute und Technologieparks und die renommierten Hochschulen fördern Innovationen. Folglich werden fast nirgendwo in 20 Europa mehr Patente angemeldet als in Baden-Württemberg.

Den Südweststaat gibt es erst seit 1952 als politische Einheit. Da schlossen sich Baden und Württemberg sowie das kleine dazwischen liegende Hohenzollern zu einem 25 Bundesland zusammen. Trotz ihrer gemeinsamen Geschichte seit Mitte des 20. Jahrhunderts identifizieren sich viele Württemberger noch heute als Schwaben, die Badener als Badener oder Alemannen. Bis heute besteht 30 sogar noch eine spielerische Rivalität zwischen ihnen. Im nördlichen Teil beider Regionen leben auch Franken und im süd-

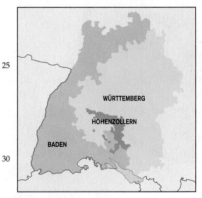

Das Gebiet bis 1945

westlichen Bayern leben Schwaben. So ist dieser Staat ein gutes Beispiel dafür, wie wenig politische Grenzen alten regionalen Zugehörigkeiten° entsprechen. 35 Historisch gesehen stammen die Badener, Schwaben und deutschsprachigen Schweizer alle vom Stamm° der Alemannen, die diesen Raum seit der Römerzeit bewohnten. Die geopolitische Fragmentierung der Region ließ die Kulturen – die Bräuche, die Küchen, die Mundarten sowie die Identität der Menschen – während der Jahrhunderte sich unterschiedlich entwickeln. 40

Der Werbespruch des Bundeslandes Baden-Württemberg lautet: „Wir können alles. Außer Hochdeutsch." Die Südweststaatler sind stolz auf ihre Leistungen als „Ländle", ohne dass sie ihre jeweilige regionale Herkunft vergessen.

Answers for *Fragen zum Text*. 1. Es ist das südwestlichste und nach Einwohnern das drittgrößte Bundesland. **2.** Hügel, Wälder und die Flüsse Rhein, Donau und Neckar; **3.** Die wirtschaftliche Stärke des Landes beruht auf dem ideenreichen Charakter der Menschen. **4.** Maschinen- und Fahrzeugbau und Elektrotechnik, Bio- und

Fragen zum Text

1. Wie ist Baden-Württemberg in Vergleich zu anderen Bundesländern?
2. Welche Landschaften findet man hier?
3. Wie konnte das Land ohne Bodenschätze zu einem hochindustrialisierten Gebiet werden?
4. In welchen Bereichen ist das Land wirtschaftlich besonders stark?
5. Was sagt der Name des Landes über seine Geschichte aus?
6. Welche Beziehung besteht zwischen Badenern, Württembergern und Schweizerdeutschen?

Informationstechnologie, Energie- und Umwelttechnik sind in Baden-Württemberg besonders ausgeprägt. **5.** Nach dem Zweiten Weltkrieg wurden hier verschiedene ethnisch-kulturelle Menschengruppen zusammengelegt. **6.** Sie stammen ursprünglich alle vom Stamm der Alemannen ab.

DIALEKTTIPP: Schwäbisch

Hören Sie ein Beispiel dieses Dialekts.

Der gemeinsame alemannische Ursprung der Badener, Württemberger und Schweizer ist heute noch an den jeweiligen Dialekten – Badisch, Schwäbisch und Schweizerdeutsch – zu erkennen, denn diese Dialekte sind alle Varianten der alemannischen Mundartfamilie. Werfen wir an dieser Stelle einen näheren Blick auf das Schwäbische, das vorwiegend in der südlichen Hälfte Württembergs aber auch im Südwesten Bayerns gesprochen wird.

Zwischen dem Hochdeutschen und dem Schwäbischen gibt es enorme Unterschiede in der Grammatik, im Wortschatz und in der Aussprache. Das Schwäbische ist für Nicht-Schwaben manchmal nur mit Schwierigkeit zu verstehen. Dennoch zählt es zu den deutschen Dialekten, die die Deutschen am liebsten hören. Die Schwaben selbst sind sehr stolz auf ihren Dialekt.

Dialekttipp. After they have read the text, ask students: *Zu welcher Mundartfamilie gehört Schwäbisch? Welche anderen Dialekte gehören zu dieser Gruppe? Wo wird Schwäbisch gesprochen? Warum ist Schwäbisch für Nicht-Schwaben schwer zu verstehen?* Then after they have completed the *Zum Dialekt* activity, write the following Swabian words and expressions on the board: *Keendle, Dia Muader isch miad,* the cities *Schduagrd* and *Tibenga.* Ask students to guess what they mean. Answers: *Keendle = Kindle/Kindchen; Dia Muader isch miad = Die Mutter ist müde. Schduagrd = Stuttgart, Tibenga = Tübingen.*

Zum Dialekt

Wie sagt man das? Wählen Sie die richtigen Erklärungen der Unterschiede zwischen Schwäbisch und Hochdeutsch.

Hochdeutsch → Schwäbisch

_f_	1.	Blümchen, Häuschen → Bliamle, Heisle
_g_	2.	geputzt, Teppich, schicken → butzd, Deppich, schigga
_k_	3.	Australien, Vesper → Auschdralien, Veschbr
_b_	4.	lassen, sparen, meckern → lassa, schbara, mäggra
_d_	5.	ein Ei, Leid → oi Oi, Leute
_j_	6.	lieb, gut → liab, guat
_h_	7.	König, böse, Glück → Keenich, bais, Glick
_e_	8.	Lampen, Namen → Lampa, Nehma
_i_	9.	wir/sie machen, ihr macht → mir/ihr/sie machad
_c_	10.	man isst → ma' tuat essa
_a_	11.	wir waren, ich machte → mr send gwä, i han gmachd

a. Perfekt statt Präteritum

b. *-en → -a*

c. *tun* als Hilfswort im Präsens

d. *ei → oi, eu → ei*

e. andere Pluralformen bei Nomen

f. Verkleinerungsform *-chen → -le*

g. *p, t, k → b, d, g*

h. *ö → e/ai, ü → i(a)*

i. einfachere Konjugation

j. längere Monophthonge

k. *sp, st → häufiger schp, scht*

Lese- und Hörtexte

Lesetext 1

Schwäbische Küche: Kochen mit Tradition (Kochbuch-Vorwort und Rezepte)

Introduction to *Lesetext 1.* Introduce students to the topic by asking about their own experiences. *Kochen Sie manchmal? Wenn ja, was kochen Sie gern? Für wen kochen Sie? Benutzen Sie Kochbücher? Folgen Sie Rezepten genau?* Then ask students what they glean from the text introduction: *Was sind Michelin-Sterne-Restaurants? Wie bekommt ein Restaurant wohl Sterne? Wie kann man die Küche des Südwestens beschreiben? Was hat die Entwicklung der badischen Küche beeinflusst?*

stronghold

identities

Information for text introduction. The famous Michelin Guides award one, two, or three stars to a small number of restaurants of outstanding quality each year.

Unter Gourmands und Genießern gilt der Südwesten Deutschlands als kulinarische Hochburg°. In Baden-Württemberg befinden sich nämlich 53 der 210 deutschen Michelin-Sterne-Restaurants. Das Angebot zeichnet sich durch seine Qualität aber auch seine Vielfältigkeit aus, denn neben der diversen internationalen Küche gibt es eine ebenso vielfältige und traditionsreiche Regionalküche. Ein Blick in die badischen und schwäbischen Kochtöpfe lässt erkennen, wie sehr die beiden Regionen ihre kulinarischen Eigenheiten° bewahrt haben, nicht zuletzt wegen der geografischen Unterschiede. Das warme Klima und der fruchtbare Boden Badens sowie die Nähe zu Frankreich führten zu einer feinen, leichten Küche, die von einer großen Auswahl an vorhandenen Lebensmitteln begünstigt wird. Bei den Schwaben ist es ganz anders, wie Sie im folgenden Vorwort zum Kochbuch über deren traditionelle Küche lesen können.

Vor dem Lesen

1. Welche Gerichte und Speisen assoziieren Sie mit welchen Regionen?

| Italien | Frankreich | Indien | Mexiko | Louisiana | Neuengland |

2. Besitzen Sie Kochbücher? Wenn ja, was für Kochbücher?

Beim Lesen

Unterstreichen Sie die Namen aller schwäbischen Gerichte und Mahlzeiten im Lesetext.

Schwäbische Küche: Kochen mit Tradition
Vorwort

08-04 to 08-06

Siehe **Kulturtipps**: Schwäbische Alb

fertile

native

„Bei de Reiche lernt ma s'spara, bei de Arme s'kocha." (Bei den Reichen lernt man das Sparen, bei den Armen das Kochen.) So eine schwäbische Weisheit. Auch wenn man es sich heute angesichts eines wohlhabenden Württembergs kaum noch vorstellen kann – Schwaben war bis ins 20. Jahrhundert ein armes Land. Die Bauern hatten kleine Höfe und besonders auf 5 der Schwäbischen Alb war der Boden nicht ertragreich°. Aber Not macht erfinderisch, und so entstand – wie könnte es im Land der Tüftler anders sein – eine deftige, solide und bodenständige° Küche. So sehr die Zeiten sich verändert haben, basiert die Küche des „Schwoabeländles" heute noch größtenteils auf dem unkomplizierten „Arme-Leute-Essen" von einst. 10

Teigwaren – billig herzustellen, nahrhaft und vielseitig einsetzbar° – spielen in Schwaben eine so wichtige Rolle wie in keiner anderen Region Deutschlands. Dabei lässt sich ein gewisser italienischer Einfluss auf die schwäbische Küche nicht verleugnen. Die schwäbischen Schupfnudeln bestehen beispielsweise aus der gleichen Mehl-Kartoffel-Teigmasse wie die italienischen Gnocchi, die schwäbischen Maultaschen haben eine große Ähnlichkeit mit den italienischen Ravioli und Spätzle scheint die schwäbische Antwort auf italienische Spaghetti zu sein. Maultaschen, die ursprünglich erfunden wurden, um während der Fastenzeit das verbotene Fleisch vor dem lieben Gott zu verstecken, begeistern inzwischen Liebhaber über die Landesgrenzen hinaus. Ihre Füllung besteht traditionsgemäß aus Hackfleisch, Spinat und Gewürzen, lässt sich aber beliebig variieren. Ähnlich sieht es bei den Spätzle aus. Die gibt es bekannterweise als Beilage zu Linsen und Saitenwürsten („Linsen und Spätzle") oder mit Käse überbacken („Käs'spätzle"), aber auch in zahlreichen anderen Kombinationen und Varianten. Inzwischen sind Spätzle in ganz Deutschland – und außerhalb – zu finden, auch als Fertigprodukt im Supermarkt. Aber zu Hause zubereitet schmecken sie natürlich am besten.

Auch gehaltvolle° Suppen und Eintöpfe° sind typisch für die schwäbische Küche. Die Schwaben sind überhaupt Nassesser, alles wird nämlich gern in eine Brühe° oder Soße getunkt. Als Einlage° dienen ihnen Spätzle und Maultaschen, aber auch Fleisch, Gemüse und Flädle – dünne, in Streifen geschnittene Pfannkuchen, die den französischen Crêpes ähneln. Schon Hans Sachs schreibt: „So sind die Suppen der Schwaben Schatz." Diese Vorliebe hat den Schwaben auch den Spitznamen „Subbaschwobe" (Suppenschwaben) eingebracht.

Ein großer Teil der schwäbischen Freude am Essen gilt der Vesper, einer kalten Zwischenmahlzeit vormittags bzw. nachmittags, auf die der Schwabe nur ungern verzichtet. Landesspezifische Würste wie die Saitenwurst, Schinkenwurst oder Landjäger werden einfach auf einem Vesperteller angerichtet oder zu einem Wurstsalat verarbeitet. Dazu darf dann auch die Laugenbrezel nicht fehlen, die in Schwaben ihren Ursprung hat.

Natürlich gehören Fleisch- und Fischgerichte, Gemüse und Salate ebenso wie süße Speisen und Kuchen zur Palette der einheimischen Speisen. In diesen Seiten lernen Sie Küche, Land und Leute kennen und werden mit den typischen Rezepten aus dem Schwabenland eine traditionsreiche und schmackhafte Küche auf den Tisch bringen können. Wir wünschen gutes Gelingen!

---

vielseitig einsetzbar
versatile

substantial / stews

broth / solid ingredient added to a soup

Siehe **Kulturtipps**:
Hans Sachs

Siehe **Kulturtipps**:
Laugenbrezel

Schbäddzla (Spätzle) Grundrezept

500 g Mehl   1 TL Salz
2-6 Eier   Wasser

Die Zutaten zu einem festen, glatten Teig anrühren. Je mehr Eier man nimmt, desto weniger Wasser ist nötig.

Eine kleine Menge Teig auf ein nasses Holzbrett streichen und mit einem langen Messer oder Spätzleschaber von der vorderen Brettkante rasch dünne Teigstreifen direkt in kochendes Salzwasser schaben.

Sobald die Spätzle an die Wasseroberfläche kommen, herausnehmen und kurz in lauwarmem Salzwasser schwenken. Danach abtropfen lassen und auf eine Platte legen.

Variationen:

Leberspätzle: Zusätzlich ca. 300 g sehr fein gehackte Rinds- oder Kalbsleber in den Teig einarbeiten.

Petersilienspätzle: Zusätzlich ein Bund frische, fein gehackte Petersilie[a] in den Teig einarbeiten.

Haselnussspätzle: 200 g gemahlene Haselnüsse mit 200 g Butter in einer Pfanne anrösten, anschließend die Spätzle hinzugeben und alles gut durchmischen.

Mauldascha (Maultaschen)

Teig: 500 g Mehl, 4 Eier, Salz
Füllung: 1 Zwiebel, 4 Brötchen vom Vortag, etwas Petersilie, Butter
2 Landjäger (oder ersatzweise Speck), 300 g Hackfleisch, 250 g gekochter Spinat
Pfeffer, Salz, Muskatnuss[b], 3 Eier

Aus den Zutaten einen glatten Teig kneten und eine Rolle formen. Diese in sechs gleich große Teile zerschneiden und die Teile hauchdünn ausrollen. Danach in Quadrate einteilen und schneiden.

Zwiebeln, Petersilie und in Wasser eingeweichte und danach ausgedrückte Brötchen in Butter dämpfen, mit dem Hackfleisch, den kleingeschnittenen Landjägern und Spinat vermengen und mit Pfeffer, Salz und Muskatnuss würzen. Eier dazu geben.

Die Teigstücke nun mit der Füllung bestreichen. Dann Rand auf Rand legen und mit dem Finger oder einer Gabel festdrücken. Die Maultaschen sofort in kochendes Salzwasser geben und zehn Minuten ziehen lassen. Danach herausnehmen und kalt werden lassen.

---

[a]*parsley*   [b]*nutmeg*

 Neue Vokabeln

Nomen

der Boden, ∵   *soil, ground*
die Freude, -n   *joy, pleasure*
der Liebhaber, -/die
   Liebhaberin, -nen   *fan, devotee*
die Not, ∴e   *need, trouble*
der Schatz, ∴e   *treasure; darling*
die Speise, -n   *food, dish*
die Vorliebe, -n   *preference*

Verben

bestehen aus, bestand,
   bestanden   *to consist of*
erfinden, erfand, erfunden   *to invent*
sparen   *to save*
sich verändern   *to change*
sich (etwas) vor·stellen
   to imagine (something)

Adjektive und Adverbien

ähnlich   *similar*
beliebig   *as one likes, at will*
ebenso wie   *as well as*
gewiss   *certain*
inzwischen   *in the meantime*
nahrhaft   *nutritious*
wohlhabend   *affluent, wealthy*

Kulturtipps

■ Schwäbische Alb

Die Schwäbische Alb ist ein etwas 200 km langes, 40 km breites Mittelgebirge, das sich vom südlichen Baden-Württemberg nach Nordosten zwischen Stuttgart und Ulm bis ins Bayrisch-Schwaben erstreckt.

■ Hans Sachs

Hans Sachs (1494–1576), Schuhmeister und Meistersinger aus Nürnberg, galt zu seinen Lebzeiten als berühmtester deutscher Dichter. Er verfasste über 6.000 Werke, meist Lieder und Gedichte aber auch Fastnachtspiele (*Carnival plays*), Komödien und Tragödien. Er ist heute wohl nach Martin Luther der bekannteste deutsche Schriftsteller des 16. Jahrhunderts.

■ Laugenbrezel (pretzel)

Die Laugenbrezel ist ein typisch süddeutsches Gebäck. Die schwäbisch-badische Variante hat meist einen dicken, eingeschnittenen Bauch und dünne Ärmchen. In den verschiedenen Regionen Baden-Württembergs und zu verschiedenen Anlässen wird die Laugenbrezel allerdings unterschiedlich zubereitet und geformt.

8-1 Textarbeit: Schwäbisch essen! Welche schwäbische Speisen oder Mahlzeiten sind das?

1. eine Teigware aus Mehl und Kartoffeln
2. gefüllte Teigtaschen wie italienische Ravioli
3. Teigwaren, die man oft mit Käse überbäckt oder zu Linsen isst
4. dünne Pfannkuchen, wie französische Crêpes
5. eine Zwischenmahlzeit
6. ein brotähnliches Gebäck
7. eine Wurstsorte

Answers for 8-1. 1. Schupfnudeln; 2. Maultaschen; 3. Spätzle; 4. Flädle; 5. Vesper; 6. Laugenbrezel; 7. Saitenwurst, Schinkenwurst oder Landjäger

8-2 Textarbeit: Fragen zum Inhalt. Beantworten Sie die Fragen zum Text.

1. Inwiefern soll die schwäbische Küche den Charakter der Schwaben widerspiegeln?
2. Woran kann man einen italienischen Einfluss auf die schwäbische Küche merken?
3. Warum hat man Maultaschen zuerst gemacht?

Answers for 8-2. 1. Schwaben war eine arme Region, und dass sie aus wenig viel machen konnten, zeigt ihren Erfindergeist. 2. Es besteht eine Ähnlichkeit zwischen Schupfnudeln und Gnocchi, Maultaschen und Ravioli, Spätzle und Spaghetti. 3. um das Fleisch während der Fastenzeit vor Gott zu verstecken

4. als Beilage zu Linsen und Saitenwürsten oder mit Käse überbacken; **5.** weil sie Nassesser sind und alles in eine Brühe oder Soße tunken wollen; **6.** Vesper kann vormittags oder nachmittags stattfinden. Dazu gehören Wurst und eine Brezel. **7.** Der Teig für beide Rezepte besteht aus Mehl, Eiern und Salz. Beide werden im Salzwasser gekocht. In einigen Variationen für Spätzle kann nach Wunsch auch Fleisch oder Petersilie hinzukommen, genau wie bei Maultaschen.

4. Wie isst man traditionell Spätzle?
5. Warum nennt man die Schwaben „Suppenschwaben"?
6. Wann ist Vesper und was isst man zur Vesper?
7. Inwiefern sind sich die Rezepte für Maultaschen und Spätzle ähnlich?

8-3 Vokabelarbeit. Ergänzen Sie die Sätze mit Wörtern aus den *Neuen Vokabeln*. Achten Sie dabei auch auf die Wortform.

1. Obwohl Schwaben einst ein armes Land war, ist es heute eine ___wohlhabende___ Region.

2. Das Fleisch war einst für die meisten Schwaben zu teuer, aber ___inzwischen___ gehören auch Fleischgerichte zur regionalen Küche.

3. Reichhaltige Suppen und Eintöpfe ___ebenso___ ___wie___ verschiedene Teigwaren haben eine zentrale Bedeutung in der schwäbischen Küche.

4. Die schwäbische Spezialität Gaisburger Marsch ___besteht___ ___aus___ Spätzle und Kartoffeln in einer Fleischbrühe.

5. Spätzle ist eine ___Speise___, die man in vielen Restaurants findet.

6. ___Liebhaber___ von Süßigkeiten kommen beim Ofenschlupfer oder Pfitzauf auch auf ihre Kosten.

7. Die berühmte Schwarzwälder Kirschtorte hat man in Tübingen ___erfunden___.

8-4 Zur Diskussion. Besprechen Sie die Fragen.

1. Glauben Sie, dass Ihnen die traditionelle schwäbische Küche schmeckt? Warum (nicht)?

2. Könnten Sie Maultaschen oder Spätzle kochen? Was können Sie besonders gut kochen?

3. Für welche Agrargüter oder Lebensmittel ist die Region, wo Sie wohnen oder herkommen, bekannt?

Expansion for 8-5. Follow up with a writing activity by having students design a dinner invitation containing all the important information: occasion, time, place, the menu and any other details they deem important.

8-5 Eine Mahlzeit. Sie und ein/e Mitstudent/in laden die ganze Deutschklasse zum Essen ein. Was kochen Sie? Welche Getränke bieten Sie an? Was sollen die anderen Studenten mitbringen? Wo und wann wird die Mahlzeit stattfinden?

8-6 Mein Kochbuch. Sie schreiben ein Kochbuch. Entscheiden Sie sich, was für ein Thema das Kochbuch hat (z. B. Nachspeisen, italienische Küche, Brot backen usw.). Denken Sie sich einen Titel aus und schreiben Sie dann ein Vorwort für das Buch, das den Inhalt des Buches beschreibt.

8-7 Noch mehr Rezepte. Suchen Sie im Internet nach einem zusätzlichen schwäbischen oder badischen Rezept und beantworten Sie die Fragen dazu.

1. Wie heißt das Gericht?
2. Wenn es ein Bild gibt, beschreiben sie, wie das fertige Gericht aussieht.
3. Aus welchen Zutaten besteht das Rezept?
4. Wie bereitet man das Gericht zu? Z. B. Muss man etwas schneiden? Mischen? Kochen? Braten? Backen? eine Soße darüber gießen? usw.
5. Möchten Sie dieses Gericht gern probieren? Warum (nicht)?

Note for 8-7. Relevant web addresses for Internet research activities can be found in *MyGermanLab* and on the Companion Website.

Lesetext 2

Daimler startet Mobilitätskonzept „car2go" in Ulm (Pressemitteilung)

Deutschland ist neben den USA und Japan einer der weltgrößten Produzenten von Automobilen, und deutsche Autos sind weltweit für ihre Qualität bekannt. Ein Viertel aller Arbeitsplätze der deutschen Automobilbranche befinden sich in Baden-Württemberg. Neben den Herstellern Daimler, Porsche und Audi gibt es hier zahlreiche Unternehmen wie Bosch, Behr, Mahle und die ZF-Gruppe, die der Automobilindustrie zuliefern°. Wenn man vom „Autoland" spricht, dann weiß man in Deutschland, dass von Baden-Württemberg die Rede ist.

Der Stand des Bundeslands als Herz der Automobilindustrie geht schon auf die Geburtsstunde des Autos zurück, denn das Automobil wurde gleichzeitig an zwei Orten in Baden-Württemberg erfunden. Ende des 19. Jahrhunderts erschufen Carl Benz im badischen Mannheim und Gottlieb Daimler im schwäbischen Cannstatt bei Stuttgart unabhängig voneinander die ersten Automobile der Welt. Seit den Pioniertagen hat man hier das Auto mit zahlreichen Innovationen – z. B. ABS°, Airbag, Abstandsregler°, Tempomat°, Tiptronic° – weiterentwickelt.

Mit der aktuellen Forschung versucht man die Mobilität nicht nur sicherer, schneller und komfortabler, sondern auch umweltfreundlicher und besser geeignet für moderne Lebensweisen zu machen. In der folgenden Pressemitteilung beschreibt das Unternehmen Daimler AG ein Projekt, mit dem es versucht, den neuen Herausforderungen des 21. Jahrhunderts entgegenzukommen.

Vor dem Lesen

1. Besitzen Sie ein Auto? Braucht man unbedingt ein Auto (oder Freunde oder Verwandte mit Auto), wo Sie wohnen?
2. Was ist eine Pressemitteilung? Wer schreibt eine Pressemitteilung? Welche Informationen erwarten Sie in einer Pressemitteilung und welche nicht?

Introduction to *Lesetext 2*. Ask students what they know about Daimler, then what they know about German cars. *Kennen Sie den Namen Daimler? Was wissen Sie darüber? Kennen Sie andere deutsche Autohersteller? Welchen Ruf haben deutsche Autos?* Then ask what they learned from the introductory text. *Warum kennt man Baden-Württemberg als Autoland? Wo wurde das Automobil erfunden und von wem? Worauf zielt die Forschung heute?* supply

anti-lock brake system / collision control system / cruise control / automatic transmission with manual upshift/downshift feature

Blick auf Ulm

Beim Lesen

Ordnen Sie die Überschriften den Absätzen
des Lesetextes zu.

_5_ Mietzeit, Parken und Kosten

_7_ Pflege und Tanken

_1_ Projekt für die Zukunft

_8_ Und wie geht's weiter?

_2_ Warum in Ulm?

_4_ Wie erhält man ein Auto?

_3_ Wie es im allgemeinen funktioniert

_6_ Preise und Bezahlung

08-07 to 08-09

Daimler startet Mobilitätskonzept „car2go" in Ulm

Stuttgart/Ulm, 21.10.2008

[1] Mit car2go startet Daimler ein völlig neues Mobilitätskonzept und gibt eine zukunftsweisende Antwort auf das steigende Verkehrsaufkommen in Ballungsgebieten°.

Verkehrsaufkommen in Ballungsgebieten volume of traffic in metropolitan areas

[2] Am 24. Oktober startet in Ulm die erste Pilotphase. „Ulm ist seit vielen 5
Jahren einer unserer bedeutendsten Forschungsstandorte und eignet sich deshalb besonders zur Erprobung dieses zukunftsweisenden Mobilitätskonzepts", sagt Dr. Thomas Weber, Forschungs- und Entwicklungsvorstand der Daimler AG. Die Stadt Ulm unterstützt das car2go Projektteam insbesondere bei Fragen der Verkehrsplanung. 10

Siehe **Kulturtipps**: Aktiengesellschaft (AG)

regionwide
Siehe **Kulturtipps**: *smart*

[3] Und so funktioniert es: Im Stadtgebiet werden flächendeckend° *smart fortwo* Fahrzeuge bereitgestellt, die rund um die Uhr von jedem Interessierten gemietet werden können. Nach einmaliger Registrierung haben die Kunden die Möglichkeit, spontan oder mit Vorbuchung auf die Fahrzeuge zuzugreifen und beliebig lange zu nutzen. Der Kunde 15
steigt ein, kann sofort losfahren und stellt den Miet-*smart* nach Fahrtende einfach auf einen Stellplatz innerhalb des Stadtgebiets zurück.

windshield

[4] Bei der Anmeldung zu car2go wird der Führerschein des Kunden mit einem elektronischen Siegel versehen, der das Öffnen des Fahrzeugs ermöglicht. Wo immer ein freier *smart* steht, kann er diesen sofort „vom Fleck weg" mieten. 20
Dazu hält der Kunde seinen Führerschein an ein Lesegerät im Bereich der Windschutzscheibe°, steigt ein, tippt im Fahrzeug seine persönliche Geheimzahl ein und fährt los. Sollte mal keiner der 50 *smarts* in Sicht sein, kann einfach über das Internet oder per Telefon ein *smart* in der Nähe lokalisiert werden. Alternativ zur Spontanmiete ist eine Buchung bis zu 24 Stunden im Voraus möglich. In 25

diesem Fall erhält der Kunde rechtzeitig vor der geplanten Abfahrt eine SMS mit dem genauen Standort des reservierten Fahrzeuges.

[5] Die Mietzeit kann beliebig lange dauern. Während Zwischenstopps – wie etwa beim Einkaufen – bleibt das Fahrzeug für den Teilnehmer reserviert. Möchte der Kunde sein car2go zurückgeben, stellt er das 30 Fahrzeug einfach auf einen Parkplatz im Stadtgebiet ab. Darüber hinaus werden zum Beispiel an Bahnhöfen oder Flughäfen speziell gekennzeichnete car2go Parkplätze bereitgestellt.

[6] car2go zeichnet sich durch ein einfaches und transparentes Bezahlsystem aus: Abgerechnet wird nicht nach Fahrtstrecke, sondern nach Zeit und zwar 35 im Minutentakt – ähnlich wie beim Mobilfunk. Für 19 Cent pro Minute kann der Kunde in Ulm ein car2go nutzen – inklusive aller Nebenkosten wie Kraftstoff°, Versicherung und Steuern. Bei längerer Nutzung gelten günstige Stunden- oder Tagestarife. Als besonderen Anreiz° dafür, car2go auszuprobieren, wird auf eine Aufnahmegebühr° verzichtet. Bezahlt werden die tatsächlich durchgeführten Fahrten bequem per Monatsrechnung.

fuel
40 *incentive*
enrollment fee

[7] Ein Serviceteam reinigt die Fahrzeuge regelmäßig und führt technische Wartungsarbeiten° durch. So ist gewährleistet, dass jeder Kunde bei jeder Fahrt ein einwandfrei sauberes, gepflegtes und schadenfreies° Fahrzeug 50 erhält. Die Betankung erfolgt ebenfalls über das Serviceteam. Übernimmt der Kunde das Tanken mit Hilfe einer vorbezahlten Tankkarte, die sich im Handschuhfach des car2go befindet, werden ihm Freiminuten für die nächste Fahrt gutgeschrieben.

maintenance work
damage-free

[8] Die erste Phase des Projektes mit 50 s*mart fortwo* startet am 24. Oktober 55 in Ulm, zunächst ausschließlich mit Mitarbeitern der Daimler AG. „Unser Ziel dabei ist es, praktische Erfahrungen beim Einsatz von car2go zu gewinnen", sagt Robert Henrich, verantwortlicher Projektleiter im Bereich Business Innovation der Daimler AG. Im Frühjahr des kommenden Jahres wird die Flotte in Ulm auf 200 Fahrzeuge erhöht und die Gruppe der mögli- 60 chen car2go Nutzer auf alle Bewohner und Besucher der Stadt erweitert.

Die Daimler AG ist ein deutscher Hersteller von PKW° und Nutzfahrzeugen sowie Anbieter von Finanzdienstleistungen mit Firmenzentrale in Stuttgart.

= ***Personenkraftwagen***
cars

Kulturtipps

▬ Aktiengesellschaft (AG)

Die Abkürzung AG im Namen eines Unternehmens bedeutet, dass die Firma eine Aktiengesellschaft (*stock corporation*) ist, d. h. ein Unternehmen, in dem Aktionäre (*shareholders*) ihr Kapital investieren und dafür Aktien besitzen, Dividenden erhalten, aber für die Schulden und Pflichten des Unternehmens nicht persönlich haften (*be liable*) müssen.

smart

Der *smart* ist ein zweisitziges Stadtauto von Daimler, das erst 1998 als *smart city-coupé* auf dem Markt erschien und seit 2004 als *smart fortwo* weiter produziert wird. Das ursprünglich 2,5 m und seit 2007 2,69 m lange Fahrzeug fährt bis zu 145 km/h, ist aber insbesondere im Stadtverkehr zu sehen, wo es in enge Straßen und in die kleinsten Parklücken passt. Der *smart* ist zum Kultauto geworden. Über 1,2 Millionen Exemplare wurden schon in mehr als 45 Ländern verkauft.

 ## Neue Vokabeln

Nomen

die Anmeldung, -en   *registration*
die Fahrt, -en   *drive, trip*
das Fahrzeug, -e   *vehicle*
der Fleck, -e   *spot*
der Flughafen, ⸚   *airport*
der Führerschein, -e   *driver's license*
die (persönliche) Geheimzahl, -en   *(personal) identification number (PIN)*

der Kunde, -n, -n/die Kundin, -nen   *customer, client*
die Steuer, -n   *tax*
die Versicherung, -en   *insurance*

Verben

sich eignen (zu)   *to be suitable (for), lend itself (to)*
mieten   *to rent*
reinigen   *to clean*

Adjektive und Adverbien

ausschließlich   *exclusively*
darüber hinaus   *furthermore*
insbesondere   *especially*
rechtzeitig   *in a timely manner*
tatsächlich   *real(ly), actual(ly)*
zunächst   *first, at first, for now*

Ausdrücke

im Voraus   *beforehand, in advance*

Answers for 8-8. 1. Ulm ist ein wichtiger Forschungsstandort von Daimler. **2.** Man muss sich erst anmelden. Dann bekommt man ein Siegel auf den Führerschein, mit dem man Autos öffnen kann und eine persönliche Geheimzahl, die das Fahren der Autos ermöglicht. **3.** € 5,70; **4.** nein; **5.** vom Serviceteam oder vom Kunden mit der vorbezahlten Tankkarte im Handschuhfach; **6.** zunächst nur Daimler-Mitarbeiter, aber nach der Pilotphase alle Bewohner und Besucher Ulms

8-8 Textarbeit: Fragen zum Inhalt. Beantworten Sie die Fragen in Bezug auf den Text.

1. Warum wurde Ulm als Standort für den Pilotversuch des car2go Projekts gewählt?
2. Was muss man tun, bevor man ein car2go Fahrzeug mieten kann?
3. Wie viel kostet eine Mietzeit von 30 Minuten?
4. Gibt es außer der Mietzeit zusätzliche Kosten?
5. Wie und von wem werden die Autos getankt?
6. Wer darf am Projekt teilnehmen?

8-9 Vokabelarbeit. Ergänzen Sie die Sätze mit Wörtern aus den *Neuen Vokabeln*. Achten Sie dabei auch auf die Wortform.

1. Wer ein Auto braucht aber keines besitzt, kann ein Auto ____mieten____.
2. Um ein Auto fahren zu dürfen, muss man einen gültigen ____Führerschein____ besitzen.
3. Gleich nach der ____Anmeldung____ kann man in ein freies car2go einsteigen.
4. Bevor man das car2go fahren kann, muss man eine ____persönliche____ ____Geheimzahl____ eingeben.

5. _____Kunden_____ dürfen ein Fahrzeug beliebig lange benutzen.

6. Zunächst wird das car2go Projekt _____ausschließlich_____ in Ulm eingeführt.

7. Ob das car2go _____sich_____ auch für andere Städte _____eignet_____, wird man erst nach der Testphase entscheiden.

8-10 Zur Diskussion. Besprechen Sie die Fragen.

1. Die Pressemitteilung von Daimler präsentiert natürlich das Positive am car2go Projekt. Was sagt die Pressemitteilung nicht? Welche Probleme könnten entstehen? Halten Sie car2go für eine gute Idee?

2. Welche Vorteile hat car2go für Kunden? Für die Stadt Ulm? Für die Umwelt? Würden Sie an dem Programm teilnehmen, wenn Sie die Möglichkeit hätten?

3. Ist der *smart* ein gutes Auto für dieses Projekt? Warum stellt Daimler Ihrer Meinung nach nicht verschiedene Autos zur Verfügung?

4. Besitzen Sie ein Fahrzeug? Wenn ja, beschreiben Sie es. Welche Vorteile hat ein eigenes Auto? Welche Pflichten und Verantwortungen hat man, wenn man ein Fahrzeug besitzt?

8-11 Welches Transportmittel? Sie sind gerade nach Ulm gezogen und müssen sich für ein Transportmittel für Ihre tägliche Fahrt – zur Uni und Arbeit, zum Einkaufen und um Freunde zu besuchen – entscheiden.

1. Vergleichen Sie mit einem Mitstudenten/einer Mitstudentin die Teilnahme am car2go Projekt mit anderen Möglichkeiten:

	Vorteile	Nachteile
car2go Fahrzeuge mieten		
ein Auto kaufen		
mit öffentlichen Verkehrsmitteln fahren		
mit dem Fahrrad fahren		

2. Besprechen Sie: Unter welchen Umständen ist das car2go vielleicht die beste Möglichkeit? Unter welchen Umständen wäre es keine gute Wahl?

08-51 8-12 Meine Pressemitteilung. Sie sind Pressesprecher für ein Unternehmen, das ein neues Produkt oder Projekt entwickelt hat. Denken Sie sich ein Produkt oder Projekt aus. Dann schreiben Sie eine Pressemitteilung über dieses Produkt oder Projekt, um mögliche Kunden dafür zu gewinnen.

8-13 Wie geht's weiter? Schauen Sie auf die Internetseite des car2go Projekts, um das Neueste darüber herauszufinden. Welche Aspekte des Projekts sind seit dem Start gleich geblieben? Was hat sich verändert? Machen Sie zwei Listen, eine mit den gleich gebliebenen Programmbedingungen und eine mit den Veränderungen. **Note for 8-13.** Relevant web addresses for Internet research activities can be found in *MyGermanLab* and on the Companion Website.

Additional writing activity for *Lesetext 2*. Sie sind Mitarbeiter/in der Daimler AG in Ulm und nehmen seit einem Monat am car2go Projekt teil. Die Projektleiter möchten nun Ihr Feedback. Schreiben Sie einen Bericht über Ihre bisherigen Erfahrungen mit car2go.

Teaching suggestion for 8-13. Once students have compiled their lists, have them compare results. Then have them discuss whether the program changes they identified represent improvements to the program.

Introduction to *Hörtext 1.*
Before reading the text introduction, activate students' knowledge and have them speculate about what they might hear. *Welche Musik hören Sie gern? Kennen Sie einige aktuelle deutsche Musiker? Was halten Sie von der Idee einer Hochschule für Popmusik? Was lernt man wohl dort? Wie unterscheidet sich wohl eine Popakademie von einer Musikhochschule?* Then ask when they learned from the introductory text. *Wodurch zeichnet sich Baden-Württemberg in der Bildung aus? In der Popmusik?*

Die Popakademie Baden-Württemberg (Interview)

Die Bildung hat in Baden-Württemberg eine lange Tradition, denn die älteste Universität Deutschlands wurde 1385 Heidelberg gegründet. Heute hat das Bundesland neun Universitäten, sechs pädagogische Hochschulen, 29 Fachhochschulen sowie eine Reihe von spezialisierten Kunst- und Musikhochschulen. Hier stehen vier von Deutschlands Elite-Universitäten und nach den Rankings von *Focus Magazin* befinden sich sieben der elf besten deutschen Unis im Südweststaat.

Die Popmusik in Baden-Württemberg hat ebenfalls eine reiche, wenn auch viel kürzere Geschichte. Einige der besten Produzenten Deutschlands arbeiten hier und aus dem Ländle stammen sehr erfolgreiche Popmusiker wie etwa die Bands PUR, Die Fantastischen Vier, Massive Töne, Freundeskreis und der Sänger Xavier Naidoo. Die Zahl der aktiven Rock- und Popbands im Land wird heute auf rund 5.000 geschätzt. Die regionale Popmusikszene wird vom Bundesland bewusst gefördert durch eine Reihe von Einrichtungen, Projekten, Festen und nicht zuletzt die 2003 gegründete Popakademie, in der sich die neuesten Musiktrends an die Bildungstradition des Landes anknüpfen.

Im folgenden Interview auf der Musikmesse Frankfurt spricht Steffi, Vertreterin° der Popakademie Baden-Württemberg, mit Marc Weissenberger von localheroes-radio.de über das Studium an der Popakademie.

representative

Vor dem Hören

Was möchten Sie über die Popakademie wissen? Denken Sie sich drei Fragen aus.

Beim Hören

Während des Interviews hören Sie folgende Vokabeln.

Die Popakademie
Baden-Württemberg

08-10 to 08-11

Abitur   *final exam in the college-preparatory secondary school*
mittlere Bildungsabschlüsse   *degrees from non-college preparatory secondary schools*
Zusatzprüfung   *additional test*
Studiengebühren   *tuition fees*
Dozenten   *lecturers*
Zweigstellen   *satellite branches*
Studiengang   *major*
Schlagzeuger   *drummer*
Kontakte knüpfen   *network, make business contacts*
Praktikum   *internship*

Hören Sie sich den Bericht an, und merken Sie, ob die Fragen, die Sie sich im *Vor dem Lesen* ausgedacht haben, im Laufe des Interviews beantwortet werden.

Kulturtipps

BAFöG

Das Bundesausbildungsförderungsgesetz, als BAFöG allgemein bekannt, regelt die finanzielle Förderung von Studenten durch den Staat. BAFöG bezeichnet auch das Geld, das man infolge dieses Gesetzes erhält.

Xavier Naidoo

Xavier Naidoo ist ein erfolgreicher deutscher Soul-/Hip-Hop-Sänger, der 1971 in Mannheim als Sohn einer Südafrikanerin und eines Vaters deutsch-indischer Abstammung geboren wurde. Seine Lieder behandeln oft solche Themen wie Fremdenhass (*hatred of foreigners*), Nächstenliebe (*charity*) und das Christentum. Parallel zur Solokarriere ist er Gründungsmitglied der Musikgruppe „Söhne Mannheims", besitzt ein eigenes Plattenlabel und ist sehr engagiert in unterschiedlichen Projekten.

 8-14 Textarbeit: Was stimmt? Kreuzen Sie an, was Sie hören.

Die Popakademie …
- __x__ bietet zwei Studiengänge an.
- __x__ kostet 500 Euro pro Semester.
- __x__ ist eine staatliche Hochschule.
- _____ möchte die Studiengebühren in Zukunft reduzieren.
- __x__ hat Dozenten aus der Musikbranche.
- __x__ ist in Mannheim.
- _____ öffnet bald eine Zweigstelle in Stuttgart.
- _____ wird in Zukunft noch weitere Studiengänge anbieten.
- _____ bietet den Master-Abschluss für Studierende.
- _____ hat Xavier Naidoo für seine Karriere ausgebildet.
- __x__ erfordert Praktika für ihre Studenten.
- __x__ arbeitet mit Universal Music zusammen.

 8-15 Zum Nachdenken. Besprechen Sie die Themen in Gruppen.

1. Beschreiben Sie den idealen Bewerber auf einen Studienplatz an der Popakademie.
2. Was meinen Sie: Was machen Absolventen der Popakademie, nachdem sie ihr Studium abgeschlossen haben?
3. Die Idee einer Popakademie wird von einigen gelobt, aber von anderen auch kritisiert. Was meinen Sie: Was kritisiert man an der Popakademie?
4. Die Popakademie wird teilweise vom Land und von der Stadt, teilweise durch private Mittel finanziert. Welche Konflikte und Schwierigkeiten können entstehen, wenn eine Hochschule durch öffentliche und private Mittel gleichzeitig unterstützt wird?

8-16 Eine neue Akademie. Sie wollen eine neue Akademie eröffnen, die auf einem bestimmten Gebiet spezialisiert. Entscheiden Sie sich, was für eine Akademie Sie gründen wollen, indem Sie die Fragen beantworten. Dann stellen Sie Ihren Plan in der Deutschklasse vor.

- Wie heißt die neue Akademie?
- Was kann man hier studieren?
- Welche Qualifikationen brauchen Bewerber?
- Wie lange dauert das Studium?
- Welche Qualifikationen und Erfahrungen brauchen Dozenten?
- Wie und wo finden Sie Dozenten?
- Warum kann man hier studieren?
- Welchen Abschluss haben Absolventen? Welche Berufsaussichten?

8-17 Studieren in Baden-Württemberg. Besuchen Sie die Internetseite einer Hochschule in Baden-Württemberg und ergänzen Sie die Tabelle. Dann tauschen Sie Informationen mit einem Mitstudenten/einer Mitstudentin aus.

Teaching Suggestion for 8-17. Have students work in pairs and assign each pair a different school. Then have student pairs compare the schools they researched.

Note for 8-17. Relevant web addresses for Internet research activities can be found in *MyGermanLab* and on the Companion Website.

Name der Hochschule: _____

Standort: _____

Anzahl der Studierenden: _____

Studiengänge: _____

Abschlüsse: _____

Jahr der Gründung: _____

Informationen für ausländische Studierende? _____

Anderes: _____

Introduction to *Lesetext* 3. Ask students if they already know something about the Black Forest. *Haben Sie schon einmal vom Schwarzwald gehört? Was assoziieren Sie damit?* Have them read the first sentence of the introduction while looking at the map of Germany on the inside front cover and ask them to determine the exact location of the *Schwarzwald*. Then ask them what else they learned from the introduction. *Welche Landschaften findet man im Schwarzwald? Wovon leben die Menschen im Schwarzwald? Wer besucht gern den Schwarzwald?*

Lesetext 3

Unser Wochenende im Schwarzwald (Blog mit Kommentaren)

Der Schwarzwald, höchstes und meistbesuchtes Gebirge Deutschlands, befindet sich im badischen Teil des Landes. Er erstreckt sich von der südlichen Grenze Deutschlands nach Norden entlang der Grenze zu Frankreich. Anmutige° Hügel im Norden, alpine Gipfel im Süden, abwechselnd Wälder und Wiesen, zahlreiche Nadelbäume°, ungezähmte Flüsse und Bäche und kristallklare Seen prägen die Landschaft des Schwarzwaldes. Mehr als die Hälfte der 11.400 km² Region ist als Naturpark ausgewiesen.

Wichtig für die Wirtschaft des Gebiets sind Forstwirtschaft (Holzhandel, Papierindustrie usw.) und Landwirtschaft (vor allem Vieh°, Getreide°, Kartoffeln, Obst- und Weinbau), die Herstellung von Uhren und Musikinstrumenten sowie andere traditionelle Handwerke. Mit über 6,5 Millionen Besuchern jährlich ist der Tourismus ein ebenfalls sehr bedeutender Wirtschaftsfaktor. Von außen her ist das Gebiet besonders für Kuckucksuhren, Kirschtorten und die typischen

graceful

conifers

livestock / grain crops

strohgedeckten° Bauernhäuser bekannt, aber auch innerhalb Deutschlands ist der Schwarzwald ein beliebtes Urlaubsgebiet, denn deutsche Gäste machen hier über 85 Prozent aller Urlaubsgäste aus.

thatched

Über einen jüngst verbrachten Kurzurlaub im Schwarzwald berichtet das deutsche Ehepaar Annegret und Jürgen K. aus Frankfurt a. M. auf ihrer Blogseite.

Vor dem Lesen

Gibt es touristische Orte bei Ihrem Wohnort? Haben Sie diese Orte schon mal besucht? Warum (nicht)?

Beim Lesen

1. Verfolgen Sie die Route von Annegret und Jürgens Reise auf der Karte.

2. Was haben Annegret und Jürgen während ihres Wochenendes im Schwarzwald erlebt? Machen Sie sich Notizen zu den Erlebnissen, die sie an folgenden Orten gehabt haben:

> in Todtnau
>
> auf dem Feldberg
>
> am Titisee
>
> am Schluchsee
>
> in Furtwangen
>
> auf der Autofahrt nach Hause
>
> zu Hause

Possible answers for *Beim Lesen (2)*. in Todtnau: in einer Pension übernachtet; auf dem Feldberg: gewandert; am Titisee: eine Seerundfahrt gemacht; am Schluchsee: am Ufer gefaulenzt, Segelbooten und Windsurfern zugesehen, gewandert; in Furtwangen: ins Deutsche Uhrenmuseum gegangen; auf der Autofahrt nach Hause: den Fallerhof besucht, badischen Wein gekauft; zu Hause: ein Glas Wein getrunken, ferngesehen

08-12 to 08-15

9. Juni

Wir sind vorgestern von unserem Wochenende im Südschwarzwald zurückgekehrt. Drei herrliche Tage haben wir dort verbracht und sind erfrischt wieder heimgekommen. In kurzer Zeit haben wir eine Menge erlebt.

Angekommen sind wir Freitag früh in Todtnau, wo Jürgen im Internet eine günstige Pension gefunden hatte – eine Übernachtung ab 30 Euro inkl. Frühstück. Zusätzlich überzeugte uns das Angebot der vielen umliegenden Sehenswürdigkeiten und Attraktionen.

5

Blick vom Feldberg auf den Feldsee

Nach der Autofahrt war gleich am ersten Tag eine Wanderung angesagt. Vom kleinen Dorf Feldberg aus konnten wir auf einem Schotterweg[a] sehr gut zum Feldsee hinunterlaufen. Es gibt die Möglichkeit, ihn zu 10 umrunden, was wir auch taten. Dann ging es wieder in die Höhe zum Haus der Natur, dem Naturschutzzentrum des Südschwarzwaldes. Hier ist nämlich alles Naturschutzgebiet, übrigens das größte und älteste Deutschlands. Von da aus kann man für sechs Euro 15 mit der Feldbergbahn auf den Berg Seebuck fahren, die paar hundert Meter sind wir aber lieber gelaufen. Vom Seebuck ist es nur noch ein Katzensprung (3 km) auf den 1493 m hohen Feldberg, den höchsten Gipfel des Schwarzwaldes. Der Weg verläuft auf der Anhöhe und die Rundumsicht ist phänomenal. Wenn man Glück hat, soll man an klaren Tagen sogar den Mont Blanc[1] sehen können! Ein solches 20 Glück hatten wir aber leider nicht. Nach dieser herrlichen Aussicht haben wir in der Gaststätte Todtnauer Hütte ein kleines Mittagessen zu uns genommen, bevor wir wieder zurück zum Ort Feldberg herunter gewandert sind.

Ausflugsziel des zweiten Tages war der Titisee. Wir hatten schon viel von diesem beliebten Urlaubsort gehört und wollten ihn unbedingt mal erleben. Wir haben für vier Euro eine 25 Seerundfahrt gemacht und haben viel Interessantes über den See erfahren. Überrascht hat es uns nicht, dass der kleine Ort an warmen Sommertagen bis zu 20.000 Touristen zählt. Zum einen ist der vom Wald umgebene See mit Blick auf den Feldberg auf jeden Fall einen Besuch wert. Zum anderen war an diesem Tag die Uferpromenade voller Touristen, die den Blick und die frische Luft genossen oder in den vielen Souvenirläden nach Kuckucksuhren 30 oder regional produzierter Keramik, Glaskunst oder Holzschnitzerei[b] schauten. Sucht man Ruhe, ist dieser Ort also nicht unbedingt die beste Wahl. Ein Einheimischer, der uns im Boot angesprochen hatte, meinte, der Schluchsee soll weniger touristisch sein, wir haben uns

Kinder paddeln auf dem Schluchsee

also entschieden, den kurzen Weg dahin zu fahren. Welch ein Glück! Er ist nicht so überlaufen und viel weniger vom 35 Massentourismus geprägt und wirkt einfach unberührter[c]. Es liegt bestimmt auch daran, dass der Schluchsee viel größer ist. Da findet man leicht ein ruhiges Fleckchen für sich. So genossen wir einige stille Stunden am Ufer, haben den Segelbooten und Windsurfern zugesehen und 40 erfreuten uns am herrlichen Blick auf Wiesen und Wälder,

---

[a]*gravel path*   [b]*woodcarving*   [c]*more pristine*

[1]Der Mont Blanc liegt an der Grenze zwischen Italien und Frankreich und ist der höchste Berg der Alpen.

sandig-felsige Ufer und kleine Inseln. Rund um den See gibt es einen 18 km langen Wanderweg, den wir auch zum Teil begangen haben.

Am Sonntag stand die Heimreise schon an. Wir brachen früh genug auf, um eine Zeitlang in Furt-wangen verweilen zu können. Der Besuch im Deutschen Uhrenmuseum, das mit über 8.000 Exem-plaren die größte deutsche Uhrensammlung darstellt, war sehr unterhaltsam. Wie erfuhren dort, dass Furtwangen im 19. Jahrhundert ein bedeutendes Zentrum der Uhrenproduktion war, und an diesem Ort wird heute noch eine Uhrmacherschule betrieben. Von Furtwangen aus haben wir auf der Fahrt Richtung B3[d] einen kleinen Abstecher gemacht, um den Bauernhof der Fernseh-Familie Faller aufzusuchen. Der Drehort soll irgendwo zwischen Furtwangen und Gütenbach liegen, finden konnten wir ihn jedoch leider nicht. Wir sind aber rechtzeitig wieder heimgekommen, um den Fallerhof* am Abend bei einem köstlichen Glas badischen Weißweins[†], den wir auf dem Heimweg gekauft hatten, im Fernsehen zu sehen.

Wer hätte gedacht, dass man in nur 250 km Entfernung einen so reizvollen[e] Urlaubsort finden kann. Danke, Lars für die Empfehlung! Alles in allem war es ein wunderschönes Wochenende, das viel zu schnell zu Ende ging.

---

3 Kommentare:

Erika: 11. Juni

Freut mich, dass euch die Gegend gefallen hat. Lars und ich waren im Winter dort, sind auf dem Titisee Schlittschuhlaufen gegangen und haben Skilanglauf machen können. Es gab eine grandiose Aussicht auf schneebedeckte Berge und Tannen[f]. Man sieht ihn also in den Wintermonaten von einer ganz anderen, aber genauso schönen Seite.

Niels: 10. Juni

Habt ihr den Todtnauer Wasserfall nicht gefunden? Ihr wart ja ganz in der Nähe. Der soll Deutschlands höchster Naturwasserfall sein, stürzt etwa 100 m ins Tal. Trotzdem ein tolles Wochenende, wie es sich anhört und wie man an den großartigen Fotos sieht. Ich wäre gerne mitgekommen.

Julia: 10. Juni

Habt ihr da Spuren von Lothar zu sehen bekommen? Ich war vor ein paar Jahren mal auf dem Lotharpfad[‡], da kann man die Zerstörung, die umgeworfenen Bäume, aber auch die Waldregenerierung ohne Zutun des Menschen hautnah[g] erleben. Sehr beeindruckend! Das liegt im nördlichen Schwarzwald, aber solche Gegenden kann man sicherlich im ganzen Schwarzwald sehen, nehme ich an.

---

[d] = *Bundesstraße 3 interstate highway*   [e]*attractive*   [f]*fir trees*   [g]*up close*

*Siehe **Kulturtipps**: Fallerhof

†Siehe **Kulturtipps**: Badischer Wein

‡Siehe **Kulturtipps**: Lothar

Kulturtipps

Fallerhof

„Die Fallers – Eine Schwarzwaldfamilie" ist eine beliebte Familien- und TV-Serie, die seit 1994 im Raum Furtwangen gedreht wird. Die Serie erzählt vom Leben einer fiktiven Familie mit vier Generationen auf einem Bauernhof – dem Fallerhof – im Schwarzwald. Behandelt werden Familienkonflikte und alltägliche Ereignisse, aber auch typische landwirtschaftliche Themen. Der Drehort (*filming location*) ist ein echter Bauernhof, der von einer wirklichen Familie bewohnt und bewirtschaftet wird. Aus Rücksicht auf die Familie versuchen die Produzenten den genauen Drehort geheim zu halten.

Badischer Wein

Baden ist eines von den 13 Weinanbaugebieten Deutschlands. Das Gebiet, das sich etwa 400 km lang von Heidelberg bis zum Bodensee erstreckt, umfasst beträchtliche geologische und klimatische Unterschiede und produziert daher Weine von unterschiedlichem Geschmack. Im Vergleich zu den anderen Weinregionen Deutschlands zeichnet sich Baden durch seine überdurchschnittlich hohen Temperaturen aus und ist daher ideal für den Weinanbau.

Lothar

1999 hat Orkan (*hurricane*) Lothar, einer der schwersten Stürme des Jahrhunderts, weite Teile des Schwarzwalds verwüstet (*devastated*). Inzwischen hat man die meisten Spuren der Naturkatastrophe beseitigt. Aber auf einer zehn Hektar großen Sturmfläche hat man die umgestürzten, entwurzelten Bäume liegen lassen und dort den Lotharpfad errichtet.

 Neue Vokabeln

Nomen

der Abstecher, -   *side trip*
die Aussicht, -en   *view*
der Baum, ⸚e   *tree*
die Gegend, -en   *area, region*
der Gipfel, -   *peak, summit*
die Menge, -n   *quantity, amount (colloq.)*

das Tal, ⸚er   *valley*
die Wiese, -n   *meadow*

Verben

erfahren (erfährt), erfuhr, erfahren   *to experience, find out*
heim·kommen, kam heim, ist heimgekommen   *to come home*
überraschen   *to surprise*

zurück·kehren, ist zurückgekehrt   *to return*

Adjektive und Adverbien

übrigens   *by the way*

Ausdrücke

auf jeden Fall   *in any case, definitely*

8-18 Textarbeit: Was ist das? In ihrem Blog nennen Annegret und Jürgen viele Orte. Welche Beschreibungen passen zu welchen Orten?

<u>c</u> 1. Todtnau

<u>f</u> 2. Feldsee

<u>k</u> 3. Haus der Natur

<u>d</u> 4. Seebuck

<u>j</u> 5. Feldberg

<u>i</u> 6. Todtnauer Hütte

<u>g</u> 7. Mont Blanc

<u>e</u> 8. Titisee

<u>a</u> 9. Schluchsee

<u>b</u> 10. Furtwangen

<u>h</u> 11. Lotharpfad

a. See, der sich zum Segelbootfahren, Windsurfen und Wandern eignet

b. Standort einer Uhrmacherschule

c. Ort, wo Annegret und Jürgen übernachtet haben

d. Berg, auf den man mit einer Feldbergbahn fahren kann

e. ein beliebter Urlaubsort, der viele Touristen anlockt

f. der See am Fuße des Feldbergs

g. Berg an der Grenze zwischen Frankreich und Italien, den man beim guten Wetter vom Gipfel des Feldberges sehen kann

h. Weg durch eine nicht geräumte Sturmfläche im Wald

i. ein Restaurant auf dem Feldberg

j. der höchste Berg des Schwarzwaldes

k. das Naturschutzzentrum des Südschwarzwaldes

8-19 Textarbeit: Fragen zum Inhalt. Beantworten Sie die Fragen in Bezug auf den Text.

1. Wie lange haben Jürgen und Annegret im Schwarzwald verbracht?
2. Wo haben sie übernachtet und wie viel haben sie bezahlt?
3. Wie sind sie auf den Feldberg gekommen?
4. Was machen Besucher am Titisee?
5. Wie unterscheidet sich der Schluchsee vom Titisee?
6. Was ist in Furtwangen?
7. Warum sind sie von Furtwangen aus nicht direkt nach Hause gefahren?
8. Was haben sie gemacht, nachdem sie zu Hause angekommen waren?

Answers for 8-19. **1.** drei Tage; **2.** in einer Pension in Todtnau für 30 Euro pro Nacht mit Frühstück; **3.** Sie sind gewandert. **4.** Sie machen Seerundfahrten, genießen den Blick und die frische Luft von der Uferpromenade aus, kaufen Souvenirs. **5.** Der Ort Schluchsee ist ruhiger, weniger von Touristen überlaufen, größer und wirkt unberührter. **6.** In Furtwangen sind das Deutsche Uhrenmuseum und eine Uhrmacherschule. **7.** Sie wollten den Fallerhof suchen. **8.** Sie haben badischen Wein getrunken und ferngesehen.

8-20 Vokabelarbeit. Ergänzen Sie die Sätze mit Wörtern aus den *Neuen Vokabeln*. Achten Sie dabei auch auf die Wortform.

1. Wenn man sich längere Zeit im Schwarzwald aufhält, kann man gut einen <u>Abstecher</u> nach Frankreich oder in die Schweiz machen.

2. Ein Wald besteht aus <u>Bäumen</u>.

3. Das tiefe Land zwischen zwei oder mehr Bergen ist ein <u>Tal</u>.

4. Der höchste Punkt eines Berges ist der <u>Gipfel</u>.

5. Von dort oben hat man bei gutem Wetter eine schöne <u>Aussicht</u>.

6. Bei einer Führung kann man viel Interessantes über die Geschichte und die Kultur eines Ortes ___erfahren___ .

7. Es ist schön, in Urlaub zu fahren, aber nach einem langen Urlaub will man gern auch wieder ___heimkehren___ .

 8-21 Dies oder das? Besprechen Sie, was Sie lieber machen würden, und sagen Sie warum.

Möchten Sie lieber …

1. im Sommer oder im Winter in den Schwarzwald fahren?
2. in einer Pension übernachten oder auf einem Campingplatz unter den Sternen schlafen?
3. den Titisee oder den Schluchsee besuchen?
4. eine Kuckucksuhr oder badische Weine kaufen?
5. den Todtnauer Wasserfall oder den Lotharpfad besichtigen?
6. ins Deutsche Uhrenmuseum gehen oder eine Seerundfahrt machen?

 8-22 Mein Ausflug. Besprechen Sie einen Ausflug, den Sie einmal in der Nähe von zu Hause gemacht haben. Ergänzen Sie die Tabelle.

	Mitstudent/in 1	**Mitstudent/in 2**
Wohin?		
Mit wem?		
Mit welchem Transportmittel?		
Wann?		
Für wie lange?		
Was gesehen und gemacht?		

8-23 Mein Blog. Sie haben ein eigenes Blog, das Ihre Familie und Freunde regelmäßig lesen. Schreiben Sie einen Blogeintrag über den Ausflug, den Sie in *Übung 8-22* besprochen haben.

8-24 Kommentar. Einige von Annegret und Jürgens Freunden haben auf dem Blog Kommentare hinterlassen. Schreiben Sie auch ein Kommentar zu ihrem Blogeintrag vom 9. Juni.

Introduction to Hörtext 2. Ask students what they know about Freiburg and to speculate about what "Green City" might refer to. *Wo liegt Freiburg? Was könnte das Label vielleicht bedeuten?* Then have students read the introduction and ask them what they learned. *Wie begann die ökologische Bewegung in Freiburg? Warum steht Freiburg in Sachen Umwelt weit vorne? Was könnten Stadtbürger gegen das Motto „Green City" einzuwenden haben?*

nuclear power plant

Hörtext 2

Green City Freiburg? (Umfrage)

Freiburg, südlichste Großstadt Deutschlands am Westrand des südlichen Schwarzwaldes gelegen, nennt sich gerne die heimliche Öko-Stadt. Der Beginn der ökologischen Bewegung in Freiburg liegt einige Jahrzehnte zurück. In den 70er-Jahren demonstrierten Menschen in der Region zu Tausenden gegen den geplanten Bau des Kernkraftwerks° Wyhl, so dass Bauarbeiten eingestellt werden mussten. Schon im Jahr nach dem Protest fand eine Sonnenenergieausstellung in Freiburg statt.

Seitdem hat sich die Stadt durch zahlreiche Projekte im Umweltbereich international einen Namen gemacht. Hier wurde die erste Plusenergie-Siedlung° Deutschlands gebaut. Hier wurde ein ganzer Stadtteil (Vauban) als ökologischer Modellstadtteil entwickelt. Schon dreimal ging der renommierte Deutsche Umweltpreis nach Freiburg. Und heute liegt Freiburg in der Entwicklung der Sonnenenergie in Deutschland an der Spitze.

Die Stadtverwaltung und die Freiburg Wirtschaft Touristik und Messe GmbH (FWTM) hat ein Konzept entwickelt, um das umweltpolitische Profil der Stadt zu fördern. Seit Anfang 2007 trägt Freiburg das Label „Green City". Und in der Tat kommen aus der ganzen Welt Delegationen nach Freiburg, um sich vorbildliche° Projekte im Bereich der erneuerbaren Energien, der Energieeffizienz oder des öffentlichen Nahverkehrs anzuschauen. Doch die Stadtbürger selbst sind verschiedener Meinung über das neue Stadtmotto. In dieser Umfrage hören Sie die Ansichten einiger Freiburger zum Label „Green City".

settlement consisting of houses that produce more energy than they use

Siehe **Kulturtipps**: Vauban

Teaching suggestion for *Hörtext 2.* Freiburg boasts 1800 hours of sunlight annually, making it one of Germany's sunniest regions. Have students look online *exemplary* to determine how many hours of sunshine their own region has annually. Maps of the United States containing this data are readily available online. Almost the entire United States has more annual hours of sunshine than „Solarregion Freiburg" and some regions of the U.S. even receive twice the amount of sunshine. Discuss with students the implications of their findings for the potential of solar energy in their region.

Vor dem Hören

Welche Funktion hat ein Motto für eine Stadt oder einen Staat? Brauchen Städte Mottos? Hat Ihre Stadt ein Motto?

Beim Hören

In dieser Umfrage hören Sie folgende Vokabeln.

griffig	*catchy*	sich … einfallen lassen	*came up with*
Plusenergiehäuser	*energy-plus houses*	verweist … auf	*refers to*
		kommt zu kurz	*is shortchanged*
berücksichtigt	*takes into account*	aufdrängt	*imposing*

Green City Freiburg?
08-16

Hören Sie sich die Umfrage an und merken Sie an, wie jeder Befragte das Motto bewertet: positiv, negativ oder ambivalent?

Dieter Haller	positiv
Irene Huber	positiv, aber negativ über den Gebrauch des Englischen
Erik Schiele	ambivalent
Annetta Bertucci	positiv
Michael Horn	negativ

Kulturtipps

▬Vauban

Vauban ist ein seit 1997 bestehender Stadtteil Freiburgs, bei dem ein innovatives Wohnkonzept gefördert wird und das als Modellprojekt für eine nachhaltige (*sustainable*) und ökologische Stadtplanung gilt. Zum Projekt gehören z. B. ein autofreies Wohngebiet, energiebewusstes Bauen, intensive Nutzung der Sonnenenergie, kooperative Planungsprozesse, an denen die Einwohner selbst beteiligt sind, eigene Geschäfte und Schulen, um das Fahren ins Stadtzentrum zu begrenzen, u. v .a.

Grüne Politik

„Grün" bezeichnet eine politische Richtung, die u. a. auf umweltbewusstes Handeln gerichtet ist. Die politische Partei „Die Grünen" entstand aus den Ökologie- und Bürgerinitiativbewegungen der 70er-Jahre. 2002 wählte Freiburg als erste deutsche Großstadt einen „grünen" Oberbürgermeister.

Münster und Bächle

Münster und Bächle befinden sich beide in der Altstadt Freiburgs und sind Wahrzeichen der Stadt. Das Münster ist eine mittelalterliche Kirche und das höchste Bauwerk der Stadt. Die Bächle sind kleine Kanäle, die durch die Straßen und Gassen der Stadt fließen. Diese versorgten im Mittelalter die Stadtbewohner mit Wasser für den Haushalt und gehören heute zu den Einmaligkeiten Freiburgs.

Das Freiburger Münster

Zwei Mädchen im Bächle

 8-25 Textarbeit: Wer sagt was? Wie reagieren die Freiburger auf ihr Motto? Finden Sie die Zusammenfassung, die die Meinung jeder Person am besten vertritt.

c	1.	Dieter Haller
e	2.	Irene Huber
b	3.	Erik Schiele
a	4.	Annetta Bertucci
d	5.	Michael Horn

a. Touristen wollen nicht nur die Freiburger Altstadt sehen. Sie interessieren sich ebenfalls für Freiburg als ökologisch bewusste Stadt.

b. Das Motto betont die ökologische Seite der Stadt, aber Freiburg ist nicht die einzige grüne Stadt. Die Geschichte der Stadt ist aber einmalig. Ein Slogan sollte beides – das Neue und das Alte – beachten.

c. So ein Motto ist international verständlich und das Thema Ökologie ist jetzt total „in". In Zukunft muss die Stadt an ökologischen Problemen aber noch weiter arbeiten.

d. Das Motto ist zu einseitig und ignoriert das Menschliche und das Kulturelle. Und warum ist das gleich auf English? Die Einwohner der Stadt sollten das Motto wählen.

e. Der Slogan passt ganz gut, weil „grün" mehrere Aspekte der Stadt umfasst. Nur frage ich mich, warum der Slogan nicht auf Deutsch ist.

8-26 Fragen zur Diskussion. Besprechen Sie die Fragen.

1. Halten Sie „Green City" für ein gutes Motto für Freiburg? Was spricht dafür? Was dagegen? Mit welcher Meinung aus der Umfrage stimmen Sie am meisten überein?

2. Wer soll ein Stadtmotto wählen: die Politiker, die Bürger oder jemand anders?

3. Sollte das Motto einer deutschen Stadt auf Deutsch sein? Wie ist das in Nordamerika? In welcher Sprache sind die Stadt- und Staatmottos, die Sie in Nordamerika kennen? Für wen ist ein Stadt- oder Staatmotto gemeint?

8-27 Ein Motto für meine Stadt. Sie sitzen auf einer Kommission, die ein neues Motto für Ihre Stadt erfinden möchte. Denken Sie sich ein passendes Motto für die Stadt aus und besprechen Sie, warum es ein passendes Motto ist. Dann stellen Sie das Motto der Klasse vor.

Teaching suggestion for 8-27. After all groups have presented their ideas to the class, have the the class vote on the best motto.

8-28 Meine Umfrage. Sie machen ein Praktikum bei Radio Dreieck und sollen eine Umfrage durchführen. Denken Sie sich ein interessantes Thema aus. Dann interviewen Sie mindestens fünf Mitstudenten in Ihrem Deutschkurs. Machen Sie sich Notizen und fassen Sie dann Ihre Resultate zusammen.

Follow-up for 8-28. You can have students report their results orally to the rest of the class or in small groups. Or you can have them prepare a written summary that would appear as a brief report on the website for Radio Dreieck.

8-29 Freiburg ist … Sie haben nun einiges über Freiburg erfahren. Beschreiben Sie die Stadt für eine Tourgruppe, die Interesse an einer Reise nach Freiburg hat.

Lesetext 4

„Das verlorene Taschenmesser" von Hermann Hesse (Autobiografie)

Hermann Hesse

Hermann Hesse (1877–1962), der 1946 den Nobelpreis für Literatur erhielt, ist einer der erfolgreichsten deutschsprachigen Schriftsteller des 20. Jahrhunderts. Geboren wurde er in der schwäbischen Schwarzwaldstadt Calw, hier und in der schweizerischen Stadt Basel wuchs er auf. Er besuchte dann die Schule in der Nähe von Stuttgart. Nach turbulenten Jugendjahren studierte er in Maulbronn, machte eine Buchhändlerlehre in Tübingen und arbeitete in Basel. Als er seinen literarischen Durchbruch erlebte und freier Schriftsteller werden konnte, zog er an den Bodensee, wo er von 1904 bis 1912 lebte. Danach siedelte er als Schweizer Staatsbürger in die Schweiz über, erst nach Bern und dann, als er sich von seiner an einer schweren Psychose leidenden Frau trennte, allein in ein Dorf im schweizerischen Tessin, wo er die letzte Hälfte seines Lebens verbrachte.

Alle Werke Hesses sind stark autobiografisch geprägt und die Orte, wo er lebte, finden sich in seinen Schriften wieder. Hesse betrachtete sich vor allem als Alemanne, womit er seine „Zugehörigkeit zu einem Lebens- und Kulturkreis,

Introduction to *Lesetext 4*. Ask students if they have ever heard of Hesse. *Kennen Sie den Namen Hermann Hesse? Was wissen Sie schon über ihn?* They may know him as the author of *Der Steppenwolf*, his best-known work internationally. Then ask what they learned from the introductory text. *Welche Verbindung hat Hesse zu Baden-Württemberg? Welchen Ort hielt er für seine Heimat?*

Siehe **Kulturtipps**: Bodensee

Vosges Mountains, in northeastern France, across the Rhine from the Schwarzwald

der von Bern bis zum nördlichen Schwarzwald, von Zürich und dem Bodensee bis an die Vogesen° reicht" meinte. Weiter schrieb er: „Dies südwestdeutsch-schweizerische Gebiet ist mir Heimat, … ob das Land nun Schweiz, Baden oder Württemberg hieß".[2] Heute werden der Schriftsteller und sein Werk in zwei baden-württembergischen Museen – einem in Calw und einem in Gaienhofen auf der Bodenseehalbinsel Höri – gewürdigt.

In „Das verlorene Taschenmesser", das zuerst 1924 in der *Vossischen Zeitung* in Berlin erschien, verarbeitet Hesse mit Bezug auf ein Taschenmesser seine Zeit in Gaienhofen am Bodensee und die darauffolgenden Jahre.

Vor dem Lesen

Der folgende Text heißt „Das verlorene Taschenmesser". Was erwarten Sie von diesem Text?

Beim Lesen

Im Laufe des Textes lernen wir etwas über verschiedene Aspekte von Hesses Leben. Machen Sie sich Notizen zu den folgenden Themen.

das Taschenmesser

seine Familie

sein Besitz

seine Wohnorte

seine Freizeit

Orthography. Hesse's text uses orthographical standards current at the 08-17 to 08-19 time of its publication.

„Das verlorene Taschenmesser"

von Hermann Hesse

preparedness to deal with fate

[1] Gestern habe ich ein Taschenmesser verloren und habe dabei die Erfahrung gemacht, daß meine Philosophie und Schicksalsbereitschaft° auf schwachen Füßen stehen, denn der kleine Verlust hat mich unverhältnismäßig betrübt, und ich bin auch heute noch mit meinen Gedanken bei jenem verlorenen Messer, nicht ohne mich selbst wegen solcher Sentimentalitäten auszulachen. 5

quirks

discomfort

[2] Es ist ein schlechtes Zeichen, daß der Verlust dieses Messers mich so betrüben konnte. Es gehört zu meinen Schrulligkeiten°, die ich wohl kritisieren und bekämpfen, nicht aber völlig abtun kann, daß ich an Dingen, die ich eine Weile besessen, mit großer Anhänglichkeit festhalte, und es 10 ist mir jedesmal ein Unbehagen°, zuweilen sogar ein kleiner Schmerz, wenn ich mich von einem lang getragenen Kleide oder Hut oder Stock trennen muß oder gar von einer Wohnung, in der ich lange gewohnt habe, um von schlimmeren Trennungen und Abschieden ganz zu schweigen. Und jenes Messer gehörte nun zu den ganz wenigen Gegen- 15 ständen, die bisher die Veränderungen meines Lebens überdauert und mich durch alle Wechsel jahrzehntelang begleitet haben.

---

[2]Aus: „Alemannische Bekenntnisse" in: Hermann Hesse, *Bodensee. Betrachtungen, Erzählungen, Gedichte*, hrsg. von Volker Michels, 7. Aufl. (Stuttgart: Jan Thorbecke Verlag, 2001), S. 15.

[3] Zwar besitze ich noch einigen geheiligten Trödel° aus fernerer Vergangenheit, einen Ring meiner Mutter, eine Uhr meines Vaters, ein paar Photographien und Andenken aus meiner frühen Kinderzeit, aber alle diese Dinge sind ja eigentlich tot, sind Museum, liegen im Schrank und werden kaum alle Jahre einmal betrachtet. Das Messer aber ist viele Jahre lang ein beinahe täglich gebrauchtes Ding gewesen, ich habe es viele tausend Male in meine Tasche gesteckt, aus der Tasche gezogen, es zu Arbeit und Spielerei benutzt, habe es hundertmal mit dem Abziehstein nachgeschliffen°, habe es in früheren Zeiten mehrmals verloren und wiedergefunden. Es war mir lieb, dies Messer, und es ist wohl eines Klageliedes wert°.

[4] Es war kein gewöhnliches Taschenmesser – deren habe ich in meinem Leben sehr viele besessen und verbraucht. Es war ein Gartenmesser, eine einzige, sehr starke, halbmondförmig gebogene Klinge° in festem, glattem Holzgriff°, kein Gegenstand des Luxus und der Spielerei, sondern eine ernste, solide Waffe, ein gediegenes Werkzeug von uralter, bewährter Form. […]

[5] Des Tages, an welchem ich den Besitz meines schönen sichelförmigen Gartenmessers antrat, kann ich mich noch wohl entsinnen. Ich war damals sehr auf der Höhe, in jeder Hinsicht und fühlte mich dementsprechend. Ich war seit kurzem verheiratet, ich war der Stadt und dem Gefängnis eines Brotberufes entronnen° und saß unabhängig und nur mir selber verantwortlich in einem schönen Dorf am Bodensee, ich hatte Erfolg mit Büchern, die ich schrieb und die mir sehr gut schienen, ich hatte auf dem See ein Ruderboot schwimmen, meine Frau erwartete ihr erstes Kind, und nun ging ich eben an eine große Unternehmung, deren Wichtigkeit mich ganz erfüllte: an den Bau eines eigenen Hauses und die Anlage eines eigenen Gartens. Der Boden war schon gekauft und die Maße abgesteckt, und wenn ich über das Grundstück ging, empfand ich manchmal feierlich die Schönheit und Würde° dieses Tuns, es schien mir, daß ich da einen Grundstein für alle Zeiten lege und für mich, meine Frau und meine Kinder hier eine Heimat und Zuflucht gründe. Die Hauspläne waren fertig, und der Garten nahm in meiner Vorstellung allmählich Gestalt an, mit dem breiten langen Mittelweg, dem Brunnen, der Wiese mit den Kastanienbäumen.

[6] Damals, ich mochte so gegen dreißig Jahre alt sein, kam eines Tages ein schweres Frachtstück° für mich mit dem Dampfer° an, und ich half es vom Landungssteg° mit heraufschleppen. Es kam von einer Gartenbaufirma und enthielt lauter Gartenwerkzeuge: Spaten, Schaufeln, Pickel, Rechen, Hacken (unter denen namentlich die mit dem Schwanenhals mich sehr entzückte) und manche andere solche Dinge. Dazwischen lagen, sorgfältig in Lappen eingeschlagen, einige kleinere und zartere Gegenstände, die ich mit Freude enthüllte und besichtigte, und unter ihnen war auch das krumme Messer, das ich sogleich öffnete und prüfte. Blank funkelte mir sein neuer Stahl entgegen, hart und straff sprang

trinkets

mit … nachgeschliffen resharpened with the whetstone
eines … wert worthy of an elegy

blade
wooden handle

dem … entronnen escaped the prison of a bread-and-butter job

dignity

package / steamboat
pier

spring / metal fittings on the handle / accessory

die Rückenfeder°, und die vernickelten Heftbeschläge° blitzten. Damals war es ein kleines Anhängsel°, ein winziges Nebenstück meiner Einrichtung. Ich dachte nicht, daß einmal dies Messer von all meinem schönen jungen Besitz, von Haus und Garten, Familie und Heimat das einzige kleine Stück sein würde, das noch mir gehörte und bei mir blieb.

[7] Es dauerte nicht lange, so schnitt ich mir mit dem neuen Messer beinahe einen Finger ab, die Narbe° trage ich noch heute. Und inzwischen war der Garten angelegt und bepflanzt, das Haus gebaut, und viele Jahre lang war das Messer mein Begleiter, sooft ich in den Garten ging. Ich habe mit ihm meine Obstbäume beschnitten und Sonnenblumen und Dahlien zu Sträußen abgeschnitten, habe Peitschenstiele und Pfeilbögen° für meine kleinen Söhne damit geschnitzt. Täglich, mit Ausnahme kurzer Reisezeiten, brachte ich einige Stunden im Garten zu, den ich alle die Jahre hindurch selbst besorgt habe, mit Graben und Pflanzen, Säen und Begießen, Düngen und Ernten, und in den kühleren Jahreszeiten hatte ich stets ein Feuerlein in einer Gartenecke brennen, wo Unkraut und alte Wurzelstöcke und Abfall jeder Art zu Asche gebrannt wurden. Meine Söhne waren gern dabei, steckten ihre Gerten und Schilfrohre° ins Feuer, brieten Kartoffeln und Kastanien darin. Dabei fiel mir einmal das Messer ins Feuer, und am Heft entstand ein kleiner Brandfleck, den es von da an trug und an dem ich es aus allen Messern der Welt heraus erkannt hätte.

[…]

[8] […] Es kamen Zeiten, wo ich mein Messer wenig mehr brauchte, es war allzuviel andere Arbeit zu tun. Und es kam so allmählich alles ins Rutschen°, zuerst das Deutsche Reich und sein Krieg, dem vom Auslande her zuzuschauen damals eine Qual° ohnegleichen war. Und als der Krieg zu Ende war, da war auch in meinem Leben allerlei gewendet und verändert, ich besaß keinen Garten und kein Haus mehr und mußte mich auch von der Familie trennen und mußte Jahre der Einsamkeit und Besinnung° antreten und durchkosten. Da saß ich oft, in den langen, langen Wintern der Verbannung, im kalten Zimmer vor dem kleinen Kamin, verbrannte Briefe und Zeitungen und schnitzelte mit meinem alten Messer am Holz herum, ehe ich es ins Feuer steckte, und sah in die Flammen, und sah mein Leben und meinen Ehrgeiz und mein Wissen und mein ganzes Ich allmählich verbrennen und zu reinlicher Asche werden. Und wenn auch das Ich, der Ehrgeiz, die Eitelkeit und der ganze trübe Lebenszauber mich nachher wieder und wieder einspann°, so war doch eine Zuflucht gefunden, eine Wahrheit erkannt, und die Heimat, die zu gründen und zu besitzen mir im Leben nie hatte glücken wollen, begann mir im eigenen Herzen zu wachsen.

[9] Wenn ich nun das Gartenmesser, das mich diesen langen Weg begleitet hat, so sehr vermisse, so ist das weder heroisch noch weise. Ich will aber heute nun einmal weder heroisch noch weise sein, dazu ist morgen wieder Zeit.

Margin glossary notes:

scar

whip handles and archery bows

switches and reeds

Siehe **Kulturtipps**: Deutsches Reich

kam ins Rutschen *began to crumble / agony*

loneliness and reflection

der Ehrgeiz … einspann *ambition, vanity, and the whole dull allure of living captivated me afterwards again and again*

Kulturtipps

Bodensee

Meersburg am Bodensee

Der Bodensee liegt im südlichen Baden-Württemberg und Bayern und ist der größte See Deutschlands. Die Grenzen zwischen Deutschland, Österreich und der Schweiz verlaufen durch den See, damit gehören Anteile des Sees zu den drei Ländern. Der Bodensee hat große Bedeutung für die Wasserversorgung des Stuttgarter Ballungsraums (*agglomeration*), als wichtiger Transportweg und als beliebtes Touristenziel.

Deutsches Reich

Das Deutsche Kaiserreich wurde 1871 gegründet und war somit die politische Form Deutschlands, die Hesse die ersten 30 Jahre seines Lebens kannte. Das Reich war eine konstitutionelle Monarchie, die nach dem Ersten Weltkrieg mit der Abdankung Kaiser Wilhelms II. 1918 endete. Darauf folgte die Weimarer Republik.

 Neue Vokabeln

Nomen

der Abfall, ⁻e   *waste, trash*

der Abschied, -e   *departure, parting*

der Erfolg, -e   *success*

das Grundstück, -e   *plot of land*

der Schmerz, -en   *pain, grief*

der Verlust, -e   *loss*

die Waffe, -n   *weapon*

der Wechsel, -   *change*

die Zuflucht, -en   *refuge, sanctuary*

Verben

ab·schneiden, schnitt ab, abgeschnitten   *to cut off*

begleiten   *to accompany*

besichtigen   *to visit, view, inspect*

besitzen, besaß, besessen   *to own, have*

betrachten   *to look at, consider*

betrüben   *to sadden*

erkennen, erkannte, erkannt   *to recognize, admit*

stecken   *to put; be located*

(sich) trennen (von)   *to separate (oneself) (from)*

verbrauchen   *to use, consume*

verbrennen, verbrannte, verbrannt   *to burn*

verlieren, verlor, verloren   *to lose*

vermissen   *to miss*

Adjektive und Adverbien

blank   *shiny*

gewöhnlich   *usual*

glatt   *smooth*

krumm   *bent*

mehrmals   *repeatedly*

verantwortlich   *responsible*

Ausdrücke

Es war mir lieb.   *It was dear to me.*

in jeder Hinsicht   *in every respect*

weder ... noch   *neither ... nor*

8-30 **Textarbeit: Zusammenfassung.** Jeder Satz fasst einen Absatz im Lesetext zusammen. Bringen Sie die Zusammenfassung in die richtige Reihenfolge.

___3___ Im Gegensatz zu anderen aufbewahrten Dingen hat er das Messer fast täglich benutzt.

___4___ Das Messer war kein einfaches, gewöhnliches Messer, sondern hatte eine altbewährte Form.

___1___ Der Verlust seines Taschenmessers hat ihn traurig gemacht.

___9___ Er erlaubt sich heute die Zeit, das Taschenmesser zu vermissen.

___6___ Das Messer kam in einem Paket mit anderen Gartenwerkzeugen an.

___5___ Er erhielt das Messer während einer sehr glücklichen Zeit seines Lebens.

___2___ Er hängt an seinem Besitz mit großer Anhänglichkeit fest.

___8___ Als er keinen Garten, kein Haus und keine Familie mehr hatte, schnitzte er mit dem Messer Holz.

___7___ Das Messer hat er fast täglich im Garten benutzt.

8-31 **Textarbeit: Fragen zum Inhalt und zur Interpretation.**
Beantworten Sie die Fragen.

Answers for 8-31. **1.** Es hat ihn betrübt. **2.** Er trennt sich nur schwer von seinem Besitz. **3.** Das Messer hat er beinahe täglich benutzt. **4.** Aus vielen Gründen: Er war frisch verheiratet, hatte Erfolg in seinem Beruf, hatte ein Ruderboot, erwartete sein erstes Kind und baute gerade ein eigenes Haus. **5.** für seine Gartenarbeit; **6.** Er hatte keinen Garten und kein Haus mehr und war nicht mehr bei seiner Familie. **7.** Answers will vary.

1. Wie reagierte er auf den Verlust des Taschenmessers?
2. Wie fühlt er sich, wenn er sich von den Dingen, die er besitzt, trennen muss?
3. Wie unterscheidet sich sein Messer von den anderen Andenken, die er die Jahre hindurch gesammelt hat?
4. Warum war die Zeit, in der er das Messer bekam, eine der glücklichsten seines Lebens?
5. Wozu hat er das Taschenmesser benutzt?
6. Wie hat sich sein Leben nach dem Ersten Weltkrieg verändert?
7. Warum schätzte er das Taschenmesser so sehr?

8-32 **Vokabelarbeit.** Ergänzen Sie die Sätze mit Wörtern aus den *Neuen Vokabeln*. Achten Sie dabei auch auf die Wortform.

1. Hesse ___besaß___ einst ein Grundstück in Gaienhofen am Bodensee.
2. Er hatte damals schon ___Erfolg___ als Schriftsteller.
3. Der Schreibtisch, an dem er hier schrieb, ___begleitete___ ihn auch später zunächst nach Bern und dann nach Montagnola.
4. Das Gartenmesser benutzte er vor allem als Werkzeug und nicht als ___Waffe___.
5. Dieses Messer konnte man am Brandfleck am Holzgriff ___erkennen___.
6. Durch die Jahre hindurch hat er das Messer ___mehrmals___ benutzt.
7. Mit dem Messer hat er Blumen ___abgeschnitten___.
8. Er hatte bestimmt große ___Schmerzen___, als er sich mit dem Messer tief in den Finger schnitt.
9. Das Messer war klein genug, dass er es sich in die Tasche ___stecken___ konnte.
10. Nachdem er sein Messer verloren hatte, ___vermisste___ er es sehr.

8-33 Zur Diskussion. Besprechen Sie die Fragen.

1. Welche Gegenstände in Ihrem Besitz sind Ihnen besonders wichtig oder wertvoll?
2. Haben Sie gerade etwas bei sich, was Sie täglich bei sich haben?
3. Das Messer ist hier mehr als ein Messer. Wofür steht es?
4. Haben Sie jemals etwas Wertvolles oder Wichtiges verloren? Wenn ja, erzählen Sie davon. Was haben Sie dann gemacht? Wie haben Sie sich gefühlt? Haben Sie den Gegenstand je wieder gefunden?
5. Hesse fühlt sich durch und durch als Alemanne. Das zeigt sich aber nicht unbedingt an seiner Schreibweise. Warum schreibt Hesse wohl im Hochdeutschen und nicht in seiner Mundart?
6. Was war bisher die glücklichste Zeit Ihres Lebens? Warum?

 8-34 Am Bodensee. Spekulieren Sie über das Leben am Bodensee. Besprechen Sie die Möglichkeiten und machen Sie zusammen eine Liste aller Aktivitäten, die man am Bodensee wohl machen kann.

8-35 Suchplakat. Sie haben etwas verloren – z. B. einen Ring, Ihr Handy, Ihr Fahrrad, Ihr Portemonnaie, oder etwas anderes. Schreiben Sie ein Suchplakat, das Sie überall aufhängen werden. Beschreiben Sie den Gegenstand, wie und wo Sie ihn wohl verloren haben, und ob Sie auch eine Belohnung geben, wenn jemand ihn zurückgibt.

Beginnen Sie so: *Hilfe! Ich habe mein/e/n _____ verloren! …*

8-36 Das gefundene Taschenmesser. Schreiben Sie für die Literaturseiten der *Stuttgarter Zeitung* eine neue Erinnerung aus der Perspektive Hesses, in der er das geliebte Taschenmesser wieder findet.

Beginnen Sie so: *Ich erinnere mich sehr wohl an den Tag, an dem ich mein verlorenes Taschenmesser wiedergefunden habe. …*

Expansion for 8-33 (5). First, no common written standards exist for any of the dialects. Second, authors who hope to reach a broader market must write in a language that is understood by a wider public. At the same time, in several dialect regions there are *Mundartdichter* and singers who perform in local theaters in their local dialects. Ask students to consider why public performers would write or speak in dialect and/or have students discuss the advantages and disadvantages of using dialect for public productions vs. using standard German.

Teaching suggestions for 8-34. After students have compiled their lists, have them decide which of the activities Hesse might have engaged in during his time at the *Bodensee* and which would have been impossible 100 years ago. If time allows, you could have them visit the official homepage of the Bodensee to verify which of their activities is indeed possible and to discover others they might have missed.

Grammatik

 ## 1. Infinitives without *zu* (Infinitive ohne *zu*)

08-27 to 08-29 The verb infinitive is the basic form of the verb found in vocabulary lists and dictionaries. All German infinitives end in **-en** or, less commonly, **-n**. Infinitives are dependent verb forms, meaning they can only appear in sentences in combination with other verbs. The infinitive commonly appears with the present and simple past tenses of:

- conjugated modal verbs (**können, müssen, dürfen, sollen, wollen, mögen**) (see *Kapitel 1 Grammatik*)

- some verbs of perception (e.g., **hören, sehen, spüren**)
- a few other verbs (e.g., **lassen, gehen, bleiben, helfen, lehren**)

When used with a conjugated verb, the accompanying infinitive appears at the end of a sentence or independent clause.

Ich **darf** keine Kontaktlinsen **tragen.**	*I may not wear contact lenses.*
Wann **gehen** wir **schwimmen?**	*When are we going swimming?*
Meine Oma **hörte** das Kind **weinen.**	*My grandma heard the child crying.*

Note that German infinitives are not always effectively translated using English infinitives (*to* + simple verb). The preposition *to* is sometimes omitted and sometimes the verb form ending in *-ing* is the best equivalent of the German infinitive.

Answers for 8-37 A. 1. Da lernt man badisch kochen. **2.** Ich kann schon Buebespitzli kochen. **3.** Ich will auch badische Schneckensuppe kochen. **4.** Maximal zwölf Personen dürfen am Kurs teilnehmen. **5.** Wir sollen auch einheimische Weine probieren. **6.** Wir helfen auch eine Schwarzwälder Kirschtorte backen. **7.** Der Kurs soll an der Volkshochschule stattfinden. **8.** Wir müssen für den Kurs nicht viel bezahlen.

Answers for 8-37 B. 1. Da lernte man badisch kochen. **2.** Ich konnte schon Buebespitzli kochen. **3.** Ich wollte auch badische Schneckensuppe kochen. **4.** Maximal zwölf Personen durften am Kurs teilnehmen. **6.** Wir halfen auch eine Schwarzwälder Kirschtorte backen. **8.** Wir mussten für den Kurs nicht viel bezahlen.

Information for 8-37 B. Sentences 5 and 7 are omitted because the simple past and present subjunctive forms of *sollen* are identical (*sollte*) and most German speakers would use the perfect in place of the simple past tense to eliminate ambiguity: 5. *Wir haben … probieren sollen.* 7. *Der Kurs hat … stattfinden sollen.* These forms are discussed in the next section.

8-37 Badisch kochen. Sie nehmen an einem Kurs über die badische Küche teil.

A. **Präsens.** Setzen Sie das in Klammern stehende Verb in den Satz ein. Achten Sie dabei auf die Konjugation und die Wortstellung!

Beispiel: Ich nehme an einem Kochkurs teil. (wollen)
> Ich **will** an einem Kochkurs *teilnehmen.*

1. Da kocht man badisch. (lernen)
2. Ich koche schon Buebespitzli (*Baden variation on Swabian* **Schupfnudeln**). (können)
3. Ich koche auch badische Schneckensuppe (*snail soup*). (wollen)
4. Maximal zwölf Personen nehmen am Kurs teil. (dürfen)
5. Wir probieren auch einheimische Weine. (sollen)
6. Wir backen auch eine Schwarzwälder Kirschtorte. (helfen)
7. Der Kurs findet an der Volkshochschule statt. (sollen)
8. Wir bezahlen nicht viel für den Kurs (müssen)

B. **Präteritum.** Sie haben vor kurzem am Kurs teilgenommen und erzählen darüber. Schreiben Sie die neuen Sätze (Nr. 1, 2, 3, 4, 6, 8) aus Teil A ins Präteritum um.

Beispiel: Ich nehme an einem Kochkurs teil. (wollen)
> Ich **wollte** an einem Kochkurs *teilnehmen.*

Double infinitives: Modal verbs in perfect and future tenses
(Der Doppelinfinitiv: Modalverben im Perfekt und Futur)

The perfect tenses of modal verbs use the past participle only when the sentence has no other verb.

Ich **habe** sie immer **gemocht.**	*I have always liked her.*
Wir **haben** es schon immer **gewollt.**	*We have always wanted it.*

When a modal verb appears with another verb in the present perfect tense, a *double infinitive* construction is used. The perfect tense auxiliary **haben** is conjugated and the other two verbs appear in their infinitive forms at the end of the sentence. The simple past tense of modal verbs, which is more concise, is often used instead. The meanings are the same.

Ich **habe** damals **reisen dürfen.**
Ich **durfte** damals **reisen.** } *I was allowed to travel then.*

The future tense is similarly formed using a double infinitive construction when a modal verb is present. Here, the future tense auxiliary **werden** is conjugated and the infinitive forms of the main verb and modal verb appear at the end of the sentence.

Sie **werden** früh **aufstehen müssen.**	*They will have to get up early.*
Ihr **werdet** wohl nicht **mitkommen können.**	*You probably won't be able to come.*

The *double infinitive* construction is also used with the perfect and future tenses of the verbs that behave like modal verbs.

Der Lehrer **hat** ihn **spielen sehen.**	*The teacher saw him playing.*
Wir **werden** morgen früh **spazieren gehen.**	*We will go walking tomorrow morning.*

When double infinitive constructions appear in a dependent clause, the conjugated auxiliary does not appear at the end of the clause as one might expect, but rather it *precedes* the two infinitives.

Er hat wohl gewusst, dass er hier keinen Zwiebelkuchen <u>hat</u> **bestellen können.**

Obwohl ich die größere Wohnung <u>habe</u> **mieten wollen,** habe ich die kleinere, billigere genommen.

8-38 Geschäftsreise nach Stuttgart. Sie arbeiten für eine amerikanische Firma mit einer Zweigstelle in Stuttgart.

A. **Futur.** Sie werden nächsten Monat eine Geschäftsreise nach Stuttgart machen. Beantworten Sie die Fragen **im Futur.**

Beispiel: Sehen Sie die VfB Stuttgart° spielen?
  *Nein, ich **werde** die VfB Stuttgart nicht **spielen sehen.***

° *name of professional soccer team in German national league*

1. Wie lange dürfen Sie nach Ihrem Meeting in Stuttgart bleiben?
2. Wollen Sie in die Staatsgalerie Stuttgart oder das Mercedes-Benz-Museum gehen?
3. Was müssen Sie unbedingt kaufen?
4. Was wollen Sie dort essen?
5. Können Sie und Ihre Kollegen auch andere Orte besuchen?

B. Perfekt. Sie sind jetzt von Ihrer Geschäftsreise in Stuttgart zurückgekehrt. Dort haben Sie mit einem Geschäftskollegen in einer Gaststätte gegessen. Beantworten Sie die Fragen zum Restaurantbesuch **im Perfekt**.

Answers for 8-38. (A) 1. Ich werde … bleiben dürfen. **2.** Ich werde … gehen wollen. **3.** Ich werde … kaufen müssen. **4.** Ich werde … essen wollen. **5.** Wir werden … besuchen können. **(B) 1.** Ich habe die Gäste … sprechen hören. **2.** Ich habe … bestellen können. **3.** Ich habe … auf das Essen warten müssen. **4.** Der Kollege hat … probieren dürfen. **5.** Ich habe … essen wollen.

Beispiel: Konnten Sie die Mundart der Stuttgarter verstehen?
> Ich **habe** sie teilweise **verstehen können.**

1. Hörten Sie die anderen Gäste Mundart sprechen?
2. Konnten Sie auf Deutsch bestellen?
3. Wie lange mussten Sie auf das Essen warten?
4. Durfte der Kollege Ihr Gericht probieren?
5. Was wollten Sie nicht essen?

2. Infinitive clauses with *zu* (Infinitivsätze)

08-32 to 08-33

When infinitives are used in combination with verbs other than those described above, the word **zu** must be added to the infinitive and it becomes known as an *infinitive clause*. While the simplest infinitive clause consists of **zu** plus the infinitive, the clause can also include objects and other modifiers, in which case it may be set off from the main clause by a comma.

> Meine Eltern haben aufgehört **zu arbeiten.**
> *My parents have stopped working.*

> Jeder Bürger hat das Recht(,) seine Meinung **zu sagen.**
> *Every citizen has the right to state his opinion.*

If the infinitive is a separable prefix verb, then **zu** is inserted between the prefix and the verb.

> Es ist uns gelungen(,) zwei neue Mitarbeiter **anzustellen.**
> *We succeeded in hiring two new employees.*

*See Grammatik 1: Infinitives without **zu**.*

The verbs that do not require the use of **zu** in main clauses can also be used in infinitive clauses. Here, however, they are infinitives rather than conjugated verbs, and they do require the addition of **zu.**

> Sie hoffen(,) an dem Forschungsprojekt **teilnehmen zu können.**
> *They hope to be able to participate in the research project.*

8-39 Die baden-württembergische Autoindustrie. Ergänzen Sie jeden Satz mit dem passenden Infinitivsatz. Setzen Sie dabei **zu** ein, um den Infinitivsatz zu bilden.

1. Bis 1883 war Gottlieb Daimler damit beschäftigt,
2. 1886 kam Carl Friedrich Benz dazu,
3. 1926 gelang es den zwei Erfindern,
4. Der Verlust seiner Stelle bei Daimler-Benz war für Ferdinand Porsche Anlass,
5. Im Mercedes-Benz-Museum haben Besucher die Möglichkeit,
6. Die Aufgabe des Allgemeinen Deutschen Automobilclubs (ADAC) ist es,
7. Mit mehr als 17 Millionen Mitgliedern behauptet der ADAC,
8. Die Hochschule Pforzheim ist stolz darauf,
9. Motorsportfans freuen sich,

a. viel über die Geschichte des Automobils erfahren.
b. auf dem Hockenheimring Formel-1-Autorennen sehen können.
c. sich zu Daimler-Benz fusionieren.
d. die Interessen deutscher Autofahrer vertreten.
e. Topdesigner für die Autoindustrie ausbilden können.
f. den Benzinmotor entwickeln.
g. der größte Automobilclub Europas sein.
h. das erste Benzinauto in Mannheim vorstellen.
i. seine eigene Firma gründen.

Answer for 8-39. 1. ... den Benzinmotor **zu** entwickeln. **2.** ... das erste Benzinauto in Mannheim vor**zu**stellen. **3.** ... sich zu Daimler-Benz **zu** fusionieren. **4.** ... seine eigene Firma **zu** gründen. **5.** ... viel über die Geschichte des Automobils **zu** erfahren. **6.** ... die Interessen deutscher Autofahrer **zu** vertreten. **7.** ... der größte Automobilclub Europas **zu** sein. **8.** ... Topdesigner für die Autoindustrie ausbilden **zu** können. **9.** ... auf dem Hockenheimring Formel-1-Autorennen sehen **zu** können.

08-34 to 08-35

Infinitive clauses beginning with *(an)statt, außer, ohne, um* (*Infinitivsätze mit [an]statt, außer, ohne, um*)

Four prepositions other than **zu** may be used to begin an infinitive clause: **außer, (an)statt, ohne, um.** These prepositions do not take prepositional objects when they begin an infinitive clause. These clauses sometimes appear at the beginning of a sentence. Unlike in other infinitive clauses with **zu,** the comma is required.

- **außer ... zu** *besides, except for (doing something).*
  Wir konnten nichts tun, **außer** auf den Anruf **zu warten.**
  We couldn't do anything except to wait for the call.

- **(an)statt ... zu** *instead of (doing something).* **Statt** and **anstatt** are interchangeable.
  Anstatt ein Auto **zu mieten,** sind wir mit der Bahn gefahren.
  Instead of renting a car we took the train.

- **ohne ... zu** *without (doing something)*
  Ich bekam eine zweite Tasse Kaffee, **ohne** dafür **bezahlen zu müssen.**
  I got a second cup of coffee without having to pay for it.

- **um ... zu** *in order to (do something)*
  Wir haben uns beeilt, **um** rechtzeitig **anzukommen.**
  We hurried in order to arrive on time.

8-40 Xavier Naidoo. Setzen Sie **anstatt, außer, ohne** oder **um** in die Lücken ein, um die Sätze zur Biografie des Mannheimer Popmusikers Xavier Naidoo zu ergänzen.

1. _____Außer_____ in einem Gospelchor zu singen, war er als Jugendlicher auch in einer Schülerband.

2. Er brach seine Lehre als Koch ab, _____um_____ seiner Musikkarriere nachzugehen.

3. _____Anstatt_____ in Mannheim zu bleiben, nahm er zunächst ein Angebot in den USA an.

4. Er kehrte nach kurzer Zeit nach Mannheim zurück, _____ohne_____ sich in den USA einen Namen gemacht zu haben.

5. Xavier Naidoo wurde Mitglied der Band „Söhne Mannheims", _____ohne_____ seine Solokarriere aufzugeben.

6. _____Um_____ sein erfolgreiches Debüt-Album voranzutreiben, organisierte der Soulsänger größtenteils selbst eine Solotournee.

7. Er verfasste das Lied „Danke", _____um_____ der deutschen Fußballnationalmannschaft für ihre Erfolge bei der WM 2006 zu danken.

8. _____Außer_____ an der Popakademie zu unterrichten, unterstützt er das Projekt auch finanziell.

---

3. Review: Verb tenses (Wiederholung: Zeitformen von Verben)

08-36 to 08-43 German has two one-word tenses: the present tense and the simple past tense.

Present: Wir **besitzen** einen neuen Wagen.
We own a new car.

Unser alter Wagen **steht** noch in der Garage.
Our old car is still in the garage.

Simple past: Wir **verkauften** alle unsere DVDs auf eBay.
We sold all of our DVDs on eBay.

Unsere Sammlung **bestand** hauptsächlich aus ausländischen Filmen.
Our collection consisted mostly of foreign films.

Present tense (Präsens)

The forms of some very common verbs – **sein, haben, werden,** and **wissen** – are irregular in the present tense. See *Kapitel 1 Grammatik* to review their forms.

08-36 to 08-37 The present tense of verbs is formed with the infinitive stem plus the present tense personal endings: **-e, -(e)st, -(e)t, -en, -(e)t, -en.** *Stem-changing verbs* use different stems in the **du-** and **er/sie/es**-forms. There are four possible types of stem changes: **a** to **ä, au** to **äu, e** to **i,** or **e** to **ie.**

Modal verbs have a stem change in their singular forms and omit personal endings in the **ich**- and **er/sie/es**-forms.

	Regular verbs		Stem-changing verbs	Modal verbs
	sparen	*erfinden*	*sehen*	*können*
ich	spare	erfinde	sehe	kann
du	sparst	erfindest	siehst	kannst
er, sie, es	spart	erfindet	sieht	kann
wir	sparen	erfinden	sehen	können
ihr	spart	erfindet	seht	könnt
Sie, sie	sparen	erfinden	sehen	können

Simple past tense (Präteritum)

08-38

The simple past tense is created using the simple past stem plus the simple past personal endings: **-, -st, -, -en, -t, -en.** The form of the simple past stem depends on whether the verb is weak, strong, or mixed. Weak verbs use the infinitive stem plus the suffix **-te**. Strong and mixed verbs have changed stems. Mixed verbs also add **-te**.

For more on the present and simple past tenses, see *Kapitel 1 Grammatik*.

	Weak	Strong	Mixed
	sparen	*verlieren*	*erkennen*
Simple past stem	sparte	verlor	erkannte
ich	sparte	verlor	erkannte
du	spartest	verlorst	erkanntest
er, sie, es	sparte	verlor	erkannte
wir	sparten	verloren	erkannten
ihr	spartet	verlort	erkanntet
Sie, sie	sparten	verloren	erkannten

Present and simple past tenses: Separable-prefix verbs

In both the present and simple past tenses, separable prefixes are separated from the main verb and are placed at the end of the sentence or clause.

heim·kommen	Klaus **kommt** morgen **heim.**	*Klaus is coming home tomorrow.*
	Klaus **kam** gestern **heim.**	*Klaus came home yesterday.*

Answers for 8-41. 1. Der Kosmos-Verlag in Stuttgart **entwickelte** das Spiel „Die Siedler von Catan". **2.** Das Spiel **bekam** nach seiner Erscheinung 1995 diverse Preise. **3.** In diesem Simulationsspiel **bauen** die Spieler Siedlungen **auf** und **sammeln** Punkte. **4.** Heute **kennt** man das Spiel in 20 Sprachen und 40 Ländern. **5.** Mitarbeiter von Ravensburger **erfanden** das Spiel „Scottland Yard". **6.** Wenn ein Spieler den Verbrecher Mister X **fängt, hört** das Spiel **auf**. **7.** Es **gibt** seit 1985 auch eine englischsprachige Version des Spiels. **8.** Der Heidelberger Spielverlag **stellt** viele Kartenspiele **her**. **9.** Der Verlag **brachte** in den letzten Jahren mehrere ausländische Spiele nach Deutschland.

8-41 Made in Baden-Württemberg: Brettspiele (*board games*). In Baden-Württemberg werden viele Spielzeuge hergestellt. Darunter befinden sich auch einige Brettspiele. Ersetzen Sie die fett gedruckten Verben mit den Verben in Klammern. Die Sätze sollen ihre Zeitformen – Präsens oder Präteritum – beibehalten.

1. Der Kosmos-Verlag in Stuttgart **gab** das Spiel „Die Siedler von Catan" (*The Settlers of Catan*) **heraus.** (entwickeln)

2. Das Spiel **erhielt** nach seiner Erscheinung 1995 diverse Preise. (bekommen)

3. In diesem Simulationsspiel **gründen** die Spieler Siedlungen und **gewinnen** Punkte. (aufbauen, sammeln)

4. Heute **spielt** man das Spiel in 20 Sprachen und 40 Ländern. (kennen)

5. Mitarbeiter von Ravensburger **entwarfen** das Spiel „Scottland Yard". (erfinden)

6. Wenn ein Spieler den Verbrecher Mister X **findet, endet** das Spiel. (fangen, aufhören)

7. Es **existiert** seit 1985 auch eine englischsprachige Version des Spiels. (geben)

8. Der Heidelberger Spielverlag **produziert** viele Kartenspiele. (herstellen)

9. Der Verlag **importierte** in den letzten Jahren mehrere ausländische Spiele nach Deutschland. (bringen)

Present perfect tense and past perfect tense (Perfekt und Plusquamperfekt)

08-39 to 08-43

For more information on the present perfect and past perfect tenses, see *Kapitel 2 Grammatik*.

The German perfect tenses are compound tenses. They are formed using an auxiliary verb, either **haben** or **sein,** plus the past participle of the main verb.

Gestern **habe** ich meinen Eltern **geholfen.**	*I helped my parents yesterday.*
Sie **sind** in eine neue Wohnung **gezogen.**	*They moved into a new apartment.*

Auxiliary verbs (Hilfsverben)

Most verbs use **haben** as their auxiliary in the perfect tenses. The verb **sein** is used mainly with intransitive verbs that express a change of location or condition (e.g., **gehen, reisen, aufstehen, einschlafen**). In the present perfect tense, the auxiliary is conjugated in the present tense. In the past perfect tense, the auxiliary is conjugated in the simple past tense.

Ich **habe** viel **gegessen.**	*I ate (have eaten) too much.*
Ich **hatte** viel **gegessen.**	*I had eaten too much.*
Unsere Eltern **sind** früh **angekommen.**	*Our parents (have) arrived early.*
Unsere Eltern **waren** früh **angekommen.**	*Our parents had arrived early.*

Past participles (Partizip II)

The form of a verb's past participle depends on whether the verb is weak, strong, or mixed. In general, past participles are formed as follows:

weak verb   **ge-** + infinitive stem   +   **-(e)t**

strong verb   **ge-** + (irregular) stem   +   **-en**

mixed verb   **ge-** + irregular stem   +   **-t**

However, there are variations on these forms for verbs with prefixes and verbs ending in **-ieren.**

	Weak	**Strong**	**Mixed**
Basic form	prüfen: geprüft	treffen: getroffen	rennen: gerannt
-ieren verbs	interessieren: interessiert	_____	_____
Separable prefix	vor·stellen: vorgestellt	ab·schneiden: abgeschnitten	nach·denken: nachgedacht
Inseparable prefix	begleiten: begleitet	erfinden: erfunden	verbrennen: verbrannt

8-42 Ein Wochenende in Heidelberg. Anna, Lisa und Brian, amerikanische Austauschstudenten an der Universität Freiburg, erzählen von einem Ausflug nach Heidelberg. Ergänzen Sie die Sätze mit den Partizipien der passenden Verben aus der Liste. Benutzen Sie jedes Verb nur einmal.

Heidelberg

besichtigen	genießen	hören	sitzen	verbringen
erzählen	herunterfahren	schlafen	studieren	
gefallen	hinaufsteigen	sein	teilnehmen	

1. Neulich haben wir ein Wochenende in Heidelberg ____verbracht____ .

2. Wir haben zwei Nächte in einer Jugendherberge direkt am Fluss ____geschlafen____ .

3. Zunächst haben wir das berühmte Heidelberger Schloss ____besichtigt____ .

4. Vom Schloss hatten wir schon viele Geschichten ____gehört____ .

5. Das riesige Weinfass und das Apothekenmuseum haben uns besonders ____gefallen____ .

6. Wir waren die steile Treppe zum Schloss ____hinaufgestiegen____ und sind dann mit der Bergbahn ____heruntergefahren____ .

7. Am zweiten Tag haben wir an einer Stadtführung ____teilgenommen____ .

8. Man hat uns ____erzählt____ , dass viele berühmte Personen an der Universität ____studiert____ haben.

9. Wir haben anschließend in einem Straßencafé ____gesessen____ und das schöne Wetter ____genossen____ .

10. Alles in allem ist es ein sehr angenehmes Wochenende ____gewesen____ .

Future tense (Futur I)

For more information on the future tense, see *Kapitel 1 Grammatik*.

The future tense is a compound tense formed by using the present tense of the auxiliary verb **werden** plus the infinitive of the main verb.

> Wegen seines neuen Haarschnitts **wirst** du ihn kaum **erkennen**.
> *Because of his new haircut you will hardly recognize him.*

Note that the forms of the auxiliary **werden** are irregular: **ich werde, du wirst, er/sie/es wird, wir werden, ihr werdet, Sie/sie werden**.

The future tense is also frequently used with **schon** or **wohl** to express probability in the present or future.

> Der Regenschirm **wird wohl** in der Ecke **stehen**.
> *The umbrella is probably in the corner.*

> Die Liebhaber dieser Musik **werden** das Album **schon besitzen**.
> *The fans of this music probably already own the album.*

Teaching suggestion for 8-43. This can be done as an oral activity in class or completed as a written assignment, in which case students could write either both the question and the response or only the response.

8-43 Sie wird wohl aufgeregt sein! Tante Karin ist in Friedrichshafen geboren, aber ist als junges Mädchen in die USA ausgewandert. Sie reist jetzt zum ersten Mal wieder nach Friedrichshafen. Sie sprechen über die Erfahrungen, die die Tante wohl während der Reise machen wird. Stellen und beantworten Sie abwechselnd Fragen.

Beispiel: einen deutschen Pass besitzen
    S1: *Besitzt sie einen deutschen Pass?*
    S2: *Sie wird wohl einen deutschen Pass besitzen.*

Answers for 8-43. Sie wird wohl heute in Friedrichshafen sein. Sie wird ihr altes Haus wohl erkennen. Sie wird wohl über gute Deutschkenntnisse verfügen. Sie wird die Mundart wohl immer noch verstehen können. Sie wird sich wohl an den Bodensee erinnern. Sie wird dort wohl Verwandte haben. Sie wird wohl noch andere Menschen dort kennen. Sie wird sich wohl für die Museen interessieren. Sie wird wohl in Deutschland bleiben wollen.

einen deutschen Pass besitzen
heute in Friedrichshafen sein
ihr altes Haus erkennen
über gute Deutschkenntnisse
    verfügen
die Mundart immer noch verstehen
    können
sich an den Bodensee erinnern
dort Verwandte haben
noch andere Menschen dort kennen
sich für die Museen interessieren
in Deutschland bleiben wollen

Friedrichshafen am Bodensee

4. Expansion: Future perfect tense (Erweiterung: Futur II)

08-45

The future perfect tense, the last of the six verb tenses, is used relatively infrequently in German. It is used to express that an action will have happened, typically within a certain time frame or within a given set of circumstances. The future perfect is a compound tense formed with the present tense of **werden**, the past participle of the main verb, and the infinitive **haben** or **sein**, depending which of the two verbs is the perfect tense auxiliary for the main verb.

> Bis morgen **werde** ich den Brief **geschrieben haben.**
> *I **will have written** the letter by tomorrow.*

> In zwei Wochen **werden** sie schon **umgezogen sein.**
> *In two weeks they **will have** already **moved.***

The future perfect tense is most commonly used to express probability in the past—that is, the idea that something has probably taken place. Probability is most often indicated by **schon, wohl, sicherlich,** or **wahrscheinlich.**

> Die alte Kirche **wird wohl** früher hier **gestanden haben.**
> *The old church probably stood here at one time.*

> Das Paket **wird schon** gestern **angekommen sein.**
> *The package probably arrived yesterday.*

8-44 Das wird Hesse wohl gemacht haben. Sie haben einiges über das Leben Hermann Hesses gelernt. Spekulieren Sie nun über sein Leben zu Beginn des 20. Jahrhunderts. Benutzen Sie das Futur II.

Beispiele: Er wird wohl im Garten gearbeitet haben.
Er wird früh aufgewacht sein.

im Garten arbeiten
mit seinen Kindern spielen
auf dem See rudern
am Seeufer spazieren gehen
früh aufwachen
Konstanz besuchen
am Schreibtisch sitzen und schreiben
ein Luftschiff sehen
ein Automobil kaufen
mit Freunden reisen
Schwarzwälder Kirschtorte essen
?

Answers for 8-44. Er wird mit seinen Kindern gespielt haben. Er wird am Seeufer spazieren gegangen sein. Er wird auf dem See gerudert haben. Er wird Konstanz besucht haben. Er wird am Schreibtisch gesessen und geschrieben haben. Er wird ein Luftschiff gesehen haben. Er wird ein Automobil gekauft haben. Er wird mit Freunden gereist sein. Er wird Schwarzwälder Kirschtorte gegessen haben.

Immer weiter!

8-45 Zur Diskussion. Besprechen Sie die Themen.

1. Wodurch zeichnet sich der Südwesten Deutschlands aus? Besprechen Sie, inwiefern jedes der folgenden Adjektive auf Baden-Württemberg und seine Menschen zutrifft. Geben Sie Gründe an. Fallen Ihnen auch andere Adjektive ein, die passend sind?

traditionell	zukunftsorientiert	umweltfreundlich	innovativ
wohlhabend	vielfältig	stolz	produktiv
weltbekannt	erfolgreich		

2. Laut Umfragen gehören die Baden-Württemberger zu den zufriedensten Menschen Deutschlands. Es behaupten beispielsweise acht von zehn Einwohnern im Ländle, dass man in ihrer Region sehr gut oder gut leben kann. Warum, glauben Sie, gehören sie zu den zufriedensten Bundesbürgern? Denken Sie sich fünf Gründe aus.

8-46 Zum Schreiben: „Wir können alles. Außer Hochdeutsch". Sie arbeiten im Akademischen Austauschbüro der Uni Tübingen. Schreiben sie einen Text für die Webseite der Universität, in dem Sie ausländischen Studierenden, die nach Tübingen kommen wollen, den Werbespruch des Landes erklären.

Beginnen Sie so: *„Wir können alles. Außer Hochdeutsch." So heißt der offizielle Slogan von Baden-Württemberg. ...*

Weitere Themen

Baden-Baden	Heidelberger Schloss
Rolf Disch	Hockenheimring
Donaueschinger Musiktage	Ravensburger AG
Europa-Park Rust	Ritter Sport
Otto Dix	Sea Life Konstanz
Karl Drais	Schauinsland
Die Fantastichen Vier	„Schwarzwaldklinik" (Fernsehserie)
Fernsehturm Stuttgart	Die Söhne Mannheims
Filmakademie Baden-Württemberg	Martin Walser
Gaisburger Marsch	Zeppelin

Nordsee

Ostsee

Nordrhein-Westfalen

Deutschland

Österreich

Schweiz

Liechtenstein

KAPITEL

9

Nordrhein-Westfalen

NIEDERSACHSEN

Mittellandkanal

NIEDERLANDE

Ems

TEUTOBURGER WALD

Münster

Bielefeld

Rhein

NORDRHEIN-WESTFALEN

Gelsenkirchen

Essen

Bottrop

Recklinghausen

Hamm

Oberhausen

Herne

Dortmund

Duisburg

Bochum

Ruhr

Moers

Witten

Hagen

Krefeld

Mühlheim an der Ruhr

Wuppertal

Mönchen-gladbach

Remscheid

⭐ Düsseldorf

SAUERLAND

Köln

Bergisch Gladbach

HESSEN

Aachen

N

Bonn

E I F E L

BELGIEN

RHEINLAND-PFALZ

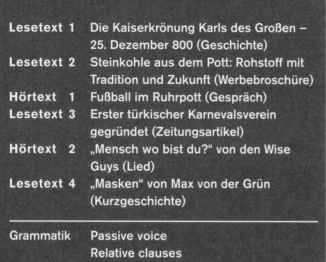

Warm-up. Set the scene by having the students look at the maps. Ask them to describe the geographical position of Nordrhe-
-Westfalen. *Wo liegt Nordrhein-Westfalen innerhalb Deutschlands? An welche anderen Bundesländer und Länder grenzt das
and? Welche Flüsse fließen durch dieses Land? Von welchen Städten und Flüssen in diesem Land haben Sie schon einmal
twas gehört?* Have students look more closely at the region map and describe what the map and photos reveal about the state.

09-01 to 09-02

Einführung

Nordrhein-Westfalen liegt im Westen Deutschlands und ist mit seinen 18 Millionen Einwohnern das bevölkerungsreichste der 16 deutschen Bundesländer. Die Landeshauptstadt Düsseldorf hat 600.000 Einwohner, aber Köln mit einer Million Einwohner ist die größte Stadt des Landes. In Bonn, der ehemaligen Hauptstadt der BRD, hatte von 1949 bis 1990 die Bundesregierung ihren Sitz. 5

Federal Ministries

Heute befinden sich hier noch einige der Bundesministerien°. In Köln und in anderen Städten und Dörfern des Landes wird der Karneval groß gefeiert. Das Land hat zahlreiche hervorragende Theater, Konzerthäuser, über 700 Museen und auch viele Monumente, die bis in die Römerzeit zurückgehen.

Read the *Sprachanalyse: Writing style* in SAM 09-02, which explores stylistics techniques used in the *Einführung*. As you read the *Lesetexte* in this chapter, do the *Sprachanalyse* activities in the SAM (09-05, 09-09, 09-15, 09-16, 09-20, 09-23) to practice identifying connections between writing style and content.

Das Land Nordrhein-Westfalen 10 gibt es erst seit 1947, als man zu der Provinz Westfalen und der Rheinprovinz die Region Lippe hinzufügte. Die britische Besatzungsmacht wollte das wirtschaftlich starke Ruhrgebiet, das 15 sich über Westfalen und die Rheinprovinz erstreckt, nicht aufteilen. Durch die Zusammenlegung wurde zwar ein Bundesland geschaffen, doch betonen die Bürger der drei Regionen heute 20

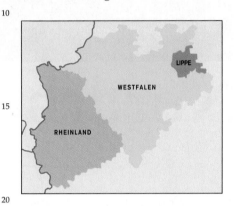

noch ihre unterschiedliche Geschichte und Kultur. Die neue nordrhein-westfälische Identität hat sich in den letzten 60 Jahren deswegen nur langsam und manchmal schwerfällig entwickelt.

Das Ruhrgebiet, auch (Kohlen-)Pott genannt, erstreckt sich um die Städte Bochum, Bottrop, Dortmund, Duisburg, Essen, Gelsenkirchen, Hagen, Hamm, 25 Herne, Mülheim an der Ruhr und Oberhausen, die während der Industrialisierung im 19. und 20. Jahrhundert zusammengewachsen sind. Zurückzuführen ist der Boom dieser Städte auf die Kohle- und Stahlindustrie, die die Wirtschaft dieser Region lange bestimmte. Seit den 1970er-Jahren erlebt das Ruhrgebiet den Rückgang der Schwerindustrie und damit 30 auch eine wirtschaftliche Umstrukturierung. Durch neue Industrie- und Dienstleistungszweige° und Sanierungsprogramme° versucht man dieser Gegend ein neues Gesicht zu geben. Mit 5,1 Millionen Einwohnern und einer Größe von 4.435 Quadratkilometern bleibt das Ruhrgebiet der größte Ballungsraum° Deutschlands. Es gehört zur größeren Metropolregion 35 Rhein-Ruhr, so genannt nach den beiden großen Flüssen, die das Land durchlaufen: der Rhein und die Ruhr. Im Rhein-Ruhr-Raum befinden sich heute mehr als ein Drittel der 100 größten Unternehmen Deutschlands.

Industrie- und Dienstleistungszweige manufacturing and service industries / redevelopment programs / agglomeration

Nordrhein-Westfalen besteht nicht nur aus großen Städten. Im relativ flachen Norden ist viel Landwirtschaft und im südlichen Landesteil sind 40 Hügellandschaften mit ausgedehnten Wäldern zu finden. Durch die Rekultivierung ehemalig industrieller Gebiete entstehen auch neue Gartenanlagen,

recreation areas

Parklandschaften und Erholungsgebiete°.

Possible answers for *Fragen zum Text.* **1.** 18 Millionen; **2.** Erst war es Hauptstadt der BRD und nun ist es nicht mehr Hauptstadt. Es gibt aber noch einige Bundesministerien in Bonn. **3.** aus der Provinz Westfalen, der Rheinprovinz und der Region Lippe; **4.** Eine Gegend mit vielen zusammengewachsenen Städten, die von der Kohle- und Stahlindustrie geprägt ist und die der größte Ballungsraum Deutschlands ist. **5.** wegen des Rückgangs der Schwerindustrie seit den 70er-Jahren; **6.** von den Flüssen Rhein und Ruhr, die das Land durchfließen; **7.** Landwirtschaft, Hügel, Wälder, Naturgebiete

Fragen zum Text

1. Wie viele Menschen leben in Nordrhein-Westfalen?
2. Welche Veränderung hat Bonn in den letzten Jahrzehnten erlebt? Was befindet sich heute noch in der Stadt?
3. Aus welchen Ländern hat man das Bundesland geschaffen?
4. Was ist das Ruhrgebiet?
5. Warum gibt es im Ruhrgebiet eine wirtschaftliche Umstrukturierung?
6. Woher hat die Metropolregion Rhein-Ruhr ihren Namen?
7. Was findet man außerhalb der Großstädte?

DIALEKTTIPP: Kölsch

Hören Sie ein Beispiel dieses Dialekts.

Das Bundesland Nordrhein-Westfalen zeichnet sich durch seine große dialektische Vielfalt aus. Im westfälischen und im lippischen Teil sind niederdeutsche Mundarten vorzufinden. Im rheinischen Gebiet findet man überwiegend fränkische Dialekte. Schauen wir uns eine dieser fränkischen Mundarten – Kölsch – näher an.

Kölsch wird hauptsächlich in und um Köln gesprochen. In der Region genießt es ein hohes Ansehen und selbst Zugezogene° versuchen, diese Mundart zu erlernen. Das Kulturprogramm des Westdeutschen Rundfunks° (WDR) trägt viel zur Pflege und regionalen Verbreitung° der Kölner Mundart bei.

Die Grammatik ist einfach im Vergleich zum Hochdeutschen. In der Aussprache und im Wortschatz gibt es viele Unterschiede. Dazu kommen auch viele Wörter aus dem Niederdeutschen wie *Aap* (Affe), aus dem Französischen wie *Bajasch* [fr. *bagage*] (Gepäck) und aus dem Niederländischen wie *Spruute* (Rosenkohl), was das Verstehen weiter erschwert.

newcomers

West German Broadcasting, a regional public broadcasting agency seated in Cologne / spread

Dialekttipp. Ask students what they learned. *Was für Dialekte findet man in Nordrhein-Westfalen? Wo wird Kölsch gesprochen? Was trägt dazu bei, dass der Dialekt erhalten bleibt? Welche Sprachen haben ihre Spuren im Wortschatz des Kölsch hinterlassen?* After students have completed the activity, write the following *Kölsch* phrases on the board: *Dat jläuv ich nit.* Personen: *Fründ, Buur;* Essen: *Jemöszupp, Appelpannekooche.* Ask students to surmise what they mean. Answers: *Dat jläuv ich nit* = Das glaube ich nicht. *Fründ* = Freund, *Buur* = Bauer. *Jemöszupp* = Gemüsesuppe, *Appelpannekooche* = Apfelpfannkuchen.

Zum Dialekt

Wie sagt man das? Wählen Sie die richtigen Erklärungen der Unterschiede zwischen Kölsch und Hochdeutsch.

Hochdeutsch → Kölsch

f	1.	Guten Morgen, Tag → Jode Morje, Tach
c	2.	ab, geben → aff, gewe
e	3.	Pfeife, Pflanze → Pief, Flanz
g	4.	treten, Traube → tredde, Druve
a	5.	Vögelchen, Tässchen → Fujjelscher, Täßje
i	6.	Schlaf, Lust, tun → Schlof, Loss, donn
d	7.	ich, Milch → isch, Millsch
j	8.	Sprache, ist, ärgern → Sproch, es, ärjere
b	9.	ich ging → ish ben jejange

a. Verkleinerungsform *-sche (r)/-je*
b. Perfekt statt Präteritum
c. *b → f* oder *w*
d. *ch → sch*
e. *pf → p* oder *f*
f. *g → j* oder *ch*
g. *t → d*
h. Monophthonge → Diphthonge
i. *a, u → o*
j. Wortendungen fehlen

Introduction to *Lesetext 1.* Introduce students to this historical topic by asking about their in knowledge of royalty and its role in contemporary society. *Wo findet man heute noch Länder mit Königen und Königinnen? Haben Sie einmal den Namen Karl den Großen oder Charlemagne gehört? Was wissen Sie über ihn?* Have students read the text introduction and share what they learned about him. *Was hat Karl als König der Franken erreicht? Warum ist er im Jahre 800 nach Rom gereist? Was ist in Rom passiert? Warum wurde der Karlspreis nach ihm benannt?*

Lese- und Hörtexte

Lesetext 1

Die Kaiserkrönung Karls des Großen –
25. Dezember 800 (Geschichte)

Siehe **Kulturtipps**:
Fränkisches Reich

Karl der Große

Karl der Große, auch als Charlemagne bekannt, wurde 747 oder 748 in Aachen geboren und starb dort im Jahre 814. Er wurde 768 König des Fränkischen Reiches. Unter seiner Herrschaft wurde Westfalen (und damit auch Lippe, das damals noch nicht existiert hat) Teil des Frankenreichs. Über drei Jahrzehnte gelang es Karl, die Grenzen des Frankenreichs so zu erweitern, dass es zum bedeutendsten europäischen Großreich des Mittelalters wurde. Der Papst, der in Rom unbeliebt war, suchte gegen Ende des 8. Jahrhunderts den Schutz des Frankenkönigs, der daraufhin nach Rom reiste. Während dieses Besuchs im Jahre 800 wurde Karl zum Kaiser des Heiligen Römischen Reiches gekrönt. Mit der Krönung wurde die Tradition des Römischen Reichs wieder aufgenommen und mit dem fränkischen Königtum verbunden.

Schon zu seinen Lebzeiten hat man Karl den Beinamen „den Großen" gegeben. Auch heute noch findet man Spuren von ihm in der Kunst, der Wissenschaft und der Politik. Seine bevorzugte Residenzstadt Aachen vergibt seit 1950 jährlich in Anerkennung° seiner Leistungen den Internationalen Karlspreis, mit dem Personen geehrt werden, die sich um die Einigung Europas verdient gemacht haben, so wie es auch Karl der Große getan hat. Seitdem haben z. B. der britische Ministerpräsident Winston Churchill (1955), der amerikanische Präsident William Jefferson Clinton (2000) und die deutsche Bundeskanzlerin Angela Merkel (2008) diesen Preis erhalten.

Wie es zu der Kaiserkrönung Karls gekommen ist und welche Bedeutung die Herrschaft Karls für die Entwicklung der abendländischen° Kultur hatte, erfahren Sie im folgenden historischen Überblick.

recognition

Western

Map legend:
das Frankenreich (768)
Eroberungen Karls des Großen (768–814)
abhängige Gebiete

Bremen
Aachen • Köln
Trier • Frankfurt
• Paris
Regensburg •
Salzburg
Lyon • Genf
Bordeaux
Venedig
Marseille
Barcelona
• Rom
• Neapel

Vor dem Lesen

1. Welche Aufgaben und Rechte hat ein/e König/in heute? Welche Aufgaben und Rechte hatte ein/e König/in in der Vergangenheit?
2. Lesen Sie gern Romane oder Biografien über wichtige historische Personen? Warum (nicht)?

Beim Lesen

Der Lesetext enthält Informationen über vier wichtige Personen. Machen Sie eine Liste der Namen und schreiben Sie auch auf, wann diese Personen lebten und welchen Beruf sie hatten.

Answers for *Beim Lesen*.
1. Karl der Große (747–814), Kaiser; **2.** Leo III. (ca. 750–816), Papst; **3.** Einhart (780–840), Hofschreiber; **4.** Alkuin (735–804), Gelehrter

Die Kaiserkrönung Karls des Großen – 25. Dezember 800

09-03 to 09-05

Der Frankenkönig Karl wurde am Abend des 1. Weihnachtstags 800 im Petersdom in Rom von Papst Leo III. zum römischen Kaiser des Heiligen Römischen Reiches gekrönt. Damit war er einer der mächtigsten Herrscher seiner Zeit.

Im November 799 war Karl (ca. 747–814) nach Rom aufgebrochen. Der Papst hatte ihn zu Hilfe gerufen, weil er sich gegen die Opposition in der Stadt nicht mehr zur Wehr setzen konnte. Nachdem Karl die Verhältnisse entschärft° und Leo III. (ca. 750–816) durch einen Reinigungseid die Gemüter besänftigt hatte°, besuchten beide einen Weihnachtsgottesdienst im Petersdom. Den anwesenden Bürgern Roms und dem Episkopat° bot sich an diesem heiligen Abend ein Schauspiel von historischer Dimension.

Siehe **Kulturtipps:** Weihnachtsfeiertage

defused

durch ... hatte had calmed things down with an oath of innocence / episcopacy (all bishops)

Unverhoffte Krönung zum Kaiser?

Karl habe sich – so sein Hofschreiber° Einhart (ca. 780–840) – vor dem Altar kniend in andächtiger° Haltung befunden, als Papst Leo III. ihm von hinten die Krone des römischen Kaisers auf den Kopf gesetzt habe. Scheinbar war Karl überrascht von der Krönung – so jedenfalls will es sein Biograph uns glauben machen. Vermutlich hat Karl jedoch mit der Kaiserkrone spekuliert, schließlich war der Papst auf weltliche Hilfe angewiesen und die konnte in Europa nur der Frankenkönig garantieren. Kaum hatte er die Krone auf dem Kopf, warf sich der Papst auf die Knie und salbte° dem neuen Kaiser die Füße. Im gleichen Moment begannen die Geistlichen mit der Krönungslitanei° und die anwesenden Bürger Roms mit heftigem Applaus. Mit dieser Zeremonie war aus dem König der Franken ein römischer Kaiser geworden, dessen Machtbereich sich über weite Teile Europas ausbreitete. Das Kerngebiet seines neuen Riesenreiches umfasste jene Länder, die rund 1.150 Jahre später die Europäische Wirtschaftsgemeinschaft gründen sollten: Frankreich, die Benelux-Staaten, Deutschland und Italien.

court scribe

devout

anointed

litany used at the time of coronation

Grundlage für kulturelle Blüte des Frankenreichs

weight measurements

Sofort nach der Krönung führte Karl im Frankenreich eine gemeinsame Währung, eine einheitliche Schrift und gleiche Gewichtsmaße° ein. Er ließ in Aachen Bauwerke errichten, deren heute noch vorhandenen Reste erahnen

deren ... lassen *from whose portions that are still standing one can surmise*

lassen°, wie aus dieser Stadt ein „zweites Rom" werden sollte. Karl war aber nicht nur ein großer Feldherr, Christianisierer und Modernisierer Europas, sondern auch ein Förderer der Wissenschaften. Er sammelte die bedeutend-sten Gelehrten seiner Zeit um sich und beauftragte sie mit der Sammlung des damals bekannten Wissens. Damit schuf er die Grundlage für eine kul-turelle Blüte des Frankenreiches. Diese „Kulturrevolution" war eng verbun-den mit Alkuin (735–804), einem britischen Gelehrten, den Karl schon 781 in Parma getroffen hatte. In der Aachener Hofschule richtete Alkuin eine Bibliothek ein, in der die antiken Autoren zu finden waren. Ihre Werke wur-

Siehe **Kulturtipps**: Karolingische Minuskel

den in der „karolingischen Minuskel" abgeschrieben und archiviert. Auch die Architektur der karolingischen Zeit griff auf die Antike zurück. Die Aachener Pfalzkapelle sollte an die „kleine Hagia Sophia", die Sergios- und Bakchos-Kirche, in Konstantinopel erinnern. Andere Regierungsbauten in

Siehe **Kulturtipps**: Kaiserpfalz

der Aachener Kaiserpfalz waren Kopien von Bauwerken in Rom.

Erbe der Antike ins Mittelalter gerettet

paramount

Diese „karolingische Renaissance" ist von überragender° Bedeutung, denn durch sie wurde das Frankenreich zum Verbindungsglied zwischen der Antike und dem mittelalterlichen Europa. Die „mittelalterliche Moderne" wurde fortan maßgeblich beeinflusst von den Gedanken der antiken Ge-lehrten, von der römischen Architektur der vorchristlichen Zeit oder den religiösen Vorstellungen aus Rom und Konstantinopel.

Indem Karl der Große auf diese Weise das Altertum mit dem Mittelalter verband, stellte er sich selbst in eine Reihe mit den antiken Heroen. Die Ret-tung des antiken Erbes war ein bewusster Vorgang, weil die Gelehrten von einem linearen Zusammenhang in Kultur und Politik ausgingen. Da die eigene Kultur auf der vorherigen aufbaute, war es sinnvoll, so viel wie möglich über die antiken Kulturen zu bewahren. Auch Karl war von der Theorie der „Vier

Theorie ... Reiche *the belief, according to Biblical prophecy, that the world would end after the decline of the fourth world empire* / decline / transfer of rule

Reiche"° überzeugt, nach deren Untergang° das Ende der Welt drohe. Mit der Übertragung der Kaiserwürde durch den Papst an ihn waren das römische Kaisertum und das Römische Reich am Leben erhalten worden. Mit dieser „translatio imperii"° war der Weltenuntergang verhindert. Im Sinne dieser politischen Vorstellung war es auch logisch römische Kultur und Architektur, Rechtsprechung, Literatur und Wissenschaft zu bewahren und teilweise zu

arrived

übernehmen. So gelangte° das Wissen der Antike nach Europa. Alles, was die moderne Welt von heute über die Antike weiß, weiß sie, weil deren kultu-relles Erbe durch die „karolingische Renaissance" vor dem endgültigen Ver-lust gerettet wurde.

Kulturtipps

Fränkisches Reich

Chlodwig I. (466–511) regierte das Fränkische Reich oder Frankenreich und erweiterte es, so dass es sich über Gebiete des heutigen Deutschlands, Belgiens, die Niederlande und Frankreich erstreckte. Unter Karl dem Großen erlangte das Frankenreich seinen kulturellen Höhepunkt. Als Franken bezeichnen sich heute nur noch die Bewohner der Region Franken, die sich von Südthüringen über Nordbayern bis ins nördliche Baden-Württemberg erstreckt.

Weihnachtsfeiertage

Der 25. Dezember ist der sogenannte erste und der 26. der zweite Weihnachtsfeiertag. In Deutschland, Österreich und der Schweiz sind diese beiden Tage heute gesetzliche Feiertage und fast alle Geschäfte und alle staatlichen Einrichtungen (*government agencies*) sind geschlossen. Am Abend des 24. Dezembers – dem sogenannten Heiligen Abend oder Heiligabend – tauscht man Geschenke aus und das Christkind oder der Weihnachtsmann kommt mit Geschenken.

Karolingische Minuskel

Als karolingische Minuskel bezeichnet man die Schreibart, die unter Karl dem Großen im Frankenreich entwickelt und danach verbreitet wurde. Sie brachte eine Standardisierung der Schreibart und leichtere Lesbarkeit aller Dokumente in Karls Reich. Die karolingische Minuskel sieht man als die Grundlage der heutigen westlichen Schreibschrift.

Kaiserpfalz

Eine Pfalz war im Mittelalter ein vorübergehender (*temporary*) Aufenthaltsort für einen Herrscher. Sie konnte je nach Titel des Herrschers Kaiserpfalz, Königspfalz oder Bischofspfalz sein. Sie bestand meist aus einem Palais, einem Gutshof (*manor*) und einer Kirche. Auf den Pfalzen haben Herrscher kirchliche Feste gefeiert, ihr Land regiert, Audienzen gegeben und oft auch den Winter verbracht. Zwei wichtige Pfalzen für Karl den Großen waren in Aachen, wo er die meiste Zeit verbrachte, und im westfälischen Paderborn.

Der Aachener Dom mit der achteckigen Pfalzkapelle

Neue Vokabeln

Nomen

der/die Geistliche, -n (*adj. noun*) *clergyman, clergywoman*

der Glaube, -ns, (*no pl.*) *faith, belief*

die Grundlage, -n *basis*

die Haltung, -en *posture, attitude*

die Hilfe, -n *help*

der Kaiser, -/die Kaiserin, -nen *emperor/empress*

die Währung, -en *currency*

Verben

auf·brechen (bricht auf), brach auf, ist aufgebrochen *to set out (for a destination), to leave (a place)*

sich aus·breiten *to extend, spread out*

beauftragen mit *to charge with (a task)*

retten *to save, rescue*

umfassen *to include, encompass*

zurück·greifen auf (+ *acc.*), griff zurück, zurückgegriffen *to draw on, go back to*

Adjektive und Adverbien

angewiesen auf (+ *acc.*) *dependent on*

anwesend *present*

heilig *holy*

maßgeblich *significantly*

sinnvoll *sensible, meaningful*

Ausdrücke

sich zur Wehr setzen *to defend oneself*

9-1 Textarbeit: Wer macht was? Ordnen Sie die Sätze den passenden Personen oder der Gruppe zu.

_g_ 1. Gelehrte aus aller Welt

_a, b_ 2. Papst Leo III.

_e, h, i_ 3. Karl der Große

_f_ 4. Einhart

_c_ 5. Alkuin

_d_ 6. die Bürger Roms

a. vollzog die Krönung in Rom

b. bat um Hilfe gegen seine Feinde

c. ließ die Werke der Antike in einer Bibliothek aufbewahren

d. waren bei der Krönung im Petersdom anwesend

e. war der Name des Kaisers

f. schrieb über das Leben des Frankenkönigs

g. kamen aus verschiedenen Ländern an den Hof

h. herrschte während einer kulturellen Blütezeit im Frankenreich

i. ist heute bekannt als Retter des Erbes der Antike

Possible answers for 9-2.
1. Er war (angeblich) überrascht. **2.** Karl war der König der Franken. **3.** die Benelux-Staaten, Deutschland Frankreich und Italien; **4.** Er vereinheitlichte Währung, Schrift und die Gewichtsmaße. **5.** Er ließ sie in der karolingischen Minuskel abschreiben. **6.** Die Kaiserkrönung verhinderte den Weltuntergang. **7.** *Answers will vary.*

9-2 Textarbeit: Fragen zum Inhalt. Beantworten Sie die Fragen in Bezug auf den Text.

1. Was war die Reaktion Karls, als ihm der Papst die Krone auf den Kopf setzte?

2. Welchen Titel hatte Karl bis zur Krönung durch den Papst?

3. Welche Gebiete, die heute zur EU gehören, waren in Karls großem Reich?

4. Was machte Karl gleich nach seiner Krönung im Frankenreich?

5. In welcher neuen Form ließ Karl die Werke der Antike übertragen?

6. Was ist nach der Meinung Karls durch seine Krönung zum Kaiser des Heiligen Römischen Reiches verhindert worden?

7. Warum ist die karolingische Renaissance wichtig?

9-3 Vokabelarbeit. Ergänzen Sie die Sätze mit Wörtern aus den *Neuen Vokabeln.* Achten Sie dabei auch auf die Wortform.

1. Mit _____Hilfe_____ von Karl dem Großen gelang es dem Papst, seine Stellung zu behalten.

2. Der Papst musste sich wegen seines unchristlichen Verhaltens gegen seine Kritiker _____zur_____ _____Wehr_____ _____setzen_____.

3. Unter Karl bekam das gesamte Frankenreich dieselbe _____Währung_____, was gut für den Handel und die Wirtschaft war.

4. Karl _____beauftragte_____ Architekten damit, neue Regierungsbauten im Stil der Antike zu bauen.

5. Seine Gelehrten am Hof _____retteten_____ die Kultur der Antike.

6. Das _____riesige_____ Reich Karls des Großen beinhaltete große Teile des heutigen Europas.

7. Die karolingische Renaissance ist die _____Grundlage_____ der „mittelalterlichen Moderne."

8. Ein anderer bekannter deutscher Herrscher, der von 1871 bis 1888 den Titel _____Kaiser_____ führte, war Wilhelm I.

9-4 Zur Diskussion. Besprechen Sie die Fragen.

1. Hat Karl Ihrer Meinung nach den Beinamen „den Großen" verdient? Warum (nicht)?

2. Was meinen Sie: Welchen Effekt wollten Architekten erreichen, die Karls Regierungsgebäude im Stil der Antike bauen ließen?

3. Inwiefern war das Leben zu Zeiten Karls des Großen anders als heute?

9-5 Veränderungen im Leben. Machen Sie eine Liste mit allen im Lesetext erwähnten Innovationen, die während der Herrschaft Karls eingeführt wurden. Dann besprechen Sie, warum jede bedeutend war. Zum Schluss entscheiden und erklären Sie, welche Innovation damals wohl am wichtigsten war.

9-6 Am Hofe von Karl dem Großen. Sie und ein/e Mitstudent/in lernen einander am Hof Karls kennen, denn Karl hat Sie beide wegen Ihrer hervorragenden Talente an seinen Hof eingeladen! Besprechen Sie, welche Talente Sie haben, welchen Auftrag Sie für Karl ausführen und was Sie am Hof Karls tagtäglich tun.

9-7 Internationaler Preis für Politik. Sie sind Reporter für ein bekanntes Politikmagazin, das jedes Jahr einen Preis an eine hervorragende politische Persönlichkeit vergibt. Nominieren Sie einen Politiker/eine Politikerin und erklären Sie, warum er/sie diesen Preis verdient hat.

Ansicht nach die sichersten Energiequellen? Welche halten Sie für besonders gefährlich? Then ask students what they learned from the text introduction. *Was ist das Ruhrgebiet? Was bestimmte hier die Industrie für über 100 Jahre? Welche Rolle spielt der Bergbau heute in der Industrie der Region? Was meinen Sie: Aus welchen Gründen wohl will die Bundesregierung die Subventionen für Steinkohlenbergbau beenden?*

Lesetext 2

Steinkohle aus dem Pott: Rohstoff mit Tradition und Zukunft (Werbebroschüre)

Das Ruhrgebiet ist eine Unterregion von Nordrhein-Westfalen, deren Grenzen sich nicht genau definieren lassen. Wenn man durch das Ruhrgebiet fährt, bekommt man das Gefühl sich in einer endlosen Stadt zu befinden. Tatsächlich ist das Gebiet jedoch eine Ansammlung von zusammengewachsenen Städten, die mit 1.167 Einwohnern pro km² die bevölkerungsdichteste Gegend von ganz Deutschland ist.

industrial plants where solid carbon fuel is distilled from coal / mines

Vom 19. Jahrhundert bis in die Mitte des 20. Jahrhunderts bestimmten der Bergbau und Kokereien° hier die Industrie. Einst gab es rund 300 Zechen° im Ruhrgebiet. Bald sollen nur noch drei Bergwerke und eine Kokerei in Nordrhein-Westfalen in Betrieb sein, und auch deren Zukunft ist nicht klar. Es ist nämlich momentan geplant, bis 2018 die öffentlichen Subventionen für Steinkohlenbergbau° zu beenden.

coal mining

advantages

Die folgende Werbebroschüre über die Steinkohle aus dem Ruhrgebiet soll den Leser von den Vorzügen° der Steinkohlenindustrie im Ruhrgebiet überzeugen.

Bergarbeiter bei der Arbeit unter Tage

Vor dem Lesen

1. Wofür braucht man Kohle?
2. Der Text ist eine Werbebroschüre. Was ist der Zweck einer solchen Broschüre?

Beim Lesen

Answers for *Beim Lesen*. Kohle (Steinkohle), Erdöl, Erdgas, erneuerbare Energien, Atomenergie

Finden Sie alle im Lesetext genannten Energiequellen.

Kokerei im Ruhrgebiet

Steinkohle aus dem Pott:

📖 Rohstoff mit Tradition und Zukunft

09-06 to 09-09

Strom ist die Energiequelle für viele alltägliche Bedürfnisse. Wir benutzen sie z. B. zum Kochen, Fernsehen, bei der Arbeit und für den Transport.
5 Und ohne U-Bahnen und Straßenbahnen wären unsere Städte völlig vom Autoverkehr überlastet. Jedoch erst wenn der Strom ausfällt, merkt man, dass ohne ihn nichts geht. Ohne
10 Strom gibt es Chaos. Man denke nur an die katastrophalen Stromausfälle im Hochsommer 2010 in vielen Städten der USA wie z. B. Washington, D. C. Die Folgen waren Ausfall
15 von Klimaanlagen und der Zusammenbruch[a] des Verkehrs. Es entstanden lebensgefährdende[b] Situationen und natürlich enorme Verluste für die Wirtschaft.

20 Je abhängiger das moderne Leben von zuverlässigen Energieressourcen wird, desto wichtiger wird die Sicherheit dieser Quellen. Deutschland importiert fast 100 Prozent seines
25 nötigen Erdöls und 85 Prozent des Erdgases. Der Import dieser Rohstoffe ist bedenklich, da die verfügbaren Vorräte in Krisengebieten wie dem Nahosten und Russland liegen. Durch
30 die Einfuhr dieser Rohstoffe verliert Deutschland seine wirtschaftliche

Unabhängigkeit und kann von politisch instabilen Ländern abhängig werden.
35 Außerdem werden die weltweiten Ölvorräte wahrscheinlich in ca. 40 Jahren, die Vorräte von Gas in etwa 65 Jahren erschöpft sein. Steinkohle bietet dagegen eine zuverlässige und
40 heimische Versorgungsoption[c].

Natürlich müssen auch ökologische Aspekte beachtet werden. Deswegen ist man dabei, erneuerbare Energien zu entwickeln. Das
45 Potential dieser Energieträger ist aber noch nicht voll erschlossen. Diese zum Teil noch ungeprüften Versuchsgebiete[d] müssen von der Bundesregierung noch über viele
50 Jahre stark subventioniert werden. So wird man erst in Zukunft diese noch sehr kostspieligen und experimentellen Methoden der Energiegewinnung voll nutzen können.

55 Atomenergie liefert gegenwärtig ca. 25 Prozent des deutschen Stroms. Doch hat diese saubere Quelle den Nachteil von potentiellen horrenden Katastrophen wie Tschernobyl
60 und Three Mile Island. Außerdem ist die Lagerung des Atommülls problematisch. Das voraussichtliche

Ende der Kernenergie* fordert zudem, dass wir für die Stromversor-
65 gung Quellen mit Zukunft benutzen.

Kohle ist ein Energieträger mit Tradition. Über Jahrhunderte hat sie sich als sichere und zuverlässige Energiequelle bewährt. Im Jahre 1800 gab
70 es 229 Bergwerke im Ruhrgebiet. Die hier abgebaute Kohle diente als heimischer Energielieferant für Haushalte und Industrie. Gegenwärtig liegt noch die Hälfte der gesamten
75 Steinkohlevorräte der EU in Deutschland. Die RAG Deutsche Steinkohle[e] zählt heute immerhin 24.000 Mitarbeiter und fördert 12,6 Millionen Tonnen Kohle in ihren Bergwerken.

80 Natürlich müssen Umweltschutz und Klimaziele weiterhin im Vordergrund stehen. Fortschritte beim Klimaschutz verdanken wir modernen Kohlekraftwerken[f] mit ihren emissionsarmen,
85 effizienten Verbrennungsanlagen. Statistisch und praktisch gesehen, verursacht Kohle aus dem Ruhrgebiet weltweit nur 0,3 Prozent der CO_2-Emissionen. China ist das Land,
90 welches den größten Prozentsatz von CO_2-Emissionen verursacht. Die USA liegt auf Platz zwei. Gemeinsam

---

[a]collapse [b]life-threatening [c]supply option [d]experimental areas [e]RAG Deutsche Steinkohle company in charge of all German coal mining activities [f]coal-burning power plants

*Siehe **Kulturtipps**: Das Ende der Kernenergie

sind diese beiden Länder für fast die Hälfte der weltweiten CO_2-Emissionen verantwortlich. Ganz Deutschland verursacht nur 2,76 Prozent der CO_2-Emissionen.

Der Strombedarf[g] wird in Deutschland auch weiterhin zunehmen. Die Verfügbarkeit von Kohle hierzulande, zusammen mit den neuentwickelten emissionsarmen Technologien, lässt

nur den einzigen logischen Schluss zu: Modern verarbeitete deutsche Steinkohle ist auf jeder Ebene eine tragbare, zukunftsfähige[h] und notwendige Energiequelle.

[g] *demand for electricity*   [h] *sustainable*

Kulturtipps

Das Ende der Kernenergie

Die Nutzung von Kernkraftwerken ist in Deutschland ein häufig diskutiertes und sehr umstrittenes Thema. Mehr als die Hälfte der Deutschen ist gegen die Nutzung von Kernkraft für Energieversorgung und weist auf Unfälle wie Tschernobyl (1986) und Fukushima Daiichi (2011) hin. Seit 1961 wurden hier 37 Kernkraftwerke gebaut. Im Jahre 2002 hat die Bundesregierung beschlossen und 2011 erneut bekräftigt, bis 2022 nach und nach auf Kernkraft zu verzichten und die noch existierenden 9 Kernkraftwerke zu schließen.

 ## Neue Vokabeln

Nomen

der Ausfall, ⸚e   *failure, loss*

das Bedürfnis, -se   *need*

die Ebene, -n   *level, plane*

die Kernkraft   *nuclear power*

der Klimaschutz   *climate protection*

die Kohle, -n   *coal*

der Nachteil, -e   *disadvantage*

die Quelle, -n   *source*

der Rohstoff, -e   *raw material*

die Unabhängigkeit   *independence, autonomy*

der Vorrat, ⸚e   *supply*

Verben

beachten   *to observe, pay attention to*

erfordern   *to require, demand*

verdanken (+ dat.)   *to owe thanks to*

verursachen   *to cause*

zu·lassen (lässt zu), ließ zu, zugelassen   *to allow, permit*

zu·nehmen (nimmt zu), nahm zu, zugenommen   *to increase*

Adjektive und Adverbien

bedenklich   *concerning, alarming*

immerhin   *after all*

verfügbar   *available*

zuverlässig   *reliable*

9-8 Textarbeit: Was passt zusammen? Wie kann man es anders sagen?
Ordnen Sie die Erklärungen den Sätzen aus dem Text zu.

___d___ 1. Ohne Strom gibt es Chaos.

___c___ 2. Durch die Einfuhr dieser Rohstoffe verliert Deutschland seine wirtschaftliche Unabhängigkeit und kann von politisch instabilen Ländern abhängig werden.

___a___ 3. Steinkohle bietet dagegen eine zuverlässige und heimische Versorgungsoption.

___e___ 4. Fortschritte beim Klimaschutz verdanken wir modernen Kohlekraftwerken mit ihren emissionsarmen, effizienten Verbrennungsanlagen.

___b___ 5. Das voraussichtliche Ende der Kernenergie fordert zudem, dass wir für die Stromversorgung Quellen mit Zukunft benutzen.

a. In Deutschland gibt es genug Kohlevorräte für lange Zeit.

b. Wenn es keine Atomkraft mehr gibt, dann brauchen wir Kohle.

c. Öl und Erdgas werden aus Regionen importiert, in denen es potentiell Unruhen und Kriege gibt.

d. Wir brauchen Elektrizität für unser hoch technologisiertes Leben.

e. Steinkohle ist eine umweltfreundliche Energiequelle.

9-9 Textarbeit: Kohle als Rohstoff der Zukunft. Beenden Sie die Sätze so, dass sie die Standpunkte wiedergeben, die im Lesetext vertreten sind.

1. Öffentliche Verkehrsmittel brauchen auch …
2. Deutschland ist seit vielen Jahren abhängig von …
3. Anders als Erdöl und Erdgas ist Kohle …
4. Erneuerbare Energiequellen sind aber …
5. Kernkraftwerke liefern viel Strom, aber …
6. Moderne Kohlekraftwerke …
7. Steinkohle ist somit …

Possible answers for 9-9.
1. Strom; **2.** zuverlässigen Energieressourcen/dem Import von Erdöl und Erdgas; **3.** eine heimische Versorgungsoption; **4.** Versuchsgebiete/stark subventioniert; **5.** Katastrophen können entstehen/eine Mehrheit der Deutschen ist dagegen; **6.** sind emissionsarm und effizient/ verursachen sehr geringe CO_2-Emissionen; **7.** eine notwendige Energiequelle

9-10 Vokabelarbeit. Ergänzen Sie die Sätze mit Wörtern aus den *Neuen Vokabeln.* Achten Sie dabei auch auf die Wortform.

1. Gas, Öl, Wind und Sonne sind mögliche ___Quellen___ für Energie.

2. Windenergie ___erfordert___ große Windgeneratoren, die viele Vögel gefährden.

3. Die Nutzung von Sonnenenergie hat in vielen Ländern in den letzten Jahren stark ___zugenommen___.

4. Der ___Vorrat___ an natürlichen Stoffen wie Kohle wird eines Tages verbraucht sein.

5. Der Sonne und dem Wind ___verdanken___ wir saubere Energie.

6. Die Diskussionen um den ___Klimaschutz___ sind weltweit von großer Wichtigkeit.

7. Viele Länder wollen ihre ___Unabhängigkeit___ behalten und ziehen deshalb eigene Energiequellen vor.

8. Anders als Deutschland hat Frankreich viele Kernkraftwerke und ___lässt___ auch weiterhin ___zu___, dass noch mehr gebaut werden.

9-11 Tatsachen und Meinungen. Im Lesetext gibt es Tatsachen über Kohle und Energieverbrauch, aber auch Meinungen, die den Leser beeinflussen sollen. Finden Sie jeweils zwei Sätze im Lesetext, die eine Meinung ausdrücken, und zwei, die eine Tatsache wiedergeben. Diskutieren Sie dann, ob diese Argumente Sie überzeugen.

Teaching suggestions for 9-12 (1). Direct students to think about the purpose of the *Werbebroschüre* in the context they learned of in the text introduction. If students don't pick up on the contradiction, point out that while the author dismisses renewable energies as sources that need hefty government subsidies to be viable, the coal industry has depended on government subsidies since the 1960s.

9-12 Zur Diskussion. Besprechen Sie die Fragen.

1. Welche Argumente bietet die Werbebroschüre für die Nutzung von Steinkohle? Welche Argumente gegen die Nutzung von Steinkohle werden nicht erwähnt? Was will der Autor wohl mit dieser Werbebroschüre erreichen?
2. Halten Sie es für problematisch, dass Deutschland und Europa immer abhängiger von Energieimporten werden? Warum (nicht)?
3. Halten Sie Kohle für eine Energiequelle der Zukunft? Warum (nicht)?
4. Verhalten Sie sich umweltfreundlich? Wenn ja, wie machen Sie das?

9-13 Umweltschutz beginnt zu Hause. Sie wollen in Ihrer Wohngemeinschaft aktiv am Umweltschutz teilnehmen. Besprechen Sie, was man zu Hause machen kann, um umweltfreundlich zu leben. Diskutieren Sie auch, was sie nur ungern tun würden (z. B. kurz duschen, weil Sie gern lange duschen).

Activity 9-14. SAM 09-49 guides students through the process of writing an *Imagebroschüre* in more detail.

09-49

9-14 Werbebroschüre: Energie der Zukunft! Welche Energiequelle halten Sie für die beste? Machen Sie erst eine Liste mit den Vor- und Nachteilen dieser Energiequelle und schreiben Sie dann eine kurze Werbebroschüre, die die Vorteile betont und die Nachteile in den Hintergrund stellt.

Hörtext 1

Fußball im Ruhrpott (Gespräch)

Introduction to *Hörtext 1*. Ask students about their experiences with soccer. *Spielen Sie Fußball? Sehen Sie gern Fußball live oder im Fernsehen? Kennen Sie bekannte Fußballspieler und -vereine? Aus welchem Land kommen sie? In welchen Ländern ist Fußball eine wichtige Sportart? Warum gehen Menschen zu großen Sportveranstaltungen?* Then ask students what they learned from the text introduction. *Woran sieht man, dass gerade im Ruhrgebiet Fußball besonders beliebt ist? Werden Fußballprofispieler in Deutschland gut bezahlt?*

Siehe **Kulturtipps**: Bundesligaskandal

Fußball ist heute der beliebteste deutsche Mannschaftssport. Ungefähr sieben Prozent der Deutschen spielen in einem Verein und Millionen verfolgen wöchentlich die Spiele im Fernsehen und in den Fußballstadien.

Der Deutsche Fußball-Bund wurde im Jahre 1900 gegründet. Besonders beliebt wurde der Sport im Ruhrgebiet, wo es heute mehr Fußballvereinsmitglieder gibt und mehr Menschen jede Woche zu den Spielen gehen als in den anderen Bundesländern. Zu Beginn war Fußball ein Spiel für Schüler aus reichen Familien, die mehr Freizeit hatten. Doch Anfang der 20er-Jahre wurde dieser Sport auch unter Bergarbeitern und deren Söhnen beliebt. Die Ruhrgebietsvereine Schalke 04 und Fortuna Düsseldorf waren 1933 die beiden besten Mannschaften Deutschlands und hatten schon damals viele Fans. Die Schließung von Zechen im Ruhrgebiet seit den 60ern und der Bundesligaskandal 1970/71 führten zum Abstieg vieler Vereine in der Region. Doch heute erfreut sich der Sport wieder weltweit allgemeiner Beliebtheit und Profispieler in Deutschland verdienen viele Millionen Euro pro Jahr.

Im folgenden Gespräch unterhält sich Christian mit seinem Freund Joachim. Christian ist in Dortmund aufgewachsen und sein Freund Joachim ist vor ein paar Jahren von Bremen in das Ruhrgebiet gezogen und kann die Fußballleidenschaft der Dortmunder noch nicht so ganz verstehen. Hören Sie sich das Gespräch an, in dem Christian über diese Tradition spricht und seinen Freund für diese Sportart zu begeistern versucht.

Vor dem Hören

Was verbinden Sie mit dem Begriff Fußball?

Beim Hören

Während des Gesprächs hören Sie folgende Vokabeln und Ausdrücke.

seit eh und je *for a long time*	fand Anklang bei *found favor with*
Anpfiff *starting whistle*	das ist schon Spitze *that is brilliant*
Grubenarbeiter *miner*	

Fußball im Ruhrpott
09-10 to 09-12

Hören Sie sich das Gespräch an und markieren Sie, welche Fußballteams genannt werden.

____ Werder Bremen	_X_ Borussia Dortmund
_X_ FC Bayern München	____ FC Köln
____ Schalke 04	____ Fortuna Düsseldorf
____ Hertha BSC	_X_ Eintracht Frankfurt

Spieler von Borussia Dortmund und Hertha BSC

Kulturtipps

■ Bundesligaskandal

In der Saison 1970–1971 manipulierte eine Reihe von Fußballvereinen insgesamt 18 Spiele. Als die Manipulation aufgedeckt wurde, kam es zu Strafen gegen Spieler und Trainer. 1973 wurde die gesamte Mannschaft des Vereins von FC Schalke 04 zu einer Geldstrafe (*fine*) und Spielsperren (*suspensions*) verurteilt. Viele der Fußballfans gingen vor Ärger nicht mehr zu den Spielen. Erst als Deutschland 1974 Fußballweltmeister wurde, begann das Interesse am Fußball wieder zu wachsen.

9-15 Textarbeit: Wer macht was? Geben Sie an, ob die Aussage aus dem Gespräch auf Christian, Joachim oder auf beide passt.

1. Er will das Spiel zwischen Borussia Dortmund und Werder Bremen im Fernsehen ansehen.
2. Er versteht die Fußballleidenschaft von seinem Freund nicht.

Answers for 9-15. 1. Christian und Joachim 2. Joachim
3. Joachim 4.Christian
5. Christian 6.Christian 7.Christian 8. Joachim 9. Christian
10. Joachim

3. Das Spiel hat noch nicht begonnen, als er ankommt.

4. Sein Urgroßvater war Grubenarbeiter.

5. 1970 haben seine Eltern geheiratet.

6. Sein Onkel hat für den Fußballverein Borussia Dortmund gearbeitet.

7. Er sieht Fußball als menschlichen Sport.

8. Er versteht den Lokalpatriotismus nicht so ganz.

9. Er glaubt, dass es auch in Bremen Dinge gibt, die man nur versteht, wenn man dort lebt.

10. Er verspricht nächste Woche zu einem Spiel mitzugehen.

9-16 Zur Diskussion. Besprechen Sie die Fragen.

1. Sehen Sie sich gern Sport im Fernsehen oder live an? Warum (nicht)?

2. Was für Sport treiben Sie? Welche Sportart würden Sie gern einmal ausprobieren und warum?

3. Warum spielen so viele Menschen gern in einer Mannschaft?

4. Berühmte Sportler verdienen sehr viel Geld. Finden Sie das richtig? Warum (nicht)?

Note for 9-17. Relevant web addresses for Internet research activities can be found in *MyGermanLab* and on the Companion Website.

9-17 Große deutsche Sportler. Berichten Sie von einer bekannten deutschen Sportpersönlichkeit. Wen die Deutschen als groß ansehen, können Sie im Internet recherchieren. Suchen Sie dann Informationen zu einer dieser Personen und berichten Sie über sie.

9-18 Mein Lieblingssport. Sehen Sie gern Sport im Fernsehen? Wenn ja, beschreiben Sie in einer E-Mail an Ihre Freunde, warum Ihnen „Ihre" Sportart so wichtig ist. Oder wenn Sie sich keinen Sport gern ansehen, beschreiben Sie in einer E-Mail an Ihre Freunde, die gern Sport sehen, warum Sie es nicht gern tun.

Introduction to *Lesetext 3*. Ask students what they know about the tradition of Carnival and if they participate in this celebration. *Wissen Sie, woher die Karnevalstradition kommt? Wann ist der Karneval vorbei?*

Lesetext 3

Erster türkischer Karnevalsverein gegründet (Zeitungsartikel)

Der Karneval – an anderen Orten in Deutschland auch als Fastnacht oder Fasching bekannt – ist die traditionelle Zeit der Feiern vor Aschermittwoch. Früher gab der Karneval dem Volk eine letzte Möglichkeit, vor dem Beginn der 40-tägigen Fastenzeit sich irdischen Genüssen° hinzugeben. Heutzutage hat das Fest kaum noch die religiöse Bedeutung wie früher, sondern ist hauptsächlich ein Anlass zum fröhlichen Feiern. Dennoch findet der Karneval hauptsächlich im katholisch geprägten Rheinland und kaum noch – außer in vereinzelten Städten wie Münster und Paderborn – im protestantisch geprägten westfälischen Landesteil statt.

irdischen Genüssen
earthly pleasures

Tanzmariechen in
Uniform

Zu dieser sogenannten „fünften Jahreszeit" verkleidet man sich in Kostümen und nimmt an Bällen und Partys teil. Eine wichtige Rolle spielen dabei die Karnevalsvereine. Sie organisieren die Umzüge und Feiern und wählen ihre Karnevalsprinzen und -prinzessinnen. Die Vereinsmitglieder tragen Narrenkappen° oder sie verkleiden sich in lustigen Kostümen. Für Unterhaltung sorgen Reden, Komödianten und auch die Tanzmariechen, die als Tanzteams in den Vereinsfarben auftreten.

jester's caps

Jecken (*revelers*) beim
Kölner Karneval

Am Rosenmontag° findet man dann gerade in den Karnevalszentren wie Köln, Mainz, Düsseldorf und Aachen die Umzüge. Dort werden Bonbons, auch Kamellen genannt, von den Wagen ins Publikum geworfen. Jeder darf Bützen oder Bützchen austeilen. Diese kleinen Küsse gelten als Ausdruck von Spaß und Freude. Die meisten Schulen und Geschäfte haben an diesem Tag sogar geschlossen, damit alle Bürger mitmachen können.

Shrove Monday

Wie die Migranten, die im Ruhrgebiet leben, ihre eigenen Traditionen in den Karneval einbringen, erfahren Sie in dem folgenden Zeitungsartikel der WDR-Online-Zeitung.

Vor dem Lesen

Das wissen Sie schon über den Karneval. Finden Sie zu jedem Begriff die passende Definition.

Vor dem Lesen. Students will find these terms explained in the text introduction.

___b___ 1. Karnevalsverein

___d___ 2. Karnevalsprinz

___c___ 3. Kamelle

___f___ 4. Bützen

___a___ 5. Funkenmariechen

___e___ 6. Narrenkappe

a. Person, die in einem Kostüm tanzt

b. Gruppe, die Feste und Feiern während der Karnevalszeit organisiert

c. Bonbons, die von den Wagen geworfen werden

d. Person, die beim dem Karnevalsumzug eine Krone trägt

e. Mütze, die eine Person im Karneval trägt

f. kleine Küsse, die man im Karneval bekommt

Beim Lesen

Finden Sie die Namen aller Personen im Artikel und schreiben Sie auf, wer jede Person ist oder welchen Titel sie im Karneval hat.

Answers for *Beim Lesen*.
Aylin – Prinzessin; Aykut Akköse – Vater von Aylin, Vereinsvorsitzender, erster Karnevalsprinz Westfalens; Aytac Arman – Sprecher des Vereins; Brings und Höhner-Musiker

09-13 to 09-16

Erster Türkischer Karnevalsverein gegründet

Türkisch – nicht getürkt°. In Dortmund hat sich der weltweit erste türkische Karnevalsverein gegründet. Der will zeigen, dass die Türken den traditionellen, deutschen Karneval drauf haben°. So richtig mit Bützen, Kamelle und Funkenmariechen.

(colloq.) pretended

***drauf haben** (colloq.) are able to do*

= *Karnevalsverein /
greeting used during Kar-
neval parades and festivities
/ swarm*

Türkische Narrenzunft° – Helau!°

Bonbonregen, aufgeregtes Gewusel°. Kinder mit bunt geschminkten Gesichtern winken, sammeln, rufen. Es ist Kinderkarneval in Dortmund und die kleine Prinzessin Aylin ist Kamelle-schmeißend mittendrin. „Seit unsere Kinder laufen können, laufen sie auch beim Zug mit", erklärt ihr stolzer Vater Aykut Akköse. Seine sechsjährige Tochter sei auch Funken- mariechen im Heimatort Beckum. Und das alles habe nichts mit Integration zu tun, das sei „total normal".

Der Karnevalswagen eines türkischen Vereins

Siehe **Kulturtipps**:
Türkische Migranten

Ungewöhnliche Premiere

Es ist der erste offizielle Auftritt der „1. Türkischen Narrenzunft Dortmund 09 e. V." Ein Verein, den eine Gruppe befreundeter türkischer Migranten gegründet hat. Am Mittwoch wurde ein höchstoffizieller Antrag auf Eintrag in das Vereinsregister gestellt – soweit so deutsch. Und trotzdem, die Welle, die nach der Vereinsgründung über die Gruppe türkischer Karnevalisten hereingebrochen ist, überrascht Sprecher Aytac Arman immer noch. Einla- dungen von deutschen Karnevalsvereinen, Mails aus aller Welt und Dut- zende Presseanfragen. „Warum der ganze Trubel°? Wir machen doch nichts Außergewöhnliches!", betont Arman.

hubbub

Riesiger Medienrummel, sympathischer Auftritt

Irgendwie doch. Denn der türkische Karnevalsverein ist weltweit noch einmalig. Wobei der Vorsitzende Akköse immer wieder betont, dass sie eigentlich kein türkischer Verein seien, sondern türkische Migranten, die einen deutschen Verein gegründet haben. Das sei nicht politisch, nicht religiös – nur Karneval! Jeder kann eintreten, soll eintreten: Ita- liener, Afroamerikaner, Spanier. Ein Karnevalsverein für alle Nationali- täten. Auch viele Deutsche haben über die Internetseite des Vereins schon Interesse bekundet. „Wir wollen niemanden ausgrenzen, wir wollen nur die Hemmschwelle° senken." So dass mehr Menschen mit Migrationshintergrund den deutschen Karneval mitfeiern. Sie seien nicht exklusiv, im Gegensatz: Sie wollen Nachahmer finden. Menschen, die den „Mumm° haben mitzumachen", so Akköse.

inhibition threshold

(colloq.) guts

Ein bisschen Spaß muss sein

Warum entsteht so ein Karnevalsverein in Dortmund und nicht in einer der Frohsinns-Hochburgen wie Düsseldorf oder Köln? Ganz einfach, findet Arman: Die Stadt habe das Potenzial an verschiedenen Kulturen. „Das Ruhrgebiet ist ein Paradebeispiel für gelungene Integration." Sein Ziel: Der ganzen Welt zeigen, dass auch Türken aus dem Ruhrpott den tra- ditionellen Karneval feiern können. Mit oder ohne Alkohol. Auf den Spaß kommt es an.

Stolzer Vereinsnachwuchs

„Ich hab' 'ne Zwiebel auf dem Kopf, ich bin ein Döner …", singt dann auch der erste Vorsitzende in die Mikros. Auch das Vereinswappen ist schön selbstironisch. Ein Dönerspieß mit Tomatenaugen und Karnevalskappe. Die Idee einen eigenen Verein zu gründen, gab es schon lange, ein PR-Gag gab letztendlich den Ausschlag. Im Januar hatte sich in Köln der angeblich „erste türkische Karnevalsverein" medienwirksam° der Öffentlichkeit präsentiert. Das Ganze entpuppte sich° danach als Satire eines Privatsenders°.

Siehe **Kulturtipps**: Döner

45

well-covered by the media
turned out to be /
commercial radio station

Echtheitszertifikat?

Jetzt wird Satire zu Wirklichkeit. Das Motto: Echt türkisch statt getürkt. Doch die Journalisten sind dieses Mal misstrauisch. Clown, Prinz und Pirat da vorne müssen beweisen, dass sie echte Türken sin d. Es folgen Sprachtests, Beteuerungen° und Beweise in Form von Prinzenorden°. Denn Aykut Akköse hatte im vergangenen Jahr schon mal eine karnevalistische Premiere gefeiert. Er war der erste türkische Karnevalsprinz Westfalens. In Beckum hat er Bauchtänzerinnen für traditionelle Karnevalssitzungen engagiert und türkische Pop-Songs unter die immer gleiche Musik der Brings und Höhner gemischt. Für den 33-jährigen Unternehmer ist Karneval Herzensangelegenheit, abschalten und man selbst sein: „Im Karneval setzt man die eigentliche Maske ab, man lebt wie man möchte." Sein zehnjähriger Sohn will heute als mutierte Comic-Schildkröte° leben. Aber irgendwann will er auch mal ein echter Prinz sein, wie der Papa.

50

declarations / medals for the
prince

55

Siehe **Kulturtipps**: Brings und Höhner

Mutant Ninja Turtle

60

Kulturtipps

Türkische Migranten

Beginnend in den 50er-Jahren, als die deutsche Wirtschaft im Aufschwung war, kamen viele ausländische Arbeiter nach Deutschland, um Arbeit zu finden. Sie kamen z. B. aus Italien, Griechenland und später vor allem aus der Türkei. Heute leben knapp zwei Millionen Türken in der Bundesrepublik. Nordrhein-Westfalen ist heute das Bundesland mit dem höchsten Migrantenanteil. Doch die Integration der ausländischen Mitbürger ist immer noch problematisch und man findet noch viele Vorurteile und kulturelle Barrieren.

Döner

Döner oder Dönerkebab ist ein türkisches Gericht, das seit seiner Einführung in Berlin in den 70ern ganz Deutschland erobert hat. Heute ist es einer der beliebtesten Imbisse in Deutschland. Ein Döner besteht aus dünn geschnittenem Fleisch, das man auf Fladenbrot legt. Dazu kann man dann noch Zwiebeln, Tomaten und Salat auf das Brot tun. Die Variationen von Döner sind heute endlos und jede Dönerbude bietet seine eigene Variante an.

Koch beim Schneiden von Dönerfleisch

Brings und Höhner

Dies sind die Namen von zwei Rockgruppen, die Rockmusik für den Karneval machen. Brings, deren Name wie „Bring es!" (*Bring it on!*) klingt, wurde 1991 gegründet. Höhner, die kölsche Aussprache von „Hühner", entstand schon 1972. Beide Gruppen singen hauptsächlich im Kölner Dialekt, dem Kölsch. Die Lieder der beiden Gruppen gehören heute fest zum Karnevalsrepertoire. Darüber hinaus sind sie auch für ihre Nicht-Karnevalslieder in ganz Deutschland bekannt.

Information for *Kulturtipp: Türkische Migranten.* In recent years, the inaccurate and controversial term *Gastarbeiter*, which was used for decades to designate these foreign workers, has been replaced by the word *Migranten*. You might want to give students this information and have them discuss the differences in terminology and then surmise why such a change matters or is perceived as necessary.

 ## Neue Vokabeln

Nomen

der Antrag, ⸚e   *request, application*

die Einladung, -en   *invitation*

die Öffentlichkeit   *public*

der Umzug, ⸚e   *parade*

der/die Vorsitzende, -n (*adj. noun*)   *chairperson*

das Wappen, -   *coat of arms*

die Welle, -n   *wave*

die Wirklichkeit   *reality*

die Zwiebel, -n   *onion*

Verben

ab·schalten   *to cut off, (colloq.) to kick back*

ein·treten (tritt ein), trat ein, ist eingetreten   *to join, enter*

ein·sammeln   *to collect, to gather*

Adjektive und Adverbien

geschminkt   *made up, painted*

misstrauisch   *distrustful, wary*

mittendrin   *in the middle of it*

riesig   *gigantic*

Ausdrücke

Interesse bekunden   *to show interest*

9-19 Textarbeit: Mitmachen! Was machen die Mitglieder des Türkischen Karnevalvereins? Ergänzen Sie die Sätze mit Informationen aus dem Lesetext.

1. Sie werfen _____Kamellen_____.

2. Sie tragen _Karnevalskostüme/Narrenkappen_.

3. Die Tochter von Akköse ist ein _____Funkenmariechen_____.

4. Sie haben keinen türkischen, sondern einen _____deutschen_____ Verein gegründet.

5. Sie wollen einen Verein für alle _____Nationalitäten_____.

6. Der Verein zeigt, dass im Ruhrgebiet die _____Integration_____ der Migranten funktioniert.

7. Der Verein hat natürlich auch einen eigenen _____Schlachtruf/Spruch_____.

8. Bei den Sitzungen spielt man türkische Lieder zu der Musik von _____Brings_____ und _____Höhner_____.

9-20 Textarbeit: Was ist damit gemeint? Der Artikel über den türkischen Karneval ist in sechs Abschnitte eingeteilt. Jeder Abschnitt hat eine Überschrift. Erzählen Sie in Ihren eigenen Worten und in jeweils ein bis zwei Sätzen, was hier berichtet wird.

Beispiel: Türkische Narrenzunft – Helau!

Die Kinder türkischer Eltern nehmen auch am Karneval teil. Das ist nichts Besonderes, sondern das ist für sie selbstverständlich.

1. Ungewöhnliche Premiere

2. Riesiger Medienrummel, sympathischer Auftritt

3. Ein bisschen Spaß muss sein

4. Stolzer Vereinsnachwuchs

5. Echtheitszertifikat?

Possible answers for 9-20.
1. Der erste türkische Narrenverein wurde gegründet. Die Vereinsgründer verstehen den großen Trubel nicht. **2.** Die Gründer halten ihren Verein für einen deutschen Verein für alle Nationalitäten. Sie hoffen, dass mehr solche Vereine entstehen. **3.** Das Ruhrgebiet eignet sich für einen solchen Verein, weil hier so viele Menschen aus verschiedenen Kulturen leben. **4.** Nach einem PR-Gag entschied man, einen wirklichen türkischen Verein zu gründen. **5.** Die Medien waren diesmal misstrauisch. In diesem Verein vermischen sich Aspekte deutscher und türkischer Kultur.

9-21 Vokabelarbeit. Ergänzen Sie die Sätze mit Wörtern aus den *Neuen Vokabeln.* Achten Sie dabei auch auf die Wortform.

1. Der ___Vorsitzende___ des neuen türkischen Karnevalsvereins heißt Aykut Akköse.

2. Bei den Karnevalsumzügen können die Zuschauer die Bonbons ___einsammeln___, die von den Wagen geworfen werden.

3. Die Kinder sind oft bunt ___geschminkt___ und tragen lustige Kostüme.

4. Der Türkische Karnevalsverein möchte, dass Bürger aller Migrationshintergründe in ihn ___eintreten___.

5. Nicht nur Türken, sondern auch viele andere Migranten haben schon ___Interesse___ an dem neuen Verein ___bekundet___.

6. Während der Umzüge können die Zuschauer die ___Wirklichkeit___ für ein paar Stunden vergessen.

7. Die Presse war in diesem Jahr noch etwas ___misstrauisch___ gegenüber den türkischen Organisatoren, da sich dieser Verein letztes Jahr als Scherz herausstellte.

8. Der türkische Karnevalsverein hat jetzt schon Pläne, wie unter der Fahne mit den Tomaten und der ___Zwiebel___ auch nächstes Jahr wieder gefeiert wird.

9-22 Zur Diskussion. Besprechen Sie die Fragen.

1. Feiert man in Ihrem Land Fasching? Wenn ja, was macht man? Welche anderen Feste kennen Sie, die als religiöse Feste begannen und heute damit nicht mehr viel zu tun haben?

2. Verkleiden Sie sich gern? Zu welchen Anlässen? Als was? Was sagt ein Kostüm über die Person aus, die es trägt?

3. Gibt es in Ihrem Land Probleme mit der Integration anderer Nationalitäten? Wenn ja, wie zeigt sich das?

4. Was macht Ihr Heimatland, um Migranten zu integrieren? Was kann man tun, um bei der Integration von Migranten mitzuhelfen?

Follow-up for 9-22 (4).
Glauben Sie, dass Migranten durch Teilnahme an traditionellen Festen in die deutsche Gesellschaft integriert werden können? Sollten die Deutschen versuchen, an den Traditionen der Migranten teilzunehmen?

9-23 Karnevalsbesuch. Es ist wieder Karnevalszeit und Sie freuen sich darauf, weil es dann viele Dinge gibt, die Ihnen Spaß machen. Stellen Sie mit einem Mitstudenten/einer Mitstudentin eine Liste auf. Vergleichen Sie sie dann im Kurs die Resultate.

9-24 Mein Karnevalsverein! Sie wollen jetzt einen Karnevalsverein gründen, der Ihre eigene Kultur mit der deutschen Karnevalskultur verbindet. Um ein offizieller Verein zu sein, müssen Sie einen Vereinsantrag stellen. Ergänzen Sie das Formular.

Vereinsantrag

Name des Vereins: _____ Ansprechpartner: _____

Adresse: _____

Telefon: _____ E-Mail: _____

Bitte ankreuzen. Ist das ein Projekt aus dem Bereich …

_____ „Integration"? _____ „Gesundheit"? _____ „Erziehung"?

Projektbeschreibung (Ihr Spruch, wie Ihr Karnevalswagen aussieht, was für Uniformen Sie tragen, Art der Unterhaltung bei Ihren Karnevalsfeiern usw.)

_____

_____

_____

_____

_____

_____   _____
Ort/Datum   Unterschrift

Bitte bis zum 31. Mai an die Stadtverwaltung, Große Straße 3, 45127 Essen, Fax: 0201-8342-284 senden.

9-25 Weiteres zum Karneval. Recherchieren Sie im Internet über den letzten Karneval in Düsseldorf oder Köln. Suchen Sie Informationen zu Karnevals-vereinen und -umzügen. Sehen Sie sich die Bilder an und beschreiben Sie, was die Menschen bei den Umzügen und dazugehörenden Feierlichkeiten machen und tragen.

Note for 9-25. Relevant web addresses for Internet research activities can be found in *MyGermanLab* and on the Companion Website.

Hörtext 2

„Mensch wo bist du?" von den Wise Guys (Lied)

Die in ganz Deutschland bekannte und beliebte a-cappella-Gruppe, die Wise Guys, existiert seit 1990. Die fünf hauptsächlich auf Deutsch singenden Gründer der Gruppe stammen aus der Stadt Köln. Im Jahre 2008 wurde allerdings der Sänger Clemens Tewinkel von Nils Olfert aus Kiel ersetzt. Da die Gruppe hauptsächlich auf Deutsch singt, beschränken sie ihre Auftritte

überwiegend auf Deutschland, Österreich und die Schweiz. Sie füllen hier Konzerthallen jeder Größe und begeistern Menschen aller Altersgruppen und aus den verschiedenen gesellschaftlichen Schichten.

Doch die populären Sänger aus Köln meinen, dass sie auch eine wichtige Aufgabe als verantwortliche Bürger haben. Sie sehen ihre Heimat, in der es einen hohen Ausländeranteil gibt und die in den letzten Jahrzehnten wirtschaftlich große Verluste erlitt, liebevoll aber auch kritisch. So setzen sie sich sozial ein, indem sie regelmäßig Benefizkonzerte veranstalten und das dabei verdiente Geld jeweils an eine lokale und eine internationale Einrichtung spenden. In ihren Liedern und Aktionen betont die Gruppe immer wieder ihre Verbundenheit mit der Heimatstadt Köln und zeigt gleichzeitig, dass man mit Popularität Menschen der eigenen Region, aber auch darüber hinaus helfen kann und soll.

Das Lied „Mensch wo bist du?" hat die Gruppe als Mottolied für den Deutschen Evangelischen Kirchentag 2009 verfasst. Hören Sie sich das Lied an, in dem es um wichtige Fragen des Lebens geht.

Vor dem Hören

Spekulieren Sie: Welche Themen nennen die Wise Guys wohl in einem Lied, das sie für einen Kirchentag geschrieben haben?

Beim Hören

Hören Sie sich das Lied an und setzen Sie dabei die fehlenden Wörter ein.

Nomen		Andere Wörter	
Alltag	Sinn	andere	fremden
Bild	Spaß	ändern	gerechtem (*fair*)
Kluft (*gap*)	Stimmung	bestimmt	gewöhnt
Reise	Streben (*ambition*)	endlich	machen
Religion	Weg	fassen	völlig
Sachen	Zeit		
Schritt			

Introduction to *Hörtext 2*. Ask students if they know any German music. *Kennen Sie deutsche Musiker oder Musikgruppen? Was für Musik machen diese Gruppen? Woher kennen Sie sie? Kennen Sie deutsche Musiker, die auf Deutsch singen? Sind diese Gruppen oder Personen hier in Amerika bekannt?* Then ask students what they learned from the text introduction. *Woher kommt die Gruppe? Was ist an der Gruppe besonders interessant?*

Mensch wo bist du?

Text & Musik: DÄN 07/08

Refrain: Mensch wo bist du?

Wo geht die _____Reise_____ hin?
Bist du noch auf der Suche nach _____gerechtem_____ Leben?
Mensch wo bist du?
Suchst du noch nach dem _____Sinn_____? 5
Und was _____bestimmt_____ für dich dein Handeln und dein _____Streben_____?

Die _____Kluft_____ wird größer zwischen Arm und Reich,
und offenbar _____gewöhnt_____ man sich dran.
Sind mir die Anderen, wenn's mir gutgeht, _____völlig_____ gleich,
weil ich ja doch nix _____ändern_____ kann? 10
Hab ich Angst vor der anderen _____Religion_____?
Wann wage ich den ersten _____Schritt_____
hin zum _____fremden_____ Nachbarn, neben dem ich wohn',
und nehme _____andere_____ mit?

Refrain: Mensch wo bist du? 15

Jetzt sind wir hier, und die _____Stimmung_____ ist gut,
wir feiern, singen, haben _____Spaß_____.
Wir denken nach, und wir _____fassen_____ neuen Mut.

Sturm im Wasserglas Ist das der Sturm im Wasserglas°?
tempest in a teapot Was passiert, wenn der _____Alltag_____ uns erfasst? 20
Was bleibt von dieser _____Zeit_____ bestehn?
Wir wollen auch, wenn manches _____Bild_____ schon verblasst,
den _____Weg_____ des Suchens weitergehn!

Refrain: Mensch wo bist du?

Man könnte mal, man sollte mal, man müsste eigentlich … 25
viel zu viele nie erledigte _____Sachen_____.
Es ist Zeit, sich _____endlich_____ ein paar Fragen zu stellen
und auf die Suche nach den Antworten zu _____machen_____.

Refrain: Mensch wo bist du?

9-26 Textarbeit: Was bedeutet das? Das Lied greift verschiedene soziale Probleme auf. Welche Liedzeile oder -zeilen passt zu jedem Satz?

1. Die reichen Menschen werden immer reicher während immer mehr Menschen weniger haben.
2. Wir alle müssen uns jetzt mit diesen Fragen befassen.
3. Der einzelne Mensch kann die Situation anderer nicht ändern.
4. Wir müssen auch, wenn es uns gut geht, immer weiter nach Verbesserungen suchen.
5. Fürchte ich mich vor Menschen, die eine andere Religion haben?
6. Wann versuchen wir endlich unsere ausländischen Nachbarn kennenzulernen?

Answers 9-26.
1. Die Kluft wird größer zwischen Arm und Reich. (Z. 7) 2. Es ist Zeit, sich endlich ein paar Fragen zu stellen (Z. 27) 3. weil ich ja doch nix ändern kann (Z. 10) 4. Wir wollen auch, wenn manches Bild schon verblasst, den Weg des Suchens weitergehn! (Z. 22) 5. Hab ich Angst vor der anderen Religion (Z. 11) 6. Wann wage ich den ersten Schritt hin zum fremden Nachbarn, neben dem ich wohn', und nehme andere mit? (Z. 12)

9-27 Textarbeit: Richtig oder falsch? Wenn eine Aussage falsch ist, geben Sie eine richtige Aussage, die auf den Liedtext basiert.

1. Das Lied spricht Menschen aus allen Altersgruppen an.
2. Das Lied stellt viele Fragen.
3. In der zweiten Strophe sagen die Wise Guys, dass sie bei Spaß und Musik neue Hoffnung finden.
4. In der letzten Strophe sagen sie, dass die meisten Fragen schon beantwortet sind.
5. Das Lied ist von Witz und Humor geprägt.
6. Das Lied ist im Kölner Dialekt.

Answers for 9-27.
1. R; 2. R; 3. R; 4. F – Sie sagen, dass wir uns die Fragen endlich stellen müssen. 5. F – Das Lied ist sehr ernst. 6. F – Das Lied ist auf Hochdeutsch.

9-28 Zur Diskussion. Besprechen Sie die Fragen.

1. Das Lied der Wise Guys greift soziale Probleme auf. Welche sind das? Warum sind gerade diese Probleme wichtig für die Gruppe aus dieser Region?
2. Wie können Künstler ihre Verbindung zu einer Region oder einem Land ausdrücken?
3. Glauben Sie, dass Musiker und andere Künstler politisch oder sozial engagiert sein sollen? Warum (nicht)?
4. Glauben Sie, dass Musiker die Meinungen von anderen Menschen beeinflussen können?

9-29 Konzertblog. Stellen Sie sich vor, Sie haben dieses Lied auf dem Kirchentag gehört. Nach Ihrer Heimkehr posten Sie auf der Internetseite der Wise Guys einen Kommentar zu dem Lied. Beschreiben Sie dabei, ob Ihnen das Lied gefällt und ob Sie glauben, dass es Einfluss haben kann.

Introduction to *Lesetext 4.*
Ask students how they feel about
returning to their hometowns
and catching up with old friends.
*Fahren Sie am Wochenende und in
den Ferien nach Hause? Treffen Sie
dort alte Freunde und Bekannte?*
Then ask them what they learned
from the text introduction. *Wo hat
Max von der Grün gelebt? Welche
Themen behandelt er besonders
gern? Woher kam sein Interesse an
der Arbeitswelt wohl?*

Lesetext 4

„Masken" von Max von der Grün (Kurzgeschichte)

Max von der Grün wurde 1926 im bayrischen Bayreuth geboren und starb 2005 im westfälischen Dortmund, wo er vier Jahrzehnte lang gelebt hatte. Während des Zweiten Weltkrieges geriet er in amerikanische Kriegsgefangenschaft und verbrachte drei Jahre in Lagern in den USA. Nach seiner Rückkehr machte er eine Umschulung zum Maurer° und von 1951 bis 1954 arbeitete er im Ruhrgebiet als Hauer°. 1955 begann er seine Tätigkeit als Schriftsteller. In seinen Romanen setzt er sich kritisch mit der industriellen Arbeitswelt und den schlechten Arbeitsbedingungen der Bergleute auseinander. 1961

Max von der Grün

gründete Max von der Grün gemeinsam mit dem Schriftsteller Paul Polte und dem Gewerkschaftler° Walter Köpping die Dortmunder *Gruppe 61.* Das Ziel der Gruppe war es, Schriftsteller, Journalisten und Kritiker zusammenzubringen, um die sozialen Probleme der Arbeiter zu diskutieren und ans Tageslicht zu bringen.

Die Kurzgeschichte „Masken" ist 1980 erschienen. Die Geschichte handelt von dem überraschenden Treffen von zwei alten Freunden und regt den Leser zum Nachdenken über das eigene Leben an.

mason

miner

unionist

Vor dem Lesen

1. Wenn Sie alte Freunde treffen, worüber reden Sie dann? Sind diese Gespräche immer positiv? Erklären Sie.
2. Wann tragen Menschen Masken? Warum trägt man eine Maske?

Answers for *Beim Lesen.*
1. Erich und Renate; **2.** Erich;
3. Erich und Renate; **4.** Erich
und Renate; **5.** Erich und Renate;
6. Erich; **7.** Renate und Erich;
8. Erich; **9.** Renate **10.** Renate
und Erich

Beim Lesen

Passt der Satz zu Erich, Renate oder zu beiden?

1. _____ freut sich über das überraschende Treffen.
2. _____ ist eine ungeduldige Person.
3. _____ ist nicht verheiratet.
4. _____ glaubt, dass die andere Person einen guten Job hat.
5. _____ hat Angst nach so langer Zeit zu fragen, ob man es noch einmal miteinander versuchen soll.
6. _____ raucht.
7. _____ hat Falten im Gesicht.
8. _____ kann wunderbar lachen.
9. _____ weint nach dem Abschied.
10. _____ glaubt, dass die Wahrheit nicht gut genug ist.

„Masken"

Orthography. The story uses orthographical conventions current at the time of its publication.

von Max von der Grün

Sie fielen sich unsanft auf dem Bahnsteig 3a des Kölner Hauptbahnhofes in die Arme und riefen gleichzeitig: Du?! Es war ein heißer Julivormittag und Renate wollte in den D-Zug° nach Amsterdam über Aachen. Erich verließ diesen Zug, der von Hamburg kam. Menschen drängten aus den Wagen auf den Bahnsteig, Menschen vom Bahnsteig in die Wagen, die beiden aber standen in dem Gewühl°, spürten weder Püffe noch Rempeleien° und hörten auch nicht, daß Vorübergehende° sich beschwerten, weil sie ausgerechnet vor den Treppen standen und viele dadurch gezwungen wurden, um sie herumzugehen. Sie hörten auch nicht, daß der Zug nach Aachen abfahrbereit war, und es störte Renate nicht, daß er wenige Sekunden später aus der Halle fuhr.

Die beiden standen stumm, jeder forschte im Gesicht des anderen. Endlich nahm der Mann die Frau am Arm und führte sie die Treppen hinunter, durch die Sperre°, und in einem Café in der Nähe des Doms tranken sie Tee.

Nun erzähle, Renate. Wie geht es dir? Mein Gott, als ich dich so plötzlich sah… du… ich war richtig erschrocken. Es ist so lange her, aber als du auf dem Bahnsteig fast auf mich gefallen bist …

Nein, lachte sie, du auf mich.

Da war es mir, als hätte ich dich gestern zum letzten Male gesehen, so nah warst du mir. Und dabei ist es so lange her …

Ja, sagte sie. Fünfzehn Jahre.

Fünfzehn Jahre? Wie du das so genau weißt. Fünfzehn Jahre, das ist ja eine Ewigkeit. Erzähle, was machst du jetzt? Bist du verheiratet? Hast du Kinder? Wo fährst du hin? …

Langsam, Erich, langsam, du bist noch genauso ungeduldig wie vor fünfzehn Jahren. Nein, verheiratet bin ich nicht, die Arbeit, weißt du. Wenn man es zu etwas bringen will, weißt du, da hat man eben keine Zeit für Männer.

Und was ist das für Arbeit, die dich von den Männern fern hält? Er lachte sie an, aber sie sah aus dem Fenster auf die Tauben. Ich bin jetzt Leiterin eines Textilversandhauses° hier in Köln, du kannst dir denken, daß man da von morgens bis abends zu tun hat und …

Donnerwetter! rief er und klopfte mehrmals mit der flachen Hand auf den Tisch° Donnerwetter! Ich gratuliere.

Ach, sagte sie und sah ihn an. Sie war rot geworden.

Du hast es ja weit gebracht. Donnerwetter, alle Achtung°. Und jetzt? Fährst du in Urlaub?

Ja, vier Wochen nach Holland. Ich habe es nötig, bin ganz durchgedreht. Und du, Erich, was machst du? Erzähle. Du siehst gesund aus.

Schade, dachte er, wenn sie nicht so eine Bombenstellung° hätte, würde ich sie jetzt fragen, ob sie mich noch haben will. Aber so? Nein, das geht nicht, sie würde mich auslachen, wie damals.

express train

*in the thick of it / **weder … Rempeleien** neither pushing nor jostling / passers-by*

Siehe **Kulturtipps**: Kölner Dom

gate

mail-order textile company

klopfte … Tisch expression of surprise and admiration

well done

very good job

Ich?, sagte er gedehnt°, und brannte sich eine neue Zigarette an. Ich …
ich … Ach, weißt du, ich habe ein bißchen Glück gehabt. Habe hier in Köln

zu tun. Habe umgesattelt°, bin seit vier Jahren Einkaufsleiter einer Ham- 45
burger Werft°, na ja, was Besonderes ist das nun wieder auch nicht.

Oh, sagte sie und sah ihn starr an und ihr Blick streifte° seine großen
Hände, aber sie fand keinen Ring. Sie erinnerte sich, daß sie vor fünfzehn
Jahren nach einem kleinen Streit auseinander gelaufen waren, ohne sich bis
heute wieder zu sehen. Er hatte ihr damals nicht genügt, der schmal verdie- 50

nende und immer ölverschmierte Schlosser°. Er solle es erst zu etwas bringen, hatte sie ihm damals nachgerufen, vielleicht könne man später wieder
darüber sprechen. So gedankenlos jung waren sie damals. Ach ja, die Worte
waren im Streit gefallen und trotzdem nicht böse gemeint. Beide aber fanden danach keine Brücke mehr zueinander. Sie wollten und wollten doch 55
nicht. Und nun? Nun hatte er es zu etwas gebracht.

Dann haben wir ja beide Glück gehabt, sagte sie und dachte, daß er
immer noch gut aussieht. Gewiß, er war älter geworden, aber das steht ihm
gut. Schade, wenn er nicht so eine Bombenstellung hätte, ich würde ihn
fragen, ja, ich ihn, ob er noch an den dummen Streit von damals denkt und 60
ob er mich noch haben will. Ja, ich würde ihn fragen. Aber jetzt?

Jetzt habe ich dir einen halben Tag deines Urlaubs gestohlen, sagte er
und wagte nicht, sie anzusehen.

Aber Erich, das ist doch nicht so wichtig, ich fahre mit dem Zug um
fünfzehn Uhr. Aber ich, ich halte dich bestimmt auf, du hast gewiß einen 65
Termin hier.

Mach dir keine Sorgen, ich werde vom Hotel abgeholt. Weißt du, meinen Wagen lasse ich immer zu Hause, wenn ich längere Strecken fahren
muss. Bei dem Verkehr heute, da kommt man nur durchgedreht an.

Ja, sagte sie. Ganz recht, das mache ich auch immer so. Sie sah ihm nun 70
direkt ins Gesicht und fragte: Du bist nicht verheiratet? Oder lässt du Frau
und Ring zu Hause? Sie lachte etwas zu laut für dieses vornehme Lokal.

Weißt du, antwortete er, das hat seine Schwierigkeiten. Die ich haben
will, sind nicht zu haben oder nicht mehr, und die mich haben wollen, sind
nicht der Rede wert. Zeit müßte man eben haben. Zum Suchen, meine ich. 75
Zeit müßte man haben. Jetzt müßte ich ihr sagen, daß ich sie noch immer
liebe, daß es nie eine andere Frau für mich gegeben hat, daß ich sie all die
Jahre nicht vergessen konnte. Wie viel? Fünfzehn Jahre? Eine lange Zeit.
Mein Gott, welch eine lange Zeit. Und jetzt? Ich kann sie doch nicht mehr
fragen, vorbei, jetzt, wo sie so eine Stellung hat. Nun ist es zu spät, sie 80
würde mich auslachen, ich kenne ihr Lachen, ich habe es im Ohr gehabt, all
die Jahre. Fünfzehn? Kaum zu glauben.

Wem sagst du das? Sie lächelte.

Entweder die Arbeit oder das andere, erwiderte er.

Jetzt müßte ich ihm eigentlich sagen, daß er der einzige Mann ist, dem 85
ich blind folgen würde, wenn er mich darum bäte, daß ich jeden Mann, der

mir begegnete, sofort mit ihm verglich. Ich sollte ihm das sagen. Aber jetzt? Jetzt hat er eine Bombenstellung und er würde mich nur auslachen, nicht laut, er würde sagen, daß … ach … es ist alles so sinnlos geworden.

Sie aßen in demselben Lokal Mittag und tranken anschließend jeder zwei Kognak. Sie erzählten sich Geschichten aus ihren Kindertagen und später aus ihren Schultagen. Dann sprachen sie über ihr Berufsleben, und sie bekamen Respekt voreinander, als sie erfuhren, wie schwer es der andere gehabt hatte bei seinem Aufstieg. Jaja, sagte sie; genau wie bei mir, sagte er.

Aber jetzt haben wir es geschafft, sagte er laut und rauchte hastig.

Ja, nickte sie. Jetzt haben wir es geschafft. Hastig trank sie ihr Glas leer.

Sie hat schon ein paar Krähenfüßchen°, dachte er. Aber die stehen ihr nicht einmal schlecht.

crow's feet

Noch einmal bestellte er zwei Schalen Kognak und sie lachten viel und laut.

Er kann immer noch so herrlich lachen, genau wie früher, als er alle Menschen einfing mit seiner ansteckenden Heiterkeit°. Um seinen Mund sind zwei steile Falten°, trotzdem sieht er wie ein Junge aus, er wird immer wie ein Junge aussehen, und die zwei steilen Falten stehen ihm nicht einmal schlecht. Vielleicht ist er jetzt ein richtiger Mann, aber nein, er wird immer ein Junge bleiben.

contagious cheerfulness
wrinkles

Kurz vor drei brachte er sie zum Bahnhof.

Ich brauche den Amsterdamer Zug nicht zu nehmen, sagte sie. Fahre bis Aachen und steige dort um. Ich wollte sowieso schon lange einmal das Rathaus besichtigen.

Wieder standen sie auf dem Bahnsteig und sahen aneinander vorbei. Mit leeren Worten versuchten sie die Augen des andern einzufangen, und wenn sich dann doch ihre Blicke trafen, erschraken sie und musterten die Bögen der Halle.

Wenn sie jetzt ein Wort sagen würde, dachte er, dann …

Ich muß jetzt einsteigen, sagte sie. Es war schön, dich wieder einmal zu sehen. Und dann so unverhofft° …

unexpected

Ja, das war es. Er half ihr beim Einsteigen und fragte nach ihrem Gepäck.

Als Reisegepäck aufgegeben.

Natürlich, das ist bequemer, sagte er.

Wenn er jetzt ein Wort sagen würde, dachte sie, ich stiege sofort wieder aus, sofort.

Sie reichte ihm aus dem Abteil erster Klasse die Hand. Auf Wiedersehen, Erich … und weiterhin … viel Glück.

Wie schön sie immer noch ist. Warum nur sagt sie kein Wort. Danke, Renate. Hoffentlich hast du schönes Wetter.

Ach, das ist nicht so wichtig, Hauptsache ist das Faulenzen, das kann man auch bei Regen.

Der Zug ruckte an. Sie winkten nicht, sie sahen sich nur in die Augen, solange dies möglich war.

Als der Zug aus der Halle gefahren war, ging Renate in einen Wagen 130
zweiter Klasse und setzte sich dort an ein Fenster. Sie weinte hinter einer
ausgebreiteten Illustrierten.

Wie dumm von mir, ich hätte ihm sagen sollen, daß ich immer noch
die kleine Verkäuferin bin. Ja, in einem anderen Laden, mit zweihundert
Mark mehr als früher, aber ich verkaufe immer noch Herrenoberhemden, 135
wie früher, und Socken und Unterwäsche. Alles für den Herrn. Ich hätte
ihm das sagen sollen. Aber dann hätte er mich ausgelacht, jetzt, wo er ein
Herr geworden ist. Nein, das ging doch nicht. Aber ich hätte wenigstens
nach seiner Adresse fragen sollen. Wie dumm von mir, ich war aufgeregt
wie ein kleines Mädchen, und ich habe gelogen wie ein kleines Mädchen, 140
das imponieren° will. Wie dumm von mir.

impress

Erich verließ den Bahnhof und fuhr mit der Straßenbahn nach Ostheim
auf eine Großbaustelle. Dort meldete er sich beim Bauführer.

Ich bin der neue Kranführer°.

crane operator

Na, sind Sie endlich da? Mensch, wir haben schon gestern auf Sie 145
gewartet. Also dann, der Polier° zeigt Ihnen Ihre Bude°, dort drüben in den
Baracken. Komfortabel ist es nicht, aber warmes Wasser haben wir trotzdem. Also dann, morgen früh, pünktlich sieben Uhr.

foreman / (colloq.) room

Ein Schnellzug fuhr Richtung Deutz. Ob der auch nach Aachen
fährt? Ich hätte ihr sagen sollen, daß ich jetzt Kranführer bin. Ach, Blöd- 150
sinn, sie hätte mich nur ausgelacht, sie kann so verletzend lachen. Nein,
das ging nicht, jetzt, wo sie eine Dame geworden ist und eine Bombenstellung hat.

Kulturtipps

Kölner Dom

Der Kölner Dom (die Hohe Domkirche St. Peter und
Maria) steht nur 250 Meter vom Rhein entfernt und
direkt neben dem Kölner Hauptbahnhof. Diese römisch-
katholische Kirche ist die zweithöchste Kirche Europas
und die dritthöchste in der Welt. Mit dem Dombau
begann man im Jahre 1248. Fertig wurde der Dom
allerdings erst 1880. Seit 1996 ist er auf der Liste der
UNESCO für Weltkulturerbe.

Kölner Dom mit Hohenzollernbrücke

Nomen

der Aufstieg, -e *promotion, advancement*

der Bahnsteig, -e *train platform*

die Illustrierte, -n *magazine*

die Strecke, -n *distance, route*

der Streit, -e *argument*

Verben

auf·halten (hält auf), hielt auf, aufgehalten *to delay*

aus·lachen *to laugh at*

sich beschweren *to complain*

ein·fangen (fängt ein), fing ein, eingefangen *to catch*

imponieren (+ *dat.*) *to impress someone*

klopfen *to knock, to beat*

sich melden (bei) *to report (to)*

stören *to bother, disturb*

zwingen, zwang, gezwungen *to force, compel*

Adjektive und Adverbien

aufgeregt *excited, nervous*

ausgerechnet *of all things*

durchgedreht (*colloq.*) *nuts*

starr *stiff, rigid, paralyzed*

stumm *in silence, silently*

ungeduldig *impatient*

Ausdrücke

Das steht ihm gut. *It suits him well.*

Donnerwetter! *Oh, my goodness!*

Ich habe es nötig. *I really need it.*

9-30 **Textarbeit: Zum Inhalt.** Beenden Sie die Sätze mit Informationen aus dem Text

1. Die Geschichte spielt in …

2. Die Jahreszeit ist …

3. Renate sagt, sie ist auf der Reise nach …

4. Erich kommt gerade …

5. Sie gehen zusammen in …

6. Sie haben sich … nicht gesehen.

7. Renate ist nicht verheiratet, sagt sie, weil …

8. Erich sagt, sein Beruf ist …

9. Vor vielen Jahren hat Renate an Erich nicht gefallen, dass …

10. Erich ist nicht verheiratet, sagt er, weil …

11. Sie sprechen dann noch über …

12. In Wirklichkeit ist Renate … und Erich … von Beruf.

Possible answers for 9-30.
1. Köln; 2. Sommer; 3. Amsterdam; 4. aus Hamburg; 5. ein Café; 6. 15 Jahre; 7. sie sehr viel arbeitet, und wenn man es zu etwas bringen will, muss man eben viel arbeiten; 8. Einkaufsleiter bei einer Hamburger Werft; 9. er nur Schlosser war; 10. die er will nicht zu haben und die anderen nicht der Rede wert sind; 11. ihre Kindheit und ihr Berufsleben; 12. Verkäuferin; Kranführer

9-31 Textarbeit: **Kurz gesagt.** In der Geschichte gibt es nicht viel Handlung. Schreiben Sie eine kurze Zusammenfassung des Handlungsablaufs in etwa fünf oder sechs Sätzen.

Possible answer for 9-31.
Ein Liebespaar trifft sich nach 15-jähriger Trennung zufällig im Kölner Hauptbahnhof wieder. In einem Café unterhalten sie sich über alte Zeiten und ihre jetzige Lebenssituation. Renate und Erich lügen und sagen, dass sie Karriere gemacht haben, denn sie haben Angst, vom anderen nicht akzeptiert zu werden. Sie haben noch Gefühle für einander, aber sie gehen auseinander, ohne die Wahrheit gesagt zu haben.

9-32 Textarbeit: **Wer sagt, denkt oder schreibt das?** Bestimmen Sie, ob die folgenden Sätze von Renate oder Erich gedacht oder gesagt werden oder ob es Zugaben des Erzählers sind.

was Renate denkt	was Erich denkt	Zugabe des Erzählers
was Renate sagt	was Erich sagt	

1. Da war es mir, als hätte ich dich gestern zum letzten Male gesehen, so nah warst du mir.

2. Bist du verheiratet? Hast du Kinder? Wo fährst du hin?

Answers for 9-32. 1. was Erich sagt; 2. was Erich sagt; 3. was Renate sagt; 4. Zugabe des Erzählers; 5. was Erich denkt; 6. Zugabe des Erzählers; 7. was Renate denkt; 8. was Erich denkt

3. Nein, verheiratet bin ich nicht, die Arbeit, weißt du.

4. Sie erinnerte sich, daß sie vor fünfzehn Jahren nach einem kleinen Streit auseinander gelaufen waren, ohne sich bis heute wieder zu sehen.

5. Jetzt müßte ich ihr sagen, daß ich sie noch immer liebe, daß es nie eine andere Frau für mich gegeben hat, daß ich sie all die Jahre nicht vergessen konnte.

6. Sie aßen in demselben Lokal Mittag und tranken anschließend jeder zwei Kognak.

7. Aber ich hätte wenigstens nach seiner Adresse fragen sollen.

8. Ach, Blödsinn, sie hätte mich nur ausgelacht, sie kann so verletzend lachen.

9-33 Vokabelarbeit. Ergänzen Sie die Sätze mit Wörtern aus den *Neuen Vokabeln.* Achten Sie dabei auch auf die Wortform.

1. Renate und Erich treffen sich auf einem ___Bahnsteig___ in Köln.

2. Sie wollen sich nicht gegenseitig ___aufhalten___, aber sie wollen gern miteinander sprechen.

3. Sie hatten sich vor Jahren nach einem ___Streit___ getrennt.

4. Renate hatte sich an einem Kiosk im Bahnhof eine ___Illustrierte___ gekauft.

5. Erich und Renate sind von dem Treffen sehr ___aufgeregt___.

6. Erich und Renate ___beschweren___ ___sich___ nicht darüber, dass sie nicht verheiratet sind.

7. Als Erich ___sich___ dann bei seinem neuen Arbeitgeber ___meldet___, denkt er immer noch an Renate.

9-34 Zur Diskussion und Interpretation. Besprechen Sie die Fragen.

1. Wie war wohl die frühere Beziehung von Erich und Renate?

2. Warum erzählen Renate und Erich einander nicht die Wahrheit?

3. Welchen Effekt wird dieses Treffen für die beiden auf ihr weiteres Leben wohl haben?

4. Wenn Sie alte Freunde und Bekannte treffen, worüber reden Sie dann?

5. Warum ist es vielen Menschen wichtig, dass sie andere beeindrucken?

6. Was können wir aus dieser Geschichte lernen?

Teaching suggestion for 9-35. Remind students that they reviewed the future tense in the *Kapitel 8 Grammatik.*

9-35 Meine Zukunft. Besprechen Sie, wie Sie sich Ihr Leben in 20 Jahren vorstellen. Denken Sie dabei an Ihren Beruf, Ihre Familiensituation, Ihre finanzielle Lage und auch, was Sie gern in Ihrer Freizeit und in den Ferien machen.

Beginnen Sie so: *In 20 Jahren werde ich wohl ...*

Variation for 9-36. Have students rewrite the ending in the form of a dialog between Erich and Renate.

9-36 Es kann auch ganz anders enden. Erich und Renate hätten sich bei ihrem Treffen auch anders verhalten können und dann wäre die Geschichte anders ausgegangen. Schreiben Sie ein neues Ende für diese Geschichte ab Z. 115.

Grammatik

1. Passive voice (Passiv)

09-28 to 09-36 German and English have two voices: active and passive. In the active voice, the focus is on the subject—the entity that performs the action of the verb. In the passive voice, the focus is on the recipient of the action. When an active voice sentence is rewritten in the passive voice, the direct object becomes the subject and the subject becomes the so-called *agent*.

Active: **Dieser Verlag** druckt **das historische Buch.**
This publisher is printing the historic book.

(subject / direct object)

Passive: **Das historische Buch** wird <u>von diesem Verlag</u> gedruckt.
The historic book is being printed by this publisher.

(subject / agent)

In the passive voice, the source of the action (the agent) may or may not be expressed, but if it is, it appears in a prepositional phrase. If the agent is a person, the preposition **von** (+ *dat.*) is used. If the agent is a means or medium by which the action occurs, the preposition **durch** (+ *acc.*) is used.

> Karl der Große <u>wurde</u> **vom Papst** zum Kaiser <u>gekrönt</u>.
> *Karl was crowned emperor by the pope.*

> Das Kulturgut der Antike <u>wurde</u> **durch die Bemühungen Karls des Großen** <u>gerettet</u>.
> *The cultural artifacts of antiquity were saved through Charlemagne's efforts.*

Passive voice tenses (*Zeitformen des Passivs*)

In German, the passive voice is formed with the auxiliary **werden** plus the past participle of the main verb. Like the active voice, the passive voice has six tenses.

Tense	German passive voice	English passive voice
	(**werden** + past participle)	(*to be* + past participle)
Present (Präsens)	Es **wird** gebaut.	*It is being built.*
Simple past (Präteritum)	Es **wurde** gebaut.	*It was being built. / It was built.*
Present perfect (Perfekt)	Es **ist** gebaut **worden.**	*It has been built. / It was built.*
Past perfect (Plusquamperfekt)	Es **war** gebaut **worden.**	*It had been built.*
Future (Futur I)	Es **wird** gebaut **werden.**	*It will be built.*
Future perfect (Futur II)	Es **wird** gebaut **worden sein.**	*It will have been built.*

The past participle **geworden** is reduced to **worden** in the passive voice perfect tenses. The auxiliary verb for the perfect tenses of the passive voice is always **sein.**

The present and simple past are the most commonly used tenses in the passive voice. The present perfect and especially the past perfect of the passive are used less often, and the future and future perfect passive are even less common. Therefore, this book will focus primarily on the present, simple past, and present perfect passive forms.

9-37 Duisburg: Großstadt am Rhein. Lesen Sie die kurze Geschichte Duisburgs und setzen Sie in jeden Satz **von** oder **durch** mit dem passenden Agenten ein. Achten Sie dabei auf den Kasus des Objekts mit der Präposition.

die Römer	ein Kanal (*m.*)	Historiker	ihre Einwohner
ein Brand	die Verlagerung	Bombenangriffe	der damalige König

1. Duisburg wurde ____von den Römern____ im 1. Jahrhundert an der Mündung der Ruhr in den Rhein gegründet.

2. Der erste schriftliche Beweis wird ____von Historikern____ auf 883 datiert.

3. Im 10. Jahrhundert wurde hier ____vom damaligen König____ eine Königspfalz errichtet.

4. 1283 wurde die ganze Königspfalz ____durch einen Brand____ zerstört.

5. Im 13. Jahrhundert wurde die Stadt ____durch die Verlagerung____ des Rheins nach Westen wirtschaftlich unwichtig.

6. Duisburg wurde erst wieder im 19. Jahrhundert ____durch einen Kanal____ mit dem Rhein verbunden.

7. 1945 wurde die Industriestadt ____durch Bombenangriffe____ schwer beschädigt.

8. Auch in Zukunft wird die Stadt ____von ihren Einwohnern____ als moderner und attraktiver Wohnsitz gesehen werden.

9-38 Das Privatleben Karls des Großen. Karls persönlicher Geschichtsschreiber Einhart berichtet aus dem Leben des Herrschers. Setzen Sie jeweils die korrekte Form von **werden** und ein passendes Verb aus der Liste ein. Benutzen Sie das Passiv Präsens.

besuchen	diskutieren	essen	feiern	spielen	schreiben

1. Die Thermen (*thermal baths*) in Aachen ____werden____ täglich von Karl dem Großen ____besucht____ .

2. Das Frühstück ____wird____ danach in seiner Wohnung zusammen mit der ganzen Familie ____gegessen____ .

3. Danach ____werden____ von Karl Briefe an Gelehrte in der ganzen Welt ____geschrieben____ .

4. Am Nachmittag ____wird____ von Karls Kindern Musik ____gespielt____ , um die Eltern zu unterhalten.

5. Feste ____werden____ oft am Abend mit vielen Gästen ____gefeiert____ .

6. Politik ____wird____ auf den Festen von Karl und seinen Ministern gern ____diskutiert____ .

9-39 Die Kaiserpfalzen. In einer Broschüre über die Kaiserpfalzen gibt es viele Beschreibungen im Aktiv. Schreiben Sie sie ins Passiv um.

A. Setzen Sie die Sätze ins Passiv Präteritum.

Beispiel: Karl der Große lud viele Gelehrte nach Aachen ein.

*Viele Gelehrte **wurden** von Karl dem Großen nach Aachen **eingeladen**.*

1. Karl der Große baute mehr als hundert Kaiserpfalzen.
2. Karl brauchte sie für sehr verschiedene Anlässe.
3. Die Arbeiter legten die Böden der Kaiserpfalz in Ingelheim mit Marmor aus.
4. Im Jahre 807 besuchte Karl Ingelheim zum letzten Mal.
5. Karl gründete auch die Kaiserpfalz in Paderborn.
6. Barbarossa errichtete die Kaiserpfalz Kaiserswerth in Düsseldorf.

B. Noch einmal bitte: Schreiben Sie die Sätze ins Passiv Perfekt um.

Beispiel: Karl der Große lud viele Gelehrte in seine Residenz in Aachen ein.

*Viele Gelehrte **sind** von Karl dem Großen in seine Residenz in Aachen **eingeladen worden**.*

Answers for 9-39, part A.
1. Mehr als hundert Kaiserpfalzen wurden von Karl dem Großen gebaut. **2.** Sie wurden von Karl für sehr verschiedene Anlässe gebraucht. **3.** Die Böden der Kaiserpfalz in Ingelheim wurden von den Arbeitern mit Marmor ausgelegt. **4.** Ingelheim wurde von Karl im Jahre 807 zum letzten Mal besucht. **5.** Die Kaiserpfalz in Paderborn wurde auch von Karl gegründet. **6.** Die Kaiserpfalz Kaiserswerth in Düsseldorf wurde von Barbarossa errichtet.

Answers for 9-39, part B.
1. Mehr als hundert Kaiserpfalzen sind von Karl dem Großen gebaut worden. **2.** Sie sind von Karl für sehr verschiedene Anlässe gebraucht worden. **3.** Die Böden der Kaiserpfalz in Ingelheim sind von den Arbeitern mit Marmor ausgelegt worden. **4.** Ingelheim ist von Karl im Jahre 807 zum letzten Mal besucht worden. **5.** Die Kaiserpfalz in Paderborn ist auch von Karl gegründet worden. **6.** Die Kaiserpfalz Kaiserswerth in Düsseldorf ist von Barbarossa errichtet worden.

9-40 Im Bergbau-Museum Bochum. Sie berichten einer Freundin, was sie im Bergbau-Museum über die Arbeit der Bergleute gelernt haben. Ergänzen Sie jeden Satz mit einem Verb aus der Liste im Passiv mit der angegebenen Zeitform.

~~bauen~~	bewahren	singen	verursachen	ziehen
beschreiben	machen	verbringen	vergessen	

Beispiel: Das Museum _____ von der Stadt Bochum _____. (Präsens)

Das Museum **wird** von der Stadt Bochum **gebaut**.

1. In der Ausstellung ____wird____ die Arbeit der Bergarbeiter anschaulich ____gemacht____. (Präsens)
2. Lieder ____wurden____ bei der Arbeit in den Gruben von den Bergleuten ____gesungen____. (Präteritum)
3. Sogar die Pausen ____wurden____ unter Tage ____verbracht____. (Präteritum)
4. Die Arbeiter ____wurden____ nach der Arbeit mit Fahrstühlen aus dem Bergwerk ____gezogen____. (Präteritum)
5. Ein Unfall in einem Bergwerk ____ist____ in der Ausstellung „Auf breiten Schultern" von einem Bergmann ____beschrieben____ ____worden____. (Perfekt)
6. Der Unfall ____war____ durch eine Explosion ____verursacht____ ____worden____. (Plusquamperfekt)

7. Ein Einblick in das tägliche Leben der Bergarbeiter _____ wird _____ durch dieses Museum für kommende Generationen _____ bewahrt _____ _____ werden _____ . (Futur I)

8. So _____ werden _____ der Bergbau und seine Tradition nicht _____ vergessen _____ _____ worden _____ _____ sein _____ , falls es zum Ende dieser Energiequelle kommt. (Futur II)

Passive with modal verbs (Passiv mit Modalverben)

09-35 to 09-36

Modal verbs may be used with the passive voice, but they are used mainly in the present and simple past tenses. When a modal verb is used, it is the conjugated verb. It is in the second position and the auxiliary **werden** appears as an infinitive at the end of the sentence, preceded by the past participle.

Present passive	Energie **wird** aus verschiedenen Quellen **hergestellt.** *Energy is produced from various sources.*
Present passive with modal	Energie **kann** aus verschiedenen Quellen **hergestellt werden.** *Energy can be produced from various sources.*
Simple past passive with modal	Energie **konnte** aus verschiedenen Quellen **hergestellt werden.** *Energy could be produced from various sources.*

Teaching suggestion for 9-41.
Have students rewrite some of the sentences in the simple past tense.

Possible answers for 9-41.
1. Kernkraft kann für die Stromerzeugung eingesetzt werden. **2.** Atomenergie darf von der Industrie nicht als einzige Energiequelle benutzt werden. **3.** Kraftwerke müssen nicht nur in Deutschland überprüft werden. **4.** Atommüll muss unter Grund gelagert werden. **5.** Kernenergie kann weltweit genutzt werden. **6.** Kohle soll eines Tages nicht länger in Deutschland abgebaut werden. **7.** Erfinder neuer Energiequellen können als Retter der Energiekrise gesehen werden. **8.** Eine Lösung dieses Problems muss endlich gefunden werden.

9-41 Kernkraft – Energie der Zukunft? Bilden Sie aus den Elementen logische Sätze im Passiv Präsens mit Modalverben.

Beispiel: Kernkraft / von den Umweltschützern / ablehnen / müssen
*Kernkraft **muss** von den Umweltschützern **abgelehnt werden.***

1. Kernkraft / für die Stromerzeugung / einsetzen / können
2. Atomenergie / von der Industrie / nicht als einzige Energiequelle / benutzen / dürfen
3. Kraftwerke / nicht nur in Deutschland / überprüfen / müssen
4. Atommüll / unter Grund / lagern / müssen
5. Kernenergie / weltweit / nutzen / können
6. Kohle / eines Tages / nicht länger in Deutschland / abbauen / sollen
7. Erfinder neuer Energiequellen / als Retter der Energiekrise / sehen / können
8. eine Lösung / dieses Problems / endlich / finden / müssen

2. Relative clauses (Relativsätze)

In both German and English, relative clauses provide additional information about a previously mentioned person, idea, or thing. Relative clauses are joined to the main clause by a relative pronoun that refers to the antecedent (**Beziehungswort**), a noun or pronoun mentioned in the preceding clause.

Main clause	**Relative clause**
Hier ist **der Brief,**	**den** wir vom Bundeskanzler bekommen haben.
Here is the letter	*(that) we received from the chancellor.*
Das ist **die Schauspielerin,**	mit **der** ich zur Schule gegangen bin.
That is the actress	*with whom I went to school.*

English relative pronouns are the words *who, whom, whose, which,* and *that.* German relative pronouns are identical to the demonstrative pronouns and resemble the definite articles, except for the genitive forms and the dative plural.

	Masculine	**Feminine**	**Neuter**	**Plural**
Nominative	der	die	das	die
Accusative	den	die	das	die
Dative	dem	der	dem	**denen**
Genitive	**dessen**	**deren**	**dessen**	**deren**

Like most German pronouns, relative pronouns show gender, number, and case. The gender and number of the pronoun are the same as those of its antecedent. The case of the relative pronoun is determined by the function of the pronoun within its clause.

> Kommt **die Studentin, die** neben dir sitzt, aus Wuppertal?
> *Is the female student who sits next to you from Wuppertal?*

The relative pronoun **die** refers to the antecedent **Studentin** (*feminine singular*) and is the subject of the relative clause (*nominative*).

> Ist das **der Rucksack, den** ich gestern gekauft habe?
> *Is that the backpack that I bought yesterday?*

The relative pronoun **den** refers to the antecedent **Rucksack** (*masculine singular*) and is the direct object in the relative clause (*accusative case*).

> Sind das **die Frauen,** mit **denen** du arbeitest?
> *Are those the women with whom you work?*

The relative pronoun **denen** refers to the antecedent **Frauen** (*plural*) and is the object of a dative preposition (**mit**).

In German, all relative clauses are set off from the main clause by commas. They use dependent word order, with the inflected verb in the final position. The relative pronoun is the first word in a relative clause unless it is the object of a preposition, in which case it follows the preposition. Unlike English, the relative pronoun can never be omitted from the sentence.

Answers for 9-42. 1. Akkusativ, Maskulin; **2.** Nominativ, Plural; **3.** Dativ, Maskulin; **4.** Genitiv, Plural; **5.** Akkusativ, Plural; **6.** Dativ, Feminin; **7.** Dativ, Plural; **8.** Genitiv, Maskulin.

9-42 Ich spiele gern Fußball. Markus erzählt von seiner Mannschaft. Identifizieren Sie die Relativpronomen und sein Beziehungswort und geben Sie Kasus und Geschlecht (oder einfach Numerus, wenn Plural) von jedem Relativpronomen an.

1. Fußball ist der Sport, den ich am liebsten mag.

2. In meiner Mannschaft gibt es elf Spieler und zwei Ersatzspieler, die alle sehr gut sind.

3. Wir haben einen Trainer, von dem ich mich gern beraten lasse.

4. Wir haben für das Team auch Sponsoren, deren Trikots wir bei den Spielen tragen, um so Werbung für die Firmen zu machen.

5. Beim letzten Spiel waren auch meine Eltern da, für die ich dann immer besonders gut zu spielen versuche.

6. Unser nächstes Spiel ist gegen eine starke Mannschaft, von der ich schon viel gehört habe.

7. Wir werden zum Spiel unsere Glücksschuhe tragen, mit denen wir sehr oft gewinnen.

8. Vor dem Spiel bekommen wir immer gute Ratschläge von unserem Trainer, dessen Erfahrung uns hilft, gut zu spielen und oft zu gewinnen.

Teaching suggestion for 9-43. This can be completed as an oral or written activity. As an oral activity, have students alternate asking (for example: *Was ist Düsseldorf?*) and answering questions.

9-43 Was ist das? Erklären Sie die Begriffe mit Relativsätzen.

Beispiele: Düsseldorf / eine Stadt

Düsseldorf ist eine Stadt, **die** eine Fußballmanschaft hat.

Düsseldorf ist eine Stadt, **in der** viele Menschen wohnen.

1. Kölsch / eine Mundart
2. die Kohle / eine Energiequelle
3. ein Lokal / ein Restaurant
4. der Euro / eine Währung
5. ein Krimi / ein Buch
6. der Rhein / ein Fluss
7. ein Computer / ein Gegenstand
8. Februar / ein Monat
9. das Mittelalter / eine Zeit
10. Fußball / eine Sportart

09-41 to 09-42

Interrogative pronouns as relative pronouns (Interrogativpronomen als Relativpronomen)

If a relative pronoun has no specific antecedent or if the antecedent is an entire clause, it can be expressed by forms of the interrogative pronouns **wer** (*who*): **wer** [*nom.*], **wen** [*acc.*], **wem** [*dat.*], **wessen** (*whose*) [*gen.*], or by **was** (*what, which*) [*nom.* or *acc.*].

Ich weiß nicht, **wer** das Spiel gewonnen hat.	*I don't know who won the game.*
Bitte erklären Sie uns, für **wen** diese Energiequelle wichtig ist.	*Please explain to us for whom this energy source is important.*
Sie kommt heute nicht, **was** mich sehr traurig macht.	*She is not coming today, which makes me very sad.*

9-44 Weißt du, wer oder was? Fragen Sie einen Mitstudenten/eine Mitstudentin, ob er/sie den Namen einer Person oder eines Ortes in Nordrhein-Westfalen kennt. Benutzen Sie einen Relativsatz mit **wer** oder **was** in Ihrer Frage. Dann beantwortet er/sie die Frage.

Konrad Adenauer	Düsseldorf	Nena	das Ruhrgebiet	Ludwig van Beethoven
Köln	der Rhein	Clara Schumann	Dortmund	~~Karl der Große~~

Beispiel: der erste Kaiser des Heiligen Römischen Reichs

      S1: *Weißt du, **wer** der erste Kaiser des Heiligen Römischen Reichs war?*

      S2: *Das war Karl der Große.*

1. der erste Bundeskanzler der Bundesrepublik
2. die wohl berühmteste Pianistin und Komponistin des 19. Jahrhunderts
3. der größte Ballungsraum Deutschlands
4. der wichtigste Fluss Nordrhein-Westfalens
5. die größte Stadt in Nordrhein-Westfalen
6. die Hauptstadt von Nordrhein-Westfalen
7. die Sängerin des Hits „99 Luftballons"
8. der berühmteste Sohn Bonns
9. die größte Stadt des Ruhrgebiets

9-45 Karneval in Köln. Karin freut sich auf die Karnevalszeit in ihrer Heimatstadt Köln. Ergänzen Sie die Sätze mit den passenden Interrogativpronomen.

1. Ich weiß noch nicht, mit _____wem_____ ich die Straßenumzüge am Rosenmontag ansehen werde.

2. Ich muss erst fragen, _____wer_____ an dem Tag noch nichts vorhat.

3. Man weiß am Rosenmontag nie genau, _____was_____ so alles passieren kann.

Possible answers for 9-44.
1. Weißt du, wer der erste Bundeskanzler der Bundesrepublik war? / Das war Konrad Adenauer. **2.** Weißt du, wer die wohl berühmteste Pianistin und Komponistin des 19. Jahrhunderts war? / Das war Clara Schumann. **3.** Weißt du, was der größte Ballungsraum Deutschlands ist? / Das ist das Ruhrgebiet. **4.** Weißt du, was der wichtigste Fluss Nordrhein-Westfalens ist? / Das ist der Rhein. **5.** Weißt du, was die größte Stadt Nordrhein-Westfalens ist? / Das ist Köln. **6.** Weißt du, was die Hauptstadt von Nordrhein-Westfalen ist? / Das ist Düsseldorf. **7.** Weißt du, wer die Sängerin des Hits „99 Luftballons" ist? / Das ist Nena. **8.** Weißt du, wer der berühmteste Sohn Bonns ist? / Das ist Ludwig van Beethoven. **9.** Weißt du, was die größte Stadt des Ruhrgebiets ist? / Das ist Dortmund.

4. Fremde Leute bützen einander, _____was_____ für Außenseiter bestimmt recht merkwürdig scheint.

5. Man weiß auch nie, _____wen_____ man auf einem der Wagen überraschend als Prinzen sieht.

6. Letztes Jahr war mein Bekannter Peter auf einmal Prinz Peter III., und ich wusste nicht, _____wer_____ seine Prinzessin war.

7. Von allen Wagen werfen die Prinzen und Prinzessinnen Kamellen in Richtung Zuschauer, aber ich bin mir nie sicher, _____wessen_____ Kamellen am besten schmecken.

8. Seit letztem Jahr bin ich nun auch Mitglied in einem Karnevalsverein und weiß noch nicht, für _____wen_____ ich bei der Prinzenwahl stimmen werde, ob für Karl oder lieber für Richard.

Immer weiter!

9-46 Zur Diskussion. Besprechen Sie die Themen.

1. Die Menschen in Nordrhein-Westfalen begeistern sich unter anderem für Fußball, den Karneval und ihre Geschichte. Beschreiben Sie, wie sich diese Vorlieben im Leben der Bürger zeigt.

2. Überlegen Sie sich, was in den kommenden Jahren wohl mit der Kohleindustrie geschehen wird und beschreiben Sie, wie das das Leben der Menschen im Ruhrgebiet beeinflussen wird.

9-47 Zum Schreiben: Ein neuer Job in NRW? Sie haben kürzlich ein Stellenangebot von einer Firma in Essen, mitten im Ruhrpott, angenommen. Sie wohnen jetzt seit einer Woche in Essen. Schreiben Sie eine E-Mail an Ihren Deutschprofessor/Ihre Deutschprofessorin und berichten Sie über die Menschen und ob Sie sich hier wohlfühlen.

Weitere Themen

BAP (Rockband)	Gustav Heinemann	Otto Schily
Bayer AG	Hermannsdenkmal	Schloss Hugenpoet
Heinrich Böll	Kölner Dom	Alice Schwarzer
Brauereimuseum Dortmund	Krupp	Teutoburger Wald
Friedrich Arnold Brockhaus	Lippe	August Thyssen
Annette von Droste-Hülshoff	der Rhein	Wuppertaler Schwebebahn
Herbert Grönemeyer	die Ruhr	

Nordsee

Deutschland

Hessen

Schweiz

Österreich

Liechtenstein

KAPITEL

10

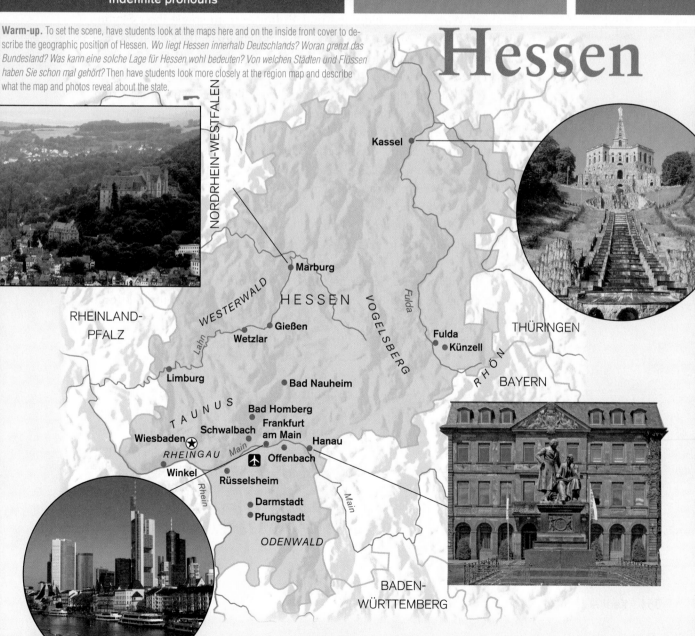

Warm-up. To set the scene, have students look at the maps here and on the inside front cover to describe the geographic position of Hessen. *Wo liegt Hessen innerhalb Deutschlands? Woran grenzt das Bundesland? Was kann eine solche Lage für Hessen wohl bedeuten? Von welchen Städten und Flüssen haben Sie schon mal gehört?* Then have students look more closely at the region map and describe what the map and photos reveal about the state.

Hessen

NORDRHEIN-WESTFALEN

Kassel

THÜRINGEN

RHEINLAND-PFALZ

WESTERWALD

HESSEN

VOGELSBERG

Fulda

Marburg

Gießen

Wetzlar

Fulda

Künzell

RHÖN

BAYERN

Limburg

Bad Nauheim

Lahn

TAUNUS

Bad Homberg

Schwalbach

Frankfurt am Main

Hanau

Wiesbaden

RHEINGAU

Main

Offenbach

Winkel

Rüsselsheim

Rhein

Darmstadt

Pfungstadt

Main

ODENWALD

BADEN-WÜRTTEMBERG

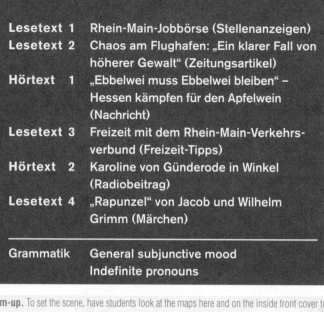

Einführung

10-01 to 10-02

Mitten in Deutschland liegt das Bundesland Hessen, eines der wichtigsten Wirtschaftszentren Deutschlands. Schon im Mittelalter zog die internationale Handelsroute zwischen Paris und Russland durch Hessen. Heute hat sich das Land zu einem wichtigen Verkehrsknotenpunkt° entwickelt, denn hier

transportation hub befinden sich das verkehrsreichste Autobahnkreuz Europas und der meistfre- 5
quentierte Hauptbahnhof und Flughafen sowie die wichtigsten Wasserwege Deutschlands. Die Behauptung, kein Weg führe an Hessen vorbei, scheint also

justified berechtigt° zu sein, ob auf Straße, Schiene, zu Luft oder Wasser.

Read the *Sprachanalyse: Indirect discourse* in SAM 10-02, which explains the forms used in the *Einführung* to convey indirect speech. As you read the *Lesetexte* in this chapter, do the *Sprachanalyse* activities in the SAM (10-08, 10-13, 10-17, 10-20) to practice recognizing and understanding the special subjunctive mood.

Die meisten der über sechs Millionen Einwohner leben im Süden Hessens entlang der Gebiete um die Flüsse Rhein und Main. Kern des Rhein- 10
Main-Gebiets ist Frankfurt am Main mit seinen 690.000 Einwohnern. Diese Großstadt trägt den Beinamen „Mainhattan" wegen ihrer Bedeutung als Handels-, Wirtschafts-, Bildungs- und Kulturzentrum sowie ihrer Skyline mit rund 80 Hochhäusern. Diese Banken- und Finanzmetropole ist Sitz der Deutschen Bundesbank, der Europäischen Zentralbank und Deutschlands 15

stock exchange größter Börse° sowie über 400 weitere Banken. Die meisten anderen hessischen Großstädte befinden sich auch in der südlichen Rhein-Main-Region:

spa town die Landeshauptstadt und der Kurort° Wiesbaden, dann Darmstadt mit seinen vier Hochschulen und schließlich Offenbach, besonders wichtig als

service center Dienstleistungszentrum°. Auch bedeutend ist der etwas kleinere Industrie- 20
und Technologiestandort Hanau. Als einzige hessische Großstadt außerhalb

urban agglomeration des Frankfurter Ballungsraums° liegt in Nordhessen Kassel. Die Mitte und der Norden des Bundeslandes sind eher ländlich und waldreich, obwohl sich hier auch kleinere urbane Zentren wie die Universitätsstädte Marburg und Gießen befinden. In ganz Hessen findet man mehrere Mittelgebirge. 25

In seiner heutigen Gestalt existiert Hessen erst seit 1945. Seitdem der

Philipp the Magnanimous Landgraf Philipp der Großmütige° 1568 Hessen unter seine vier Söhne aufteilte, entwickelten sich die Regionen politisch, wirtschaftlich und kulturell auseinander. Die Geschichte Hessens ist eine Geschichte des Teilens, Zusammenfügens und erneuten Teilens, sodass man ständig darüber stritt, wel- 30
ches das wirkliche Hessen sei. Spürbar sind diese regionalen Unterschiede etwa in den verschiedenen hessischen Mundartvarianten und darin, dass man sich eher als Wiesbadener, Marburger oder Frankfurter und weniger als Hesse identifiziert. 1961 hat man den seitdem jährlich stattfindenden Hessentag gegründet. Der damalige Ministerpräsident erklärte, er habe damit 35
die Menschen des Landes zusammenbringen und ihnen ein Zusammengehörigkeitsgefühl verschaffen wollen. Die Bürger Hessens sollen an diesem Tag die Vielfalt ihres Landes feiern und gleichzeitig Gemeinsamkeiten entdecken. Zu den letzteren zählen die Leistungen und Erfahrungen des modernen Landes, das nun seit über 60 Jahren besteht. 40

Possible answers for *Fragen zum Text*. **1.** Hessen ist Verkehrsknotenpunkt zu Luft und Wasser, auf Straße und Schiene. Mehr Menschen reisen durch Hessen als durch andere Gegenden in Deutschland. **2.** Frankfurt ist als Handels-, Wirtschafts-, Bildungs- und Kulturzentrum sowie als Bank- und Finanzzentrum bekannt. **3.** Frankfurt, Wiesbaden, Darmstadt, Offenbach, Hanau; **4.** Die Flüsse Rhein und Main fließen durch den südlichen Teil des Landes, hier befindet sich ein Großteil der Einwohner und der Städte. Die Mitte und der Norden sind ländlich und waldreich. Die Landschaft besteht aus mehreren Mittelgebirgen. **5.** Hessen wurde im Laufe der Jahrhunderte mehrmals aufgeteilt und dann erneut wieder zusammengefügt. Die Dialekte und die regionalen Identitäten der Menschen sind Ergebnis ihrer Geschichte. **6.** Es ist ein jährlicher Feiertag, der das moderne Land Hessen feiert und der den Bürgern Hessens eine gemeinsame Identität verschaffen soll.

Fragen zum Text

1. Erklären Sie das Motto „Kein Weg führt an Hessen vorbei".
2. Wofür ist Frankfurt bekannt?
3. Welche Städte liegen im Rhein-Main-Gebiet?
4. Beschreiben Sie die Geografie und Demografie des Landes.
5. Warum gibt es regionale Unterschiede innerhalb Hessens? Welche Unterschiede kann man erkennen?
6. Was ist der Hessentag?

DIALEKTTIPP: Hessisch

Hören Sie ein Beispiel dieses Dialekts.

Hessisch ist ein fränkischer Dialekt, der im größten Teil Hessens und in angrenzenden Gebieten gesprochen wird. Es gibt fünf teilweise sehr unterschiedliche Varianten des Hessischen, aber oft wird die südhessische Mundart des Rhein-Main-Gebiets als das einzige Hessisch betrachtet, denn Regionalprogramme des Hessischen Rundfunks (HR), die teilweise auch außerhalb Hessens übertragen werden, sind häufig von der Sprache des Frankfurter Raums gefärbt.

Im hessischen Sprachraum hört man charakteristische Wörter wie *Bembel* (Apfelweinkrug), *Schnibbelsche* (kleines Stück), *hogge* (sitzen [hocken]) und *babbele* (sprechen [babbeln]). In der Grammatik und der Aussprache gibt es ebenfalls Unterschiede.

Dialekttipp. Ask students: *Wo wird Hessisch gesprochen? Warum wird die Frankfurter Mundart für das Hessische schlechthin gehalten? Welche Unterschiede gibt es zwischen Hochdeutsch und Hessisch?* After students have completed the activity, write the dialect phrases on the board and ask: *Wann ist für einen Hessen „Sunndachaawend"? Was isst er, wenn er „Lewwerworscht" isst? Und wie ist das Wetter, wenn er es als „rischdisch herrlisch" beschreibt?* Answers: *„Sunndachaawend"* = Sonntagabend; *„Lewwerworscht"* = Leberwurst; *„rischdisch herrlisch"* = richtig herrlich.

Zum Dialekt

Wie sagt man das? Wählen Sie die richtigen Erklärungen der Unterschiede zwischen Hessisch und Hochdeutsch.

Hochdeutsch → Hessisch

_g_	1.	Wiese, Karte → Wies, Kart
_l_	2.	Magen, auch, klein → Maache, aach, klaa
_h_	3.	wichtig, verzichten → wischtisch, verzischde
_b_	4.	Papa, Tasche, Zucker → Babba, Dasch, Zugger
_f_	5.	er schläft → er duud schlafe
_e_	6.	Häuschen, Blümchen → Häusje/Häusersche, Blümmelsche
_a_	7.	Wiesen, Karten, Würmer → Wisse, Karde, Wemscher
_k_	8.	Regen, Säge → Reesche, Sääch
_i_	9.	Bäumchen, lesen, hören → Beemsch, leese, heere
_k_	10.	Küche, drüben → Kisch, dribbe
_d_	11.	Frankfurt, Blut → Frankfort, Bluud
_c_	12.	Stube, habe → Stuwe, hawwe

a. andere Pluralformen bei Nomen

b. *p, t, k* → oft *b, d, g*

c. *b* → *w*

d. *u* → manchmal *o, uu*

e. Verkleinerungsform *-(er/el)sche/-je*

f. *tun* als Hilfswort im Präsens

g. *-e* Endung fällt weg

h. *-ich* → *-isch*

i. *eu, e, ö* → manchmal *ee*

j. *ü* → manchmal *i*

k. *g* → *(s)ch*

l. *a, au, ei* → manchmal *aa*

Lese- und Hörtexte

Lesetext 1 ────────────

Rhein-Main-Jobbörse (Stellenanzeigen)

urban agglomeration

Das Rhein-Main-Gebiet ist der Ballungsraum°, der etwa die südliche Hälfte Hessens umfasst und auch die an Hessen angrenzenden Städte Aschaffenburg in Bayern und Mainz in Rheinland-Pfalz einschließt. Das städtische Gebiet ist eines der wichtigsten Wirtschaftszentren Deutschlands und besitzt nach dem

concentration of industry

Ruhrgebiet die zweithöchste Industriedichte° Deutschlands. 400.000 Unternehmen in vielen Branchen beschäftigen hier rund 2 Millionen Arbeitnehmer. Vorrangig zu nennen sind chemisch-pharmazeutische Industrie, Maschinen- und Fahrzeugbau und vor allem im führenden Finanz- und Messeplatz Frankfurt

service sector

am Main Dienstleistungsunternehmen°. Große Arbeitgeber in der Region sind etwa der Automobilhersteller Opel in Rüsselsheim, die weltgrößte Versicherungsgesellschaft Allianz, die deutsche Fluggesellschaft Lufthansa und die Deutsche Bank. Zahlreiche andere weltweit bekannte Unternehmen wie Proctor & Gamble, Kraft, Nestlé, Merck und Siemens, um nur einige wenige zu nennen, sind hier

commuters

in der Region vertreten. Etwa 390.000 Pendler° fahren jeden Tag teilweise mehr als hundert Kilometer zur Arbeit in das Rhein-Main-Gebiet.

In den folgenden Stellenanzeigen aus der Rhein-Main-Region bekommen Sie einen Einblick in den Arbeitsmarkt der Region. Sie können gleichzeitig sehen, wie deutsche Stellenanzeigen aussehen.

Geschäftsmann vor dem Hauptsitz der Deutschen Bank

Vor dem Lesen

Was für Informationen erwarten Sie in einer Stellenanzeige? Was gehört nicht in eine Stellenanzeige?

Beim Lesen

Ergänzen Sie die Tabelle mit Informationen aus dem Text, soweit die Infos vorhanden sind.

Stelle	Standort	befristet oder unbefristet?	Information zum Gehalt?
Bauleiter/in	Pfungstadt	unbefristet	attraktives Gehalt
Rechtsanwalt/-anwältin	Darmstadt	unbefristet	keine Informationen zum Gehalt
Elektriker/in	Frankfurt a. M.	auf 4–5 Wochen befristet	Gehalt nach Tarifvertrag
Kundenberater/in	Hanau	unbefristet	Gehalt nach Tarifvertrag
Erzieher/in	Schwalbach am Taunus	befristet	Gehalt nach Tarifvertrag

Rhein-Main-Jobbörse

Als erfolgreiches mittelständisches Bauunternehmen mit Hauptsitz in der Rhein-Main-Region sind wir mit über 800 Mitarbeitern in allen Bereichen des Hoch-, Tief- und Straßenbaus tätig.

Zur Verstärkung unseres Teams suchen wir für unsere **Tiefbau-Niederlassung**[a] in **Pfungstadt** zum nächstmöglichen Termin einen engagierten

Bauleiter (m/w) Dipl.-Ing. FH/TU*

Sie übernehmen eigenverantwortlich Projekte im Erd-, Kanal- und Straßenbau und sind u. a. für die Bauleitung, Abrechnung[b] und die Nachtragskalkulation zuständig.

Wir bieten eine Dauerstellung in einem zukunftsorientierten Unternehmen bei offener und angenehmer Arbeitsatmosphäre. Unterstützt werden Sie von einem leistungsorientierten Team.

Neben einem attraktiven Gehalt steht Ihnen ein Firmenwagen zur Verfügung.

Wenn Sie diese berufliche Herausforderung reizt, senden Sie Ihre Bewerbungsunterlagen bitte an:

Robert Klein GmbH & Co. KG / Dudweilerstraße 151 / 64319 Pfungstadt / Telefon: 06894-15 303 / Fax: 06894-15 319

[a]*civil engineering branch office*   [b]*billing*

*Siehe **Kulturtipps**: Dipl.-Ing. FH/TU

Wir sind eine in Deutschland fest etablierte Kanzlei[a] und suchen

einen Rechtsanwalt (m/w) im Bereich Arbeitsrecht

in Festanstellung[b] für unseren Standort in Darmstadt

Ihre Aufgaben:
Ihnen wird als Berufsanfänger oder Rechtsanwalt mit bis zu zwei Jahren Erfahrung die Möglichkeit gegeben, Ihre Expertise auszubauen. Sie werden namhafte in- und ausländische Unternehmen aus Industrie und Handel sowie die öffentliche Hand[c] beraten. Sie werden dabei in Ihrer Weiterbildung gefördert, um so langfristig Ihre Karriere als Anwalt zu planen.

Ihre Qualifikationen:
- 2. Staatsexamen[d] mit in der Summe aus beiden mindestens 17 Punkte[e]
- nachweisbar gute Englischkenntnisse
- einen Lebenslauf, in dem das Arbeitsrecht als roter Faden zu erkennen ist
- gerne eine Promotion und/oder einen LL.M.[f]

Interessiert? Dann freuen wir uns auf Ihre aussagekräftige Bewerbung. Ihre Bewerbungsunterlagen sollten Anschreiben, Lebenslauf und Zeugnisse enthalten. Bitte geben Sie auch den gewünschten Arbeitsbeginn an.

Kanzlei Gaßmann, Brauer, Ostheim, Rainer Ostheim, Rechtsanwalt, Fachanwalt für Arbeitsrecht, Wilhelminenstraße 10, 64283 Darmstadt, Telefon: 0 61 51/1 01 42 63, Telefax: 0 61 51/1 01 42 65

[a]*law office*   [b]*permanent position*   [c]*public authorities*   [d]*bar exam*   [e]*17 points (out of possible 18)*
[f]*Legum Magister (Master of Laws)*

Für unser erfolgreiches Unternehmen der Elektrobranche im Großraum Frankfurt a. M. suchen wir ab sofort vorerst für 4–5 Wochen

zwei Elektriker/-innen für die Frankfurter Messe*

in Vollzeit mit 45 Wochenstunden.

Ihre Aufgaben:
- Vorbereiten von Anschlüssen[a] für techn. Geräte und Lichtquellen
- Anschließen von techn. Geräten und Lichtquellen
- Führerschein ist von Vorteil aber kein Muss

Sie haben eine abgeschlossene Berufsausbildung† in der Elektrobranche, sind flexibel, arbeiten gerne im Team und freuen sich auf Herausforderungen?–Dann freuen wir uns auf Ihre Bewerbung!

Wir bieten:
- Leistungsgerechte[b] Bezahlung nach BZA-DGB-Tarifvertrag[c]
- Einsatz mit der Option zur Übernahme bei nachgewiesener Eignung

Bei Tätigkeiten außerhalb des Wohnortes übernehmen wir Unterkunftskosten[d], vergüten Ihnen die Kosten für die Heimfahrt am Wochenende und VMA[e].

Wir erwarten Ihre Bewerbung mit Anschreiben, Lebenslauf, Zeugnissen an:

Herrn Michael Brauns / Klingerstraße 25 60313 Frankfurt / Telefon +49-69-920377-0 / Fax +49-69-920377-55

---

[a]*connections* [b]*commensurate with performance* [c]*collective bargaining agreement between the Federal Association for Temporary Employment and the German Federation of Trade Unions* [d]*cost of housing*
[e]*= Verpflegungsmehrwaufwand per diems*

*Siehe **Kulturtipps**: Frankfurter Messe
†Siehe **Kulturtipps**: Berufsausbildung

Wir suchen eine/n KundenberaterIn.

Als erfolgreiche Privatkundenbank wissen wir auch, wie wir als engagierter Arbeitgeber begeistern können. Entdecken Sie bei einer interessanten und vielseitigen Tätigkeit im Allfinanzbereich neue berufliche Perspektiven in unserer Filiale in Hanau.

Ihr Profil:
- abgeschlossene kaufmännische Berufsausbildung
- niederländische Sprachkenntnisse auf muttersprachlichem Niveau
- gute Deutschkenntnisse in Wort und Schrift
- weitere Fremdsprachen von Vorteil
- Erfahrung im Umgang mit Kunden
- gute Kenntnisse in MS-Office
- sorgfältige und verantwortungsvolle Arbeitsweise
- Teamfähigkeit

Wir bieten Ihnen:
- einen sehr interessanten Arbeitsplatz
- attraktive Bezahlung nach TvöD[a]
- volle soziale Absicherung[b]
- unbefristeter Arbeitsvertrag

Wie Sie sich bewerben:

Bitte bewerben Sie sich mit Ihren vollständigen Bewerbungsunterlagen inkl. Eintrittstermin. Nutzen Sie am besten unseren Online-Bewerbungsbogen. Alternativ können Sie Ihre Unterlagen an unser Recruiting Center, Postfach 12 94 01, 60311 Frankfurt am Main schicken. Bitte geben Sie dabei folgende Referenznummer an: DB-1309-7328. Für Fragen steht Ihnen Herr Eric Meyer, Personalreferent, unter der Telefonnummer 040 / 30 29 44 61 gerne zur Verfügung.

---

[a]*= Tarifvertrag für den öffentlichen Dienst collective bargaining agreement for civil servants* [b]*benefits*

Die Stadt Schwalbach am Taunus mit 14.700 Einwohnern und verkehrsgünstig im Main-Taunus-Kreis gelegen sucht für eine Kindertagesstätte[a] zum 1. August eine Elternzeitvertretung* für die Position

Erzieher/in

Sie haben eine abgeschlossene Ausbildung als staatlich anerkannte/n Erzieher/in, haben pädagogische, soziale und kommunikative Kompetenzen, sind sehr flexibel und sehr zuverlässig, haben Erfahrungen mit altersübergreifenden[b] Gruppen (wünschenswert) und können ein Instrument spielen (wünschenswert).

Diese abwechslungsreiche und anspruchsvolle Teilzeit-Beschäftigung (27,5 Stunden/Woche) ist zunächst befristet auf 1 Jahr. Die Arbeitszeit liegt in der Regel von Montag bis Freitag zwischen 7.30 und 13.00 Uhr.

Das Bezahlung richtet sich nach TvöD. Bei gleicher Eignung werden Schwerbehinderte bevorzugt.

Sollten wir Ihr Interesse an dieser Stelle geweckt haben, freuen wir uns über Ihre aussagefähige Bewerbung mit Lebenslauf, Zeugnissen und Lichtbild bis spätestens 15.05. an den Magistrat der Stadt Schwalbach, Badener Straße 25, 65824 Schwalbach am Taunus, Tel.: 06196/317682

---

[a] *daycare facility* [b]*of mixed age*

*Siehe **Kulturtipps:** Elternzeit

Kulturtipps

▪ Dipl.-Ing. FH/TH

Die Abkürzung Dipl.-Ing. FH/TH bezeichnet den Hochschulabschluss „Diplom" im Bereich Ingenieurwesen an einer Fachhochschule (FH) oder einer Technischen Hochschule (TH). Weil die EU auf ein einheitliches Hochschulwesen zielt, sollten die traditionellen deutschen Diplom- und Magister-Abschlüsse bis 2010 durch Bachelor/Master-Studiengänge ersetzt worden sein. Trotzdem wollen viele Deutsche noch den Titel „Diplomingenieur" neben den neuen Abschlüssen beibehalten, denn er gilt weltweit als Zeichen von Qualität.

▪ Frankfurter Messe

Frankfurt ist schon seit dem Mittelalter ein bedeutender Messeplatz. Heute ist die Messe Frankfurt GmbH das größte deutsche Messeunternehmen. In den neun Hallen und dem angeschlossenen Kongresszentrum finden zahlreiche bekannte Messen und viele der weltweit größten Ausstellungen in den Bereichen Konsumgüter, Schreibwaren, Architektur, Automobiltechnik und Bücher statt. Zu den Dutzenden von Messen und weit über hundert Kongressen, Konzerten und kulturellen, wirtschaftlichen sowie sportlichen Veranstaltungen kommen jährlich rund drei Millionen Besucher.

Automobilmesse Frankfurt

▪ Berufsausbildung

Eine Berufsausbildung ist eine zwei- oder dreijährige Lehre, in der der/die Auszubildende (Azubi) neben dem Besuch einer Berufsschule in einem Betrieb praktische Erfahrung erhält. Es gibt rund 340 staatlich anerkannte Ausbildungsberufe, bei denen der Staat Lehrzeit und Lehrinhalte regelt, die mit einer staatlichen Prüfung abgeschlossen werden. Etwa 60 Prozent der deutschen Jugendlichen entscheiden sich für eine staatlich anerkannte Berufsausbildung statt eines Studiums an einer Hochschule.

Junge Frau macht Ausbildung als Metallbauerin

▪ Elternzeit

Die Elternzeit bietet arbeitenden Eltern die Möglichkeit, sich ihrem neugeborenen Kind zu widmen und gleichzeitig Kontakt zum Beruf zu bewahren. Mütter und Väter haben dadurch das Recht auf eine völlige Freistellung von der Arbeit, bis das Kind drei Jahre alt wird. Während dieser Zeit besteht Kündigungsschutz (*protection from job termination*) und ein Recht auf Teilzeitarbeit. Nach Ende der Elternzeit haben die Eltern Anspruch auf ihren oder einen gleichwertigen Arbeitsplatz.

Nomen

der Bauleiter, -/die Bauleiterin,
-nen *construction manager*

der Erzieher, -/die Erzieherin,
-nen *preschool teacher/
caregiver*

die Kenntnis, -se *knowledge*

der Kundenberater, -/
die Kundenberaterin,
-nen *customer service
representative*

der Lebenslauf, ⁻e *resume*

die Promotion, -en *doctorate
(PhD, MD, LLD, etc.)*

der Rechtsanwalt, ⁻e/die
Rechtsanwältin, -nen *lawyer*

der/die Schwerbehinderte, -n
(adj. noun) handicapped person

die Stelle, -n *job, position; place*

die Tätigkeit, -en *activity; job*

die Unterlagen *(pl.) documents*

der Vorteil, -e *advantage*

das Zeugnis, -se *academic record*

Verben

beraten (berät), beriet,
beraten *to advise*

bevorzugen *to prefer*

reizen *to tempt, provoke*

sich bewerben (bewirbt), bewarb,
beworben (um) *to apply (for)*

Adjektive und Adverbien

anspruchsvoll *challenging*

befristet *fixed-term; temporary*

verantwortungsvoll *responsible*

zuständig für *responsible for*

Ausdrücke

der rote Faden *thread, recurring
theme*

10-1 Textarbeit: Mehr zu den Stellen. Erweitern Sie die Informationen, die Sie in der *Beim-Lesen*-Übung gesammelt haben. Einige Informationen nur indirekt zu vermuten.

Stelle	Arbeitgeber	Arbeitsbeginn	Teilzeit oder Vollzeit?	benötigter Abschluss
Bauleiter/in	Robert Klein GmbH & Co. KG	zum nächstmöglichen Termin	Vollzeit	Dipl.-Ing. FH/TH
Rechtsanwalt/-anwältin	Kanzlei Gassmann, Brauer, Ostheim	Bewerber soll den Arbeitsbeginn angeben	Vollzeit	Staatsexamen, gerne auch Promotion oder LL.M.
Elektriker/in	ein erfolgreiches Unternehmen der Elektrobranche	ab sofort	Vollzeit	Ausbildung in der Elektrobranche
Kundenberater/in	eine erfolgreiche Privatkundenbank	Bewerber soll den Eintrittstermin nennen	Vollzeit	kaufmännische Berufsausbildung
Erzieher/in	die Stadt Schwalbach am Taunus	zum 1. August	Teilzeit	Ausbildung als staatlich anerkannter Erzieher/anerkannte Erzieherin

10-2 Textarbeit: Welche Stelle? Welche Beschreibung passt zu welcher Stelle?

Bauleiter/in	Elektriker/in	Erzieher/in
Kundenberater/in	Rechtsanwalt/-anwältin	

Answers for 10-2. **1.** Rechtsanwalt; **2.** Kundenberater; **3.** Bauleiter; **4.** Elektriker; **5.** Bauleiter; **6.** Erzieher; **7.** Rechtsanwalt; **8.** Elektriker; **9.** Erzieher; **10.** Kundenberater; **11.** Elektriker; **12.** Erzieher

1. Diese Stelle ist für Berufsanfänger.
2. Für diese Stelle muss man Niederländisch sprechen können.
3. Man bekommt ein Auto der Firma.
4. Man installiert Lichter.
5. Bei dieser Stelle baut man Brücken und Straßen auf und ab.
6. Ein Musikinstrument zu spielen wäre von Vorteil.

7. Bei dieser Stelle berät man Klienten in deutschen und ausländischen Unternehmen.

8. Einen Führerschein zu besitzen, wäre von Vorteil, ist aber nicht unbedingt notwendig.

9. Man muss flexibel und zuverlässig sein.

10. Für diese Stelle kann man sich online bewerben.

11. Obwohl diese Tätigkeit befristet ist, besteht die Möglichkeit zur festen Anstellung.

12. Qualifizierte Schwerbehinderte werden für diese Position bevorzugt.

10-3 Vokabelarbeit. Ergänzen Sie die Sätze mit Wörtern aus den *Neuen Vokabeln.* Achten Sie dabei auch auf die Wortform.

1. Oliver möchte _____ Erzieher _____ werden, denn er arbeitet gerne mit Kindern.

2. Britta hat ihren Abschluss gemacht und _____ bewirbt _____ _____ sich _____ nun um eine Stelle als Tierpflegerin.

3. Ein Tischler braucht gute _____ Kenntnisse _____ im Bereich Holzverarbeitung.

4. Der Kundenberater, Herr Beckmann, ist _____ zuständig _____ _____ für _____ unsere Kunden in China.

5. Stephanie langweilt sich bei ihrer Arbeit im Café. Sie möchte lieber eine _____ anspruchsvolle _____ Stelle.

6. Obwohl mich die Stelle in Offenbach _____ reizt _____, möchte ich nicht so weit pendeln müssen.

7. Zu den _____ Vorteilen _____ des Pilotenberufes zählt die Möglichkeit, die Welt zu sehen und immer wieder Neues zu erleben.

8. Monikas neue Tätigkeit als Rechtsanwältin ist auf ein Jahr _____ befristet _____.

 10-4 Zur Diskussion. Besprechen Sie die Fragen.

1. Wie weist man in den Stellenanzeigen darauf hin, dass sich Frauen wie Männer für die Position bewerben sollen? Wo gibt es Hinweise auf das Alter der Bewerber? Inwiefern sind Stellenanzeigen in Ihrem Land ähnlich oder anders?

2. Welche dieser Stellen interessiert Sie am meisten? Warum? Welche interessiert Sie am wenigsten?

3. Arbeiten Sie jetzt? Wenn ja, welche Aufgaben gehören zu Ihrem Job? Wie lange arbeiten Sie schon in dieser Stelle? Was mussten Sie tun, um sich für die Stelle zu bewerben? Wenn Sie zurzeit nicht arbeiten, beschreiben Sie Ihren letzten Job.

4. Was wäre für Sie der ideale Beruf? Welche Qualifikationen und Fähigkeiten braucht man für diesen Beruf?

10-5 Tutor/in für Deutsch gesucht! Sie haben die Aufgabe, einen neuen Tutor/eine neue Tutorin für das Deutschprogramm Ihrer Universität anzustellen. Besprechen Sie, welche Ausbildung, Fähigkeiten und Erfahrungen Bewerber haben sollten. Dann entwerfen Sie eine Stellenanzeige für die Position. Benutzen Sie die Stellenanzeigen oben als Modell.

10-6 Der/Die ideale Kandidat/in. Wählen Sie eine der Stellenanzeigen, und stellen Sie sich vor, Sie sind der ideale Bewerber/die ideale Bewerberin dafür. Stellen Sie sich dem Arbeitsgeber zunächst schriftlich vor, indem Sie sich beschreiben und Ihre besonderen Fähigkeiten für diese Stelle erklären.

Beispiel für die Position Elektriker/in:

Ich heiße Kurt Strohmeyer, bin 26 Jahre alt und habe eine abgeschlossene Berufsausbildung als Elektriker. Ich wohne nicht in Frankfurt, sondern ganz nah in Mainz, …

Ich bin für diese Position besonders geeignet, weil …

Ich möchte diese Stelle, weil …

In meiner letzten Stelle habe ich …

Note for 10-7. Relevant web addresses for Internet research activities can be found in *MyGermanLab* and on the Companion Website.

Introduction to *Lesetext 2*. Ask students what they learned from the text introduction and to speculate using information from the introduction. *Welche Superlative nimmt der Flughafen für sich in Anspruch? Wie kommt man wohl vom Flughafen in die Stadt? Wie viele Passagiere benutzen pro Jahr/Tag den Flughafen? Was findet man wohl am Flughafen außer Passagieren?*

10-7 Eine Stelle für mich. Benutzen Sie die Suchfunktion einer online Jobbörse, um im Rhein-Main-Gebiet eine Stelle zu finden, die für Sie geeignet wäre. Dann beschreiben Sie dem Arbeitgeber schriftlich wie oben in **10-6**, warum er/sie Sie anstellen sollte.

Lesetext 2

Chaos am Flughafen: „Ein klarer Fall von höherer Gewalt" (Zeitungsartikel)

Als größte lokale Arbeitsstätte in ganz Deutschland ist der Flughafen Frankfurt ein bedeutender Wirtschaftsfaktor für die Rhein-Main-Region. Im und am Flughafen sind über 500 Firmen vertreten, bei denen über 70.000 Menschen beschäftigt sind. Aber natürlich auch als Verkehrsknotenpunkt° trägt der Flughafen, der mit Abstand größte und verkehrsreichste Deutschlands und der drittgrößte Europas, zum wirtschaftlichen Erfolg des Rhein-Main-Gebiets bei. Zu der sehr gut ausgebauten Verkehrsinfrastruktur des Flughafens gehören drei Bahnhöfe und direkte Anbindung an die zwei meistbefahrenen Autobahnen Europas, die nordsüdlich verlaufende A5 und die ostwestlich verlaufende A3.

transportation hub

Eine Boeing 747 fliegt über die Autobahn vor der Landung in Frankfurt.

Jährlich werden über 50 Millionen Passagiere und über zwei Millionen Tonnen Fracht und Post durch den internationalen Rhein-Main-Flughafen befördert. Es kommen täglich 145.000 Reisende durch den Flughafen, eine Zahl, die Jahr für Jahr steigt. Für diesen Artikel aus der *Frankfurter Allgemeinen Zeitung* wurden Reisende am Flughafen an einem Nachmittag interviewt, wo nicht alles nach Plan verlief.

Siehe **Kulturtipps**: Frankfurter Allgemeine Zeitung

Vor dem Lesen

1. Sind Sie schon mal mit dem Flugzeug gereist? Wenn ja, wohin? Mussten Sie lange auf Ihren Flug warten? Was haben Sie während Ihrer Wartezeit gemacht?

2. Aus welchen Gründen können Verzögerungen im Flugverkehr entstehen? Wie reagieren Sie auf Verzögerungen im öffentlichen Verkehr (Flugzeuge, Bus, Bahn)?

Beim Lesen

Suchen Sie im Lesetext die Namen der interviewten Passagiere, wo diese herkommen und wohin sie reisen. In einigen Fällen wird die Information nicht direkt gegeben, lässt sich aber vermuten.

Passagier(e)	Wohnort	Reiseziel
Christopher Blanks	England	London
Ian, Jason, Katie und Bennett	Utah	Utah
Chinesin	China	London
Volkmar Schmidt	Frankfurt	Berlin

10-05 to 10-08

Chaos am Flughafen: „Ein klarer Fall von höherer Gewalt"

von Katharina Iskandar und Jochen Remmert

Christopher Blanks wartet schon seit Stunden. Er will nach London, und eigentlich wäre der Engländer auch schon längst dort. Um zwölf Uhr sollte seine Maschine starten – jetzt ist es fast vier. Blanks steht in der Abflughalle des Terminal 1, umgeben von tausenden anderen Passagieren, die nicht so gute Laune haben wie er.

„Was soll ich machen?", fragt er, zuckt die Schultern und trinkt einen Schluck Wasser aus einer Flasche, die er in der drückenden Hitze der Halle fest umklammert hält. Irgendwann werde er heute Nacht schon nach Haus kommen, meint er. Aber dass wegen eines Regens gleich 200 Flüge gestrichen werden müssen, das kann er dann doch nicht so ganz verstehen. „In England regnet es schließlich ständig. Ich dachte, das sei nichts Besonderes für den Flugverkehr."

200 Flüge mussten gestrichen werden

Doch genau das ist es offenbar. Flughafenbetreiber Fraport lässt jedenfalls verlauten, dass es zu gefährlich sei, die Flugzeuge während des Unwetters starten und landen zu lassen. Der Regen sei zu heftig, der böige Wind zu stark. „Ein klarer Fall von höherer Gewalt", das Wetter könne man schließlich nicht kontrollieren. Insgesamt 200 Flüge mussten gestrichen werden, etwa 120 allein bei der Lufthansa. Erste Verzögerungen im Flugbetrieb hatte es schon am frühen Morgen gegen 6.30 Uhr gegeben, als ein erstes starkes Gewitter mit heftigem Blitzschlag die auf dem Vorfeld 20

processing beschäftigten Arbeiter gefährdete: Die Abfertigung° der Maschinen wurde dort eingestellt – später der gesamte Flugverkehr.

Am Rande eines Buchladens sitzen Ian, Jason, Katie und Bennett, Schüler der Logan High School aus dem amerikanischen Bundesstaat Utah. Sie haben kaum noch Hoffnung, dass ihr Flieger Richtung Heimat an diesem 25 Nachmittag noch starten wird und freuen sich stattdessen über den Service des Bodenpersonals, das ihnen fast stündlich etwas zu Essen bringt. „Für uns ist das ein Abenteuer", sagt Ian. Die anderen nicken. Müde sind sie zwar, aber zu aufgeregt, um zu schlafen.

Ihre Eltern hätten am Telefon geraten, das Beste aus der Situation zu 30 machen. Doch das liegt für die Schüler an diesem Nachmittag etwa fünfzehn Kilometer entfernt und bleibt unerreichbar. „Frankfurt angucken, das wäre doch auch mal interessant", meint Katie, die mit ihren 14 Jahren die Jüngste in der Gruppe ist. Weil sie zum Französisch lernen nach Europa gekommen seien, hätten sie außer London und Rom „nur" Paris 35 kennengelernt.

baggage handling system ## Gepäckförderanlage° beschädigt

Was die vier jungen Amerikaner ebenso wie die anderen wartenden Passagiere zu dieser Zeit noch nicht wissen: Die Regenfälle haben auch die insgesamt rund 68 Kilometer lange Gepäckförderanlage unter den

in ... gezogen affected Flughafen-Gebäuden in Mitleidenschaft gezogen°. „Ich habe keine Ahnung, 40 wo mein Gepäck geblieben ist", sagt eine Chinesin, die nur zwischengelandet ist und wie Christopher Blanks auf dem Weg nach London ist. Aber darüber will sie sich auch gar keine Gedanken machen – „es wird sich schon einfinden."

Volkmar Schmidt hat sein Gepäck noch in der Hand, einen kleinen 45 schwarzen Trolli. Er wollte geschäftlich nach Berlin, sein Flug wurde von 16.45 auf 17.50 Uhr verlegt – und damit gehört der Siebenundvierzigjährige zu den Passagieren mit den kürzesten Wartezeiten. Trotzdem wird er vielleicht doch mit dem Zug fahren – seine Firma lasse gerade prüfen, ob es um diese Uhrzeit noch eine vernünftige Verbindung gebe, sagt er. So viel Glück 50 haben Christoffer Blanks und die High School-Schüler aus Utah nicht. Sie müssen warten. Wenn nötig, die ganze Nacht.

Kulturtipps

Frankfurter Allgemeine Zeitung

Die 1949 gegründete *Frankfurter Allgemeine Zeitung* (*F.A.Z.*) ist eine unabhängige überregionale Tageszeitung und eine der einflussreichsten Deutschlands. Mit einer Auflage von 360.000 Exemplaren ist sie auch eine der meistgelesenen Zeitungen des Landes. Sie wird außerdem in 145 Länder der Welt geliefert und hat damit die höchste Auslandsverbreitung aller deutschsprachigen Tageszeitungen.

Nomen

der Flug, ̈e *flight*

das Gepäck *luggage*

die Gewalt *power, authority*

das Gewitter, - *thunderstorm*

die Hoffnung, -en *hope*

die Laune, -n *mood*

das Unwetter, - *severe weather*

die Verbindung, -en
connection

die Verzögerung, -en *delay*

Verben

an·gucken (*colloq.*) *to look at*

ein·stellen *to discontinue*

gefährden *to endanger*

streichen, strich,
gestrichen *to cancel*

verlegen *to postone;*
to relocate

Adjektive und Adverbien

entfernt *distant, away*

gefährlich *dangerous*

gesamt *whole, entire*

heftig *heavy, violent*

nötig *necessary*

offenbar *apparently*

ständig *constant*

stattdessen *instead of that*

vernünftig *reasonable,*
sensible

Ausdrücke

Ich habe keine Ahnung. *I have*
no clue.

die Schultern zucken *to shrug*
(one's shoulders)

10-8 Textarbeit: Fragen zum Inhalt. Beantworten Sie die Fragen in Bezug auf den Lesetext.

1. Wie lange wartet Herr Blanks schon auf einen Flug?
2. Wie viele Flüge wurden gestrichen? Warum?
3. Welches Ereignis brachte die ersten Verzögerungen?
4. Worüber freuen sich die amerikanischen Schüler?
5. Warum waren die Schüler in Europa?
6. Was hindert den Flugverkehr außer dem Wetter?
7. Was will Herr Schmidt wegen der Verzögerung seines Fluges vielleicht tun?

Possible answers for 10-8.
1. Vor vier Stunden hat sein Flugzeug starten sollen. **2.** 200 Flüge wurden angeblich wegen des Regens gestrichen. **3.** Ein erstes starkes Gewitter gefährdete Arbeiter auf dem Vorfeld. **4.** Sie freuen sich über das Essen, das das Bodenpersonal ihnen ständig bringt. **5.** Sie haben Französisch gelernt. **6.** Die Gepäckförderanlage wurde durch das Unwetter beschädigt. **7.** Er will vielleicht stattdessen mit dem Zug nach Berlin reisen.

10-9 Textarbeit: Begriffe im Text. Erklären Sie, welche Bedeutung folgende Begriffe in Bezug auf den Artikel haben.

Beispiel: „Ein klarer Fall von höherer Gewalt"
Der Flughafen will damit sagen, man kann das Wetter nicht kontrollieren.

1. 120 Flüge
2. 6.30 Uhr
3. ein Buchladen
4. 15 Kilometer
5. London, Rom und Paris
6. ein Trolli
7. Berlin

Possible answers for 10-9.
1. Anzahl der Flüge, die von Lufthansa gestrichen wurden;
2. die ersten Verzögerungen;
3. Am Rande des Buchladens sitzen die Schüler und warten.
4. Distanz vom Flughafen in die Stadt; **5.** die Städte, die die Schüler aus Utah kennengelernt haben; **6.** das Gepäck von Volkmar Schmidt, das er noch in der Hand hat; **7.** das Reiseziel von Volkmar Schmidt

10-10 Vokabelarbeit. Ergänzen Sie die Sätze mit Wörtern aus den *Neuen Vokabeln.* Achten Sie dabei auch auf die Wortform.

1. Seit seiner Eröffnung 1936 wurde der Flughafen ___ständig___ vergrößert.

2. Von der Besucherterrasse im Flughafen können wir uns die Flugzeuge bei Starts und Landungen ___angucken___ .

3. Bei Gewitter oder heftigem Schneefall muss der gesamte Flugbetrieb ___eingestellt___ werden.

4. Manche Passagiere haben bei solchen Verzögerungen schlechte ___Laune___ .

5. Unser Flug nach Hongkong wurde ___gestrichen___ , und der nächstmögliche Flug fliegt erst in zwei Tagen.

6. Wenn sich der Flug nach London verspätet, verpasse ich dort meine ___Verbindung___ nach Toronto.

7. Bei einer längeren Verzögerung wollen wir nicht am Flughafen bleiben. ___Stattdessen___ fahren wir die kurze Strecke in die Stadt und sehen uns um.

8. Anstatt im Flughafen zu schlafen, hielten wir es für ___vernünftig___ , in einem Hotel zu übernachten.

9. Nicht nur Unwetter, sondern auch Vogelschwärme oder Vulkanausbrüche können Flugzeuge ___gefährden___ .

10-11 Situationen im Verkehr. Besprechen Sie, wie Sie in den folgenden Situationen reagieren oder was Sie machen würden.

1. Sie sind am Frankfurter Flughafen gelandet, aber später als erwartet. Ihr Anschlussflug nach Tokio fliegt in 15 Minuten ab, das Gate ist aber auf der anderen Seite des Flughafens.

2. Sie fliegen auf Geschäftsreise nach München und sind in Frankfurt zwischengelandet. Es ist 14.00 Uhr. Ihr Flug nach München wurde gestrichen und die nächstmögliche Verbindung ist erst morgen früh um 7.30 Uhr.

3. Sie sind nach zwei Wochen Urlaub in Deutschland und einem langen transatlantischen Flug endlich wieder nach Hause gekommen. Ihr Gepäck ist aber nicht mitgekommen.

4. Heute Morgen haben Sie eine große Prüfung in Mathematik. Aber Sie haben gerade den Bus verpasst.

5. Sie hatten einen langen Tag an der Uni und wollen jetzt nach Hause fahren. Aber offenbar hat jemand Ihr Fahrrad gestohlen!

10-12 Liebe Renate! Volkmar Schmidt hat wegen der Verzögerung im Flughafen seine Reisepläne geändert und schreibt seiner Frau vom Flughafen aus eine SMS auf seinem Handy, um sie über die Änderung zu informieren. Was sagt er ihr? Sie sind Herr Schmidt. Schreiben Sie die SMS.

10-13 Reisepanne. Schreiben Sie einen Artikel für die *Frankfurter Allgemeine Zeitung* über ein Reiseerlebnis, wo etwas Unerwartetes und Ungeplantes passiert ist. Wählen Sie eine der Ideen unten oder erfinden Sie eine Situation.

Alternative for 10-13. Have students write about a real travel experience they had.

Streik im Hotel	Grippe auf der Urlaubsinsel
Unfall auf der Autobahn	Flug landet am falschen Reiseziel

Hörtext 1

„Ebbelwei muss Ebbelwei bleiben" – Hessen kämpfen für den Apfelwein (Nachricht)

Introduction to *Hörtext 1*. After having students read the title and introduction, ask them to speculate what they might hear in the news piece. *Was meinen Sie: Was hört man vielleicht in dieser Nachricht? Was sagt uns der Titel? Was für ein Streit könnte das sein? Wer ist wohl am Streit beteiligt?* Then ask them what they learned from the introduction: *Was ist Apfelwein? Wie unterscheidet sich der hessische Apfelwein von anderen Getränken, die aus Äpfeln gemacht werden?*

Zu den traditionellen kulinarischen Spezialitäten Hessens gehört der Apfelwein. Das leicht alkholisches Getränk, der in den hessischen Dialekten „Ebbelwoi", „Äppelwei", „Äppler" oder „Stöffche" genannt wird, ist in der Regel eine Mischung verschiedener Apfelsorten und ist saurer als die leicht süßlichen Variationen, die man größtenteils im Rest der Welt kennt.

Apfelwein mit Bembel und Geripptem

Die Hessen haben eine ganze Kultur um ihren Stöffche entwickelt. Rund 55 hessische Keltereien° produzieren 40 Millionen Liter jährlich. Es wird traditionell in einem „Bembel", einem besonderen Tonkrug°, der das Getränk kalt hält, serviert und aus einem „Gerippten", einem leicht geriffelten 0,25-Liter Glas, getrunken. Es gibt auch Gerichte, wie etwa Rippchen° mit Kraut, Handkäs mit Musik oder Kartoffeln mit grüner Soße, zu denen es zu trinken gilt.

2007 war der hessische Apfelwein in den Nachrichten. Hier erfahren Sie über den Streit, der damals wegen eines Vorhabens der Europäischen Kommission° entfacht wurde.

fruit crushing and pressing house

earthenware jug

smoked ribs

Siehe **Kulturtipps:** Handkäs mit Musik

European Commission; executive body of the EU

Vor dem Hören

Gibt es Lebensmittelgesetze in Ihrem Land? Was wird zum Beispiel durch solche Gesetze geregelt?

Beim Hören

Während des Hörens kommen folgende Vokabeln vor:

„Ebbelwei muss Ebbelwei bleiben" - Hessen kämpfen für den Apfelwein
10-09

Verordnung *regulation*
Rebkrankheiten *vine diseases*
beeinträchtigten *impaired*
Wirte *tavern keepers*
behördliche Genehmigung
    official license
Gebräu *brew*

SPD (Sozialdemokratische Partei
    Deutschlands) *Social
    Democratic Party of Germany*
keltern *press wine*
Empörung *outrage*
FDP (Freie Demokratische
    Partei) *Free Democratic Party*
beharren auf *insist on*

Hören Sie sich den Bericht an. Finden Sie für jede Bezeichnung für den Apfelwein die richtige Erläuterung.

__e__ 1. Apfelwein

__d__ 2. Cidre

__c__ 3. Sidra

__a__ 4. Viez

__b__ 5. das hessische
        Traditionsgetränk

__h__ 6. Ebbelwei

__g__ 7. Stöffche

__f__ 8. das hessische
        Nationalgetränk

a. wie der Apfelwein in den Regionen Saar und Mosel heißt

b. wie der hessische Ministerpräsident den Apfelwein bezeichnet

c. die spanische Bezeichnung für Apfelwein

d. die französische Bezeichnung für Apfelwein

e. der hochdeutsche Begriff für das hessische Getränk

f. wie ein Bürger aus Hanau den Apfelwein bezeichnet

g. was die Frankfurter Oberbürgermeisterin den Apfelwein nennt

h. wie die SPD-Chefin den Apfelwein nennt

Kulturtipps

Ebbelwoi-Viertel Sachsenhausen

Gegenüber der Innenstadt am südlichen Ufer des Mains liegt der Frankfurter Stadtteil Sachsenhausen, dessen historischer Teil von schmalen Gassen und mittelalterlichen Fachwerkhäusern geprägt ist. Hier befinden sich mehr Lokale als sonst wo, die selbst gekelterten (*pressed*) Apfelwein ausschenken und auch Frankfurter Spezialitäten servieren.

Handkäs mit Musik

Handkäs, ein weicher Sauermilchkäse, der mit der Hand geformt wird, ist eine hessische Spezialität, die oft mit Apfewein gepaart wird. Er wird traditionell „mit Musik", d. h. in einer Soße aus klein gehackten Zwiebeln, Essig, Öl, Kümmel (*caraway seeds*), Pfeffer und Salz serviert.

10-14 Textarbeit: Wer ist wer? Es kommen in der Nachricht eine Reihe von Namen und Bezeichnungen vor. Finden Sie für jeden Gruppen- oder Personennamen die richtige Erläuterung.

Answers for 10-14. 1. b; 2. f; 3. i; 4. a; 5. h; 6. g; 7. c; 8. e; 9. d

1. die Europäische Kommission
2. Wirte
3. Roland Koch
4. Andrea Ypsilanti
5. Petra Roth
6. Jörg-Uwe Hahn
7. Reinhard Schifferle
8. Natascha Engels
9. Hans-Jürgen Wiedemeyer

a. SPD-Chefin
b. die Exekutive der EU
c. ein Hesse aus Hanau
d. ein hessischer Bürger aus Maintal
e. eine Hessin aus Bad Nauheim
f. Betreiber der Apfelweinlokale
g. FDP-Landesvorsitzender
h. Frankfurter Oberbürgermeisterin
i. der hessische Ministerpräsident

10-15 Textarbeit: Richtig oder falsch? Wenn eine Aussage falsch ist, korrigieren Sie und ergänzen Sie sie mit Informationen aus dem Text.

1. Die Europäische Kommission will die Herstellung von Apfelwein verbieten.
2. Seit dem 16. Jahrhundert ist Frankfurt Zentrum des Apfelweins.
3. Apfelwein wurde beliebt, als sich das Klima für den Anbau von Weintrauben nicht mehr eignete.
4. Wirte in Hessen haben Apfelwein aus Frankreich und Spanien importiert.
5. Außerhalb von Hessen ist der Apfelwein unbekannt.
6. Der Ministerpräsident Hessens hat vor, sich für den Apfelwein einzusetzen.
7. Die Oberbürgermeisterin Frankfurts weist auf die 250 Jahre lange Tradition des Apfelweins in Hessen hin.
8. Ein hessischer Bürger hält die Diskussion über Wein für ein unwichtiges Geschäft für die EU.
9. Heutzutage keltert man den eigenen Apfelwein nicht mehr.
10. Hessen tritt aus der EU aus, wenn Apfelwein nicht mehr Apfelwein heißen darf.

Answers for 10-15. 1. F – Die Europäische Kommission will die Bezeichnung „Apfelwein" verbieten. 2. R; 3. R; 4. F – Wirte in Hessen haben selbst Apfelwein gekeltert. 5. F – Außerhalb von Hessen ist der Apfelwein unter anderen Namen bekannt. 6. R; 7. R; 8. R; 9. F – Einige Hessen pflegen diese Tradition und geben es an die Kinder weiter. 10. F – Der FDP-Landesvorsitzende Jörg-Uwe Hahn prophezeit, dass Hessen aus der EU austreten sollte, wenn Apfelwein nicht mehr Apfelwein heißen darf.

10-16 Zur Diskussion. Besprechen Sie die Fragen.

1. Warum will die EU wohl Gesetze über die Bezeichnung „Wein" machen? Was halten Sie von diesem Vorhaben der EU?
2. Wie wichtig ist die Bezeichnung einer Sache? Können Sie an Begriffe aus Ihrer Sprache denken, bei denen eine solche Aktion der Regierung ähnliche Reaktionen auslösen würde?
3. Was können Bürger eines demokratischen Landes tun, wenn sie gegen die Aktionen ihrer Regierung sind?
4. Was gehört zur Identität einer Region? Wie unterscheidet sich die Region, in der Sie leben, von anderen Regionen?

Teaching Suggestions for 10-17. Follow up the discussion with an in-class spontaneous free-writing activity on the same topic. Or have students decide on a new name for *Apfelwein*. Have them work in groups and be prepared to justify their name choice. Then have each group present its suggestion to the class and let the class vote on the best alternative.

Teaching Suggestion for 10-18. Share with students that in the final version of the wine regulation, the European Commission included wording that allowed the use of the term *Apfelwein* with reference to the Hessian specialty. You could also instead have students research the outcome of the conflict and report on their findings.

Introduction to *Lesetext 3*. Ask students what they learned from the introduction to the text. *Welche Funktion hat der Rhein-Main-Verkehrsverbund (RMV)? Wie wäre es wohl, mit öffentlichen*

transportation network
counties

Verkehrsmitteln in Hessen zu fahren, wenn der RMV nicht existieren würde? Students may need

short-range public
transportation

help understanding the differences between the trains mentioned in the introduction. *Regionalzüge* are local or regional trains whose

coordinated

lines traverse multiple cities within a region. *S-Bahnen* provide rapid transit within a suburban area. *U-Bahnen* are subway trains. *Straßenbahnen* are streetcars or electric trams that travel on rails through city streets.

extensive

10-17 „Apfelwein" verboten! Stellen Sie sich vor, die EU-Verordnung zum Begriff „Wein" wird Gesetz. Was passiert dann wohl? Wie reagieren die Hessen darauf? Was wird aus dem Apfelwein? Besprechen Sie die Möglichkeiten und entwerfen Sie ein Szenario für diesen Fall.

10-18 Rette den Apfelwein! Sie wollen einen Kommentar zu dieser Nachricht auf die Internetseite des Hessischen Rundfunks geben, um für den Begriff „Apfelwein" zu plädieren. Geben Sie in Ihrem Kommentar mindestens drei Argumente dafür.

Beginnen Sie so: *Apfelwein muss Apfelwein bleiben!* ...

Lesetext 3

Freizeit mit dem Rhein-Main-Verkehrsverbund (Freizeit-Tipps)

Der Rhein-Main-Verkehrsverbund° (RMV), der 1995 von 15 Landkreisen°, elf Städten und dem Land Hessen gebildet wurde, organisiert den öffentlichen Personennahverkehr° in Mittel- und Südhessen. Er koordiniert die Zusammenarbeit von mehr als 150 Verkehrsunternehmen und fördert dadurch die Nutzung öffentlicher Verkehrsmittel durch ein einheitliches Tarif-

S-Bahn der RMV

system mit einheitlichen Fahrscheinen und abgestimmten° Fahrplänen. Mit nur einer Fahrkarte kann man also jedes Nahverkehrsmittel im Verbundgebiet – Regionalzüge, S-Bahnen, U-Bahnen, Straßenbahnen und regionale wie lokale Busse – nutzen. Im nördlichen Drittel des Landes ist der viel kleinere Nordhessische Verkehrsverbund (NVV) zuständig für die Koordinierung des öffentlichen Nahverkehrs dort.

Das Gebiet des RMVs schließt 368 Gemeinden und eine Fläche von 14.000 Quadratkilometer ein und ist damit der zweitgrößte Verkehrsverbund in Deutschland. Das umfangreiche° Netz von Bahn- und Buslinien lässt eine Reihe von interessanten Zielen in Hessen relativ leicht erreichen. Auf seiner Internetseite empfiehlt der Rhein-Main-Verkehrsbund eine Menge solcher Ausflugsziele. Hier befindet sich eine Auswahl.

Vor dem Lesen

Gibt es in Ihrer Stadt ein öffentliches Verkehrsnetz? Wie breit ist das Netz der öffentlichen Verkehrsmittel? Wohin können Sie damit fahren? Was in Ihrer Gegend können Sie damit nicht erreichen?

Beim Lesen

1. Schauen Sie sich die Freizeit-Tipps an. Was für Informationen enthält jeder Tipp? Welche Informationen sind nicht dabei, die Sie trotzdem wichtig fänden?

2. Geben Sie die Adressen der Standorte in Google-Maps ein, um zu sehen, wo sie im Verhältnis zueinander liegen.

Freizeit mit dem Rhein-Main-Verkehrsbund

Freizeit-Tipps

Das RMV-Gebiet bietet spannende Ausflugsziele und tolle Möglichkeiten zur Freizeitgestaltung. Der RMV und seine Partner unterstützen viele davon. Auf diesen Seiten finden Sie schnell ein Ausflugsziel ganz nach Ihrem Geschmack.

Unsere Freizeit-Tipps beinhalten einen Link für nähere Informationen und selbstverständlich die passende Haltestelle mit Verknüpfung zur Verbindungsauskunft.
                                                                                                          5

Wir wünschen Ihnen viel Spaß!

1 Frankfurt im Überblick

Main Tower

Blick vom Main Tower auf Frankfurt

Der Panoramablick von der 200 Meter hoch gelegenen Aussichtsterrasse zählt zu den Höhepunkten eines Frankfurtbesuchs.

Von der Main Tower Terrasse sehen Sie nahezu alle historischen und modernen Sehenswürdigkeiten wie Dom und   10
Paulskirche, Alte Oper und Festhalle, Museumsufer, Henninger Turm und Messegelände und das Bankenviertel. Mit dem Aufzug gelangen Sie zur Aussichtsplattform, zum Restaurant oder in die Bar des Main Towers.

Der Eintritt ist kostenpflichtig.   15

Zu erreichen am besten über die Haltestellen „Taunusanlage" und „Willy-Brandt-Platz".

Zeilgalerie

Eine gute Alternative, um Frankfurt mal von oben zu betrachten, ist die Terrasse der Zeilgalerie. Der Zugang zu dieser Aussichtsterrasse ist kostenlos und bietet einen interessanten Blick über die Zeil* und das Stadtzentrum.

Die nächste Haltestelle ist „Hauptwache".   20

*Siehe **Kulturtipps**: Zeil

10-10 to 10-13

Main Tower / Neue Mainzer Straße 52-58 / 60311 Frankfurt / www.maintower.de

Zeilgalerie / Zeil 112-114 / 60313 Frankfurt / www.zeilgalerie.de

Ⓗ ▰▰▰▰▲ Frankfurt (Main) Taunusanlage

Ⓗ ▰▰▰▰▲ Frankfurt (Main) Willy-Brandt-Platz

Ⓗ ▰▰▰▰▲ Frankfurt (Main) Hauptwache   25

2 Hessisches Puppenmuseum Hanau-Wilhelmsbad

Spielzeug von der Antike bis zur Barbie

Im Mittelpunkt der ständigen Ausstellung steht die Entwicklung der europäischen Spielpuppe von der Antike bis in die Gegenwart, daneben „Puppen aus aller Welt" und „Zirkus und Jahrmarkt".

Kindern bietet das museumspädagogische Programm Veranstaltungsreihen und Entdeckungsreisen ins Museum an. Ob „Museumssafari", „Auf den Spuren von Indiana Jones" oder der nächtlichen Führung „Was machen Puppen eigentlich nachts?" – für jede Altersgruppe ist etwas dabei. Dazu   30 steht in jedem Raum Spielzeug für die Kinder bereit – ein großes Holzhaus, Plüschtiere, ein Kasperletheater* und vieles mehr.

Hessisches Puppenmuseum Hanau / Parkpromenade 5 / 63454 Hanau-Wilhelmsbad / www.hessisches-puppenmuseum.de

Ⓗ ▰▰▰▰▲ Hanau Wilhelmsbad Bahnhof   35

Ⓗ ▰▰▰▰▲ Hanau Bismarckturm

3 Goethe-Haus und Goethe-Museum Frankfurt

Das Leben gehört dem Lebendigen

Am 28. August 1749 kam im Großen Hirschgraben Johann Wolfgang Goethe zur Welt. Sein Elternhaus und die Stadt Frankfurt prägten den jungen Goethe. Das Elternhaus des Dichters zählt zu den bedeutendsten und beliebtesten Gedenkstätten[a] Deutschlands. Mit seinem alten Mobiliar und den Bildern erinnert es an das Leben der Familie Goethe.   40

Denn was wäre die Welt ohne Kunst?

Das Goethe-Museum, eine Gemäldegalerie der Goethezeit, zeigt das Verhältnis des Dichters zu Kunst und Künstlern seiner Zeit. Das Spektrum reicht von den Frankfurter Malern des Spätbarocks bis zur deutschen Romantik[††].

Goethe-Haus und Goethe-Museum / Hauptwache / Großer Hirschgraben 23-25 / 60311 Frankfurt / 45 *www.goethehaus-frankfurt.de*

Ⓗ ▰▰▰▰▲ Frankfurt (Main)

Ⓗ ▰▰▰▰▲ Frankfurt (Main) Willy-Brandt-Platz

---

[a]*memorials*

*Siehe **Kulturtipps**: Kasperletheater

†Siehe **Kulturtipps**: Goethe

‡Siehe **Kulturtipps**: Romantik

4 Rhön-Therme in Künzell

Hinein ins Bade- und Freizeitparadies

Eine fast unbegrenzte Auswahl an Freizeitmöglichkeiten für die ganze Familie finden Sie hier. Squash, Tennis und Kegeln[b] stehen genauso auf dem Programm wie eine große Saunawelt mit acht 50 verschiedenen Saunen.

Für alle, die eher das kühle Nass bevorzugen, ist die Rhön-Therme ein wahres Paradies. Europas längste überdachte[c] Wildwasserrutsche mit einer Gesamtlänge von 380 Meter ist ein Renner bei Groß und Klein. Und zum Entspannen gibt's eine Vielzahl von Solarien und sprudelnden Whirlpools.

Rhön-Therme / Harbacher Weg 166 / 36093 Künzell / www.rhoen-therme.de   55

Ⓗ ▮▰▰▰▲ Künzell Rhön-Therme

5 Saalburg – Römerkastell[d] und Museum bei Bad Homburg

Schutz vor den wilden Germanen

Der Limes[e], ein rund 550 km langer Schutzwall, sicherte in den ersten Jahrhunderten unserer Zeitrechnung das römische Reich im Norden gegen die germanischen Feinde. Die Saalburg war damals eines von rund 60 60 Limes-Kastellen. Heute ist das weltweit einzige rekonstruierte Römerkastell sowohl Freilichtmuseum als auch Ausstellungsraum.

Die alten Römer–wie sie lebten und kämpften

Ob Gegenstände des Alltags aus Bronze, Eisen und Glas oder steinerne Monumente wie Grab- 65 und Weihesteine[f]: Die Saalburg bietet ein anschauliches Bild des Lebens zur Römerzeit am Limes. Besonders gezeigt wird in einer ehemaligen Grenzbefestigung[g], wie die dort stationierten Soldaten lebten und welche Waffen zur Ausrüstung[h] zählten. Und ein breit gefächertes Angebot an Veranstaltungen macht Geschichte erlebbar.

Haltestellen

Direkt an der Saalburg liegt die Haltestelle „Saalburg", sie wird von Bussen angefahren. Vom 70 Bahnhof „Wehrheim Saalburg/Lochmühle" an der Taunusbahn (RMV-Bahnlinie 15) führt ein Fußweg entlang des Limes zur Saalburg – Gehzeit etwa 45 Minuten.

Saalburg / Kastell und Museum / 61350 Bad Homburg / www.saalburgmuseum.de

Ⓗ ▮▰▰▰▲ Bad Homburg v.d.H. Saalburg

Ⓗ ▮▰▰▰▲ Wehrheim Saalburg/Lochmühle Bahnhof   75

---

[b]*bowling*   [c]*roofed*   [d]*Roman fort*   [e]*fortified border wall built by the Romans*   [f]*tombstones and sacred stones*
[g]*border fortification*   [h]*equipment*

Kulturtipps

Zeil

Die Zeil ist eine Straße in der Frankfurter Innenstadt, deren westlicher Teil Fußgängerzone und Einkaufsmeile ist. Die sich hier befindende Zeilgalerie ist ein Einkaufszentrum mit sieben Stockwerken und über 50 Geschäften.

Kasperletheater

Das Kasperletheater, das seit Ende des 18. Jahrhunderts existiert, ist ein Puppentheater mit Hand- oder Stockpuppen (*stick puppets*) um die Figur des Kaspers, auch Kasperle genannt. Der Kasperle ist immer der komische Held, der dem Harlekin ähnlich sieht und mit derbem (*crude*) Humor ausgestattet ist. Außer ihm gehören Hexe, Teufel, Prinzessin, König, Zauberer und Drache zum üblichen Personal. Seit Anfang des 20. Jahrhunderts setzt man das Kasperletheater an Schulen und in Kindergärten als didaktisches Medium ein.

Goethe (1749–1832)

Der Dichter, Kritiker und Naturforscher Johann Wolfgang von Goethe, von dem Sie schon in *Kapitel 3* gehört haben, gilt als eine der bedeutendsten Gestalten der deutschen Literatur und als einer der Großen der Weltliteratur. Sein voluminöses Schaffen spannt und bestimmte mehrere Epochen – Sturm und Drang, Klassik, Romantik, die zusammen oft als die Goethezeit bezeichnet werden. Seine feste Rolle als große Ikone der deutschen Kultur wird nicht nur durch zahlreiche Denkmäler und Statuen bestätigt, sondern auch durch die vielen Straßen, Schulen, Preise und Kulturinstitute, die seinen Namen heute noch tragen.

Romantik

Die Romantik ist ein Begriff, mit dem man die kulturgeschichtlichen Entwicklungen zwischen etwa 1790 und 1840 vor allem in der Musik, der Literatur und der Kunst in Europa bezeichnet. Sie entstand als Gegenbewegung zum Rationalismus mit dessen Formstrenge und Kälte. Dagegen betont die Romantik Fantasie, Gefühl und individuelles Erlebnis.

Nomen

der Ausflug, ⸚e *excursion*

der Aufzug, ⸚e *elevator*

der Eintritt, -e *entry, admission*

der Feind, -e/die Feindin,
  -nen *enemy*

die Gemeinde, -n *town,
  community*

die Haltestelle, -n *(bus or train)
  stop*

der Renner, - *(colloq.)* *hit,
  blockbuster*

die Puppe, -n *doll; puppet*

die Rutsche, -n *slide*

das Spielzeug, -e *toy*

Verben

gelangen (zu/nach/in + *acc.*)
  to get to, arrive at

sichern *to secure*

Adjektive und Adverbien

anschaulich *vivid(ly)*

10-19 Textarbeit: Hier kann man … Ergänzen Sie die Sätze mit Informationen aus dem Lesetext.

1. Mit dem Aufzug des Main Towers erreicht man …
2. Auf der Aussichtsterrasse der Zeilgalerie …
3. Im Puppenmuseum können Kinder …
4. Das Goethe-Haus ist das Haus, in dem …
5. Im Goethe-Museum findet man …
6. Für Wasserliebhaber hat die Rhön-Therme …
7. Die Saalburg ist heute …

10-20 Textarbeit: Fragen zum Inhalt. Beantworten Sie die Fragen in Bezug auf den Lesetext.

1. Welche Möglichkeiten gibt es für Sportliche?
2. Aus welchen Gründen würde man vielleicht die Aussichtsterrasse der Zeilgalerie anstatt die des Main Towers besuchen? Warum würde man vielleicht den Main Tower stattdessen bevorzugen?
3. Wie macht man das Puppenmuseum für Kinder interessant?
4. Welche Verbindung hat die Kunst im Goethe-Museum zu dem Dichter?
5. Wo kann man sich gut entspannen?
6. Warum haben die Römer den Limes gebaut?
7. Kommt man am besten mit dem Bus oder mit der Bahn an die Saalburg? Erklären Sie.

10-21 Vokabelarbeit. Ergänzen Sie die Sätze mit Wörtern aus den *Neuen Vokabeln*. Achten Sie dabei auch auf die Wortform.

1. Künzell ist eine ___Gemeinde___ in der Nähe von Fulda.
2. Um das Goethe-Haus zu erreichen, steigt man an der ___Haltestelle___ „Hauptwache" aus.
3. Im Heimatmuseum Heuchelheim wird ___anschaulich___ demonstriert, wie man in früheren Zeiten gelebt hat.

Possible answers for 10-19.
1. die Aussichtsplattform, das Restaurant und die Bar. 2. hat man einen Blick über die Zeil und das Stadtzentrum. 3. an Veranstaltungen und Entdeckungsreisen teilnehmen, mit Spielzeugen spielen. 4. Goethe geboren wurde. 5. Gemälde aus der Goethezeit. 6. eine lange Wildwasserrutsche und Whirlpools. 7. ein rekonstruiertes Römerkastell und Freilichtmuseum mit Ausstellungsraum.

Possible answers for 10-20.
1. Die Rhön-Therme bietet Squash, Tennis, Kegeln. 2. Die Aussichtsterrasse der Zeilgalerie ist kostenlos. Vom Main Tower kann man viel mehr sehen. 3. Durch interessante Veranstaltungen und interaktives Spielen. 4. Gezeigt werden die Werke von Künstlern, die eine Verbindung zu Goethe hatten. 5. In den Saunen, Solarien oder Whirlpools der Rhön-Therme. Im Restaurant oder der Bar des Main Towers. 6. Um sich gegen die germanischen Feinde im Norden zu schützen. 7. Mit dem Bus, denn damit kommt man direkt an die Saalburg. Von der nächsten Bahnstation muss man noch 45 Minuten zu Fuß gehen.

4. Bei Wanderfreunden sowie Radfahrern ist auch das schöne Rhöngebirge immer ein _____Renner_____ .

5. In den Titus Thermen Frankfurts kann man auf der 50 Meter langen _____Rutsche_____ ins Schwimmbecken sausen.

6. Der _____Eintritt_____ ins Deutsche Geldmuseum, wo man alles über die Herstellung und die Funktion des Geldes lernen kann, ist kostenlos.

7. Mit den Bahnen und Bussen des RMVs kann man bei vielen _____Ausflügen_____ im Rhein-Main-Gebiet aufs Auto verzichten.

10-22 Was man alles machen kann. Besprechen Sie, warum oder unter welchen Umständen Sie die verschiedenen Orte besuchen.

> Beispiele: *Wenn ich mich entspannen möchte, besuche ich die Rhön-Therme.*
> *Ich gehe in den Main Tower, um beim Abendessen die schöne*
> *Aussicht zu genießen.*

10-23 Wohin? Heute ist der letzte Tag Ihres Aufenthalts in Deutschland, denn morgen früh fliegen Sie und ein/e Mitstudent/in vom Frankfurter Flughafen ab nach Hause. Wie verbringen Sie Ihren letzten Tag hier in Hessen? Besprechen Sie die Möglichkeiten und planen Sie gemeinsam Ihren letzten Tag.

Teaching Suggestion for 10-25. Additionally or alternatively, have students research the cultural sites that are mentioned in the descriptions: *Frankfurter Dom, Paulskirche, Alte Oper, Festhalle, Museumsufer, Henninger Turm, Messegelände* and the *Limes.*

10-24 Mein Freizeit-Tipp. Schreiben Sie für deutsche Touristen, die Ihre Region besuchen, einen Freizeit-Tipp. Benutzen Sie die RMV-Freizeit-Tipps als Modell.

Introduction to *Hörtext 2*. To get students thinking about the context of the radio broadcast, ask them about the cultural heritage of their own regions. *Welche Persönlichkeiten/ Leistungen/Traditionen gehören zur Kulturgeschichte Ihrer Heimat/Ihrer Stadt/Ihres Staates? Welche Rolle spielen diese noch heute?* Then have them extract information from the text introduction. *Warum hat das Land die Bezeichnung „Literaturland Hessen" verdient? Wie kann man sich am Tag der Literatur beteiligen?* Well-known authors who were born in/ resided in Hessen include(d) Hans Jakob Christoffel von Grimmelshausen, Sophie von La Roche, Johann Wolfgang von Goethe, Georg Büchner, and the Grimm Brothers as well as contemporaries such as Peter Härtling, Bodo Kirchhoff and Gabriele Wohmann.

10-25 Noch ausführlicher, bitte! Besuchen Sie die Internetseite eines der Orte im Lesetext, um Bilder zu sehen und mehr darüber herauszufinden. Dann überarbeiten und erweitern Sie den Tipp im Lesetext, um eine detailliertere Beschreibung des Ortes zu geben.

10-26 Mehr Ausflugstipps. Suchen Sie auf der Internetseite des RMVs nach anderen Freizeit-Tipps. Dann wählen Sie drei Ausflugsziele aus und schreiben Sie auf Ihrer persönlichen Blogseite, warum diese Sie interessieren und was Sie an jedem Ort erleben wollen. **Note for 10-25 and 10-26.** Relevant web addresses for Internet research activities can be found in *MyGermanLab* and on the Companion Website.

Hörtext 2

Karoline von Günderode in Winkel (Radiobeitrag)

Wie bei manchen deutschen Regionen basiert die Identität der Hessen teilweise auf dem gemeinsamen kulturellen Erbe. Die starke und lange Literaturtradition des Gebiets hat in dieser Hinsicht viel zu bieten. „Das Hildebrandslied" – das älteste Zeugnis deutscher Literatur überhaupt – entstand um 830 im Kloster Fulda und befindet sich heute in der Universitätsbibliothek Kassel. Verschiedene Orte am Rhein dienten Romantikern als literarische wie künstlerische

Inspiration und Marburg war Aufenthaltsort sowie Werkstatt vieler Romanti-ker. Die Region, die das heutige Hessen umfasst, ist seit jeher Geburtsort oder Wahlheimat ungezählter namhafter Schriftsteller und Dichter.

Um die reiche Literaturtradition des Landes zu pflegen und zu feiern, ver-anstaltet das Literaturland Hessen seit 2007 den „Tag für die Literatur". Es finden an einem Sonntag im Mai in ehemaligen Dichterhäusern, Bibliotheken, Museen, Schulen und auf Stadtrundgängen an literarisch bedeutenden Orten überall in Hessen Lesungen, Ausstellungen, Vorträge und andere Veranstaltun-gen statt. Der Hessische Rundfunk° hat diesen Literaturtag ins Leben gerufen und auch im Radio begleitet. Sie hören jetzt einen Beitrag aus dem Programm des Hessischen Rundfunks, der im Rahmen des Literaturtags gesendet wurde, über das Leben und Tun in einem romantischen Bekanntenkreis in Winkel am Rhein.

Karoline von Günderode um 1800

name of the regional public broadcasting agency seated in Frankfurt

Vor dem Hören

1. Woran denken Sie, wenn sie das Wort „Romantik" hören?
2. Was wissen Sie über Frauenrechte zu Beginn des 19. Jahrhunderts?

Beim Hören

Während des Beitrags hören Sie folgende Vokabeln.

10-14　Karoline von Günderode in Winkel

Dolch *dagger*
Irrtum *mistake*
Selbstmord *suicide*
Verzweiflungstat *act of desperation*
zerrissen *torn*
beanspruchen *claim*
Gemächer *chambers*
Plaisir *pleasure*

griechisch drapiert *in ancient Greek dress*
Geschwätz *chatter*
verschwärmt *prattled away*
verträumt *dreamy*
herablassend *condescendingly*
Eilfer *legendary 1811 vintage from the Brentano vineyard*

Hören Sie sich die Radiosendung an und identifizieren Sie die Personen.

c	1. Karoline von Günderode	a. Dichter mit einem eigenen Stu-dierzimmer im Brentanohaus
g	2. Friedrich Creuzer	
f	3. Bettina Brentano	b. Jurist und Freund von Clemens Brentano
d	4. Clemens Brentano	c. Dichterin, die Selbstmord begangen hat
b	5. Friedrich Carl von Savigny	
i	6. Achim von Arnim	d. Bruder von Bettina
e	7. Christoph Martin Wieland	e. Dichter, der aus Weimar anreiste
a	8. Johann Wolfgang von Goethe	f. Freundin von Karoline
		g. Liebhaber von Karoline
h	9. Antonie Brentano	h. Hausherrin und Schwägerin von Bettina und Clemens
		i. Schwager von Clemens Brentano

Kulturtipps

Rheingau

Der Rheingau ist ein Weinanbaugebiet in der westlichen Rhein-Main-Region, das sich über 30 km den Rhein entlang erstreckt und somit zu den kleineren Weinanbaugebieten Deutschlands gehört. Besonders für seine Riesling-Weine ist der Rheingau weltberühmt. Schon seit der Römerzeit wird der Wein hier angebaut. So prägt der Weinbau die Kultur dieser Region wesentlich.

Burgruine Ehrenfels und Weinberg

10-27 Textarbeit: Wer spricht da? Man hört im Beitrag vier Frauenstimmen: die von Karoline, Bettina, Antonie und der Moderatorin. Wer sagt was?

Answers for 10-27.
1. Karoline; 2. Bettina; 3. Moderatorin; 4. Moderatorin; 5. Bettina; 6. Moderatorin; 7. Bettina; 8. Antonie; 9. Moderatorin; 10. Karoline; 11. Moderatorin; 12. Antonie

1. Ich bin lebensmüde.
2. Ich lese aus dem Homer vor.
3. Wahrscheinlich hat sie gewusst, dass sie früh sterben würde.
4. Man kam aus entfernten Orten ins Rheingau gereist.
5. Am Abend spazieren wir an den Ufern des Rheins entlang.
6. Mit der Auswanderung der Großfamilie Brentano nach Winkel begann ein romantisches Jahrzehnt am Rhein.
7. Wir verbringen den Tag beim launischen Geschwätz.
8. Goethe schöpfte seinen Teller voll Speisen.
9. Die Ereignisse des Sommers haben die Erinnerungen und die traurigen Gedanken wohl bald fortgespült.
10. Ich lebe nur durch einen Irrtum der Natur fort.
11. Sie konnte nie eine klare Identität für sich beanspruchen.
12. Von unserem guten Rheinweine konnte er fürchterlich viel trinken.

10-28 Textarbeit: Fragen zum Inhalt. Beantworten Sie die Fragen in Bezug auf den Beitrag.

Possible answers for 10-28.
1. aus enttäuschter Liebe und Verzweiflung am Leben; 2. Hier sammelten sich viele zeitgenössische Künstler und die Freunde und Bekannten der Brentanos. Die Zeit verbrachte man beim Gespräch, Gesang, Lesungen, Spaziergängen und Genuss der Landschaft. 3. Goethe war ein anstrengender Gast. Er verhielt sich herablassend, hat zu große Portionen auf seinen Teller genommen, ohne es aufzuessen und viel Wein getrunken. 4. Ja, aber es ist kein öffentliches Museum. Man muss einen Termin telefonisch vereinbaren. 5. Sie ist auf dem Friedhof begraben und dort auf ihrem Grabstein kann man ihr Abschiedsgedicht lesen.

1. Warum hat Karoline von Günderode Selbstmord begangen?
2. Beschreiben Sie das Leben im Brentanohaus in Winkel am Rhein.
3. Wie hat sich Goethe dort verhalten?
4. Kann man das Brentanohaus heute besuchen? Erklären Sie.
5. Welche Erinnerung an Karoline von Günderode gibt es heute noch in Winkel?

10-29 Zur Diskussion. Besprechen Sie die Fragen.

1. Gibt es einen Ort, den Sie jedes Jahr wiederholt besuchen? Wenn ja, was machen Sie dort? Was zieht Sie immer wieder hin?

2. Wie haben Frauen Anfang des 19. Jahrhunderts gelebt und was haben sie nicht machen dürfen? Inwiefern hat sich die Rolle der Frau seitdem verändert? Inwiefern hat sich die Rolle des Mannes verändert?

10-30 Rheinleben im 19. Jahrhundert. Bettina Brentano beschreibt das Leben einer vornehmen Familie zu Beginn des 19. Jahrhunderts. Wie hätten Sie damals wohl gelebt? Was hätten Sie im Brentanohaus wohl gemacht und erlebt?

Note for 10-30. The subjunctive mood is covered in the *Grammatik* in this chapter.

Beispiele: *Ich hätte abends bei Kerzenlicht gelesen.*

Ich hätte als Frau kein Buch schreiben dürfen.

Ich wäre mit berühmten Künstlern am Rhein spazieren gegangen.

10-31 Abschiedsbrief. Karoline von Günderode hat kurz vor ihrem Tod einen Abschiedsbrief von ihrem Geliebten erhalten. Wie war wohl der Inhalt des Abschiedsbriefs? Schreiben Sie den Brief, wie Sie sich ihn vorstellen.

Alternative for 10-31. Have the students write a Dear John letter between a pair of their own choosing.

Beginnen Sie so: *Meine liebste Karoline, …*

Enden Sie so: *Dein Friedrich*

Note for 10-32. Relevant web addresses for Internet research activities can be found in *MyGermanLab* and on the Companion Website.

10-32 Romantik am Rhein. Suchen Sie im Internet nach weiteren Informationen zu den folgenden Menschen und Orten aus dem Hörtext. Sammeln Sie Basisinformationen (Daten, kurze Beschreibung von Leistungen) und dann drei interessante Tatsachen zu Ihrem Thema. Dann berichten Sie darüber.

Alternatives for 10-32. Have students work in small groups to find information and to prepare a presentation. You could also expand the range of topics to include those mentioned in the text introduction and organize your own mini "Hessischer Tag der Literatur." Or alternatively, you could have students create manuscripts and record their own simulated radio broadcasts and save them in MyGermanLab for the entire class to access.

Karoline von Günderode	Achim von Arnim	Winkel am Rhein
Bettina Brentano	Friedrich Carl Savigny	Brentanohaus
Clemens Brentano		

Lesetext 4

„Rapunzel" von Jacob und Wilhelm Grimm (Märchen)

Der Name der Brüder Grimm ist untrennbar verbunden mit der Märchensammlung, die ihren Namen trägt. Jacob und der ein Jahr jüngere Wilhelm kamen in der südhessischen Stadt Hanau zur Welt, wuchsen in Steinau auf und besuchten die Schule in Kassel. An der Universität Marburg studierten beide Rechtswissenschaft und sie verbrachten anschließend 23 Jahre in Kassel, wo beide an der Bibliothek beschäftigt waren. Während ihrer Kasseler Zeit fingen die Brüder an, Märchen zu sammeln.

Die *Kinder- und Hausmärchen* erschienen 1812 und 1815 in zwei Bänden. Die Brüder sammelten mehr als 150 Märchen aus mündlicher Überlieferung° und

Introduction to *Lesetext 4*. Ask students what they already know of the Grimm Brothers. *Kennen Sie den Namen Grimm? Womit verbinden Sie den Namen? Welche Märchen kennen Sie schon?* Then have them glean information from the text introduction. *Warum sind die Märchen der Grimms so bekannt? Wie lange liest man ihre Märchen schon? Welche Verbindungen haben die Brüder zu Hessen? Welche Bindung haben ihre Märchen zu Hessen?*

from oral tradition

fast nur in ihrem hessischen Umkreis, wo sie einige Märchenerzähler fanden. So betonten sie wiederholt in ihren Vorreden°, dass es sich dabei um „echt hessische Märchen" handele. Heute erkennt man jedoch, dass die Märchen eher allgemein europäischen Kulturguts sind. Dass die Grimms die Geschichten auch frei bearbeitet und teilweise wesentlich verändert haben, ist in den verschiedenen Editionen ihres Werkes zu erkennen. Den Erfolg der Brüder ist dennoch nicht zu bestreiten. Zu ihren Lebzeiten allein gab es sieben Auflagen° des Werkes und bis heute wurden ihre Märchen in 160 Sprachen übersetzt. So ist die Sammlung neben Martin Luthers Bibelübersetzung das meistgelesene Werk und die Brüder zwei der bekanntesten Persönlichkeiten der deutschen Kulturgeschichte.

prefaces

editions

Wilhelm und Jacob Grimm (ca. 1850)

„Rapunzel" erschien zuerst in der 1812 veröffentlichten Märchenausgabe. Die Fassung des Märchens, die hier wiedergeben wird, ist die von den Grimms selbst überarbeitete Version, die 1857 in der 7. Auflage erschien.

Vor dem Lesen

Welche Figuren und Motive sind typisch für ein Märchen?

Beim Lesen

1. Listen Sie alle Figuren auf, die in dem Märchen vorkommen, und schreiben Sie einige Stichwörter zu jeder Person und ihrem Handeln.

2. Es gab in der DDR eine Briefmarkenserie zu dem Märchen „Rapunzel". Schreiben Sie für jede Szene einen Satz, der das abgebildete Geschehen beschreibt.

10-15 to 10-17

„Rapunzel"

von Jacob und Wilhelm Grimm

Note. The fairy tale reflects the orthography current at its time of publication. Students examine the differences between the Grimms' spelling and the current standard spelling in SAM 10-16.

Es war einmal ein Mann und eine Frau, die wünschten sich schon lange vergeblich ein Kind, endlich machte sich die Frau Hoffnung der liebe Gott werde ihren Wunsch erfüllen. Die Leute hatten in ihrem Hinterhaus ein kleines Fenster, daraus konnte man in einen prächtigen Garten sehen, der voll der schönsten Blumen und Kräuter stand; er war aber von einer hohen Mauer umgeben, und niemand wagte hinein zu gehen, weil er einer Zauberin gehörte, die große Macht hatte und von aller Welt gefürchtet ward. Eines Tags stand die Frau an diesem Fenster und sah in den Garten hinab, da erblickte sie ein Beet°, das mit den schönsten Rapunzeln° bepflanzt war: und sie sahen so frisch und grün aus, daß sie lüstern° ward und das größte Verlangen empfand von den Rapunzeln zu essen. Das Verlangen nahm jeden Tag zu, und da sie wußte daß sie keine davon bekommen konnte, so fiel sie ganz ab, sah blaß und elend aus. Da erschrack der Mann und fragte „was fehlt dir, liebe Frau?" „Ach," antwortete sie, „wenn ich keine Rapunzeln aus dem Garten hinter unserm Hause zu essen kriege, so sterbe ich." Der Mann, der sie lieb hatte, dachte „eh du deine Frau sterben lässest, holst du ihr von den Rapunzeln, es mag kosten was es will." In der Abenddämmerung stieg er also über die Mauer in den Garten der Zauberin, stach in aller Eile eine Hand voll Rapunzeln und brachte sie seiner Frau. Sie machte sich sogleich Salat daraus und aß sie in voller Begierde auf. Sie hatten ihr aber so gut, so gut geschmeckt, daß sie den andern Tag noch dreimal so viel Lust bekam. Sollte sie Ruhe haben, so mußte der Mann noch einmal in den Garten steigen. Er machte sich also in der Abenddämmerung wieder hinab, als er aber die Mauer herabgeklettert war, erschrack er gewaltig, denn er sah die Zauberin vor sich stehen. „Wie kannst du es wagen," sprach sie mit zornigem Blick, „in meinen Garten zu steigen und wie ein Dieb mir meine Rapunzeln zu stehlen? das soll dir schlecht bekommen." „Ach," antwortete er, „laßt Gnade für Recht ergehen°, ich habe mich nur aus Noth dazu entschlossen: meine Frau hat eure Rapunzeln aus dem Fenster erblickt, und empfindet ein so großes Gelüsten, daß sie sterben würde, wenn sie nicht davon zu essen bekäme." Da ließ die Zauberin in ihrem Zorne nach und sprach zu ihm „verhält es sich so, wie du sagst, so will ich dir gestatten Rapunzeln mitzunehmen so viel du willst, allein ich mache eine Bedingung: du mußt mir das Kind geben, das deine Frau zur Welt bringen wird. Es soll ihm gut gehen, und ich will für es sorgen wie eine Mutter." Der Mann sagte in der Angst alles zu, und als die Frau in Wochen kam°, so erschien sogleich die Zauberin, gab dem Kinde den Namen Rapunzel und nahm es mit sich fort.

Rapunzel ward das schönste Kind unter der Sonne. Als es zwölf Jahre alt war, schloß es die Zauberin in einen Thurm, der in einem Walde lag, und weder Treppe noch Thüre hatte, nur ganz oben war ein kleines Fensterchen. Wenn die Zauberin hinein wollte, so stellte sie sich unten hin, und rief

patch / lamb's lettuce; mâche (a wild salad green) / lustful

laßt... ergehen temper justice with mercy

(obs.) gave birth

„Rapunzel, Rapunzel,
laß mir dein Haar herunter.“

Rapunzel hatte lange prächtige Haare, fein wie gesponnen Gold. 45
Wenn sie nun die Stimme der Zauberin vernahm, so band sie ihre Zöpfe
los, wickelte° sie oben um einen Fensterhaken°, und dann fielen die Haare
zwanzig Ellen° tief herunter, und die Zauberin stieg daran hinauf. Nach
ein paar Jahren trug es sich zu, daß der Sohn des Königs durch den Wald
ritt und an dem Thurm vorüber kam. Da hörte er einen Gesang, der war so 50
lieblich, daß er still hielt und horchte. Das war Rapunzel, die in ihrer Einsamkeit sich die Zeit damit vertrieb, ihre süße Stimme erschallen zu lassen.
Der Königssohn wollte zu ihr hinauf steigen und suchte nach einer Thüre
des Thurms, aber es war keine zu finden. Er ritt heim, doch der Gesang
hatte ihm so sehr das Herz gerührt, daß er jeden Tag hinaus in den Wald 55
gieng und zuhörte. Als er einmal so hinter einem Baum stand, sah er daß
eine Zauberin heran kam und hörte wie sie hinauf rief

„Rapunzel, Rapunzel,
laß dein Haar herunter.“

Da ließ Rapunzel die Haarflechten herab, und die Zauberin stieg zu 60
ihr hinauf. „Ist das die Leiter, auf welcher man hinauf kommt, so will ich
auch einmal mein Glück versuchen.“ Und den folgenden Tag, als es anfieng
dunkel zu werden, gieng er zu dem Thurme und rief

„Rapunzel, Rapunzel,
laß dein Haar herunter.“ 65

Alsbald fielen die Haare herab und der Königssohn stieg hinauf.
Anfangs erschrack Rapunzel gewaltig als ein Mann zu ihr herein kam,
wie ihre Augen noch nie einen erblickt hatten, doch der Königssohn fing an
ganz freundlich mit ihr zu reden und erzählte ihr daß von ihrem Gesang
sein Herz so sehr sei bewegt worden, daß es ihm keine Ruhe gelassen, und 70
er sie selbst habe sehen müssen. Da verlor Rapunzel ihre Angst, und als er
sie fragte ob sie ihn zum Manne nehmen wollte, und sie sah daß er jung
und schön war, so dachte sie „der wird mich lieber haben als die alte Frau
Gothel,“ und sagte ja und legte ihre Hand in seine Hand. Sie sprach „ich
will gerne mit dir gehen, aber ich weiß nicht wie ich herab kommen kann. 75
Wenn du kommst, so bring jedesmal einen Strang Seide° mit, daraus will
ich eine Leiter flechten° und wenn die fertig ist, so steige ich herunter und
du nimmst mich auf dein Pferd.“ Sie verabredeten daß er bis dahin alle
Abend zu ihr kommen sollte, denn bei Tag kam die Alte. Die Zauberin
merkte auch nichts davon, bis einmal Rapunzel anfieng und zu ihr sagte 80
„sag sie mir doch, Frau Gothel, wie kommt es nur, sie wird mir viel schwe-
rer heraufzuziehen, als der junge Königssohn, der ist in einem Augenblick
bei mir.“ „Ach du gottloses Kind,“ rief die Zauberin, „was muß ich von
dir hören, ich dachte ich hätte dich von aller Welt geschieden, und du hast
mich doch betrogen!“ In ihrem Zorne packte sie die schönen Haare der 85

Rapunzel, schlug sie ein paar mal um ihre linke Hand, griff eine Scheere mit der rechten, und ritsch, ratsch, waren sie abgeschnitten, und die schönen Flechten lagen auf der Erde. Und sie war so unbarmherzig daß sie die arme Rapunzel in eine Wüstenei° brachte, wo sie in großem Jammer und Elend leben mußte.

wasteland

90

Denselben Tag aber, wo sie Rapunzel verstoßen hatte, machte Abends die Zauberin die abgeschnittenen Flechten oben am Fensterhaken fest, und als der Königssohn kam und rief

„Rapunzel, Rapunzel,
laß dein Haar herunter,"

95

so ließ sie die Haare hinab. Der Königssohn stieg hinauf, aber er fand oben nicht seine liebste Rapunzel, sondern die Zauberin, die ihn mit bösen und giftigen Blicken ansah. „Aha," rief sie höhnisch, „du willst die Frau Liebste holen, aber der schöne Vogel sitzt nicht mehr im Nest und singt nicht mehr, die Katze hat ihn geholt und wird dir auch noch die Augen auskratzen. Für dich ist Rapunzel verloren, du wirst sie nie wieder erblicken." Der Königssohn gerieth außer sich° vor Schmerz, und in der Verzweiflung sprang er den Thurm herab: das Leben brachte er davon, aber die Dornen, in die er fiel, zerstachen ihm die Augen. Da irrte er blind im Walde umher, aß nichts als Wurzeln und Beeren, und that nichts als jammern und weinen über den Verlust seiner liebsten Frau. So wanderte er einige Jahre im Elend umher und gerieth endlich in die Wüstenei, wo Rapunzel mit den Zwillingen, die sie geboren hatte, einem Knaben und Mädchen, kümmerlich° lebte. Er vernahm eine Stimme, und sie däuchte° ihn so bekannt: da gieng er darauf zu, und wie er heran kam, erkannte ihn Rapunzel und fiel ihm um den Hals und weinte. Zwei von ihren Thränen aber benetzten° seine Augen, da wurden sie wieder klar, und er konnte damit sehen wie sonst. Er führte sie in sein Reich, wo er mit Freude empfangen ward, und sie lebten noch lange glücklich und vergnügt.

100

gerieth... sich went wild

105

miserably
seemed

110

moistened

Neue Vokabeln

Nomen

der Dorn, -en *thorn*
das Elend *misery*
die Leiter, -n *ladder*
die Schere, -n *scissors*
die Träne, -n *tear*
die Treppe, -n *stairs*
das Verlangen, - *desire, demand*
der Zauberer, -/die Zauberin, -nen *sorcerer/sorceress*

der Zopf, ¨e *braid*
der Zorn *rage, wrath*

Verben

betrügen, betrog, betrogen *to deceive*
gestatten *to allow, permit*
greifen, griff, gegriffen *to grab*
kriegen (*colloq.*) *to get*
reiten, ritt, ist geritten *to ride (an animal)*

rühren *to stir, move*
scheiden, schied, geschieden *to separate*
stehlen (stiehlt), stahl, gestohlen *to steal*
zu·sagen *to accept, consent*

Adjektive und Adverbien

prächtig *magnificent*
unbarmherzig *merciless*

Possible answers for 10-33.
1. Sie ist schwanger und sieht die Rapunzeln im Garten der Zauberin. **2.** Er holt sie am Abend, damit ihn keiner sieht. **3.** Er darf sie pflücken, wenn er der Zauberin sein erstes Kind verspricht. **4.** *Answers will vary.* **5.** *Answers will vary.* **6.** Er hört sie singen. **7.** Er kommt am Abend, da die Zauberin sie am Tag besucht. **8.** Sie wollen heiraten, aber zuerst muss Rapunzel aus dem Turm kommen. Er soll ihr Seide mitbringen, damit sie eine Leiter daraus flechten kann. **9.** Die Zauberin entdeckt das Geheimnis und bringt Rapunzel in eine Wüstenei. **10.** Sie entdecken sich in der Wüstenei. **11.** *Answers will vary.* **12.** *Answers will vary.*

Possible answers for 10-34. fantastische Charaktere: die Zauberin; wunderbare Ereignisse: Rapunzels Haare sind sehr lang und sehr stark, Rapunzels Tränen heilen die Blindheit; eine Notsituation: Rapunzel wird in einen Turm verschlossen, dann in eine Wüstenei verbannt, der Königssohn erblindet; Erlösung aus der Not: Rapunzel und der Königssohn finden sich wieder und ziehen in sein Reich, ihre Tränen heilen seine Blindheit; Wiederholungen: der Mann steigt zweimal in den Garten, der Königssohn kommt dreimal zum Turm, dreimal der Spruch: Rapunzel, Rapunzel, laß (mir) dein Haar herunter; das Gute wird belohnt: Rapunzel und der Königssohn finden das Glück

10-33 Textarbeit: Fragen zum Inhalt und zur Interpretation. Beantworten Sie die Fragen in Bezug auf den Lesetext.

1. Wodurch entsteht das Verlangen der Frau?
2. Zu welcher Tageszeit holt der Mann die Rapunzeln? Warum?
3. Unter welcher Bedingung darf der Mann Rapunzeln pflücken?
4. Beschreiben Sie Rapunzels Leben im Turm.
5. Was für eine Frau ist die Zauberin? Rapunzel?
6. Wie wird der Königssohn auf Rapunzel aufmerksam?
7. Zu welcher Tageszeit besucht der Königssohn Rapunzel? Warum?
8. Welchen Plan machen Rapunzel und der Königssohn?
9. Warum ist der Plan nicht erfolgreich?
10. Wie kommt das Paar am Ende zusammen?
11. Über wie viele Jahre zieht sich wohl die Märchenhandlung hin?
12. Welche Aspekte der Handlung sind unrealistisch?

10-34 Textarbeit: Märchenland. Welche der folgenden typischen Märchenelemente sind in „Rapunzel" zu finden? Nennen Sie Spezifisches aus dem Märchen als Beweis.

fantastische Charaktere	sprechende Tiere
wunderbare Ereignisse mitten im Alltag	Wiederholungen
drei Wünsche	das Gute wird belohnt
eine Notsituation	das Böse wird bestraft
Erlösung aus der Not	

10-35 Vokabelarbeit. Ergänzen Sie die Sätze zum Märchen „Aschenputtel" mit Wörtern aus den *Neuen Vokabeln*. Achten Sie dabei auch auf die Wortform.

1. Als Aschenputtels Mutter stirbt und der Vater eine neue Frau nimmt, lebt das junge Mädchen im ____Elend____.
2. Das Verhalten der Stiefmutter und Stiefschwestern gegenüber dem armen Aschenputtel ist ___unbarmherzig___.
3. Aschenputtel weint am Grab der Mutter und ihre ____Tränen____ lassen einen Zweig zu einem schönen Baum wachsen.
4. Aschenputtel möchte mit ihren Stiefschwestern zu dem Fest des Königs, aber die Stiefmutter ___gestattet___ es ihr nicht.
5. Als Aschenputtel vor dem Baum ihren Wunsch ausspricht, so ___kriegt___ sie plötzlich schöne Kleidung für das Fest.
6. Als das Fest zu Ende geht, muss sie vom Prinzen ___scheiden___.
7. Als sie die ___Treppe___ herunterkommt, fällt ihr allerdings der Schuh vom linken Fuß.
8. Auf das ___Verlangen___ des Prinzen probieren alle drei Frauen den Schuh an.
9. Der Schuh passt nur Aschenputtel und sie ___reitet___ mit dem Prinzen zu ihrer Hochzeit.

10-36 Was wäre gewesen, wenn? Besprechen Sie, wie alles unter anderen Umständen wohl anders gekommen wäre.

1. Wenn die Zauberin den Mann im Garten nicht entdeckt hätte, …
2. Wenn der Mann der Zauberin das Kind nicht versprochen hätte, …
3. Wenn Rapunzel kürzere Haare gehabt hätte, …
4. Wenn der Königssohn nicht an dem Turm vorbeigeritten wäre, …
5. Wenn Rapunzel der Zauberin ihr Geheimnis nicht verraten hätte, …
6. Wenn der Königssohn nicht in die Wüstenei gekommen wäre, …
7. Wenn …

 10-37 Wer ist schuld daran? Rapunzel hat viele Jahre im Turm verbracht. Entscheiden Sie sich, wer die Schuld für ihre jahrelange Gefangenschaft trägt: ihre Mutter, ihr Vater, die Zauberin oder Rapunzel selbst. Dann präsentieren Sie Ihre Argumente.

10-38 Arme Rapunzel. Sie sind Rapunzel. Da andere Frauen sich für Ihre Lebensgeschichte interessieren, will das Frauenmagazin *Petra* einen Exklusiv-bericht zu Ihrem Leben in der nächsten Ausgabe veröffentlichen. Schreiben Sie also eine kurze Autobiografie für das Magazin.

10-39 Eine moderne Rapunzel. Die Märchen der Brüder Grimm werden in einer neuen Ausgabe für die Kinder von heute aktualisiert. Schreiben Sie dafür eine moderne Version der Geschichte von Rapunzel.

Teaching Suggestion for 10-37. Divide the class into four groups and assign each group a character. Each group should then develop arguments supporting the guilt (or innocence) of their assigned character. After a set period of time, a representative for each group presents the arguments to the class. Then the class votes on whom they believe to be the guilty party.

Alternative for 10-39. Have students write a new section of the story to fill in missing information, e.g., what happens to Rapunzel's parents, what happens to the sorceress, what goes on in the twelve years before Rapunzel is brought to the tower, what Rapunzel does in the years she spends in the wasteland, what Rapunzel and the prince do in their new life together in his kingdom, etc.

Grammatik

10-25 to 10-29

1. General subjunctive mood (Konjunktiv II)

German has three moods—the imperative, the indicative, and the subjunctive. The imperative mood is used when giving commands. Most of the time we speak and write in the indicative mood, which is used to state facts and talk about real events. The general subjunctive mood is used to make hypothetical or conditional statements, to express wishes, and to make polite requests and statements.

Indicative:	Ich trinke einen Kaffee.
	I'm drinking coffee.
Subjunctive:	Wenn es nicht so spät wäre, tränke ich einen Kaffee. (CONDITION)
	If it weren't so late, I would drink coffee.
	Wenn ich nur einen Kaffee trinken könnte! (WISH)
	If only I could drink coffee!
	Ich möchte einen Kaffee trinken. (POLITE REQUEST)
	I would like to drink coffee.

Special subjunctive (Konjunktiv I). Students will learn about the special subjunctive, also known as the subjunctive of indirect discourse, in the *Sprachanalyse* activities in the *Kapitel 10* SAM. There they will also learn that the general subjunctive usually substitutes for the special subjunctive when the latter form is ambiguous.

Remember that you cannot tell whether a verb is weak, strong, or mixed simply by looking at its infinitive. You must look it up in a dictionary or verb chart if you are unsure of its principal parts.

Present tense general subjunctive (Konjunktiv II: Gegenwart)

The six verb tenses we have examined thus far are tenses in the indicative mood. The general subjunctive mood primarily uses two tenses: present and past. The forms of the present tense general subjunctive are based on the simple past tense. Variations depend on whether verbs are weak, strong, or mixed.

	Weak verbs	Mixed verbs	Strong verbs		
Infinitive	leben	müssen	sein	fliegen	bleiben
Simple past stem	lebte	musste	war	flog	blieb
ich	lebte	müsste	wäre	flöge	bliebe
du	lebtest	müsstest	wär(e)st	flögest	bliebest
er, sie, es	lebte	müsste	wäre	flöge	bliebe
wir	lebten	müssten	wären	flögen	blieben
ihr	lebtet	müsstet	wär(e)t	flöget	bliebet
Sie, sie	lebten	müssten	wären	flögen	blieben

- The present subjunctive forms of weak verbs and the modal verbs **wollen** and **sollen** are identical to their simple past tense forms.

- The present subjunctive of mixed verbs is also identical to the simple past tense, except that an umlaut is added if the stem vowel is **a, o,** or **u.**[1] The modal verbs with umlauts in their infinitives retain the umlaut in the present subjunctive.

General subjunctive of *sein*. The *e* in the *du*- and *ihr*-form personal endings is often omitted.

- The present subjunctive of strong verbs is created from the simple past stem, plus an umlaut when the stem verb has an **a, o,** or **u,** plus the following subjunctive endings: **-e, -est, -e, -en, -et, -en.**[2]

---

[1]Six of the mixed verbs (**brennen, kennen, nennen, rennen, senden, wenden**) use an **e** instead of an **ä** in the subjunctive forms. These irregular forms are generally avoided; the **würde**-construction is used instead (see below).

[2]A few strong verbs verbs have a different stem vowel in the present subjunctive than in the simple past tense. Of that group, the most common verbs are **helfen, stehen,** and **sterben,** which all replace the simple past **a** with **ü.** Exceptional forms are generally avoided in favor of the alternative with **würde** (see below).

10-40 Ich möchte lieber ... Nicolas Werner ist nicht ganz zufrieden mit seinem Leben. Benutzen Sie die Informationen in Klammern, um zu sagen, wie er alles lieber wollte. Benutzen Sie den Konjunktiv II.

Beispiel: Ich heiße Nicolas. (Jakob)

Ich hieße lieber Jakob.

Schwache Verben

1. Ich arbeite als Kundenberater in einer Bank. (als Bankdirektor)

2. Ich verdiene 34.000 Euro im Jahr. (100.000 Euro)

3. Ich wohne in Offenbach. (in Wiesbaden)

4. In den Ferien reise ich nach Frankreich. (nach Spanien)

Gemischte Verben

5. Ich verbringe mein Wochenende zu Hause. (in den Bergen)

Starke Verben

6. Ich fahre mit der S-Bahn zur Arbeit. (mit dem Auto)

7. Während der Fahrt lese ich Zeitung. (einen spannenden Roman)

8. Zur Arbeit trage ich einen Anzug mit Krawatte. (Jeans und ein T-Shirt)

9. Ich gehe nach der Arbeit zum Supermarkt. (direkt nach Hause)

10. Ich besitze ein Fahrrad. (einen *smart*)

Answers for 10-40. 1. Ich arbeitete lieber als Bankdirektor. 2. Ich verdiente lieber 100.000 Euro im Jahr. 3. Ich wohnte lieber in Wiesbaden. 4. In den Ferien reiste ich lieber nach Spanien. 5. Ich verbrächte mein Wochenende lieber in den Bergen. 6. Ich führe lieber mit dem Auto zur Arbeit. 7. Während der Fahrt läse ich lieber einen spannenden Roman. 8. Zur Arbeit trüge ich lieber Jeans und ein T-Shirt. 9. Ich ginge nach der Arbeit lieber direkt nach Hause. 10. Ich besäße lieber einen *smart*.

10-41 Interview auf der Jobmesse. Auf der Jobmesse Wiesbaden hat man Herrn Waldauer von der Allianz Gruppe interviewt. Er beschrieb, was man als Kundenberater in seinem Versicherungsunternehmen macht und wie der ideale Bewerber für diese Stelle aussähe. Setzen Sie für alle fett gedruckten Verben im Indikativ den Konjunktiv II ein.

Answers for 10-41. 1. wäre; 2. Könnten; 3. machte; 4. wären; 5. beantworteten; 6. verkauften; 7. gewännen; 8. pflegten; 9. berieten; 10. sähe ... aus; 11. verfügte; 12. schriebe; 13. spräche; 14. müsste; 15. erwarteten; 16. hätte; 17. böten; 18. gehörten

Interviewer: Stellen Sie sich vor, ich (1) **bin** Kundenberater bei Ihnen. (2) **Können** Sie mir sagen, was ich bei Ihnen als Kundenberater (3) **mache?**

Herr Waldauer: Die Tätigkeiten (4) **sind** vielseitig. Zum Beispiel: Sie (5) **beantworten** komplexe Kundenanfragen, persönlich sowie telefonisch. Sie (6) **verkaufen** Produkte und Leistungen. Sie (7) **gewinnen** neue Kunden. Kurz gesagt, Sie (8) **pflegen** Beziehungen zu Kunden und (9) **beraten** sie umfassend.

Interviewer: Wie (10) **sieht** der ideale Bewerber **aus?**

Herr Waldauer: Die ideale Person (11) **verfügt** über eine abgeschlossene Ausbildung als Bankkaufmann oder -frau. Er oder sie (12) **schreibt** und (13) **spricht** fließendes Englisch und (14) **muss** gute PC Kenntnisse haben. Wir (15) **erwarten** außerdem einige Erfahrungen in der Kundenberatung.

Interviewer: Welche Vorteile (16) **hat** man in dieser Stelle?

Herr Waldauer: Wir (17) **bieten** einen Arbeitsvertrag in Vollzeit mit allen sozialen Leistungen und beste Aufstiegschancen. Eine angenehme Arbeitsatmosphäre und ein attraktives Gehalt (18) **gehören** auch dazu.

Interviewer: Danke für das Interview, Herr Waldauer.

Note on usage of *würde*-construction. 10-30 to 10-32 Until recently, the use of *würde* in the *wenn*-clause was considered poor style. This is no longer necessarily the case. For example: *Wenn du uns helfen würdest, könnten wir schneller fertig werden. (If you would help us we could finish more quickly.)* However, the more common verbs (i.e., *haben, sein, werden, wissen,* and the modals) are almost never replaced with the *würde* alternative.

The *würde*-construction (Alternative mit *würde*)

You may encounter the present tense general subjunctive (**Konjunktiv II**) of many verbs in formal written German. In everyday speech, however, only the subjunctive forms of **haben (hätte)**, **sein (wäre)**, **werden (würde)**, **wissen (wüsste)**, and the modals are commonly used.[3] For most other verbs in the spoken language, the **würde** + *infinitive* alternative is the preferred form. Because the present subjunctive of weak verbs is identical to the simple past forms, the **würde**-construction can also be used to eliminate ambiguity.

The **würde**-construction is created using the subjunctive form of the verb **werden** plus the infinitive of the main verb:

ich	würde … mieten	wir	würden … mieten
du	würdest … mieten	ihr	würdet … mieten
er, sie, es	würde … mieten	Sie, sie	würden … mieten

The **würde**-form corresponds to the English *would*. For any verb, the **würde**-construction and the present subjunctive form have the same meaning.

Subjunctive: Wenn ich Zeit hätte, **besuchte** ich den Dom in Limburg.
If I had the time, I would visit the cathedral in Limburg.

würde-**construction** Wenn ich Zeit hätte, **würde** ich den Dom in Limburg **besuchen**.
If I had the time, I would visit the cathedral in Limburg.

10-42 Ich würde lieber … Sie haben in **Übung 10-40** gehört, dass Nicolas Werner mit seinem Leben unzufrieden ist. Nun erzählen Sie Nicolas, was Sie an seiner Stelle machen würden. Benutzen Sie die Alternative zum Konjunktiv II mit **würde**.

Beispiel: Ich hieße lieber Jacob.

An deiner Stelle würde ich lieber Anthony heißen.

---

[3]Also sometimes used in spoken German, though to a lesser extent, are the present general subjunctive forms of: **finden (fände)**, **geben (gäbe)**, **gehen (ginge)**, **halten (hielte)**, **kommen (käme)**, **lassen (ließe)**, **stehen (stünde)**, and **tun (täte)**.

10-43 Was wäre, wenn … Besprechen Sie, was Sie in diesen Situationen wohl machen würden. Benutzen Sie den Konjunktiv II oder **würde** + Infinitiv, wo das die bessere Wahl ist.

Beispiel: wenn Sie eine neue Arbeitsstelle in Wiesbaden fänden

> *Wenn ich eine neue Arbeitsstelle in Wiesbaden fände, würde ich mich freuen.*
> *Ich müsste für die neue Arbeit nach Deutschland ziehen. Dort würde ich*
> *täglich Deutsch sprechen.*

1. wenn Sie in zwei Wochen nach Wiesbaden ziehen müssten
2. wenn Sie als Sportler/in bei der nächsten Olympiade teilnehmen sollten
3. wenn Sie Musiker/in in einer erfolgreichen Band wären
4. wenn Sie eine Million Euro im Lotto gewinnen würden
5. wenn Ihre Familie eine mittelalterliche Burg am Rhein besäße

10-33 to 10-35

Past tense general subjunctive (Konjunktiv II: Vergangenheit)

The past tense general subjunctive is formed using the present subjunctive of the auxiliary verb **haben** or **sein** and the past participle of the main verb. If a modal verb is used in the past subjunctive, the double infinitive construction is used in lieu of the past participle.

You learned about double infinitive constructions in *Kapitel 8 Grammatik.*

Infinitive	sparen	fahren	schreiben müssen
ich	hätte gespart	wäre gefahren	hätte schreiben müssen
du	hättest gespart	wär(e)st gefahren	hättest schreiben müssen
er, sie, es	hätte gespart	wäre gefahren	hätte schreiben müssen
wir	hätten gespart	wären gefahren	hätten schreiben müssen
ihr	hättet gespart	wär(e)t gefahren	hättet schreiben müssen
Sie, sie	hätten gespart	wären gefahren	hätten schreiben müssen

The past subjunctive indicates a situation that could have happened in the past but did not.

> Wenn ich genug Zeit **gehabt hätte, wäre** ich länger in Fulda **geblieben.** (CONDITION)
> *If I had had enough time, I would have stayed in Fulda longer.*

> An deiner Stelle **hätte** ich ihn **angerufen.** (HYPOTHETICAL, CONTRARY-TO-FACT STATEMENT)
> *If I were you, I would have called him.*

> Wenn sie nur nicht so früh **gegangen wären!** (WISH)
> *If only they hadn't left so early!*

Answers for 10-44. 1. Sie hätte spannende Vorlesungen gehört. **2.** Sie hätte ihr Deutsch verbessert. **3.** Sie wäre während der Ferien gereist. **4.** Sie hätte Fahrradtouren gemacht. **5.** Sie hätte Apfelwein probiert. **6.** Sie hätte viele Deutsche kennengelernt. **7.** Sie wäre manchmal durch den Botanischen Garten gegangen. **8.** Sie hätte jeden Tag das Alte Schloss gesehen. **9.** Sie wäre im Wald um Gießen gewandert. **10.** Sie hätte ihre Freunde aus Amerika einladen können.

10-44 Was hätte sie alles erlebt? Nach zwei Jahren Deutschunterricht an Ihrer Universität hatte Ashley die Möglichkeit, ein Jahr an der Universität Gießen zu studieren. Sie hat sich aber dagegen entschieden. Was hätte sie wohl alles erleben können, wenn sie nach Gießen gegangen wäre? Bilden Sie Sätze mit Konjunktiv II.

Beispiel: an den Wochenenden manchmal nach Frankfurt oder Kassel fahren
Ashley wäre an den Wochenende manchmal nach Frankfurt gefahren.

1. spannende Vorlesungen hören
2. ihr Deutsch verbessern
3. während der Ferien reisen
4. Fahrradtouren machen
5. Apfelwein probieren
6. viele Deutsche kennenlernen
7. manchmal durch den Botanischen Garten gehen
8. jeden Tag das Alte Schloss sehen
9. im Wald um Gießen wandern
10. ihre Freunde aus Amerika einladen können

10-45 Geschäftsreise gestrichen! Letzte Woche haben Sie für eine Geschäftsreise nach Frankfurt reisen sollen, aber das Meeting ist ausgefallen und Sie sind nicht hingeflogen. Sie sind enttäuscht, denn Sie hatten viele Pläne. Sagen Sie, was Sie an den folgenden Orten in und um Frankfurt gemacht hätten, wenn Ihre Reise stattgefunden hätte.

Beispiele: *Am Bahnhof hätte ich eine Zeitung gekauft.*
Ich wäre im Flugzeug eingeschlafen.

am Bahnhof	im Frankfurter Goethe-Haus	im Main Tower
in der Frankfurter Altstadt	in einem Lokal	am Fluss
in der Zeilgalerie	im Buchladen	in der Alten Oper
im Hotel	im Deutschen Filmmuseum	im Flugzeug

10-36 to 10-37

2. Indefinite pronouns (Indefinitpronomen)

Indefinite pronouns designate unspecified people and things. In English, indefinite pronouns include such words as *anybody, one, nothing, something, much, neither*, etc.

In German, the most frequently used singular indefinite pronouns that refer to people are **man** (*one*), **jeder** (*each, every*), **jemand** (*somebody, someone*), and **niemand** (*nobody, no one*). Each of these pronouns is always singular and refers to both males and females. They are declined for case, but the optional endings on **jemand** and **niemand** are frequently omitted.

Nominative	man	jeder	jemand	niemand
Accusative	einen	jeden	jemand(en)	niemand(en)
Dative	einem	jedem	jemand(em)	niemand(em)
Genitive	eines	jedes	jemand(es)	niemand(es)

The words **ein** and **kein** can also function as pronouns with reference to either people or things. As pronouns, they take the same endings as **der**-words and mean *one* and *none* respectively. When the referent is unknown, the masculine forms are used to denote a person, the neuter forms for a thing.

	Masculine	Feminine	Neuter	Plural
Nominative	einer	eine	ein(e)s	—
	keiner	keine	kein(e)s	keine
Accusative	einen	einen	ein(e)s	—
	keinen	keine	kein(e)s	keine
Dative	einem	einer	einem	—
	keinem	keiner	keinem	keinen
Genitive	eines	einer	eines	—
	keines	keiner	keines	keiner

Some other indefinite pronouns refer exclusively to things and ideas. Common examples of such pronouns are **alles** (*everything*), **etwas** (*something*), **nichts** (*nothing*), **viel** (*much*) und **wenig** (*little*).

- The pronoun **alles** is declined using neuter endings (**allem** in the dative, **alles** in all other cases)

- For **viel** and **wenig** the endings are optional.

- The pronouns **etwas** and **nichts** are not declined at all. These singular, neuter indefinite pronouns can accompany adjectival nouns that refer to abstract qualities: **nichts Interessantes**, **etwas Gutes**.

See *Kapitel 7 Grammatik*: Adjectival nouns.

Indefinite pronouns in the plural form designate an indeterminate number of people or things. Common examples are **alle** (*all, everyone*), **einige** (*some*), **manche** (*some*), **mehrere** (*several*), **andere** (*others*), **viele** (*many*), and **wenige** (*few*). When declined, these pronouns add **-n** in the dative and **-r** in the genitive.

> **Viele** sind geblieben, aber **mehrere** sind ausgewandert.
> *Many remained, but several emigrated.*

> Habt ihr schon von **allen** gehört?
> *Have you already heard from everyone?*

> Zur Überraschung **vieler** kam er schon heute an.
> *To the surprise of many, he arrived today already.*

Note that several of the words that can be used as indefinite pronouns can also function as determiners or adjectives when used in combination with nouns.

Michael: jemand (*nom.*), man (*nom.*); *Sarah:* jemanden (*acc.*), nichts (*acc.*); *Michael:* einige (*nom.*), etwas (*acc.*); *Ulrike:* man (*nom.*), keiner (*nom.*), vieles (*acc.*), keinem (*dat.*); *Michael:* viel (*acc.*), Manche (*nom.*); *Sarah:* Viele (*nom.*), wenige (*nom.*), nichts (*acc.*), jemand (*nom.*)

Teaching suggestion for 10-46. Have students identify the cases of the indefinite pronouns as well.

10-46 Studiengebühren in Hessen. Michael, Sarah und Ulrike sprechen über Studiengebühren in Hessen. Unterstreichen Sie in ihrem Gespräch 16 Indefinitpronomen.

Michael: Weiß jemand, ob man für das Studium in Gießen zahlen muss?

Sarah: Ich kenne jemanden, der in Darmstadt studiert und nichts zahlt.

Michael: Vor ein paar Jahren mussten einige etwas zahlen. Ich glaube, es waren 500 Euro pro Semester.

Ulrike: Jetzt hat man die Studiengebühren in Hessen abgeschafft. Aber keiner weiß, ob sie wieder eingeführt werden. Die Politiker versprechen vieles, aber wir können keinem von ihnen trauen.

Michael: Was sollen Studenten machen, wenn es so viel kostet? Manche können solche Gebühren sicherlich nicht zahlen.

Sarah: Viele wollen studieren, aber wenige wollen Studiengebühren zahlen. Ihr sollt aber bedenken: Wenn die Studenten selber nichts zahlen, muss der Staat oder sonst jemand dafür aufkommen.

Immer weiter!

10-38 to 10-44

10-47 Zur Diskussion. Besprechen Sie die Themen.

1. Was macht Hessen zu einem attraktiven Wohnort? Nennen Sie drei Faktoren und erklären Sie, wie jeder zur Lebensqualität in Hessen beiträgt.

2. Ein Freund von Ihnen hat gerade eine Stelle bei einem Unternehmen im Rhein-Main-Gebiet angenommen. Besprechen Sie, was Sie diesem Freund von seinem neuen Wohn- und Arbeitsort erzählen können. Was muss er unbedingt wissen? Welche Geheimtipps haben Sie für ihn?

10-48 Zum Schreiben: An Hessen führt kein Weg vorbei. In einem Wettbewerb des Hessischen Rundfunks sollte man das Motto „An Hessen führt kein Weg vorbei" erklären. Schreiben Sie einen Beitrag für diesen Wettbewerb. Gewinner erhalten ein bezahltes Wochenende in einem Frankfurter Luxushotel und die Aufsätze erscheinen auf der HR Internetseite!

Beginnen Sie so: *Hessen ist aus vielen Gründen ein Land, an dem kein Weg vorbeiführt. …*

Weitere Themen

Alte Oper	Hessentag	Opel
Christine Brückner	Hessische Soldaten	Paulskirche
Deutsche Märchenstraße	im amerikanischen	Philipp der Großmütige
documenta	Unabhängigkeitskrieg	Struwwelpeter
Eintracht Frankfurt	Hildebrandslied	Wilhelmshöhe
Frankfurter Buchmesse	Limes	Wolkenkratzerfest
Fulda	Kurhaus	
Hessenlied	Museumsufer	

Appendix

Principal parts of irregular verbs

The following list contains the principal parts of the most common strong and mixed verbs. With a few exceptions, separable and inseparable prefix verbs are not included since the stem changes are the same as for the basic verb (e.g., **zu·geben – geben, besprechen – sprechen**). Note, however, that the perfect tense auxiliary verb can differ for verbs created from the same root (e.g., **gehen – ist gegangen, begehen – hat begangen**).

Perfect tense auxiliary verbs are given only for verbs conjugated with **sein**. Verbs that can use either **sein** or **haben** as auxiliaries often have two different meanings, an intransitive meaning (i.e., lacking a direct object) with **sein** and a transitive one (i.e., using a direct object) with **haben**. Compare, for example: **Er <u>ist</u> nach Hause <u>gefahren</u>** (intransitive) and **Er <u>hat</u> einen Sportwagen <u>gefahren</u>** (transitive).

Infinitive	Irregular present tense	Simple past stem	Past participle	Definition
backen	bäckt *or* backt	buk *or* backte	gebacken	*to bake*
befehlen	befiehlt	befahl	befohlen	*to command*
beginnen		begann	begonnen	*to begin*
beißen		biss	gebissen	*to bite*
betrügen		betrog	betrogen	*to deceive*
biegen		bog	gebogen	*to bend*
bieten		bot	geboten	*to offer*
binden		band	gebunden	*to bind, tie*
bitten		bat	gebeten	*to ask, request*
blasen	bläst	blies	geblasen	*to blow*
bleiben		blieb	ist geblieben	*to stay*
braten	brät	briet	gebraten	*to fry*
brechen	bricht	brach	gebrochen	*to break*
brennen		brannte	gebrannt	*to burn*
bringen		brachte	gebracht	*to bring*
denken		dachte	gedacht	*to think*
dürfen	darf	durfte	gedurft	*may, to be allowed*
empfehlen	empfiehlt	empfahl	empfohlen	*to recommend*
essen	isst	aß	gegessen	*to eat*
fahren	fährt	fuhr	ist/hat gefahren	*to go, ride; to drive*
fallen	fällt	fiel	ist gefallen	*to fall*
fangen	fängt	fing	gefangen	*to catch*
finden		fand	gefunden	*to find*
fliegen		flog	ist/hat geflogen	*to fly*
fliehen		floh	ist geflohen	*to flee*

(continued)

Infinitive	Irregular present tense	Simple past stem	Past participle		Definition
fließen		floss	ist	geflossen	*to flow*
frieren		fror	ist/hat	gefroren	*to freeze*
geben	gibt	gab		gegeben	*to give*
gehen		ging	ist	gegangen	*to go*
gelingen		gelang	ist	gelungen	*to succeed*
gelten	gilt	galt		gegolten	*to be valid, apply*
genießen		genoss		genossen	*to enjoy*
geschehen	geschieht	geschah	ist	geschehen	*to happen*
gewinnen		gewann		gewonnen	*to win*
gießen		goss		gegossen	*to pour*
gleichen		glich		geglichen	*to resemble*
gleiten		glitt	ist	geglitten	*to glide, slide*
greifen		griff		gegriffen	*to seize*
haben	hat	hatte		gehabt	*to have*
halten	hält	hielt		gehalten	*to hold, stop*
hängen		hing		gehangen	*to hang*
heißen		hieß		geheißen	*to be called*
helfen	hilft	half		geholfen	*to help*
kennen		kannte		gekannt	*to know*
klingen		klang		geklungen	*to sound*
kneifen		kniff		gekniffen	*to pinch*
kommen		kam	ist	gekommen	*to come*
können	kann	konnte		gekonnt	*can, to be able*
kriechen		kroch	ist	gekrochen	*to crawl, creep*
laden	lädt	lud		geladen	*to load*
lassen	lässt	ließ		gelassen	*to let, leave*
laufen	läuft	lief	ist	gelaufen	*to run*
leiden		litt		gelitten	*to suffer*
leihen		lieh		geliehen	*to lend*
lesen	liest	las		gelesen	*to read*
liegen		lag		gelegen	*to lie, be lying*
lügen		log		gelogen	*to (tell a) lie*
mahlen		mahlte		gemahlen	*to grind*
meiden		mied		gemieden	*to avoid*
messen	misst	maß		gemessen	*to measure*
mögen	mag	mochte		gemocht	*to like*
müssen	muss	musste		gemusst	*must, to have to*
nehmen	nimmt	nahm		genommen	*to take*

Infinitive	Irregular present tense	Simple past stem	Past participle		Definition
nennen		nannte		genannt	to name, call
pfeifen		pfiff		gepfiffen	to whistle
raten	rät	riet		geraten	to advise, guess
reißen		riss	ist/hat	gerissen	to rip
reiten		ritt	ist	geritten	to ride
rennen		rannte	ist	gerannt	to run
riechen		roch		gerochen	to smell
ringen		rang		gerungen	to wrestle
rufen		rief		gerufen	to call
schaffen[1]		schuf		geschaffen	to create
scheiden		schied	ist/hat	geschieden	to depart; to separate
scheinen		schien		geschienen	to shine
schieben		schob		geschoben	to push, shove
schießen		schoss		geschossen	to shoot
schlafen	schläft	schlief		geschlafen	to sleep
schlagen	schlägt	schlug		geschlagen	to hit, beat
schließen		schloss		geschlossen	to close, shut
schmelzen	schmilzt	schmolz	ist/hat	geschmolzen	to melt
schneiden		schnitt		geschnitten	to cut
schreiben		schrieb		geschrieben	to write
schreien		schrie		geschrieen	to scream, shout
schreiten		schritt	ist	geschritten	to stride
schweigen		schwieg		geschwiegen	to be silent
schwimmen		schwamm	ist/hat	geschwommen	to swim
schwören		schwor		geschworen	to swear
sehen	sieht	sah		gesehen	to see
sein	ist	war	ist	gewesen	to be
senden[2]		sandte		gesandt	to send
singen		sang		gesungen	to sing
sinken		sank	ist	gesunken	to sink
sitzen		saß		gesessen	to sit
sollen	soll	sollte		gesollt	shall, to be supposed to
sprechen	spricht	sprach		gesprochen	to speak
springen		sprang	ist	gesprungen	to jump

[1]When conjugated as a weak verb, **schaffen** means *to manage (to do something), work.*
[2]When conjugated as a weak verb, **senden** means *to broadcast.*

(continued)

Infinitive	Irregular present tense	Simple past stem	Past participle		Definition
stechen	sticht	stach		gestochen	to prick, sting
stehen		stand		gestanden	to stand
stehlen	stiehlt	stahl		gestohlen	to steal
steigen		stieg	ist	gestiegen	to climb
sterben	stirbt	starb	ist	gestorben	to die
stinken		stank		gestunken	to stink
stoßen	stößt	stieß	ist/hat	gestoßen	to bump; to push
streichen		strich		gestrichen	to stroke
streiten		stritt		gestritten	to quarrel
tragen	trägt	trug		getragen	to wear, carry
treffen	trifft	traf		getroffen	to meet
treiben		trieb	ist/hat	getrieben	to drive; to drift
treten	tritt	trat	ist/hat	getreten	to step
trinken		trank		getrunken	to drink
tun		tat		getan	to do
verderben	verdirbt	verdarb	ist/hat	verdorben	to spoil; to ruin
vergessen	vergisst	vergaß		vergessen	to forget
verlieren		verloren		verloren	to lose
verschwinden		verschwand	ist	verschwunden	to disappear
verzeihen		verzieh		verziehen	to excuse
wachsen	wächst	wuchs	ist	gewachsen	to grow
waschen	wäscht	wusch		gewaschen	to wash
weisen		wies		gewiesen	to point
wenden[3]		wandte		gewandt	to turn
werben	wirbt	warb		geworben	to advertise, recruit
werden	wird	wurde	ist	geworden	to become
werfen	wirft	warf		geworfen	to throw
wiegen		wog		gewogen	to weigh
wissen	weiß	wusste		gewusst	to know
wollen	will	wollte		gewollt	to want
ziehen		zog	ist/hat	gezogen	to move; to pull
zwingen		zwang		gezwungen	to force

[3]**Wenden** may be used as a weak verb, especially to mean *to turn over, turn around.*

German-English Glossary

The German-English Glossary contains all words from the chapter *Neue Vokabeln* as well as relevant lexical items that appear in the text but are not presented for active mastery. Chapter numbers are given in parentheses for all items appearing in the *Neue Vokabeln* to indicate where they are first introduced. Words typically learned during the first year are not included.

Nouns are listed with their plural forms: **die Geschichte, -n.** No plural entry is given if the plural is rarely used or nonexistent. Masculine weak nouns are listed with both genitive singular and nominative plural endings, as is customary in dictionaries: **der Held, -en, -en.**

Weak verbs are given only in their infinitive form. Strong and mixed verbs are listed with their principal parts: **bieten, bot, geboten.** Vowel changes in the present tense are noted in parentheses: **erfahren (erfährt), erfuhr, erfahren.** Perfect tense auxiliary verbs are given only for verbs conjugated with **sein: ziehen, zog, ist gezogen.** Separable prefixes are indicated by a raised dot between the prefix and the verb stem: **an·stellen.**

The following abbreviations are used:

acc.	accusative	*def. art.*	definite article	*m.*	masculine
adj. noun	adjectival noun	*f.*	feminine	*pl.*	plural
colloq.	colloquial	*fig.*	figurative	*sing.*	singular
dat.	dative	*gen.*	genitive		

ab und zu (6) from time to time

der Abbau (2) dismantling

das Abenteuer, - (5) adventure

der Aberglaube, -ns, *(no pl.).* superstition

der Abfall, ⸚e (8) waste, trash

ab·hängen: Es hängt davon ab (, ob...) (2) It depends (on whether . . .)

das Abitur, -e secondary school leaving exam (in Germany)

ab·reißen, riss ab, abgerissen to tear down

der Abriss, -e sketch, outline

der Absatz, ⸚e (2) sales, turnover; paragraph

ab·schalten (9) to cut off, *(colloq.)* to kick back

der Abschied, -e (8) departure, parting

der Abschluss, ⸚e (1) conclusion, completion; school degree

ab·schneiden, schnitt ab, abgeschnitten (8) to cut off

der Abschnitt, -e section, part

der Absolvent, -en, -en/die Absolventin, -nen (7) graduate

der Abstecher, - (8) side trip

achten (auf + *acc.***)** to pay attention (to)

das Adjektiv, -e adjective

die Adjektivendung, -en adjective ending

das Adjektivnomen, - adjectival noun

der Adventskranz, ⸚e Advent wreath

das Adverb, -ien adverb

ahnen (5) to suspect

Ahnung: Ich habe keine Ahnung. (10) I have no clue.

ähnlich (8) similar

die Ähnlichkeit, -en similarity

aktuell current, latest

der Alemanne, -n, -n/die Alemannin, -nen Alemannian

alemannisch Alemannic

allerdings (1) though, indeed, certainly

Alles in Maßen! (4) Everything in moderation!

Alles in Ordnung! (6) All's well!

allgemein (4) general

allmählich (6) gradually

das Alter age

sich amüsieren (5) to have fun

an·bieten, bot an, angeboten (3) to offer

der Anblick, -e (4) sight

das Andenken, - souvenir

ändern to change

andererseits (1) on the other hand

anders, ander- different

die Anfrage: auf Anfrage (2) by request, on demand

das Angebot, -e (2) offer, offering

angemessen appropriate

der/die Angestellte, -n *(adj. noun)* (3) employee

angewiesen auf (+ *acc.*) (9) dependent on

der Angriff, -e (6) attack

an·gucken (*colloq.*) (10) to look at

der Anhänger, -/die Anhängerin, -nen (6) supporter, fan

an·knüpfen an (+ *acc.*) to link to; to resume

an·kommen, kam an, ist angekommen to arrive

Es kommt darauf an. (2) It depends.

der Anlass, ̈e (4) occasion

die Anmeldung, -en (8) registration

an·nehmen (nimmt an), nahm an, angenommen (6) to accept

die Anrede, -n form of address

an·regen to encourage, stimulate

der Anruf, -e telephone call

anschaulich (10) vivid(ly)

das Ansehen, - (2) reputation

die Ansicht, -en opinion, view

der Ansicht sein (6) to be of the opinion

an·sprechen (spricht an), sprach an, angesprochen to address, appeal to

der Anspruch, ̈e (auf + acc.) claim (to)

in Anspruch nehmen to claim for oneself

anspruchsvoll (10) challenging

anstelle (+ *gen.*) in place of

an·stellen (5) to hire

anstrengend (5) exhausting

der Anteil, -e portion, proportion

der Antrag, ̈e (9) request, application

die Antwort, -en answer

anwesend (9) present

die Anzahl, -en number, quantity

an·ziehen, zog an, angezogen to attract

der Ärger (7) trouble, annoyance

die Art, -en kind, type; way, manner

Art und Weise method, manner

der Artikel, - article

der Aschermittwoch Ash Wednesday

atemlos (4) breathless

auf·bauen (4) to build (up)

auf·brechen (bricht auf), brach auf, ist aufgebrochen (9) to set out (for a destination), to leave (a place)

der Aufenthalt, -e (3) stay, residence

auf·fordern to challenge, call upon

die Aufführung, -en (5) performance

die Aufgabe, -n assignment

auf·geben (gibt auf), gab auf, aufgegeben to give up

aufgeregt (9) excited, nervous

auf·halten (hält auf), hielt auf, aufgehalten (9) to delay

auf·kommen, kam auf, ist aufgekommen to arise, come up

die Aufmerksamkeit (5) attention

aufregend (5) exciting

die Aufregung, -en (5) excitement

der Aufsatz, ̈e essay

auf·schreiben, schrieb auf, aufgeschrieben to write down

der Aufstieg, -e (9) promotion, advancement

auf·teilen to divide up

der Auftrag, ̈e (3) job, order

der Auftritt, -e (2) appearance

auf·wachsen (wächst auf), wuchs auf, ist aufgewachsen (1) to grow up

auf·weisen, wies auf, aufgewiesen to exhibit, boast

aufwendig (5) extravagant, costly

der Aufzug, ̈e (10) elevator

die Ausbeutung, -en exploitation

aus·bilden (3) to train, educate

der Ausblick, -e (5) view

sich aus·breiten (9) to extend, to spread out

der Ausdruck, ̈e (3) expression

aus·drücken (2) to express

der Ausfall, ̈e (9) failure, loss

der Ausflug, ̈e (10) excursion

die Ausgabe, -n issue, edition

ausgerechnet (9) of all things

ausgestattet (mit) (2) equipped (with)

aus·lachen (9) to laugh at

ausländisch foreign

aus·lösen to activate, trigger

aus·reißen, riss aus, ausgerissen (7) to pull out

die Aussage, -n statement

aus·schenken (4) to pour, to serve (a drink)

ausschließlich (8) exclusively

aus·sehen wie (sieht aus), sah aus, ausgesehen to look like

außerdem (7) besides, in addition

außergewöhnlich (3) exceptional, extraordinary

außerordentlich (1) extraordinary; extraordinarily

äußerst (7) extremely

die Aussicht, -en (8) view

die Aussprache, -n pronunciation

die Ausstellung, -en (6) exhibit

aus·tauschen (7) to exchange

aus·üben: Druck aus·üben auf (+ *acc.*) (4) to put pressure on (someone)

die Auswahl, -en (7) selection

aus·wandern, ist ausgewandert to emigrate

auswärtig (2) external, from outside

der Ausweis, -e (4) identification card, ID

die Auswirkung, -en (1) effect

sich aus·zeichnen (2) to distinguish oneself

der Auszug, ̈e excerpt

badisch associated with Baden

die Bahn, -en train

der Bahnhof, ⸚e (1) train station

der Bahnsteig, -e (9) train platform

der Band, ⸚e (3) volume (book)

die Bank, ⸚e (6) bench

barfuß (4) barefoot

der Bau, Bauten (3) building, construction

der Bauer, -n, -n/die Bäue-rin, -nen (5) farmer

der Bauernhof, ⸚e (5) farm

der Bauleiter, -/die Bauleiterin, -nen (10) construction manager

der Baum, ⸚e (8) tree

bayerisch Bavarian

(das) Bayern Bavaria

beachten (9) to observe, pay attention to

beantworten to answer

beauftragen mit (9) to charge with (a task)

bedenklich (9) concerning, alarming

bedeuten to mean

die Bedeutung, -en (4) importance, relevance

die Bedingung, -en (6) condition

das Bedürfnis, -se (9) need

beeindruckt (von) (7) impressed (by/with)

sich befinden, befand, befunden (3) to be located

befristet (10) fixed-term; temporary

begeistert (von) (6) enthusiastic (about)

begleiten (8) to accompany

der Begriff, -e term, concept

begründen to justify, substantiate

behalten: den Kopf klar behalten (2) to keep a clear head

behandeln to treat, deal with

behaupten to claim, maintain

die Beilage, -n side dish

der Beiname, -ns, -n epithet

das Beispiel, -e example

der Beitrag, ⸚e contribution; article

bei·tragen (trägt bei), trug bei, beigetragen (zu) (2) to contribute, to add (to)

bekannt (1) known

bekunden: Interesse bekunden (9) to show interest

die Belletristik (6) literary fiction

beliebig (8) as one likes, at will

beliebt (1) popular, favored

belohnen (6) to reward

beobachten (6) to observe

bemerkenswert noteworthy

benennen, benannte, benannt to name

beraten (berät), beriet, beraten (10) to advise

der Bereich, -e (5) area, region

bereits (5) already

die Bereitschaft (2) willingness

der Berg, -e mountain

der Bergbau mining

das Bergwerk, -e mine

der Bericht, -e (3) report

berichten (2) to report

der Beruf, -e profession

berühmt (1) famous

die Besatzungszone, -n occupation zone

beschädigen (4) to damage

beschäftigen (7) to employ, engage

Bescheid: Bescheid wissen (5) to be in the know

beschließen, beschloss, beschlossen to decide

beschreiben, beschrieb, beschrieben to describe

sich beschweren (9) to complain

besetzt occupied

besichtigen (8) to visit, view, inspect

besitzen, besaß, besessen (8) to own, have

besonders especially

besorgen (6) to obtain

besprechen (bespricht), besprach, besprochen to discuss

bestehen, bestand, bestanden to exist

bestehen aus (8) to consist of

bestimmen (6) to decide, determine

bestimmt definite, certain

sich beteiligen (an + *dat.*) (1) to participate (in)

betrachten (8) to look at, consider

betreiben, betrieb, betrieben (4) to operate

der Betrieb, -e (7) business, operation

betrüben (8) to sadden

betrügen, betrog, betrogen (10) to deceive

beurteilen (7) to assess, judge

die Bevölkerung, -en population

bevorzugen (10) to prefer

bewahren (4) to conserve, preserve

bewährt (6) tried and true

die Bewegung, -en (4) movement

der Beweis, -e (7) evidence

sich bewerben (bewirbt), bewarb, beworben (um) (10) to apply (for)

bewusst consciously, deliberately

bezeichnen (als) (3) to label (as)

sich beziehen auf (+ *acc.*), bezog, bezogen to refer to

die Beziehung, -en relationship, connection

das Beziehungswort, ⸚er antecedent

der Bezug, ⸚e (6) connection

in Bezug auf (+ *acc.*) (6) in relation to

bieten, bot, geboten (1) to offer

bilden to form, create; to educate

die Bildung, -en education

bitten um, bat, gebeten to ask for

blank (8) shiny

blass pale

der Blick, -e (4) glance, look

einen Blick werfen to take a look

das Blut (7) blood

die Blüte, -n; die Blütezeit, -en blossoming, height

der Boden, ⸚ (8) soil, ground

der Bodensee Lake Constance

der Brand, ⸚e (4) fire

der Brauch, ⸚e custom, tradition**

die Brauerei, -en brewery

brav (5) well-behaved

die BRD (Bundesrepublik Deutschland) Federal Republic of Germany, West Germany

brennen, brannte, gebrannt to burn

die Brücke, -n (1) bridge

der Brunnen, - fountain, well

der Buchtipp, -s book recommendation

die Bühne, -n stage

bummeln, ist gebummelt (5) to stroll

der Bundeskanzler, -/die Bundeskanzlerin, -nen (2) Federal Chancellor

das Bundesland, ¨er federal state (in Germany or Austria)

die Bundesregierung (1) federal government

bunt (6) colorful

die Burg, -en (3) castle, fortress

der Bürger, -/die Bürgerin, -nen (5) citizen

bürgerlich (3) middle-class, bourgeois

der Bürgermeister, -/die Bürgermeisterin, -nen (2) mayor

bzw. = beziehungsweise (4) and/or

ca. = circa (1) approximately

dagegen: etwas dagegen haben (4) to object to something

damals (6) back then, at that time

die Dampfnudel, -n sweet or savory yeast dumpling

die Darstellung, -en (3) depiction

darüber hinaus (8) furthermore

das Datum, Daten date

die Dauer (1) duration, length of time

auf die Dauer (1) in the long run

die da-Verbindung, -en da-compound

die DDR (Deutsche Demokratische Republik) German Democratic Republic, East Germany

decken to cover

das Denkmal, ¨er (3) monument

dennoch nevertheless

deshalb therefore, because of that

(das) Deutschland Germany

deswegen therefore, because of that

deutlich (1) clearly

dicht (4) close together

dienen (+ dat.) to serve

der Dichter, -/die Dichterin, -nen (3) poet

das Ding, -e thing

das Dirndl, - traditional Alpine dress with a tight bodice and full skirt

der Dom, -e (4) cathedral

Donnerwetter! (9) Oh, my goodness!

doof (colloq.) (5) dumb, stupid

das Dorf, ¨er village, small town

der Dorn, -en (10) thorn

dran sein (5) to have a turn

Ich bin dran. (5) It's my turn.

draußen (5) outside

das Drittel, - third

drüben (2) over there

der Druck: Druck aus·üben auf (+ acc.) (4) to put pressure on (someone)

drucken (3) to publish, print

dünn thin(ly)

durchaus (7) absolutely

durch·führen (4) to carry out

durchgedreht (colloq.) (9) nuts

der Durchschnitt, -e (7) average

eben (7) just, simply, precisely

die Ebene, -n (9) level, plane

ebenfalls (7) likewise

ebenso wie (8) as well as

echt (7) genuine

ehemalig (6) former

eher rather; more likely

die Ehre, -n honor

zu Ehren (+ gen.) in honor of

eigen (6) one's own

die Eigenart, -en unique character

die Eigenschaft, -en characteristic

eigentlich (3) actually

sich eignen (zu) (8) to be suitable (for), lend itself (to)

der Einblick, -e (5) insight; glimpse

der Eindruck, ¨e (2) impression

einerseits (1) on the one hand

ein·fangen (fängt ein), fing ein, eingefangen (9) to catch

der Einfluss, ¨e (1) influence

die Einführung, -en introduction

eingerichtet (4) furnished

einheimisch (7) local, native

die Einheit (3) unity

einige some

sich einigen to agree

die Einigkeit unity

ein·laden (lädt ein), lud ein, eingeladen (3) to invite

die Einladung, -en (9) invitation

sich ein·lassen auf (+ acc.) to get involved in

einmalig (7) unique

ein·ordnen to arrange in order

die Einrichtung, -en organization, institution; furnishing

ein·sammeln (9) to collect, to gather

ein·schätzen (4) to estimate, to assess

ein·setzen to insert

einst (3) once, at one time (in the past)

ein·stellen (10) to cancel

ein·treffen (trifft ein), traf ein, ist eingetroffen (6) to arrive

ein·treten (tritt ein), trat ein, ist eingetreten (9) to join, enter

der Eintritt, -e (10) entry, admission

die Einwanderung, -en immigration

der Einwohner, -/die Einwohnerin, -nen inhabitant

einzig (3) only, sole

einzigartig unique

der Eisbär, -en, -en (2) polar bear

das Elend (10) misery

empfehlen (empfiehlt), empfahl, empfohlen (2) to recommend

empfindlich sensitive

endgültig (4) finally

eng close(ly)

der Engel, - angel

der Enkel, -/die Enkelin, -nen (1) grandson/ granddaughter

entdecken to discover

entfernt (10) distant, away

enthalten (enthält), enthielt, enthalten (7) to contain

entscheiden, entschied, entschieden (1) to decide

die Entscheidung, -en (5) decision

sich entspannen to relax

die Entspannung (2) relaxation

entsprechen (entspricht), entsprach, entsprochen (+ *dat.*) (2) to correspond to

entstehen, entstand, ist entstanden (1) to arise, originate

enttäuschen (7) to disappoint

sich entwickeln (1) to develop

entweder ... oder either . . . or

entwerfen (entwirft), entwarf, entworfen to design, create

die Entwicklung, -en (1) development

das Erbe heritage

der Erbe, -n, -n/die Erbin, -nen (1) heir/heiress

das Ereignis, -se (3) event, occurrence

erfahren (erfährt), erfuhr, erfahren (8) to experience, find out

die Erfahrung, -en (1) experience

der Erfahrungsbericht, -e personal report, field report

erfinden, erfand, erfunden (8) to invent

der Erfolg, -e (8) success

erfolgreich (2) successful

erfordern (9) to require, demand

ergänzen (4) to complete, to add

erhalten (erhält), erhielt, erhalten (2) to receive; to preserve

erheblich considerably

erhöhen (5) to increase

sich erholen (5) to recuperate

erinnern (an + *acc.***)** (7) to remind (of)

sich erinnern an (+ *acc.***)** (6) to remember

die Erinnerung, -en (2) memory

erkennen, erkannte, erkannt (8) to recognize, admit

erklären (4) to explain

die Erklärung, -en explanation

erkunden (5) to explore

erläutern to explain

erleben (1) to experience

das Erlebnis, -se (7) experience

ermöglichen to make possible

ermorden (3) to murder

die erneuerbare Energie, die erneuerbaren Energien (1) renewable energy

eröffnen (7) to open, start

erregt (4) excited, agitated

erreichen (1) to reach

erscheinen, erschien, ist erschienen (4) to appear

erschöpft (5) exhausted

erschrecken (erschrickt), erschrak, erschrocken (7) to frighten, be startled

ersetzen to replace

sich erstrecken to stretch, extend

der/die Erwachsene, -n (*adj. noun*) adult

erwähnen to mention

erwarten (2) to expect

die Erwartung, -en (2) expectation

die Erweiterung, -en expansion

der Erzieher, -/die Erzieherin, -nen (10) preschool teacher, caregiver

die Erziehung, -en upbringing, education

etliche (5) several

eventuell (6) perhaps

das Fach, ̈er subject of study

Faden: der rote Faden (10) thread, recurring theme

die Fähigkeit, -en (7) ability

die Fahrt, -en (8) drive, trip

das Fahrzeug, -e (8) vehicle

Fall: auf jeden Fall (8) in any case, definitely

faul (5) lazy

fehlen (+ *dat.***)** (4) to lack, be absent

feiern (4) to celebrate

der Feiertag, -e (4) holiday

der Feind, -e/die Feindin, -nen (10) enemy

das Feld, -er (5) field

fern (1) distant

fertig (6) finished

fest·halten an (+ *dat.***) (hält fest), hielt fest,**

festgehalten (6) to hold fast to

das Festspiele (*pl.*) festival

fett gedruckt boldface

der Fleck, -e (8) spot

die Flexion, -en inflection, declension

die Flucht, ̈e (6) escape

der Flug, ̈e (10) flight

der Flughafen, ̈ (8) airport

der Fluss, ̈e (1) river

die Folge, -n (2) consequence

folgen (+ *dat.***), ist gefolgt** (3) to follow

fördern (2) to foster, promote

fordern to demand

die Förderung, -en (1) support

der Forscher, -/die Forscherin, -nen (2) researcher

die Forschung, -en (2) research

fort·setzen to continue

die Fracht, -en freight, cargo

der Franke, -n, -n/die Fränkin, -nen Franconian (person)

(das) Franken Franconia

der Franken franc (unit of currency)

fränkisch Franconian

französisch French

die Freiheit freedom

freiwillig (7) voluntarily

der Fremdenverkehr tourism

fremdsprachig (7) foreign language-speaking

die Freude, -n (8) joy, pleasure

sich freuen auf (+ *acc.*) (7) to look forward to

der Frieden (2) peace

friedlich peaceful

führen (zu) (1) to lead (to)

der Führerschein,- e (8) driver's license

die Führung, -en (5) guided tour

fürchten (1) to fear

das Fürstentum, ¨er (1) principality

die Fußgängerzone, -n (5) pedestrian area

füttern (5) to feed (an animal)

das Futur I future tense

das Futur II future perfect tense

der Gang, ¨e (6) path

ganz complete; quite

die Gaststätte, -n (3) restaurant

das Gebäck baked goods

das Gebäude, - (3) building

das Gebiet, -e (1) region

das Gebirge, - mountain range

gebrauchen to use

die Gebühr, -en fee

der Geburtstag, -e birthday

der Gedanke, -ns, -n thought

das Gedicht, -e poem

geeignet (für) (5) suitable, fitting (for)

gefährden (10) to endanger

gefährlich (10) dangerous

gefallen (gefällt), gefiel, gefallen (+ *dat.*) to be pleasing to

das Gefühl, -e feeling

die Gegend, -en (8) area, region

der Gegensatz, ¨e opposite, contrast

gegenseitig (4) mutually

der Gegenstand, ¨e (4) object, thing

gegenüber (+ *dat.*) opposite, across from; in comparision with

die Gegenwart (6) present (time)

das Gehalt, ¨er (7) salary

das Geheimnis, -se (6) secret

der Geheimtipp, -s insiders' tip

die (persönliche) Geheimzahl, -en (8) personal identification number (PIN)

gehören (+ *dat.*) (7) to belong (to)

gehören zu (7) to be part of, to rank among

der Geiger, -/die Geigerin, -nen (3) violinist

der Geist, -er (3) intellectual (person); mind, spirit

geistig (2) intellectually, spiritually

der/die Geistliche, -n (*adj. noun*) (9) clergyman, clergywoman

geistreich (4) witty

gelangen (zu/nach/in + *acc.*) (10) to get to, arrive at

die Gelegenheit, -en (7) opportunity, occasion

gelingen (+ *dat.*), gelang, ist gelungen (3) to succeed

gelten (gilt), galt, gegolten (1) to be valid, apply

gelten als (1) to be considered to be (something)

das Gemälde, - (6) painting, picture

die Gemeinde, -n (10) town, community

gemeinsam (5) common, mutual

gemischt mixed

gemütlich (5) comfortable, cozy

genießen, genoss, genossen (7) to enjoy

das Genitivattribut, -e genitive modifier (expressing possession and relationships)

genügend (6) sufficient

das Gepäck (10) luggage

das Gerät, -e (3) tool, equipment

das Gericht, -e (7) dish (food)

der Geruch, ¨e smell, odor

das Gerücht, -e (4) rumor

gesamt (10) whole, entire

das Geschäft, -e business

geschehen (+ *dat.*), (geschieht), geschah, ist geschehen (3) to happen, occur

das Geschenk, -e gift, present

die Geschichte, -n (3) history; story

geschichtlich (3) historical

das Geschlecht, -er gender

der Geschmack, ¨er (3) taste

geschminkt (9) made up, painted

geschweige denn (5) let alone, much less

der Geselle, -n, -n (7) journeyman

die Gesellschaft, -en society; company

gesellschaftlich (4) social

das Gesetz, -e (2) law

das Gespräch, -e conversation

gestatten (10) to allow, permit

das Getränk, -e drink, beverage

das Getreide, - grain

getrennt (2) separated

die Gewalt (10) power, authority

gewinnen, gewann, gewonnen to win

gewiss (8) certain

das Gewitter, - (10) thunderstorm

gewöhnlich (8) usual

das Gewürz, -e spice

der Gipfel, - (8) peak, summit

glatt (8) smooth

der Glaube, -ns, (*no pl.*) (9) faith, belief

gleichen (+ *dat.*), glich, geglichen (6) to resemble

gleichzeitig (7) simultaneously

die Glocke, -n (4) bell

gotisch Gothic

die Grammatik grammar

gratis (4) for free

greifen, griff, gegriffen (10) to grab

die Grenze, -n (2) border

großartig (7) splendid, superb

die Größe, -n (6) size

die Großschreibung
capitalization

der Grund, ⸚e reason

gründen (2)
to found

die Grundlage, -n (9)
basis

das Grundstück, -e (8) plot
of land

der Gruß, ⸚e greeting

günstig (4) inexpensive

das Gut, ⸚er (3) good(s)

**das Gymnasium,
Gymnasien** college-
preparatory secondary
school

der Hafen, ⸚ (1) harbor

halten (hält), hielt, gehalten
(5) to hold, stop

halten für (5) to deem,
regard as

Was halten Sie von …?
(5) What do you think
of . . . ?

die Haltestelle, -n (10) (bus
or train) stop

die Haltung, -en (9)
posture, attitude

der Handel (1) trade

sich handeln um (7) to be
about something, to
concern

handeln von to be about,
deal with

der Harz northernmost
mountain range in
Germany

der Hase, -n, -n hare,
rabbit

häufig (5) frequently

hauptsächlich (1) mainly

der Hauptsatz, ⸚e main
clause

die Hauptstadt, ⸚e capital
city

die Hausaufgabe, -n
homework assignment

heftig (10) heavy, violent

heilig (9) holy

die Heimat, -en (1)
hometown, homeland

**heim·kommen, kam heim, ist
heimgekommen** (8) to
come home

heimlich secret

**der Held, -en, -en/die Heldin,
-nen** (6) hero/ heroine

**heraus·finden, fand heraus,
herausgefunden** to find
out

die Herausforderung, -en
(2) challenge

herkömmlich (6)
conventional

die Herrschaft, -en rule

her·stellen (3) to produce

der Hersteller, - (2) producer

die Herstellung (3)
production

hervorragend (3)
outstanding, eminent

**der Herzog, ⸚e/die Herzogin,
-nen** (5) duke/duchess

(das) Hessen Hesse

heutzutage nowadays

die Hilfe, -n (9) help

das Hilfsverb, -en auxiliary
verb

**die Hinsicht: in jeder
Hinsicht** (8) in every
respect

der Hintergrund, ⸚e (4)
background

**hin·weisen auf, wies hin,
hingewiesen** (6) to point
out, make
aware of

hinzu·fügen (zu) to add (to)

das Hochdeutsch High
German, standard
German

die Hochschule, -n (3)
institution of higher
education

die Hochzeit, -en (5)
wedding

die Hoffnung, -en (10) hope

der Höhepunkt, -e (2)
highlight; pinnacle

holen (7) to get

das Holz (7) wood

der Hügel, - (5) hill

die Illustrierte, -n
(9) magazine

der Imbiss, -e snack, light
meal

immerhin (9) after all

der Imperativ, -e
imperative mood

imponieren (+ *dat.*) (9) to
impress someone

inhaftiert (3) imprisoned

inbegriffen included

insbesondere (8)
especially

das Indefinitpronomen, -
indefinite pronoun

der Indikativ, -e
indicative mood

der Infinitiv, -e infinitive

der Infinitivsatz, ⸚e
infinitive clause

der Inhalt, -e contents

die Insel, -n (1) island

inszenieren to stage

Interesse bekunden (9) to
show interest

sich interessieren für (7) to
be interested in

**das Interrogativ
pronomen, -**
interrogative pronoun

inwiefern how, in what way

inzwischen (8) in the
meantime

das Jahrhundert, -e (1)
century

jährlich (2) annually

je (7) ever, each

jedoch however,
nevertheless

jemals ever

jemand someone

jen- (*def. art.*) that, those, the
former

jeweils each,
respectively

die Jobbörse, -n job search
website

der Jude, -n, -n (7) Jew

jüdisch Jewish

die Jugend (1) youth

der/die Jugendliche, -n (*adj.
noun*) (4) young person,
adolescent

**der Kaiser, -/die Kaiserin,
-nen** (9) emperor/
empress

das Kapitel, - chapter

**die Kardinalzahl,
-en** cardinal number

der Kasus, - case

der Kaufmann, Kaufleute
(*pl.*)/**die Kauffrau, -en**
(1) businessman,
merchant/
businesswoman

kaum (2) hardly

die Kenntnis, -se (10)
knowledge

kennzeichnen to distinguish

der Kern, -e core, heart (*fig.*)

die Kernkraft (9) nuclear
power

die Kerze, -n (4) candle

die Kindheit, -en childhood

das Kissen, - (4) pillow

die Klammer, -n parenthesis

klappen (7) to go as planned

klettern, ist geklettert (5) to climb

der Klimaschutz (9) climate protection

der Klimawandel, - climate change

der Klingelton, ¨e (2) ringtone

klingen to sound

klopfen (9) to knock, to beat

knapp almost; narrow, close; scarce

der Knödel, - dumpling

knuddelig (2) cuddly

knusprig crispy

das Kochbuch, ¨er cookbook

die Kohle, -n (9) coal

(das) Köln Cologne

komponieren (3) to compose

das Kompositum, Komposita compound word

der Konditor, -en confectioner, pastry chef

die Konjunktion, -en conjunction

der Konjunktiv, -e subjunctive mood

die Konkurrenz, -en competition

der König, -e/die Königin, -nen king/queen

konkurrieren (um) (1) to compete for

der Konsonant, -en, -en consonant

die Kontrolle, -n (4) inspection

koordinierend coordinating

der Kopf, ¨e head

den Kopf klar behalten (2) to keep a clear head

der Korb, ¨e (6) basket

der Körper, - body

die Kosten: Sie kommen auf ihre Kosten. (2) They get their money's worth.

kostenlos (5) (for) free

die Köstlichkeit, -en (5) delicacy

die Kraft, ¨e (3) strength, power

der Krieg, -e (2) war

kriegen (*colloq.*) (10) to get

der Krimi, -s (6) mystery novel, crime thriller

die Krippe, -n crib, manger; daycare

die Krone, -n crown

krumm (8) bent

die Küche, -n (7) cuisine; kitchen

das Kulturerbe cultural heritage

sich kümmern um to take care of

der Kunde, -n, -n/die Kundin, -nen (8) customer, client

der Kundenberater, -/die Kundenberaterin, -nen (10) customer service representative

künftig (1) future, in the future

die Kunst, ¨e (3) art

die Kunstkritik, -en art criticism

der Künstler, -/die Künstlerin, -nen (3) artist

die Kürze: in Kürze (5) shortly, soon

die Kurzgeschichte, -n short story

das Kurzporträt, -s brief profile

die Küste, -n (1) coast

lachen (4) to laugh

die Lage, -n (3) position

das Land, ¨er (1) land; country; countryside

die Landkarte, -n map

die Landschaft, -en landscape

die Landwirtschaft agriculture

langfristig (2) long-term

langweilig boring

der Lärm (4) noise

der Lauf: im Laufe (+ *gen.*) over the course of

die Laune, -n (10) mood

der Laut, -e sound

das Leben, - life

ums Leben kommen to lose one's life

der Lebenslauf, ¨e (10) resume

das Lebensmittel, - (3) food; groceries (*pl.*)

die Lederhose, -n leather pants

leer (2) empty

die Lehre, -n (7) apprenticeship, lesson; teaching

der Leib, -er (4) body

leicht easy, light

die Leidenschaft, -en passion

die Leinwand, ¨e (5) projection screen

leisten (2) to achieve

die Leistung, -en (2) service, offerings; achievement

der Leiter, -/die Leiterin, -nen (3) leader, director

die Leiter, -n (10) ladder

lieb: Es war mir lieb. (8) It was dear to me.

der Liebhaber, -/die Liebhaberin, -nen (8) fan, devotee

der Liebling, -e favorite

das Lied, -er song

liefern (2) to deliver

die Linse, -n lentil

das Lob, -e (4) praise

locker loose

lockig (5) curly

sich lohnen: Es lohnt sich. (2) It's worth it.

das Lokal, -e (7) restaurant, bar, venue

die Lücke, -n (6) gap, hole

die Luft (1) air

lügen, log, gelogen (7) to lie; tell a lie

lustig (5) funny, amusing

die Macht, ¨e (1) power

mächtig (1) powerful, influential

mahlen to grind

die Mahlzeit, -en meal

der Maler, -/die Malerin, -nen (6) painter

die Malerei, -en (6) painting

manch- (*def. art.*) many, some, several

die Mandel, -n (6) almond

die Mannschaft, -en team

die Marke, -n (2) brand

maßgeblich (9) significantly

die Mauer, -n (2) (free-standing) wall

(das) Mecklenburg-Vorpommern Mecklenburg-West Pomerania

das Meer, -e (1) sea

das Mehl (6) flour

die Mehrheit, -en (7) majority

mehrmals (8) repeatedly

die Meinung, -en opinion, view

meiner Meinung nach (5) in my opinion

sich melden (bei) (9) to report (to)

die Menge, -n (8) quantity, amount (*colloq.*)

merkwürdig (4) strange

die Messe, -n (6) trade fair, exhibition

mieten (8) to rent

mindestens at least

misstrauisch (9) distrustful, wary

der Mitarbeiter, -/die Mitarbeiterin, -nen (7) co-worker, colleague

das Mitglied, -er (1) member

mit·machen to participate in, experience

der Mitstudent, -en, -en/die Mitstudentin, -nen fellow student

mit·teilen to share (information)

die Mitteilung, -en, -en notification, announcement

das Mittelalter (1) Middle Ages

mittelalterlich (3) medieval

das Mittelgebirge, - low mountain range

mittendrin (9) in the middle of it

mittlerweile (2) meanwhile; in the meantime

die Möbel (*pl.*) furniture

das Modalverb, -en modal verb

die Mode, -n fashion

aus der Mode kommen (6) to go out of style

möglich possible

die Möglichkeit, -en possibility

(das) München Munich

die Mundart, -en (7) dialect

mündlich orally

na ja (5) oh well

nach·denken (über), dachte nach, nachgedacht (4) to reflect (about), to ponder

die Nachfrage, -n (2) demand

die Nachricht, -en message, news

die Nachspeise, -n dessert

der Nachteil, -e (9) disadvantage

nah close, near

die Nähe (2) closeness, vicinity

in der Nähe von near

nahrhaft (8) nutritious

nass wet

der Nebensatz, ⸚e dependent clause

nennen, nannte, genannt to name, call

neugierig (4) curious

nicken (4) to nod

das Niederdeutsch Low German

die Niederlassung, -en branch office

(das) Niedersachsen Lower Saxony

niedrig low

niemand (3) nobody

noch still

noch nicht not yet

weder ... noch (8) neither ... nor

das Nomen, - noun

der Norden north

(das) Nordrhein-Westfalen North Rhine-Westphalia

normalerweise usually

die Not, ⸚e (8) need, trouble

nötig (10) necessary

Ich habe es nötig. (9) I really need it.

notwendig (1) necessary

der Numerus number (of a noun, i.e., *sing.* or *pl.*)

nutzen (1) to use

oberdeutsch Upper German (i.e., Southern German)

offenbar (10) apparently

öffentlich (2) public

die Öffentlichkeit (9) public

ohne weiteres readily, without further ado

die Oper, -n (3) opera

die Ordinalzahl, -en ordinal number

die Orgel, -n (3) organ

der Ort, -e (2) place

vor Ort (6) on site, on the spot

der Osten east

(das) Ostern (4) Easter

(das) Österreich Austria

das Partizip I, -ien present participle

das Partizip II, -ien past participle

der Passant, -en, -en/die Passantin, -nen passer-by

passen (+ *dat.*) (7) to fit

passen zu (7) to be suited to

passend suitable, fitting

das Passiv passive voice

peinlich (5) embarrassing

das Perfekt present perfect tense

das Personalpronomen, - personal pronoun

das Pferd, -e (5) horse

pflegen (7) to maintain, care for

die Pflicht, -en (2) duty

plädieren für to plead for

das Plattdeutsch Low German

die Pluralform, -en plural form

das Plüschtier, -e (2) stuffed animal

das Plusquamperfekt past perfect tense

das Portemonnaie, -s wallet

prächtig (3) magnificent, grand

das Prädikatsnomen, - predicate nominative

das Präfix, -e prefix

prägen (1) to mold, shape

das Praktikum, Praktika internship

das Präsens present tense

das Präteritum simple past tense

die Pressemitteilung, -en press release

die Probe: auf die Probe stellen (2) to put to the test

probieren (3) to try; to have a taste

die Promotion, -en (10) doctorate (PhD, MD, LLD, etc.)

die Prüfung, -en (3) test, inspection

die Puppe, -n (10) doll; puppet

die Quelle, -n (9) source

der Rang: ersten Ranges first-rate

raten (rät), riet, geraten (5) to guess

reagieren (auf + *acc.*) to react (to)

recherchieren to research

das Recht, -e (3) right

mit Recht justifiably

der Rechtsanwalt, ¨e/die Rechtsanwältin, -nen (10) lawyer

rechtzeitig (8) in a timely manner

die Rede, -n speech

Es ist von … die Rede. There is talk of …

Es kann von … keine Rede sein. … is out of the question.

reden (von) to talk, speak (of)

das Referat, -e presentation, oral report

ein Referat halten to give a presentation

das Reflexivpronomen, - reflexive pronoun

das Reflexivverb, -en reflexive verb

die Regel, -n rule, regulation

regelmäßig (3) regular(ly)

regieren to rule, govern

die Regierung, -en (1) government

der Regisseur, -e/die Regisseurin, -nen (5) director

das Reich, -e (1) empire, realm, kingdom

reichen (7) to reach, to hand

reichhaltig (2) substantial, extensive

die Reihe: an der Reihe sein (5) to have one's turn

eine ganze Reihe (3) a whole series

eine Reihe von a number of

die Reihenfolge, -n order, sequence

reinigen (8) to clean

der Reiseführer, - travel guide

das Reisejournal, -e travel journal

reiten, ritt, ist geritten (10) to ride (an animal)

reizen (10) to tempt, provoke

das Relativpronomen, - relative pronoun

der Relativsatz, ¨e relative clause

der Renner, - (*colloq.*) (10) hit, blockbuster

renommiert renowned

die Reportage, -n report, feature

die Residenzstadt, ¨e seat of royal power

der Restaurantführer, - restaurant guide

restaurieren to restore

retten (9) to save, to rescue

das Rezept, -e recipe

riechen, roch, gerochen (5) to smell

riesig (9) gigantic

das Risiko, Risiken (1) risk

der Ritter, - (5) knight

der Rohstoff, -e (9) raw material

das Rollenspiel, -e role play

der Roman, -e novel

romanisch Romanesque

die Rosine, -n (6) raisin

der Ruf, -e (3) reputation; call

rühren (10) to stir, move

das Ruhrgebiet Ruhr region

der Rundfunk broadcasting

der Rundgang, ¨e walking tour

die Rutsche, -n (10) slide

das Sachbuch, ¨er (6) non-fiction book

die Sachertorte, -n Vienesse chocolate cake with an apricot marmelade filling

(das) Sachsen Saxony

sächsisch Saxon

die Sahne cream

sammeln to collect

die Sammlung, -en (3) collection

sämtlich (4) all

sanft (5) gentle, mild

der Satz, ¨e sentence

die Satzklammer, -n verbal bracketing (in a sentence)

der Satzteil, -e clause, phrase

die S-Bahn, -en suburban train

Schade! (6) What a pity!

der Schaden, ¨ (1) damage

schaffen (4) to manage (to do something)

schaffen, schuf, geschaffen (3) to create

der Schatz, ¨e (8) treasure; darling

schätzen (7) to value; to estimate

schauen to look

der Schauplatz, ¨e scene, setting, stage

der Schauspieler, -/die Schauspielerin, -nen (5) actor/actress

scheiden, schied, geschieden (10) to separate

die Schere, -n (10) scissors

die Schicht, -en (7) social class; layer

das Schicksal, -e fate

das Schild, -er (4) sign

schließlich (4) after all, finally

der Schmerz, -en (8) pain, grief

schmücken to decorate

der Schrecken, - horror, terror

die Schrift, -en (3) writing

der Schriftsteller, -/die Schriftstellerin, -nen (3) author

der Schritt, -e (4) step, stride

schuld: Ich bin nicht schuld (daran). (7) I am not to blame (for it).

die Schuld, -en (*sing.*) blame, guilt; (*pl.*) debt

die Schulter, -n shoulder

die Schultern zucken (10) to shrug (one's shoulders)

Schutt und Asche (4) rubble and ashes

schützen (1) to protect

(das) Schwaben Swabia

schwäbisch Swabian

schwach weak

schweigen, schwieg, geschwiegen (6) to remain silent

die Schweiz Switzerland

der/die Schwerbehinderte, -n (*adj. noun*) (10) handicapped person

schwerhörig (4) hard of hearing

der Schwerpunkt, -e (6) main emphasis, focus

die Schwierigkeit, -en (1) difficulty

schwören, schwor, geschworen (6) to swear, pledge

der See, -n (1) lake

die See, -n (1) sea

segeln (1) to sail

die Seele, -n (4) soul

die Sehenswürdigkeit, -en sight, place of interest

die Sehnsucht, ˙e (nach) (5) desire, longing (for)

selbstverständlich of course

die Sendung, -en (5) show, broadcast

der Senf mustard

sicher (4) safe, secure; surely, certainly

sichern (10) to secure

die Sicht, -en sight, point of view

sichtbar visible

der Sieger, -/die Siegerin, -nen winner, victor

der Sinn, -e (7) sense, meaning

in den Sinn kommen to spring to mind

sinnvoll (9) sensible, meaningful

der Sitz, -e (1) seat

slawisch Slavic

die SMS, - text message

solch- (*def. art.*) such

sonst otherwise, else

sorgfältig (6) carefully

sowie as well as

spannend (6) exciting

die Spannung, -en (2) tension; suspense

sparen (8) to save

die Speise, -n (8) food, dish

die Spende, -n (4) donation

das Spielzeug, -e (10) toy

die Spitze, -n tip; top position

spotten (4) to joke

die Sprachanalyse, -n linguistic analysis

die Spur, -en trace, vestige

die Stadtrundfahrt, -en city sightseeing tour

der Stadtteil, -e district, part of the city

stammen aus (6) to originate from

der Stammwechsel, - stem-vowel change

ständig (10) constant

der Standort, -e (7) site, location

stark strong

starr (9) stiff, rigid, paralyzed

stattdessen (10) instead of that

statt·finden, fand statt, stattgefunden (1) to take place

stecken (8) to put; be located

stehen: Das steht ihm gut. (9) It suits him well.

stehlen (stiehlt), stahl, gestohlen (10) to steal

steigen, stieg, ist gestiegen (2) to climb, rise

die Steigerung, -en degree, gradation (of adjectives and adverb)

die Stelle, -n (10) job, position; place

an deiner Stelle in your place; if I were you

die Stellenanzeige, -n job advertisement

die Stellung, -en position

Stellung nehmen to give one's opinion

sterben (stirbt), starb, ist gestorben (1) to die

sterben an (+ *dat.*) (1) to die of

stets (4) always

die Steuer, -n (8) tax

das Stichwort, ˙er cue, keyword

die Stimme, -n (6) voice

stimmen: Das stimmt (nicht). (4) That is (not) correct/right.

die Stimmung, -en mood, atmosphere

die Stirn, -en (4) forehead

der Stock, Stockwerke (4) floor, story (of a building); **der Stock, ˙e** stick

stolz auf (+ *acc.*) (3) proud of

stören (9) to bother, to disturb

der Strand, ˙e (1) beach

die Straßenbahn, -en streetcar, tram

die Strecke, -n (9) distance, route

streichen, strich, gestrichen (10) to cancel

der Streit, -e (9) argument

der Strom (1) electricity, current

strömen to stream, pour

das Studienfach, ˙er subject of study

die Studiengebühr, -en tuition fee

der/die Studierende, -n (*adj. noun*) (2) student

das Studium, Studien course of studies

die Stufe, -e (4) stair, step

stumm (9) in silence, silently

die Stunde, -n (3) hour

subordinierend subordinating

die Subvention, -en subsidy

der Süden south

süß sweet

das Tal, ˙er (8) valley

die Tasche, -n (4) bag; pocket

das Taschenmesser, - pocket knife

die Tat, -en act, deed

in der Tat actually, indeed

tätig active, employed

die Tätigkeit, -en (10) activity; job

die Tatsache, -n fact

tatsächlich (8) real(ly), actual(ly)

tauchen to dip, dive

tauschen (5) to exchange

der Teig (6) dough

der Teil, -e part

teilen to share

teil·nehmen (nimmt teil), nahm teil, teilgenommen (1) to participate, take part

teilnehmen an (+ *dat.*) (1) to take part in (something)

die Teilung, -en (2) separation

teilweise (7) partly

der Termin, -e (6) appointment, fixed date

das Thema, Themen theme, topic

(das) Thüringen Thuringia

thüringisch Thuringian

der Tiefpunkt, -e low point

das Tier, -e animal

der Tischler, - (7) carpenter

das Tor, -e (1) gate, gateway

die **Tracht, -en** traditional costume

die **Träne, -n** (10) tear

der **Traum, ̈e** dream

(sich) **treffen (trifft), traf, getroffen** (7) to meet (each other)

der **Treffpunkt, ̈e** (6) meeting place

treiben to do; to herd

trennbar separable

(sich) **trennen (von)** (8) to separate (oneself) (from)

die **Treppe, -n** (10) stairs

trösten (7) to comfort

trotzdem (3) nevertheless

die **Trümmer** (*pl.*) (7) debris, rubble

das **Tuch, ̈er** (4) cloth

tun, tat, getan to do

der **Türke, -n, -n/die Türkin, -nen** Turk

die **Türkei** Turkey

der **Turm, ̈e** (1) steeple, tower

die **U-Bahn, -en** subway

der **Überblick, -e** overview

der **Übergang, ̈e** transition

überhaupt (3) in general, at all

überleben to survive

übernachten to spend the night

übernehmen (übernimmt), übernahm, übernommen (3) to take over

überprüfen (4) to check

überraschen (8) to surprise

die **Überraschung, -en** (6) surprise

die **Überschrift, -en** heading, title

übersetzen (3) to translate

übertragen (überträgt), übertrug, übertragen (5) to transmit, broadcast, transfer

überwiegend (7) predominantly

überwinden, überwand, überwunden (2) to conquer

überzeugen (6) to convince

üblich common, usual

übrigens (8) by the way

das **Ufer, -** (1) shore, bank

umfangreich extensive

umfassen (9) to include, to encompass

die **Umfrage, -n** survey, questionnaire

der **Umgang** (7) contact, dealings

umgeben (5) surrounded

die **Umgebung, -en** surrounding area

um·gehen mit, ging um, ist umgegangen to treat, handle

um·schreiben, schrieb um, umgeschrieben rewrite

sich **um·sehen (sieht um), sah um, umgesehen** to look around

der **Umstand, ̈e** circumstance

umstritten (7) controversial

die **Umwelt** (1) environment

der **Umweltschützer, -/die Umweltschützerin, -nen** (2) protector of the environment

der **Umzug, ̈e** (9) parade

unabhängig (von) (2) independent (from)

die **Unabhängigkeit** (9) independence, autonomy

unbarmherzig (10) merciless

unbedingt (5) at all costs, necessarily, absolutely

unbestimmt indefinite, uncertain

unbestritten undisputed

der **Unfall, ̈e** accident

ungeduldig (9) impatient

ungefähr (1) approximately

ungewöhnlich (6) unusual

unmittelbar (6) immediate(ly)

unregelmäßig irregular

unter anderem (2) among other things

unterhalten (unterhält), unterhielt, unterhalten (5) to entertain, amuse

sich **unterhalten (unterhält), unterhielt, unterhalten** (7) to chat

die **Unterlagen** (*pl.*) (10) documents

unternehmen (unternimmt), unternahm, unternommen to undertake

das **Unternehmen, -** (2) company, enterprise

der **Unterricht** (3) instruction

unterrichten (7) to teach

(sich) **unterscheiden, unterschied, unterschieden** (7) to differentiate (oneself)

der **Unterschied, -e** difference

unterschiedlich varied, different

unterstreichen, unterstrich, unterstrichen to underline

unterstützen (7) to support

die **Unterstützung** (2) support

die **Untersuchung, -en** (4) study, investigation

unterwegs on the way

untrennbar inseparable

unverändert (5) unchanged

unvorhergesehen (5) unexpected

das **Unwetter, -** (10) severe weather

unzufrieden dissatisfied

der **Urlaub, -e** vacation

der **Ursprung, ̈e** (3) origin

ursprünglich (1) original(ly)

u. v. a. = und viele(s) andere (3) and many others

sich **verändern** (8) to change

die **Veränderung, -en** (2) change

veranstalten (3) to organize (an event)

die **Veranstaltung, -en** (1) event, activity

verantwortlich (8) responsible

die **Verantwortung, -en** (6) responsibility

verantwortungsvoll (10) responsible

verbessern to improve

die **Verbindung, -en** (10) connection

verbrauchen (8) to use, consume

verbreitet common, widespread

verbrennen, verbrannte, verbrannt (8) to burn

verbringen, verbrachte, verbracht (5) to spend (time)

verbunden: mit ... verbunden sein (2) to be affiliated with . . .

verdanken (+ *dat.*) (9) to owe thanks to

der Verein, -e (3) association, club

vereinigt (2) united

der Verfall (4) decay

verfassen (3) to write

verfügbar (9) available

verfügen über (+ *acc.*) (7) to have at one's disposal or command

die Verfügung: zur Verfügung stehen (3) to be at one's disposal

vergangen (3) past

die Vergangenheit (6) past (time)

vergeblich (7) in vain, futilely

der Vergleich, -e (4) comparison

vergleichen, verglich, verglichen (5) to compare

das Vergnügen, - (4) pleasure

sich verhalten (verhält), verhielt, verhalten to behave, act (in a certain way)

das Verhältnis, -se (2) relationship

verhältnismäßig (1) relatively, comparatively

verhindern (4) to prevent

der Verkehr (5) traffic

verkleidet (6) dressed up, disguised

verknüpft (mit) linked (to)

der Verlag, -e (6) publishing house

das Verlangen, - (10) desire, demand

verlassen (verlässt), verließ, verlassen (1) to leave (a person or place)

verlegen (10) to postpone; to relocate

sich verlieben in (+ *acc.*) to fall in love with

verlieren, verlor, verloren (8) to lose

der/die Verlobte, -n (*adj. noun*) fiancé (*m.*)/fiancée (*f.*)

der Verlust, -e (8) loss

vermeintlich supposed

vermissen (8) to miss

vermögen (vermag), vermochte, vermocht (5) to be capable

vermuten to surmise

vermutlich (3) presumably

vernünftig (10) reasonable, sensible

veröffentlichen to publish

verpassen to miss, miss out on

sich verraten (verrät), verriet, verraten (7) to betray (oneself), give (oneself) away

die Versammlung, -en (6) meeting, gathering

verschenken (5) to give something away

die Verschiebung, -en shift

verschieden (1) different, various

verschlossen closed

versorgen to supply

verschwinden, verschwand, ist verschwunden (4) to disappear

die Versicherung, -en (8) insurance

verständlich (5) comprehensible

verstecken (6) to hide

der Versuch, -e (3) attempt

versuchen to try

verteilen (5) to distribute, spread

der Vertrag, ⁻e (5) contract, agreement

vertreten (vertritt) vertrat, vertreten to represent

verursachen (9) to cause

die Verwaltung, -en (2) administration

sich verwandeln in (+ *acc.*) (6) to transform oneself into

der/die Verwandte, -n (*adj. noun*) relative

verwenden (2) to use

verzichten auf (+ *acc.*) (7) to do without

die Verzögerung, -en (10) delay

die Vielfalt (7) diversity

vielfältig diverse

das Viertel, - quarter

der Vogel, ⁻ bird

der Vokal, -e vowel

das Volk, ⁻er people, populace

vollenden to complete

völlig (7) completely

vollständig complete(ly)

Voraus: im Voraus (8) beforehand, in advance

die Voraussetzung, -en (5) condition, requirement

das Vorbild, -er model, example

vorbei·führen an (+ *dat.*) to go past, to go around

vor·bereiten auf (+ *acc.*) to prepare for

die Vorbereitung, -en (5) preparation

der Vorgang, ⁻e (6) process, occurrence

vor·haben (5) to plan, intend (to do something)

vorhanden present, existent

vor·lesen (liest vor), las vor, vorgelesen (6) to read (something) to (somebody)

die Vorlesung, -en lecture

die Vorliebe, -n (8) preference

vornehm distinguished

(das) Vorpommern West Pomerania

der Vorrat, ⁻e (9) supply

der Vorschlag, ⁻e (6) suggestion

vor·schlagen (schlägt vor), schlug vor, vorgeschlagen to suggest

der/die Vorsitzende, -n (*adj. noun*) (9) chairperson

sich (etwas) vor·stellen (8) to imagine (something)

die Vorstellung, -en (6) idea; performance

der Vorteil, -e (10) advantage

der Vortrag, ⸚e speech, lecture

der Vorurteil, -e (7) prejudice

vorwiegend predominantly

das Vorwort, -e preface

vorzeitig (4) before its time, prematurely

wachsen (wächst), wuchs, ist gewachsen (7) to grow

die Waffe, -n (8) weapon

wagen (5) to dare

die Wahl, -en (3) choice, selection

wählen to choose

die Wahrheit, -en (7) truth

wahrscheinlich (3) probable; probably

die Währung, -en (9) currency

das Wahrzeichen, - emblem

der Wald, ⸚er (3) forest

das Wappen, - (9) coat of arms

die Ware, -n (1) product; (pl.) goods

der Wechsel, - (8) change

wechseln (7) to change, alternate

die Wechselpräposition, -en two-way preposition

weder ... noch (8) neither . . . nor

die Wehr: sich zur Wehr setzen (9) to defend oneself

die Weide, -n (5) meadow

(das) Weihnachten (4) Christmas

weinen (7) to cry

die Weise, -n way, manner

Art und Weise method, manner

auf welche Weise? in what way?

weit far

weitgehend extensive

die Welle, -n (9) wave

die Welt, -en (1) world

das Weltkulturerbe world cultural heritage

weltlich (3) worldly, secular

die Wende (2) turn; here: 1990, German reunification

wenden, wandte, gewandt (4) to turn

die Wendung, -en expression

wenigstens at least

werben (wirbt), warb, geworben (2) to advertise

werben für (2) to promote

der Werbespruch, ⸚e advertising slogan

die Werbung, -en advertisement

werfen (wirft), warf, geworfen (4) to throw

die Werkstatt, ⸚en (4) workshop, garage

das Werkzeug, -e (5) tool

der Wert, -e (7) value

wesentlich (1) essential, fundamental

der Westen west

westfälisch Westphalian

der Wettbewerb, -e (2) competition

wichtig (1) important

wider·spiegeln to reflect

der Widerstand, ⸚e (7) resistance, opposition

widmen to dedicate

wiederholen (6) to repeat

die Wiederholung, -en review

die Wiedervereinignung, -en (2) reunification

(das) Wien Vienna

Wiener (adj.) Viennese

die Wiese, -n (8) meadow

wieso (7) why

winken (4) to wave

wirken (3) to have an effect, to work

die Wirklichkeit (9) reality

die Wirtschaft, -en (1) economy

das Wissen (7) knowledge

wissen (weiß), wusste, gewusst to know

Bescheid wissen (5) to be in the know

der Wissenschaftler, -/die Wissenschaftlerin, -nen (3) scholar, scientist

der Witz, -e (4) joke

wohl probably

wohlhabend (8) affluent, wealthy

der Wohlstand prosperity, wealth

das Wort word; (pl.) ⸚er words in a list; (pl.) -e words in a text

das Wörterbuch, ⸚er dictionary

der Wortschatz, ⸚e vocabulary

die Wortstellung word order

die wo-Verbindung, -en wo-compound

der Wunsch, ⸚e wish

würdigen to acknowledge

der Wurzel, -n root

die Zahl, -en number

zahlreich (3) numerous

der Zauberer, -/die Zauberin, -nen (10) sorcerer/ sorceress

z. B. = zum Beispiel (1) for example

die Zeit, -en time

die Zeitform, -en tense

zeitgenössisch (3) contemporary

zerstören (5) to destroy

zeugen (von) (3) to be evidence (of), to bear witness (to)

das Zeugnis, -se (10) academic record

ziehen, zog, ist gezogen (2) to move

das Ziel, -e (3) destination, goal

zögern (4) to hesitate

der Zopf, ⸚e (10) braid

der Zorn (10) rage, wrath

zucken: die Schultern zucken (10) to shrug (one's shoulders)

die Zuflucht, -en (8) refuge, sanctuary

zufrieden content

der Zug, ⸚e characteristic; train

zugänglich (5) accessible

zu·geben (gibt zu), gab zu, zugegeben (7) to admit

die Zugehörigkeit, -en belonging

der Zuhörer, -/die Zuhörerin, -nen listener

die Zukunft (1) future

zu·lassen (lässt zu), ließ zu, zugelassen (9) to allow, to permit

die Zulassung, -en (2) admission

zumindest (4) at least

zunächst (8) first, at first, for now

zu·nehmen (nimmt zu), nahm zu, zugenommen (9) to increase

zu·ordnen to match, assign

zurück·gehen, ging zurück, ist zurückgegangen (1) to recede, decline

zurück·greifen auf (+ *acc.*), **griff zurück, zurückgegriffen** (9) to draw on, go back to

zurück·kehren, ist zurückgekehrt (8) to return

zu·sagen (10) to accept, consent

die Zusammenfassung, -en summary

der Zusammenhang, ̈e (6) connection, context

zusammen·rücken, ist zusammengerückt (2) to come together

zusätzlich (5) additionally

zu·schauen (+ *dat.*) (7) to observe, watch

der Zuschlag, ̈e (2) surcharge

der Zustand, ̈e condition, state

zuständig für (10) responsible for

die Zutat, -en (6) ingredient

zu·treffen (trifft zu), traf zu, zugetroffen (7) to apply to, be correct

zwar (7) admittedly, to be precise

der Zweck, -e (4) purpose

Es hat keinen Zweck. (7) It serves no purpose.

die Zwiebel, -n (9) onion

der Zwilling, -e (5) twin

zwingen, zwang, gezwungen (9) to force, to compel

Index

Bold page numbers show where relevant grammar charts can be found.

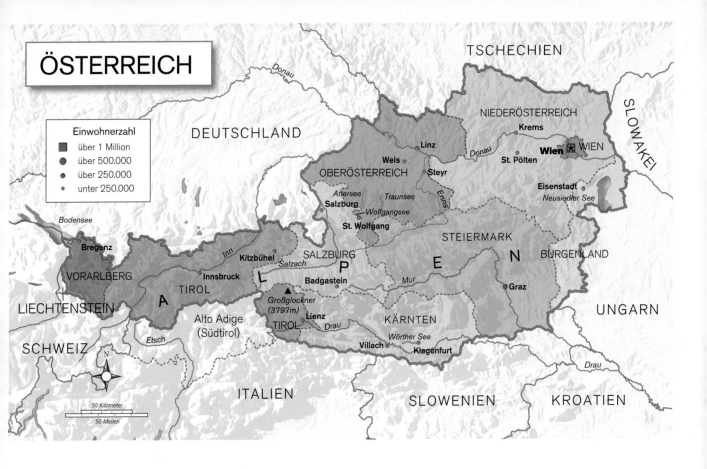

ÖSTERREICH

Einwohnerzahl
- über 1 Million
- über 500.000
- über 250.000
- unter 250.000

TSCHECHIEN

SLOWAKEI

DEUTSCHLAND

NIEDERÖSTERREICH

Krems

Linz

Donau

Wien · WIEN

St. Pölten

Wels

OBERÖSTERREICH

Steyr

Eisenstadt

Attersee

Traunsee

Salzburg

Neusiedler See

Wolfgangsee

St. Wolfgang

STEIERMARK

BURGENLAND

Bodensee

Bregenz

Inn

Kitzbühel

SALZBURG

A L P E N

VORARLBERG

Innsbruck

Salzach

Badgastein

Mur

Graz

LIECHTENSTEIN

TIROL

Großglockner
(3797m)

UNGARN

Alto Adige
(Südtirol)

Lienz

KÄRNTEN

SCHWEIZ

Etsch

TIROL

Drau

Wörther See

Villach

Klagenfurt

N

ITALIEN

Drau

SLOWENIEN

KROATIEN

50 Kilometer
50 Meilen

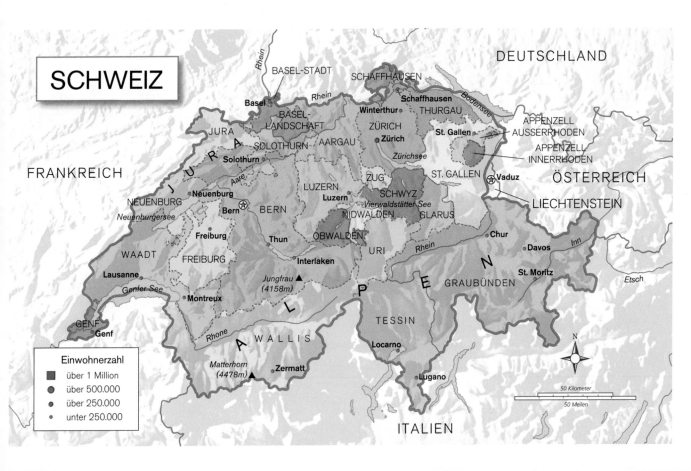

SCHWEIZ

DEUTSCHLAND

Rhein

BASEL-STADT

SCHAFFHAUSEN

Rhein

Schaffhausen

Bodensee

Basel

Winterthur

THURGAU

APPENZELL
AUSSERRHODEN

BASEL-
LANDSCHAFT

ZÜRICH

JURA

SOLOTHURN

AARGAU

St. Gallen

APPENZELL
INNERRHODEN

J U R A

Zürich

Zürichsee

FRANKREICH

Solothurn

Aare

ZUG

ST. GALLEN

Vaduz

ÖSTERREICH

NEUENBURG

Neuenburg

LUZERN

SCHWYZ

LIECHTENSTEIN

Bern

BERN

Luzern

Vierwaldstätter See

GLARUS

Neuenburgersee

NIDWALDEN

Freiburg

Thun

OBWALDEN

Chur

Inn

WAADT

FREIBURG

Interlaken

URI

Rhein

Davos

Lausanne

Jungfrau
(4158m)

St. Moritz

GRAUBÜNDEN

Etsch

Genfer See

Montreux

A L P E N

GENF

Rhone

TESSIN

Genf

Locarno

A   WALLIS

N

Matterhorn
(4478m)

Zermatt

Lugano

Einwohnerzahl
- über 1 Million
- über 500.000
- über 250.000
- unter 250.000

50 Kilometer
50 Meilen

ITALIEN

EUROPA 2012

Mitglieder der Europäischen Union (EU-27)

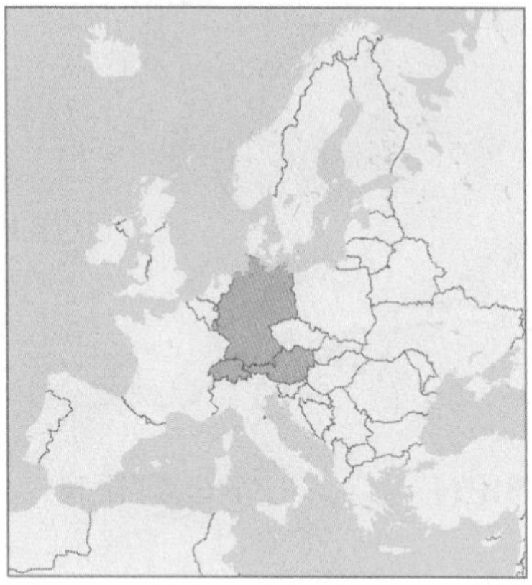

Deutschsprachige Länder

ISLAND

⊛ Reykjavik

SCHWE

NORWEGEN

Oslo ⊛

Stock

NORDSEE

DÄNEMARK

Kopenhag ⊛

IRLAND

Dublin ⊛

GROSS-
BRITANNIEN

NIEDERLANDE

Amsterdam ⊛

Berlin ⊛

London ⊛

Brüssel ⊛

DEUTSCHLAND

BELGIEN ⊛

⊛ Prag

LUXEMBURG

TSCHECH

Paris ⊛

Luxemburg ⊛

Wien ⊛

ATLANTISCHER

OZEAN

FRANKREICH

Bern ⊛ Vaduz

ÖSTERREICH

SCHWEIZ

SLOWENIEN

LIECHTENSTEIN

Ljubljana ⊛

KROATIEN

BOSNIE
HERZEGOWI

PORTUGAL

ITALIEN

MONTE

Lissabon ⊛

Madrid ⊛

⊛ Rom

SPANIEN

MITTELMEER

⊛ Rabat

Algier ⊛

Tunis ⊛

MAROKKO

ALGERIEN

MALTA

TUNESIEN